VICTORIAN MATERIAL CULTURE

VICTORIAN MATERIAL CULTURE

General Editors:
Tatiana Kontou and Victoria Mills

Volume IV

Manufactured Things

Edited by Deborah Wynne
and Louisa Yates

Routledge
Taylor & Francis Group
LONDON AND NEW YORK

First published 2023
by Routledge
4 Park Square, Milton Park, Abingdon, Oxon OX14 4RN

and by Routledge
605 Third Avenue, New York, NY 10158

Routledge is an imprint of the Taylor & Francis Group, an informa business

British Library Cataloguing-in-Publication Data
A catalogue record for this book is available from the British Library

Library of Congress Cataloging-in-Publication Data
A catalog record for this book has been requested

ISBN: 978-1-138-22526-8 (set)
eISBN: 978-1-315-40038-9 (set)
ISBN: 978-1-138-22537-4 (volume IV)
eISBN: 978-1-315-40010-5 (volume IV)

DOI: 10.4324/9781315400105

Typeset in Times New Roman
by Apex CoVantage, LLC

Publisher's Note
References within each chapter are as they appear in the original complete work

For Product Safety Concerns and Information please contact our EU representative:
GPSR@taylorandfrancis.com
Taylor & Francis Verlag GmbH, Kaufingerstraße 24, 80331 München, Germany

CONTENTS

ACKNOWLEDGEMENTS

We would like to thank Unilever Collections at Unilever Art, Archives and Records Management, Port Sunlight for permission to reproduce 'Vinolia Soap'. The following institutions, and particularly their staff, have offered invaluable assistance, guidance and support:

Bishopsgate Institute, London, UK (Stefan Dickers, Library and Archive Manager)
Gladstone's Library, Hawarden, Wales, UK (Peter Francis, Warden)
Special Collections and Archives, University of Liverpool, UK (Robyn Orr, Library Assistant and Jenny Higham, Special Collections and Archive Manager)
The Leeds Library, Leeds, UK (Assistant Librarian Anna Goodridge, Librarian Jane Riley, and Chief Executive Carl Hutton)
Museums Sheffield, Sheffield, UK (Leigh-Anne Baldridge and Jennifer Cocker)
Thanks to Unilever Collections at Unilever Art, Archives and Records Management Port Sunlight, UK (Ruth Loughrey, Art, Archives and Records Management Service Operations Manager)
Wellcome Library, London, UK

This project benefited from two research grants from the Faculty of Arts and Humanities, University of Chester, and we would like to express our thanks for this support. We would also like to thank the series editors, Tatiana Kontou and Victoria Mills, both of whom have offered us much needed advice. We also would like to thank colleagues at Gladstone's Library and the English Department, University of Chester, for their support and encouragement throughout. Special thanks are due to Naomi Walker for her efficiency and thoroughness as our research assistant during the final stages of the project.

BIBLIOGRAPHY

Primary sources

A. L. O. E., *The Story of a Needle* (London: T. Nelson and Sons, 1874), pp. 7–10.

Anon, 'The Age of the Electro-Plate', *Fun*, Vol. 5 (March 1867), p. 8.

Anon, 'Cigarette', *London Journal* (1 November 1869), p. 229.

Anon, 'A Crinoline Manufactory', *Once a Week* (23 January 1864), pp. 124–126.

Anon, 'A Day at the Nottingham Lace Manufactories', *The Penny Magazine* (26 March 1843), pp. 113, 115–120.

Anon, 'A Day at the Sheffield Cutlery-Works', *The Penny Magazine of the Society for the Diffusion of Useful Knowledge*, Vol. 13 (27 April 1844), pp. 161–168.

Anon, 'A Day at a Soap and Candle Factory', *Penny Magazine for the Diffusion of Useful Knowledge*, Vol. 11 (29 January 1842), pp. 41–47.

Anon, 'Electro-Deposition', *The National Encyclopaedia: A Dictionary of Universal Knowledge*, Vol. 5 (London: [n.p], c.1870), pp. 782–786.

Anon, 'The Falcon Glass-Works', in *The Busy Hives Around Us: A Variety of Trips and Visits to the Mine, the Workshop, and the Factory* (London: James Hogg and Sons, c.1850), pp. 165–168.

Anon, 'A Few Thoughts on Keys', *Cornhill Magazine*, Vol. 12 (November 1865), pp. 623–628.

Anon, 'Fraudulent Trade Marks', *Once a Week*, Vol. 8 (7 February 1863), pp. 177–179.

Anon, 'French Lace', *Bow Bells* (9 November 1894), p. 467.

Anon, 'A Glass Manufactory', pp. 197–201 [bound pamphlet].

Anon, 'Gloves', *All The Year Round*, Vol. 9 (27 June 1863), pp. 425, 428–430.

Anon, 'Help for Women', *National Magazine* (May 1861), pp. 32–34.

Anon, 'Honiton Lace', *The Gentleman's Magazine* (January 1871), pp. 164–171.

Anon, 'Joseph Rodgers & Sons, Limited', *The New Monthly Magazine*, Vol. 121 (July 1882), pp. 551–557.

Anon, 'Made in Germany', *The New Review*, Vol. 14 (March 1896), pp. 258–261.

Anon, 'A Midland Tour; XVII – Wolverhampton', *The Leisure Hour: A Family Journal of Instruction and Recreation* (20 July 1872), pp. 462–463.

Anon, 'Musgrave & Co. (Limited), Stable Fitting and Stove Manufacturers, Belfast, London, Manchester, and Paris', in *Wyman's Commercial Encyclopædia of Leading Manufacturers of Great Britain and Their Productions; Being a Guide to Merchant Buyers All Over the World* (London: Wyman, 1888), pp. 450–451.

Anon, 'Pin-Making (from Sir George Head's Home Tour)', *The Mirror*, Vol. 28 (9 July 1836), pp. 29–30.

Anon, 'Pins', *Belgravia: A London Magazine*, Vol. 6 (August 1868), pp. 300–302.
Anon, 'A Second Day at the Birmingham Factories', *Penny Magazine of the Society for the Diffusion of Useful Knowledge*, Vol. 13 (28 December 1844), pp. 501–502.
Anon, 'Sewing Machines', *All the Year Round*, Vol. 1 (new series) (27 March 1869), pp. 395–397.
Anon, 'William S. Burton, General Furnishing Ironmonger', *The Athenaeum*, no. 2171 (5 June 1869), p. 780.
Baines, Edward, *History of Cotton Manufacture in Great Britain* (London, 1835).
Baines, Edward, 'On the Woollen Manufacture of England; With Special Reference to the Leeds Clothing District', *Journal of the Statistical Society of London*, Vol. 22, no. 1 (March 1859), pp. 1–9, 11–14.
Beaver, Stanley H. 'The Potteries: A Study in the Evolution of a Cultural Landscape: Presidential Address', *Transactions and Papers (Institute of British Geographers)*, No. 34 (June 1964), pp. 1–31.
Capper, John, 'British Cotton', *Household Words*, Vol. 5, no. 106 (3 April 1852), pp. 51–54.
Capper, John, 'The Northern Wizard', *Household Words*, Vol. 3, no. 189 (5 November 1853), pp. 225–228.
Charles Chubb, *Chubb's Improved Patent Detector Lock* ([n. p.], 1832, 4pp.
Cox, Harold, 'How Real Axminster is Made – A Visit to the Only Factory in England', *Time: A Monthly Magazine* (October 1890), pp. 1067–1071.
Crookes, William, 'Preface', in Michael Faraday (ed.), *The Chemical History of a Candle: A Course of Lectures Delivered Before an Audience at the Royal Institution* (London: Chatto and Windus, 1875), pp. v–vii.
Crowquill, Alfred, 'The Service of Plate', *Temple Bar*, Vol. 20 (May 1867), pp. 272–277.
Dickens, Charles and Mark Lemon, 'A Paper-Mill', *Household Words*, Vol. 1 (31 August 1850), pp. 529–531.
Dickens, Charles and W. H. Wills, 'Spitalfields', *Household Words*, Vol. 3 (5 April 1851), pp. 25–30.
Disraeli, Benjamin, *Sybil; or, the Two Nations* (London: Henry Colburn, 1845).
Dodd, George, *Days at the Factories, or the Manufacturing Industries of Great Britain Described* [extract] (London, 1843).
Gaskell, Elizabeth, *North and South* (1855) (London: Smith, Elder, and Co., 1897).
Hatton, Joseph, 'Candle-Making', *The English Illustrated Magazine*, Vol. 105 (Jun 1892), pp. 703–712.
Heather-Bigg, Ada, 'Women and the Glove Trade', *The Nineteenth Century*, Vol. 30 (December 1891), pp. 939–944, 946–947.
Herbert, Luke, 'Glass', in *The Engineer's and Mechanics Encyclopeadia, Comprehending Practical Illustrations of the Machinery and Processes Employed in Every Description of Manufacture in the British Empire*, Vol. 1 (London: Thomas Kelly, 1836), pp. 635–639.
Hood, Thomas, 'The Song of the Shirt' *Punch* (1843).
Horne, Richard H., 'The Female School of Design in the Capital of the World', *Household Words*, Vol. 2 (15 March 1851), pp. 578–581.
Image: 'By Order of the Bath', *Pears Soap, Unilever Archives, ref. GB1752.AFP 12/3/1* [n.d.], Unilever Collections, Unilever Art, Archives and Records Management, Port Sunlight.
Image: 'Calico Printing', in Charles Tomlinson (ed.), *Tomlinson's Cyclopaedia of Useful Arts and Manufactures*, Vol. 2 (1852–1854), p. 279.

Image: 'Cotton Printing', in *The National Encyclopaedia: A Dictionary of Universal Knowledge*, Vol. 5 (London: [n.p.], c. 1870).

Image: 'Fish-slice and Fork, and Dessert-knife (Messrs. J. Rodgers & Sons, of Sheffield)', in *Art Journal Illustrated Catalogue of the Industry of All Nations* (London: Bradbury & Evans, George Virtue, n.d.), p. 278.

Image: James McNeill Whistler, 'Price's Candle-Works' 1876/77, The Metropolitan Museum of Art.

Image: Joseph Rodgers & Sons, selections from the 'Old Table Day Book' (date approx. late 1800s), Museums Sheffield.

Image: 'Lock' [Plate], *The National Encyclopaedia: A Dictionary of Universal Knowledge*, Vol. 8 (London: n.p., c. 1870).

Image: 'Vinolia Soap', *Unilever Collections*, Unilever Art, Archives and Records Management, Port Sunlight, Archive ref. GB1752. AFP 12/4/125 [c. 1890].

Image: Wallpaper, *The Art Journal Illustrated Catalogue: The Industry of All Nations* (London, 1851), pp. 129, 143.

Image: 'Weaving Looms', *The National Encyclopaedia: A Dictionary of Universal Knowledge*, Vol. 4 (London: [n.p.], c. 1870).

Image: 'Wool Machinery', in *The National Encyclopaedia: A Dictionary of Universal Knowledge*, Vol. 4 (London: [n.p.], c. 1870).

Martineau, Harriet, 'Household Scenery', *Household Words*, Vol. 5 (14 August 1852), pp. 513–519.

Martineau, Harriet, 'How to Get Paper', *Household Words*, Vol. 10 (28 October 1854), pp. 241–245.

Martineau, Harriet, 'Needles', *Household Words*, Vol. 4 (28 February 1852), pp. 540–546.

Martineau, Harriet, 'Rainbow Making', *Household Words*, Vol. 4 (14 February 1852), pp. 485–490.

Marx, Karl, 'The Fetishism of Commodities and the Secret Thereof', in *Capital* (1867) (London: Swan Sonnenschein and Co. Ltd., 1902), pp. 41–50.

Moisley, H. A. 'The Industrial and Urban Development of the North Staffordshire Conurbation', *Transactions and Papers, Institute of British Geographers*, Vol. 17 (1951), pp. 151–165.

Mokyr, Joel, *The Enlightened Economy: An Economic History of Britain, 1700–1850* (New Haven: Yale University Press, 2009).

Morfit, Campbell, *A Treatise on Chemistry Applied to the Manufacture of Soap and Candles* (Philadelphia: [n.p], 1856).

Morris, William, 'Textile Fabrics' [1884] in William Morris (ed.), *Architecture, Industry and Wealth: Collected Papers* (London: Longmans, Green S and Co., 1902), pp. 133–163.

Palmer, Henry J., 'Cutlery and Cutlers at Sheffield', *The English Illustrated Magazine*, Vol. 11 (August 1884), pp. 667–669.

Paterson, David, *The Colour Printing of Carpet Yarns: A Useful Manual for Colour-Chemists and Textile Printers* (London: Scott and Greenwood, 1900).

Playfair, Lyon, 'On Patents and the New Patent Bill', *Nineteenth Century* (April 1877), pp. 317–319, 321–323, 325–326.

Porter, G. R., 'On the Manufacture of Crown-Glass, Broad Glass, and Bottle Glass', in *Treatise on the Origin, Progressive Improvement, and Present State of the Manufacture of Porcelain and Glass* (London: Longman, Brown and Green, 1832), pp. 182–187.

Professor Archer, 'On the Progress of Our Art Industries: Textile Manufacturers – The Carpet Works of Messrs. J. Templeton & Co., Glasgow', *The Art Journal* (June 1875), pp. 177–178.

Richardson, B. W., 'Health at Home', *Good Words*, Vol. 21 (January 1880), pp. 98–101.

Sidney, Samuel, 'A Ladies' Warehouse', *Household Words*, Vol. 12 (27 October 1855), pp. 301–305.

Simcox, Edith, 'Eight Years of Co-operative Shirtmaking', *The Nineteenth Century*, Vol. 15 (June 1884), pp. 1037–1054.

Slugg, J. T., *Reminiscences of Manchester Fifty Years Ago* (Manchester, 1881).

Smiles, Samuel, *Industrial Biography: Iron Workers and Tool Makers* (London: John Murray, 1863).

Tildesley, J. C., 'A Chapter on Locks and Keys', *Once a Week*, Vol. 4 (9 November 1867), pp. 560–563.

Wood, Henry, *Mrs Halliburton's Troubles* [1862] (London and New York: The Walter Scott Publishing Co., n.d.).

Wynne, Deborah, 'Arnold Bennett and Material Culture', in John Shapcott (ed.), *A Companion to Arnold Bennett* (Leek: Churnet Valley Press, 2015), pp. 193–207.

Secondary sources

Alexander, Lynn M., *Women, Work and Representation: Needlewomen in Victorian Art and Literature* (Athens, OH: Ohio University Press, 2003).

Anon., 'Social, Sanitary and Municipal Progress', *Household Narrative: A Monthly Supplement to Household Words* (May 1851), pp. 112–115.

Anon., 'Locks and Picklocks', *Chambers's Edinburgh Journal* (Dec 25, 1852), pp. 405–8.

Anon. (1866) 'The Resources, Products, and Industrial History of Birmingham and the Midland Hardware District', *Birmingham Daily Post*, 3 September [n.p.] *British Library Newspapers, Part 1*, accessed 15th August 2018.

Anon, 'Paper and Pins', D. F. Tayler & Co, <http://collections.vam.ac.uk/item/O361504/pins-d-f-tayler/> [accessed 6th April 2018].

Anon, 'Visits to British Manufactories', *The Art-Union* (Jan 1847), pp. 29–31.

Anon, *The Art Journal Illustrated Catalogue: The Industry of all Nations 1851* (London: Bradbury and Evans, 1851).

Anon, 'The Carpet and its History', *Sharpe's London Magazine of Entertainment and Instruction for General Reading* (Jul 1858), pp. 269–271.

Armstrong, Isobel, *Victorian Glassworlds: Glass Culture and the Imagination 1830–1880* (Oxford: Oxford University Press, 2008).

Auerbach, Jeffrey A. and Peter H. Hoffenberg (eds.), *Britain, the Empire, and the World at the Great Exhibition of 1851* (London: Routledge, 2008).

Babbage, Charles, *On the Economy of Machinery and Manufactures* [1832] (digital rept. Cambridge: Cambridge University Press, 2009).

Beaudry, Mary C., *Findings: The Material Culture of Needlework and Sewing* (New Haven, CT, and London: Yale University Press, 2006).

Beaver, Stanley H., 'The Potteries: A Study in the Evolution of a Cultural Landscape: Presidential Address', *Transactions and Papers (Institute of British Geographers)*, no. 34 (June 1964), pp. 1–31.

Beckert, Sven, *The Empire of Cotton: A Global History* (New York: Vintage Books, 2014).

Beeton, Isabella (ed.), *Beeton's Book of Household Management* (London, S. O. Beeton, 1861).

Berg, Maxine, *The Age of Manufactures, 1700–1820: Industry, Innovation and Work in Britain* (London: Routledge, 1994).

Berg, Maxine, *Luxury and Pleasure in Eighteenth-Century Britain* (Oxford: Oxford University Press, 2007).

Bizup, Joseph, *Manufacturing Culture: Vindications of Early Victorian Industry* (Charlottesville and London: University of Virginia Press, 2003).

Broomfield, Andrea, *Food and Cooking in Victorian England: A History* (Westport: Greenwood Publishing Group, 2007).

Cantor, Geoffrey, 'Emotional Reactions to the Great Exhibition of 1851', *Journal of Victorian Culture*, 20: 2 (2015): 230–245.

Chambers, J.D., *The Workshop of the World: British Economic History from 1820–1880* (London: Oxford University Press, 1961).

Churchill, David, 'The Spectacle of Security: Lock-Picking Competitions and the Security Industry in mid-Victorian Britain', *History Workshop Journal*, 80:1 (Autumn 2015), pp. 52–74.

Cohen, Deborah, *Household Gods: The British and their Possessions* (New Haven and London: Yale University Press, 2006).

Crawford, Iain, '"Faithful Sympathy": Dickens, the *Edinburgh Review*, and Editing *Household Words*', *Victorian Periodicals Review*, 44:1 (Spring 2011): 42–68.

de Réamur, René-Antoine Ferchault, *Art de l'epinglier* (1761).

Dickens, Charles, *Great Expectations*, Vol. II (London: Chapman and Hall, 1861).

Disraeli, Benjamin, *Sybil; or, the Two Nations*, Vol. II (London: Henry Colburn, 1845).

Dobson Collet, Collet, *History of the Taxes on Knowledge: Their Origins and Repeal* [1899] (London: Watts & Co, 1933).

Elliott, Simon, 'Reading by Artificial Light in the Victorian Age', in Matthew Bradley and Juliet John (eds.), *Reading and the Victorians* (Farnham: Ashgate, 2015), pp. 15–30.

Eskilson, Stephen, *The Age of Glass: A Cultural History of Glass in Modern and Contemporary Architecture* (London and New York: Bloomsbury Academic, 2018).

Flanders, Judith, *Inside the Victorian Home* (New York: W. W. Norton & Company, 2004).

Flanders, Judith, *Consuming Passions: Leisure and Pleasure in Victorian Britain* (London: Harper Collins, 2006).

Forty, Adrian, *Objects of Desire: Design and Society since 1750* (London: Pantheon Books, 1986).

Freedgood, Elaine, 'What Objects Know: Circulation, Omniscience and the Comedy of Dispossession in Victorian It-Narratives', *Journal of Victorian Culture*, 15: 1 (April 2010), 83–100.

Freedgood, Elaine, 'Cultures of Commodities, Cultures of Things' in *The Victorian World* (ed.) Martin Hewitt (London: Routledge, 2012), pp. 225–240.

Gaskell, Elizabeth, *Cranford* (London, Macmillan & Co., 1892).

Griffin, Emma. *A Short History of the British Industrial Revolution* (Basingstoke: Palgrave Macmillan, 2010).

Gurney, Peter, 'An Appropriated Space: The Great Exhibition, the Crystal Palace and the Working Class' in Louise Purbrick (ed.), *The Great Exhibition of 1851* (Manchester: Manchester University Press, 2001), pp. 114–145.

Gurney, Peter, *Wanting and Having: Popular Politics and Liberal Consumerism in England, 1830–1870* (Manchester: Manchester University Press, 2015).

Habib, Vanessa, 'The Printed Tapestry Carpet: the Pioneering Work of Richard Whytock of Edinburgh, 1784–1857', *Review of Scottish Culture* (Vol. 14), pp. 14–17.

Hamlett, Jane. *Material Relations: Domestic Interiors and Middle-Class Families in England, 1850–1910* (Manchester: Manchester University Press, 2010).

Hansard, Gladstone repeals soap duty (1853): https://api.parliament.uk/historic-hansard/commons/1853/apr/18/the-financial-statement-the-budget#S3V0125P0_18530418_HOC_15

Harskamp, Jaap, 'In Praise of Pins: from Tool to Metaphor', *History Workshop Journal*, 70 (2010), pp. 47–66.

Helsinger, Elizabeth K., Robin L. Sheets and William Veeder (eds.), *The Woman Question: Society and Literature in Britain and America, 1837–1883*, Vol. 2 (Manchester: Manchester University Press, 1983).

Henchman, Anna, 'Tallow Candles and Meaty Air in *Bleak House*', *19: Interdisciplinary Studies in the Long Nineteenth Century*, 25, <doi: 10.16995/ntn.794> [accessed 12th January 2018].

Higgins, David, and Geoffrey Tweedale, 'Asset or Liability? Trade Marks in the Sheffield Cutlery and Tool Trades', *Business History*, 37:3 (1995), pp. 1–27.

Holmes, Rachel, *Eleanor Marx: A Life* (London: Bloomsbury, 2014).

Horowitz, Evan, 'Industrialism and the Victorian Novel' in *The Oxford Handbook of the Victorian Novel* Lisa Rodensky (ed.) (Oxford: Oxford University Press, 2013): 357–375.

Huett, Lorna, 'Among the Unknown Public: *Household Words*, *All the Year Round* and the Mass-Market Weekly Periodical in the Mid-Nineteenth Century', *Victorian Periodicals Review*, 38:1 (Spring 2005): 61–82.

Hughes, Kathryn, *The Short Life & Long Times of Mrs Beeton* (London: Fourth Estate, 2011).

Jenkins, David, (ed.) *The Cambridge History of Western Textiles* vol. II, David Jenkins (Cambridge: Cambridge University Press, 2003).

Kelley, Victoria, *Soap and Water: Cleanliness, Dirt, and the Working Classes in Victorian and Edwardian Britain* (London: IB Tauris, 2010).

Ketabgian, Tamara, *The Lives of Machines: The Industrial Imaginary in Victorian Literature and Culture* (Ann Arbor: University of Michigan Press and the University of Michigan Library, 2011).

Kidd, Alan, *Manchester: A History* 4th ed. (Lancaster: Carnegie Publishing, 2011).

Livesey, Joseph (ed.), *The Moral Reformer, and Protestor Against the Vices, Abuses, and Corruptions of the Age*, vol. 2, issue 4 (Apr 1832), 118.

Logan, Thad, *The Victorian Parlor* (Cambridge: Cambridge University Press, 2001).

Lohrli, Anne, '*Household Words* and its Office Book', *The Princeton University Library Chronicle* 26:1 (Autumn 1964), pp. 27–47.

Marx, Karl, *Capital: A Critical Analysis of Capitalist Production*, Vol. II, trans. by Samuel Moore and Edward Aveling, ed. Frederick Engels (London: Swan Sonnershein, Lowrey, & Co., 1887).

Marx, Karl, 'Economic and Philosophical Manuscripts', in *Early Writings*, trans. by Rodney Livingstone and Gregor Benton (London: Penguin, 1992), pp. 279–400.

Maw, Peter, Terry Wyke and Alan Kidd, 'Canals, Rivers, and the Industrial City: Manchester's industrial waterfront, 1790–1850', *Economic History Review* 65: 4 (2012): 1495–1523.

Message, Kylie and Ewan Johnston, 'The World Within the City: The Great Exhibition, Race, Class and Social Reform' in *Britain, the Empire, and the World at the Great Exhibition of 1851*, Jeffrey A. Auerbach and Peter H. Hoffenberg (eds) (London: Routledge, 2008), pp. 27–46.

Moisley, H. A. 'The Industrial and Urban Development of the North Staffordshire Conurbation'. *Transactions and Papers*, Institute of British Geographers, vol. 17 (1951), pp. 151–65.

Mokyr, Joel, *The Enlightened Economy: An Economic History of Britain 1700–1850* (New Haven and London: Yale University Press, 2009).

Morley, Henry, 'A House Full of Horrors', *Household Words*, Vol. 6 (4 December 1852), pp. 265–270.

Mosley, Stephen, 'Fresh Air and Foul: The Role of the Open Fireplace in Ventilating the British Home, 1837–1910, *Planning Perspectives*, 18:1 (2003), pp. 1–21.

Murtha, Hillary, 'Man, Machine and Refined Dining in Victorian America', in *Food for Thought: Essays on Eating and Culture*, Lawrence C. Rubin (ed.) (Jefferson: McFarland & Company, Inc., Publishers, 2008), pp. 16–30.

Otter, Chris, *The Victorian Eye: A Political History of Light and Vision in Britain, 1800–1910* (Chicago: University of Chicago Press, 2008).

Plotz, John, *Portable Property: Victorian Culture on the Move* (Princeton: Princeton University Press, 2008).

Price, Leah, *How to Do Things with Books in Victorian Britain* (Princeton, NJ: Princeton University Press, 2012).

Richards, Thomas. *The Commodity Culture of Victorian England: Advertising and Spectacle*. (Stanford, CA: Stanford University Press, 1990).

Riello, Giorgio, *Cotton: The Fabric that Made the Modern World* (Cambridge: Cambridge University Press, 2013).

Ruskin, George, *General Statement Explaining the Nature and Purpose of St George's Guild* (Kent: G. Allen, 1882).

Shears, Jonathon ed. *The Great Exhibition, 1851: A Sourcebook*. (Manchester: Manchester University Press, 2017).

Skrabec, Quentin R., *The Metallurgic Age: The Victorian Flowering of Invention and Industrial Science* (North Carolina: McFarland & Company, Inc, 2006).

Smith, Adam *The Wealth of Nations*. (London, W. Strahan and T. Cadell, 1776).

Stavenow-Hidemark, Elisabet, 'Textile Design and Furnishings, c. 1780–1914' in David Jenkins, (ed.) *The Cambridge History of Western Textiles* vol. II, (CUP, 2003), pp. 860–881.

Stonewell, N. S., 'Popular Carpets', *The Decorator and Furnisher*, 11:2 (Nov 1887), pp. 50–51.

Sussman, Herbert, *Victorian Technologies: Invention, Innovation and the Rise of the Machine* (California: Praeger, 2009).

Tayler, D. F. (c. 1840), Paper of Pins. http://collections.vam.ac.uk/item/O361504/pins-d-f-tayler/

Thwaite, B. H., 'The Commercial War Between Germany and England', *The Nineteenth Century: A Monthly Review* (March 1877), pp. 925–931.

Trentmann, Frank, *The Empire of Things: How We Became a World of Consumers from the Fifteenth century to the Twenty-first* (London: Penguin, 2017).

'Tumbler', *Oxford English Dictionary Online*, <www.oed.com/view/Entry/207355?redirectedFrom=tumbler#eid> [accessed 21st April 2020].

Tweedale, Geoffrey, *Steel City: Entrepreneurship, Strategy, and Technology in Sheffield 1743–1993* (Oxford: Oxford University Press, 1995).

Waters, Catherine. *Commodity Culture in Dickens's* Household Words: *The Social Life of Goods*. Aldershot, UK: Ashgate, 2008.

Wynne, Deborah, 'Reading Victorian Rags: Recycling, Redemption and Dickens's Ragged Children', *Journal of Victorian Culture*, Vol. 20, no. 1 (2015), pp. 34–49.

Wynne, Deborah. "Responses to the 1851 Great Exhibition in Household Words." *The Dickensian* 455.97, Part 3 (Winter 2001–2002): 228–234.

Wynne, Deborah. *The Sensation Novel and the Victorian Family Magazine* (Basingstoke: Palgrave Macmillan, 2001).

Young, Paul. *Globalization and the Great Exhibition: The Victorian New World Order*. (Basingstoke, UK: Palgrave, 2009).

INTRODUCTION TO VOLUME IV

The industrial revolution and the mass production of commodities

Between 1750 and 1850, Britain's Industrial Revolution brought about 'deep and irreversible' changes, including the mass production of goods on an unprecedented scale (Mokyr, 2009: 4–5; see also Jenkins, 2003: 718). Practical science combined with entrepreneurship flourished during this period, resulting in machine-made goods being produced at a rate greatly surpassing the capacities of hand labour. This, added to the availability of skilled workers, a flexible credit system, good transport networks, and an empire from which raw materials could be sourced cheaply and markets for goods found, ensured the ideal conditions for the proliferation of manufactured objects (see Maw, Wyke & Kidd, 2012: 1495, and Riello, 2013: 285). Understandings of the Industrial Revolution as the rapid expansion of technology and the development of factory production have, until recently, tended to overshadow the equally significant developments in consumerism which characterised this period. Vast distribution networks channelled mass-produced commodities from the factory to the shop, transforming people's lives in terms of increased access to the ownership of objects (Gurney, 2015: 3–4; Trentmann, 2017; and Waters, 2008). Indeed, because mass production was matched by mass consumption, many contemporary observers, such as Andrew Ure and Edward Baines, saw before them 'social progress' in action, 'a stimulus to national culture', which appeared to herald a new economic miracle (Bizup, 2003: 25; see also Gurney, 2001: 116 and Stavenow-Hidemark, 2003: 860). Utopian visions such as these did not materialise, however, for Britain's industrial project was 'a period of painful transition' beset by problems; nevertheless, there were benefits for some of the labouring poor in terms of a slow but steady increase in living standards (Griffin, 2010: 161). Such improvements meant that more people than ever before had the potential to consume non-essential goods (see Freedgood, 2012: 228).

Through its careful selection of primary sources pertaining to the cultural role of manufactured objects, this volume contributes a unique insight into the way Victorians responded to the production and consumption of manufactured goods. Mass production had significant social and cultural consequences; indeed, the geography of Britain changed dramatically with previously small settlements such as Manchester and Birmingham becoming, by the early nineteenth century, globally significant cities dominated by factories, textile mills, workshops and

DOI: 10.4324/9781315400105-1

retail centres, all visible symbols of the power of commodities to create wealth. Indeed, Manchester in particular, the home of the nation's massive cotton industry, 'acquired an almost mythical status as the emblem of a new order of things' (Kidd, 2011: 14). The mass production of ordinary objects such as cotton, cups and saucers, glass, soap, candles, buttons, pins, cutlery and paper, often cheap and usually available to consumers from all but the very poorest sections of society, led to changes in dress, hygiene, domestic habits, literacy and taste. Indeed, working-class people, exploited as they were in a fluctuating capitalist marketplace and frequently suffering poor working conditions for much of the century, were nevertheless able to make some improvements to their lives by buying the cheap goods they were collectively involved in producing (see Horowitz, 2013: 365). It is unsurprising that Victorian writers found the dynamic processes of industrial change and new developments in consumer culture a source of fascination, and the making of simple, everyday objects appeared to be almost magical to some who visited the factories, with many references to 'alchemy' at the sight of raw materials, such as rags, being transformed into white paper or evil-smelling brews of chemicals being processed into bright dyes for fabrics or fragrant soaps. Similarly, the fact that workshops and mills appeared to turn out incessantly vast quantities of goods for home consumption and export was noted as miraculous by some observers. 'Industrial tourists' or 'factory tourists', those writers, often London-based, who travelled to industrial regions to report on how objects were made, produced an abundance of popular 'process articles', Dickens' term for essays describing in detail the processes of manufacture (Waters, 2008: 85, and Armstrong, 2008: 19–36). The periodical press had itself undergone considerable expansion in the 1840s and 1850s, and the 'process article' was a staple of many new family magazines, along with serialised novels, short stories and features on current affairs (see Wynne, 2001: 1–22), suggesting that such articles were informative leisure-time reading. This volume sets out to convey the considerable range of views expressed in nineteenth-century print culture on the subjects of consumerism, material culture and the processes of manufacturing.

There were inevitably political consequences ensuing from the rapid social changes that occurred in the Victorian period, and a number of the sources selected in this volume refer to debates surrounding free trade; factory reform; child labour; health and safety standards; slave labour in the United States; anxieties surrounding female labour outside the home; environmental damage; the decline of traditional working practices and crafts; along with the growth of trade unionism, highlighting the fact that each object produced had associations with stories of exploited workers, shifting global trade networks, government levies and a radicalised workforce. Some of the discussions of manufactured objects in the periodical press and other print media combine a sense of wonder at how objects are manufactured with a sense of dismay at the political, social, environmental and cultural costs of mass production. As Armstrong has argued in relation to the writing of industrial tourists, their 'narrative[s] of progress had to be reconciled with a narrative of suffering' (Armstrong, 2008: 19).

Interest in manufacturing processes and the objects produced was intensified around the time of the Great Exhibition of 1851, a display of 'The Works of Industry of all Nations' housed in the so-called 'Crystal Palace' in London's Hyde Park. The Earl of Carlisle, in May 1851 when the exhibition opened, spoke of it as 'a shrine to labour' (Anon, 1851: 115); more recently Capuana has argued that the thousands of 'industrially produced products at the Crystal Palace' offered a 'comprehensive display of contemporary machine culture' (Capuana, 2015: 204). Many of the sources in this volume celebrate the power of machinery and the efficiency of workers, inventors and entrepreneurs, as well as the cornucopia of goods produced. Despite its ostensible aim to offer a peaceful bringing together of all nations to celebrate material culture in all its forms, the Great Exhibition, whose organisational committee was headed by Prince Albert, appeared to some commentators, particularly those from abroad, to be largely a showcase for Britain as 'the workshop of the world' (Chambers, 1961; see also Richards, 1990; Shears, 2017; Wynne, 2001–2002; and Young, 2009). For many, however, it was the idea of 'consumption, rather than production' that attracted people to the exhibition, as though the Crystal Palace was a vast shopping emporium, despite the 'goods' on display not being for sale (Message & Johnston, 2008: 42). Between May and October 1851, there were over 2 million visitors (see Cantor, 2015). Despite its successful presentation of Britain as the world leader in the mass production of goods, the exhibition also exposed the poor quality of British design, an issue which is discussed in some of the sources included in this volume; indeed, the Great Exhibition showed that most 'designs of English applied arts, including wallpaper and textiles, were regarded as beneath contempt' (Stavenow-Hidemark, 2003: 873). Nevertheless, this was seen as one of the few shortcomings of the British exhibits; the verdict of the world in 1851 was that British machine culture was second to none (see Gurney, 2001: 114–116, and Chambers, 1961).

Many of the texts from the 1840s and 1850s collected in this volume are largely celebratory in tone, and most have been chosen because they reveal the widespread interest in how ordinary things were manufactured. Later features are more ambivalent about mass production, and, from the 1860s onwards, a nostalgia for hand-made and antique goods is evinced. The selection of sources here includes only a very small number of the texts available, and inevitably many interesting and relevant sources have had to be omitted for reasons of space. The manufactured objects we have chosen to represent in this volume are items in general use in most Victorian households, rather than unusual or specialised products. The highlighting of ordinary domestic objects seemed to us a priority for two reasons: firstly, the majority of 'process' texts and accounts of industrial tourism focus on the manufacture of familiar things. Secondly, a focus on ordinary things reveals a snapshot of human-object relations at this period. The value of the sources selected here is that they offer information which is often missing from later histories of the Industrial Revolution and Victorian consumer culture. Few general readers today demand detailed descriptions of manufacturing processes, and recent histories of the period tend to examine the bigger picture of Victorian manufacturing culture, rather than how specific items were made (see Armstrong, 2008: 20). Yet Victorian readers, particularly between 1840 and 1870, possessed an insatiable desire to understand the science behind what often appeared to be the mysterious processes of industrial production. This resulted in an enormous number of 'process' articles appearing in popular weekly and monthly periodicals devoted to showing how to manufacture a candle, or machine-made lace, or locks and keys, carpets, cigarettes, soap, paper, silks, ceramics, sewing machines, wall-paper and so on. Indeed, no object was too humble to be ignored, and many books were published with titles such as *Days at the Factories* (1843); *The Busy Hives Around Us: A Variety of Trips and Visits to the Mine, Workshop, and the Factory* (c. 1850); and *The Romance of Manufacture* (1910), suggesting both the possibility of pleasurable tourism combined with a sense of wonder.

The majority of sources in this volume were first published in Victorian periodicals. Some popular weekly magazines aimed at a broad readership, such as Charles Dickens' *Household Words*, established in 1850, and its successor *All the Year Round*, established in 1859, along with the *Penny Magazine of the Society for the Diffusion of Useful Knowledge*, edited by Charles Knight in the 1840s, were particularly keen to represent and explain to their readers the new age of mass production, its various processes and the characteristics of the objects manufactured. This has resulted in a high proportion of articles from these magazines in our selection. As Iain Crawford has explained, *Household Words* was 'committed to demonstrating the "Romance" to be found "in all familiar things"', including mass-produced consumable objects (Crawford, 2011: 42; see also Huett, 2005, and Waters, 2008: 16–17).[1] The journalist, political economist and novelist Harriet Martineau, an advocate of free trade and champion of the dignity of labour, was a prolific contributor of 'process' articles to *Household Words*. Waters argues that Martineau 'sought to restore the history of the production of a commodity, as if to combat the process of its fetishization, seeing in the objects described the labour invested in their manufacture' (Waters, 2008: 85). Among the popular periodicals represented in our selection (other than the previously mentioned *Household Words*, *All The Year Round* and *The Penny Magazine*) are *Once A Week*; *Belgravia*; *The Nineteenth Century*; *The Leisure Hour: A Family Journal of Instruction and Recreation*; *The New Monthly Magazine*; *Good Words*; *Temple Bar*; *The Gentleman's Magazine* and *Bow Bells*. Also included are extracts from non-fiction books, novels, poetry, encyclopaedia entries, pamphlets and advertisements, along with images. The sources we have chosen appeared between the 1830s and the early 1900s, thus representing the whole of the Victorian period, and are presented chronologically in each section in order to show how the discussion of specific items developed over time, as well as how they were represented in different media and contexts.

Manufactured objects in Victorian Britain: the sources

The sources are divided under four main headings: 'The context of manufacturing in Victorian Britain'; 'Textiles': 'Fabrics', 'Clothing', 'Carpets' and 'Paper'; 'Metal goods': 'Pins and needles', 'Cutlery', 'Locks and keys' and 'Fire

Ironmongery'; and 'Household goods': 'Ceramics', 'Glassware', 'Plate', 'Soap' and 'Candles'. These categories cover the majority of household items familiar to most Victorians (see Logan, 2001, and Hamlett, 2010). Missing from the selection are accounts of specialised, small-scale manufactured items, such as jewellery, ornaments and art objects, items which feature in other volumes in this series. However, a few specialised goods, such as toys and musical instruments feature, albeit briefly and in passing. There is inevitably some crossover between these categories, with some extracts offering different, yet related, perspectives on the same item. Also included is a selection of images from magazines, books, encyclopaedias and advertisements which help to show the ubiquity of visual representations of manufactured items during this period.

The introductory selection of sources, 'The context of manufacturing in Victorian Britain', reveals some of the key debates surrounding the manufacture of goods. They include discussions on free trade ('The Velveteen Correspondence' in *Punch*, 1843); the inadequacies of British design ('The Female School of Design in the Capital of the World' in *Household Words*, 1851); the processes of invention and patenting ('Sewing Machines' in *All The Year Round*, 1869, and 'On Patents and the New Patents Bill' in *Nineteenth Century*, 1877); the factory system (Dodd's *Days at the Factories*, 1843); issues relating to political economy (the extract from Marx's *Capital*, 1867); and gender ('Help for Women', *National Magazine*, 1861). This selection of texts is designed to show that complex political, legal and cultural issues were involved in the production and consumption of manufactured objects and that developments in the quality of lived experience of material culture were a major preoccupation of many British writers.

Responses to industrial production differed considerably, depending on factors such as an individual's class position, political views and economic interests. Ketabgian argues that while some people associated machines with 'sterility, alienation, and dehumanization', others rejected the idea that they were 'lifeless, predictable, and unidimensional . . . not simply reductive material objects' and saw them as contributing to 'habits, feelings, communities, and subjectivities' (2011: 2–3). This section indicates the awareness of manufactured objects as not only important to the British economy but also able to convey political messages, signify identities and evoke strong emotions. Among the psychological impacts of mass-produced commodities is the tendency to fetishise them, as the extract from Karl Marx's *Capital* (1867) reveals in which he critiques the ways in which a pseudo-religious significance is conferred upon objects, while the labour that went into their manufacture is elided (see Freedgood, 2012: 229). Among the items referred to in this section are fabrics, sewing machines, bleaches and dyes; however, most of the sources have been selected because they emphasise the unusual and sometimes unforeseen effects of manufactured objects and the cultural and political debates in which they are implicated.

The second section of the volume, 'Textiles', including 'Fabrics', 'Clothing', 'Carpets' and 'Paper', focuses on the importance of the textile industry. Britain's place as the first industrial nation was based on its massive output of cotton textiles, a point which cannot be overemphasised (Jenkins, 2003: 717). Previously, woollen textile production had been the nation's staple industry. However, by the nineteenth century, cotton textiles, made mainly in Lancashire, rapidly took over as the mainstay of the British economy and export industry. As Sven Beckert maintains, 'The factory itself was an invention of the cotton industry', going on to claim that 'cotton provides the key to understanding the modern world' (Beckert, 2014: xvii). Certainly, many of the sources in this section illustrate the international importance of the cotton goods made in Manchester and other Lancashire towns. However, also included here are sources discussing woollen goods made in Yorkshire, which remained significant despite the dominance of 'King Cotton', as well as sources focused on lace, another traditional British product which had undergone a major transformation when cheaper, machine-made lace came onto the market.

The section on 'Fabrics' also includes an extract from the work of the socialist writer, textile artist and manufacturer William Morris, who established Morris & Co. in 1861 to design and make artistic home furnishings, most notably textiles. Although Morris largely believed industrialisation to be a 'tragedy' because workers were alienated from their labour (see Stavenow-Hidemark, 2003: 874), Morris & Co.'s beautifully designed, handcrafted goods were actually too expensive for all but the wealthiest consumers. The extract here from Morris' essay 'Textiles' helps to show the ethical and economic tensions generated by a culture based on mass production and the mass consumption of textiles, where workers tended inexhaustible machines rather than used their skills and imagination to make products by hand. Morris influenced a reaction to machine-made goods in the wealthy middle classes, who sought his beautiful but expensive products and despised cheap, factory-made goods. Yet, the fact that the majority of the population could only afford mass-produced goods was central to Morris' awareness of the 'tragedy' of the industrial age.

Other sources in the 'Textiles' section include discussions of many subsidiary branches of Victorian textile manufacturing, namely, the clothing trades, carpet making and the manufacture of paper from rags. A scarcity of rags in the 1850s led to a serious paper shortage, and the importance of recycling, not only in terms of paper manufacture but also of wool into the cheaper fabrics of mungo and shoddy, is featured in some of the extracts in this section. We have also included here discussions of the manufacture of ribbons, gloves, shirts, luxury carpets and cheaper machine-made ones, wallpaper and cardboard.

The third section, 'Metal goods', which includes 'Pins and needles', 'Cutlery', 'Locks and keys' and 'Fire ironmongery', confirms that iron was one of industrial Britain's most significant raw materials. It was transformed into buildings, bridges and structures associated with the railway network, as well as consumer goods (Sussman, 2009: 28). The Crystal Palace's dazzling lightness was achieved through the use of plate glass contained within a cast-iron skeleton, and later in the century iron monuments such as the Eiffel Tower, built for the International Exhibition of Paris in 1889, reveal this metal's profound importance in terms of both art and engineering across the century (Skrabec, 2013: 51). The sources reprinted here, however, feature metal objects found in domestic rather than civic contexts, and most tend to focus on the relationship between British innovation and British domestic habits and tastes.

The metallurgical industries were mainly centred in Birmingham and the Midlands. Birmingham's workshops produced nails, brass tubes, metal bedsteads, steel pens and other metal objects. Elsewhere, Sheffield was the centre of cutlery, scythes and sickle manufacture, while Redditch was chiefly known for producing the best needles, pins and fishhooks. The 'process' narrative is well represented here, with many of the sources offering detailed accounts of each manufacturing stage from raw material to finished product. Machine-assisted production lines made the speed and volume of production dizzying. Many writers profess astonishment at the proficiency of the production process. Pins, for example, were produced in the tens of thousands every day, while Sheffield consumed raw materials by the tonne daily to meet the demand for cutlery.

Adam Smith's *The Wealth of Nations* (1776) used pin manufacture to prove the benefits of the division of labour in terms of increased productivity, a point later emphasised by Charles Babbage in his *On the Economy of Machinery and Manufactures* (1832). Production lines, in which an item passed through a series of sequential operations, meant that workers making the same object could vary from unskilled, temporary labourers to skilled artisans. The hierarchy of skilled and unskilled labour was usually gendered; many of the writers witness people of both sexes and all ages working in Britain's factories, with no account presenting this as remarkable. All of the objects discussed here were manufactured to meet most levels of household income. Even as early as 1844, with significant increases in manufacturing output yet to come, the *Penny Magazine* is firm in contending that only the very poorest households would be without a knife. Fire-resistant metal goods were essential in every household, dependent as they were upon burning coal for heat and cooking; as well as cooking utensils (see Broomfield, 2007), coal scuttles and 'companion sets' consisting of small shovels, fire tongs and pokers were sold to aid the tending of multiple household hearths. Locks and keys of many different designs were manufactured en masse to allay society's fears of burglary, and company names like Chubb and Bramah rapidly became widely understood as shorthand for the word 'lock'. One intriguing form of public fascination with manufactured items was the Victorian craze of competitive lock picking, whereby lock manufacturers challenged people to pick their locks for prizes. In 1852, *Chambers's Edinburgh Journal* observed that lock making – and lock breaking – had become 'invested with a dignity not before accorded to it: it has risen almost to the rank of a science' (see Anon, 1852: p. 405).

As well as home security, the increase in the availability of household goods from the mid-Victorian period led to anxieties about their correct usage. *Beeton's Book of Household Management* (1861) is clear on how a table should be dressed. Each diner must have butter knife, a table knife and fork, and a dessert knife and fork, while a carving knife and fork as well as a fish slice and gravy spoon should be available at the head of the table (see Beeton, 1861: 905). Yet even the comprehensive Beeton is silent on how the cutlery should look or what materials are most stylish or durable. Consumers often relied on advertising and price to understand which goods were 'tasteful' and which were 'vulgar'. Apprehensions around dining are humorously strewn through Victorian literature; for example, how one deploys a knife and fork can reveal much about conceptions of social class. When Mary Smith, Miss Matty and Miss Pole dine with Mr Holbrook in Elizabeth Gaskell's novel *Cranford* (1851–1853), originally published in *Household Words*, they 'looked at each other in dismay; we had only two-pronged, black-handled forks. It is true, the steel was as bright as silver; but what were we to do?' (Gaskell, 1892: 61). Cutlery fashions could thus contribute to anxieties about genteel behaviour.

Alongside security and etiquette, writers took the opportunity to discuss other national anxieties via the country's manufactured objects. Needles and pins are disposable in a way unique to this collection; it is perhaps no coincidence that they are consistently associated with women and their work. Needlework was evidence of desirable feminine industry, which is represented here in the extract from an it-narrative, *The Story of a Needle* (1878). As Elaine Freedgood has observed, it-narratives helped the Victorians 'come to terms with new ideas about the commonalities between subjects and objects' (Freedgood, 2010: 83), for the object narrates the story from its own perspective, thus defamiliarising ordinary things.

The final section in this volume, 'Household goods', including 'Ceramics', 'Glassware', 'Plate', 'Soap' and 'Candles', reveals additional information about the qualities of the material culture of domestic life. The ideal Victorian home contained numerous objects associated with practical uses, such as cups and soap and candles; however, ambitious householders aimed to buy non-essential decorative items, such as ornaments for the mantelpiece. Some objects were, of course, both useful and decorative, such as attractive tea sets and candlesticks. Since the eighteenth century, when the fashion for drinking tea and coffee spread across the social spectrum, British ceramics had been manufactured on an industrial scale in Stoke-on-Trent, Staffordshire, a region known as the 'Potteries'. There were a few other significant centres of ceramics production in Britain, such as Shropshire and Derbyshire, but it was the Staffordshire Potteries which dominated the mass production of ceramic items for the home (see Moisley, 1951: 151–153). Among the sources in the 'Ceramics' subsection is an extract from Arnold Bennett's 1902 novel *Anna of the Five Towns*, set in the 1870s, which takes readers inside a 'pot-bank' to see through the eyes of the heroine Anna how cups and saucers are made. This example shows that the 'process' narrative was not limited to non-fiction articles and books.

The sections here have been chosen to demonstrate the ways in which manufactured items brought about wholesale changes in domestic life. The categories also speak to the Victorian pastime of shopping, with the shop as a conduit between manufactory and home. In her analysis of Victorian leisure time, Judith Flanders characterises the nineteenth-century shopping environment as a 'paradise', with even working-class shoppers catered for with an array of products (Flanders,

2006: 78–122). As with all of our sections, the objects reveal much about their owners, current fashions and tastes, social class, anxieties and aspirations. John Plotz' analysis of 'portability' suggests that Victorians acquired masses of small objects in which they invested a complex mix of sentimental, fiscal and transcendent values (see Plotz, 2008: 1–23). The selection we have chosen here demonstrates that mass-manufactured objects were subject to a remarkable range of cultural and emotional investments.

Our choice of sources also reveals the manufacturing boom generated by the abolition of duties on items such as paper and glass. The mass production of glass items, for example, increased significantly when the glass duties (1745–1845) were repealed. Prior to 1845, all glass was subject to excise duties, and glass windows had long been taxed because of a notorious levy imposed in 1696. It was only repealed in 1851, in time for the construction of Victorian Britain's most significant glass structure, the Crystal Palace in Hyde Park. With untaxed windows and cheaply produced candles, as well as the repeal of the paper duties, the impediments to reading were alleviated, and working people were more easily able to read and study (see Dobson Collett, 1933). Similarly, personal and domestic cleanliness improved when the soap duties 'on an article so essential to the health and comfort of the poor' were repealed by Gladstone in 1853 (see Livesey, 1832: 18, and also Hansard, 1853).

Conclusion

The sources we have chosen reveal how the mass production of household goods contributed to an aspirational society and gave rise to debates about quality, taste and etiquette, which featured in conduct books and articles in the periodical press. The sheer quantity of manufactured goods available meant that consumers could amass 'vulgar' decorative items which failed to harmonise with one another. Deborah Cohen has linked the 'bounty of industrial manufacture' with 'a new cast of advice-givers', helping the British navigate 'the perilous waters of moral decoration' (Cohen, 2006: x–xi). While many 'process articles' from the 1840s and 1850s, when the manufacturing sector appeared to promise affluence and an extension of civilising values, are reprinted in this volume, there are also examples of later writers urging their readers to avoid mass-produced or newly manufactured items, an indication of disenchantment with mass manufacture characteristic of the late-Victorian period on the part of middle-class people, who were concerned that cheap replicas would allow those below them on the social scale to emulate their possessions. This volume aims to reveal how a broad selection of objects became important to everyday life in the Victorian era. It also reveals the political and cultural debates which were raised in relation to even the most mundane of items. For example, questions relating to imitation and authenticity, cheapness and value, and aesthetics and practicality are shown across the sections.

Manufacturing methods also come under scrutiny in some sources included here. For example, patent carpet methods such as that developed by Wytock, which brought expensive items within reach of middle- and working-class consumers, were praised and rewarded with a medal at the Great Exhibition, where the company's 'thrifty' production methods were formally recognised. Detractors of modern processes also existed; one visitor reported in *Time* magazine a suspicion of new-fangled methods at an Axminster factory, expressing the conviction that traditional, labour-intensive ways of manufacturing carpets resulted in better quality. Other manufactured objects, like candles, are discussed in terms of a hierarchy of value. Cities and some wealthy homes started to be lit by gas around 1850, with electricity networks present in many British towns only by 1900 (see Otter, 2008: 215). Candles were thus ubiquitous, providing at least some of the light in most homes across the nineteenth century. A household's budget could be revealed by the smell of its candles: only expensive beeswax burned cleanly, with cheaper tallow burning smoky, pungent and dim. The invention of affordable, bright-burning stearin candles collapsed these visible markers of wealth.

Some of the sources show manufacturers exploiting Victorian concerns over health and cleanliness, with a particular fear of dirt and polluted air, as an effective advertising technique. Household advice books warned against smoke, vermin, insects and even dust; in some of the sources included here, dirt itself is characterised as an invader, threatening the skin and lungs. Victoria Kelley writes that such fears profoundly influenced Victorian perceptions of social class, with the working classes particularly subject to narratives of contagion (Kelley, 2010: 24–26). As this volume reveals, advances in science and technology are presented largely as moral and technological marvels, making domestic life brighter, lighter and more hygienic through the use of newly manufactured objects. The increasing fascination with science corresponded with the fashion for 'process' articles which attempted to explain every stage of production, such as the mysterious processes of saponification and combustion, and involved visits to factory tanks filled with inert, inactive liquids that would be transformed into ordinary soaps and bleaches used within the home. This volume presents a small selection of what was available to Victorian readers keen to understand the things they owned and used. It was clearly important that people understood their country's progress in research, invention and industrial development, and many learned about this by reading the abundant narratives published on manufacturing and its products.

Note

1 It should be noted here that all of the features in *Household Words* were published anonymously; however, the editor's 'Office Book', now in Princeton University Library, makes it easy to identify the contributors (see Lorhli, 1964).

Sources

Anon., 'Social, Sanitary and Municipal Progress', *Household Narrative: A Monthly Supplement to Household Words* (May 1851): 112–115.

Anon., 'Locks and Picklocks', *Chambers's Edinburgh Journal* (Dec 25, 1852), pp. 405–8.

Anon. (1866) 'The Resources, Products, and Industrial History of Birmingham and the Midland Hardware District', *Birmingham Daily Post*, 3 September [n.p.] *British Library Newspapers, Part 1*, accessed 15th August 2018.

Armstrong, Isobel, *Victorian Glassworlds: Glass Culture and the Imagination 1830–1880* (Oxford: Oxford University Press, 2008).

Babbage, Charles, *On the Economy of Machinery and Manufactures* [1832] (digital rept. Cambridge: Cambridge University Press, 2009).

Beaver, Stanley H., 'The Potteries: A Study in the Evolution of a Cultural Landscape: Presidential Address', *Transactions and Papers (Institute of British Geographers)*, no. 34 (June 1964): 1–31.

Beckert, Sven, *The Empire of Cotton: A Global History* (New York: Vintage Books, 2014).

Beeton, Isabella (ed.), *Beeton's Book of Household Management* (London, S. O. Beeton, 1861).

Bizup, Joseph, *Manufacturing Culture: Vindications of Early Victorian Industry* (Charlottesville and London: University of Virginia Press, 2003).

Broomfield, Andrea, *Food and Cooking in Victorian England: A History* (Westport: Greenwood Publishing Group, 2007).

Cantor, Geoffrey, 'Emotional Reactions to the Great Exhibition of 1851', *Journal of Victorian Culture*, 20: 2 (2015): 230–245.

Chambers, J.D., *The Workshop of the World: British Economic History from 1820–1880* (London: Oxford University Press, 1961).

Cohen, Deborah, *Household Gods: The British and their Possessions* (New Haven and London: Yale University Press, 2006).

Crawford, Iain, '"Faithful Sympathy": Dickens, the *Edinburgh Review*, and Editing *Household Words*', *Victorian Periodicals Review*, 44:1 (Spring 2011): 42–68.

Dobson Collet, Collet, *History of the Taxes on Knowledge: Their Origins and Repeal* [1899] (London: Watts & Co, 1933).

Flanders, Judith, *Consuming Passions: Leisure and Pleasure in Victorian Britain* (London: Harper Collins, 2006).

Freedgood, Elaine, 'What Objects Know: Circulation, Omniscience and the Comedy of Dispossession in Victorian It-Narratives', *Journal of Victorian Culture*, 15: 1 (April 2010), 83–100.

Freedgood, Elaine, 'Cultures of Commodities, Cultures of Things' in *The Victorian World* (ed.) Martin Hewitt (London: Routledge, 2012): 225–240.

Gaskell, Elizabeth, *Cranford* (London, Macmillan & Co., 1892).

Griffin, Emma. *A Short History of the British Industrial Revolution* (Basingstoke: Palgrave Macmillan, 2010).

Gurney, Peter, 'An Appropriated Space: The Great Exhibition, the Crystal Palace and the Working Class' in Louise Purbrick (ed.), *The Great Exhibition of 1851* (Manchester: Manchester University Press, 2001): 114–145.

Gurney, Peter, *Wanting and Having: Popular Politics and Liberal Consumerism in England, 1830–1870* (Manchester: Manchester University Press, 2015).

Hamlett, Jane. *Material Relations: Domestic Interiors and Middle-Class Families in England, 1850–1910*. Manchester: Manchester University Press, 2010.

Hansard, Gladstone repeals soap duty (1853): https://api.parliament.uk/historic-hansard/commons/1853/apr/18/the-financial-statement-the-budget#S3V0125P0_18530418_HOC_15

Horowitz, Evan, 'Industrialism and the Victorian Novel' in *The Oxford Handbook of the Victorian Novel* (ed.) Lisa Rodensky (Oxford: Oxford University Press, 2013): 357–375.

Huett, Lorna, 'Among the Unknown Public: *Household Words, All the Year Round* and the Mass-Market Weekly Periodical in the Mid-Nineteenth Century', *Victorian Periodicals Review*, 38:1 (Spring 2005): 61–82.

Jenkins, David, 'Introduction' to *The Cambridge History of Western Textiles* vol. II, ed. David Jenkins (Cambridge: Cambridge University Press, 2003): 717–720.

Kelley, Victoria, *Soap and Water: Cleanliness, Dirt, and the Working Classes in Victorian and Edwardian Britain* (London: IB Tauris, 2010).

Ketabgian, Tamara, *The Lives of Machines: The Industrial Imaginary in Victorian Literature and Culture* (Ann Arbor: University of Michigan Press and the University of Michigan Library, 2011).

Kidd, Alan, *Manchester: A History* 4th ed. (Lancaster: Carnegie Publishing, 2011).

Livesey, Joseph (ed.), *The Moral Reformer, and Protestor Against the Vices, Abuses, and Corruptions of the Age*, vol. 2, issue 4 (Apr 1832), 118.

Logan, Thad, *The Victorian Parlor* (Cambridge: Cambridge University Press, 2001).

Lohrli, Anne, '*Household Words* and its Office Book', *The Princeton University Library Chronicle* 26:1 (Autumn 1964): 27–47.

Maw, Peter, Terry Wyke and Alan Kidd, 'Canals, Rivers, and the Industrial City: Manchester's industrial waterfront, 1790–1850', *Economic History Review* 65: 4 (2012): 1495–1523.

Message, Kylie and Ewan Johnston, 'The World Within the City: The Great Exhibition, Race, Class and Social Reform' in *Britain, the Empire, and the World at the Great Exhibition of 1851*, (eds) Jeffrey A. Auerbach and Peter H. Hoffenberg (London: Routledge, 2008): 27–46.

Moisley, H. A. 'The Industrial and Urban Development of the North Staffordshire Conurbation'. *Transactions and Papers*, Institute of British Geographers, vol. 17 (1951): 151–65.

Mokyr, Joel, *The Enlightened Economy: An Economic History of Britain 1700–1850* (New Haven and London: Yale University Press, 2009).

Otter, Chris, *The Victorian Eye: A Political History of Light and Vision in Britain, 1800–1910* (Chicago: University of Chicago Press, 2008).

Plotz, John, *Portable Property: Victorian Culture on the Move* (Princeton: Princeton University Press, 2008).

Richards, Thomas. *The Commodity Culture of Victorian England: Advertising and Spectacle.* (Stanford, CA: Stanford University Press, 1990).

Riello, Giorgio, *Cotton: The Fabric that Made the Modern World* (Cambridge: Cambridge University Press, 2013).

Shears, Jonathon ed. *The Great Exhibition, 1851: A Sourcebook.* (Manchester: Manchester University Press, 2017).

Skrabec, Quentin R., *The Metallurgic Age: The Victorian Flowering of Invention and Industrial Science* (North Carolina: McFarland & Company, Inc, 2006).

Smith, Adam *The Wealth of Nations.* (London, W. Strahan and T. Cadell, 1776).

Stavenow-Hidemark, Elisabet, 'Textile Design and Furnishings, c. 1780–1914' in *The Cambridge History of Western Textiles* vol. II, ed. David Jenkins (CUP, 2003): 860–881.

Sussman, Herbert, *Victorian Technologies: Invention, Innovation and the Rise of the Machine* (California: Praeger, 2009).

Tayler, D. F. (c. 1840), Paper of Pins. http://collections.vam.ac.uk/item/O361504/pins-d-f-tayler/

Trentmann, Frank, *The Empire of Things: How We Became a World of Consumers from the Fifteenth century to the Twenty-first* (London: Penguin, 2017).

Waters, Catherine. *Commodity Culture in Dickens's* Household Words: *The Social Life of Goods*. Aldershot, UK: Ashgate, 2008.
Wynne, Deborah. "Responses to the 1851 Great Exhibition in Household Words." *The Dickensian* 455.97, Part 3 (Winter 2001–2002): 228–234.
Wynne, Deborah. *The Sensation Novel and the Victorian Family Magazine* (Basingstoke: Palgrave Macmillan, 2001).
Young, Paul. *Globalization and the Great Exhibition: The Victorian New World Order*. (Basingstoke, UK: Palgrave, 2009).

PART 1

The context of manufacturing in Victorian Britain

'Peel's Velveteens', *Punch*, Vol. 4 (1843), p. 36.

George Dodd, *Days at the Factories, or the Manufacturing Industries of Great Britain Described* [extract] (London, 1843), pp. 1–16.

Richard H. Horne, 'The Female School of Design in the Capital of the World', *Household Words*, Vol. 2 (15 March 1851), pp. 578–581.

Image: 'Calico Printing' in Charles Tomlinson (ed.), *Tomlinson's Cyclopaedia of Useful Arts and Manufactures*, Vol. 2 (1852–1854), p. 279.

John Capper, 'The Northern Wizard', *Household Words*, Vol. 3, no. 189 (5 November 1853), pp. 225–228.

Anon, 'Help for Women', *National Magazine* (May 1861), pp. 32–34.

Karl Marx, 'The Fetishism of Commodities and the Secret Thereof', *Capital* (1867) (London: Swan Sonnenschein and Co. Ltd., 1902), pp. 41–50.

Anon, 'Sewing Machines', *All The Year Round*, Vol. 1 (new series), 27 March 1869, pp. 395–397.

Lyon Playfair, 'On Patents and the New Patent Bill', *Nineteenth Century* (April 1877), pp. 317–319, 321–323, 325–326.

J. T. Slugg, *Reminiscences of Manchester Fifty Years Ago* (Manchester, 1881), pp. 27–28, 37–38.

This section presents a selection of sources discussing some of the key features of manufacturing in the Victorian period, including legal interventions, finance and capital, urban development, labour and design, and the intellectual property associated with new inventions.[1] Legislation in the form of import and export duties, along with a variety of taxes on goods, including windows and paper, informed the debates surrounding manufacturing in the first half of the nineteenth century. The Corn Laws of 1815 became a source of irritation to the manufacturing sector because they protected British farmers at the expense of free trade. The powerful Anti-Corn Law League, based in Manchester, lobbied Parliament tirelessly between 1838 and 1846 for changes in the law. The tactics of the League are evident in 'Peel's Velveteens', published in *Punch* (1843), which reports a practical joke played on the Prime Minister, Sir Robert Peel, who received a roll of printed 'velveteen' made by the Manchester manufacturer W. Barlow. Peel gratefully accepted the cloth as a gift, not realising that it was actually a political statement sent by the members of the Anti-Corn Law League, as the pattern on the fabric depicted ears of corn and the word 'free' in tiny letters. Once he discovered the trick played on him, Peel returned the cloth. This article highlights how manufacturing interests acted as a powerful political force in this period. The League's 'velveteen' message is also referred to in the short extract from J. T. Slugg's *Reminiscences of Manchester Fifty Years Ago* (1881), in which the author looks back nostalgically to the rapid expansion of calico manufacturing in Manchester in the 1830s and 1840s.[2] The image 'Calico Printing' from *Tomlinson's Cyclopedia* (1852–1854) depicts a worker operating a cylinder printing machine which prints an elaborate pattern on cotton.

Other sources in this section discuss political debates relating to the manufacture of goods. The dominance of mass production is emphasised by Karl Marx in his influential book, *Capital: A Critique of Political Economy*, first published in

German in 1867 and translated into English in 1887. Marx exposes the vagaries and exploitative nature of capitalism and, in the short extract reprinted here, analyses commodity fetishism, arguing that the realities of human labour are overshadowed by society's obsession with the 'magical' properties of commodities. *Capital* was one of the first texts to analyse the social implications of mass production, and Marx's approach to the analysis of manufactured objects as a component of commodity culture is rare in nineteenth-century writing. However, his ideas on the role of commodities, labour and capital became enormously influential as the twentieth century progressed. Manufacturing, entrepreneurship, intellectual property and the social role of the inventor are discussed in Lyon Playfair's 1877 article, 'On Patents and the New Patent Bill'. Playfair points up the anomaly whereby inventors receive little reward in comparison to the manufacturers who exploit their inventions. He highlights the need to reform the patent system in order to acknowledge fully the intellectual property of the inventor.

While Britain excelled in the development of machinery, the Great Exhibition of 1851 exposed to the world the inferiority of British-designed goods.[3] This issue is raised in 'The Female School of Design in the Capital of the World', originally published anonymously in *Household Words* in 1851 (later identified as the work of Richard H. Horne). Narrated by a fictional Northern manufacturer who, seeking examples of good British design, visits a government-supported school of design for girls and young women in London. The article exposes how the good training the pupils receive and the high quality of their designs are not matched by the conditions in which they work, with the school being run in dilapidated rooms above a shop in an insalubrious area of the city. The narrator condemns the lack of interest in good design shown by manufacturers who are wedded to those 'vulgar' designs considered archetypically 'British'.

Women's relationships to manufacturing are also featured in two anonymous articles about sewing machines, 'Help for Women' in the *National Magazine* (1861) and 'Sewing Machines' in *All The Year Round* (1869). 'Help for Women' celebrates the invention of the sewing machine, arguing that women are freed from bondage 'to the loom and the [spinning] wheel' now that the '[s]ewing [m]achine does all that was wearisome and fatiguing in the manufacture of garments'.[4] This view is contradicted in the later article 'Sewing Machines', which complains that women are now in bondage to this machine, forced to press pedals and 'exert muscular efforts, to a degree never before required of them'. The author sees the additional food required to fuel this extra labour as a hidden cost, while the health of the seamstress is placed in 'permanent danger' by the effort of powering the machine. Plans to develop an electric motor are seen as a welcome innovation. These articles reveal anxieties surrounding women's relationship to machinery and the processes of mass production.

The extracts from Dodd's book *Days at the Factories* (1843) and the anonymous 'The Northern Wizard' in *Household Words* (1853) reveal the tone of wonder and curiosity characteristic of so much writing on manufactured items during the period. Both concern visits to factories and describe manufacturing processes in detail. 'The Northern Wizard' considers the manufacture of dyes, acids and bleaches in Glasgow, while the extract from *Days at the Factories* focuses on objects manufactured in London, including toys, musical instruments, printing and watchmaking. London is revealed as the financial powerhouse of northern manufacturing, rather than a centre of mass-produced goods. Many of the sources in this section reveal a north-south divide in the nation's industrial life.

Notes

1 For good overviews of the social, economic and cultural development of industrial Britain, see Emma Griffin, *A Short History of the British Industrial Revolution* (Basingstoke: Palgrave Macmillan, 2010), and Joel Mokyr, *The Enlightened Economy: An Economic History of Britain 1700–1850* (New Haven, CT, and London: Yale University Press, 2009).

2 For a detailed discussion of the important role of Manchester in the development of British manufacturing see Alan Kidd, *Manchester: A History*, 4th ed. (Lancaster: Carnegie Publishing, 2011).

3 For comprehensive discussions of the 1851 Great Exhibition, see the essays in Jeffrey A. Auerbach and Peter H. Hoffenberg (eds.), *Britain, the Empire, and the World at the Great Exhibition of 1851* (London: Routledge, 2008).

4 For a discussion of the development of the sewing machine, see Adrian Forty, *Objects of Desire: Design and Society since 1750* (London: Pantheon Books, 1986), pp. 94–95.

1

'PEEL'S VELVETEENS'

Punch, Vol. 4 (1843), p. 36

THE ingenuous Sir ROBERT has been the victim of a shameful trick. For ourselves, we have not the slightest doubt that the Corn-Law Leaguers are at the bottom of the transaction, which we only hope it is within the reach of Parliament to punish. The conspiracy displays such subtlety – has in it such a wicked *animus* – that did we merely consult our own feelings, we should devote the whole of our present number to discuss the iniquity, in its every shade of turpitude; in its depth, length, and width. The careless world, however, has not the same interest as PUNCH in the feelings of a Prime Minister – has, of course, not the same intimate sympathies with the private emotions of a politician. We shall therefore narrate, with all our characteristic brevity, the circumstances of as dark a political conspiracy as ever blackened the human heart – will show how the peace – nay, more the consistency of a Prime Minister, has been aimed at in his hour of social confidence, threatened in his whole anatomy.

A week or two since, Mr. W. BARLOW of Ancoats-vale having – we are convinced of this truth – by the instigation of the Corn-Law League, perfected "some printed velveteens" of a most novel and beautiful fabric, sent a few yards of his handiwork as a present to Sir ROBERT PEEL. Gracious, unsuspecting Minister! No artless milkmaid on Drayton Manor could have received with less suspicion a bunch of ribands from Hodge, the carter; albeit given for the basest after-purposes by the designing clown. Sir ROBERT gazed upon the velveteen "made to look like silk," although of cotton, – gazed, and was lost. (Mr. BARLOW has the honesty to allow that one of the excellences of the fabric is, that it appears much better than it really is; that it has a glossy, silky outside look, to captivate unthinking eyes; although, indeed, the stuff itself be of an inferior yarn – a thing of very cotton. Why, believing this, Mr. BARLOW should have thought fit to select such a politician as Sir ROBERT to patronize his velveteen, we leave to the man's conscience to answer; and proceed with our story.) Sir ROBERT – courteous victim! – lost no time in acknowledging the present of velveteen, and – (how the Corn-Law League must have chuckled!) – further assured Mr. BARLOW, that Lady PEEL was so delighted with the stuff, that she purposed "*having a cloak*" made of part of it, whilst he, Sir ROBERT, would devote the remnant to his own bodily comfort, in some other fashion!

DOI: 10.4324/9781315400105-3

Reader, pause for a moment, and imagine the smothered laugh shaking the ribs of the League! How the master manufacturer grinned with all his heart and all his soul! Nay, it is said, that feeble smiles did "shoot and circulate" in the tax-ground faces of the tenants of Manchester cellars – that the very ghastliness of want was irradiated with the dim sense of a joke played upon the Prime Minister! Indeed, everywhere throughout Manchester, laughter abandoned. It is said, the very knockers on the manufacturers' doors were dimpled with smiles – that the church vanes no longer creaked, but laughed audibly! Wherefore? Why this exultation at the courtesy of the most courteous of Prime Ministers? Why this rudeness of merriment at an act of gentlemanly condescension? With mingled feelings of contempt and pity for our species, we tell the why.

The velveteen was made into a cloak – (this we know from Lady PEEL's milliner,) – the remainder stuff was worked into trousers for the Prime Minister – (this we know from Sir ROBERT's tailor, the same man who has made our own motley for many years), – when the fraud, the iniquity, lurking in the fatal gift was discovered.

It appears that some *ears of wheat* were gracefully worked into the pattern adorning the velveteen, and further, that the dreaded mono-syllable "FREE," – those four damning letters, like tares and poppies, threw among the corn, thus insidiously presented to the Minister. Lady PEEL, with the quick feminine eye, discovered the device at once. Why, then, it may be asked, did so many days elapse ere Sir ROBERT returned the stuff – for return it, he did – to Mr. BARLOW? Ere we answer, we subjoin the missive that accompanied the rejected velveteen: –

> "Drayton Manor, Jan. 7, 1843. – Sir: I was not aware, until to-day, that the specimen manufacture which you requested me to accept bore any allusion to matters that are a subject of public controversy. No mention whatever was made of this in the letter you addressed to me; and I thought it would be ungracious to reject what appeared to be a pure act of civility on your part. I must beg leave to return to you that which I accepted under an erroneous impression.
>
> I am, Sir, your obedient servant, ROBERT PEEL – W. Barlow, Esq."

Lady PEEL, like an excellent, devoted wife as she is, with a full knowledge of the wheat, and of those "idle weeds," the letters f. r. e. e. that "grew among the sustaining corn," – ordered her cloak to be made; and wherefore? Simply, because she knew that Sir ROBERT had, at the last election, used a cloak with some sort of corn-ear device upon it, and that therefore, like a good wife, she could do no better than follow the example of a virtuous and beloved husband. How different the case with Sir ROBERT, the Prime Minister!

We have no doubt whatever, that as far as a cloak might have been got out of the stuff for himself, Sir ROBERT would have had no objection to retain the velveteen as a provision for future accidental keeping it on, or putting it off as the wind might blow, or the sun might shine; but when once the velveteen was made into trousers when once the minister had donned so succinct a garment, it must become to him a sort of tight-fitting principle, not under any circumstances to be cast aside, with the least respect for the usages of honourable society. It was then Sir ROBERT saw the trap that had been laid for him; it was then that, looking with an instructed eye upon the velveteen, he felt the full force of the political plot got up in a pair of trousers:

> "The seed was cursèd that did grow the web,
> And it was dyed in mummy, which the Corn Laws
> Conserved of broken hearts!"

Such, then, appeared the velveteen presented by Mr. W. BARLOW, and the Prime Minister immediately resolved to put no foot in it.

We hope there is no admirer of Sir ROBERT who will not feel grateful for the escape of the Minister. Spells and incantations have been woven in a web ere now; and these, we are convinced of it, lurked in every ear of law-taxed corn.

> "See the griesly texture grow,
> (*'Tis of human entrails made,*)
> And the weights that play below,
> Each a ſtarving Briton's head!"

Might not the velveteen, the produce of Corn-law looms, have been manufactured from such horrid materials – by such ghastly machinery? Indeed, we fear it.

And then that fatal word "FREE." In the *Gesta Romanorum* there is a story of a beautiful girl who, having been nurtured upon serpents, was sent as a slave to a certain king; the monarch kissed the rosy venom, and straightway died. We have not the slightest doubt that the word "free" in PEEL's velveteen was composed of serpents – and that no sooner should the Prime Minister have taken the trousers to himself, than that the petty reptiles would have grown into boa-constrictors, and poor Sir ROBERT, the unwilling Laocoön of "free" corn, would, as Minister, have been strangled by opposing principles!

However, thanks to the late sagacity of Sir ROBERT, our minister is saved. We have, let us be grateful for it, another plot to add to the unsuccessful machinations of democrats and knaves. We have had the Gunpowder Plot – the

Rye-house Plot – the Thistlewood Plot – and now, as a crowning escape – the Velveteen Plot! Great, indeed, would have been the triumph of the League, if the Minister had donned the insidious trousers, and, taking his seat in them in the House of Commons, had, without knowing it, based his Ministry upon – "free" corn!

Q.

2

GEORGE DODD, *DAYS AT THE FACTORIES, OR THE MANUFACTURING INDUSTRIES OF GREAT BRITAIN DESCRIBED* [EXTRACT]

(London, 1843), pp. 1–16

Extract from 'Introductory Chapter on the Trades of London', pp. 1–16

The bulk of the inhabitants of a great city, such as London, have very indistinct notions of the means whereby the necessaries, the comforts, or the luxuries of life are furnished. The simple fact, that he who has money can command every variety of exchangeable produce, seems to act as a veil which hides the producer from the consumer. The coined piece of gold is the general agent, the factor, the broker, through whose medium the labours of all become available to all; and, as in the case of other agencies, the principals have but a vague knowledge of the sources whence the supply is obtained. Who, if he were to catalogue the articles of food, or of clothing, or of furniture, or other commodities which contribute to his daily comfort, could enumerate the sources whence they are obtained, and the general character of the processes by which they are manufactured? The number of such is probably very small. And yet the inquiry is an interesting and a valuable one: for the social features of a city or town are largely dependent on these two questions, – whether manufactures are carried on therein to a notable extent, and whether the mode of production partakes more of the *factory* or of the *handicraft* character. Again, the means of transit from one town to another depend in a striking degree on the relative positions of the two towns with respect to manufactures: if each consumes largely the produce of the other, their mutual wants will not fail to lead to the construction of roads, of canals, of railroads, of shipping, and other facilities for transit; and these again give activity to various departments of commercial industry.

[. . .]

When we consider how large a portion of the modern attire of both sexes is formed of the textile fabrics – silk, cotton, linen, woollen, and worsted – and how small an

DOI: 10.4324/9781315400105-4

amount of this is manufactured in London, we begin to appreciate the dependence of the metropolis on the country districts for a supply. Let man enumerate the various articles which form his dress, and he will probably find that the woven and fulled material from his coat comes from the West Riding of Yorkshire, or from the West of England; that the linen for his shirt is of Irish manufacture; his gloves, if of silk, probably came from Derby, and his leather gloves from Worcester; to Nottingham he is indebted for his stockings, and to Glasgow for his 'Bandana' hand-kerchief. The materials for female dress, too, are dependent in an equally large degree on the labours of the provinces. In the district of which Manchester is the centre are produced enormous quantities of the various cotton fabrics, while Norwich contributes its crape, Derby its silks, Coventry its ribbons, Nottingham its bobbinet and machine-made lace, and Bedfordshire its straw-plait – omitting mention of the infinite variety of materials obtained from the Continent.

[. . .]

But although scarcely any woven fabrics are produced in London (and those which are can hardly come within the class of factory produce), the arrangements for working up these materials into garments are here developed to an extraordinary extent. Tailors and dress-makers are to be reckoned, not by thousands, but by tens of thousands. So it may likewise be said in reference to boots and shoes, for shoe-makers are among the most numerous of London artisans; but here another feature is observed, for the leather used in this manufacture is made in London more extensively than in any other part of England: – indeed the large district of Bermondsey derives its chief importance from its tanneries and leather-factories. We have no 'coat-factories' nor 'boot-factories,' no assemblages of men in large many-storied buildings, manufacturing coats and boots with those appliances of machinery and division of labour which distinguish a factory. There was at one time, during the last war, a shoe-factory strictly deserving of the name, established by Mr Brunel for making shoes for the army by machinery; but taking it as a branch of national industry, shoe-making is almost independent of machinery.

To a man's *hat* the same remark cannot be applied as to his coat or his boots. The whole article is made from the raw material, and to a greater extent in London than anywhere else, by a connected series of processes in one establishment: the sheep's wool and the beaver's furry pelt are brought to London, and from these materials the glossy beaver hat is mainly formed by a chain of processes whose links have much of a factory characters about them.

In what manner female labour is bestowed in making articles of dress is too well known to need recital. Here, from the Stepney seamstresses who wear out life by making shirts at a penny a-piece, to the court milliner who is surrounded by the luxuries of life, all produce their results by the slender needle and the supple thread, by dexterity of finger, by patience and endurance, and by such lengthened hours of labour as men would rebel against. In some few occupations, such as artificial flower-making, feather working, and so forth, other implements besides the needle and thread and scissors are required; but in the large bulk of female employments, as directed to dress, there is a singular uniformity of working apparatus, of posture, and of general procedure.

If we leave the textile materials of dress, and notice the various appendages and ornaments which modern taste deems indispensable to it, we find that a large number of manufacturers at once come before us. The trifling *pin* which assists in the toilet, as well as the needle and thread employed in making a dress, all come from distant parts of England. The pin, it is probable, was brought from Gloucestershire; the needle from Redditch; the sewing cotton and silk from Derby; – the manufacture of these articles being almost unknown in London. Then again, buttons and buckles, clasps and studs, hooks and eyes, and the numerous small articles of metal pertaining more or less to dress, are brought principally from the north. Those decorative appendages which remind us that 'all is not gold that glitters,' such as chains, guards, bracelets, rings, &c., are largely manufactured at Birmingham, as well as a portion of the really valuable jewellery: but it is probable that the larger portion of the gold, silver, and jewel manufacture, in its highest and most costly form, is carried on in London.

[. . .]

As cleansing agents in connection with the person and the dress, we must not forget soap, and soda, and pearl-ash, and blacking. All these are manufactured on what may be deemed a large scale, the first and the last principally in London. Indeed the other two are also largely made here, but they may be more appropriately associated with the north of England, especially since the changes which modern chemistry has wrought in the modes of producing these alkalis.

A glance may next be taken at some of the manufacturing operations by which our dwellings are built and stocked with useful furniture and implements. The raw materials, in this as in other cases, are brought from distant parts; the stone from Yorkshire or from Portland, or some other rocky district; the slate from Westmoreland or Wales; the timber from Norway or Canada; while the bricks and tiles are made in the fields in the neighbourhood of London. The brick-layer, the mason, the carpenter, the joiner, the slater, – all are artisans or handicraftsmen, in the usual meaning of these terms, and do not generally work together on anything like a factory system. Marble-working has within the last few years been brought under the operation of machinery, which in some degree sets it apart from the occupations just named. Glass-making has always been one of the most notable of our manufactures, and is carried on, in some of its branches, on a large scale in London; although window-glass and plate-glass are more extensively produced in the north of England. Saw-mills for timber have come prominently into use; but this can scarcely be called a branch of manufacture.

[. . .]

When we turn our attention to the innumerable articles which come under the denomination of 'household furniture,' we found how largely the inhabitants of London are indebted to country manufacturers for the supply. Our carpets and rugs, our grates and fenders, our fire-irons, and the variety of implements and vessels made of iron and brass, found in every house, our plates and dishes, cups and saucers, knives and forks – all are brought from the north of England; or at least if any are made in London, the number is too limited to allow of these branches of manufacture being ranked among those belonging to London. Floor-cloth and paper-hangings are London manufactures, carried on in large premises, and by a routine of processes very similar throughout. The tables, the chairs, the bedsteads, the beds, the mattresses, the glass-frames, the picture-frames, the window cornices, – all are made to a vast extent in London, but not generally in large factories: they are the productions of tradesmen, each of whom can carry on a tolerably extensive business without great extent of room, or a large number of workmen. Clocks, time-pieces, and watches may perhaps be included in our present category. These are assuredly manufactured to a large extent in London; one entire district, that of Clerkenwell, being chiefly occupied by artisans in these departments of labour – some of whom, such as those engaged in the manufacture of church clocks, carry on their operations on a large scale. Yet even here we have a curious instance of the dependence of the London makers on the workmen of the north of England; for it is understood that the 'movement' or wheel and pinion work of almost every watch said to be made in London is actually produced in Lancashire, the London watchmaker being merely the workman who puts together the separate parts made by others. Proposals have recently been made to establish what might correctly be termed a watch factory; but up to the present time nothing has been known in London which can in any sense come under that designation.

Taking up next that item in our classification which relates to *instruction and amusement*, the mind at once dwells upon the printing-machine, and the agency by which it is brought to bear upon the spread of information, as occupying a prominent position in respect to this matter. Whether we regard the arrangements connected with the printing of a book, of a newspaper, or of parliamentary proceedings, London undoubtedly takes the lead among the cities of the empire. In no other British town or city are there printing-offices on so large a scale, or so many printing-machines congregated in one spot, or so many workmen contributing to this object by their combined exertions. Yet at the same time it is observable that the *paper* which is thus brought into useful requisition is not a London manufacture: there are no paper-mills in the metropolis, nor within several miles of it. The ink employed is made in London, but does not involve manufacturing arrangements on a large scale. The printing of books is, like the printing, a department of labour essentially metropolitan: there is probably no other town in England where the extent of book-binding is such as to warrant the construction and arrangement of a large building, on factory principles, for this purpose.

The number of occupations in London whose tendency is to contribute to the instruction and amusement of the inhabitants is extremely large; but it does not appear that many large manufacturing arrangements are involved in them. Take, for instance, a pair of globes, a case of drawing instruments, a telescope, a microscope, a set of instruments used by the surveyor – all these require mechanical ingenuity of a very high order; but it is the ingenuity of the individual workman, who could exercise his vocation as well in a small room as in a large factory, and perhaps better. The implements and instruments employed in scientific investigations of every kind are similarly dependent, for their production, on manual dexterity, and not on factory combinations; while those conducive to education, in schools, mechanics' institutions, colleges, and universities, are still less complex than the others.

Amusement, like instruction, presents one prominent instance wherein factory arrangements on a large scale are involved. *Books* and *piano-fortes* are each, in London, produced on a scale which totally eclipses the productions of the provinces. Nay, there is perhaps not one occupation, throughout the whole range of productive industry, in which the metropolis maintains a more marked pre-eminence than in the manufacture of piano-fortes; for these instruments are classed among those wherein a kind of commercial halo envelops the names of the principal manufacturers. This preference for London-made instruments, and the spread of musical taste within the present century, have led to factory arrangements on an extremely large scale in reference to piano-fortes. Other musical instruments are manufactured to a much humbler extent. Organs, indeed, from their large dimensions, require corresponding arrangements for their manufacture, which bears considerable resemblance to that of a piano-forte in many parts. Harps, guitars, violins, violoncellos, – all require more delicate skill than extensive arrangements for their production; and the same may likewise be observed of wind instruments made of wood, such as the flute, the clarinet, and the flageolet; and those made of brass, such as horns, trumpets, and bugles. Tube-drawing and cylinder-boring for steps in the manufacture of many of these instruments; but the finishing processes which follow are examples of delicate manipulation, generally carried on in small workshops.

[. . .]

Descending from the professor of the fine arts to the child, we find that toys give rise to no inconsiderable amount of manufacturing enterprise. The ball and the bat, the whistle and the drum, the rocking-horse and the mimic cart, the hoop, the doll, the humming-top, the skipping-rope – all are sold so very largely as to render the employment of a considerable number of persons necessary to the maintenance of the supply. A wholesale toy warehouse would surprise those who for the first time were to visit it, by the magnitude of its arrangements, the classification of its contents, and the indication which it affords of the importance of trifles when large in number. But although the warehousing is thus extensive, the manufacture of these articles is not conducted in large factories. The dealer collects his store from a large number of persons, each of whom, perhaps in a very humble dwelling, fashions some of the numerous kinds of children's toys; the little fragments of wood, of coloured paper, of leather, of tinsel, which enter so largely into the construction of these humble articles, are cut out and prepared principally by children, – indeed the price at which the toys are sold sufficiently indicates that the wages of labour in their manufacture much be insufficient for adult workmen, except in the better kinds of toys. Could we dive into the alleys and narrow streets of the East End of London, we should probably find many whole families – father, mother, and children – employed in making toys under their own poor roof; but a toy-factory, properly so called, does not perhaps exist in London.

[. . .]

Whoever were to attempt to classify all the trades and occupations of London, and were to consult a directory with a view to determine their number, would perhaps be somewhat startled to find it amount to something like thirteen or fourteen hundred, and would admit that any classification of them under five or six headings much necessarily be very imperfect. It is not pretended that the arrangement given in the preceding pages is anything more than an approximate aid, or that we have glanced at more than the chief in each class; but it may perhaps have been shown that, numerous as are the London trades, the number which involve large factory arrangements and are *characteristic* of London, is not so considerable as would at first appear.

3

RICHARD H. HORNE, 'THE FEMALE SCHOOL OF DESIGN IN THE CAPITAL OF THE WORLD'

Household Words, Vol. 2 (15 March 1851), pp. 578–581

I heard a great Manchester manufacturer lamenting, only a few days ago, the want of new and good designers in our own country. I told him I had been informed that there were two Schools of Design in London – a male school, and a female school – where the students continually produced first-rate designs. He said he had never been there, nor seen any of their designs, that he knew of; and again lamented the want of new patterns. Another, a great ribbon manufacturer of my acquaintance – in fact, he married my aunt – expends at least a thousand a year in getting foreign designs, and he has never once taken a design from any of these Schools. When I told him I had seen good things that came from them, he looked incredulous and vacant, and said that I was young in the business. Not a word about going to see them, or sending up for a few specimens. Another great manufacturer, with whom our firm often has large dealings, dined with us last week. He knew of these Schools, and showed us a beautiful design for a carpet which he had obtained from one of them, in which the colours were all finely harmonised. "It will sell very well," said he, "after I have altered it a little to my own taste." "Why, what will you do to it?" I inquired. "I must *vulgarise* it," said he, touching my elbow; "where they have put grey, I shall put scarlet; and where you see purple here, I shall put green and yellow, or such like." Another manufacturer, whose warehouse I was visiting only the other day, showed me a table cover of a most chaste and handsome design – a broad, rich, gothic border, with a dark centre quite plain, which of course made the deep border look all the richer. "This is very good," said he, "but we always like something catching in the centre. I shall have a good bunch of peony roses and tulips, or something of that sort, for the middle."

These rebuffs, however, added to the excellence of several designs I had seen, which had come both from the male and female schools, determined me to go to London forthwith and visit them. It is only justice to say that I did this with the full approval and, indeed, the wish, of my senior partners.

During the journey by rail, I thought very much about these Schools – and especially the Female School, as it seemed to me to include many questions of

DOI: 10.4324/9781315400105-5

social interest, which one now so often sees discussed in periodicals, and even in newspapers. Many of these young persons, thought I, are, no doubt, of highly respectable families, well educated, and who once had very different expectations; though now, for the purpose of making designs, they are learning drawing, perhaps, to sell them – perhaps that they may become teachers – but in all cases to help some scanty income at home. Perhaps, also some of them are orphans. But the Government takes charge of them. As the manufacturers have not yet learnt the importance of supporting these Schools, by employing some of the students, or making selections from their designs, a paternal Government has kindly and wisely taken charge of these industrious and praiseworthy young women.

Having made known to Mrs. Mc Ian – the lady superintending the school – that I was a manufacturer, and a partner in an influential firm, I received a polite attention, and was conducted into the largest of the rooms appropriated to the students.

This room was the first-floor front, exactly over the shop below. It could not have been above eleven or twelve feet high. I do not know how many students were there; but the room was full to crowding. They were packed close together on forms, just like children at a Sunday School, in our manufacturing towns. The elbows, and, in some cases, the shoulders of one student touching those of her next door neighbours, on each side. The drawing desks, or stands, with the forms, were arranged in rows across the room, and so closely that to pass along between was not possible without frequently scraping oneself against the desk behind, or causing the student in front to bend and pack herself forward against her own drawing-board. This was the junior class. They were copying from the "flat" and the "round," (prints or drawings, and bas-reliefs); but, though it was only two o'clock, the light was so bad, owing to the fog, and the dusty, uncleaned windows, that to distinguish anything accurately was out of the question. I asked a student why they did not have drawing-lamps, but was informed that none were allowed. By bending down, with a close scrutiny, to the drawings of two or three of those nearest the windows, I could see that they were very well done; and the copies of several of the casts of scrollwork, flowers, and fruit, in high relief, were excellent. In the imperfect light, the drawings really looked almost as tangible and round as the casts themselves. Some drew in chalk, and some painted in oil, some in watercolour; but the majority painted in what is called *tempera*, or body colour, and of the same kind in which Cartoons are painted. Though the fire was small, the room was very hot and close, and there was no sort of provision for ventilation.

In the back room, on the second floor, which was much smaller, there was similar crowding, and with greater injury, as the higher class of students were here; and these, frequently having large designs, were continually in each other's way. For a young lady to have a blow on the cheek, or the side of her head, from the corner of a wooden-frame – an easel to be upset – a cast knocked down – a freshly-painted design smeared across, or a hole knocked in a canvas, were things of almost every-day occurrence. One of these rents in a design for a carpet, and half finished, I myself saw. The hole was so large I could have crept through it; and on this very day of my visit, a valuable porcelain vase has been knocked down and broken, sheerly from the impossibility of any one being able to move without jostling somebody or something. Here also, the room was very hot and close – nothing in the shape of ventilation.

Impossible as it was, from the state of the atmosphere, added to the extreme dirtiness of the windows, all crusted over, as they were, with London dust and smuts, to judge well of colours, in themselves, I could yet see that the best had been selected, and the best harmonies employed. I here saw designs for table-covers, chintz, ladies' muslin, or other figured dresses, groups of flowers, fruit, carpets, paper-hangings, models in clay and wax, &c.

The designs were handsome, beautiful, chaste, and original, and would do any English manufacturer's heart good to see them, if he only had the good sense to set a just value on the advantage of finding such things close to hand in his own country.

The two attics above are arranged in the same way as the rooms on the second floor, the senior students being packed in the little back room, while the junior are in the larger room in front. These rooms are only eight feet high. In the front attic there are twenty students. The oppressive atmosphere was scarcely endurable on first entering. No ventilation whatever had been provided. It reminded me of what we read of the "sweating system" among the poor journeymen tailors.

The principal designs in the attics were similar to those below, viz., for carpets, rugs, skreens, ladies' dresses, table covers, lace handkerchiefs, ribbons, shawls, &c., and I am quite sure, from the excellence displayed in many of them, that the instructions and assiduity of Mrs. M'Ian must be of the highest order. The day being so very dark, I took my leave, proposing to make another visit when the light should be favourable.

This School has now been established eight years, and comprises seventy students. Considering that the majority of them on first entering the School could not draw at all, and had to be instructed in the first rudiments, the progress displayed by so many confers the greatest credit upon their instructor. The merits of this institution ought to be much better known than they are, and the example should be followed in the provinces.

I leave London to-night by the express train, and shall present myself before my partners tomorrow morning in the warehouse, with uplifted hands and eyes; but I'm quite sure our firm will speedily avail itself of some of the designs of those industrious young ladies.

4

IMAGE: 'CALICO PRINTING'

Tomlinson's Cyclopaedia of Useful Arts and Manufactures, Vol. 2 (1852–1854), p. 279

Fig. 410. CYLINDER PRINTING MACHINE.

Figure 4.1 Cylinder printing machine.

DOI: 10.4324/9781315400105-6

5

JOHN CAPPER, 'THE NORTHERN WIZARD'

Household Words, Vol. 3, no. 189 (5 November 1853), pp. 225–228

MY Wizard presides over by far the greater portion of our manufactures. He is the prime minister of your wealthy sugar-refiners; he is the right hand of your opulent brewers; the confidential adviser of all sensible farmers; the factotum of the iron manufacturers; the enamellers and papier-mâché makers cannot possibly do without him; he is always in demand amongst calico-printers; and dyers, bleachers, and calenders can no more do without him than they could dispense with the air they breathe. They would not offend him for half their wealth. My Wizard is a worker in huge caverns of smoke, in gulfs of fire and in oceans of insidious gases – a philosopher, who if he does not by a touch of his wand convert stones into pure gold; yet he transmutes the ugliest, most unseemly blocks of useless rock and mineral into potent agents of good, into wonder-working subtle fluids, or deadly gases, or brightly shining crystals.

My Wizard is employed in the vicinity of such cities as Manchester and Glasgow, in the productions of dyes and dye-tests, of salts, acids, and bleaching substances necessary in the different stages of the manufacture of cotton yarn or cotton goods. The vast extent of his works, the enormous quantities of chemicals he produces, and the astonishing results of his labours, are well worthy a few moments' consideration, as affording perhaps the best guide to the magnitude of those other branches of industry of which these are but the incidental offshoots.

A wizard of whose operations I am now writing is to be found busily employed in the wonder-workings of his craft within the city of Glasgow. Amidst the busy life, the ceaseless din, the undying smoke of that large town, his temple rears its lofty head high above the roofs of other tenements. Far out at sea, for many a league by land, the traveller sees what seems at first a giant finger pointing to the clouds. Looking at this nearer one might imagine it to be the Old Monument gone down from Fish Street Hill for change of air, and taken to smoking. I have no sort of hesitation in affirming that there is not such another chimney as that in the wide world, and I don't care where you look for it. If ever Cheops had wanted to give a little ventilation to the dwellers in the Gizeh Pyramids; if ever any Ninevite Soyer had commenced making soup for the million, in the great halls of Koyunjik,

DOI: 10.4324/9781315400105-7

most assuredly they would have erected some such monster shaft as that which overtops the Old Cathedral church of the good city of Glasgow. Those of my readers who may not have seen this Titan piece of brickwork may perhaps form some conception of its dimensions, when I mention that it measures one hundred and twenty feet in circumference at its base, and cost the enormous sum of fifteen thousand pounds in its erection. So gigantic is it and its subsidiary feeding-flues, that a coach and four might easily be driven along the main tunnel which connects this structure with the many fiery furnaces in my Wizard's establishment – ay, and with plenty of luggage on the roof too.

The traveller who takes his leisure along the busy wharves on the banks of the Clyde may see among the many ships discharging their cargoes there, one or two from which strange looking lumps of a dirty rough stone-like substance are being removed. Waggons are being loaded with it in rapid succession, as though it had been some product of great value. It is too earthy to be a building material, it can't be anything to eat, and the spectator feels certain that it is not guano. If we follow these heavily loaded waggons, we shall find that they are driven towards the King of the Chimneys – right into my Wizard's great iron-bound gates.

Within, amidst the Babel sounds and sights that meet our senses, let us endeavour to understand what all this busy world is doing. The first place is the laboratory or test room – the very inner sanctuary of this wizardom – full of curious little earthen pots, porcelain pans, glass cups and metallic dishes. There is a mysterious sort of Flemish stove in this terrible cook-shop, at which fifty kinds of supernatural stews are being concocted by the aid of as many different charcoal and gas furnaces. A quiet gentleman – my Wizard's right hand man – is stirring these pans with a glass rod as indifferently as if they contained gruel or barley broth, instead of doses that would ruin the constitutions of all the giants and ogres that ever lived in childhood's memory.

Our quiet friend hands over the charcoal fires, and the bubbling hissing pans, and the glass rod to some incipient Wizard, and leads the way to the great workshops of this strange poison factory. The laboratory is the place in which all their productions are put to the proof before being sent away, or where the earths and salts they employ are tested before use – a very necessary and delicate operation, requiring the utmost care and skill.

Covering ten acres of ground, these works present as busy a spectacle as could be met with anywhere. The number of persons employed about them is perhaps not so large as in many other kinds of manufacture; but their occupations are varied and unceasing, many of them, too, being, to the uninitiated, perfectly inexplicable. Vast sheds, enormous factories extend in every direction. The whole range of open space is intersected at all points with iron tram-ways, railroads in miniature. Along these, trains of loaded railway waggons are propelled by horses; some filled with coals, some with lime, others with salt, and many with the curious looking stony earth that we have seen discharged from the ships on the wharves.

Where they all come from, where they are going to, or what their use, are perfect mysteries. My conductor takes me through a lofty doorway, and I find myself in a huge storehouse filled on every side with leaden cisterns of enormous magnitude. There is not more than just sufficient space left between those Titanic vats for a portly man to walk in comfort. I am buried in lead; the place being in appearance a huge leaden coffin. A leaden feeling of oppression overwhelms me; I appear to be crushed under the vast expanse of metal; I try to catch a glimpse of the summit of those towering, far-spreading cisterns, and become giddy with the effort; my imagination is drowned within their metallic profundity, and I abandon the attempt. But what do these contain? Do they hold within their dusky sides a supply of water for the city of Glasgow? Not at all. They only contain vitriolic acid! Merely that. If I shudder; if I observe how thin their leaden cases are; if I feel chilly at the supposition of the consequences of one of them giving way at this particular moment, a desire to be somewhere out of scalding bounds will surely be excused.

It is a relief to step out from this chamber of horrors, to another of my Wizard's workshops; a long sort of kitchen with an innumerable quantity of little twinkling furnace doors, through which we perceive bright flames of sparkling blue rising in circling columns to some regions far out of sight. One of these warm looking cooking places is opened; and peeping cautiously in, I perceive the interior to be one long brick chamber, in which are rows of grotesque vessels blazing blue and white flames like so many incantation accessories in Der Freischütz. Can they be making soup from a collection of Chinese fireworks, or a warm *potage* from lucifer matches?

I am told that those earthen cauldrons contain portions of nitre or saltpetre mixed with the dirty-looking earthy stone before alluded to – in other words, rough sulphur. These are burnt together; their fumes ascend into a chimney perfectly air tight; whence they are conducted by means of earthen tubes into the huge leaden cisterns in the room just visited, and which contain a certain quantity of water. There the nitrosulphuric fume or gas is absorbed by water: and, combining with it, forms sulphuric acid or oil of vitriol. Of this destructive yet highly necessary acid, there are not less than half a million of tons manufactured every year in this country by my Wizard and his numerous brethren.

The sulphur stone is brought from one of the westerly districts of Ireland, whence the supply is almost unlimited. Every week a shipload of it is discharged on the banks of the Clyde, to supply the fiery requirements of this one particular northerly Wizard. Every week half a ship's cargo of saltpetre is poured into his capacious jaws of brickwork, and every week these rough, unseemly substances are forced by the magic craft of chemical science to yield three hundred tons of potent burning acid.

The larger portion of this terrible liquid is consumed on the premises in the manufacture of muriatic acid – better known amongst housekeepers by the name of spirits of salts – this acid being required in large quantities for the production of chlorine gas, forming the basis of a bleaching powder in extensive use amongst cotton and linen manufacturers. Sulphuric acid is also employed in the make of crystallised soda, produced in immense quantities by our friends the Wizards for the use of their manufacturing friends in Glasgow, Manchester, and other places. A considerable quantity – not less than four hundred tons a week – of this acid is concentrated by distillation in a platinum retort or still; and, in that state, is sold for many chemical and domestic purposes.

From the acid rooms I pass forward through extensive yards teeming with life, and coals, and sulphur; until I reach a vast range of hot and smoky buildings, though devoid of any visible signs of fire. There are huge, grim chambers of solid masonry guarded by sooty mortals in the deep silence of Ethiopic mutes waiting for victims. They hold cabalistic wands of metal in their hands. A sign from the deputy Wizard, and one of these ugly genii flings open an iron doorway of yawning dimensions, from which glare out fiercely upon us long spires of red flickering flame, dancing and twisting about us in hungry savageness as if they were the tortured spirits of so many original sea-serpents.

These warm places are the furnaces in which shiploads of common salt are blended with tons of the potent liquor from the leaden cisterns; and, in that condition, subjected to violent heat, sufficient to form from the mixture a substance called sulphate of soda, or commonly, Glauber Salts. In other chambers a similar fiery process is going on, except that there the saline materials are combined with large quantities of lime and coal-dust, all of which, being ignited, send forth terrific flames of a white heat until they make the beholder wink and blink again.

During this latter ordeal the Wizard contrives to effect a clever change in the composition of the substances blended together. In the last process the sulphuric acid had seized the soda of the muriate of soda or common salt so tightly and resolutely, that the muriatic part of it felt compelled to yield up possession; the consequence was that, instead of muriate of soda, the chemist finds he has a sulphate of soda. But now a retribution awaits the acid. The lime, naturally voracious for all acidulous matter, has its appetite quickened by the great heat applied; and which, whilst it renders the sulphate of soda easily acted upon, gives the lime a more powerful hold of the acid which it instantly and remorselessly seizes, becoming, in doing so, a new body – sulphate of lime. The soda thus set free is supplied with carbon from the burning coal, though not to any large extent, and is transmuted into sub-carbonate of soda, or common washing soda.

Looking on whilst a number of hot, half-clad, sooty people are raking with enormous instruments interminable heaps of glowing red-hot soda-ashes, from fiery furnaces that appear to have no end or bottom to their flaming abysses, I cannot believe that the scorching soda-ash is the same substance as the pure shining crystals so often beheld in the hands of laundresses – identical in nature with the beautiful white soda-powder which forms the leading feature in the refreshing Seidlitz draught; but all doubts are removed by being shown the succeeding process which completes the transformation. Another large building, hotter and more sooty than the last, is furnished with what have the appearance of bakers' ovens, on a very extensive scale. I am requested to peep into one of these wholesale bakeries, and I do so; but draw back rather more quickly than anticipated. I had often read of that theory which supposes the centre of our globe to be composed of a torrid sea of liquid fire – an ocean of the essence of Etna; here the very hot waters of that ocean seemed to be realized.

Another cautious peep at this wondrous lake of phosphorus and flame – at this restless rolling tide of flickering, hungry, remorseless fire. I learn that this cavern is filled with a solution of the soda-ash previously seen, for the purpose of being evaporated to a state of crystalline dryness. In ordinary cases of evaporation by heat, the calorific agency is applied below the matters to be acted upon. But here the liquid, requiring to be reduced to a state of solidity, is placed in a long shallow receptacle, over the surface of which a rolling flame of intense heat is driven by a restless blast. This fiery agency sweeps from end to end of the saline stream; and, as it darts on its way, lifts up and bears on its molten wings the lighter particles of moisture, which accompany it through many subterranean vaults of giant magnitude, and finally find their way up the towering chimney.

The thirsty flame is allowed to feed upon the liquor, until the latter becomes so concentrated that, upon cooling, it deposits the salt held by it in solution in the shape of fine, white, solid, many-sided crystals. In another and far cooler factory we find this solidifying liquor in the course of doing what we thus learn about it. Wooden cisterns or vats are standing about us, brim full of the bright, clear liquor. At the bottom of these tanks we perceive, on peeping down, a collection of the crystals; whilst in a further corner of the shed a number of men are busily occupied in shovelling quantities of these same crystals of soda into casks ready for sale, the waste liquor having been first run off. Those who are in the habit of seeing "washing-soda" in handfuls at a time have small conception of the vast importance of the manufacture for general purposes. The trade in this simple article – which may be bought retail for something like a farthing a pound – amounts in the aggregate to the yearly value of a million sterling; a hundred and fifty thousand tons being annually produced of this and the ordinary soda-ash. These articles are chiefly employed in the manufacture of soap and glass; and for the cleaning and bleaching cotton and linen goods.

There is now the muriatic acid room, a department smaller than the other. Magazines of salt are stored up in the vicinity. This, indeed, is the basis of the acid. Here again, the Wizard is all-powerful. The salt, or muriate of soda is blended with sulphuric acid, which possessing a greater power over the soda of the salt than its muriatic fellow, seizes it, appropriates it, and by the violence of its proceedings, compels the remaining acid to mount up in the form of acidulous vapour, which, passing away through stoneware channels into reservoirs, becomes muriatic acid.

This fighting and mastery of the acids; this gaseous flight of the muriatic particles of the salt, is going on all day long. It is at its height as we enter the scene of the conflict. A sharp puncturing in the nostrils, which darts up as it were to the very brain, a twingeing as if a thousand needles were perforating my throat, a winking of the eyes similar to that produced by hot blasts of sand in the great African wilderness, combine to make me regret having ventured within such unpleasant precincts. It is impossible to stand acid-proof against the horrid vapour that permeates my inmost man. I am blinded, choked and wretched, I look in vain for some exit from this inferno. The deputy Wizard is perfectly indifferent to any such sensation as I suffer from. He is adamant, and wishes to detain me to explain the process; but I intimate that I know all about it; that the thing is perfectly clear; and that I will pass on at once. I enter another capacious desert; but pass from discomfort to torture; from choking to strangulation. It is in vain I apply handkerchiefs to my nostrils and mouth; the subtle poison defies every effort. Death is in the air: the upas tree was an olive-branch to this destroying atmosphere; and, heedless of the unruffled guide, I rush out by the first opening I can find; knocking over half-a-dozen young stokers who impede my progress.

The terrible sense of strangulation is produced by the chlorine gas yielded by a mixture of muriatic acid and manganese; and which gas, being passed through tubes into a chamber half-filled with finely powdered lime, combines with it, and makes chloride of lime or bleaching powder, used most extensively for whitening many substances. The annual production of this is fully one hundred and fifty thousand tons: of which a hundred and twenty tons are made weekly at this one establishment.

The raising so lofty a chimney at such a large outlay was at the time a work of necessity, in order to convey the spent vapours of the acid works beyond the reach of human lungs. Singular to relate, within a month of its completion a method was discovered by which these vapours could be rendered perfectly harmless. Thus the enormous expense of the huge fabric might have been saved, had the inventor been but a little earlier in the field.

The Wizard's hungry furnaces burn so fiercely, that a shipload of coals is daily consumed within their devouring jaws; equal in one year to not less than a hundred thousand tons. His wondrous products are wafted to all parts of the habitable globe by ship, by railroad, by canal. Not a country but is indebted to him for some gift from out his precious storehouse. All profit by his skill; all are indebted to his science for more or less of good; and yet how few know, or knowing recognise, the mind which by its potency works out the marvels of this daily magic, converting earths, and stones, and refuse matter to things that scatter riches in their after course through many lands.

6

ANON, 'HELP FOR WOMEN'

National Magazine (May 1861), pp. 32–34

Our sisters and wives and daughters have, where the family is large, and a good stock of clothes is required, and the family exchequer is limited, a terrible amount of drudgery to endure. They have no time for reading, for attending lectures, for self-improvement. Very often they are denied the ordinary intercourse of society; ofttimes many a mother in the middle ranks of life is little better than a slave. In America they manage these things better. Where machinery can be used, and human labour saved, it is always introduced. Men and women are as much as possible relieved of mechanical toil. Science can never be better applied than when it comes to set men and women free – free for the higher modes of life and for the nobler purposes of creation. Women are under deep obligations to science; they are no longer sent to the loom and the wheel as in days when the garments of the household were woven and spun. And now another step has been taken for her self-emancipation; another of her wearisome and monotonous employments is gone. The solitary needle must pass into disuse. The Sewing Machine does all that was wearisome and fatiguing in the manufacture of garments.

The history of the Sewing Machine may be soon told. It was discovered in America, the country where labour is scarce and machinery is doubly welcome. The discoverer, Mr. Howe, took out a patent for the United States. Since that time great improvements have been made, and Wheeler and Wilson, whose London agency is 462 Oxford Street, have brought the machine to a perfection which really leaves nothing to be desired.

Prior to Mr. Howe's invention, patented in 1846, all attempts to adapt machinery to sewing had proved abortive. His is the basis of all successful machines. Their differences, however, are marked and important. The Committee of the American Institute classified them according to the stitch made and the purpose to which the machine is to be applied, in four classes, 1st, 2nd, 3rd, and 4th – a classification indicating the general order of merit and importance. Class 1st includes the "Lock Stitch" Machine for family use, and for manufacturers in the same range of purpose and material. The Committee has assigned this class the highest rank, on account of the "elasticity, permanence, beauty, and general desirableness of the stitching when done," and the wide range of its application. At the head of this class they place the Wheeler and Wilson Machine, and award it the highest

DOI: 10.4324/9781315400105-8

premium. The machine of Wheeler and Wilson is the most popular. Up to 1859 they had sold no less than 38,991 machines, thus distancing by many thousands the remaining manufacturers of sewing machines. The following figures show the extent and increase of the sales of Sewing Machines for the last seven years in the United States: – 1853, 2509; 1854, 4469; 1855, 3513; 1856, 7223; 1857, 12,713; 1858, 17,589; 1859, 46,243. Not only are the wants of the housekeeper met, but the Sewing Machine is found a necessity to the seamstress, dressmaker, tailor, manufacturers of shirts, collars, cloaks, mantles, clothing, hats, caps, corsets, ladies' boots, linen and silk goods, umbrellas, parasols, boots, shoes, harness, upholstery, &c. Some of the branches of business have increased to gigantic proportions. In the manufacture of men and boys' clothing in America it is estimated the machines save £15,000 on every £40,000. Annually it is estimated the saving effected on caps is £17,500; sundry hats, £76,000; shirt fronts, £170,000. It is calculated the whole saving for the United States is £42,000,000. It is not unusual to find from 100 to 400 Sewing Machines used in a single manufactory. Mothers support families thereby, and young women become capitalists. Contrary to the prediction of many on the first introduction of Sewing Machines, the needlewomen have been greatly benefited. New branches of needlework have been introduced, and the old ones greatly extended, resulting to the operator in better remuneration, lighter and more healthful toil. It is not unusual to find the owner of a Sewing Machine earning from £20 to £30 per month. The Sewing Machine will ultimately perform the greater part of the sewing in this country, as in America; and wise are they who, heeding the signs of the times, early avail themselves of its advantages.

The hygienic importance of the Sewing Machine is not less than its commercial. The unhealthful nature of ordinary needlework is proverbial. The cramped posture, the strain of the eyes, the derangement of the digestive organs and the nerves, over a monotonous task, have told with fearful effects upon the health and character of needlewomen.

The efficiency of the Sewing Machine is equal to about ten hands. The speed varies from 500 to 2000 stitches per minute. The actual time saved by the use of it has been determined by a series of experiments. Carefully conducted Tables are furnished by the Wheeler and Wilson Sewing Machine Company, giving the exact time required to stitch each part of a garment by hand, and with the Machine. Subjoined is a summary of several of these Tables:

	BY MACHINE.		BY HAND.	
	Hours.	Minutes.	Hours.	Minutes.
Gentlemen's Shirts . .	1	16	14	26
Coats	2	38	16	35
Satin Vests.	1	14	7	19
Linen Vests	0	48	5	14
Cloth Trousers.	0	51	5	10
Summer Trousers . . .	0	38	2	50
Silk Dress	1	13	10	22

	BY MACHINE.		BY HAND.	
	Hours.	Minutes.	Hours.	Minutes.
Merino Dress	1	4	8	27
Calico Dress.	0	57	6	37
Chemise	1	1	10	31
Moreen Skirt	0	35	7	28
Muslin Skirt	0	30	6	1
Drawers	0	28	4	6
Night Dress	1	7	10	2
Silk Apron.	0	15	4	16
Plain Apron	0	9	1	26

Seams of considerable length are ordinarily sewed with the best machines, at the rate of a yard a minute, and that too in a manner far superior to hand sewing. Saving of time, superiority in work, and healthfulness, are three strong recommendations.

Of the various stitches made by Sewing Machines, that best adapted to the ordinary purposes of sewing is known as the "Lock Stitch." It is the only stitch that cannot be raveled, and that presents the same appearance upon each side of the seam. It is made with two threads, one upon each side of the fabric, and interlocked in the centre. From two and one half to three yards of thread are required for each yard of seam. This is the only stitch that has commended itself fully to public favour, forming as it does a beautiful, firm, and elastic seam.

But we have not yet described the machine. Indeed we know not that we can. To be understood and appreciated and admired, as it deserves to be, it must be seen, and we are sure that Mr. Hunting, the manager of the depôt in Oxford Street, will be able to explain as clearly to others as he did to us in what the value of the machine consists. To work it the young lady seats herself at a small table, as in the following cut, on which the machine is placed, with her feet upon the sandal treadles by which it is driven; the fabric to be sewed is placed upon the cloth plate beneath, the needle to pass from left to right. The machine is then set in motion by a gentle pressure of the feet upon the sandals. The motion is communicated directly by a band to the mandril which drives the whole machinery. The needle, with the thread, passing through the eye near the point, from left to right, descends through the fabric, carrying with it the thread, forming a loop, which is gently taken from the right of the needle by the rotating hook. The rotating hook, in its revolution, enlarges the loop of thread, and at the same time carries it around the bobbin containing the under thread, which is enclosed by the rotating hook, and confined in its place by a simple slide ring. By this method the upper and under threads are locked together, when the rise of the needle arm draws up both, making in the centre of the fabric a firm "Lock Stitch," presenting the same smooth appearance on both sides, and forming a seam much stronger and more beautiful than can possibly be made by hand-sewing. The fabric is moved forward by the "feed" under the "cloth-plate," and the stitches are easily graduated by the operator. Three yards of thread are a fair average for a seam. The bearings and friction surfaces are so constructed, that the propelling power required is merely nominal, and the wear of the parts so trifling, that machines used continually in manufactories for five or six years are nearly as good as new.

The machine is very sightly, and may be an ornament to a drawing-room. In time we shall hope to see it in every decent house in the land. As it is, the sooner our poor half-starved seamstresses turn their hands to some more profitable employment the better. No one can regret the extinction of their trade, which has always been unhealthy, and always under paid.

Very pretty things have been written on needlework. Hawthorne tells us: –

"There is something pleasant, and even touching – least, of very sweet, soft, and winning effect – in the peculiarity of needlework, distinguishing women from men. Our own sex is incapable of any such by-play aside from the main business of life; but women – be they of what earthly rank they may, however gifted with intellect of genius, or endowed with awful beauty – have always some little handiwork ready to fill the tiny gap of every vacant moment. A needle is familiar to the fingers of them all. A queen, no doubt, plies it on occasion; the woman-poet can use it as adroitly as her pen; the woman's eye that has discovered a new star, turns from its glory to send the polished little instrument gleaming along the hem of her kerchief, or to darn a casual fray in her dress. And they have greatly the advantage of us in this respect. The slender thread of silk or cotton keeps them united with the small, familiar, gentle interests of life, the continually operating influences of which do so much for the health of the character, and carry off what would otherwise be a dangerous accumulation of morbid sensibility. A vast deal of human sympathy runs along this electric line, stretching from the throne to the wicker-chair of the humblest seamstress, and keeping high and low in a species of communion with their kindred beings. Methinks it is a token of healthy and gentle characteristics, when women of high thoughts and accomplishments love to sew, especially as they are never more at home with their own hearts than while so occupied." Is not this nice writing, reader? nevertheless needlework is doomed. Wheeler and Wilson have given it a death-blow.

7

KARL MARX, 'THE FETISHISM OF COMMODITIES AND THE SECRET THEREOF'

Capital (1867) (London: Swan Sonnenschein and Co. Ltd., 1902), pp. 41–50

A commodity appears, at first sight, a very trivial thing, and easily understood. Its analysis shows that it is, in reality, a very queer thing, abounding in metaphysical subtleties and theological niceties. So far as it is a value in use, there is nothing mysterious about it, whether we consider it from the point of view that by its properties it is capable of satisfying human wants, or from the point that those properties are the product of human labour. It is as clear as noon-day, that man, by his industry, changes the forms of the materials furnished by nature, in such a way as to make them useful to him. The form of wood, for instance, is altered, by making a table out of it. Yet, for all that the table continues to be that common, every-day thing, wood. But, so soon as it steps forth as a commodity, it is changed into something transcendent. It not only stands with its feet on the ground, but, in relation to all other commodities, it stands on its head, and evolves out of its wooden brain grotesque ideas, far more wonderful than "table-turning" ever was.

The mystical character of commodities does not originate, therefore, in their use-value. Just as little does it proceed from the nature of the determining factors of value. For, in the first place, however varied the useful kinds of labour, or productive activities, may be, it is a physiological fact, that they are functions of the human organism, and that each such function, whatever may be its nature or form, is essentially the expenditure of human brain, nerves, muscles, &c. Secondly, with regard to that which forms the ground-work for the quantitative determination of value, namely, the duration of that expenditure, or the quantity of labour, it is quite clear that there is a palpable difference between its quantity and quality. In all states of society, the labour-time that it costs to produce the means of subsistence, must necessarily be an object of interest to mankind, though not of equal interest in different stages of development.[1] And lastly, from the moment that men in any way work for one another, their labour assumes a social form.

Whence, then, arises the enigmatical character of the product of labour, so soon as it assumes the form of commodities? Clearly from this form itself. The equality of all sorts of human labour is expressed objectively by their products all being

DOI: 10.4324/9781315400105-9

equally values; the measure of the expenditure of labour-power by the duration of that expenditure, takes the form of the quantity of value of the products of labour; and finally, the mutual relations of the producers, within which the social character of their labour affirms itself, take the form of a social relation between the products.

A commodity is therefore a mysterious thing, simply because in it the social character of men's labour appears to them as an objective character stamped upon the product of that labour; because the relation of the producers to the sum total of their own labour is presented to them as a social relation, existing not between themselves, but between the products of their labour. This is the reason why the products of labour become commodities, social things whose qualities are at the same time perceptible and imperceptible by the senses. In the same way the light from an object is perceived by us not as the subjective excitation of our optic nerve, but as the objective form of something outside the eye itself. But, in the act of seeing, there is at all events, an actual passage of light from one thing to another, from the external object to the eye. There is a physical relation between physical things. But it is different with commodities. There, the existence of the things *quâ* commodities, and the value relation between the products of labour which stamps them as commodities, have absolutely no connection with their physical properties and with the material relations arising therefrom. There it is a definite social relation between men, that assumes, in their eyes, the fantastic form of a relation between things. In order, therefore, to find an analogy, we must have recourse to the mist-enveloped regions of the religious world. In that world the productions of the human brain appear as independent beings endowed with life, and entering into relation both with one another and the human race. So it is in the world of commodities with the products of men's hands. This I call the Fetishism which attaches itself to the products of labour, so soon as they are produced as commodities, and which is therefore inseparable from the production of commodities.

This Fetishism of commodities has its origin, as the foregoing analysis has already shown, in the peculiar social character of the labour that produces them.

As a general rule, articles of utility become commodities, only because they are products of the labour of private individuals or groups of individuals who carry on their work independently of each other. The sum total of the labour of all these private individuals forms the aggregate labour of society. Since the producers do not come into social contact with each other until they exchange their products, the specific social character of each producer's labour does not show itself except in the act of exchange. In other words, the labour of the individual asserts itself as a part of the labour of society, only by means of the relations which the act of exchange establishes directly between the products, and indirectly, through them, between the producers. To the latter, therefore, the relations connecting the labour of one individual with that of the rest appear, not as direct social relations between individuals at work, but as what they really are, material relations between persons and social relations between things. It is only by being exchanged that the products of labour acquire, as values, one uniform social status, distinct from their varied forms of existence as objects of utility. This division of a product into a useful thing and a value becomes practically important, only when exchange has acquired such an extension that useful articles are produced for the purpose of being exchanged, and their character as values has therefore to be taken into account, beforehand, during production. From this moment the labour of the individual producer acquires socially a two-fold character. On the one hand, it must, as a definite useful kind of labour, satisfy a definite social want, and thus hold its place as part and parcel of the collective labour of all, as a branch of a social division of labour that has sprung up spontaneously. On the other hand, it can satisfy the manifold wants of the individual producer himself, only in so far as the mutual exchangeability of all kinds of useful private labour is an established social fact, and therefore the private useful labour of each producer ranks on an equality with that of all others. The equalisation of the most different kinds of labour can be the result only of an abstraction from their inequalities, or of reducing them to their common denominator, viz., expenditure of human labour power or human labour in the abstract. The two-fold social character of the labour of the individual appears to him, when reflected in his brain, only under those forms which are impressed upon that labour in everyday practice by the exchange of products. In this way, the character that his own labour possesses of being socially useful takes the form of the condition, that the product must be not only useful, but useful for others, and the social character that his particular labour has of being the equal of all other particular kinds of labour, takes the form that all the physically different articles that are the products of labour, have one common quality, viz., that of having value.

Hence, when we bring the products of our labour into relation with each other as values, it is not because we see in these articles the material receptacles of homogeneous human labour. Quite the contrary; whenever, by an exchange, we equate as values our different products, by that very act, we also equate, as human labour, the different kinds of labour expended upon them. We are not aware of this, nevertheless we do it.[2] Value, therefore, does not stalk about with a label describing what it is. It is value, rather, that converts every product into a social hieroglyphic. Later on, we try to decipher the hieroglyphic, to get behind the secret of our own social products; for to stamp an object of utility as a value, is just as much a social product as language. The recent scientific discovery, that the products of labour, so far as they are values, are but material expressions of the human labour spent in their production, marks, indeed, an epoch in the history of the development of the human race, but, by no means, dissipates the mist through which the social character of labour appears to us to be an objective character of the products themselves. The fact, that in the particular form of production with which we are dealing, viz., the production of commodities, the specific social character of private labour carried on independently, consists in the equality of every kind of that labour, by virtue of its being human labour, which character, therefore, assumes in the product the form of value – this fact appears to the producers, notwithstanding the discovery above referred to, to be just as real and final, as the fact, that, after the discovery by science of the component gases of air, the atmosphere itself remained unaltered.

What, first of all, practically concerns producers when they make an exchange, is the question, how much of some other product they get for their own? in what proportions the products are exchangeable? When these proportions have, by custom, attained a certain stability, they appear to result from the nature of the products, so that, for instance, one ton of iron and two ounces of gold appear as naturally to be of equal value as a pound of gold and a pound of iron in spite of their different physical and chemical qualities appear to be of equal weight. The character of having value, when once impressed upon products, obtains fixity only by reason of their acting and re-acting upon each other as quantities of value. These quantities vary continually, independently of the will, foresight and action of the producers. To them, their own social action takes the form of the action of objects, which rule the producers instead of being ruled by them. It requires a fully developed production of commodities before, from accumulated experience alone, the scientific conviction springs up, that all the different kinds of private labour, which are carried on independently of each other, and yet as spontaneously developed branches of the social division of labour, are continually being reduced to the quantitative proportions in which society requires them. And why? Because, in the midst of all the accidental and ever fluctuating exchange-relations between the products, the labour-time socially necessary for their production forcibly asserts itself like an over-riding law of nature. The law of gravity thus asserts itself when a house falls about our ears.[3] The determination of the magnitude of value by labour-time is therefore a secret, hidden under the apparent fluctuations in the relative values of commodities. Its discovery, while removing all appearance of mere accidentality from the determination of the magnitude of the values of products, yet in no way alters the mode in which that determination takes place.

Man's reflections on the forms of social life, and consequently, also, his scientific analysis of those forms, take a course directly opposite to that of their actual historical development. He begins, post festum, with the results of the process of development ready to hand before him. The characters that stamp products as commodities, and whose establishment is a necessary preliminary to the circulation of commodities, have already acquired the stability of natural, self-understood forms of social life, before man seeks to decipher, not their historical character, for in his eyes they are immutable, but their meaning. Consequently it was the analysis of the prices of commodities that alone led to the determination of the magnitude of value, and it was the common expression of all commodities in money that alone led to the establishment of their characters as values. It is, however, just this ultimate money form of the world of commodities that actually conceals, instead of disclosing, the social character of private labour, and the social relations between the individual producers. When I state that coats or boots stand in a relation to linen, because it is the universal incarnation of abstract human labour, the absurdity of the statement is self-evident. Nevertheless, when the producers of coats and boots compare those articles with linen, or, what is the same thing, with gold or silver, as the universal equivalent, they express the relation between their own private labour and the collective labour of society in the same absurd form.

The categories of bourgeois economy consist of such like forms. They are forms of thought expressing with social validity the conditions and relations of a definite, historically determined mode of production, viz., the production of commodities. The whole mystery of commodities, all the magic and necromancy that surrounds the products of labour as long as they take the form of commodities, vanishes therefore, so soon as we come to other forms of production.

Since Robinson Crusoe's experiences are a favourite theme with political economists,[4] let us take a look at him on his island. Moderate though he be, yet some few wants he has to satisfy, and must therefore do a little useful work of various sorts, such as making tools and furniture, taming goats, fishing and hunting. Of his prayers and the like we take no account, since they are a source of pleasure to him, and he looks upon them as so much recreation. In spite of the variety of his work, he knows that his labour, whatever its form, is but the activity of one and the same Robinson, and consequently, that it consists of nothing but different modes of human labour. Necessity itself compels him to apportion his time accurately between his different kinds of work. Whether one kind occupies a greater space in his general activity than another, depends on the difficulties, greater or less as the case may be, to be overcome in attaining the useful effect aimed at. This our friend Robinson soon learns by experience, and having rescued a watch, ledger, and pen and ink from the wreck, commences, like a true-born Briton, to keep a set of books. His stock-book contains a list of the objects of utility that belong to him, of the operations necessary for their production; and lastly, of the labour time that definite quantities of those objects have, on an average, cost him. All the relations between Robinson and the objects that form this wealth of his own creation, are here so simple and clear as to be intelligible without exertion, even to Mr. Sedley Taylor. And yet those relations contain all that is essential to the determination of value.

Let us now transport ourselves from Robinson's island bathed in light to the European middle ages shrouded in darkness. Here, instead of the independent man, we find everyone dependent, serfs and lords, vassals and suzerains, laymen and clergy. Personal dependence here characterises the social relations of production just as much as it does the other spheres of life organized on the basis of that production. But for the very reason that personal dependence forms the groundwork of society, there is no necessity for labour and its products to assume a fantastic form different from their reality. They take the shape, in the transactions of society, of services in kind and payments in kind. Here the particular and natural form of labour, and not, as in a society based on production of commodities, its general abstract form is the immediate social form of labour. Compulsory labour is just as properly measured by time, as commodity-producing labour; but every serf knows that what he expends in the service of his lord, is a definite quantity of his own personal labour-power. The tithe to be rendered to the priest is more matter of fact than his blessing. No matter, then, what we may think of the parts played by the different classes of people themselves in this society, the social relations between individuals in the performance of their labour, appear at all events as their own mutual personal relations, and are not disguised under the shape of social relations between the products of labour.

For an example of labour in common or directly associated labour, we have no occasion to go back to that spontaneously developed form which we find on the threshold of the history of all civilized races.[5] We have one close at hand in the patriarchal industries of a peasant family, that produces corn, cattle, yarn, linen, and clothing for home use. These different articles are, as regards the family, so many products of its labour, but as between themselves, they are not commodities. The different kinds of labour, such as tillage, cattle tending, spinning, weaving and making clothes, which result in the various products, are in themselves, and such as they are, direct social functions, because functions of the family, which, just as much as a society based on the production of commodities, possesses a spontaneously developed system of division of labour. The distribution of the work within the family, and the regulation of the labour-time of the several members, depend as well upon differences of age and sex as upon natural conditions varying with the seasons. The labour-power of each individual, by its very nature, operates in this case merely as a definite portion of the whole labour-power of the family, and therefore, the measure of the expenditure of individual labour-power by its duration, appears here by its very nature as a social character of their labour.

Notes

1 Among the ancient Germans the unit for measuring land was what could be harvested in a day, and was called Tagwerk, Tagwanne (jurnale, or terra jurnalis, or diornalis), Mannsmaad, &c. (See G. L. von Maurer Einleitung zur Geschichte der Mark – , &c. Verfassung, München, 1859, p. 129–59.)

2 When, therefore, Galiani says: Value is a relation between persons – "La Ricchezza è una ragione tra due persone," – he ought to have added: a relation between persons expressed as a relation between things. (Galiani: Della Moneta, p. 221, V. III of Custodi's collection of "Scrittori Classici Italiani di Economia Politica." Parte Moderna, Milano, 1803.)

3 "What are we to think of a law that asserts itself only by periodical revolutions? It is just nothing but a law of Nature, founded on the want of knowledge of those whose action is the subject of it." (Friedrich Engels: Umrisse zu einer Kritik der Nation lökonomie," in the "Deutsch-französische Jahrbücher," edited by Arnold Ruge and Karl Marx. Paris, 1844.)

4 Even Ricardo has his stories à la Robinson. "He makes the primitive hunter and the primitive fisher straightway, as owners of commodities, exchange fish and game in the proportion in which labour-time is incorporated in these exchange values. On this occasion he commits the anachronism of making these men apply to the calculation, so far as their implements have to be taken into account, the annuity tables in current use on the London Exchange in the year 1817. 'The parallelograms of Mr. Owen' appear to be the only form of society, besides the bourgeois form, with which he was acquainted." (Karl Marx: "Zur Kritik," &c., p. 38, 39.)

5 "A ridiculous presumption has latterly got abroad that common property in its primitive form is specifically a Slavonian, or even exclusively Russian form. It is the primitive form that we can prove to have existed amongst Romans, Teutons, and Celts, and even to this day we find numerous examples, ruins though they be, in India. A more exhaustive study of Asiatic, and especially of Indian forms of common property, would show how from the different forms of primitive common property, different forms of its dissolution have been developed. Thus, for instance, the various original types of Roman and Teutonic private property are deducible from different forms of Indian common property." (Karl Marx. "Zur Kritik," &c., p. 10.)

8

ANON, 'SEWING MACHINES'

All the Year Round, Vol. 1 (new series), No. 17 27 March 1869, pp. 395–397

Well-made in general, simple, giving marvellous results of speed, sewing machines have found their way everywhere; into factories, work-rooms, drawing-rooms. They have brought about a complete revolution in the process of sewing. A good seamstress could make her twenty-five or thirty stitches per minute; a sewing machine will now do eight hundred. It is an increase of speed unparalleled in industrial history. The economical results immediately showed themselves by a general drop in the price of the most essential articles of clothing. We have all reaped the benefit of the invention; and how many have ever heard of Thimonnier's name?

And now for the physical and moral effects. The commercial results are palpable, immense; the hygienic consequences are the reverse of advantageous. For, the sewing machine is a tool, and so is the needle. But the needle is so light, so essentially feminine; the machine so heavy, so fatiguing to work! It illustrates the mechanical axiom, "What you gain in speed, you expend in strength." You get on wonderfully faster than with the needle, but you must employ quite a different degree of force to work this charming little implement. Has the idea ever struck anybody at any time or place?

One would hardly think it, to see poor girls fixed to their sewing machine as no other motive power ever was before. Riding-school horses are changed every three hours; omnibus horses every two hours; but here is no change. For ten or twelve hours a day, and sometimes more, the feet have to press alternately on the pedals, and the frame has to be shaken by the same continuous and regular movements.

The object of all machinery ought to be to replace manual labour by mechanical labour; but sewing by machinery leads to the very reverse.

It compels women to exert muscular efforts, to a degree never before required of them. It is an absolute contradiction to common sense. Instead of advancing in respect to hygienic considerations, we have actually gone backward. It has been seen that the implement beats the needle in speed, but by a greater expenditure of muscular power. Now, who supplies this muscular power? Who, except the workwoman? And do we fancy that muscular power is to be had gratuitously, without something to sustain it? Nothing in this world comes of nothing. Our bodies are machines, consuming fuel, quite as much as steam engines are. There is a close

DOI: 10.4324/9781315400105-10

connection between the work turned off by the human machine, and the alimentary substances with which it is fed. If you increase the work, and do not wish exhaustion and death to be the consequence, you must also augment the daily allowance of food. If the labour required be excessive, overtaxing the supply of strength which the organisation is able to furnish, a morbid condition of the frame is speedily induced.

To the increased production which we so much admire, there corresponds, in fact, an increased expenditure of the workwoman's strength, which she must meet by a fuller and more generous diet. If the fatigue be more than *that* can resist, there ensues a derangement of health and a decay of the natural powers. We can only transform or transmit force; we cannot *create* the strength to lift a feather. Every mode of exercise we take, costs some grains of alimentary substance, and we cannot lift our hand to our head without an expenditure of the provision laid in at breakfast or dinner.

These facts are confirmed by experiment. In 1866, Dr. Guibout gave the alarm in a report to the Hospital Medical Society. While attending the Hospital Saint Louis, he had to prescribe for several workwomen, whose weakness and exhaustion were more than suspicious: these evils were evinced in pale and hollow cheeks, bowed backs, epigastric pains, &c. Afterwards, the same symptoms were noticed in the provinces as well as in Paris. Consumption even was a possible consequence. It cannot be denied that the sewing machine may threaten permanent danger to the workwoman's health and morality. She *must* be better fed than ordinary workwomen; if her earnings do not supply the means, great cities offer only too many other resources. Female prisoners who worked at sewing machines, have not been able to stand the fatigue with the ordinary prison diet. They were obliged to be allowed supplementary rations; broth and boiled beef every day, roast meat twice a week.

The danger is greatly diminished when the machine is only employed temporarily or occasionally. Still, there ought to be limits for delicate young persons. By the way, similar symptoms have been observed in young ladies who regularly practise the piano for several consecutive hours per day. With sewing machines, having ascertained the exact cause of evil, the remedy becomes easier to indicate. We must consider the sewing machine as a simple implement; and, like all implements rapid in their action, we must make it work by means of a motor.

In large work-rooms, like those of M. Godillot, where five hundred sewing machines are at work at once, the motive power employed is steam. Each workwoman, by means of a pedal pressing on the communicator of motion, can regulate the velocity of her machine, or stop it altogether. But in small establishments steam is inapplicable, still less in chamber work. What is wanted to make the sewing machine uninjurious to health, is to couple with it a motive power inconsiderable in size, to be set going or stopped at will, a supplier of artifical muscular power, dispensing with that of the workwoman. We want a sewing machine capable of setting itself agoing. The desideratum is now realised to such an extent that it is quite possible for everybody to have their automaton or self-acting sewing machine.

A French engineer, Monsieur H. Cazal, has invented a little electric motor which, by its combination with the sewing machine, resolves the problem. On touching a button, the machinery turns, exactly as if an invisible workwoman were treading the pedals. Electricity does the work, and the woman superintends it. A pile stuck in a corner, or concealed in a footstool, supplies the motive force required.

The workwoman, to work, must be liberally fed: the electric motor, too, must be supplied with victuals, and luckily its digestion is never out of order, while its appetite is considerable. The pile is its stomach, which assimilates zinc, exactly as the steam engine consumes coal. Electric work costs about thirty times as much as steam work; notwithstanding which, its expense is low enough to allow of its employment in domestic industry.

M. Cazal, by attaching his little motor directly to the implement, suppresses the ordinary modes of transmitting force by which much power is unavoidably lost. He also thus diminishes the first effort which has to be made to set the thing a going. Four Bunsen's elements, for instance, suffice to put the motor in action. Now each one of these consumes about the fifth of a pennyworth of zinc per hour, making the expense for a day about sevenpence halfpenny or eightpence. For those who want to work only several hours per day, a few pence cover the cost. Now if the workwoman, or her employer, remembers that she must spend more than that on extra diet to keep up her strength, it will be found that there is a manifest advantage in employing the electric motive power, not to mention the question of health. Moreover, there are times when mothers of families cannot without danger work at a sewing machine. At such periods, a self-acting machine will afford invaluable assistance. The machines, besides, are furnished with pedals, so that they can be set in action either by electricity or by human strength. Finally, the electro-motor is so ingeniously contrived, that it will probably be found applicable to other things besides sewing machines.

9

LYON PLAYFAIR, 'ON PATENTS AND THE NEW PATENT BILL'

Nineteenth Century (April 1877), pp. 317–319, 321–323, 325–326

Some thirty years ago, I had the pleasure of making a tour in England and Scotland with some very agreeable travelling companions, among whom were Baron Liebig, Dean Buckland, and Professor Daubeny. Shortly before our tour, Buckland had proved that certain nodules found in both secondary and tertiary strata were really the fossil exuviæ of ancient reptiles, and he took us to see this fossil dung *in situ*. During our inspection of the coprolites, Liebig suggested that they might still preserve the valuable bone earth or phosphate of lime of ordinary dung, and if so he prophesied that the time would come when England would enrich her fields with the fossil dung of the old saurians. Subsequent analysis in my laboratory proved the correctness of this idea. Some time before this occurrence, Liebig had shown how bone earth might be made a soluble manure by mixing it with sulphuric acid. Of course it was a mere childish extension of the idea that the same thing would do for the bone earth in coprolites. The coprolites of commerce consist of two kinds, those which are really intestinal excretions from extinct animals, and others which seem to be mere mineral accretions without any immediate animal origin. The manure manufacturers patented the preparation of these by sulphuric acid, and held a monopoly for fourteen years. The application of the idea could scarcely be called the slightest advance on the knowledge given as common property to the world by Liebig, and yet agriculture was taxed for fourteen years by an abstraction from common right. The original discoverer, Baron Liebig, who had given to the world every idea which we yet possess on the subject, was left unrewarded, while the manufacturer who made a petty and obvious application of his conceptions is allowed to abstract a portion of the philosopher's discoveries from common right. The advocates of patent right would contend that the patent in this case was just, because a new material was brought into productive use. But the law is very uncertain in admitting this as a claim. There is a celebrated case in point. When madder is treated with sulphuric acid, it produces commercial garancin, a body of high tinctorial power. Some one found out that fresh madder was not the only material required for this purpose, but that the spent or exhausted madder of the dyeing baths might be converted into an inferior garancin by a like

DOI: 10.4324/9781315400105-11

process. Here was a great economy. Spent madder was a waste product, which accumulated in great heaps in calico print works, and it was possible to convert these heaps into a commercial utility. But the same law, which upheld the application of sulphuric acid from modern bone earth to fossil bone earth, denied the application of sulphuric acid from fresh madder to waste madder, and the patent was abrogated. Generally, however, the law looks with favour upon any even the most obvious application of a scientific discovery, but leaves unregarded the discoverer, who has to content himself with a tardy public gratitude. This is strikingly the case when the application leads to large and momentous consequences. The fundamental scientific laws which laid the foundation of modern telegraphy were determined by a Danish philosopher Oersted, a Swiss philosopher De la Rive, and our English philosopher Faraday. After their discoveries, various men began to apply them to useful purposes, such as electrotype and telegraphy. The semaphore was then, weather permitting, waving its cumbrous arms and repeating its sluggish messages from station to station. The patents which now appeared in quick succession to apply electricity to telegraphy have been among the most legitimate illustrations of the uses and purposes of patents, and yet how small has been their benefit to mankind compared with the original discoveries of the illustrious philosophers which led to them! The applications are indeed important, but they are an offshoot from the discoveries, and are confined to a single purpose, while the latter are universal and endure for all time; and yet the law recognises only the inventors, but apportions no part of the benefits to the discoverers. It cannot then be contended that there is an inherent right of property in an idea when it is transformed into material embodiment by an industrial application, unless the admission is extended to the discoverer of the law upon which it is based as well as to the inventor.

The ardent advocates of patent rights urge the existence of copyright among authors as an admission of property in ideas. There is no doubt a similarity in the claim, but there is an essential difference in its bearings on public interest. The adjunct of the word 'right' to the word 'copy' begs the question on the ground of principle, and might tempt us to show that expediency even in this case governs the law as much as in the case of patents. But there is an essential distinction in the working of copyright and patent law. I may take out of a book any principle or idea of an author and use it as much as I like for my own and neighbours' advantage. This I cannot do with the patented idea or principle of an inventor. If this difference did not exist, the monopoly of thought by copyright would be more intolerable than the abstraction of a portion of knowledge from the common fund by patent. Let me take an instance in point. Pascal was a voluminous writer over a broad region of human thought, and possessed copyright of his works, though that fact did not prevent mankind from benefiting by his ideas when they were applicable to any particular subject under discussion. His keen and merciless attacks on the Jesuits were much used even in our Parliament, when we had to combat with despotism and concealed papal aggression. In fact, the more that Pascal's ideas were used for such purposes, the greater must have been the satisfaction of the author. Now Pascal invented as well as wrote, and is said to be the inventor of our modern form of the ordinary wheelbarrow. I do not know that he ever patented it, but let us assume for the sake of argument that he did. All parts of the wheelbarrow – the box, handles, feet, and wheel – were old, but the combination was new and therefore patentable as being a novel utility. But Pascal's wheelbarrow and Pascal's books were in a totally different position as regards the public. From his book any one could freely extract and diffuse his ideas for public use, but the wheelbarrow could not be used on a single occasion or for the most trivial purpose without the payment of a royalty. The book and the wheelbarrow are undoubted property because the law has made them so, but the public have a much freer use of the one than of the other. The difference between the copyright and the patent is that between two estates, where the owner of one throws his park freely open for public use, while the owner of the other charges a shilling every time that you enter his grounds.

The best improvements of manufacture, though open to all, are rarely used, because it is no one's interest to push them, while manufacturers are careless to substitute novelties for their regular methods. Germany has felt this evil to be so serious, that, notwithstanding the famous condemnatory memorandum of Bismarck against patents, she has at this moment a new and liberal patent law before her Chambers. In fact, public opinion in favour of patents has changed not only in England, but among nations generally; and we have arrived at a general conclusion that, whatever logic and reason may decide in the abstract, expediency is too strong in the concrete. For experience has abundantly proved that manufacturers become sluggish without a stimulus applied by inventors. The former are content to go on without change; but there are two bodies who have great interest in promoting it – the public and inventors – and the problem is how to unite them in a common interest.

England is the last country that could afford to make any experiment which might diminish the inventive faculty of her industrial population. It is quite true that invention flourished long before protection was extended to it. In ancient Egypt what marvels of inventive industry are still found in her remains! Engineering, architecture, hydraulics, metallurgy, glass-blowing, pottery, spinning, weaving, dyeing, all flourished among the ancient Egyptians. If invention were not marked among Greeks and Romans, we must recollect that where war is the occupation of the free, and labour is relegated to the mechanical operations of a servile class, invention must become stagnant. Machines do not invent machines; and slaves as mere machines cannot be inventive. But as slavery faded away, and light penetrated the darkness of the Middle Ages, the inventive faculty received a great development. Even two centuries before the patent law of James the First, the art of printing, paper, guns, watches, telescopes, wire-drawing machines, table-forks, knitting needles, horseshoes, and glass mirrors had been invented. If this be so, the question may be asked, what need is there now of a patent law? The answer is obvious, that England has no other source of wealth than the industry of her people. Her land is insufficient to feed half her population, and their means of support must be found in an active development of industry. Improved means of communication by land and sea have reduced the raw materials of manufacture to be the lowest factor of production, and competition among nations is now a competition of intellect and not of local advantages. When the patent law was passed in 1624, Manchester was a hamlet surrounded by an undrained moss, and Birmingham was a village on the top of a bleak hill. The machinery which since then has added so largely to production has filled these towns with teeming populations, and they can only be supported by renewed inventions which will retain the superiority of England in the growing active competition of the world. Though previous to the patent laws important inventions, such as those we have mentioned, were made, they are as nothing compared to the triumphs of industry in modern times. There is no leisure now to let invention flow on in a sluggish stream, as it would undoubtedly do whether there were patent laws or not. Prizes in the form of rewards for successful venture must be offered to all who have inventive faculties, in order that there may be a constant effort for improvement and progress. These prizes are the royalties for successful patents, and expediency is their justification. But if expediency be the chief reason for granting monopolies to invention, we have a right to consider with what limitations patents should be given in the public interest.

The bill before the House is founded on the necessity of protecting public interests while it accords private monopolies to inventors, and it is well that we should examine its guiding principles. These are that only good and substantial patents should be encouraged, but that bad and frivolous ones should be repressed. The latter are to be sifted out by examiners, and the worthy patents are to be tested by their utility and by an increasing money payment as evidence that there is a practical interest to keep them upon the roll. The bill also compels the inventor to supply the public with the products of his invention, or to grant licenses within a moderate time and at reasonable rates. Patentees object to this condition of use. They contend that there are very few 'dog in the manger' patents, and that no one has a right to dictate the use of property. For example, a man may cultivate his fields as he likes, and even leave portions of them in fallow, without interference from the State. But patents, as we have shown, are not property in this sense. If they stand in the way of human progress, they are altogether indefensible. It is only by the right of use that the public can receive the benefit which is the justification of the monopoly. On the whole, then, the principles of the bill appear to be fair conditions in the interests of the public, though, by the manner in which they are applied in the bill, poor inventors may be much discouraged, and rich capitalists may chiefly benefit by the new legislation. This is a great merit in the eyes of rich manufacturers. A celebrated inventor said to me a few days ago, 'No patent is worth anything unless 20,000*l.* have been sunk in its preliminary stages.' The bill now before the House may give us well-tested patents of this description, but it may, on the other hand, unduly restrict invention. I have written enough to show that I do not desire to see the ground cumbered with useless inventions which trip up ordinary wayfarers in the field of industry. But I think that it is no improvement of patent law to contruct a system which has a tendency to repress invention among the poor, and only to stimulate it among the rich.

I have made no allusion to the views of those who think that patents should not be given at all, but that the State should recompense inventors by honours and pecuniary rewards. The experience of State rewards for inventions is melancholy in the extreme. It is true that there are a few instances in which such a man as Crompton, the inventor of the spinning mule, got 5,000*l*. as a wholly insufficient recompense when some five or six millions of spindles were enriching the country; but there are other records of large over-payments for the most trivial and useless inventions. Take, for instance, another reward of 5,000*l*., given to Mr. Steven, in 1739, on the recommendation of a Royal Commission, consisting of an archbishop, ten bishops, the Lord Chancellor, three Secretaries of State, five peers, and ten men of science. The reward was for a remedy to cure gravel, and the remedy proved to consist of three items – a powder, a pill, and a decoction. The powder was made of pounded egg-shells and snail-shells; the pill of egg-shells, soap, and honey; the decoction of soap and 'swines cresses.' The Government is an unfit tribunal to assess public rewards, which never could be so efficient as the results of commercial success. As to paying in honours, the time is past when that would be accepted as a discharge for public work in relation to industry or science. The State has unwisely limited these honours to combatant and more lately to civil services, while the victors of peaceful struggles in science and industry have lost their appreciation of them. At one time the sovereign was the fountain of honour to all, and three letters of the alphabet, with a few inches or a yard or two of riband, was taken as payment in full for much service rendered to the State. But by the exclusive policy of the Government, in denying honours to scientific and industrial achievements, the fountain of honour which used to spring from the throne has become dried up, and both discoverers and inventors have learned to prefer the democratic letters 'F.R.S.' to the more royal letters 'K.C.B.'

10

J. T. SLUGG, *REMINISCENCES OF MANCHESTER FIFTY YEARS AGO*

(Manchester, 1881), pp. 27–28, 37–38

Calico printers

FIFTY years ago all the ingenuity of a Chancellor of the Exchequer was employed, not in discovering how he could relieve the burden of taxation, but how many ways there were into the pocket of the British taxpayer. As a consequence we cannot be surprised that not only were newspapers and advertisements heavily taxed, but soap, leather, glass, and many other articles of general consumption, amongst them being printed calicoes, which paid a duty of 3½d. per square yard. I well remember how the tab ends of prints used to bear certain numbers and hieroglyphics which had been impressed on them by the exciseman. Of course there was a heavy penalty for either buying or selling a piece of print without such marks. Every printworks was under the supervision of an exciseman, who used to visit the place at certain times to levy the duty and impress the pieces with his stamp. Tales were rife as to excisemen visiting various printworks for this purpose, and sometimes being so well plied with liquor as to lose self-control, when their stamp would be borrowed for a short time, and used pretty freely in stamping hundreds of pieces, which were consequently admitted into the market duty-free.

I have mentioned that the second warehouse on the right-hand side of High Street, was that of Butterworth and Brooks, calico printers, whose works were at the other side of Bury. When a boy, I accompanied my father over the works, and remember being allowed to enter a room which we were told very few persons were allowed to enter, inasmuch as a new process of engraving copper rollers was carried on in it. This was by working a small steel roller, which had the pattern engraved on it, on a large copper one, by means of a press, the hard steel cutting the pattern on the softer copper, and the process being many times repeated till the whole surface of the copper roller was covered with the pattern.

The process of impressing cotton fabrics with a pattern in colours was not confined to calico, but was extended to cotton velvets. The material mostly used as a pigment was chrome yellow, of which, I remember, we used to sell a great deal to the firm of Jackson, Watson, and Greg, whose warehouse was in the neighbourhood of Watling Street. A large trade was done in these printed velvets, though what became of them, whether they were used for coats and waistcoats in the

DOI: 10.4324/9781315400105-12

agricultural districts, or were exported, I cannot say. At the time when the Anti-Corn-Law agitation was at its height, and a suspicion lurked in the minds of many, especially amongst the supporters of Protection, that Sir Robert Peel was undergoing a process of conversion, and was about to bring in a measure of free trade in corn, and whilst the country was anxiously awaiting some sign from him, Mr. Charles Ramsay, of Ancoats Vale, printed a pattern consisting of an ear of corn with the stalk and a flowing blade or leaf. On this blade was printed the word "FREE." He forwarded a piece of it to Sir Robert Peel, asking his acceptance of it as a piece of printed cotton velvet, but without drawing his attention particularly to the nature of the design. Sir Robert, of course, gracefully accepted it, and thanked the donor. In a very short time a paragraph went the round of the papers describing the pattern, and reporting Sir Robert's acceptance of it. Inferences were drawn, and the Protectionist party were up in arms, but the storm was instantly quelled by Peel's returning the piece to the donor with an explanatory note. I have in my possession a small portion of this piece of printed velvet which was the cause of so much commotion, which I had given to me at the time, and have religiously preserved ever since.

PART 2

Textiles

2.1

Fabrics

DOI: 10.4324/9781315400105-14

2.1 Fabrics

Edward Baines, *History of Cotton Manufacture in Great Britain* (London, 1835), pp. 335–337, 358.
Anon, 'A Day at the Nottingham Lace Manufactories', *The Penny Magazine* (26 March 1843), pp. 113, 115–120.
Charles Dickens and W. H. Wills, 'Spitalfields', *Household Words*, Vol. 3 (5 April 1851), pp. 25–30.
John Capper, 'British Cotton', *Household Words*, Vol. 5, no. 106 (3 April 1852), pp. 51–54.
Elizabeth Gaskell, *North and South* (1855) (London: Smith, Elder, and Co., 1897), pp. 54–55, 97–98.
Edward Baines, 'On the Woollen Manufacture of England; With Special Reference to the Leeds Clothing District', *Journal of the Statistical Society of London*, Vol. 22, no. 1 (March 1859), pp. 1–9, 11–14.
'The Diary of John Ward of Clitheroe, Weaver 1860–64', rpt. in *Transactions of the Historic Society of Lancashire and Cheshire*, Vol. 5 (1953), pp. 176–184.
Image: 'Cotton Printing', *The National Encyclopaedia: a Dictionary of Universal Knowledge*, Vol. 5 (London: [n.p.], c. 1870).
Image: 'Wool Machinery', *The National Encyclopaedia: a Dictionary of Universal Knowledge*, Vol. 4 (London: [n.p.], c. 1870).
Image: 'Weaving Looms', *The National Encyclopaedia: a Dictionary of Universal Knowledge*, Vol. 4 (London: [n.p.], c. 1870).
Anon, 'Honiton Lace', *The Gentleman's Magazine* (January 1871), pp. 164–171.
William Morris, 'Textile Fabrics' [1884] in William Morris, *Architecture, Industry and Wealth: Collected Papers* (London: Longmans, Green S and Co., 1902), pp. 133–163 (selections from pp. 148–149 & 161–163).
Anon, 'French Lace', *Bow Bells* (9 November 1894), p. 467.

Edward Baines (1800–1890), a journalist and politician born in Leeds, wrote on the textile industries of the North of England and the two extracts selected here are from his book, *History of Cotton Manufacture in Great Britain* (1835), and his later report 'On the Woollen Manufacture of England; With Special Reference to the Leeds Clothing District' which appeared in the specialised *Journal of the Statistical Society of London* (1859). His book offers a comprehensive study of the cotton industry, which he sees as wholly beneficial to the nation's wealth and prestige, as well as contributing considerably to scientific advances in chemistry and engineering. The mass production of cheap cotton allowed working-class people to be better clothed at a dramatically lower cost, a fact which is celebrated by Baines.[1] His report on woollen manufacture takes stock of the state of the industry and is useful in detailing the processes of wool manufacture, including the recycling of wool into cheap fabrics such as 'mungo' and 'shoddy'. The three images included in this section, all from the *National Encyclopaedia*, depict the machinery used in the production of wool and cotton, revealing in painstaking detail the various components of each machine.

Three of the other extracts reprinted here focus on lace manufacture, another traditional branch of the British textile industry. The anonymous article 'A Day at the Nottingham Lace Manufactories' (1843) discusses advances in machine-made lace in Nottingham, arguing that few people can distinguish between this and hand-made lace. The anonymous article 'Honiton Lace' (1871) displays nostalgia for the time when all lace was hand-made, focusing on small-scale manufacture in rural Devon. Here, the sight of women sitting outside their cottages making bobbin-lace is presented as quaint – a foreshadowing of the way the heritage industry now promotes traditional crafts and industries as a tourist experience. The 1894 anonymous article 'French Lace' in a similar vein focuses on the history of lace and the superiority of traditionally made French lace. The change signalled by these articles is typical of the way in which discussions of manufacturing from the 1830s, 40s, and 50s tend to celebrate machinery and modernity, particularly the low cost of manufactured goods, while features from the 1870s onwards evince a nostalgia for forgotten crafts and products made before the age of mass production.

British silk manufacturing is discussed in 'Spitalfields' (1851), a description of a visit to this silk weaving area in the East End of London. The article focuses on the unsuitability of unventilated workrooms, arguing that London fogs simultaneously contaminate the white satins and destroy the weaver's health. The authors urge the need for the industry to be relocated to the countryside, for white silk woven in Suffolk is 'as white as driven snow' and workers there are healthier. However, the Spitalfields weavers insist on staying in London, despite its disadvantages. Conditions endured by workers are also featured in the extract from Elizabeth Gaskell's social problem novel, *North and South* (1855), and in the extract from the diary of John Ward, a Lancashire weaver. Ward discusses the hardships he endured during the Cotton Famine of the 1860s, when embargoes imposed by North America on exports from Southern ports starved Lancashire of raw cotton. Both Gaskell's novel and Ward's diary reveal cotton as a global commodity existing in a complex network of trade routes and political situations.

An interesting article by John Capper (first published anonymously), 'British Cotton' (1852), highlights the dependency of the British cotton textile industry on slave-grown cotton from the United States. Capper discusses 'the Flax Movement', an attempt to 'cottonise' flax, a crop easily grown in Britain and traditionally used to make linen. If flax could be woven in the Lancashire cotton mills, Capper argues, then Britain's dependency upon America would cease. The article is hopeful that a new machine will be developed to convert flax into something resembling cotton fibre. However, nothing actually came of the so-called 'Flax Movement' and this article reveals the desperation of British manufacturers to source their raw materials from home, avoiding the politically volatile and unethically grown cotton crop from the Southern States of America.

Finally, the aesthetic qualities of textiles are focused on in 'Textile Fabrics' (1884) by William Morris (1834–1896), based on a lecture he delivered at the International Health Exhibition. In the extract here, Morris emphasises the 'important art of weaving', rejecting machine-made fabrics as inferior, being 'only used to get more profit out of the production of the goods'. Morris details the processes of hand weaving, championing aesthetically pleasing patterns and urging weavers to study historical fabrics in museum collections to gain inspiration. The rejection of machine-made fabrics and promotion of traditional handicrafts were central to the late-Victorian Arts and Crafts Movement, of which Morris was a central figure.[2]

Notes

1 For useful discussions of textile manufacturing during the period see Sven Beckert, *The Empire of Cotton: A Global History* (New York: Vintage Books, 2014) and Giorgio Riello, *Cotton: The Fabric that Made the Modern World* (Cambridge: Cambridge University Press, 2013).

2 See Elisabet Stavenow-Hidemark, 'Textile Design and Furnishings, c. 1780–1914' in *The Cambridge History of Western Textiles* vol. II, ed. David Jenkins (CUP, 2003): 860–881 for a useful discussion of Morris's influence.

11

EDWARD BAINES, *HISTORY OF COTTON MANUFACTURE IN GREAT BRITAIN*

(London, 1835), pp. 335–337, 358

A familiar but lively and striking description of the great change in the dress of the people, consequent on the introduction of English calicoes and muslins, is given in Macpherson's Annals of Commerce, under the year 1785. It is as follows: – "The manufacture of calicoes, which was begun in Lancashire in the year 1772, was now pretty generally established in several parts of England and Scotland. The manufacture of muslins in England was begun in the year 1781, and was rapidly increasing. In the year 1783, there were above a thousand looms set up in Glasgow for that most beneficial article, in which the skill and labour of the mechanic raise the raw material to twenty times the value it was of when imported. Bengal, which for some thousands of years stood unequalled in the fabric of muslins, figured calicoes, and other fine cotton goods, is rivalled in several parts of Great Britain. The rapid increase in the number of spinning engines, which took place in consequence of the expiration of Arkwright's patent, forms a new era, not only in manufactures and commerce, but also in the dress of both sexes. The common use of silk, if it were only to be worn while it retains its lustre, is proper only for ladies of ample fortune, and yet women of almost all ranks affected to wear it: and many in the lower classes of the middle ranks of society distressed their husbands, parents, and brothers, to procure that expensive finery. Neither was a handsome cotton gown attainable by women in humble circumstances; and thence the cottons were mixed with linen yarn, to reduce their price. But now cotton yarn is cheaper than linen yarn; and cotton goods are very much used in place of cambrics, lawns, and other expensive fabrics of flax; and they have almost totally superseded the silks. Women of all ranks, from the highest to the lowest, are clothed in British manufactures of cotton, from the muslin cap on the crown of the head, to the cotton stocking under the sole of the foot. The ingenuity of the calico printers has kept pace with the ingenuity of the weavers and others concerned in the preceding stages of the manufacture, and produced patterns of printed goods, which for elegance of drawing exceed every thing that ever was imported; and, for durability of colour, generally stand the washing so well, as to appear fresh and new every time they are washed; and give an air of neatness

DOI: 10.4324/9781315400105-15

and cleanliness to the wearer, beyond the elegance of silk in the first freshness of its transitory lustre. But even the most elegant prints are excelled by the superior beauty and virgin purity of the muslins, the growth and the manufacture of the British dominions. With the gentlemen, cotton stuffs for waistcoats have almost superseded woollen cloths; and silk stuffs, I believe, entirely: and they have the advantage, like the ladies' gowns, of having a new and fresh appearance every time they are washed. Cotton stockings have also become very general for summer wear, and have gained ground very much upon silk stockings, which are too thin for our climate, and too expensive for common wear for people of middling circumstances."

It is impossible to estimate the advantage to the bulk of the people, from the wonderful cheapness of cotton goods. The wife of a labouring man may buy at a retail shop a neat and good print as low as fourpence per yard, so that, allowing seven yards for the dress, the whole material shall only cost *two shillings and four pence*. Common plain calico may be bought for 2½d. per yard. Elegant cotton prints, for ladies' dresses, sell at from 10d. to 1s. 4d. per yard, and printed muslins at from 1s. to 4s., the higher priced having beautiful patterns, in brilliant and permanent colours. Thus the humblest classes have now the means of as great neatness, and even gaiety of dress, as the middle and upper classes of the last age. A country-wake in the nineteenth century may display as much finery as a drawing-room of the eighteenth; and the peasant's cottage may, at this day, with good management, have as handsome furniture for beds, windows, and tables, as the house of a substantial tradesman sixty years since.

The cotton manufacture, like every other extensive branch of trade, has had its seasons of depression; some of them produced by periods of national distress and exigency, and some by causes peculiar to itself; but from each of these it has recovered with surprising elasticity, and has afterwards sprung forward with an unabated rapidity of increase.

12

ANON, 'A DAY AT THE NOTTINGHAM LACE MANUFACTORIES'

The Penny Magazine (26 March 1843), pp. 113, 115–120

If the fair ladies who wear veils, 'cardinal capes,' scarfs, collars, borders, quillings, and edgings of British lace, could know the vast amount of inventive skill, of complicated machinery, and of patient endurance involved in the production of these articles, they would see how largely the well-being of thousands depends on the fluctuations of 'fashion,' and would perhaps marvel how such fabrics could be sold at such a price as the modern market indicates.

We shall perhaps be correct in saying that those who, from their sex and the form of their attire, have most concern with lace as a material for ornamental dress, are seldom in a condition to decide whether lace is in our own day made by machinery or by hand; or how far the two are combined. And there is good reason why this may be the case; for almost every year presents some new adaptation of mechanism, some new order of processes, by which a pattern is produced that could before only result from the needle of the embroiderer. In some cases the imitation is so exact, that a close inspection is necessary to determine the mode of production; while in others the machine produces a new pattern altogether, rather than an imitation of an old one worked by hand.

From the mode in which the lace-manufacture is subdivided at Nottingham, any notice of one single factory would fail to convey an idea of the general system pursued, because links would be wanting in the chain of processes. For this reason we have thought it better, instead of confining ourselves to the general arrangements of one large factory, to consider the whole town as a collective lace-manufacturing community, and to follow a piece of lace from house to house, and from factory to factory, till it is presented to us in a finished form. Several manufacturers, some of whose names we shall have to mention, have kindly furnished the facilities for this object.

In the first place, then, the cotton-thread is procured from the Manchester districts. There are probably a few cotton-mills at hand, but the main bulk of the material employed is furnished by the great Lancashire and Cheshire firms. We do not know whether flax-thread is ever now used for machine-made lace, but cotton forms the great staple, and to that we may confine our attention. The 'cotton-yarn

DOI: 10.4324/9781315400105-16

agents' are perhaps the first parties in the chain of operations at Nottingham to whom it may be necessary to refer. They come between the Manchester spinner and the Nottingham manufacturer, effecting sales of cotton thread or yarn from the former to the latter. These agents are in some cases lace-agents also, and effect sales of the manufactured articles; indeed they occasionally receive a portion of the finished lace as payment for the thread supplied.

Then comes the 'manufacturer.' A bobbin-net machine is so complex and so costly, that, unlike a common loom, the actual workman can seldom possess one of his own; he must be indebted to another man who possesses capital, for his working implements. In some cases the capitalist has a large building, containing all the requirements and resources of a regular factory, and where the machines are generally worked by steam-power. In other cases he may have a large number of machines, but instead of working them on his own premises, he lets them out at so much a day to middle-men called 'machine-holders.' These machine-holders intervene between the machine-owners and the workmen, much in the same way as a householder supplies a link between the house-owner and the lodger; he pays rent to the owner, and receives it back, with a profit, from those who occupy a subordinate position to himself. In such cases as these the machines are worked by hand-power, since steam-power only becomes available in a tolerably large building.

Mr. Drinkwater, one of the Factory Commissioners, who visited Nottingham for the purposes of the Commission in 1833, after giving a list of the machine-owners, says: – "It will be seen by this list that a very large proportion of them are proprietors of a single machine; in this case the owner generally works it himself, and so far partakes of the character of master and journeyman. It is not uncommon to find one of these costly machines, which may have occasioned an outlay of 500*l*. to 1000*l*., within a house but little removed above the degree of a cottage; but for the most part they are worked in the attics and upper stories of substantial houses, the lower parts of which are occupied as shops or lodging-houses. The centre of the town is not much filled with them; but in all the approaches and in the back streets, as well as in the better houses of the lower town, the incessant thumping of the machine is heard."

As an example of a factory on a considerable scale, we may mention one which we visited in the vicinity of Nottingham, in the possession of a Mr. Burton. The lace-manufacture is carried on not only *in* Nottingham, but throughout a circle of wide radius, of which that town is the centre. About two miles north of the town, on the road to Mansfield and Worksop, is a pretty little village called Carrington, many of the inhabitants of which are employed in this factory. The factory presents to view a double pile of buildings, exhibiting long ranges of windows, story after story, to a considerable height, and surmounted by the usual pinnacle of a factory – viz. a chimney. The entrance and the staircases occupy a middle compartment between the two ranges of buildings.

On entering some of the stories of the factory, the effect to a stranger is most deafening, for the lace-making machine is anything but a silent worker. Some of the stories of the building are filled with the machines, making broad net several yards wide, or narrower net for quillings. Some are occupied by winders, winding the yarn on the very remarkable bobbins employed in the manufacture. Some are devoted to processes subsequent to the actual formation of the net, but preparative to the sale of the commodity. In the lower part of the factory are smiths' and engineers' shops, where the machines are partially made, and wholly adjusted to working order. In a court-yard in front of the factory is an appendage which may at first seem rather remarkable, viz., a *gas-house*. The factory being a mile or two from Nottingham renders a supply of gas from thence a serious affair; while the system on which the factory is conducted renders necessary a large amount of night-work. The machinery is kept at work for twenty hours out of the twenty-four, two complete sets of workpeople being engaged; and thus a supply of artificial light is required for a great number of hours. It is to furnish this, and in sufficient quantity, that the gas-works, with the necessary apparatus of retorts, purifiers, gasometer, &c., have been constructed within the establishment.

At the factory here described, various kinds of net and lace, both plain and figured, are made. At another establishment which we visited, in Nottingham, viz. that of Mr. Beck, the machines are employed in the production of fancy net alone, that is, such as are intended to imitate the productions of hand-labour; both in the form of wide pieces, and in that of narrow quillings and borders. In a third establishment, the property of Mr. Cleaver, we found the machines wholly employed in making silk edgings; a great many widths being made at one time, and then separated by drawing out threads from between them; and some of the machines able to produce ten thousand yards of silk edging per week.

So it is throughout Nottingham and its vicinity. Some manufacturers undertake the fabrication of one kind of net or lace, and some another; but there is a general similarity of proceeding throughout, both in the mode in which the machines act, and in the preparatory and finishing processes to which the lace is subjected.

The reader may now very naturally be desirous of knowing what kind of a machine it is that produces such remarkable results. Here we have to state at once that a thorough comprehension of its action can scarcely by any possibility be acquired from a written description, unless accompanied by a large series of illustrative engravings, and studied closely by those who are accustomed to investigate the action of machinery. This is, of course, quite beyond our present purpose, which relates only to a slight exposition of the general principles involved.

Let us ask, then, what is it that the machine has to perform? It has to entwine threads one around another in such a way as to form meshes or holes, bounded by a circular, a square, a hexagonal, or an octagonal margin, according to the pattern. We may make the following supposition: – Let a number of strings be suspended from the ceiling of a room in pairs, so that when the two strings of each pair are twisted round each other by hand, they may form half as many ropes as there were strings. We will further suppose, that after two or three turns of one string round another, each string is twisted once round one string of an *adjoining* pair, and then returned again to its former companion. By this arrangement, each rope would become linked to the adjoining ropes on either side, and the whole would form a kind of net-work, presenting holes or meshes bearing some analogy to those of net-lace.

Or we may represent it pictorially, thus: – Here we have a small number of strings, fixed at one end; and each string has to be passed diagonally round and between the others, so as to form knots, links, loops, or whatever fastenings they may seem most to resemble. The reader, perhaps, could hardly bring the matter home to his own mind more clearly than by selecting a few threads of different colours, fastening them at one end, and twisting them round one another in a certain definite and pre-arranged order: he would find that the meshes produced would bear some slight resemblance to different kinds of net, according to the manner and the order in which the successive threads were brought into the twist.

Now it is to effect such convolutions as these that the machine is employed; and there is certainly much to call for admiration in the successful adaptation of parts to this end. In common weaving, it is well known that the cross threads

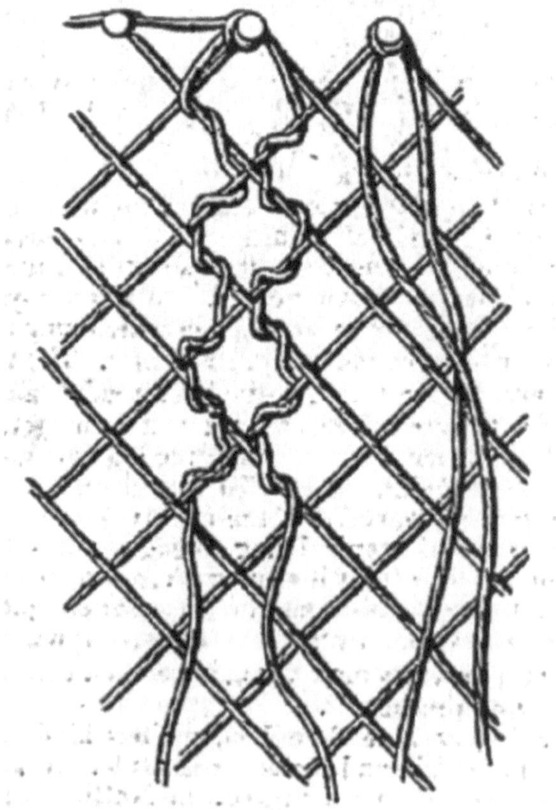

Figure 12.1 [Strings twisted in the manner of the bobbin-net.]

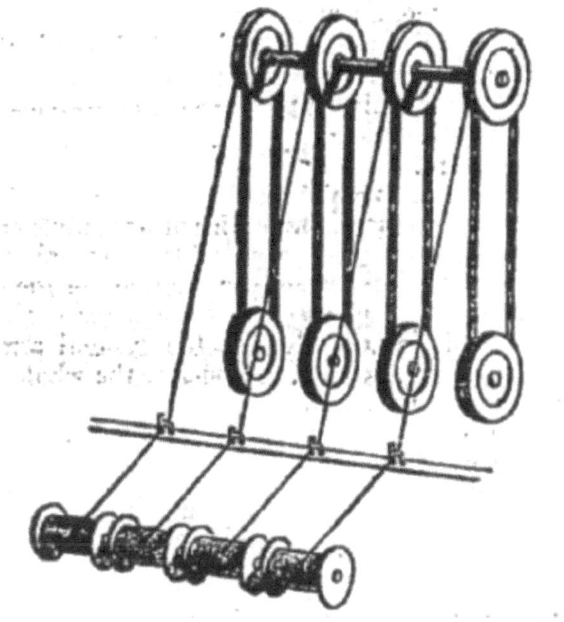

Figure 12.2 [Winding-Engine.]

pass at right angles over and under the long thread, passing over and under each thread alternately, if it be to form a plain material, or passing over several threads consecutively and under one, if it be to form a twill. But in the production of net this crossing is at the same time accompanied by a twist, so that one thread passes completely round another.

Annexed is a representation of part of a winding-engine; to which succeeds another cut portraying the essential parts of one kind of bobbin-net machine. The former winds the cotton for the latter, and is represented here to show how the cotton leaves the form of *skeins*, and is wound on a bobbin or reel.

The net-machines are infinitely more complex. There are several kinds employed by the Nottingham manufacturers, and known by the names of the 'circular-bolt machine,' the 'lever-machine,' &c., according to certain peculiarities in the mode of action; but one of these, viz. the 'circular bolt,' which is more used than any of the others, will be sufficient for our purpose. It so far bears an analogy to a common loom that there are warp-threads stretched in a parallel layer, and weft-threads wound on bobbins which pass between the warp-threads; but beyond this point the analogy is very slight indeed. In common weaving, the warp-threads lie horizontal; here they are vertical. In the former case, the bobbins are only few in number; in the latter they amount to hundreds, and even thousands. In the former the bobbin passes between and among the warp-threads in the direction of the plane in which the warp lies; in the latter it passes at right angles to that direction. In the former there is only one weft-thread, or one bobbin or shuttle, to many thousand warp-threads; in the latter, there are as many separate weft-threads and bobbins as there are warp-threads.

When we thus speak of 'bobbins' in reference to common weaving, we depart a little from common nomenclature; for the name of 'shuttle' is given to the little machine which carries the weft-thread: but the analogy of principle is observable, independent of the technical terms employed. The shuttle, in common weaving, is a kind of little boat, containing the weft-thread, wound upon a pirn or axis. But the bobbin of a net-machine is a most remarkable contrivance. The whole apparatus, including the bobbin on which the cotton weft-thread is wound, and the carriage or frame in which it is placed, is not thicker than the diameter of the meshes in the net to be made. Very frequently the thickness is not more than one-thirtieth of an inch! The bobbin consists of two thin disks of brass, about an inch and a half in diameter, laid face to face with a slight intervening space; and in this minute space the thread is wound, in quantity about fifty or sixty yards to each bobbin. The bobbin is then fitted into a kind of carriage, which conveys it between the threads of the warp, and at the same time allows the thread to be unwound from the bobbin: in short, the carriage is to the bobbin what the little boat of a shuttle is to the pirn on which the weft-thread is wound.

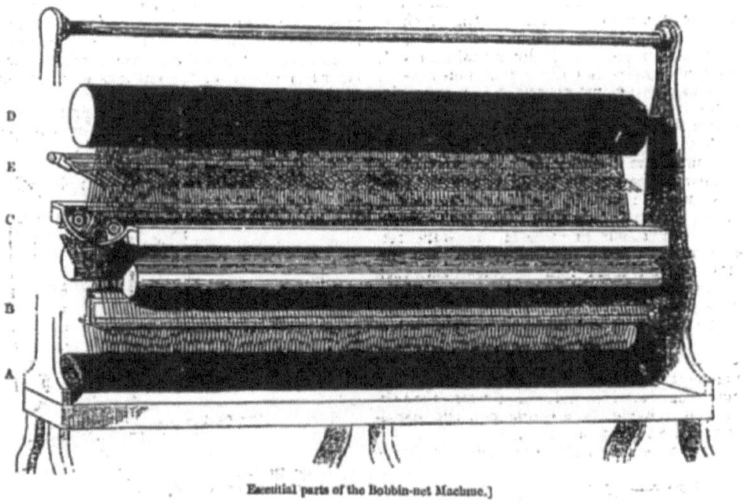

Figure 12.3 [Essential parts of the Bobbin-net Machine.]

(The warp, ascending from the beam A, passes through small holes in a guide-bar B, and thence to the point C, where the bobbins in their respective combs, driven by the ledges on the two bars beneath, traverse the warp to and fro, and interlace the threads as shown at D; the points E assisting to maintain the forms of the meshes.)

No less than three thousand six hundred of such bobbins as are here described are sometimes used in one machine! Many of the machines are twenty quarters wide – that is, fitted to the manufacture of net five yards in width; and have twenty of these bobbins to the inch. If the arrangements of the machine, as represented in the cut, be examined (the moving power being here wholly omitted), it will be seen that the warp-threads are wound on a beam in the lower part of the machine, from which they ascend to the upper part. The warp is divided into two parcels (somewhat in the same manner as the warp of a common loom by the action of the treadles), and each parcel is susceptible of a reciprocating motion, alternately to the right and left. The weft-threads, wound on the bobbins, are fastened each at one end to the upper part of the machine; and the bobbins are suspended so as to have a backward and forward motion between the warp-threads, like so many clock pendulums, being guided between the warp-threads by a very curious piece of apparatus called a 'comb.' The principle of action, then, is this: – After the bobbins have been driven between the respective warp-threads, the warp is shifted a little on one side, so that, when the bobbins return, they pass through openings different from those which they traversed in the first instance; and by this means the weft-thread, unwinding from each bobbin in the course of its movement, becomes twisted round one of the warp-threads. After this has been repeated two or three times, the comb which carries the bobbins is itself shifted to and fro laterally, by which the bobbins are brought opposite to openings between the warp-threads different from those to which they were before opposed. Herein lies the whole principle. According as the front layer of warp, or the hinder layer, or the comb carrying the bobbins, are shifted to and fro laterally, so does the weft-thread, as it becomes unwound from the bobbins, twist round the warp-threads during the passage of the bobbins across; a shifting, in one or other of several different ways, being effected immediately after each traverse of the bobbin. After a certain number of twistings have been effected, a series of points become inserted between the warp-threads, and temporarily hold up the knotted twists so as to form the meshes of the net.

It has been often said, and truly, that the bobbin-net machine is one of the most complicated which the ingenuity of man has ever devised; and it may therefore well be supposed that nothing more than the bare principle can be here exhibited. Perhaps it may assist the reader if we carry out our former supposition a little further. Let a series of strings be suspended from the ceiling in two rows, with their ends fastened to a horizontal bar; and let a number of small pendulums be suspended between the strings, and enabled to oscillate to and fro between them. Then, if after each traverse of the pendulums between the stretched threads, the rows, one or both, of threads be shifted a little on one side, so that the pendulums may return through openings different from those which they before traversed, we should have a system of movements somewhat analogous to those in the machine; and the strings by which the pendulums were suspended would be found to twist round the stretched vertical strings. If we further suppose that each row of strings is capable of being shifted independent of the other, and that the pendulum strings be fastened to a shifting bar near the ceiling, we might imitate in a rough way the series of movements by which net is made.

Not only is plain net made by these movements of the machine, but figured net also. In plain nets, all the bobbins are moved similarly at one time; but in fancy nets, some are stationary, some pass between the warp-threads, some are shifted laterally to the distance of one mesh, some to the distance of two or three meshes; some move to the right, some to the left; the warp-threads, too, instead of being divided into two parcels only, are divided into several, each of which is susceptible of the lateral movement independent of the others. It is by modifications of these lateral movements that all the numerous varieties of machine-made lace or net are produced; and if this fact be borne in mind, the principle of the machine becomes to a certain degree explicable. It is known to those who have witnessed weaving, that figured weaving results from a multiplication or extension of the same kind of movements as those whereby plain weaving is effected; and the same may be said of lace-making. It results from this, that a great portion of the complexity of the machine is due to the mechanism by which these lateral movements are produced: if the warp is divided into several parcels, each of which can be moved, either to the right or to the left, independently of the other parcels; and if the bobbins are similarly classed in several parcels, each of which shifts without reference to the others; it follows that an almost infinite variety of movements may be brought about; and it is not difficult to see that these movements must affect the manner in which the bobbin-threads twist round the warp-threads, and consequently affect the pattern produced.

It is by means of levers that the various parcels of warp and bobbin threads are shifted laterally, after each traverse of the bobbins; and the annexed cut shows one of the modern contrivances for governing the movements of the levers. This is an application of the Jacquard apparatus, which we saw at work in the establishment of Mr. Beck. Near the end of the bobbinnet machine is fixed the pentagonal bar here represented, each side of which is pierced with as many holes as there are pins or levers above, seen at the top of the cut. A number of oblong pieces of card, from two to five hundred, are connected together in an endless chain, and so arranged as to size, that when one of the cards is laid on one side of the pentagon, and the latter made to revolve, the whole series will be brought successively in contact with the pentagon, each one lying temporarily on the flat upper side. Every card is pierced with holes, varying in number and disposition according to the pattern of the lace to be produced, but never more in number than the pins or levers above; and these holes are so cut as to coincide exactly with those in the pentagon. Suppose, then, the pentagon to have an up and down motion, so as to be brought in contact with the pins, what would result? Wherever a hole occurs in the card, it permits the pin opposite to it to penetrate into the pentagon; but where a blank occurs, by the card not being perforated opposite to a particular pin, the pin cannot enter the pentagon, but is driven upwards. Now the warp and bobbin threads, and other apparatus of the machine, are so connected with these pins, that when one of the pins is driven upwards, some part of the thread-apparatus is

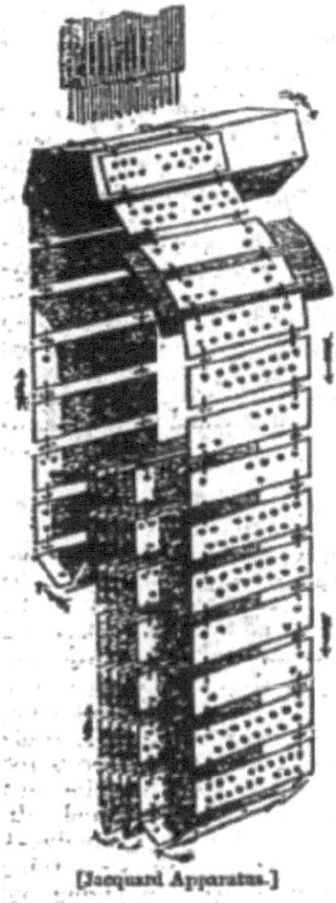

Figure 12.4 [Jacquard Apparatus.]

shifted laterally; and it hence follows that the disposition of the holes in the cards determines the order and number of the shiftings of the threads. It bears a strong analogy to the action of a barrel-organ or a musical snuff-box, where the number and disposition of the pins on the barrel determine the pipes and the springs which shall be sounded. The number of cards employed depends on the number of successive movements requisite to form one complete specimen of the pattern.

Whether the article be plain broad net, fancy broad net, sprigged net, plait net, wire-ground net, quilling net, or edging, the movements of the machine by which it is made depend pretty much on the same principles, and may therefore all be alluded to in connection. But in noticing the subsequent processes, it will be desirable to take some one kind as a standard; and for this purpose it will be well to select a specimen of 'piece-goods,' such as a collar or a cape, in which all the figures are worked by hand on a piece of plain net.

After a piece of plain net has left the machine, it undergoes the process of 'gassing,' or singeing, for the removal of the hairy filaments from the cotton. There are some firms in Nottingham which confine their attention to this operation only.

The gassing-machine is a very beautiful contrivance, in which the manufactured article is drawn between two rollers, and exposed, as it passes, to the action of a large number of minute blazes of gas, which remove the little adherent filaments without scorching or burning the net.

Supposing, as we do, the specimen to be a piece of plain net which is to be embroidered by hand, the net next receives a slight printing, with some coloured pigment, of the pattern which is to be worked upon it. There are in Nottingham a small number of artists (for so they are or ought to be) who design patterns for the lace-workers, and cut them out on wooden blocks, precisely as those for the floor-cloth manufacture. This is evidently an employment in which taste and a knowledge of the forms of natural objects are required; and it is satisfactory to find that a School of Design is about to be established at Nottingham, with the avowed object of elevating the taste and character of the lace-patterns produced. The lace is generally carried to the house of the 'designer and stamper,' who stamps the pattern very slightly on it. In the instance of a cape or collar, or any article of definite shape, the stamp gives the shape and size of the article, as well as the figures with which it is to be decorated.

When the stamper has imprinted on the net the outlines of the device, a 'pattern-setter' decides on the manner in which the pattern shall be filled up. For instance, if a leaf form part of the pattern, the stamper only gives the outline of the leaf, and it rests with the pattern-setter to determine how the needle of the embroideress shall fill up the device.

We next go to one of the humble homes of the numerous and lowly-paid 'lace-runners.' The term *embroidery* does not seem to be much used in connection with the Nottingham lace-trade, most of those who work on net with the needle being termed 'lace-runners.' Each workwoman has a frame, on which the net is stretched out horizontally, at a height of about three feet from the ground. She sits on a stool or chair, places her left hand under the stretched net, to keep it in a right position for working, and with her right hand works the pattern with needle and thread in every part where the stamper has imprinted a device. The needle is inserted between and among the meshes of the net, and stitches of greater or less length taken, until there is a body of thread laid in sufficient to mark the device conspicuously. This working round of the outline is called 'running,' while the filling-up of the interior parts is termed either 'fining' or 'open-working,' according as the original meshes of the net are brought to a smaller or a larger size by the action of the needle. How, by the work of the needle, the meshes of the net may be made larger or smaller, will be easily comprehended by the one sex, and must be taken for granted by the other.

It is sad work to see how continuously these poor females must labour before they can earn a small pittance. Little do those who see in the attractive shop-windows of London the beautiful veils and capes which Nottingham now produces, imagine how many aching fingers and eyes, and perhaps hearts, have been concerned in their production. We believe it to be pretty nearly correct to say that at the present time the earnings of the lace-runners do not, on an average, much exceed a half-penny an hour; for the weekly earnings for long days' work are not much above three shillings, and are frequently below it.

After the lace-runners have worked the collar, cape, veil, or other net-lace article, it is taken back to the manufacturer, who then employs 'lace-menders' to examine every piece, and mend, with needle and thread, every defective mesh in the net, whether produced in the machine or by any subsequent accident. This is done so skilfully, and the form of the mesh so closely imitated, that the mended part can scarcely be detected except by a practised eye. The females engaged at 'lace-mending' earn much higher wages than the lace-runners, on account of the greater skill required.

The bleaching is an important part of the net manufacture, and is carried on by several firms in the neighbourhood of Nottingham. The net, after going through the greater part of the processes, has acquired a tint nearly as dark as brown holland; and it is the office of the bleacher to give it the snowy whiteness which adds so much to the beauty of the material. This bleaching is effected by a series of processes, such as scouring, exposure to the action of bleaching liquid, drying, &c. At one bleaching establishment near Nottingham, that of Messrs. Manlove and Alliott, we witnessed a most remarkable mode of drying the net after bleaching, recently patented, we believe, by these gentlemen. Usually the bleached article is wrung or pressed, and then hung up in a hot room to dry; but in this new mode the net is wrapped round in a kind of coil, between two concentric copper cylinders, the outer one of which is perforated with holes. The apparatus is then made to rotate with extraordinary velocity, so great even as a thousand times in a minute; and the centrifugal force thus engendered drives out the water from the damp net through the holes in the cylinder, thus leaving the material nearly dry. It is expected that this invention will introduce important improvements in bleaching and analogous processes.

If the net or lace is to be black, instead of white, it is dyed instead of bleached.

After being again examined to see whether any further mending is required, the net next goes to be 'dressed,' and this takes us to the work-rooms of another class of persons. The 'lace-dressing rooms' of Nottingham are sometimes two hundred feet in length, and furnished as in the annexed cut. Long frames extend from end to end of the shop, capable of being adjusted to any width by a screw, and provided with a row of pins round the edge. The net or lace is first dipped in a mixture of gum, paste, and water, wrung out, and stretched upon the frame by means of the pins or studs. While on the frame it is rubbed well with flannels, to equalize the action of the stiffening material in different parts, and then left to dry in a warm room. It is to the nature of the solution used that the different kinds of net and lace owe their different degrees of stiffness.

If the manufactured article be a cape, a collar, or a veil, it is not till the present stage in the proceedings that it is cut from the piece. The stamping, the embroidering, the gassing, the bleaching, the dressing – all are done while the piece is yet whole, several yards in length; but when it approaches thus far towards completion, the material is cut up, according to the size and shape given by the stamp, and a 'pearl edge,' or something similar, is sewn on by hand round every edge.

After a process of rolling, pressing, ticketing, &c., the article is finished.

The kind of article which we have selected as a specimen or standard comprises within the range of its manufacture nearly all the processes involved in the other branches of the lace-trade; and will therefore serve to give an idea of them all. As regards the question, to what degree hand-labour is employed upon the different varieties, the following will be a kind of summing-up. In a plain net the whole fabric is made at the machine. In sprigged net, the groundwork and a portion of every sprig are made at the machine, and the outline of every sprig is then worked by hand. In fancy broad-net the device as well as the groundwork are made at the machine. In plait-net the same thing is observable, and also in tatting-net. In edging and lace for borders the device is now very generally worked by the machine, but in some varieties it is partly put in by hand. In 'piece-goods,' such as capes, collars, and veils, the device is almost wholly worked by hand, a very small proportion being effected by the Jacquard appendage to the lace-machine. As an exemplification of the manner in which the machine and the hand imitate each other's productions, we annex representations of two specimens, one of which was wholly worked at the machine, and the other wholly figured by hand on a machine-made net, excepting the pearl edge,' which, after being made at the machine, was sewn on by hand.

We stated, in a former part of the article, that the machine-holder, whether owner or not, buys thread from the Manchester cotton-spinner, and then works it up into net or lace. He does not do anything further to the material, but sells it at once, either to other manufacturers, or to agents and dealers. These other manufacturers carry the material through all the subsequent operations, employing and paying for the services of the gassers, the bleachers, the dyers, the dressers, the stampers, the menders, and the embroiderers. Some of these manufacturers only undertake the finishing of the plain goods, while others confine themselves to the fancy or embroidery department. One of these latter, Mr. Hickling, to whose kindness we have been much indebted, has been instrumental in the introduction of the Nottingham 'cardinal capes' of modern lady-costume; while other firms have taken up some other department in particular. Some are 'cap-manufacturers;' that is, they procure the lace from the machine-workers, dress and finish it, cut it up, and employ a number of women to make it into caps. Lastly, agents, sent by the great wholesale houses from London and elsewhere, visit Nottingham periodically, and make their purchases in lace and net; for Nottingham is the market for this commodity, whether made there or elsewhere.

Such, then, is a very brief sketch of a manufacture which may be said to have had no existence in the beginning of the present century, and of which Mr. Felkin (the greatest authority in all matters relating to the bobbin-net trade) made the following estimate in 1831: he calculated that the capital employed in Manchester in spinning thread for the bobbin-net manufacturers amounted to nearly a million sterling; and that the capital employed by the latter in various ways exceeded two millions sterling; that the number of persons employed in spinning, making, winding, embroidering, mending, &c. for the bobbin-net work, amounted to more than two hundred thousand; that the raw material (cotton and silk) used was worth about 150,000*l*. annually, in the state as imported; that this value was increased to 540,000*l*. when spun into thread; and that the final value, when manufactured into net, and ready for sale, was nearly two millions sterling per annum, or, including the wages of the embroiderers employed in different parts of England, more than three millions sterling! These results are certainly extraordinary, and could have been but little anticipated by the inventors of the machine, sanguine as they might be.

13

CHARLES DICKENS AND W. H. WILLS, 'SPITALFIELDS'

Household Words, Vol. 3 (5 April 1851), pp. 25–30

Have you any distinct idea of Spitalfields, dear reader? A general one, no doubt you have – an impression that there are certain squalid streets, lying like narrow black trenches, far below the steeples, somewhere about London, – towards the East, perhaps, – where sallow, unshorn weavers, who have nothing to do, prowl languidly about, or lean against posts, or sit brooding on door-steps, and occasionally assemble together in a crowd to petition Parliament or the Queen; after which there is a Drawing-Room, or a Court Ball, where all the great ladies wear dresses of Spitalfields manufacture; and then the weavers dine for a day or two, and so relapse into prowling about the streets, leaning against the posts, and brooding on the door-steps.

Will you come to Spitalfields?

The house to which we are bound, stands at an angle with the spot where the Pulpit-cross was anciently planted; whence, on every Easter Monday and Tuesday, the Spital sermons were preached, in presence of the Lord Mayor and Corporation, and children of Christ's Hospital. We cross the many-cornered "square" and enter a sort of gateway.

Along a narrow passage, up a dark stair, through a crazy door, into a room not very light, not very large, not in the least splendid; with queer corners, and quaint carvings, and massive chimney-pieces; with tall cupboards with prim doors, and squat counters with deep dumpy drawers; with desks behind thin rails, with aisles between thick towers of papered-up packages, out of whose ends flash all the colours of the rainbow – where all is as quiet as a playhouse at daybreak, or a church at midnight – where, in truth, there is nobody to make a noise, except one well-dressed man, one attendant porter (neither of whom seem to be doing anything particular), and one remarkably fine male cat, admiring, before the fire, the ends of his silky paws – where the door, as we enter, shuts with a deep, dull, muffled sound, that is more startling than a noise – where there is less bustle than at a Quakers' meeting, and less business going on than in a Government office – the well-dressed man threads the mazes of the piles, and desks, and cupboards, and counters, with a slow step, to greet us, and to assure us, in reply to

 DOI: 10.4324/9781315400105-17

our apology, that we have *not* made any mistake whatever, and that we are in the silk warehouse which we seek: a warehouse in which, we have previously been informed, by one whose word we never before doubted, that there is "turned over" an annual average of one hundred thousand pounds, of good and lawful money of Great Britain.

We may tell our informant, frankly, that, looking round upon the evidences of stagnation which present themselves, we utterly disbelieve his statement. Our faith, however, is soon strengthened. Somebody mounts the stairs, and enters the apartment with the deliberate air of a man who has nothing whatever to do, but to walk about in a beautifully brushed hat, a nicely-fitting coat admirably buttoned, symmetrical boots, and a stock of amazing satin; to crush his gloves tightly between his hands, and to call on his friends, to ask them – as this gentleman asks our friend – how he is getting on; and whether he has been down "yonder" lately (a jerk eastward of the glossy hat); and, if he hasn't, whether he intends going down next Sunday, because if he does, he (the visitor) means to go too, and will take him down in his "trap." He then, in a parenthetical, post-scriptum sort of way, alludes to certain "assorted Glacés," and indicates the pile of silks he means by the merest motion of his ring finger. "The figure is –" says he.

"Two and seven," replies the vendor; "How many pieces shall I put aside?"

"Well – fifty. By-the-bye, have you heard?" – Mr. Broadelle (our friend) has *not* heard, and the visitor proceeds to announce, from unimpeachable authority, that the match between Mr. Crumpley of Howell's, and Miss Lammy of Swan's, is to come off at last: in fact, next Thursday. Cordial "good bye;" graceful elevation of the polished hat to myself; and departure of, as Mr. Broadelle informs us, one of his best customers.

"Customer?"

"Yes? You heard? He has just bought fifty pieces of silk of various or 'assorted' colours."

"At two shillings and seven-pence per yard?"

"Just so. And there are eighty-four yards in a piece."

"Our trade," says our friend . . . "has been reduced to a system that enables us to transact business with the fewest possible words, and in the easiest possible way. The gentleman who has just left, is Messrs. Treacy and Mclntyre's silk-buyer. That department of their establishment is handed over to his management as unrestrictedly and unreservedly as if the whole concern were his own. In like manner, the different branches of large houses – such as cotton, woollen, hosiery, small wares, &c. – are placed under the controul of similar buyers. At the end of every half-year, an account is taken of the stewardship of each of these heads of department; and, if his particular branch has not flourished – should the stock on hand be large and unsaleable – the Buyer is called to account, and his situation jeopardised. The partners, of course, know the capabilities and peculiarities of their trade, and can tell, on investigation, how and why the Buyer has been at fault. If, on the contrary, the Buyer have narrowly watched the public taste, and fed it successfully, – if he have been vigilant in getting early possession of the most attractive patterns, or in pouncing on cheap markets, by taking advantage, for instance, of the embarrassments of a "shaky" manufacturer or a French revolution (for he scours the country at home and abroad in all directions), and if his department come out at the six-monthly settlement with marked profit – his salary is possibly raised. Should this success be repeated, he is usually taken into the firm as a partner."

"But, *no* judgment was exercised in the bargain just made. The Buyer did not even look at your goods."

"That is the result of previous study and experience. It is the art that conceals art. He need not examine the goods. He has learned the characteristics of our dyes to a shade, and the qualities of our fabrics to a thread."

"Then, as to price. I suppose your friend is lounging about, in various other Spitalfields warehouses at this moment. Perhaps by this time he has run his firm into debt for a few thousand pounds more?"

"Very likely."

"Well; suppose a neighbour of yours were to offer him the same sort of silks as those he has just chosen here, for less money, could he not – as no writing has passed between you – be off his bargain with you?"

"Too late. The thing is done, and cannot be undone," answers Mr. Broadelle, made a little serious by the bare notion of such a breach of faith. "Our bargain is as tight as if it had been written on parchment and attested by a dozen witnesses. His very existence as a Buyer, and mine as a Manufacturer, depend upon the scrupulous performance of the contract. I shall send in the silks this afternoon. And I feel as certain of a check for the cash, at our periodical settlement, as I do of death and quarter-day."

It is difficult to reconcile the immense amount of capital which flows through such a house as this – the rich stores of satins, velvets, lutestrings, brocades, damasks, and other silk textures, which Mr. Broadelle brings to light from the quaint cupboards and drawers – with the poignant and often-repeated cry of poverty that proceeds from this quarter.

What says Mr. Broadelle to it? He says this:

"Although most masters make this locality their head-quarters, and employ the neighbouring weavers, yet they nearly all have factories in the provinces: chiefly in Lancashire. The Spitalfields weaver of plain silks and velvets, therefore, keeps up a hopeless contest against machinery and cheaper labour, and struggles against overwhelming odds. Will you step round and see a family engaged in this desperate encounter?"

"Is there no remedy?" we ask, as we go out together.

"A very simple one. In the country – say in Suffolk, where we have a hand-weaving factory – food is cheaper and better; both food for the stomach, and food for the lungs."

"The air is better, so less money, you think, would be spent in drink?"

"Undoubtedly. Fancy yourself stewed up in a stifling room all day; imagine the lassitude into which your whole frame would collapse after fourteen hours' mere inhalation of a stale, bad, atmosphere – to say nothing of fourteen hours' hard work in addition; and consider what stern self-denial it would require to refrain from some stimulant – a glass of bad gin, perhaps – if you could get it. On the other hand, the fresh air which plays around country looms, exhilarates in itself, and is found to be a substitute for gin."

"I have also heard that the atmosphere of London is positively detrimental to the manufacture of silk. Is that so?"

"Why, sir," replies Mr. Broadelle, stopping short, and speaking like a deeply-injured man, "the two-days' fog we had in December last, was a dead loss to me of one hundred pounds. The blacks (London genuine particular) got into the white satins, despite the best precautions of the workpeople, and put them into an ugly, foxy, unsaleable half-mourning, sir. They would not even take a dye, decently. I had to send down, express, to our Suffolk branch to supply the deficiency; and the white satins, partly woven there on the same days, came up as white as driven snow."

Considering that both the worker and the work are deteriorated by an obstinate tenure of the present dense and unfit site, it seems wonderful that the weavers themselves are not as anxious to remove from a noxious and unprofitable neighbourhood, as their wellwishers can be to effect their removal. From fourteen to seventeen thousand looms are contained in from eleven to twelve thousand houses – although, at the time at which we write, not more than from nine to ten thousand of them are at work. The average number of houses per acre in the parish is seventeen; and the average per acre for all London being no more than five and a fifth, Spitalfields contains the densest population, perhaps, existing. Within its small boundaries, not less than eighty-five thousand human beings are huddled. "They are," says Mr. Broadelle, "so interlaced, and bound together, by debt, marriage, and prejudice, that, despite many inducements to remove to the country establishments of the masters they already serve, they prefer dragging on a miserable existence in their present abodes. Spitalfields was the Necropolis of Roman London; the Registrar-General's returns show that it is now the grave of modern Manufacturing London. The average mortality is higher in this Metropolitan district than in any other."

"And what strange streets they are, Mr. Broadelle! These high gaunt houses, all window on the upper story, and that window all small diamond panes, are like the houses in some foreign town, and have no trace ol London in them – except its soot, which is indeed a large exception. It is as if the Huguenots had brought their streets along with them, and dropped them down here. And what a number of strange shops, that seem to be open for no earthly reason, having nothing to sell! A few halfpenny bundles ot firewood, a few halfpenny kites, halfpenny battledores, and farthing shuttle-cocks, form quite an extensive stock in trade here. Eatables are so important in themselves, that there is no need to set them off. Be the loaves never so coarse in texture, and never so unattractively jumbled together in the baker's dirty window, they *are* loaves, and that is the main thing. Liver, lights, and sheep's-heads, freckled sausages, and strong black puddings, are sufficiently enticing without decoration. The mouths of Spitalfields will water for them, howsoever raw and ugly they be. Is its intellectual appetite sharp-set, I wonder, for that wolfish literature of highly-coloured show-bill and rampant wood-cut, filling the little shop-window over the way, and covering half the house? Do the poor weavers, by the dim light of their lamps, unravel those villanous fabrics, and nourish their care-worn hearts on the last strainings of the foulest filth of France?" "I can't say," replies Mr. Broadelle; "we have but little intercourse with them in their domestic lives. They are rather jealous and suspicious. We have tried Mechanics' Institutions, but they have not come to much."

"Is there any school here?"

"Yes. Here it is."

An old house, hastily adapted to the purpose, with too much darkness in it and too little air, but no want of scholars. An infant school on the ground floor, where the infants are, as usual, drowsily rubbing their noses, or poking their fore-fingers into the features of other infants on exploratory surveys. Intermediate schools above. At the top of all, in a large, long, light room – occupying the width of two dwelling-houses, as the room made for the weaving, in the old style of building, does – the "ragged school."

"Heaven send that all these boys may not grow up to be weavers here, Mr. Broadelle, nor all these girls grow up to marry them!"

"We don't increase much, now," he says. "We go for soldiers, or we go to sea, or we take to something else, or we emigrate perhaps."

Now, for a sample of the parents of these children. Can you find us a man and wife who should be in Lancashire, or Suffolk, or anywhere rather than here? Nothing easier to find in Spitalfields. Enter by this doorway.

Up a dark narrow winding public stair, such as are numerous in Lyons or in the wynds and closes of the old town of Edinburgh, and into a room where there are four looms; one idle, three at work.

A wan thin eager-eyed man, weaving in his shirt and trousers, stops the jarring of his loom. He is the master of the place. Not an Irishman himself, but of Irish descent.

"Good day!"

"Good day!" Passing his hand over his rough chin, and feeling his lean throat.

"We are walking through Spitalfields, being interested in the place. Will you allow us to look at your work."

"Oh! certainly."

"It is very beautiful. Black velvet?"

"Yes. Every time I throw the shuttle, I cut out this wire, as you see, and put it in again – so!" Jarring and clashing at the loom, and glancing at us with his eager eyes.

"It is slow work."

"Very slow." With a hard dry cough, and the glance.

"And hard work."

"Very hard." With the cough again.

After a while, he once more stops, perceiving that we really are interested, and says, laying his hand upon his hollow breast and speaking in an unusually loud voice, being used to speak through the clashing of the loom:

"It tries the chest, you see, leaning for'ard like this for fifteen or sixteen hours at a stretch."

"Do you work so long at a time?"

"Glad to do it when I can get it to do. A day's work like that, is worth a matter of three shillings."

"Eighteen shillings a week."

"Ah! But it ain't always eighteen shillings a week. I don't always get it, remember! One week with another, I hardly get more than ten, or ten-and-six."

"Is this Mr. Broadelle's loom?"

"Yes. This is. So is that one there;" the idle one.

"And that, where the man is working?"

"That's another party's. The young man working at it, pays me a shilling a week for leave to work here. That's a shilling, you know, off my rent of half-a-crown. It's rather a large room."

"Is that your wife at the other loom?"

"That's my wife. She's making a commoner sort of work, for bonnets and that."

Again his loom clashes and jars, and he leans forward over his toil. In the window by him, is a singing-bird in a little cage, which trolls its song, and seems to think the loom an instrument of music. The window, tightly closed, commands a maze of chimney-pots, and tiles, and gables. Among them, the ineffectual sun, faintly contending with the rain and mist, is going down. A yellow ray of light crossing the weaver's eager eyes and hollow white face, makes a shape something like a pike-head on the floor.

The room is unwholesome, close, and dirty. Through one part of it the staircase comes up in a bulk, and roughly partitions off a corner. In that corner are the bedstead and the fireplace, a table, a chair or two, a kettle, a tub of water, a little crockery. The looms claim all the superior space and have it. Like grim enchanters who provide the family with their scant food, they must be propitiated with the best accommodation. They bestride the room, and pitilessly squeeze the children – this heavy, watery-headed baby carried in the arms of its staggering little brother, for example – into corners. The children sleep at night between the legs of the monsters, who deafen their first cries with their whirr and rattle, and who roar the same tune to them when they die.

Come to the mother's loom.

"Have you any other children besides these?"

"I have had eight. I have six alive."

"Did we see any of them, just now, at the –"

"Ragged School? O yes! You saw four of mine at the Ragged School!"

She looks up, quite bright about it – has a mother's pride in it – is not ashamed of the name: she, working for her bread, not begging it – not in the least.

She has stopped her loom for the moment. So has her husband. So has the young man.

"Weaver's children are born in the weaver's room," says the husband, with a nod at the bedstead. "Nursed there, brought up there – sick or well – and die there."

To which, the clash and jar of all three looms – the wife's, the husband's, and the young man's, as they go again – make a chorus.

"This man's work, now, Mr. Broadelle – he can't hear us apart here, in this noise? –"

"Oh, no!"

– "requires but little skill?"

"Very little skill. He is doing now, exactly what his grandfather did. Nothing would induce him to use a simple improvement (the 'fly shuttle') to prevent that contraction of the chest of which he complains. Nothing would turn him aside from his old ways. It is the old custom to work at home, in a crowded room, instead of in a factory. *I* couldn't change it, if I were to try."

Good Heaven, is the house falling! Is there an earthquake in Spitalfields! Has a volcano burst out in the heart of London! What is this appalling rush and tremble?

It is only the railroad.

The arches of the railroad span the house; the wires of the electric telegraph stretch over the confined scene of his daily life; the engines fly past him on their errands, and outstrip the birds; and what can the man of prejudice and usage hope for, but to be overthrown and flung into oblivion! Look to it, gentlemen of precedent and custom standing, daintily opposed to progress, in the bag-wigs and embroidered coats of another generation, you may learn from the weaver in his shirt and trousers!

There, we leave him in the dark, about to kindle at the poor fire the lamp that hangs upon his loom, to help him on his labouring way into the night. The sun has gone down, the reflection has vanished from the floor. There is nothing in the gloom but his eager eyes, made hungrier by the sight of our small present; the dark shapes of his fellow-workers mingling with their stopped looms; the mute bird in its little cage, duskily expressed against the window; and the watery-headed baby crooning in a corner God knows where.

We are again in the streets.

"The fluctuations in the silk trade, and, consequently, in the condition of the Spitalfields weaver," says our friend, "are sudden and unforeseen; for they depend upon a variety of uncontrollable causes. Let us take, for example, the past four or five years."

"But does that period afford a fair average of the condition of the trade? Were not the fluctuations extreme?"

"They were. In 1846 the price of raw silk was very low. The manufacturers bought all they could, and worked up all they bought. Not a hand was idle, not a loom at rest. Enormous stocks soon accumulated, silk became dearer; but in May, 1847, there came a sudden stop."

"Was it not, then, that the last loud cry of distress arose from Spitalfields, and that public meetings were held for finding means of 're-dress?'"

"It was. The stagnation was prolonged by a dispute, in which the silk manufacturers and wholesale dealers were involved with the large retail houses. It got the name of the 'short measure question.' The retailers wanted us to give them thirty-seven inches to every yard. The autumn trade was completely crippled by this discussion; which did not end till the breaking out of the French Revolution in February 1848. West-end and wholesale buyers rushed over to Paris and Lyons, in regiments, and with unlimited capital. They bought for almost any price they chose to offer. This cut two ways; although wholesale and retail houses brought home great parcels of manufactured articles, we also bought raw silk, in France, from fifteen to twenty per cent. below the lowest price I ever knew it. What do you think, sir, of the finest French organzine for a guinea a pound?"

We answered by an exclamation of vague surprise.

"Such a price as this enabled us to set some of our looms at work for stock, and, during 1849, the French goods being exhausted, ours came into play. Indeed, during that year the British manufacturer was in a position to defy competition."

"The French had not recovered themselves?"

"Not only that – but we had bought nearly all their raw silk, and they were actually obliged to buy it back from us at advances of from twenty to fifty per cent.! From that time prices advanced here, and work kept on increasing, so that, during most of last year, Spitalfields was busy."

"A glut of stock has been again the consequence."

"Yes; and what with that and the advancing price of raw silk,[1] I have within the last fortnight been compelled to discharge one hundred hands."

Spitalfields, however, has its bright side. As yet machinery has not been taught to turn artist, or to guide the shuttle through the intricate niceties of the Jacquard loom, so as to execute designs. Figured and brocaded silks must still be done by hands, and those hands must be skilful.

"Our silks," Mr. Broadelle tells us, "have never been inferior, in quality, to those of our foreign rivals; but, we have always been beaten in taste. In the stolid assiduous pains-taking motion of the hand and treadle, the English weaver is unsurpassed; but, he has seldom exercised his fancy. Until lately, therefore, few designs originated in this country. We silk-manufacturers, like the Dramatic Authors' Society, have been content to take our novelties from the French."

"You say, 'until lately.' Has the English manufacturer improved in that respect?"

"Decidedly. Schools of Design have done something: the encouragement given by masters to those who make available patterns, has done something too; but, the great improver of the English silk trade was the last French revolution."

"How?"

"That political disaster brought the manufacturers of France to a dead-lock. During the whole of 1849, the English markets were stocked with the most splendid fashions that ever came into it. As we could not sell a yard of *our* manufacture, we had plenty of leisure to examine the different foreign goods minutely. So rich a variety had never fallen under our observation, and never before had such a flood of light been thrown on the manufactures of our greatest rivals. We profited by it.

More important improvements have been effected in the fabric of fancy silk goods since 1848, than were made, down to that time, since the days of Jacquard."

"This shows the value of national intercourse, Mr. Broadelle. Will the Great Exhibition do much service in this way?"

"I have no doubt it will. But, we are now at the door of a figure-weaver; and you will compare this visit with our last."

We knock at the door of a cheerful little house, extremely clean. We are introduced into a little parlour, where a young artist sits at work with crayons and water-colours. He is a student of the School of Design. He is at work on a new pattern for a table-cover. He has learnt to paint in oil. He has painted the portraits his sisters – and of some one who I suspect is not a sister, but who may be

A nearer one yet and a dearer one, and they decorate the room. He has painted groups of flowers. He shows us one that was in last year's Exhibition of the Royal Academy. He shows us another that he means to finish in good time to send to the next Exhibition. He does these things over and above his regular work. He don't mind work – gets up early. There are cheap casts prettily arranged about the room, and it has a little collection of cheap books of a good sort in it. The intrinsic worth of every simple article of furniture or embellishment is enhanced a hundred-fold (as it always may be) by neatness and order. Is father at home? Yes, and will be glad to see the visitors. Pray walk up!

The young artist shows us the way to the top of the house, apologising cheerfully for the ladder-staircase by which we mount at last. In a bright clean room, as pure as soap and water, scrubbing, and fresh air, can make it, we find a sister whose portrait is down stairs – we are able to claim her instantly for the original, to the general satisfaction. We find also, father, who is working at his Jacquard loom, making a pretty pattern of cravat, in blue upon a black ground. He is as cordial, sensible, intelligent a man, as any one would wish to know. He has a reason for everything he says, and everything he does. He is learned in sanitary matters among other necessary knowledge, and says the first thing you have to do, is, to make your place wholesome, or you can't expect to work heartily. Wholesome it is, as his own pleasant face, and the pleasant faces of his children well brought up. He has made various improvements in his own loom; he has made an improvement in his daughter's, who works near him, which prevents her having to contract her chest, although she is doing very ordinary work. Industry, contentment, sense, and self-respect, are the hopeful characteristics of everything animate and inanimate in this little house. If the veritable summer light were shining, and the veritable summer air were rustling, in it, which the young artist has tried to get into the sketches of green glades from Epping Forest that hang near father's loom, and can be seen by father while he is at work, it could not be more cheering to our hearts, oppressed with what we have left.

Note

1 The price of "organzine" during the month of March was: – French, 32*s*.; Piedmont, 26*s*.; China, 22*s*.

14

JOHN CAPPER, 'BRITISH COTTON'

Household Words, Vol. 5, no. 106
(3 April 1852), pp. 51–54

THE words British Cotton will perhaps sound as significantly as Gooseberry Champagne, conveying to the mind the embodiment of one of the "shams" of the present age. Some may "pooh, pooh!" the flax-cottonising process as very much akin to a discovery for converting silver into lead, linen goods being dearer than those made from cotton; whilst not a few express their astonishment at the recent "Flax Movement," and wonder why we should be so desirous of finding any substitute for what has hitherto answered, and still continues to answer our purpose remarkably well.

The annual importation of raw cotton into Great Britain has risen enormously since the commencement of the present century. In 1800, it amounted to fifty-six millions of pounds; in 1815, to one hundred millions; in 1835, to four hundred millions; and at the present time it is upwards of seven hundred millions of pounds, equal to one thousand tons a-day. Nearly the whole of this arrives at the port of Liverpool. Seventeen-twentieths of this aggregate is imported from the United States of America, the remainder from the Brazils, the East Indies, and Egypt. About one-seventh leaves the country for other places in the raw state; so that fully six hundred millions of pounds are wrought into goods in our factories, the greater portion of which are in Lancashire, affording employment to a million-and-a-half of inhabitants. The quantity manufactured is thus disposed of: – one-tenth is wasted in the process, in dirt and refuse; one-fourth is worked up for home consumption; and the balance is shipped to other countries as manufactured goods. The present yearly value of the Cotton manufacture of this country is estimated at forty-five millions sterling, of which thirty millions are believed to be paid away in wages; one-third being the original cost of the raw material. In some inferior descriptions of goods the value of the material is far beyond that of the labour and skill expended on them. In others, the labour bestowed in their production is infinitely more costly than the original value of the material operated upon. Samples of cotton yarn have been recently produced so exquisitely fine in texture, that a single thread is found to be invisible to the naked eye, unless placed upon some dark substance. A hank of cotton measures eight hundred and forty yards; yet it would require more than two thousand hanks of this gossamer to weigh one pound. Twenty-five pounds weight of such a fibre would encircle the globe at the

DOI: 10.4324/9781315400105-18

equator, whilst in value it would far exceed it own weight in gold. In the importation of the raw cotton into this country, and in the exportation of the manufactured goods, about eight hundred thousand tons of shipping are yearly employed.

Perhaps a better idea of the magnitude of this branch of our national industry can scarcely be embodied than in these two facts: – Firstly, a rise in the price of the raw material of twopence the pound, costs the manufacturers four millions sterling; Secondly, in the simple process of starching the fibres whilst being spun, two hundred and fifty thousand barrels of flour are annually used, worth about half a million sterling.

Such is the Cotton trade of England; unequalled by any industry of any other country in the world. It is not difficult, therefore, to understand how important becomes any question affecting the future supply of this great staple commodity. We are at present dependent upon another nation for the staff of our national prosperity, and that nation depends upon the labour of a race of slaves. Let any great social or physical convulsion visit that country, and England would feel the shock from Land's End to John O'Groat's. The lives of nearly two millions of our countrymen are dependent upon the cotton crops of America; their destiny may be said, without any sort of hyperbole, to hang upon a thread. Should any dire calamity befal the land of cotton, a thousand of our merchant ships would rot idly in dock; ten thousand mills must stay their busy looms; two thousand thousand mouths would starve for lack of work to feed them.

It is not, however, sufficient that we glance at the Cotton manufacture; we must say a few passing words touching that of Linen, before pointing out the operation of the present "Flax Movement." For the supply of flax, we are equally dependent upon foreign countries; not more than one-fourth of the flax required, that is, a hundred thousand tons, being grown in Great Britain. We pay to other countries for flax, for linseed, and for oil-cake, not much under seven millions sterling annually; whilst we ship linen goods to the yearly value of three millions sterling. Flax is employed in the manufacture of the most delicate French and Irish cambrics, and of the coarsest sail-cloth and tarpaulins; of the most beautiful laces from Lisle and Valenciennes, and of the heavier sacking and towelling. The folds of snowy lawn that deck a bishop's arms, and the stout storm-sail that rides out the fiercest gale, are both the produce of the same plant.

The propriety of rendering ourselves independent of other nations for the supply of cotton, is no new idea. It has been entertained for many years past. The manufacturers of Manchester have been urging the cultivation of cotton in our Indian possessions, where vast tracts of land are known to exist well suited to the cultivation. Our own chilly climate is utterly unfitted for the growth of this plant; with flax, however, the case is different, and, as already stated, about one-fourth of our requirements of this article is raised on British ground. There appears to be no reason whatever, why the remaining three-fourths should not also be grown upon our own soil. Besides which, recent experiments have demonstrated that flax may be substituted for one half of the cotton at present in use, which would give an additional demand for the article of five hundred tons daily, requiring for their growth twelve thousand acres every week. The experiments alluded to were made by the Chevalier Clausson, who has thus originated what is known as the "Flax Movement." By these he discovered a simple and at the same time beautiful and effective process, by which flax may be "cottonised" or converted into what is termed "British Cotton."

Some of the more important processes in the manufacturing arts have been the result of mere accident. It was even so with Flax Cotton. The accidental discovery of the new application of the flax-plant has been thus described, in the last edition of the Chevalier Clausson's little work on the subject of the "Movement:" –

Wandering along the luxuriant banks of one of the Brazilian rivers, his attention was attracted to a white, down-like substance, adhering to the branches of trees, overhanging and touching the stream. On obtaining a quantity of it, he was so pleased with its character, that – thinking he had discovered some vegetable product hitherto unknown – he determined to trace it, if possible, to its source, and to ascertain the plant which produced it. Pursuing his task with great ardour, he eventually found that the substance had been washed from a bed of flax-straw, the produce of some of his own land; and which, long before, he had caused to be thrown, as useless, near the banks of the river. As the swollen waters had occasional access to this heap, fermentation, and the decomposition of a portion of the plant, had taken place; and, in time, the influence of natural chemistry had so separated the filaments of the flax-fibre, as to give the mass a cotton-like appearance. Some of it having been washed by the river, had been arrested by the overhanging branches.

The process thus casually observed in a very imperfect state, Clausson afterwards imitated by the aid of chemistry; and he can now supply the factories of Lancashire with a home-grown substance, capable of being worked up with certain portions of cotton, silk, or wool, with the machinery already in use for those manufactures. And herein lies the great value of the discovery. From the peculiar structure of the flax-fibre, and the consequent nature of the machinery to work it up, it now costs tenpence per pound in the manufacture; whereas cotton is made up for threepence per pound. It is obvious, therefore, that by preparing flax, so as to be capable of being worked upon the ordinary machinery at the same cost as cotton, the process must be one of great value. Next in importance to this, is the greater yield of marketable fibre from a given quantity of straw, than by the old mode of steeping and preparing.

We will now examine the new process; which we witnessed a short time since, at the Chevalier's model establishment at Stepney. An old poorhouse has been converted into a factory; oakum-picking has been supplanted by the magic transformation of chemistry; iron soup-boilers are now busy with mysterious mixtures, producing results which, when the old fabric was built, would have consigned every man and woman concerned to the stake at Smithfield, for sorcerers and witches.

The flax plant is composed of three distinct parts, the wood, the fibre, and the gum-resin, which causes the fibres to adhere together. To remove the wood is the first object; and this, under the old system, was performed by a machine little better than a flail. Here commences the first improvement. At the Stepney factory we saw a small apparatus at work, which costing a mere trifle, removed the wood from the fibre with astonishing rapidity and cleanliness. It is proposed that growers should employ this machine on their farms; by which means they reduce the bulk by one-half, and at the same time retain the portion most useful for manure. In this state it will be brought to market for sale to the manufacturers, who will then have to free it, in the first instance, from the gum-resin. Under the old system, this was effected by steeping the flax in cold water, a process which occupied from four to six weeks, and frequently caused much discoloration of the fibres. The Chevalier's mode consists in boiling the material in a weak alkaline solution for about four hours, after which it is washed first in a slightly acidified liquor, and then in plain water. It is then dried and in a fit state for the various processes of scutching, heckling, &c., necessary to render it fit for the linen manufacture. In order to "cottonise" the flax, according to the Clausson's patent, the fibres are taken from the washing vats direct to a series of other vats, ranged side by side; and it is in these that the magic of chemistry is so brought to bear as to transmute a heavy mass of dark, harsh straw, in the course of some minutes, to a light, silky, snow-white wool.

In the first of these vats is a weak solution of carbonate of soda: here the previously boiled and washed fibres are steeped for about fifteen minutes, during which time they become completely saturated with the soda liquid. To explain the chemical action which follows, it is necessary to point out the structure of the flax fibre. These fibres, minute though they be, are cellular, composed of a number of smaller cylinders, united closely at their side. It is the separation of these finer fibres, and the consequent addition to the length and surface of the whole mass, that has now to be accomplished; a process that may well be likened to hair-splitting. These cellular fibres being thoroughly saturated with the soda in most minute quantities, are removed from the first vat, and placed in vat number two, containing water slightly acidulated with one part in five hundred of sulphuric acid. The change which now takes place is instantaneous. A rapid frothing and ebullition of the liquor may be observed, and the heavy mass of flax which, in the first liquor, sank far below the surface, is now seen floating lightly on the face of the water: it is no longer flax – it is British Cotton. And how has this happened? The acid in this liquor, finding its way into the little cylinders already saturated with the soda, immediately effects a chemical change; the sulphuric acid combines with the alkali, and forms sulphate of soda, giving out the carbonic acid gas from the carbonate of soda, which, seeking its liberation, expands and bursts open the cellular tubes. The cottonised flax is next placed in a weak solution of soda, in order to free it from any remaining acid; and thence transferred to the bleaching vat, which contains a mixture of solution of chloride of lime and sulphate of magnesia. Here it remains during two hours, at the end of which time it wears a perfectly snow-white appearance. The process is then completed by washing, first in a weak acid liquor, and afterwards in pure water. It then only remains to dry the flax-cotton, in order to fit it for the after processes, preparatory to spinning. The hopeless streets of regularly-built houses, all small and of brick. Here and there a great oblong many-windowed factory stood up, like a hen among her chickens, puffing out black "unparliamentary" smoke, and sufficiently accounting for the cloud which Margaret had taken to foretell rain. As they drove through the larger and wider streets, from the station to the hotel, they had to stop constantly; great loaded lurries blocked up the not over-wide thoroughfares. Margaret had now and then been into the city in her drives with her aunt. But there the heavy lumbering vehicles seemed various in their purposes and intent; here every van, every waggon and truck, bore cotton, either in the raw shape in bags, or the woven shape in bales of calico. People thronged the footpaths, most of them well-dressed as regarded the material, but with a slovenly looseness which struck Margaret as different from the shabby, threadbare smartness of a similar class in London.

"I used to think once that if I could have a day of doing nothing, to rest me – a day in some quiet place like that yo' speak on – it would maybe set me up. But now I've had many days o' idleness, and I'm just as weary o' them as I was o' my work. Sometimes I'm so tired out I think I cannot enjoy heaven without a piece of rest first. I'm rather afeard o' going straight there without getting a good sleep in the grave to set me up."

"Don't be afraid, Bessy," said Margaret, laying her hand on the girl's: "God can give you more perfect rest than even idleness on earth, or the dead sleep of the grave can do."

Bessy moved uneasily; then she said:

"I wish father would not speak as he does. He means well, as I telled yo' yesterday, and tell yo' again and again. But yo' see, though I don't believe him a bit by day, yet by night – when I'm in a fever, half asleep and half awake – it comes back upon me – oh! so bad! And I think, if this should be th' end of all, and if all I've been born for is just to work my heart and my life away, and to sicken i' this dree place, wi' them mill-noises in my ears for ever, until I could scream out for them to stop, and let me have a little piece o' quiet – and wi' the fluff filling my lungs, until I thirst to death for one long deep breath o' the clear air yo' speak on – and my mother gone, and I never able to tell her again how I loved her, and o' all my troubles – I think if this life is th' end, and there's no God to wipe away all tears from all eyes – yo' wench, yo'!" said she, sitting up, and clutching violently, almost fiercely, at Margaret's hand, "I could go mad, and kill yo', I could." She fell back completely worn out with her passion. Margaret knelt down by her.

"Bessy – we have a Father in Heaven."

"I know it! I know it," moaned she, turning her head uneasily from side to side. "I'm very wicked. I've spoken very wickedly. Oh! don't be frightened by me and never come again. I would not harm a hair of your head. And," opening her eyes, and looking earnestly at Margaret, "I believe, perhaps, more than yo' do o' what's to come. I read the book o' Revelations until I know it off by heart, and I never doubt when I'm waking, and in my senses, of all the glory I'm to come to."

"Don't let us talk of what fancies come into your head when you are feverish. I would rather hear something about what you used to do when you were well."

same method as has been here described can be made available for converting the refuse tow from the flax establishments into a fine white article, admirably adapted for paper-making, and at a less price than he pays for linen rags. The value of this latter preparation may be estimated, when it is known that one manufacturer of linen in the north of Ireland throws aside "refuse tow" to the yearly value of five thousand pounds sterling; all of which, at present, is utterly useless.

From what has been stated, it is evident that the objection held against this process, of its converting a dear article into a cheap one, does not hold. Not only is the value of the British cotton greatly enhanced by being rendered capable of spinning at the low cost of ordinary cotton goods, but the yield of marketable fibre is much increased, and at a much less cost of time and labour than was needed under the old method. The new fibre is so completely assimilated in character to cotton, that it readily receives the rich dyes imparted to the latter, and is, in short, capable of being printed or dyed in a precisely similar manner.

At the Stepney model factory we examined specimens of flannel, felt, and woollen cloth, manufactured of equal parts of British cotton and wool; also, a felt that was composed entirely of the former material. All of those goods had a remarkably stout feel, and appeared to be strong in their body.

Combined with silk, British cotton may be worked up with great ease on the existing silk machinery, and when so wrought, is capable of receiving the same colours in dying, and materially adding to the strength of the fabric manufactured.

We saw two other substances, which, it appears, are quite as susceptible of being "cottonised" as flax: one was a coarse species of China silk, at present of little value; the other was "Jute," or Indian hemp. Both of these fibres were materially improved in appearance and feel, and are, no doubt, in their new form, adapted to purposes for which they were not at all available, previously.

Looking at this "Flax Movement" in an agricultural point of view, we shall find as many advantages likely to arise from it in that direction as in any other. Hitherto it has been a most prevalent opinion that flax crops were exceedingly exhaustive in their effect upon the soil. Experiments fairly carried out have shown this to be a fallacy. Chemical analysis of the plant, and a series of flax crops taken from the same land, have proved beyond doubt, that not only does this cultivation not weaken the soil, but tends to keep it in a state of great productiveness.

An examination of the structure of the plant demonstrates that those portions of it which absorb the alkalies and the nutritive properties of the soil, are those which are not required for the purpose of manufacture; namely, the woody part, the resinous matter, and the seed. The fibres derive their elements almost entirely from the atmosphere, one hundred parts containing not more than two parts of mineral matters. Under the old process of steeping, the nutritive portions contained in the wood and gum, as well as the whole of the seed, were lost in the fermentation during steeping; so that nothing whatever was restored to the land. By the new method, these properties are capable of being returned whence they were taken. The seed may be either employed in feeding cattle, or crushed for oil; the oil-cake being in that case returned for the cattle-yard.

Estimates, based upon several years of actual experience, go to show that, by this cultivation, the farmer may realise a yearly profit of from fifteen pounds to eighteen pounds the acre, and that, too, upon land which has been just previously heavily cropped in cereals. Many thousands of acres which hitherto have yielded but indifferent and uncertain crops, or which have scarcely been worth cultivation, may be brought under flax without any fear of the result. Hitherto, the absence of linen manufactures, and the consequent want of markets, in so many parts of England and Scotland, have proved a serious obstacle to any attempts at extending flax culture. But now that every grower may, by the purchase of an inexpensive and simply constructed machine, convert the flax-straw into a fit condition for economical and convenient transport to a market, and now that conveyance is so much lessened in cost, and that the patent process will before long be in active operation in every agricultural county of Great Britain and Ireland, it is to be hoped that a widely extended cultivation of this article may take place, affording active employment to a vast number of persons of all ages.

Already the patent has been taken in hand in Scotland: arrangements are in progress for a similar undertaking in Ireland; and, should the like activity be manifested in England, there can be little doubt that two most important results will have been attained – the providing a great portion of our poorer population with good employment, and rendering our manufacturers less dependent upon the United States for the supply of flax and cotton.

15

ELIZABETH GASKELL, *NORTH AND SOUTH*

(London: Smith, Elder, and Co., 1897), pp. 54–55, 97–98

THE next afternoon, about twenty miles from Milton-Northern, they entered on the little branch railway that led to Heston. Heston itself was one long straggling street, running parallel to the sea-shore. It had a character of its own, as different from the little bathing-places in the south of England as they again from those of the continent. To use a Scotch word, every thing looked more "purpose-like." The country carts had more iron, and less wood and leather about the horse-gear; the people in the streets, although on pleasure bent, had yet a busy mind. The colours looked grayer – more enduring, not so gay and pretty. There were no smock-frocks, even among the country-folk; they retarded motion, and were apt to catch on machinery, and so the habit of wearing them had died out. In such towns in the south of England, Margaret had seen the shopmen, when not employed in their business, lounging a little at their doors, enjoying the fresh air, and the look up and down the street. Here, if they had any leisure from customers, they made themselves business in the shop – even, Margaret fancied, to the unnecessary unrolling and re-rolling of ribbons. All these differences struck upon her mind, as she and her mother went out next morning to look for lodgings.

One evening it was arranged that Margaret and her father should go the next day to Milton-Northern, and look out for a house. Mr. Hale had received several letters from Mr. Bell, and one or two from Mr. Thornton, and he was anxious to ascertain at once a good many particulars respecting his position and chances of success there, which he could only do by an interview with the latter gentleman. Margaret knew that they ought to be removing; but she had a repugnance to the idea of a manufacturing town, and believed that her mother was receiving benefit from Heston air, so she would willingly have deferred the expedition to Milton.

For several miles before they reached Milton, they saw a deep lead-coloured cloud hanging over the horizon in the direction in which it lay. It was all the darker from contrast with the pale gray-blue of the wintry sky; for in Heston there had been the earliest signs of frost. Nearer to the town, the air had a faint taste and smell of smoke; perhaps, after all, more a loss of the fragrance of grass and herbage than any positive taste or smell. Quick they were whirled over long, straight

DOI: 10.4324/9781315400105-19

"I think I was well when mother died, but I have never been rightly strong sin' somewhere about that time. I began to work in a carding-room soon after, and the fluff got into my lungs and poisoned me."

"Fluff?" said Margaret, inquiringly.

"Fluff," repeated Bessy. "Little bits, as fly off fro' the cotton, when they're carding it, and fill the air till it looks all fine white dust. They say it winds round the lungs, and tightens them up. Anyhow, there's many a one as works in a carding-room, that falls into a waste, coughing and spitting blood, because they're just poisoned by the fluff."

"But can't it be helped?" asked Margaret.

"I dunno. Some folk have a great wheel at one end o' their carding-rooms to make a draught, and carry off th' dust; but that wheel costs a deal of money – five or six hundred pound, maybe, and brings in no profit; so it's but a few of th' masters as will put 'em up; and I've heard tell o' men who did'nt like working in places where there was a wheel, because they said as how it made 'em hungry, at after they'd been long used to swallowing fluff, to go without it, and that their wage ought to be raised if they were to work in such places. So between masters and men th' wheels fall through. I know I wish there'd been a wheel in our place, though."

"Did not your father know about it?" asked Margaret.

"Yes! And he was sorry. But our factory were a good one on the whole; and a steady likely set o' people; and father was afeard of letting me go to a strange place, for though yo' would na think it now, many a one then used to call me a gradely lass enough. And I did na like to be reckoned nesh and soft, and Mary's schooling were to be kept up, mother said, and father he were always liking to buy books, and go to lectures o' one kind or another – all which took money – so I just worked on till I shall ne'er get the whirr out o' my ears, or the fluff out o' my throat i' this world. That's all."

"How old are you?" asked Margaret.

"Nineteen, come July."

"And I too am nineteen." She thought, more sorrowfully than Bessy did, of the contrast between them. She could not speak for a moment or two for the emotion she was trying to keep down.

16

EDWARD BAINES, 'ON THE WOOLLEN MANUFACTURE OF ENGLAND; WITH SPECIAL REFERENCE TO THE LEEDS CLOTHING DISTRICT'

Journal of the Statistical Society of London, Vol. 22, no. 1 (March 1859), pp. 1–9, 11–14

I. – Introduction

It is suitable, when the British Association honours Leeds with a visit, that its members should receive some account of that great Branch of Manufacturing industry of which Leeds is the ancient seat, and which prevails here on a larger scale than in any other part of England or of the world. It is peculiarly desirable that such an account should be rendered to this Section, because, notwithstanding the antiquity of the manufacture, its economy and statistics are by no means well ascertained. The statute-book has for centuries been loaded with enactments for the protection and regulation of this manufacture. To the present day, in the House of Lords, the Lord Chancellor and the Judges sit upon Woolsacks, as a constant memento of the duty they owe to that branch of industry which was of old pronounced to be "the flower and strength, the revenue and blood, of England." It has been nursed with superfluous and mistaken care; it has been praised with great exaggeration; it has been the subject of endless controversies; but so little attention was paid by our fathers to accurate statistical inquiry that to the present day the real magnitude and value of the Woollen Manufacture are most imperfectly known. Though a large part of the Raw Material is grown at home, we have absolutely no reliable statistics of the amount of this famous product of the British Isles. The commercial records of the manufacture are so imperfect and confused as greatly to perplex the inquirer. Until within a very few years no separation was made in official tables of exports between the two great and distinct branches of the manufactures of wool, the *Woollen* and the *Worsted* fabrics. It is hoped, therefore, that the present attempt to ascertain the facts connected with the Woollen Manufacture may not be without its use; and also that it may derive some additional interest from indicating remarkable modern changes in this department of

DOI: 10.4324/9781315400105-20

industry, and explaining some peculiarities which at first sight perplex the political economist.

The Woollen Manufacture of Yorkshire is prosperous and advancing; but it cannot fail to have been noticed that its progress is less rapid and extraordinary than that of other textile manufactures; and it may be well to show that this is to be ascribed to circumstances inherent in the nature of the fabric, and not to indifference and apathy on the part of those engaged in this branch of industry.

II. – Woollen and Worsted fabrics

It is right, and it will conduce to the understanding of important points in the economy of the manufacture, to explain in the first place the difference between the Woollen and the Worsted fabrics. The raw material of both is Sheep's Wool. It would formerly have been sufficient to say that woollens were made of short wool, and worsted goods of long wool; but owing to the improvement in the worsted spinning machinery, much short wool, both English and Colonial, is now used in that manufacture. Wool intended for woollens is prepared for spinning by the Carding machine; whilst wool intended for worsted goods, being generally of a longer staple, is prepared for spinning by the metallic Comb. But the essential distinction of woollens from worsted, cotton, linen, and every other textile fabric is, that they depend upon that peculiar property of sheep's wool, its disposition to *felt;* that is, under pressure and warm moisture to *interlock its fibres* as by strong mutual attraction, and thus to *run up* into a compact substance not easily separable. Wools differ in the degree of this felting property; but, generally speaking, the long wools possess it in a lower degree than the short wools, and the wools which felt best are the best adapted for making woollen cloth. For worsted stuffs the felting property is not required; and not only have the wools used for this purpose less of the felting property, but they are so treated in the spinning and manufacture as almost entirely to destroy it.

In every other textile fabric, when the material is spun into yarn and woven into a web, the fabric is complete. But in woollen cloth, after the process of spinning and weaving comes the essential process of felting by means of heavy pressure with soap and warm water; and so efficacious is this process that a piece of cloth under it often shrinks up to two-thirds its original length and little more than half its width. The process is called Milling or fulling, and some of the oldest traces of the Woollen Manufacture found in ancient records are in the mention of fulling mills on certain streams or estates. Before the milling, the web of the woollen cloth, when held up to the day, admits the light through its crossed threads; but after the milling, every fibre in the piece having laid hold of the neighbouring fibres, and all having firmly interlaced themselves together, the cloth becomes thick and opaque; of course it is made stouter, warmer, and more enduring in the wear; and if torn, it will be found that its tenacity has consisted not so much in the strength of the warp and weft as in the firm adhesion of all the fibres, so that it does not unravel like cotton or linen cloth.

After the cloth has been milled it undergoes the various processes of dressing or finishing, which consist mainly in these two, – first, raising up all the fibres of the wool which can be detached by violent and long-continued brushing of the cloth with teazles, so as to make a nap on the surface, and then secondly, shearing off that nap in a cutting machine so clean and smooth as to give a soft and almost velvety appearance and feel to the cloth. This nap, more or less closely cut, distinguishes woollen cloth from nearly all other fabrics; it is one of its two essential characteristics; and, combined with the felting, it makes superfine broad cloth one of the finest, warmest, richest, most useful, and most enduring of all tissues.

But in order to produce these two principal characteristics of woollen cloth, the *felting* and the *nap*, it will easily be seen that woollen yarn must not be spun so tight and hard as worsted, cotton, or linen yarn. The fibres must be left as loose as possible, first that they may felt, and afterwards that they may constitute a nap. Hence woollen yarn, both for the warp and weft, is spun into a much feebler, looser, and less-twisted thread than other kinds of yarn. But this feebleness of the yarn constitutes a principal difficulty in applying the power-loom to the Woollen Manufacture. The threads are more liable to break by the passing of the shuttle through them, and the weaving is consequently more difficult. This difficulty is increased by the great width of the web, which in broad cloth, before it is milled, is nine feet. Owing to these combined causes the Power-Loom in the Woollen Manufacture works much more slowly than in the worsted manufacture; in the latter, on the average, the shuttle flies at the rate of 160 picks per minute, whilst the power-loom in weaving broad cloth only makes 40 to 48 picks per minute, that is, just the same as the hand-loom. The weaving of woollen cloth by hand is a man's work, whereas the weaving of Cotton, Linen, or Silk cloth by hand was a woman's or a child's work. Hence the hand-loom weaver in the Woollen Manufacture has never been reduced to the miserable wages paid to the same class of operatives in other manufactures, and hence he maintains a more equal competition with the steam-loom. It is to this cause that we must principally ascribe *the continued existence of the system of domestic manufacture in the woollen trade;* and to the same cause we must ascribe the slower advances made in the woollen than in those manufactures *where all the processes can be more advantageously carried on in factories, by one vast system of machinery, under a single eye, and by the power of great capital.* Whether for good or for evil, or for a combination of both, such are the economical results which may be traced in a great measure to the peculiarities in woollen yarn and cloth.

III. – Woollen manufacture – processes

But another circumstance must be noticed, as bearing upon the same results, namely, that the processes of the Woollen Manufacture are more numerous and complex than those of any other of our textile manufactures. In one of those complete and beautiful establishments where fine cloth is both manufactured and finished, as that of Messrs. Benjamin Gott and Sons, of this town, which has long ranked with the first woollen factories of any country, the spectator who may be admitted to it will see all the following processes, namely: –

1 Sorting the wool – no less than ten different qualities being found in a single fleece.
2 Scouring it with a ley and hot water, to remove the grease and dirt.
3 Washing it with clean cold water.
4 Drying it, first in an extractor – a rapidly revolving machine full of holes, and next, by spreading it and exposing it to the heat of steam.
5 Dyeing, when the cloth is to be wool-dyed.
6 Willying, by revolving cylinders armed with teeth, to open the matted locks and free them from dust.
7 Teasing, with a teaser or devil, still further to open and clean.
8 Sprinkling plentifully with olive oil, to facilitate the working of the wool.
9 Moating, with the moating-machine, to take off the moats or burs, *i.e.*, seeds of plants or grasses which adhere to the fleece.
10 Scribbling, in a scribbling-machine, consisting of a series of cylinders clothed with cards or wire-brushes working upon each other, the effect of which is still further to disentangle the wool and draw out the fibres.
11 Plucking, in a plucking-machine, more effectually to mix up the different qualities which may remain in the wool.
12 Carding, in a carding-machine, resembling the scribbler, but more perfectly opening the wool, spreading it of a regular thickness and weight, reducing it to a light filmy substance, and then bringing it out in cardings or slivers about three feet in length.
13 Slubbing, at a frame called the billy, generally containing sixty spindles, where the cardings are joined to make a continuous yarn, drawn out, slightly twisted, and wound on bobbins.
[By a new machine, called the Condenser, attached to the carding-machine, the wool is brought off in a continuous sliver wound on cylinders, and ready to be conveyed to the mule, so as to dispense with the billy.]
14 Spinning on the mule, which contains from 300 to 1,000 spindles per pair.
15 Reeling the yarn intended for the warp.
16 Warping it, and putting it on the beam for the loom.
17 Sizing the warp with animal gelatine, to facilitate the weaving.
18 Weaving, at the power-loom or hand-loom.
19 Scouring the cloth with fuller's earth, to remove the oil and size.
20 Dyeing, when piece-dyed.
21 Burling, to pick out irregular threads, hairs, or dirt.
22 Milling or fulling, with soap and warm water, either in the fulling-stocks or in the improved milling-machine, where it is squeezed between rollers.
23 Scouring, to remove the soap.
24 Drying and stretching on tenters.

25 Raising the nap of the cloth, by brushing it strongly on the gig with teazles fixed upon cylinders.
26 Cutting or shearing off the nap in two cutting-machines, one cutting lengthwise of the piece and the other across.
27 Boiling the cloth, to give it a permanent face.
28 Brushing, in a brushing-machine.
29 Pressing in hydraulic presses, sometimes with heat.
30 Cutting the nap a second time.
31 Burling and drawing, to remove defects, and marking with the manufacturer's name.
32 Pressing a second time.
33 Steaming, to take away the liability to spot.
34 Folding or cuttling for the warehouse.

These processes, as has been said, are greatly more numerous than those required by any other textile manufacture, and they are performed by a much greater variety of machines and of workpeople. It is pretty obvious that there must be proportionate difficulty in effecting improvements which will tell materially on the quantity or the price of the goods produced.

IV. – Dearness of the raw material

There is still another fact which retards the advance of the Woollen, as compared with other manufactures, namely, the higher price of the Raw Material. The average value of the Sheep's Wool imported during the three years 1854, 1855, and 1856, was 1*s*. 4*d*. per lb., and the average price of English wool in the same years was about 1*s*. 2*d*. per lb.; but during those three years the average price of Cotton Wool imported was only 5¾*d*. per lb., and that of Flax only 5*d*. per lb.[1] So that wool is about three times the market price of the two vegetable substances which form the raw materials of the cotton and linen manufactures. Nor can sheep's wool be augmented in quantity so rapidly as raw materials which merely require the cultivation of the soil. The fleece, at least in this country, forms only a small proportion of the value of the sheep on which it grows; and the sheep farmer is more dependent on the demand for his mutton than on the demand for his wool. Now the consumption of animal food only increases, as a general rule, with the increase of population; and hence there is a natural restriction on the supply of sheep's wool, owing to which restriction the price is kept high.

V. – Factories, Woollen and Worsted

But the economist may inquire – how is it that the Worsted Manufacture has of late years increased so much more rapidly than the Woollen, seeing that it uses the same raw material, sheep's wool? I may briefly say, that it is to be ascribed in part to very remarkable improvements made within these few years in the process of *Combing*, which is now performed by machinery, and the cost of the process reduced almost to nothing, instead of by hand, – in part to the greater simplicity of the other processes, admitting of their being carried on almost entirely in large factories, – but more than all to the introduction of Cotton Warps into the manufacture, which has not only cheapened the raw material, but has introduced a vast variety of new descriptions of goods, light, beautiful, cheap, and adapted both for dress and furniture.

I am informed by a Bradford merchant of great knowledge that "out of 100 pieces of worsted goods manufactured, at least ninety-five are made with cotton warps; and a rough estimate of the cotton contained would be, that if a piece weighed 3 lb. one pound weight would be cotton and the rest wool." There is still, therefore, a greater weight of wool than of cotton in those goods; but as cotton warps are stronger than woollen, owing to their being harder spun, even when their weight is less, the cloth may be made altogether much lighter than worsted goods were formerly made, and thus the material is economized.

If we look to the last Factory Return made by the Factory Inspectors in 1856, and printed by the House of Commons in 1857, we shall find that in Yorkshire there were 445 Worsted factories and 806 Woollen factories, but the number of Operatives was 78,994 in the former and only 42,982 in the latter. The average number of operatives in the Worsted factories therefore was 177, whilst in the Woollen factories it was only 53. The whole number of operatives returned in the census of 1851 as employed in these two manufactures in the county of York was, 97,147 in the Worsted manufacture and 81,128 in the Woollen. Four-fifths of all the hands employed in the worsted trade are in factories, whilst only about half of those in the woollen trade are in factories.

Everything tends to show that the Worsted manufacture, like those of Cotton and Linen, has become an employment carried on by the machinery of Large Factories; and as mechanical improvements are constantly speeding the power-loom and the spindle, so that in worsted factories the power-loom has increased 67 per cent. in speed within the last ten years, and the spindle 114 per cent.,[2] manufactures thus situated must advance more rapidly than those which, like the woollen, are more dependent on manual labour.

VI. – Persons, &c., employed 1838 and 1856

My hearers will now be prepared to find that the Woollen Manufacture, though large, prosperous, and advancing with considerable rapidity, has within the last twenty years advanced less rapidly than any of the other great textile manufactures. It was surpassed by the cotton manufacture at the beginning of the century. It still holds the second place in regard to the number of operatives employed, though not to the number employed in factories, in which it is surpassed both by the worsted and the flax or linen trades. The following Table shows the advances made by all the textile manufactures, in respect to number of operatives, horsepower, and power-looms, from 1838 to 1856: –

(A.) – FACTORIES *of the* UNITED KINGDOM *in* 1838 *and* 1856.

Description of Factories.	Persons Employed.			Horse Power.			Power Looms.		
	1838.	1856.	Incr.	1838.	1856.	Incr.	1836.*	1856.	Incr.
	No.	No.	Pr. cnt.	No.	No.	Pr. cnt.	No.	No.	Pr. cnt.
Cotton	259,104	379,213	46	59,803	97,132	62	108,751	298,847	175
Woollen......	54,808	79,091	44	20,617	25,901	25	2,150	14,453	572
Worsted......	31,628	87,794	177	7,176	14,904	108	2,969	38,956	1,212
Flax............	43,557	80,262	84	11,089	18,322	65	1,714	9,260	440
Silk............	34,303	56,137	64	3,384	5,176	53	209	7,689	3,579
TOTALS........	423,400	682,497	61	102,069	161,435	58	115,793	369,205	219

* The first return of Power Looms was in 1836. There was also a general Factory Return in that year; but it bears evident marks of inaccuracy, as pointed out by the Factory Inspectors in their Report of October, 1856.

It will be seen that in the woollen mills, between 1838 and 1856, the number of operatives increased 44 per cent., the horse-power employed increased 25 per cent., and the number of power-looms increased 572 per cent.; but still the other manufactures advanced with greater strides in almost all these respects.

VII. – Raw material – sources of supply

I must now refer to the sources from which the Raw Material, *Sheep's Wool,* is drawn, and to the remarkable changes which the present century has witnessed in regard to it. The wool is English, Foreign, and Colonial, and comes from all the quarters of the globe. Our largest supply is from the United Kingdom, but nearly half of the domestic wools is consumed in the worsted manufacture, and the other half is used for the lower kinds of woollen goods. Within living memory Yorkshire cloth was made exclusively of English wool, though Spanish wool has long been used for the finer cloths of the West of England.[3] Now, however, English wool, from its comparative coarseness, is entirely disused in the making of broad cloth. When the late Mr. Gott, who with the late Mr. James Bischoff and others fought a hard battle for many years, first to get rid of the monstrous duty of 6*d.* per pound on foreign wool imposed in 1819, and afterwards to prevent its re-imposition, told a Committee of the House of Lords that broad cloth made of English wool would not be merchantable, and that their lordships' servants would not wear it, the statement was received with a burst of incredulity and derision. But so it was. The cloth of the present day is immensely superior both in fabric and in finish to the cloth of half a century back. Working men now wear finer cloth than gentlemen wore when Mr. Gott began his spirited improvements; and it is so in consequence of the general use of the fine and delicate wool of the Merino sheep. In the last half of the eighteenth century the import of foreign wool fluctuated from a little under to a little over two million pounds weight a-year. In 1799 it was 2,263,666 lbs.; but in the year 1857 the quantity of Foreign and Colonial wool imported was 127,390,885 lbs., of which 90,903,666 lbs. was retained for home consumption. As the exports of woollen goods did not increase in any proportion whatever to these figures, it is evident that the character of the cloth, both that worn at home and that exported, must have changed by the substitution of Foreign and Colonial for English wool.

Of the annual produce of Wool in the *United Kingdom* there are, as has been said, no reliable statistics whatever, and the judgment of those engaged in the trade varies very widely. The late Mr. John Luccock, a wool merchant of Leeds, and a careful inquirer, in a work published by him in 1800 "On the Nature and Properties of Wool," estimated the number of sheep in England and Wales at 26,147,763, and the quantity of wool produced annually at 94,376,640 lbs. weight. The late Mr. James Hubbard revised this estimate in 1828 for a Committee of the House of Lords, with the aid of Sir George Goodman, both of those gentlemen being wool merchants in this town, and raised the quantity of wool to 111,160,560 lbs. Professor Law, in his able work "On the Domesticated Animals of the British Islands," published in 1845, estimates the number of sheep in the British Islands at 35 millions, and the produce of wool at 157,500,000 lbs. Mr. Southey, an eminent wool-broker in London, who has published several works on Colonial Wool, issued a little work in 1851,[4] in which, judging from the information he received from wool merchants in Leeds, Bradford, and other places, he raised the estimate to 228,950,000 lbs.; and then, by an unreliable mode of calculating, even carried it to the enormous figure of 275,000,000 lbs. weight.

The balance of authority would dispose us to conclude that the annual produce of Domestic Wool must be between 150,000,000 lbs. and 200,000,000 lbs. If we take the medium, viz., 175,000,000 lbs., at 1*s.* 3*d.* per lb., which is about the average price of the last thirty years, the value of this great raw material produced at home will be 10,937,500*l.* The judgment thus formed from comparison of authorities has been exactly and unexpectedly confirmed by the result of careful inquiries and calculations, founded on the number of hands employed, the power of the machinery, and the estimated value of the goods manufactured. That result is, that 160,000,000 lbs. is used by the Woollen and Worsted Manufactures, whilst the quantity *Exported* in 1857 was 15,142,881 lbs., making an aggregate of 175,142,881 lbs. of English wool.

The exports of English wool, both in the raw state and in the first stage of manufacture, namely yarn, are great and rapidly increasing, as will be seen by the following Table: –

(D.) – British Wool *and* Woollen *and* Worsted Yarn Exported.

Years.	Wool.	Woollen and Worsted Yarn.
	lbs.	lbs.
1824........	53,000	12,640
1830........	2,951,000	1,108,000
1840........	4,810,000	3,796,000
1850........	12,001,000	13,794,000
1857........	15,142,000	24,654,000

Thus the farmer is deriving benefit from the freedom of trade, and English wool is resuming its flow through channels which legislation had closed for five centuries. It is for our manufacturers to take care that no other country makes a better use of their native raw material than themselves.

Of the history of this ancient manufacture up to our own times I must dispose in a few sentences.

It is probable that the fleece of the sheep afforded the first material of human clothing, and that in this pastoral country it has been manufactured from the earliest dawn of civilization. It is on record that the Romans had weaving establishments of woollen cloth at Winchester; that the mother of Alfred the Great was skilled in the spinning of wool; that Flemish woollen weavers settled in England in the time of William the Conqueror; that fresh immigrations of weavers from Flanders took place in the reigns of Henry I, Henry III, Edward I, and Edward III; that the last-named king especially encouraged the settlement of these artizans in various parts of the country, and that in this policy he was followed by Henry VII; and that at the Reformation many thousands of Woollen weavers, flying from the persecutions of the Duke of Alva in the Low Countries, found refuge in England. It is certain that the manufacture of woollen and worsted goods was carried to a high degree of perfection in Flanders, and of woollens in Italy, long before the art had made any considerable advancement in England. There are also many accounts of the exportation of English wool to those countries from very early times; and it would appear to have been of better quality than that of any other country except Spain. But the monarchs who endeavoured to establish the Woollen Manufacture in England, instead of relying on our natural advantages for that branch of industry, sought to attain the end by prohibiting the exportation of the raw material. In the years 1337 and 1341, under Edward III, the export was forbidden by statute, under penalty of life and limb: and from that time forward, for nearly five centuries, the Statute Book was loaded with Acts, equally absurd and many of them equally severe, to prevent the "running" or illegal exportation of wool. Hundreds, if not thousands of volumes and pamphlets were issued to show that this was one of the first points of national policy, and that the country would be ruined if we allowed other countries to obtain our wool instead of manufacturing it ourselves. There are few things in the history of nations showing so entire an ignorance of political economy and such outrageous blindness in statistics as the history of the English woollen manufacture. It was not till the year 1824 that English wool was allowed to be exported; and it is amusing to recall the long struggle by which freedom was obtained for the export of our own wool, the import of foreign wool, and the import of foreign cloth, – Lord Liverpool, Mr. Robinson, and Mr. Huskisson, having alternately to play off the prejudices of the manufacturers and the agriculturists against each other. The import of foreign wool was only taxed from 1819 to 1824, but the amount of the duty, namely 6*d.* per lb., was most prejudicial. The Government succeeded in persuading the manufacturers, or at least some of them, to consent to the free export of English wool on condition of the free import of foreign wool; and afterwards, with the aid of the manufacturers, they prevented the agricultural interest from reimposing the duty on foreign wool. But the struggle was a desperate one; and it is humbling to remember that Leeds, Bradford, and Huddersfield were for years on the wrong side. They were happily defeated, and, still more happily, their defeat in this matter made them victors in the next great battle against protection; for there can be no doubt that the liberation of the trade in wool was a step to the liberation of the trade in corn; and thus the great, high, ugly, and unsafe edifice, miscalled protection, fell storey after storey, and human industry in all its branches stood upon the same fair level and solid foundation of freedom.

We ought not in this Association and this Section to withhold the honour due to the high intelligence, manly spirit, and wonderful disinterestedness of Lord Milton, afterwards Earl Fitzwilliam, who, whilst representing the great seat of the Woollen Manufacture, Yorkshire, advocated the removal of protection from manufactures, and, although one of the largest landowners, contended for the removal of protection from agriculture. It is a matter of just pride for this Association and for Yorkshire to remember, that that enlightened and high-minded nobleman was the first President of the British Association.

Notes

1 It will be seen from the "Annual Statement of the Trade and Navigation of the United Kingdom" for 1856, that for the three years 1854, 1855, and 1856, the average annual import of Sheep's Wool was 107,211,277 lbs., of the computed real value of 7,230,249*l*. (showing 1*s*. 4*d*. per lb.); of Cotton, 934,323,824 lbs., of the value of 22,490,711*l*. (showing 5¾*d*. per lb.); and of Flax, 164,405,248 lbs., of the value of 3,461,899*l*. (showing 5*d*. per lb.), pp. 11 to 16. I am assured by practical men that the scales of prices by which the values are computed are very correct.

2 Ten years ago the average speed of worsted looms was 96 picks per minute; it is now 160. In the old spinning frame, called the fly frame, generally used ten years since, the spindles made 2,800 revolutions per minute: in the new frame, called the bell frame, they make 6,000.

3 It is certain from the facts stated in Smith's "Memoirs of Wool" (vol. 1., p. 196), that Spanish Wool was used in England before the year 1656.

4 "Rise, Progress, and Present State of Colonial Sheep and Wools," by Thos. Southey.

17

'THE DIARY OF JOHN WARD OF CLITHEROE, WEAVER 1860–64'

Transactions of the Historic Society of Lancashire and Cheshire, Vol. 5 (1953): 176–184

1864

April 10: It has been a very poor time for me all the time owing to the American War, which seems as far off being settled as ever. The mill I work in was stopped all last winter, during which time I had three shillings per week allowed by the relief committee, which barely kept me alive. When we went to work again it was with Surat cotton and a great number of weavers can only mind two looms. We can earn very little. I have not earned a shilling a day this last month, and there are many like me. My clothes and bedding is wearing out very fast and I have no means of getting any more, as what wages I get does hardly keep me, after paying rent, rates and firing. [. . .] It is the same all through Lancashire. [. . .] The principal reason why I did not take any notes these last two years is because I was sad and weary. One half of the time I was out of work and the other I had to work as hard as ever I wrought in my life, and can hardly keep myself living.

May 1: At our mill things are getting worse. I have given up my odd loom as I cannot keep two looms going, and last week I had only 5/1$^{1/2}$ after a very hard week's work, but they have promised us better work as soon as the cotton is done that they have on hand. They have promised so often that we can hardly believe them.

May 8: The work at our place in beginning to mend. I have got two beams in, the best I have had for twelve months, but they are for shifting the looms out of our shop into a new shed that is ready for starting, so I hope to get better on than I have done this last winter.

May 15: I have been shifted into the new shed and got two very bad looms and bad work in them, so I am no better off than I was. We are to have a holiday tomorrow, but I am too poor to go anywhere so I must stay at home.

 DOI: 10.4324/9781315400105-21

May 22: [A]t our mill things is likely to get worse. The spinners turned out, and a deputation waited upon the Masters, wanting them to mend the work as it was so bad they could scarce get a living.

August 28: I had only six shillings this last week with very hard work, and there was some had less than me; and then our machinery is running very slow owing to the great drought as [the River] Ribble is very near dry.

September 11: [I]f there should be peace, then the price of cotton must come down two shillings per pound, and that is the reason why the cotton trade is so bad just now. The merchants will not buy cloth, as they expect the price will come down one half, and the Manufacturers will not buy cotton for the same reason. There are several mills in Lancashire begun to run short time and some are stopping altogether. At our mills the cotton was done last Tuesday and no signs of any coming there is none working now but weavers, and if no cotton comes, why then we must stop next, so everything has a black look – and winter coming on!

September 25: The cotton trade is getting worse every day. There is no market whatever, and the mills are closing every day.

October 2: There is complete stagnation in trade, both in the cotton and cloth market, and nothing doing.

October 9: There is great distress all through Lancashire at present owing to so many mills stopping, and Clitheroe will soon be as bad as anywhere else.

18

IMAGE: 'COTTON PRINTING'

The National Encyclopaedia: a Dictionary of Universal Knowledge, Vol. 5 (London: [n.p.], c. 1870)

COTTON PRINTING.
SIXTEEN COLOUR PRINTING MACHINE.

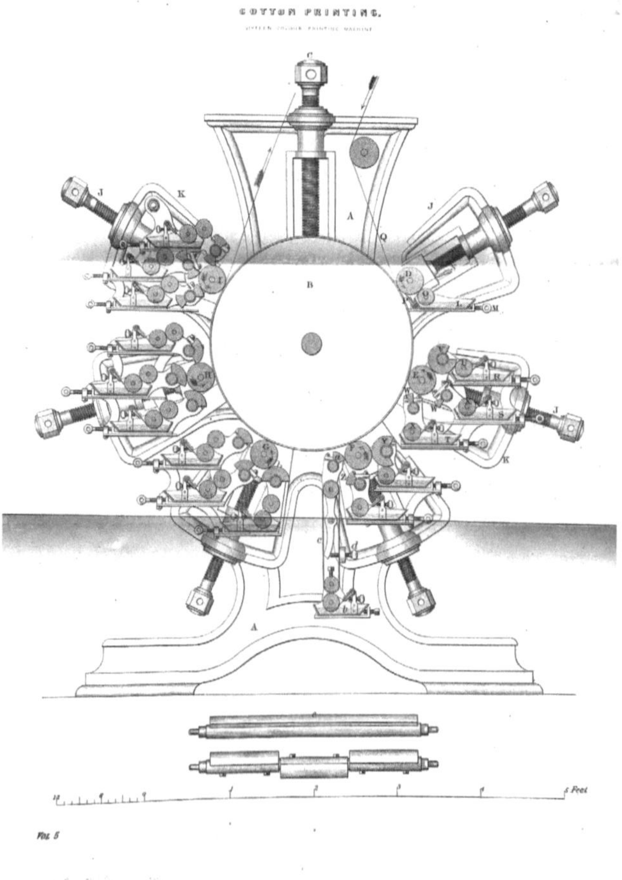

Figure 18.1

DOI: 10.4324/9781315400105-22

19

IMAGE: 'WOOL MACHINERY'

The National Encyclopaedia: a Dictionary of Universal Knowledge, Vol. 4 (London: [n.p.], c. 1870)

WEAVING.
LOOMS.

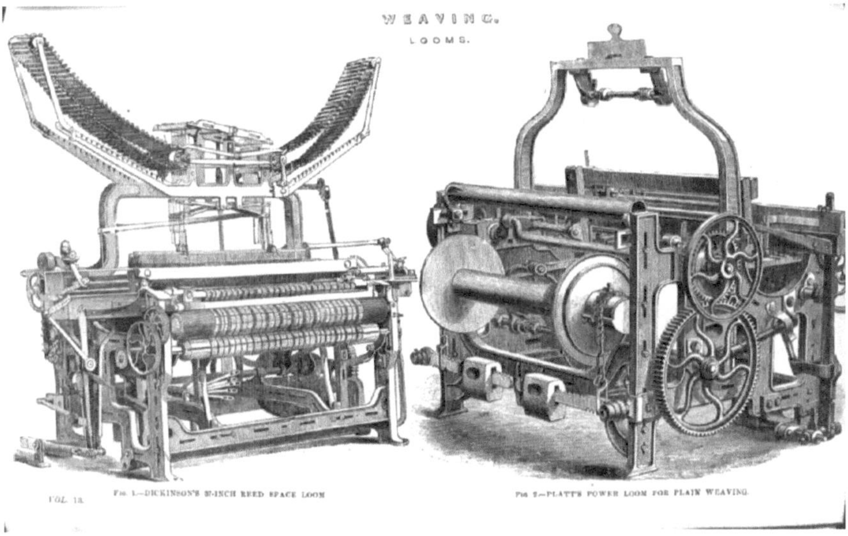

Figure 19.1 Dickinson's 37-inch reed space loom.

Figure 19.2 Platt's power loom for plain weaving.

20

IMAGE: 'WEAVING LOOMS'

The National Encyclopaedia: a Dictionary of Universal Knowledge, Vol. 4 (London: [n.p.], c. 1870)

WOOL MACHINERY.

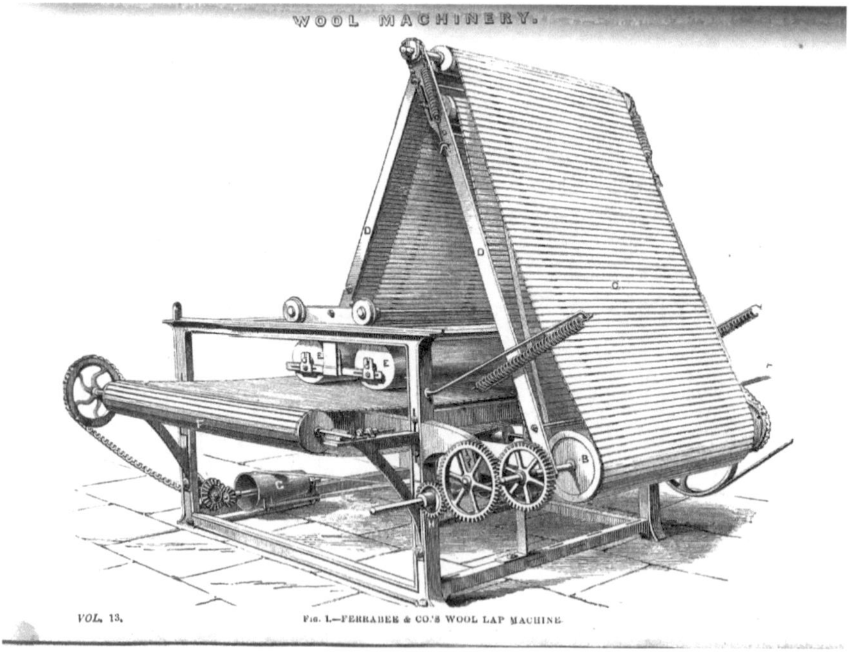

Figure 20.1 Ferrabee & Co.'s wool lap machine.

DOI: 10.4324/9781315400105-24

21

ANON, 'HONITON LACE'

The Gentleman's Magazine (January 1871), pp. 164–171

The usual type of Honiton lace consists of sprigs made separately, like Brussels lace, on a pillow, and then *appliquéd* or sewn on to a net ground. In the last century this was a plain pillow-ground made of the finest Antwerp thread, which in 1790 cost £70 per pound, though even more has been given for it. Eighteen shillings a yard, scarce two inches in width, was paid for this ground. The ordinary way of paying for veils of this fabric was (as jewellers now weigh sovereigns against gold chains) by spreading shillings over them, and giving as many as covered the lace. The last specimen of this "real" ground made in Devon was the marriage veil of the late Mrs. Marwood Tucker, about forty-five years ago. It was with the greatest difficulty that workers were procured to make it, and the ground of it alone, which resembled a series of small circular loops alternating with straight threads, cost thirty guineas. At present the sprigs are generally sewn, as they are completed by the workwomen, on blue paper, and then united by another hand, either on the pillow by "cutworks" or "purling," or else joined with the needle by various stitches. The patterns of these sprigs are in the first place pricked with needles on a kind of shining brown millboard known as "parchment paper," by women, who often devote themselves exclusively to this branch of the business. Among the commonest sights of a fine summer evening in East Devon are the lacemakers, each seated at her door, with their lace-pillows (which resemble thick circular pads) on their laps, and the small children around them on their little stools, all busily occupied in making these sprigs, whether "turkey-tails," "blackberries," or "stars." Similarly in winter the steady "click, click, click," of their pins proceeds from every cottage, just as in a Nottinghamshire village is heard the incessant jar and rattle of the stockingers' frames.

Flemish lace was formerly manufactured in England over a much larger area than at present. From Cambridge and the adjacent shires of Northampton and Herts, by Bucks, Beds, and Oxfordshire, lacemaking spread to the southern and western counties, Wilts, Hants, Somerset, and Devon. It even reached Launceston. Beyond this regular track a kindred sort of lace was made at Swansea, and a few more places in Wales, and again at Ripon, but in all probability these were relics of conventual times, when embroidery and lacemaking occupied the one sex as exclusively as illuminating and transcribing MSS. did the other. At present

DOI: 10.4324/9781315400105-25

the trade is mainly carried on over the greater parts of Beds and Northamptonshire, and in parts of Oxfordshire and Bucks. Government elicited a good deal of information on lacemaking by the Commission on the Employment of Children in Manufactures, which is to be found in their published report. The number of persons employed in the entire lace-manufacture of the Kingdom is estimated at 150,000, and in these four counties at 25,000. The business is taught to children at lace-schools, which are for the most part managed with harshness and oppression. In Beds these schools are far more considerable than those in Devon. Four or five are often found in the same village, which contain from twenty to thirty children each. They are now inspected by Government.

Like all trades, Honiton lacemaking is subject to depression. It received its first check about the beginning of the American War, 1778, when the caprices of taste in George the Third's reign diverted ladies' attention to foreign lace. To remedy this the Society of the Anti-Gallicans was founded, which distributed prizes for bone and point lace of native manufacture, and proved most beneficial to the lace trade. But the invention of machinery for lacemaking was the greatest blow administered to the genuine hand-made fabric. Mr. Heathcoat in 1809, after his machinery at Loughborough had been destroyed by the Luddites, established a factory at Tiverton for *bobbin* lace (so called because made of coarse thread by means of long bobbins) greatly to the injury of the pillow-made lace for the next twenty years. The lacemakers have employed 2,400 hands in the town and neighbourhood of Honiton (writes Lysons), but now, 1822, not above 300 are employed. It was at this period that the debased sprigs, called by the workers "turkeys' tails," "frying pans," "bullocks' hearts," and so forth, were introduced into Honiton lace, instead of the beautiful leaves and flowers copied from nature, which had hitherto distinguished it. It is difficult to induce the Devonshire workwomen even now to forego their prejudices in favour of these conventional sprigs. Mrs. Palliser tried in vain to provide some families with new patterns of roses and leaves, instead of the old senseless "Duchess of Kents," "Brunswicks," or "snowballs," which so extensively prevail.

It has been already stated that Honiton lace, like Trolly lace – which differs from it, however, in being composed of coarse thread – is made on a pillow by the aid of boxwood pins. These are often curiously marked with names or initials branded upon them. "These bone or wood bobbins," says Mrs. Palliser, "some ornamented with glass beads, the more ancient with silver let in, are the calendar of a lacemaker's life." A romance frequently lives in each pin; this one being stamped with a lover's name who presented it perhaps long years ago, this one bearing a grandmother's maiden name, another showing by its stamps that it has descended from two or three generations, and so on. In the sedentary, uneventful life of a lacemaker it is touching to note these cherished evidences of romance and sentiment.

The picturesque village of Beer, near the chalk headland of the same name, so famous of old for smugglers, is now celebrated for its exquisite Honiton lace. Here the Queen's wedding dress was made, at a cost of £1,000; it is composed of Honiton sprigs connected on the pillow by a variety of open-work stitches. The

Princess Royal, Princess Alice, and Princess of Wales also wore wedding dresses of Honiton point made at Beer and the neighbourhood. Capital workmanship in this lace was shewn at the International Exhibition of 1862, but the patterns were conventional and clumsy, arabesques, medallions, and poor imitations of nature. Hence may be traced in great measure its decline in public estimation, though its costliness must always militate against its general use. In consequence of this deficiency prizes were offered in connection with the Bath and West of England Society for natural work in Honiton lace, which produced such admirable specimens that the Queen ordered them to be sent to Windsor Castle for her inspection. Little encouragement is given to the Devon lacemaking trade by the resident gentry, not, we think, because "the air is soft and balmy, and the inhabitants an apathetic generation, alone to be roused by famine or some other calamity from the natural somnolence of their existence," as Mrs. Palliser states. There is doubtless truth to a certain extent in this, but more probable causes seem to be the costliness of the article, and a dislike in the higher classes to encourage the habits of pauperism, neglect, and improvidence engendered but too often by its fabrication, which induce the women to leave their natural sphere as housewives and adopt the lace-pillow in preference. A new branch of industry has lately been developed in Devon – viz., the restoring of old lace. Many of the exquisite mantles and flounces to be seen in the London shop-windows are made up in Devonshire of old tattered fragments of lace "needled" and *appliquéd* to one another on the lace-pillow.

Trolly lace, which, as we have said, is made of coarse British thread, unlike true Honiton, used to be manufactured by men in Devonshire, especially at the little villages of Woodbury and Salcombe, but lacemaking is now almost exclusively a feminine trade. At the former village a colony of workers fabricate imitation Maltese or Greek lace. From very tender years children are taught to make Honiton lace in what are termed lace-schools. The little things collect in a dame's room, and under her tuition, frequently seconded by a cane, are taught the mysteries of the art. They are apprenticed to the trade in Devon at eight, nine, and ten years of age (but in Bucks and Beds commonly at six years, often at four and five), earning nothing in their first year, and sixpence per week in the second. Afterwards they are paid so much per sprig, the price varying with the demand, value of cotton, &c., but being generally 1½d., 2d., or 3d. per sprig. "I can make four turkeys' tails a-day, and get 1½d. for each," a girl of ten lately told us with pardonable pride. A child of five years old will earn a penny in four hours by making six "flies." One master in the trade is said to employ as many as 3,000 of these workchildren. A clever adult hand will easily earn a shilling a-day at her lace-pillow in good times; in many parts of Devon, however, the work is paid for on the truck system. The average earnings of a quick hand may be put down at three shillings or three shillings and sixpence a-week. At Valenciennes the workers used to toil in underground cellars from four in the morning till eight at night, and scarcely earn tenpence a-day. The abuses connected with the lace schools were lately exposed by the Children's Employment Commission. It was found that the hours of work in them were generally excessive, and the atmosphere extremely bad, owing to the crowded state of the small rooms in which the children work. Discipline is rigidly enforced, and in some schools, in order that the lace may be kept clean, the children sit without shoes on brick or stone floors. These causes, coupled with the constrained position of the worker, who must bend over the pillow which rests in her lap, lay the seeds of illness and frequently of consumption in after life. The mortality amongst the laceworkers of Devon we can testify, from personal knowledge, is large. They are thin and sallow, inclined to that bold, false independence which is always engendered when women neglect the domestic virtues. The children are often defiant and disobedient to parents, and, on the whole, the occupation of lacemaking cannot be called one favourable to morality.

The trade is subject to great fluctuation in Devon, brisk demand and high prices alternating at the caprice of fashion with depression and even stagnation. The experience gained from the exhibitions of late years proves that if Honiton lace is to hold its own against foreign workmanship, it must improve in the character of its designs. It must become more artistic. This can only result from extension of educational advantages. At the Paris Exhibition two beautiful cases of Honiton lace, or, as it is known abroad, *point d'Angleterre*, were shown by Mr. Hayward of Oxford Street, and Mrs. Hayman of Sidmouth, well-known dealers in the lace, but it was remarked that to those accustomed to the lovely *point d'Alençon* of France and Belgium this style of Honiton lace appeared more like a fancy article than a work of art. If any one desires to see specimens of the best modern Honiton lace, we recommend him, after paying a visit to the fine cathedral at Exeter, to inspect the magnificent show of this lace which always adorns the windows of a shop in the Cathedral Yard. This establishment sent a noble piece of lace to the Paris Exhibition, and has still more recently introduced a novel variety of it, named Vandyke point.

Having thus indicated the chief *magasins* for this exquisite English lace, our admiration for it is so great that we shall risk the imputation of interested motives, in conclusion, by advising all male readers, if they would earn the certain approbation of the gentle sex, to give a Honiton veil or mantle when they next choose a wedding present. If we might venture on so tender a subject as advice respecting feminine attire, we would fain whisper one word of counsel to ladies. Although a great poet says that a fair form when unadorned is adorned the most, still the fairest figure need not despise the graceful addition of Honiton lace. It is not, however, necessary for a lady, even with the greatest admiration for this delicate fabric, to set an example (like Pope's Narcissa) of the ruling passion strong in death, and be laid to rest, as an instance actually occurred a few years ago, wrapped in a winding-sheet of Honiton lace.

> "Odious! in woollen! 'twould a saint provoke,"
> Were the last words that poor Narcissa spoke.
> "No, let a charming chintz and Brussels lace
> Wrap my cold limbs and shade my lifeless face:
> One would not, sure, be frightful when one's dead;
> And, Betty, give this cheek a little red!"

22

WILLIAM MORRIS, 'TEXTILE FABRICS'

William Morris, *Architecture, Industry and Wealth: Collected Papers* (London: Longmans, Green S and Co., 1902), pp. 148–149, 161–163

The sixteenth century saw the change in woven work which fell upon all the architectural arts. I have said that weaving is conservative of patterns and methods, and this is very obvious in this great period of change; one may say that the oriental-gothic feeling, which was the very well-spring of fine design in this art, lasted side by side with divers new fashions, some of which were merely the outcome of the general pseudo-classical feeling, and shown in detail rather than general arrangement of the pattern, and in some pieces of fantastic ugliness which indicated only too surely the coming degradation of the weaving art.

By the first years of the seventeenth century that degradation had befallen the art in Europe, in fact it was becoming, or had become no longer an art, but a trade, as we very properly nowadays call work, which is really but an accident of the profit-market. I need not, therefore, trace its degradation further, though that degradation was checked, to a certain extent, by the traditions of the better times; and some good work was done until the great flood of the vileness of the eighteenth century swamped everything, and prepared the way for the inanity of the nineteenth; which, in its turn, let us hope, is doomed to prepare the way for a new life once more, even in this small corner of the result of man's intelligence, the textile arts.

In the times of the degradation of the art, with the history of which I have not thought it worth while to trouble you, people gradually forgot that the material had anything to do with the design at all, in fact they often spent time and pains to make, for instance, woven silk look like printed paper and so forth. Moreover in the fine time of art what the designer thought of was always in some way to appeal to the imagination; in other words, to tell some story, however imperfectly; he had not time, therefore, for the petty ingenuities of the later days, he was determined to let us know what he had in his mind, and he, unconsciously maybe, well understood that he was to use fair colour and beautiful form in the simplest and most direct way in order to carry out his purpose. So treated, the design of even a scrap of cloth becomes elevated by human intelligence, and has in its humble way distinct intellectual value; it becomes a thing which no intelligent unprejudiced man has any right to pass by with contempt, as a piece of mere frivolity; and I must say point blank, that unless we can elevate our design into this region of fancy and imagination, we were better to have no ornament at all; for to my mind as a mere commercial necessity, a bit of trade finish, it is unspeakably contemptible. You may easily imagine that I have not time to give you any hints as to the way of elevating our ornament on wares, nor perhaps would this be quite the best place in which to treat the subject, which it seems to me if properly treated would lead us into very serious matters indeed.

One hint, however, I should like to give you; I am myself an ornamentalist, a maker of would-be pretty things. Yet I will not try to press on you the fact that there is nothing like leather; rather, I would say, be cautious of over-ornamenting your houses and your lives with cheap unenduring prettiness; have as few things as you can, for you may be sure that simplicity is the foundation of all worthy art; be sure that whatever ornament you have is proper and reasonable for the sort of life you want to lead, and don't be led by the nose by fashion into having things you don't want. In looking forward towards any utopia of the arts, I do not conceive to myself of there being a very great quantity of art of any kind, certainly not of ornament, apart from the purely intellectual arts; and even those must not swallow up too much of life. As to ornamental art (so called), I can, under our present conditions, looking forward from out of the farrago of rubbish with which we are now surrounded, chiefly see possible negative virtues in the externals of our household goods; can see them never shabby, pretentious, or ungenerous, natural and reasonable always; beautiful also, but more because they are natural and reasonable, than because we have set about to make them beautiful. We need not think that this will be an easy matter to bring about, but when it is brought about, I do believe that some sort of genuine art and ornament will accompany it, it may be in rather a Spartan way at first; from that time onward we shall have art enough, and shall have become so decent and reasonable, that every household will have become a quiet, daily, unadvertised Health Exhibition.

23

ANON, 'FRENCH LACE'

Bow Bells (9 November 1894), p. 467

LACE MAKING is a very old industry in France. The oldest documents referring to the lace trade date back to the fifteenth century. Le Velay, a little country place in Languedoe, now the department of the Haute Loire, is considered as the birthplace of the industry, and remains to-day an important centre.

About the same time the lace-making began in France the Low Countries, or Flanders – to-day known as Belgium – began the manufacture of what is to-day the well-known Point de Bruxelles, Malines, et cetera. The exceptional laws made by Henry II. against the use of lace were very prejudical to the French lace-makers, but Colbert, under Louis XIV., revived the industry.

There are two kinds of lace – pillow or bobbin lace and needle lace. Very little needle lace is made in France.

For the pillow lace all that is required is a cushion, on which is fixed a card on which the pattern to be made is drawn. According to these figures pins are stuck in to represent the pattern, then the threads are wound on bobbins. Every thread has a bobbin, and it is in twisting and crossing these threads round the pins, picking up each bobbin in turn, that the pattern is formed.

The production of lace by machinery at Calais, Nottingham and elsewhere, has very much diminished the demand for real lace, and instead of lace-making being, as it once was, a lucrative business, it is difficult to earn fifty centimes per day, and the women only turn to their cushion to fill up their leisure time, or when there is no work in the fields. This causes great difficulty to the manufacturer requiring deliveries of certain patterns in quantities at fixed dates for foreign markets, which send on their orders without consideration whether the goods can be delivered, as at Nottingham, in quantity, and it also sends up the price, as it then becomes entirely a question of supply and demand.

Le Puy, in the Haute Loire, is the chief French centre for this trade. Every manufacturer has, according to his importance, several hundred lace-makers, all of whom work in their own homes, and many of whom reside at long distances from the chief centre. It is calculated that there are as many as thirty thousand villages and hamlets in Auvergne, all making laces.

Every Saturday, which is market day, the lace-makers all come in with their work and take back the thread, to return the following week with the lace made.

DOI: 10.4324/9781315400105-27

This system makes it very difficult for the manufacturer to control his deliveries, and he is necessarily very much at the will and pleasure of his workpeople, who can please themselves, and do, entirely as to how much of what he gives them they will complete. One or two towns, such as Craponne and Le Chaise Dieu, make the fine grades which sell side by side with Belgian laces, but the staple article of the district of which Le Puy is the centre are the well-known torchons and wool laces.

Lace being very much an article of taste and fashion, the patterns are continually liable to go out of style; hence very small stocks are kept ahead, except for well-accepted staple designs for underwear and the like.

The modus operandi of this kind of lace-making is of the simplest. The design is first drawn and is copied on to as many cards as are needed for the workers who are to produce the pattern. The card is then perforated where the pins are to be put in. This is simplicity itself compared with the enormously complicated setting up of a pattern on a Calais loom, but difficulties much greater lie in wait for a Le Puy manufacturer. Machines can be made to do their work, but women workers are different, and when a difficult pattern is given out lots of "kicking" comes in and much difficulty has to be overcome. Especially is this the case when the work is plentiful. All then want to do the easy patterns which bring in the most money.

2.2

Clothing

DOI: 10.4324/9781315400105-28

2.2 Clothing

Thomas Hood, 'The Song of the Shirt' (1843).
Harriet Martineau, 'Rainbow Making', *Household Words*, Vol. 4 (14 February 1852), pp. 485–490.
Samuel Sidney, 'A Ladies' Warehouse', *Household Words*, Vol. 12 (27 October 1855), pp. 301–305. Mrs Henry Wood, *Mrs Halliburton's Troubles* [1862] (London & New York: The Walter Scott Publishing Co., n.d.), pp. 99–100, 107–108, 122, 134–135.
Anon, 'Gloves', *All The Year Round*, Vol. 9 (27 June 1863), pp. 425, 428–430.
Anon, 'A Crinoline Manufactory', *Once A Week*, 23 January 1864, pp. 124–126.
Edith Simcox, 'Eight Years of Co-operative Shirtmaking', *The Nineteenth Century*, Vol. 15 (June 1884), pp. 1037–1054.
Ada Heather-Bigg, 'Women and the Glove Trade', *The Nineteenth Century*, Vol. 30 (December 1891), pp. 939–944, 946–947.

Britain's dominance of the global trade in textile fabrics gave employment to many in the dressmaking and tailoring trades. Their working conditions, however, were notoriously poor, and rates of pay were appalling, sometimes barely sufficient to support life. Indeed, such conditions became a national scandal, and 'The Song of the Shirt', a poem by Thomas Hood (1799–1845), which was first published anonymously in 1843, expresses this well. It was inspired by reports of a widow forced to enter the workhouse because she was unable to support her children with her wages from shirtmaking. The reiterated lines 'Work – work – work' and 'Seam, and gusset, and band,/ Band, and gusset, and seam' echo the repetitive labour of sewing, while the irony of the seamstress making new shirts while working 'in unwomanly rags' is emphasised. 'The Song of the Shirt' became famous, playing an important role in raising awareness of the terrible conditions endured by some workers in the clothing trades.

The situation of the shirtmaker had improved somewhat by later in the century, as 'Eight Years of Co-operative Shirtmaking' (1884) by Edith Simcox (1844–1901) indicates. Simcox notes the increased presence of women in trade unions in her discussion of the establishment of a shirtmaking co-operative in London, a 'self-supporting clothes-making factory, where women should do all the work, and divide the profits among them[selves]'. The extract here indicates the different aspects of shirtmaking, from the cutting out of pieces, to specialised work on buttonholes, collars and wristbands, to the sewing itself. Simcox usefully highlights the political and economic realities of clothing manufacture in this period and the work being done to empower workers.

Female labour in the clothing trade also features in the sources on glove manufacture: the anonymous 'Gloves' (1863), Ada Heather-Bigg's 'Women and the Glove Trade' (1891), and an extract from the 1862 novel *Mrs Halliburton's Troubles* by Mrs Henry (Ellen) Wood (1814–1887). Set in Worcester, the centre of glove manufacturing in Britain, the eponymous heroine takes in piecework from the local factory. Both Wood and Heather-Bigg present the manufacture of gloves at home as ideal 'feminine' work, particularly suitable for married women. There had long been anxieties about women working outside the home in factories and mills, with common perceptions of this causing a deterioration in working-class domestic life.[1] Factory wages appeared to empower women, with some commentators expressing fears that they would eschew modesty in dress and behaviour. Heather-Bigg's article notes problems of mechanisation in the glove trade, which forced female glove workers out of the home and into the factory. Both extracts usefully detail how gloves are made and the different stages of their manufacture. 'Gloves', by contrast, offers a history of gloves and glove making in Britain.

Female labour is also foregrounded in 'A Crinoline Manufactory' (1864), an article in the popular journal *Once A Week* based on a factory visit. While men cut the sheets of steel into narrow strips to create the 'cages' worn beneath skirts, the skirts themselves are covered with cotton by women using sewing machines. Harriet Martineau's 'Rainbow Making', published anonymously in 1852, recounts a visit to a dye works in Coventry where silk ribbons are made. The article shows how improved dyes and the use of cotton blended with silk created more affordable, brightly coloured ribbons. The abundance of affordable clothing also features in 'A Ladies' Warehouse' (1855). The author (later identified as Samuel Sidney) asserts that the sumptuary laws are impossible to maintain in the age of machinery. Visiting a warehouse in Cheapside, he notes that it is 'a barrack and storehouse of commercial warfare on human nakedness'. The warehouse supplies the retail trade and distributes vast quantities of goods, including gowns, baby linen, millinery, lace collars, handkerchiefs, caps, ribbons and stays. All three articles celebrate the abundance and cheapness of mass-produced goods, as well as the sources of employment and revenue generated by the clothing trade.

Note

1 For discussions of female labour in factories and mills, see Maxine Berg, *The Age of Manufactures, 1700–1820: industry, innovation and work in Britain* (London: Routledge, 1994), and Helsinger, Elizabeth K., Robin L. Sheets and William Veeder (eds.), *The Woman Question: Society and Literature in Britain and America, 1837–1883*, Vol. 2 (Manchester: Manchester University Press, 1983).

24

THOMAS HOOD, 'THE SONG OF THE SHIRT' (1843)

With fingers weary and worn,
  With eyelids heavy and red,
A woman sat in unwomanly rags,
  Plying her needle and thread –
    Stitch! stitch! stitch!
In poverty, hunger, and dirt,
  And still with a voice of dolorous pitch
She sang the "Song of the Shirt."

  "Work! work! work!
While the cock is crowing aloof!
  And work – work – work,
Till the stars shine through the roof!
It's O! to be a slave
  Along with the barbarous Turk,
Where woman has never a soul to save,
  If this is Christian work!

  "Work – work – work,
Till the brain begins to swim;
  Work – work – work,
Till the eyes are heavy and dim!
Seam, and gusset, and band,
  Band, and gusset, and seam,
Till over the buttons I fall asleep,
  And sew them on in a dream!

  "O, men, with sisters dear!
  O, men, with mothers and wives!
It is not linen you're wearing out,

DOI: 10.4324/9781315400105-29

But human creatures' lives!
Stitch – stitch – stitch,
In poverty, hunger and dirt,
Sewing at once, with a double thread,
A Shroud as well as a Shirt.

"But why do I talk of death?
That phantom of grisly bone,
I hardly fear his terrible shape,
It seems so like my own –
It seems so like my own,
Because of the fasts I keep;
Oh, God! that bread should be so dear.
And flesh and blood so cheap!

"Work – work – work!
My labour never flags;
And what are its wages? A bed of straw,
A crust of bread – and rags.
That shattered roof – this naked floor –
A table – a broken chair –
And a wall so blank, my shadow I thank
For sometimes falling there!

"Work – work – work!
From weary chime to chime,
Work – work – work,
As prisoners work for crime!
Band, and gusset, and seam,
Seam, and gusset, and band,
Till the heart is sick, and the brain benumbed,
As well as the weary hand.

"Work – work – work,
In the dull December light,
And work – work – work,
When the weather is warm and bright –
While underneath the eaves
The brooding swallows cling
As if to show me their sunny backs
And twit me with the spring.

"O! but to breathe the breath
Of the cowslip and primrose sweet –

With the sky above my head,
And the grass beneath my feet;
For only one short hour
To feel as I used to feel,
Before I knew the woes of want
And the walk that costs a meal!

"O! but for one short hour!
A respite however brief!
No blessed leisure for Love or hope,
But only time for grief!
A little weeping would ease my heart,
But in their briny bed
My tears must stop, for every drop
Hinders needle and thread!"

With fingers weary and worn,
With eyelids heavy and red,
A woman sat in unwomanly rags,
Plying her needle and thread –
Stitch! stitch! stitch!
In poverty, hunger, and dirt,
And still with a voice of dolorous pitch, –
Would that its tone could reach the Rich! –
She sang this "Song of the Shirt!"

25

HARRIET MARTINEAU, 'RAINBOW MAKING'

Household Words, Vol. 4 (14 February 1852), pp. 485–490

When our Queen Mary passed a law forbidding servant-maids to wear ribbon on bonnets; and when monarch after monarch passed acts to teach how silk should be boiled, and whence it should be brought, and who should, and who should not, wear it when wrought; but the perplexity and amazement of king, lords, and commons could hardly, at any time, have exceeded that of the humblest visitor of to-day in any dye-house at Coventry. We know something of the fact of this astonishment; for we have been noting the wonders that are to be found on the premises of Messrs. Leavesley and Hands at Coventry.

On entering, we see, ranged along the counters, half round the room, bundles of glossy silk, of the most brilliant colours. Blues, rose-colours, greens, lilacs, make a rainbow of the place. It is only two days since this silk was brought in in a very different condition. The throwster (to throw, means to twist or twine), after spinning the raw silk, imported from Italy, Turkey, Bengal, and China, into thread fit for the loom, sent it here in bundles, gummy, harsh, dingy; except, indeed, the Italian, which looks, till washed, like fragments of Jason's fleece. If bundles, and regiments of bundles, like these, come into one dye-house every few days, to be prepared for the weaving of ribbons alone, and for the ribbon-weaving of a single town, it is overwhelming to think of the amount of production required for the broad silk-weaving of England, of Europe, of the world. Of the silk dyed at Coventry, about eighty per cent, is used for the ribbon-weaving of the city and neighbourhood; and the quantity averages six tons and a half weekly. Of the remaining twenty per cent., half is used for the manufacture of fringes; and the other half goes to Macclesfield, Congleton, and Derby.

The harsh gummy silk that comes in from the throwing mills is boiled, wrung out, and boiled again. If it wants bleaching, there is a sort of open oven of a house; a vault in the yard, where it is "sulphured." The heat, and the sensation in the throat, inform us in a moment where we have got to. When the hanks come forth from this process, every thread is separated from its neighbour, and the whole bundle is soft, dry, and glossy. Then follows the dyeing. To make the silk receive the colours, it is dipped in a mordant, in some diluted acid, or solution of metal,

 DOI: 10.4324/9781315400105-30

which enables the colour to bite into the fibre. To make pinks of all shades, the silk is dipped in diluted tartaric acid for the mordant, and then in a decoction of safflower for the hue. To make plum-colour or puce, indigo is the dye, with a cochineal. To make black, nitrate of iron first; then a washing follows; and then a dipping in logwood dye, mixed with soap and water. For a white, pure enough for ribbons, the silk has to pass through the three primary colours, yellow, red, and blue. The dipping, wringing, splashing, stirring, boiling, drying, go on vigorously, from end to end of the large premises, as may be supposed, when the fact is mentioned that the daily consumption of water amounts to one hundred thousand gallons. A reservoir, in the middle of the yard, formerly supplied the water; but it proved insufficient, or uncertain; and now it is about to be filled up, and an Artesian well is opened to the depth of one hundred and ninety-five feet. The dyeing sheds are paved with pebbles or bricks, crossed with gutters, and variegated with gay puddles. Stout brick-built coppers are stationed round the place. Above each copper are cocks, which let in hot and cold water from the pipes that travel round the walls of the sheds. There are wooden troughs for the dye; and to these troughs the water is conveyed by spouts. The silk hangs down into the dye from poles, smoothly turned and uniform, which are laid across the troughs by the dozen or more at once. These staves are procured from Derby. They cost from six shillings to twenty-four shillings per dozen, and constitute an independent subsidiary manufacture. The silk hanks being suspended from these poles, two men, standing on either side the trough, take up two poles, souse, and shake, and plunge the silk, and turn that which had been uppermost under the surface of the liquor, and pass on to the next two. When done enough, the silk is wrung out and pressed, and taken to the drying-house. The heat in that large chamber is about one hundred degrees. On entering it, everybody begins to cough. The place is lofty and large. The staves, which are laid across beams, to contain the suspended silk, make little moveable ceilings here and there. This chamber contains five or six hundred-weights of silk at once. Our minds glance once more towards the spinning insects on hearing this; and we ask again, how much of their produce may be woven into fabrics in Coventry alone? We think we must have made a mistake in setting down the weekly average at six tons and a half. But there was no mistake. It is really so.

While speaking of weight, we heard something which reminded us of King Charles I.'s opinions about some practices which were going forward before our eyes. It appears, that the silk which comes to the dye-house is heavy with gum, to the amount of one-fourth of its weight. This gum must be boiled out before the silk can be dyed. But the manufacturers of cheap goods require that the material shall not be so light as this process would leave it. It is dipped in well-sugared water, which adds about eight per cent, to its weight. Many tons of sugar per year are used as (what the proprietor called) "the silk-dyer's devil's dust." It was this very practice which excited the wrath of our pious King Charles, in all his horror of double-dealing. A proclamation of his, of the date of 1630, declares his fears of the consequences of "a deceitful handling" of the material, by adding to its weight in dyeing, and ordains that the whole shall be done as soft as possible; that no black shall be used but Spanish black, "and that the gum shall be fair boiled off before dyeing." He found, in time, that he had meddled with a matter that he did not understand, and had gone too far. Some of the fabrics of his day required to be made of "hard silk;" and he took back his orders in 1638, having become, as he said, "better-informed."

From trough to trough we go, breathing steam, and stepping into puddles, or reeking rivulets rippling over the stones of the pavement; but we are tempted on, like children, by the charm of the brilliant colours that flash upon the sight whichever way we turn. What a lilac this is! Is it possible that such a hue can stand? It could not stand even the drying, but for the alkali into which it is dipped. It is dyed in orchil first, and then made bluer, and somewhat more secure, by being soused in a well-soaped alkaline mixture. – That is a good red brown. It is from Brazil wood, with alum for its mordant. – This is a brilliant blue; – indigo, of course? Yes, sulphate of indigo, with tartaric acid. – Here are two yellows: how is that? One is much better than the other; moreover, it makes a better green; moreover, it wears immeasurably better. – But what is it? The inferior one is the old-fashioned turmeric, with tartaric acid. And the improved yellow? – O! we perceive. It is a secret of the establishment, and we are not to ask questions about it. But among all these men employed here, are there none accessible to a bribe from a rival in the art? There is no saying; for the men cannot be tempted. They do not know, any more than ourselves, what this mysterious yellow is. But why does it not supersede the old-fashioned turmeric? – It will, no doubt; and it is gaining rapidly upon it; but it takes time to establish improvements. The improvement in greens, however, is fast recommending the new yellow. – This deep amber is a fine colour. We find it is called California, which has a modern sound in it. – This Napoleon blue (not Louis Napoleon's) is a rich colour. It gives a good deal of trouble. There is actually a precipitation of metal, of tin, upon every fibre, to make it receive the dye; and then it has to be washed; and then dipped again, before it can take a darker shade; and afterwards washed again, over and over, till it is dark enough; when it is finally soused in water which has fuller's earth in it, to make it soft enough for working and wear. – What is doing with that dirty-white bundle? It is silk of a thoroughly bad colour. Whether it is the fault of the worm, or of the worm's food, or what, there is no saying – that is the manufacturer's affair. He sent it here. It is now to be sulphured, and dipped in a very faint shade of indigo, curdled over with soap. This will improve it, but not make it equal to a purer white silk. Next, the wet hanks have to be squeezed in the Archimedean press, and then hung up in that large, hot drying-room.

One serious matter remains unintelligible to us. Plaid ribbons – that is, all sorts of checked ribbons – have been in fashion so long now, that we have had time to speculate (which we have often done) on how they can possibly be made. About the colours of the warp (the long way of the ribbon) we are clear enough. But how, in the weft, do the colours duly return, so as to make the stripes, and therefore the checks, recur at equal distances? We are now shown how this was done formerly, and how it is done now. Formerly, the hanks were tied very tightly, at equal distances, and the alternate spaces closely wrapped round with paper, or wound round with packthread. This took up a great deal of time. We were shown a much better plan. A shallow box is made, so as to hold within it the halves of several skeins of silk; these halves being curiously twisted, so as to alternate with the other halves when the hanks are shaken back into their right position for winding. One half being within the box, and the other hanging out, the lid is bolted down so tight that the dye cannot creep into the box; and the out-hanging silk is dipped. So much can be done at once, that the saving of time is very great, and, judging by the prodigious array of plaid ribbons that we saw in the looms afterwards, the value of the invention is no trifle. The name of this novelty is the Clouding Box.

We see a bundle of cotton. What has cotton to do here? It is from Nottingham – very fine and well twisted. It is a pretty pink, and it costs one shilling and sixpence per pound to dye. But what is it for? – Ah! that is the question! It is to mix in with silk, to make a cheap ribbon. Another pinch of devil's dust!

There is a calendering process employed in the final preparation of the dried silk, by which, we believe, its gloss is improved; but it was not in operation at the time of our visit. We saw, and watched with great curiosity, a still later process – more pretty to witness than easy to achieve – the making up of the hanks. This is actually the most difficult thing the men have to learn in the whole business. Of course, therefore, it is no matter for description. The twist, the insertion of the arm, the jerk, the drawing of the mysterious knot, may be looked at for hours and days, without the spectator having the least idea how the thing is done. We went from workman to workman – from him who was making up the blue, to him who was making up the red – we saw one of the proprietors make up several hanks at the speed of twenty in four minutes and a half, and we are no more likely to be able to do it, than if we had never entered a dye-house. Peeping Tom might spy for very long before he would be much the wiser: when done, the effect is beautiful. The snaky coils of the polished silk throw off the light like fragments of mirrors.

Another mysterious process is the marking of the silk which belongs to each manufacturer. The hanks and bundles are tied with cotton string; and this string is knotted with knots at this end, at that end, in the middle, in ties at the sides, with knots numbering from one to fifteen, twenty, or whatever number may be necessary; and the manufacturer's particular system of knots is posted in the books with his name, the quantity of silk sent in, the dye required, and all other particulars.

We were amused to find that there is a particular twist and a particular dye for the fringe of brown parasols. It is desired that there should be a claret tint on this fringe, when seen against the light; and here, accordingly, we find the claret tint. The silk is somewhat dull, from being hard twisted; it is to be made more lustrous by stretching, and we accompany it to the stretching machine. There it is suspended on a barrel and moveable pin; by a man's weight applied to a wheel, the pin is drawn down, the hank stretches, and comes out two or more inches longer than it went in, and looking perceptibly brighter. A hank of bad silk snaps under this strain; a twist that will stand it is improved by it.

Looking into a little apartment, as we return through the yard, we find a man engaged in work which the daintiest lady might long to take out of his hands. He is making pattern-cards and books. He arranges the shades of all sorts of charming colours, named after a hundred pretty flowers, fruits, and other natural productions, – his lemons, lavenders, corn flowers, jonquils, cherries, fawns, pearls, and so forth; takes a pinch of each floss, knots it in the middle, spreads it at the ends, pastes down these ends, and, when he has a row complete, covers the pasted part with slips of paper, so numbered as that each number stands opposite its own shade of colour. A pattern-book is as good as a rainbow for the pocket. This looks like woman's work; but there are no women here. The men will not allow it. Women cannot be kept out of the ribbon-weaving; but in the dye-house they must not set foot, though the work, or the chief part of it, is far from laborious, and requires a good eye and tact, more than qualities less feminine. We found many apprentices in the works, receiving nearly half the amount of wages of their qualified elders. The men earn from ten shillings to thirty shillings a-week, according to their qualifications. Nearly half of the whole number earn about fifteen shillings a-week at the present time.

And, now, we are impatient to follow these pretty silk bundles to the factory, and see the weaving. It is strange to see, on our way to so thoroughly modern an establishment, such tokens of antiquity, or reminders of antiquity, as we have to pass. We pass under St. Michael's Church, and look up, amazed, to the beauty and loftiness of its tower and spire; – the spire tapering off at a height of three hundred and twenty feet. The crumbling nature of the stone gives a richness and beauty to the edifice, which we would hardly part with for such clear outlines as those of the restored Trinity Church, close at hand. And then, at an angle of the market-place, there is Tom, peeping past the corner, – looking out of his window, through his spectacles, with a stealthy air, which, however ridiculous, makes one thrill, as with a whiff of the breeze which stirred the Lady Godiva's hair, on that memorable day, so long ago. It is strange, after this, to see the factory chimney, straight, tall, and handsome, in its way, with its inlaying of coloured bricks, towering before us, to about the height of a hundred and thirty feet. No place has proved itself more unwilling than Coventry to admit such innovations. No place has made a more desperate resistance to the introduction of steam power. No place has more perseveringly struggled for protection, with groans, menaces, and supplications. Up to a late period, the Coventry weavers believed themselves safe from the inroads of steam power. A Macclesfield manufacturer said, only twenty years ago, before a Committee of the House of Commons, that he despaired of ever applying power-looms to silk. This was because so much time was employed in handling and trimming the silk, that the steam power must be largely wasted. So thought the weavers, in the days when the silk was given out in hanks or bobbins, and woven at home, or, when the work was done by handloom weavers in the factory – called the loom-shop. The day was at hand, however, when that should be done of which the Macclesfield gentleman despaired. A small factory was set up in Coventry by way of experiment, in the use of steam power, in 1831. It was burned down during a quarrel about wages, – nobody knows how or by whom. The weavers declared it was not their doing; but their enmity to steam power was strong enough to restrain the employers from the use of it. It was not till everybody saw that Coventry was losing its manufacture, – parting with it to places which made ribbons by steam, – that the manufacturers felt themselves able to do what must be done, if they were to save their trade. The state of things now is very significant. About seventy houses in Coventry make ribbons and trimmings, (fringes and the like). Of these, four make fringes and trimmings, and no ribbons; and six or eight make both. Say that fifty-eight houses make ribbons alone. It is believed that three-fourths of the ribbons are made by no more than twenty houses out of these fifty-eight. There are now thirty steam power-loom factories in Coventry, producing about seven thousand pieces of ribbons in the week, and employing about three thousand persons. It seems not to be ascertained how large a proportion of the population are employed in the ribbon manufacture: but the increase is great since the year 1838, when the number was about eight thousand, without reckoning the outlying places, which would add about three thousand to the number. The total population of the city was found, last March, to amount to nearly thirty-seven thousand. So, if we reckon the numbers employed in connexion with the throwing-mills and dye-houses, we shall see what an ascendancy the ribbon manufacture has in Coventry.

At the factory we are entering, the preparatory processes are going forward at the top and the bottom of the building. In the yard is the boiler fire, which sets the engine to work; and, from the same yard, we enter workshops, where the machinery is made and repaired. The ponderous work of the men at the forge and anvils contrasts curiously with the delicacy of the fabric which is to be produced by the agency of these masses of iron and steel. Passing up a step-ladder, we find ourselves in a long room, where turners are at work, making the wooden apparatus required, piercing the "compass boards," for the threads to pass through, and displaying to us many ingenious forms of polished wood. While the apparatus is thus preparing below, the material of the manufacture is getting arranged, four stories over-head. There, under a skylight, women and girls are winding the silk from the hanks, upon the spools, for the shuttles. Here we see, again, the clouded silk, which is to make plaid ribbons, and the bright hues which delighted our eyes at the dyeing-house. This is easy work, – many of the women sitting at their reels; and the air is pure and cool. The great shaft from the engine, passing through the midst of the building, carries off the dust, and affords excellent ventilation. Besides this, the whole edifice is crowned by an observatory, with windows all round; and no complete ceilings shut off the air between this chamber and the rooms of two stories below. In clear weather, there is a fine view from this pinnacle, extending from the house, gardens, and orchard of the Messrs. Hamerton below, over the spires of Coventry, to a wide range of country beyond.

Descending from the long room, where the winding is going on, we find ourselves in an apartment which it does one good to be in. It is furnished with long narrow tables, and benches, put there for the sake of the workpeople, who may like to have their tea at the factory, in peace and quiet. They can have hot water, and make themselves comfortable here. Against the door hangs a list of books, read, or to be read, by the people: and a very good list it is. Prints, from Raffaelle's Bible, plainly framed, are on the walls. In the middle of the room, on, and beside, a table, are four men and boys, preparing the "strapping" of a Jacquard loom for work. The cords, so called, are woven at Shrewsbury. We next enter a room where a young man is engaged in the magical work of "reading in from the draught." The draught is the pattern of the intended ribbon, drawn and painted upon diced paper, – like the patterns for carpets that we saw at Kendal, but a good deal larger, though the article to be produced here is so much smaller. The young man sits, as at a loom. Before him hangs the mass of cords he is to tie into pattern, close before his face, like the curtain of a cabinet piano. Upreared before his eyes is his pattern, supported by a slip of wood. He brings the line he has to "read in" to the edge of this wood, and then, with nimble fingers, separates the cords, by threes, by sevens, by fives, by twelves, according to the pattern, and threads through them the string which is to tie them apart. The skill and speed with which he feels out his cords, while his eyes are fixed on his pattern, appear very remarkable: but when we come to consider, it is not so complicated a process as playing at sight on the piano. The reader has to deal thus with one chapter, or series, or movement, of his pattern. A *da capo* ensues: in other words, the Jacquard cards are tied together, to begin again; and there is a revolution of the cards, and a repetition of the pattern, till the piece of ribbon is finished. In the same apartment is the press in which the Jacquard cards are prepared; – just in the way which may be seen wherever silk or carpet weaving, with Jacquard looms, goes forward.

All the preparations having been seen, – the making of the machinery, the filling of the spools, the drawing and "reading in" of the pattern, and the tying of the cords or strapping, we have to see the great process of all, – the actual weaving. We certainly had no idea how fine a spectacle it might be. Floor above floor is occupied with a long room in each, where the looms are set as close as they can work, on either hand, leaving only a narrow passage between. It may seem an odd thing to say; but there is a kind of architectural grandeur in these long lofty rooms, where the transverse cords of the looms and their shafts and beams are so uniform, as to produce the impression that symmetry, on a large scale, always gives. Looking down upon the details, there is plenty of beauty. The light glances upon the glossy coloured silks, depending, like a veil, from the backs of the looms, where women and girls are busy piercing the imperfect threads with nimble fingers. There seems to be plenty for one person to do; for there are thirteen broad ribbons, or a greater number of narrow ones, woven at once, in a single loom; yet it may sometimes be seen that one person can attend the fronts, and another the backs of two looms. In the front we see the thirteen ribbons getting made. Usually, they are of the same pattern, in different colours. The shuttles, with their gay little spools, fly to and fro, and the pattern grows, as of its own will. Below is a barrel, on which the woven ribbon is wound. Slowly revolving, it. winds off the fabric as it is finished, leaving the shuttles above room to ply their work.

The variety of ribbons is very great, though in this factory we saw no gauzes, nor, at the time of our visit, any of the extremely rich ribbons which made such a show at the Exhibition. Some had an elegant and complicated pattern, and were woven with two shuttles (called the double-batten weaving) which came forward alternately, as the details of the rich flower or leaf required the one or the other. There were satin ribbons, in weaving which only one thread in eight is taken up, – the gloss being given by the silk loop which covers the other seven. On entering, we saw some narrow scarlet satin ribbons, woven for the Queen. Wondering what Her Majesty could want with ribbon of such a colour and quality, we were set at ease by finding that it was not for ladies, but horses. It was to dress the heads of the royal horses. There were bride-like, white-figured ribbons, and narrow flimsey black ones, fit for the wear of the poor widow who strives to get together some mourning for Sundays. There were checked ribbons, of all colours and all sizes in the check. There were stripes of all varieties of width and hue. There were diced ribbons, and speckled, and frosted. There were edges which may introduce a beautiful harmony of colouring; – as primrose with a lilac edge; – green with a purple edge; rose-colour and brown; puce and amber; and so on. The loops of pearl or shell edges are given by the silk being passed round horse-hairs, which are drawn out when the thing is done. There are belts, – double ribbons, – which have other material than silk in them; and there are a good many which are plain at one edge, and ornamented at the other. These are for trimming dresses. One reason why there are so few gauzes, is that the French beat us there. They grow the kind of silk that is best for that fabric: and labour is cheap with them; so that any work in which labour bears a large proportion to the material, is particularly suitable for them.

We have spent so much time among the looms, that it is growing dusk in their shadows, though still light enough in the counting-house for us to look over the pattern-book, and admire a great many patterns, most, till we see more. Young women are weighing ribbons in large scales; and a man is measuring off some pieces, by reeling. He cuts off remnants, which he casts into a basket, where they look so pretty that, lest we should be conscious of any shop-lifting propensities, we turn away. There is a glare now through the window which separates us from the noisy weaving room. The gas is lighted, and we step in again, just to see the effect. It is really very fine. The flare of the separate jets is lost behind the screens of silken threads, which veil the backs of the looms, while the yellow light touches the beams, and gushes up to the high ceiling in a thousand caprices. Surely the ribbon manufacture is one of the prettiest that we have to show.

If the Coventry people were asked whether their chief manufacture was in a flourishing state, the most opposite answers would probably be given by different parties equally concerned. Some exult, and some complain, at this present time. As far as we can make out, the state of things is this. From the low price of provisions, multitudes have something more to spare from their weekly wages than formerly, for the purchase of finery: and the demand for cheap ribbons has increased wonderfully. As always happens when any manufacture is prosperous, the operatives engage their whole families in it. We may see the father weaving; his wife, on the verge of her confinement, winding in another room, or, perhaps, standing behind a loom, piecing the whole day long. The little girls fill the spools; the boys are weaving somewhere else. The consequences of this devotion of whole households to one business, are as bad here as among the Nottingham lace-makers, or the Leicester hosiers. Not only is there the misery before them of the whole family being adrift at once, when bad times come, but they are doing their utmost to bring on those bad times. Great as is the demand, the production has, thus far, much exceeded it. The soundest capitalists may be heard complaining that theirs is a losing trade. Less substantial capitalists have been obliged to get rid of some of their stock at any price they could obtain: and those ribbons, sold at a loss, intercept the sales of the fair-dealing manufacturer. This cannot go on. Prosperous as the working-classes of Coventry have been, for a considerable time, a season of adversity must be within ken, if the capitalists find the trade a bad one for them. We find the case strongly stated, and supported by facts, in a tract on the Census of Coventry, which has lately been published there. It might save a repetition of the misery which the Coventry people brought upon themselves formerly – by their tenacity about protective duties, and their opposition to steam power – if they would, before it is too late, ponder the facts of their case, and strive, every man in his way, to yield respect to the natural demand for the great commodity of his city; and to take care that the men of Coventry shall be fit for something else than weaving ribbons.

26

SAMUEL SIDNEY, 'A LADIES' WAREHOUSE'

Household Words, Vol. 12
(27 October 1855), pp. 301–305

The notion of a sumptuary law, after the model prescribed by that fearful bore, Mentor, in Telemachus, is still in favour with a good many well-to-do people; but they are beaten by the cheapness of machinery, which has swept away a crowd of prejudices and flooded us with comforts and luxuries and reasons for not "silting at home at ease." Nevertheless, a comical example of Queen Charlotte's principles is yet extant. Squire Raven owns the parish of Ravensburne, a fine estatein the most rural part of Lancashire. Having failed in making the social and political world around him stand still, he is obliged to be content with ruling over his own parish. In the squire's servants'-pew on Sundays is ranged a row of serving-maids in the old Lancashire costume – a calico jacket or Lancashire bedgown, and a striped lindsey-wolsey petticoat. A very pretty costume no doubt; and a costly one; for the old-fashioned chintz, in the good old days, would have cost five shillings instead of five pence a yard. No servant-maid is engaged at Raven Hall, no family allowed to live in the sqire's cottages, that does not conform in costume as well as in politics, to the immutable Ravensburne principles.

If Squire Raven's ukase had been as powerful in parliament as in his own parish; if he could have settled the costumes of the lower classes and excluded all the produce of foreigners, the long line of manufacturing towns and villages, which, beginning a few miles from that green oasis of squiredom, Ravensburne, stretches into Yorkshire and across the border – clothing the naked and feeding the hungry, placing clean linen within the reach of every labouring family – would have remained stagnant under the dominion of the spinning-wheel, in the midst of the moorland deserts, over which manufacturing power has spread turnips and corn, sheep and shorthorns.

Single examples best show what machinery and enterprise have done towards clothing the world. An accident has given us the opportunity of describing what machinery and enterprise can do to clothe womankind and babykind. The accident was a hunt-breakfast, given by Mr. Julius Lincoln (the celebrated paper-stainer), to Lord Drainland's Hunt, – a breakfast which, for admirable profusion and confusion of everything; from plain chops to Yorkshire pies; from cherry cordial to

DOI: 10.4324/9781315400105-31

champagne – will long be a green spot in the memory of the two hundred guests. We had the good fortune to make the acquaintance of a stout, fresh-complexioned, broad-shouldered, broad-brim-hatted, scarlet-coated stranger. Later in the day, a cramped stile, unjumpable for fifteen stone, gave us the opportunity of turning aside, and jogging on leisurely together; and so, during the rest of the day, we talked of horses and farming aloud, silently reckoning each other up. For my part, I thought my new friend could not be a parson – parsons don't ride in pink in Lancashire; nor a farmer, although very like a thousand-acre Lincoln Wolds man. Speculation came to an end when we parted, and the stout stranger presented me with his card – Mr. George Ahrab – and invited me to come and lunch with him any day (except two hunting days), "at number ten thousand, Cheapside, where his firm, Ashstock and Ahrab, did a little business with all parts of the world."

Wanting, lately, to show a foreign friend the showy side of England, which does not lie in palaces or public places, I remembered my adventure, and fished out the fox-hunter's card. And this was how I found my way, one fine morning, to a great warehouse – a barrack and storehouse of commercial warfare on human nakedness – which modestly obtrudes a narrow architectural front on Cheapside, and stretches many a rood into the length and breadth of the back regions of that mysterious thoroughfare.

We found Mr. Ahrab, in his brown coat and commercial den, deep in his correspondence, – a very different style of man from Ahrab mounted, top-booted, scarlet-coated, with no anxiety except about killing the fox; after a few cordial words of welcome, an intimation that his dinner and my luncheon would be ready at one o'clock "sharp," he put us under the care of a Mentor able to guide us on our voyage of discovery.

We began our investigations at a counter of pocket-handkerchiefs. A pocket-handkerchief is one of the most solid signs of civilisation – a standard waving in advance of civilised wants. Here were to be found handkerchiefs fitted for all classes; from duchesses to dairymaids; from royalty to the Lilliputian tenants of infants' schools, arranged in dozens, – an exceptional number being worth ten pounds each without lace. Thirty pounds the dozen seemed the apex of ordinary transactions; thence descending, the importance of the sales generally increasing with the descent, were the cheapest description of French at eight shillings and sixpence, Irish cambric at one shilling and ninepence, and Scotch cambric at ninepence-halfpenny the dozen. The price per dozen, in all the cheaper qualities being considerably less than the price charged for a single handkerchief before steam superseded hand-spinning.

French embroidered handkerchiefs, even of a very cheap kind, undergo a strange round of voyages and travels before they appear at evening parties. The cambric is imported into London in the piece, thence forwarded to the branch manufactory in Glasgow; there divided into proper lengths for handkerchiefs; and, with a due quantity of cotton-thread, are distributed among the peasant girls of Scotland and Ireland, to be embroidered. By this new trade of embroidering handkerchiefs, petticoat borders, muslin dresses, and under-garments, many a comely lass is able to exchange the digging-fork for the needle. When embroidered, the cambric, no longer white as driven snow, is collected and returned to Glasgow to be washed and bleached. Then, marshalled in dozens, it journeys back to Cheapside to be thence distributed

Far as the breeze can bear the billow's foam.

By meeting all tastes, and descending to pocket-handkerchiefs at a little more than three farthings a-piece, Ashstock, Ahrab and Co. manage to sell, in the course of the year, something like three million of them; that is to say rather more than three hundred and fifty acres of lawn and cambric; yet, before the spinning-jenny beat the spinning-wheel, a cambric pocket-handkerchief in the hand of a village maiden was as great a rarity as a pair of silk stockings in the days of Queen Bess.

The boxes by which ladies, on shopping thoughts intent, are craftily seduced into buying a dozen at a time, all ready marked with the name Annie or Bessie, and so on through the alphabet, are no longer of the plainest description. The march of luxury has transformed them into works of art; moulded them in elegant forms, and adorned them with coloured pictures of the interesting events of the day – royal marriages and interviews, portraits of princesses and heroes, views of shipwrecks and battles. The Great Exhibition afforded a good many subjects: the Turkish alliance, the Sultan, and Omar Pasha have had their day; as also Alma and Inkermann. At the date of our inquisitorial progress, the Emperor and Empress of the French, with scenes from the Queen's visit to Paris, were in high favour. The taking of Sebastopol will probably follow. These boxes, once given with the handkerchiefs, have now a distinct wholesale value of from sixpence to ten shillings and sixpence each.

The next step was into a snowy armoury; where a wonderful variety of embroidered muslins, dresses (from the Glasgow branch manufactory) for wedding, christening, ball, or any other occasion where white is imperative, were arranged in such numbers as to be truly distracting. Full-flounced robes, gorgeous in their blanch extravagance of tambouring and embroidery, were to be had at ten and fifteen pounds each; but, the great trade is in our favourite plain tucked robes, of which thousands were annually distributed among our rising beauties at from seven to ten shillings each. Imagine the astonishment of our grandmothers at hearing of a ball-dress at half-a-guinea! "We calculated that Ashstock and Ahrab sell annually about fifty acres of muslin dresses, without counting roods of cambric collars from fourpence halfpenny upwards, and miles of habit-shirts, chemisettes, jabots, cuffs, sleeves, mantles, and jackets.

Curtains for cottages were once an unknown luxury, unless in common calico, but we found, in the muslin department, that the march of machinery had produced embroidered muslin curtains at two shillings and sixpence per pair; while plate-glass four-windowed drawing-rooms could be accommodated at eighteen pounds.

Mourning – both light and deep affliction departments – came next; and there, amid crape in all shapes of dress and all degrees of fineness, with bugles worthy of Hamlet, we found that the largest trade was in servants' black caps at three farthings a-piece, and plain linen collars at the same price.

Marching steadily on, we successively passed the department of cap fronts, of cauls – not the natural article occasionally advertised in the Times at fifteen pounds, and specially recommended to sea-captains – but white net, supplied at fifteen pence the dozen, and nightcaps too, from the very plainest to the most insinuating that ever adorned a rosy morning face. In caps, not nightcaps, the Swedish Nightingale's seems the favourite name, judging by the trade thermometer; for the sale last year in white and black Jenny Linds was over a hundred thousand dozen. We roughly estimated the weight of caps of all kinds sold annually at this single shop at two hundred tons,

Next, ribands in all the colours of the rainbow – of silk, satin and velvet – the best work of Coventry and Lyons, made the counters gay as flower-beds. What a delightful addition to a collar is a becoming neck-riband of bright harmonious colours, Parisian women of all grades well know. The attendant in this department told us, with a professional sigh of regret, that his stock was very dead, as broad ribands were all the rage. Passing from gay ribands, a regiment of grave cloaks were reviewed. Cloaks of all materials; cotton velvet, silk velvet, satin and moiré antique, cloth, in admirable sober colours (when shall we have a revival, for the streets, of the charming red riding-hood cloaks of our youth?) alpacas, and mixed mysterious textures with names to match. All tastes and pockets were to be suited; expense-no-object could be satisfied, while the real use of a winter's cloak, warmth, was amply fulfilled in capital woollen imitation of bear-skins neatly trimmed, at five shillings each.

Baby linen came next; organised on a scale sufficiently large to provide for all the nurseries in the kingdom at a moment's notice. There were doll-like shirts at sixpence, and also at sixteen shillings; long robes at four shillings and at ten pounds each (more Scotch and Irish peasant embroidery); Lilliputian silk-embroidered merino shoes, which a young lady with a very new white bonnet pronounced perfect ducks; pincushions – those monuments of increasing nurseries – at from ninepence to a guinea; and all the other paraphernalia that are called into use by the wonder of every family, the baby! Bassinettes, at fabulous prices, and caps of satin with or without cockade, pictured babyhood in every corner of the department.

The ladies' general outfitting section came very naturally close to the baby's. The name describes it. As for the contents, it was quite plain that, if a telegraphic despatch announced the arrival at Southampton of an army of amazons a thousand strong in want of all the armoury of modern costume, there would be no hesitation in returning an answer of "All right; the clothes will be sent down by the next train." Everything was to be found there, from top to toe, except shoes. An entire room was given up to those instruments of torture, stays. A single brown wooden-busked rib-compresser was to be had at tenpence; increasing prices ended at best French, one hundred and fifty shillings a-dozen.

Millinery made its department very gorgeous in ornamental articles, the greater part of which puzzled our ignorance, and warned us not to enter into details; but one instance of the development of commerce in an insignificant branch of trade was too curious to be passed over. At a certain, or rather an uncertain, time of life, ladies take to head-dresses. Some adopt false hair, some caps, and many used to wear particoloured skull-caps of Berlin wool. These have recently been in a great measure superseded by certain dark-brown silky materials, manufactured into network coronets, marvellously resembling braided hair, and caps with pendent corkscrew curls, made of mohair, that is, the hair of a goat, chiefly imported from Syria. At first there were difficulties in the way of spinning and weaving mohair; but the attention paid, with such remarkable success, to alpaca led to the study of all kinds of goats' hair; and now, more than five hundred manufacturers, some of them little above the rank of journeymen, are engaged in supplying mohair head-dresses.

Artificial flowers, English and French, occupy two rooms, and make them gay as the parterres of Paxton. English flowers have not, as was expected, been extinguished by French taste and cheapness, but continue to afford employment to a numerous class. But, as a general rule, there is no comparison between the two in beauty. The French flower-maker is an artist; the English, a mechanic, copying from a conventional standard; although some of the English examples showed that there must be brilliant exceptions.

From French flowers at fabulous prices in the two extremes of cheapness ant costliness, we returned to the principal department in this great warehouse, lace – the department which in fact has originated all the rest, and led the firm in the course of years to consult the convenience of their customers, by concentrating all their wants and enabling them to stock a shop in one morning walk, under one roof. Thus curtains, dresses, collars, ribbons for collars bracelets, brooches, flowers, feathers, cloaks baby-linen, bonnets, millinery, and all the rest of ladies' apparel were added; and, a Glasgow muslin manufactory became the colony of the parent establishment in Nottingham.

Lace, is not a describable article, a few figures will be more expressive than any vain attempt to plunge into a labyrinth of filaments, Roods of counters and shelves were devoted to every description of every country and every kind. France and Belgium supplied handmade pillow-lace, as did our own counties of Bucks, Herts, and Northampton, and Devon; but the great trade is in machine lace and net from Nottingham, Honiton, and Tiverton; in which, besides many new uses, the finest descriptions are so well imitated that, at a yard distance, no person not in the trade, can tell the difference between costly fine hand-work and cheap machine imitation. The most fashionable collar at the present moment is Irish hand crochet, in imitation of ancient point lace, – the difference in price between the simulated and the real article being about shillings to guineas. Lace curtains and lace flounced robes in black and white have been rendered a possible luxury within the reach of the middle classes. Five-and-twenty years ago an article (in net) now sold for fourpence cost forty shillings a-yard. Changes of the same character, succeeding from year to year, have enabled the million to use goods which were once the privilege of the inactive few, have created the lace-trade of England, and given employment to the thousands who, directly or indirectly, draw their wages from the house of Ashstock and Ahrab.

The importance of the machine lace trade may be measured in millions of yards. Five kinds of it were sold in one year to the extent of more than six thousand miles, or more than the distance from Liverpool to New York and back. This trade rests, like the bulk of British trade, on cheap machine manufacture, and is daily improved and extended to new uses. Where our grandmothers were content with a pair of hereditary lace lappets of unknown age, and, in their eyes, incalculable value, our daughters and wives aspire to whole dresses and curtains, and our servants can afford a succession of clean light caps and bonnet fronts. In fact, by modern improvements, we are less afraid of wearing out than of washing; cheap clothes mean cleanliness.

There is – purse-proud beauties would be surprised to hear – no demand in England for the finest and most expensive descriptions of modern foreign hand-made lace; English ladies will rarely give one, two, three hundred pounds – as French, Spanish, Russian, and American ladies will – for a dress, a shawl, or even a veil. The most expensive laces they purchase are antiquities, or mock antiquities, dyed in coffee-grounds to the colour which enables them to pass for the point of Queen Anne. At the French Exhibition, there is a black silk-lace shawl, manufactured for the empress of the French, from an original design, by the well-known house of Lefebuvre, price six hundred pounds; and the manufacturers have more than once received orders of nearly equal cost.

At lace ended our tour through the long avenues and towering storeys of the great house, the first of some half-dozen engaged in the same operations, presenting in the vastness, completeness, and machine-like order of its operations, a sample of British commercial enterprise. Although a half-way house of distribution between the manufacturers and the retailer, nearly four hundred persons, male and female, are employed under one roof to serve, note down, correspond, pack up, and deliver the supplies required from every point of the compass – five pounds' worth to the little milliner at Penzance, a thousand pounds' worth to Madame Lafleur at Havannah, and Madame Sriggs, from Paris, at Melbourne – which amount in a year to more than a million sterling. We were glad to find that Ashstock and Ahrab – more wise than certain railway companies lately noticed in Household Words – do not disperse their staff among the chop-houses of Cheapside, but provide at a great economy of time, money, and digestion, a series of meals of roast and boiled joints, cooked by gas, which, as our luncheon told us, left nothing to be desired.

Among the elements of the progress of this many-armed establishment, penny postage had no mean share in selling, freighting, and setting in motion the railway van, the ocean steamer, and the clipper ship. The average number of letters received and answered weekly, amount to some four thousand. The electric telegraph, too, gives its help, and often saves twenty-four hours of time in the execution of an order.

What we may call outposts of attack on women's wants have been established by Ashstock and Ahrab in branches in the great cities of Manchester, Liverpool, Edinburgh, Birmingham, Plymouth, and Dublin; besides a muslin manufactory at

Glasgow and a lace factory at Nottingham. In New York and Calcutta, independent colonies – consuming nothing but the produce of the Cheapside empire – have been established; and, in the great Australian cities, like plantations have been founded. As for home consumption, Great Britain is mapped out into districts, which are periodically traversed by commercial ambassadors, travelling by road and rail. In the hilly territories of the north you may sometimes meet a neat, capacious, dark-green fourgon, driven four-in-hand. It does not contain the bed or batterie de cuisine of a foreign prince, nor any of the hounds or racehorses of a sporting peer: it is a moving warehouse of our friends Ashstock and Ahrab: one of the means by which they push their sales and afford to pay wages, directly or indirectly, to some ten thousand people, including peasant girls, in English, Scotch, and Irish counties, in France and in Belgium.

And this firm, with its princely revenues, army of assistants, thousands of dependents – its several branch establishments, and still more numerous agents, all working with a clockwork regularity incomprehensible to the muddling proceedings of Ordnance and Horseguards, Admiralty, Woods, Forests, and Public Works – is but one sample of hundreds of firms which organise the labour of the staple trades of England. Neither are the principals mere money-grabbing drudges. They can afford time, as we have seen, for healthful recreation. Neither do any of their dependents appear to be overworked.

27

MRS HENRY WOOD, *MRS HALLIBURTON'S TROUBLES*

(London & New York: The Walter Scott Publishing Co., n.d.) pp. 99–100, 107–108, 122, 134–135

Honey fair

HELSTONLEIGH abounded with glove manufactories. It is a trade that may be said to be a blessing to the localities where it is carried on, since it is one of the very few employments that furnish to the poor female population easy, clean, and profitable work *at their own homes*. The evils arising to women who go out to work in factories have been rehearsed over and over again; and the chief evil – we will put others out of sight – is, that it takes the married woman from her home and her family. Her young children drag themselves up in her absence, for worse or for better; alone they must do it, for she has to be away, toiling for daily bread. There is no home privacy, no home comfort, no home happiness; the factory is their life, and other interests give way to it. But with glove-making, the case is different. While the husbands are abroad at the manufactories, pursuing their day's work, the wives and elder daughters are earning money easily and pleasantly at home. The work is clean and profitable; all that is necessary for its accomplishment being common skill as a seamstress.

Not five minutes' walk from Mrs. Halliburton's house, nearer to Helstonleigh, a turning out of the main road led you to quite a colony of workwomen – gloveresses, as they are termed in the local phraseology. It was a long and wide lane; the houses, some larger, some smaller, built on either side of it. A road quite wide enough for health, if the inhabitants had but kept it as it ought to have been kept: which they did not. The highway was made a common receptacle for refuse. It was so much easier to open the kitchen door (most of the houses were entered at once by the kitchen), and to "chuck" things out, *pêle mêle*, rather than be at the trouble of conveying them to the proper receptacle, the dust-heap at the back. Ashes, cabbage-leaves, bones, egg-shells, potato-peelings, heads and tails of herrings, choked up the gutters in front; a dead dog or cat being often added by way of variety. Occasionally a solitary policeman would come, picking his way through the dirt, and order it to be removed; or, as the women phrased it, "blow

 DOI: 10.4324/9781315400105-32

off at them"; upon which, some slight improvement would be visible for a day or two. The euphonious name of this place was Honey Fair; though, in truth, it was redolent of nothing so pleasant as honey.

Of the occupants of these houses, the husbands and elder sons were all glove operatives; several of them in the manufactory of Mr. Ashley. The wives sewed the gloves at home. Many a similar colony to Honey Fair was there in Helstonleigh, but in hearing of one set you hear of all. The trade was extensively pursued. Some very few of the manufactories were, like Mr. Ashley's, of large extent: others there were which, in there little orbit, comprised not half a score workmen, all told; but whose masters alike dignified themselves by the title of "manufacturer."

There flourished a shop in the general line in Honey Fair, kept by a Mrs. Buffle, a great gossip. Her husband, a well-meaning, steady little man, mincing in his speech and gait, scrupulously neat and clean in his attire, and thenceforth called "the dandy," was the chief workman at one of the smallest of the establishments. He had three men and two boys under him; and so he styled himself the "foreman." Nobody knew half so much of the affairs of their neighbours as did Mrs. Buffle; nobody could tell of the ill-doings and shortcomings of Honey Fair as she could. Many a gloveress girl, running in at dusk for a halfpenny candle, did not receive it until she had first submitted to a lecture from Mrs. Buffle. Not that her custom was all of this ignoble description: some of the gentlemen's houses in the vicinity would deal with her in a chance way when out of articles at home. Her wares were good; her home-cured bacon was particularly good. Among other olfactory treats, indigenous to Honey Fair, was that of pigs and pig-sties, kept by Mrs. Buffle.

Occasionally Mrs. Halliburton would go to this shop: it was nearer to her house than any other; and, in her small way, had been extensively patronised by her. Of all her customers, Mrs. Halliburton was the one who most puzzled Mrs. Buffle. In the first place, she never gossiped; in the second, though evidently a lady, she would carry her purchases home herself. The very servants from the large houses, coming flaunting in with their smart caps, would loftily order their pound of bacon or shilling's worth of eggs sent home for them. Mrs. Halliburton took hers away in her own hand; and this puzzled Mrs. Buffle. "But her pays ready money," observed that lady, when relating this to another customer, "so 'taint my place to grumble."

During the summer weather, whenever Jane had occasion to walk through Honey Fair, on her way to this shop, she would linger to admire the women, at their open doors and windows, busy over their nice clean work. Rocking the cradle with one foot, or jogging the baby on their knees, to a tune of their own singing, their hands would be ever active at their employment. Some made the gloves; that is, seamed the fingers together and put in the thumbs, and these were called "makers." Some welted, or hemmed the gloves round the edge at the wrist; these were called "welters." Some worked the three ornamental lines at the back; and these were called "pointers." Some of the work was done in what was called a patent machine, whereby the stitches were rendered perfectly equal. And some of the stouter gloves were stitched together, instead of being sewn: stitching so beautifully regular and neat, that a stranger would look at it in admiration. In short there were, and are, different branches in the making and sewing of gloves, like there are in most trades.

The glove operatives

At the hours of going to and leaving work, Helstonleigh's streets were alive with glove operatives, some being in one branch of the trade, some in another. There were parers, grounders, leather-sorters, dyers, cutters, makers-up, and else: all being necessary, besides the sewing, to turn out one pair of gloves; though, I dare say, you did not think it. The wages varied, according to the particular work, or the men's ability and industry, from fifteen shillings per week to twenty-five: but all could earn a good living. If a man gained more than twenty-five, he had a stated salary; as was the case with the foremen. These wages, joined to what was earned by the women, were sufficient to maintain a comfortable home, and to bring up children decently. Unfortunately the same drawbacks prevailed in Helstonleigh which are too common elsewhere: and they may be classed under one general head – improvidence. The men were given to idle away at the public-houses more time than was good for them: the women to scold and to quarrel. Some were slatterns; a great many gave their husbands the welcome of a home of discomfort, ill-management, and dirt: which, of course, had the effect of sending them out all the more surely.

Just about this period, the men had their especial grievance – or thought they had: and that was, a low rate of wages and not full employment. Had they paid a visit to other places and compared their wages with some, earned by operatives of a different class, they had found less cause to complain. The men were rather given to compare present wages with those which they had earned before the dark crisis (dark so far as Helstonleigh's trade was concerned) when the British ports were opened to foreign gloves. But few, comparatively speaking, of the manufacturers had weathered that storm. Years had elapsed since; but the employment continued scanty, and the wages (I have quoted them to you) low. Altogether, the men were, many of them, dissatisfied. They even went so far as to talk of a "strike": strikes being less common in those days than they are in these.

It was Saturday night, and the streets were crowded. The hands were pouring out of the different manufactories; clean-looking, respectable workmen, as a whole: for the branches of glove-making are mostly of a cleanly nature. Some wore their white aprons; some had rolled them up round their waists. A few – very few, it must be owned – were going to their homes, but the greater portion were bound for the public-house.

The Messrs. Bankes

On the Monday morning, a group of the gloveress girls flocked into Charlotte East's. They were taking holiday, as was usual with them on Mondays. Charlotte was a favourite. It is true, she "bothered" them, as they called it, with good advice, but they liked her, in spite of it. Charlotte's kitchen was always tidy and peaceful, with a bright fire burning in it: other kitchens would be full of turmoil and dirt. Charlotte never let them hinder her; she worked away at her gloves all the time. Charlotte was a glove-maker; that is, she sewed the fingers together, and put in the thumbs, forgits, and quirks. Look at your own gloves, English make. The long strips, running up inside the fingers, are the forgits; and the little pieces between, where the fingers open, are the quirks. The gloves Charlotte was occupied on now, were of a very dark green colour, almost black, called corbeau in the trade, and they were sewn with white silk. Charlotte's stitches were as beautifully regular as though she had used a patent machine. The white silk and the fellow glove to the one she was making, lay inside a clean white handkerchief doubled upon her lap; other gloves, equally well covered, were in a basket at her side.

William was not so fortunate. He was at that period very short of his age, timid in manner, and no office could be persuaded to take him. Nothing in the least congenial presented itself, or could be found; and the result was, that he resigned himself to Samuel Lynn, who introduced him to Mr. Ashley's extensive manufactory – to be initiated by degrees into all the mysteries necessary to convert a skin into a glove. And, although his interest and curiosity were excited by what he saw, he pronounced it a "hateful" business.

When the skins came in from the leather-dressers, they were washed in a tub of cold water. The next day warm water, mixed with yolks of eggs, was poured on them, and a couple of men, barelegged to the knee, got into the tub, and danced on them, skins, and eggs, and water, for two hours. Then they were spread in a field to dry, till they were hard as lantern horn; then they were "staked," as it was called, a long process, to smooth and soften them. To the stainers next, to be stained black or coloured; next to the parers, to have the loose flesh pared from the inside, and to be smoothed again with pumice-stone – all of this being done on the outside premises. Then they came inside, to the hands of one of the foremen, who sorted and marked them for the cutters. The cutters cut the skins into tranks (the shape of the hand in outline) with the separate thumbs and forgits, and sent them into the slitters. The slitters slit the four fingers, and *shaped* the thumbs and forgits: after that, they were ready for the women: three different women, you may remember, being necessary to turn out each glove, so far as the sewing went; for one woman rarely worked at more than her own peculiar branch, or was capable of working at it. This done, and back in the manufactory again, they had to be pulled straight, and "padded," or rubbed, a process by which they were brightened. If black gloves, the seams were washed over with a black dye, or else glazed; then they were hung up to dry. This done, they went into Samuel Lynn's room, a large room next to Mr. Ashley's private room, and here they were sorted into firsts, seconds, or thirds; the sorting being always done by Samuel Lynn, or by James Meeking, the head foreman. It was called "making-up." Next they were banded round with a paper, in dozens, labelled, and placed in small boxes, ready for the warehouses in London. A great deal, you see, before one pair of gloves can be turned out.

28

ANON, 'GLOVES'

All the Year Round, Vol. 9 (27 June 1863), pp. 425, 428–430

THE old proverb goes, that for a glove to be well made, three nations must have a hand in it: Spain must dress the leather, France cut the shape, and England sew the seams. At the present time, France has the monopoly, at least in reputation; for not even the best Spanish kid would be preferred to the rat-skins of Paris, nor can the stoutest English sewing compete for favour – we will not speak of excellence – with those slender, easily loosened stitches of French needles, so sure to give way at the ball of the thumb, and in the three cornered joinings of the fingers. Though, indeed, the French glove sewers use a machine invented by an Englishman, which should secure the wearer against all such mishaps as flying ends and ripped seams; only it does not. But for all their shortcomings, French gloves are unapproachable, even in these days of general commerce and awakened wits, when everybody imitates everybody, and there is no special art left to any one; and neither Cordova nor Dent can give us such well-cut, well-fitting, well-looking, and desirable "hand shoes," as those delicately tinted marvels to be found on the Boulevards of the Circe of modern cities.

The perfection of a modern glove is its smoothness and elasticity, its unexceptionable fit, the delicacy and uniformity of its tint, and a sewing that shall be at once fine and strong: while anything like embroidery or adventitious ornament, or mixture of colours, or incongruous materials, does not count as the best taste in these modern days of luxury and utility combined. But in olden times gloves were often exceedingly costly.

In Burke's Vicissitudes there is a very curious story of a glover-nobleman, William Maclellan, sixth Lord Kirkcudbright, who was utterly ruined, retaining nothing of his earldom save the right to the name, and so became a glover for his daily bread. He used to stand in the lobby of the Edinburgh Assembly Rooms, in the old town, selling gloves, which were then wanted in greater profusion than now, it being the etiquette to wear a new pair for each dance. But the glove-seller was a lord nevertheless, and an earl in his own right and by his father's; and, more than this, he was the ancestor of that General across the Atlantic who was to have crushed the Southern Confederacy in ninety days – but didn't do it, somehow. The son of the glover-earl became a colonel, and eventually won the recognition of his condition from Parliament, May the 3rd, 1773. And there is the epigram – or what

DOI: 10.4324/9781315400105-33

would it be called in scientific poetry books? – passing between the lady and her aged lover, one Mr. Page, when he sent her a glove with this distich pinned to it:

> If from glove you take the letter G, Then Glove is Love, which I do send to thee.
> And she answered him saucily with,
> And if from Page you take the letter P, Then Page is Age, and that won't do for me;

to the eternal confusion of the ancient Philander, indignant at ridicule. Then, there are Woodstock and its dusty, powdery, sheepskin gloves, its traditions of Fair Rosamond, and its present practical skill in leather-work; and the chicken gloves of Limerick, not now to be had, packed up in a walnut-shell, fastened with fairy ribbon, and sold for five shillings the pair; and the pocket gloves of a few years back, which had a pocket in the palm, which opened when the hand was closed, and shut when the hand was opened; convenient enough for timid ladies who carry their omnibus sixpence in the palm of the hand slipped up inside the glove, but of no great reputation among the public in general, and dying out in a stifled asphyxiated kind of way. And there are the "slipskins" of Switzerland – the skins of young kids prematurely brought into the world by some unholy practices of the goatherds, and which, marvellously smooth and fine, go to make very fine ladies' very fine gloves. And there are all the old petitions and remonstrances addressed to parliament against laying on duties here, and taking off duties there, with the inevitable cry of "gloves are so many and glovers so poor," as the reason for unsound political economy. and faulty legislation. And there are the Board of Trade statistics, showing what numbers of the made article we import, and where we get our best glove-leather from; with many other curious and interesting particulars, too long to be fully detailed. But the history of gloves and glove-making, is, like all things whatever in human life and society – a very interesting matter when looked into and thoroughly traced from source to outfall; a thoroughness to which this mere surface sketch has no pretension.

29

ANON, 'A CRINOLINE MANUFACTORY'

Once A Week, 23 January 1864, pp. 124–126

"These," said Ham, "are the Montmorency Crinoline Works and Patent Crinoline Steel and Skirt Manufactories."

Neither the irregular courtyard, dark except for the lights which gleamed through a number of narrow casements, nor the very courteous gentleman who received us on entering it, struck me with that amount of awe which these high-sounding titles seemed to bespeak. The place was rather dilapidated, and decidedly dirty. The whirr of machinery, too, was, to say the least of it, unmusical. Possibly, had I been left to myself, I should not have persevered in my design of acquiring knowledge. However, I was in for it. There was Ham eager to act as showman, and the courteous gentleman all willingness to allow him. We had better begin at the beginning, he said – that is, with the tempering and "cutting" department, then proceed to the "covering" department, and finish our view with Ham's neat-handed damsels and the "fitting-up" department.

We did not give much time to the "cutting" process. The sheets of steel, untempered as yet, are brought into the works in rolls fifty or sixty feet long, and three inches broad, and are cut into strips of from a quarter of an inch to an inch wide by an apparatus not unlike that of a travelling knife-grinder. The narrower widths, not more than one-sixteenth of an inch broad, do not arrive in sheets, and consequently do not require to be cut. They go at once to the tempering-room. This, from Ham's anxiety to move on, I suspected was to afford one of the sensation effects of the place. And certainly, at first sight, it did look rather like the home of the demon of discord beneath the bowels of the earth, where he forges his bolts previous to the comic business of the pantomime. From out a nondescript mass of iron, filling up the middle of the room (I had all but said stage), glowed a murky light, which, leaving all but a confined space in darkness, reddened the grimy faces and sinewy arms of the workmen and their attendant imps as they moved to and fro within its reach. On examination, this mass proved to consist of two furnaces, separated by a kind of tank. As steel is tempered by being subjected to alternations of heat and cold, the glistening strip, when it arrives from the "cutting" shop, is first drawn slowly through one furnace; it then passes under and is pressed by vessels filled with cold water; and lastly, after being exposed to the air for a yard or two of its course, its hardness becomes elasticity during a journey

 DOI: 10.4324/9781315400105-34

through the second furnace. If the operation be successful, the elasticity will be almost perfect. For exposure to cold, immersion in oil is sometimes substituted. The steel now tempered is next wound on "bobbins," which are neither more nor less than gigantic reels of the sewing-cotton kind. It is then taken to the "covering" room, whither we accompanied it.

This room was evidently Ham's second great sensation scene. The whirr, which I have ventured to call unmusical, proceeded from it, and, when the door opened to admit us, became positively deafening. Long parallel rows of stands occupied the whole length, on each of which stands were what looked like four sets of small nine-pins, engaged in dancing circular Scotch reels after the maddest fashion.

"Ay, but there is a method in their madness," said the courteous gentleman, in answer to my expression of surprise.

Ham, possibly from a desire to reserve himself for pointing out the beauties of the neat-handed maidens, didn't seem quite equal to an explanation.

"These are the covering machines. There, that is the 'bobbin,' which you saw in the other room. Look; it is hung horizontally below what you call a set of nine-pins, and we a 'head.' The steel to be covered is passed up through the middle of the pins, and attached from above to the top of each one of them by the cotton which is to form the 'covering;' much as the centre pole of a bell tent is fastened by ropes to the circle of pegs inserted in the ground, to secure its steadiness. The nine-pins, when set in motion, act each one upon its neighbour by means of notches in the edges of the small circular discs on which they are fixed; and, as they thus whirl each other round and round, and in and out, they plait the cotton round the crinoline steel, which is all the time slowly rising and exposing a fresh surface to their efforts. The machines are, as you see, 'minded' by women and girls, whose duties are but little more than the correction of occasional accidents. Each machine will cover as many as six hundred yards of steel in the factory day of ten hours and a half. Before crinoline came into fashion, these same machines were used for making braid, whence they are still sometimes called braid machines. There are yet other methods of covering. Sometimes the cotton is not plaited, but only twisted round the steel by what we call the Derby Frame. There, that is one. The process is much simpler in this case. I will give you an idea of it. Pass a wire through the hole, which perforates longitudinally a reel of sewing cotton; fasten the cotton on the reel to the part of the wire which projects above it; keep twirling the reel round and slowly raising the steel, and you will see this process of twisting performed on a small scale. Of course, in the frame the 'spindles,' which represent the reel, are turned, and the steel raised by steam power. A frame containing twenty spindles will cover over eight thousand yards of steel in a day. The twisted covering is cheaper than the plaited, because it takes less cotton; it is inferior, because it is more easily unravelled. Again, the high price of cotton has led to the substitution of a paper covering instead of cotton. The paper is pasted over the steel by a machine for the purpose; but the exact way in which this is done is known, I believe, only to the firm which uses it."

We had now visited two of the three departments of the manufacture. There remained the insertion of the steel in the skirts in the "fitting-up" rooms, where likewise the skirts themselves are made. About this time Ham seemed to brighten up wonderfully, and to exhibit his interest in the proceedings by various surreptitious acts of personal embellishment, such as passing his fingers through his hair, flicking bits of fluff off his coat, &c. The cause of this was soon evident. An ascent up some steepish stairs introduced us to quite other scenes. Here nor red light glared, nor nine-pins whirred. These were pleasant places, illumined by a cheerful gaslight, and made musical by the buzz of female voices. In the place of grimy artisans and slovenly factory hands appeared groups of smart young women, either squatted in circles on the floor, as if they were playing at "Hunt the slipper," or side by side on tables, one and all apparently intent on embryo crinolines, in various stages of forwardness. I say apparently, because I am not quite ready to take affidavit that an occasional eye may not have wandered afield, while Ham, going through a selection of his most imposing attitudes, explained to me the not very abstruse processes by which sewing machines joined the pieces and the ordinary needle and thread secured the ribs in their destined apertures in those pieces. Whether the eyes of the young ladies wandered or not, I know that Ham's eyes did. He even went so far as to try to prolong our stay by the pretence of imparting a few facts, such as, that the number of hoops in an ordinary skirt varies from six to sixteen, though some contain as many as fifty; that there are stuff skirts and skeleton skirts, the latter consisting merely of ribs, without any stuff at all; that the goodness of a crinoline depends partly on the quantity of steel in it, partly on the perfection of the temper; and lastly, *mirabile dictu!* that the length of the steel contained in a skirt may amount to no less than one hundred and fifty yards, a distance which has ere now severely taxed the powers of long-winded pedestrians. This was a climax. Ham could not get beyond this. True, he hum'd and ha'd for a minute or two, as if casting about for some even more astounding assertion, but it was of no use. We had seen all, and, what was more important to him, his stock of facts was used up; so, darting one Parthian glance around, he jauntily led the way to the door, which was to close upon our last and brightest experience of the Montmorency Crinoline Works and Patent Crinoline Steel and Skirt Manufactories.

30

EDITH SIMCOX, 'EIGHT YEARS OF CO-OPERATIVE SHIRTMAKING'

The Nineteenth Century, Vol. 15 (June 1884), pp. 1037–1054

SOMEWHERE about December, 1874, the attention of the present writer was attracted by a short paragraph in the *Echo*, giving an account of a public meeting attended by working women, who made speeches and passed resolutions advocating the formation of a trade union for the women employed in bookbinding. This was remarkable, not to say epoch-making. The 'intelligent workingman' is an old friend – was it possible that some one had discovered the 'intelligent working-woman'? This and nothing less proved to be the purport of the newspaper report. Under the inspiration of Mrs. Paterson,[1] not only the bookbinders, but upholsteresses, shirtmakers, dressmakers, sewing machinists, tailoresses, and others, were successively invited and encouraged to form themselves into societies having the same objects as the trade unions of workmen, which had only been fully legalised three years before. And for the first time, at the Trades Congress held at Glasgow in 1875, *bonâ fide* trade unions of women were represented in the industrial parliament by women delegates, who still remember with pleasure the fraternal welcome accorded them.

Then and subsequently interesting and instructive conferences were held in different places with ladies of the above-named trades, as well as with hatmakers, umbrella-makers, nailmakers, staymakers, laundresses, and others. But space forbids us to dwell on these, which have no direct bearing upon the experiment in co-operative shirtmaking which grew out of the third women's union, established in that trade, at a public meeting held on the 1st of July, 1875, by the kindness of a clerical friend, in St. Martin's Schoolroom near Covent Garden. As it happened, public opinion had just been scandalised by two police cases, from which it had appeared that shirts were made at such prices as ¾*d.* and 1½*d.* a piece; and it was almost a matter of course that no meeting of shirtmakers would pass without allusions to, or quotations from, the *Song of the Shirt*. But these allusions, it was soon seen, were not regarded with unmixed favour. The plainly dressed, mostly middle-aged, somewhat hard-featured, ready-witted, and on the whole eminently 'respectable' looking women present, were clearly not of a class to feel flattered by allusions to 'poverty, hunger, and dirt,' as the normal conditions of their existence.

DOI: 10.4324/9781315400105-35

It is a well-known fact that the audience at a public meeting has nearly as much hand in the speeches made as the orators themselves, who can rarely resist the temptation to develope most fully the sentiments which elicit the most intelligent applause. The audience may be wrong, and in that case the orator is led astray; but when well-meaning amateurs undertake to represent the interests of the working classes, a little wholesome docility among the speakers has its advantages. The women present were not starving slop-workers, but they responded heartily to the suggestion that organisation must begin in the best paid part of the trade, in which, moreover, wages and prices were always tending to go down owing to the competition of the cheap slop-work. Somewhat to our surprise, they also gave a warm welcome to the suggestion that if shirts had to be made at a price which would not afford a subsistence both for the maker and the dealer, the makers must co-operate and do away with the dealer.

Another point upon which light was thrown by the conversational remarks of the audience was the inequality of the wages paid for substantially similar work in the West End itself. A respectable Piccadilly hosier, keeping a workroom of his own, will pay the women he employs as good wages as women of the same class can earn at any other trade. But competition is keen even among the arbiters of fashion, with whom extravagant youth delights to clothe itself on 'tick;' rents are high in the angle between Regent Street and Piccadilly where these arbiters do mostly congregate; and in the hands of a respectable tradesman who is accustomed to pay fair wages, and to spend money when necessary on his drains, a workroom *does not pay*. The cost of keeping up 'the room,' distributed over the few thousand shirts per annum made in it, represents a charge per dozen for the making alone considerably higher than the price at which a professional shirtmaker, contractor, or middle man will offer to manufacture shirts for the trade. These shirtmakers or sweaters are sometimes ex-shopmen or shirt-cutters, sometimes women of the lower middle class with a turn for managing and driving; they live mostly in Soho or similar neighbourhoods, and take in work from several shops at a time. Their expenses for rent may of course be legitimately lower than those of the hosiers; but to realise a commercial profit out of *less* than the bare cost of production in the comparatively scrupulous hands of the shopkeeper, the middle man is obviously compelled to bring all his expenses down to the lowest possible limit; to pack his workpeople in one or two rooms of a crowded house, with drainage and water-supply adapted to the requirements of one family fifty years ago; to pay them low wages for long hours when work is abundant; and to turn them on the streets the moment it is 'slack.'

All this was set forth with much vivacity and graphic detail in the picturesque language of which London shirtmakers have a great command. Our suggestion of a co-operative workshop, where the shirtmakers should be their own employers, and divide amongst themselves the whole price paid by the hosier to the contractor, was not allowed to drop. We were pressed to say how it was to be carried out: one and another said she would like to join if it *could* be carried out; and as each discussion left the ladies of the trade more hopefully interested in the project, it left the rash reformers, who were *not* (yet) of the trade more nearly pledged to realise the hopes they had helped to raise. Moreover, we had other theories as to the employment of women, which made the vision of a co-operative work-shop seductive. Idleness is the mother of misery and megrims, but not all women can go to Girton or make books, and we maintained that the true solution of the problem 'what to do with our girls' lay in an affirmative answer to good Bishop Berkeley's query, 'whether it is not to be wished that the finding of employment for themselves and others were a fashionable distinction among the ladies.' Why should not the labours of women in all feminine arts be directed by humane and intelligent persons of their own sex, instead of being abandoned to the lowest class of speculators, of which the worst-paid work seems always doomed to maintain the greatest number? Why, again, if a score of such speculators can make a living for themselves out of the labour of two or three hundred women, could not one staff of civilised managers be maintained at a less cost out of the same labour, so as to leave a margin available for raising the workers' wages? We knew that attempts had been made by Miss Barlee and others to establish workrooms for the unemployed, where government contracts could be taken, and the prices for the coarsest work given unreduced to the workers. But these were mostly charitable expedients, presupposing gratuitous management and a subscription list, and intended rather to mitigate temporary distress than to grapple with its chronic causes. Our dream was of a strictly self-supporting clothes-making factory, where women should do all the work, and divide the profits among them.

The shirtmakers had no money in hand, but they were willing to back their opinions to the extent of throwing up their present situations to join the Co-operative Society, if any of their friends would provide rooms, sewing-machines, and work for them; and in the face of this call it seemed that to refuse our own co-operation would be to earn a place with him

> Che fece per viltate il gran rifiuto.

So the eponym of the firm and its present biographer were united in the bonds of lawful partnership, and as the word 'co-operative' stinks in the nostrils of every shopkeeper, the name of 'Hamilton & Co.' was allowed to shine upon a brass plate on the door of 68 Dean Street, Soho. Commerce, indeed, is considered *infra dig.* in certain circles, but for a young lady to 'take an interest in the poor shirtmakers' was quite right and unexceptionable, and susceptible friends were easily satisfied that the brass plate was to be regarded as an emblem of social reform. Should we be equally successful in persuading hosiers and drapers to regard it as the sign of a real and competent shirtmaker?

For the encouragement of those who may wish to follow in our wake, it should be explained that our ignorance of the nature of 'business' in general and the manufacture of shirts in particular was absolute and complete. We endeavoured to improve our minds by taking in the *Warehouseman and Draper's Journal*; we studied the *Sewing Machine Gazette*; we were filled with envy of the educational advantages enjoyed by tailors, who have classes where the scientific mysteries of their craft are unveiled to students; we gazed at every shop window decorated with the garment on which our minds were set; we purchased for private contemplation and analysis a selection of, so to speak, 'representative shirts' of all grades of distinction. We welcomed the adhesion of a young lady who shared our opinions, and had had some experience in keeping her father's 'books;' and we were truly grateful when Mr. Samuel Morley introduced us to the chief of the shirt department in Wood Street, a personage of far too much importance for us to have aspired to the honour of his acquaintance without such potent intercession. Much midnight oil was burnt as the shirtmakers, after their day's work, met to confer with us as to the time and place of beginning operations, the manufacture of a specimen shirt, and the composition of our original staff; and as our first sewing-machine drove cumbrously to our meeting-place on the top of a 'four-wheeler,' the historically-minded amongst us wondered whether, in days to come, that cabload would rank in the annals of co-operation with the wheelbarrow in which the Rochdale pioneers trundled their whole stock-in-trade down Toad Lane in 1844.

Our real experience of life as a shirtmaker began with the search for rooms. Landlords and house-agents looked at us dubiously as we explained, in the most matter-of-fact tone we could command, that we required premises for 'business purposes,' and alluded, with a would-be practical air, to the importance of light and ventilation for a 'workshop.' We began our quest in what appeared superficially the most desirable streets, and, as we descended gradually in the social scale, we found that we might have been accepted had we wanted a studio, or a school, or even a milliner's shop, but as shirtmakers we must betake ourselves to humbler and more expensive quarters. As idle amateurs, we could get a good house in a quiet street for 80*l*., together with all the deferential civility due to highly 'desirable tenants.' As working shirtmakers, after refreshing our radicalism with a glimpse of 'th' oppressor's scorn, the proud man's contumely,' we were fortunate in securing half a house for 90*l*., under a landlord whose exceptional amenity explained itself afterwards when we learned that he was an admirer of George Eliot's works.

It should not be forgotten, when we are referred to private enterprise and the natural action of supply and demand to provide decent homes for the working classes, that the congestion of population and the rise of rents in certain districts are fostered and aggravated by the refusal of large landowners to let this natural action of supply and demand take its course upon their own estates. The rents of tenement houses and places of business are abnormally high, say in St. Giles's, because the ground landlord of the adjoining estate prefers to let his houses at a lower rental for residential purposes, so that the tide of population cannot find its level over the whole area, but is dammed up into the slums. The great proprietor may be able to boast that there are no rookeries on his property, but his neighbours pay for this immunity, which is secured by driving off the rooks as country parishes used to guard themselves against giving house-room to potential paupers.

After the question of workrooms came that of workers. We learned that there go to the scientific construction of shirts two sewing-machines by different makers, a shirt-cutter, a preparer of collars and wristbands, known as a 'tacker and turner,' a buttonhole-maker, a shirtmaker proper, otherwise called a 'topper,' a front-maker, a plain-worker, also a little girl to sew on buttons and 'go to shop' (*sc.* to fetch work); and unless one of the former functionaries combines the 'giving out the work' with her own department, this will employ a separate forewoman. It is by no means an easy task so to deal round the different jobs of work that the different stages shall keep pace and no time be lost while one part is waiting for another; but without this division of labour it would be impossible to make a shirt in a couple of hours, or two dozen in a day, as may have to be done on an emergency.

Of course we ought to have known beforehand exactly how few hands would suffice to do all the work in the best way, and how much work would be necessary to keep them fully employed; and we ought also to have had orders enough in hand to begin with to last for two or three weeks, instead of less than as many days. The initial losses of the co-operators were due to the fact that none of these conditions were complied with; the staff of workers at weekly wages employed at starting was much larger than the work would warrant. On the other hand, but for this overstaffing the infant firm would not have been able to turn out the best work from the first; so that the evil was not unmitigated. Apart from financial considerations the chief inconvenience arising from a dearth of 'orders' was that it left the ladies leisure for a very entertaining amount of wrangling. We had always understood that it was a common catastrophe for the cooperative associations of workmen to quarrel themselves to pieces, and certainly, but for the mediation of the partners, the shirtmakers would scarcely have escaped that early doom. To form any conception of the bitterness, the fanatical zeal, and disinterested fury of conviction with which a cutter and fitter can debate the set of a shirt-front, one must go back to the history of the early Church and its minuter and abstruser heresies. One might as well expect lucidity from an enraged theologian as from either irate lady a comprehensible statement of the points at issue. We have listened by the hour in fascination to the dramatic contest, but long months elapsed before we had quite learned what was implied by the most derogatory of imputations, that a shirt was 'tight' – which is *not* a euphemism for 'tipsy' – or before we could venture on our own responsibility to intimate that another appeared 'full to the front.' 'In and out like a dog's hind leg' struck us as a felicitous description of stitching gone astray, and a whole volume of archæological instruction opened itself before us as the cabalistic phrase 'to work for a dead horse' was explained. 'Dead horse' is work paid for before it is done, and the woman who has 'booked' and been paid on Saturday for more work than she could finish has the pleasure on Monday and maybe Tuesday of stitching away at work that will bring in no further pay. The phrase is common among shoemakers and tailors, and, according to Mr. Stevenson, is also known to seamen; according to Wakefield it is an Irish expression, and as such it becomes at once intelligible, though we have to go back to the Brehon laws for its interpretation. One of the abuses attendant on the 'giving stock' by feudal chiefs to their dependants was that the latter were expected to make good the animals that died; and in the similar state of things described by Huc as existing among the Mantchu Tartars, a tyrannical chief will give sick and dying animals to his men to herd and expect them to pay rent accordingly, even *for a dead horse*. As this discovery dawned on us, we felt that shirtmaking was really an instructive pursuit.

That there might be two opinions about its professors appeared from the remarks of our first client, a worthy hosier who had received our business card and opened negotiations by observing that 'shirt-makers were an infernal lot.' We understood that the 'lady' from whom he was withdrawing his custom was in the habit of getting drunk unseasonably, and he was kind enough before long to describe our firm as 'an excellent institution.' We had reason to doubt whether this phrase would have given more satisfaction than the other in the workroom, which was found one morning in a state of smouldering wrath, verging on rebellion. The fair partner, missing the smiles that used to greet her, looks round for an explanation. At length one bolder than the rest stood forth.

'If you please, Miss, is it true that we are a Dorcas Society?'

'A Dorcas Society! Gracious, no! Who told you that? We are honest shirtmakers, tradesmen, like everybody else.'

'Well, Miss, you see we have to hear on all hands that we are a charity workroom, and please, Miss, if I thought I had to do with a Dorcas Society, I should *put on my bonnet and go*.' This last phrase became proverbial; it resounded through tears in the most impassioned theological debates, and was seldom wholly absent from the more purely domestic differences which broke the monotony of our toils. On one occasion strife had risen high before we intervened; perhaps we were growing idle and inclined to let the ladies fight out their own quarrels for once, but a solemn embassy from the housekeeper invokes our authority. We ask philosophically 'What's the row this time?' and even our large conception of the stumbling-blocks in the way of productive co-operation is enriched by the earnest answer: 'Oh, Miss, it's all about *onions in the oven!*' The ladies, it should be explained, provide their own dinners, but have them cooked, if they please, in the common kitchen; and we deliver a Solomon's judgment to the effect that the partisans of the 'energetic bulb' must agree to enjoy their baked meats together, and leave the oven 'unimpregnated' for the rest between whiles. Sometimes the quarrel would be about a chair. Every one is familiar with the pathetic limitation that makes the so-called 'home' of the poor consist of the furniture for their one room, but there is something still more pitiful in the way the baffled instinct of appropriation fastens upon the worker's 'seat:' to sit always in the same place becomes a habit and in time a cherished right; if two chairs happen to be alike, a bit of rag or string tied round the back or leg distinguishes the twins, and the worker would be miserable if she thought the tokens were exchanged; one old hand, we had reason to believe, left us after years because a necessary displacement was not broken to her with all needful tenderness and consideration.

The turning-point in the fortunes of the firm came one morning, when the ladies were discussing an advertisement for a 'marker' wanted at a shop in 'the Arcade' not previously known to deal in shirts. With more than usual acuteness we reasoned that where garments had to be marked, they must also be made, and a devoted emissary was induced to 'put on her bonnet and go' to apply for the place. Our promptitude was rewarded by finding ourselves almost first in the field for a real good thing in the way of business. After the first step it was comparatively easy to establish a modest connection: to work for one good shop was a recommendation to others, and friendly shopmen and commercial travellers would, from time to time, give us a hint of new openings, though we set our faces against the wretched system of bribery and treating which is one of the costly accessories of competitive trading. We lived down all suspicions arising from dim rumours of the 'Dorcas' sort, and – to anticipate a few years – a time came when we were applied to by a shirt-cutter out of place; and on our asking why, as we had not advertised, he explained that he had written to a few leading West-End places on the chance, and he understood 'Hamilton's' was a 'good house.' Ye gods! had any one told us in those early days that we should live to be famed as far off as Fenchurch Street as 'a good house' in the shirt trade, we should perhaps have perished before our time of gratified vanity.

After a while our principles were put to severe tests; we found rivals willing to bid against us and 'lower the price,' and we let work go from us rather than join in the suicidal competition which paves the operative's as well as the tradesman's road to ruin. We felt at the same time how almost irresistible the temptation must be. There was a day when, borrowing epithets from our friend the hosier, we set on record that 'the struggle for existence is an infernal process.' We reached the low-water mark of desperation in bad weeks, happily few and far between, in which the old plain workers on our staff were 'setting still' half their time, and found their earnings on the Saturday sink to a miserable 5*s*. or 6*s*. One slack December, necessity proved once more the mother of invention, and we designed a 'fancy' – *n'importe quoi* – which had a momentary success, and enabled one clever machinist to take home 2*l*., and buy her consumptive husband a greatcoat. We learned in those vicissitudes to understand how it is that the strugglers for existence are not crushed by the ever-recurring hardships of their lot. Paley thought there was no happiness equal to the intermission of pain, and it is quite true that when, after days of despair, cheerful news greet the ear of 'a nice lot of work in this morning,' human nature rebounds, and, remembering no more the anguish, the workroom resumes its labours gaily. It is hard for the rich and idle to understand that the jealousies and covetousnesses of the poor all turn upon the race for work, not the race for wages, and that the call for self-denial and forethought lies not in accepting work, but in daring to refuse it, to risk present personal privation rather than become a party to enforcing more unfavourable conditions on all the workers in the trade. We could afford to keep a conscience in this respect, but we were rash as well as scrupulous; and that partner, it must be confessed, did not deserve well of the firm who was so far left to herself as to support the excusable demands of a shirtmaker for good prices by irrelevant remarks about wages, and in fact ended by talking rank trade-unionism over the counter to the scandalised hosier's manager.

As a rule, we prudently reserved our theories for the ears of private customers, who, it is needless to say, had plenty of their own to offer in exchange. We were frequently confronted with Carlyle's problem: How was it that, with all the talk about distressed needlewomen, he could never find a needlewoman, 'distressed or otherwise,' to do a periodical day's sewing at Cheyne Row; and the oftener the question was put, the better we were pleased, as it gave us the opportunity of asking in return, how did Mr. Carlyle and those who quoted him expect the said needlewoman to maintain herself on all the other days of the year when the philosopher's clothes didn't want mending? We pointed out that some ten or twenty families, offering between them not less than 250 days' work to a decent and competent sempstress, would have no difficulty in finding one; but that, without some virtual security for regular employment, any woman in her senses must prefer the poorly paid but constant employment given by the trade, where even the hardest employer will try to find or make a bit of work for his best hands in bad times, to the casual engagements offered in private families, which spend two or three months of every year out of town, and feel unfortunately in no way bound to enable their needlewoman to earn a year's wages during the nine months for which they need her services.

Other queries were of a more personal character. A young man with historic christian names wanted to know if one of us was any relation of the Miss So-and-so who 'had written a dismal book about ethics,' and had some difficulty in grasping that the nearest relation was that of identity. One pretty creature with a good sweet face wanted to know if we made shirts for the love of Christ, and as truth forced us to reply it was for the love of shirtmakers, we were fain to hope that our friend had never heard of

> Abou ben Adhem (may his tribe increase!),

so that the involuntary plagiarism might at least be innocent of presumption. In truth we found little upon which to pride ourselves in what the charitable were pleased to call 'our work.' They wished to know if we tried to do our people good. Did we read to them at their work? – a question solved by the sound as of distant thunder overhead, where four sewing-machines kept up a continuous rumble. Did we try to teach them thrift, temperance, and the rest of it? – virtues which, to tell the truth, we felt less likely to abound in our customers and ourselves than among our workers. Did we try to cultivate their intelligence and provide them with 'higher interests'? – we were, on the whole, more apt to realise our substantial inferiority to every woman with a trade and to exaggerate the intelligence implied in the skill we lacked, while we observed with awe and admiration that, by some inexplicable freemasonry, as news fly through the uninhabited desert, our shirtmakers were generally in a position to give us the earliest intelligence as to the winner of the Derby or the Oxford and Cambridge boat race, while their comments on current affairs were fully up to the customary standard of intelligence observable, say, in the nine o'clock omnibuses.

Of course we must not allow ourselves to exaggerate. Side by side with an astonishing and admirable amount of patient industry, endurance, kindness to those in trouble and scrupulous professional honesty, our shirtmaking friends have their less amiable traits. The language of workrooms is not select, and we have had to beg that nothing might be said before the children in the room that would not be said before the partners; then there are a few – we are told and can believe a diminishing number, but still some, and those not the least skilled shirtmakers – who, after working steadily for a few weeks or months, disappear some Monday, spend a few days in drinking, and then come back to their work as if nothing had happened, or with a mythical story that no one takes the trouble to question because every one knows what it means. We naturally took a more serious view of these escapades than employers made kind by fellow feeling, and there was less of this with us than in most workrooms, but the offenders we should have most liked to reclaim have a good deal of pride in their lucid intervals, and we found that after one or two lapses they preferred to go elsewhere rather than face our remonstrances. Then, again, the embittering effect of the struggle for existence shows itself in jealousies and wranglings about the distribution of work, each imagining the other to have more than herself of the easiest or the best-paid work, or more than her fair share of the work when there is not enough for everybody. But we always found them ready to respond to an explicit appeal to their sense of reason and justice. A shirtmaker does not believe 'that two and two will make five if she cries and bothers enough about it;' she does not expect to get forty-nine farthings out of a shilling; and when we found that we were in some cases dividing amongst them more farthings and halfpence for making a particular shirt than our employers paid us for it, the ladies in parliament assembled voted the necessary redistribution and reduction of prices, without, so far as we could judge, thinking us at all to blame for the unamiable limitation of arithmetical possibilities.

Thus from year to year the work went on. Customers multiplied, and were no longer drawn mainly from the ranks of private acquaintanceship. It seemed that, with all our inexperience and blundering, we blundered on the average less than the average tradesman; people who came at first out of goodnature, came again because it suited them. Whether we solved Carlyle's problem to his satisfaction or no, we made his and his brother's shirts. Our first issue of an explanatory circular brought us so many members of the House of Commons as seriously to raise our estimate of the intelligence scattered up and down on both sides in the great national palaver. Men, who in their devoted youth had bought co-operative coats of infelicitous cut under the inspiration of *Alton Locke*, rejoiced to assert their principles at less expense in shirts of unexceptionable fashion. The higher mathematics, we began to feel, would have been nowhere without us, for by a curious chance it seemed that such of their professors as did not deal with us direct were yet drawn by some elective affinity to the shops supplied with our manufactures.

The bench of bishops, of course, was represented on our books, and that the last precocious scholar of Balliol should be unable to 'go up' without our assistance seemed the most natural thing in the world, while our human sympathies were not less touched by the bereft old gentleman who abandoned himself to our care, with a belated sigh, 'My poor dear wife used to look after these things for me.' We remember, too, the gratitude, mixed with wonder, of the first little bride to whom a sympathetic partner lightened the anxieties of the trousseau with afternoon tea and counsels based on the widest experience of bridesmaidenship.

Indeed, by the time we were fully launched on our career as clothes-makers to every age and sex, we felt that Schiller had gone too far afield to seek in the *Lied von der Glocke* the accompaniment –

> Des Lebens wechselvolles Spiel –

and that in truth 'tis your outfitter who receives the earliest and most intimate confidences as to the trappings proper to whichever step, in the long journey from the cradle to the grave, lies before you next. The 'wedding order' is a symbol of universal joy, and even a dressmaker is sorry for girls whose bright new frocks have to be cast aside because there has been 'a death in the family.' The bell of the poet is a supernumerary, but besides the usual chapter of births, deaths, and marriages, the sempstress is in contact with a thousand domestic fatalities which never reach the ringers. She knows when the boys go to Eton and when their mothers are no longer trusted to buy their shirts. Illness comes to her with sudden calls for unaccustomed garments, and the climate of the future emigrant's home is known to her by his wardrobe. The dressmaker is in humble alliance with the artist if the fair one who is to sit for her portrait has a face, or the artist a brush, that will be the better for effects in costumery. The creeds, too, are represented in this microcosm, and nothing is foreign to a shirtmaker of catholic capacity, from the last fashion in surplices to the riband of blue 'put upon the fringe of the borders of the garments of the children of Israel throughout their generations.'[2] Even the larger movements of the political world have their echo in the workroom, and officers ordered to Afghanistan or diplomatists sent to the rescue of oppressed nationalities, bear with them the good wishes of all who have worked upon their orders. A shirtmaker of cynical proclivities may even observe that the washermen of the oppressed nationality have a tendency to avenge its wrongs by 'spoiling' the linen of the intrusive benefactor with a celerity suggestive of general financial disorganisation.

These glimpses of a kind of far-reaching household union, of domestic services rendered out of doors and from a distance, but yet by individual human beings to creatures of their own kind, have sometimes seemed to open to us dim visions of the industrial ideal which social reformers have laboured to construct *à priori*. The shirtmaker whose buttons don't come off is a social benefactor, saving the time of women and the temper of men in distant households. Let us for a moment imagine that the time of our customers is as valuable, as uniformly well employed, as that of mortal men should be in a much-suffering world, then the value of the services rendered them is enhanced and becomes a part of their larger services to the race, while the service itself is rendered with more faithfulness and zeal because the work is seen to be useful and the reward for it ungrudged. If we could imagine all wealth to be expended profitably, no labour would then be driven to throw itself away, bribed to do work for which the community is none the better at wages for which the worker is the worse. There is no moralising agent equal to the power of work, but, as an idle poet wrote,

> Work without hope draws water in a sieve,

and a large proportion of the work imposed upon the poor by the vagaries of industrial competition has about the moral as well as the economic value of so many months upon the treadmill.

We are much indebted to the industrious poet who preaches the right of the worker to joy as well as hope for his portion; but it may be doubted whether quite every screw and bolt in the machinery of civilisation can be wrought into a thing of beauty, and to glorify duly the commonest kinds of labour we must idealise the object rather than the product of the workman's toil. What worshipper would not rejoice to make his hero's shoes, if hero-worshippers were apt to be able to do anything half so useful? But surely not all work is worship (unless, maybe, of Mammon); to make it so in all cases, the employers of labour and the consumers of its fruits had need be worshipful.

No account of a co-operative adventure would be complete which did not touch upon the important question of profit and loss. Could co-operative shirtmaking be made to pay as well as private trading, and what are the difficulties in the way of its doing so? For the benefit of other amateurs it may be worth while to go into details which would be superfluous for those whose ignorance of the ways of commerce was less complete than ours.

We entered upon our work with the capital of a few hundred pounds, to be raised to 1,000*l.* if necessary. We were advised that the cost of articles sold should be estimated at the cost of the raw material plus the cost of the work, plus a certain percentage to cover rent, general working expenses, interest on capital, and profits. But no one explained to us, nor did it occur to us *à priori*, that, for a business to pay its way, it is first of all necessary that the amount of trade done shall be large enough for the percentage added to the cost to equal the anticipated fixed general expenses; thus, if the price is made by adding 20 per cent. to the cost of work and materials, and the general expenses are 300*l.*, the sales must reach 1,800*l.*, or there will be a loss on the year's transactions, as 20 per cent. on less than 1,500*l.* will not produce the requisite 300*l.* This is obvious as soon as stated, but such truths are by no means *innate*, and it must be confessed that, so far from being discouraged by the smallness of our turnover in 1876, we were rather proud of ourselves, and had a sense of commercial success, when we found after a few months that, with 500*l.* invested, we had actually received

800*l*. for goods and work. It is even possible that we had a dim and short-lived notion that we were already earning profits to the extent of the difference! Even the drafting of a balance-sheet does not come by nature, and in our first attempt at one the distinction between capital and revenue was still a little nebulous. Its general tendency was to indicate a loss of between 250*l*. and 300*l*. – a fact which the partners discreetly buried in the deepest recesses of their own minds beneath wreaths of cheerful remarks about the cost of the 'goodwill' of a business and the high premiums charged to learners.

In the course of that year we had gradually substituted the scale of piece-work prices ruling in the best first-hand shops for weekly wages, and in 1877 an increase of nearly fifty per cent. in our gross earnings enabled us to establish an equilibrium between receipts and expenditure. In the third year there was a falling off in the trade work, owing partly to general depression and partly to the competition already referred to, while our private customers had increased and began to grumble at the back-rooms we had thought so businesslike and appropriate to the humble shirtmaker. With some hesitation we determined to move from Soho, to take a whole house and add dressmaking to our other work; one of us wished to become a tailor, but we felt that too lofty ambitions were a snare. In its new quarters, at 27 Mortimer Street, Cavendish Square, the progress of the firm was gradual but continuous, and its earnings in 1882 and 1883 would have warranted the declaration of a dividend of eleven per cent. and eight per cent. respectively upon its modest capital. We had drawn interest at the rate of five per cent. throughout, but when there was a surplus, anything beyond that was left to make good the original losses. It should however be explained that after the first three or four years much of the clerical and other work that had been done by the partners was handed over to paid officials, so that the amount of gratuitous supervision became less and less. Before that time we used to suffer severe remonstrances from our political-economical friends, who were shocked, in a way that was at once complimentary and embarrassing, at the idea of our valuable services being given without remuneration. Commercial prudence forbade us to explain, to actual or potential customers, that perhaps the market value of our commercial services was a minus quantity, as this would have cast a slur upon the firm we represented, and yet we could not endure tamely to have our economic orthodoxy impugned. We represented that our commercial reward was in the future; no new business could be expected to pay more than five per cent. in its first years; and if it was hinted that we might employ ourselves more profitably elsewhere, and that it was uneconomic not to bring our wares to the best market, we were fortunately able to protest, with great sincerity, that shirtmaking was quite as remunerative an industry as, say, publishing books on half-profits, and much less expensive than doing the London season. Anyway in these hard times, an investment paying five per cent. was not to be despised, and the political economists must admit that the market value of commercial management is fairly measured by the dividend it realises, so that we had no reason to consider ourselves underpaid.

Our articles of partnership were drawn up originally for three years, and we had been much impressed by one of the *facetiæ* of the *Sewing Machine Gazette* which set forth the terms of a similar contract. 'So you are going into partnership with young Brown, Herr Schmidt; what are the terms of the agreement?' 'Oh, ve do go into bardnership vor dwo years, and he do vind the money and I do vind the exberience.' 'And what is to happen at the end of the three years?' 'Vy, I vill 'ave de money and he vill 'ave de exberience.' At the same time we made the acquaintance of Mr. Lawson's not very encouraging account of *Ten Years of Gentleman Farming on Cooperative Principles*, and we should hardly have ventured to predict that at the end of eight years of co-operative shirtmaking we should be left in possession both of our money and our experience, together with a faith in human nature and the feasibility of industrial co-operation unimpaired by our own rash attempt to set the world to rights. There must surely be some vitality in the ideas which have allowed us to boast at last of this result. It is the fashion now-a-days to write people's lives before they are dead; so these reminiscences must not be taken as an *oraison funèbre* celebrating, like Mr. Lawson's book, the decease of the co-operators, but rather as the legacy of a retiring partner, whose place will be more than supplied by a group of ladies and gentlemen earnestly interested alike in co-operation and clothes-making. May their record at the end of another seven years be far more brilliant than the present!

But a more important question than that of the capitalist's immunity from loss is the extent of the operatives' gain. The economists, of course, were anxious that we should pay the market rate of wages, whatever that might be – anything else was a pauperising charity; but whether the 'market rate' is the highest or the lowest rate paid in the open market or half-way between it was left to our imagination to decide. We adopted the scale of prices current in the best shops, which would presumably have been accepted by a stronger trade society as the standard towards which it was desirable to 'level up.' Economically, we were bound not to pay less, or we should not have secured the services of the best workers; socially, we should have been glad to pay more, because the best rate of wages is still too low to give an average income, after allowing for illness and slackness of trade, sufficient for the comfortable and wholesome maintenance of a family. Practically we paid all we could afford: more considerably than a private tradesman would have done in our place (nearly 13,000*l.* in the eight years); less than we might have done if we and the shirtmakers had had our present experience before we bought it; certainly not more than any one desirous of 'improving the condition of the working classes' must have wished.

By the original scheme, one-fourth of the profits, after paying five per cent. interest on capital, was to be divided as bonus among the workers, and half as dividend among the capitalists, the partners offering to accept as a loan, bearing interest without risk, and entitling the lender to a proportionate share in the half profits, any savings the employees liked to trust them with; the remaining fourth was to form a reserve fund for the benefit of the workers. From the strictly co-operative point of view, the weak point of 'Hamilton & Co.' was that the financial risks were borne by the partners, and that wages were paid in full, even when the firm was working at a loss; and the hope of profit at the end of a year is not so strong an incentive to the utmost zeal and economy as the fear of loss next Saturday. On the other hand, since our avowed object was to secure a larger proportion of the earnings of labour to the actual worker, we were right in treating wages as a first charge on the receipts; and though we might have nominally divided more profits among the workers had we spent less on wages (by working longer hours, turning off day workers in slack times, and such like familiar devices), their real share in the earnings of the shop would have been less. After all, we should not have lived in vain if one elderly sempstress owed us the earning of a spare sixpennyworth of tea and sugar for 416 weeks; and not one, but many, have certainly earned spare shillings during these years through our intervention.

As time went on, we came in contact with another difficulty, which has something to do with the lukewarmness of workmen, as a body, in taking up the cause of productive co-operation. That some workers are more skilled than others, and some kinds of skill worth a higher price than others, is admitted and acquiesced in; what is not acquiesced in is the exceptionally high price commanded by the skill of the born *exploiteur*, and hence the smallest community tends to split into two camps, of which the financial interests are not identical. Our first and most zealous co-operator began to think herself indispensable, and to feel that the prices paid for other work than hers should be so adjusted as to leave a margin for special recognition of her own peculiarly valuable services. By working harder she might indeed have increased the divisible profits, but if she was to work harder it occurred to her as more inviting to work on her own hook, so as not to have to share such profits with the rank and file, and having learned in the co-operative shop enough of the art of management to set up as a 'little master,' she left us to do so. This secession, which was not the last of its kind, is typical of the difficulty of a large development of real co-operative production. Those who are born with the knack of driving, or playing 'boss,' of getting the maximum amount of work out of their subordinates, frankly don't care to exercise their special skill *pro bono publico*; if they are to make themselves disagreeable by keeping all workers constantly up to the mark, they require to be paid as much as they could earn by driving on their own account. On the other hand, the rank and file look dubiously at so-called 'co-operation,' which means that they are to earn profits to be divided amongst the foremen who are good enough to take the trouble to drive them. Theoretically, we know, co-operation is supposed to have a magic virtue which will make driving in every grade unnecessary. But it is better to face our difficulties frankly. If all the workers are to participate in profits, and the smallest share is to be large enough to stimulate the lowest grade of workers to do their best to earn it, it will seldom happen that the proportion available for the higher grades will be as much larger as they will be disposed to claim. Most industrial partnerships make things pleasant in the higher grades, with which alone the employer comes in contact, and one has to mix unofficially with the workers to get at the view of the other side, which is that the operatives have to work rather harder than elsewhere to earn *less* than the fair value of the increased amount of work they do. And this, say the democrats, is a fraud: even the Maison Leclaire, according to such critics, is only a collection of *petits bourgeois*, like the joint-stock millowners at Oldham.[3] Rightly or wrongly, we identified ourselves with the interests of the rank and file, and let our malcontent managers go. The firm in no case suffered from the secessions, which, it should be added, did not occur till after the partners ceased to be in daily contact with the workrooms. But, in a full and true history of the firm's experience, they must be put on record among other conditions of the problem future co-operators will have to grapple with. The earnings of a firm of average capacity will not suffice to pay at the same time more than average profits, salaries, and wages to capitalists, managers, and labourers respectively; and eight years' experience of the ways of trade has only confirmed the writer's conviction that salaries need raising less than wages, while profits may be very wholesomely reduced.

There was another disputed point of economics upon which we very soon felt able to speak with the authority of personal experience: viz. the question lately reopened by Mr. George, whether wages are paid out of capital or from the fruits of labour. In 1876 our average weekly expenditure on wages was under 20*l*., so the problem was not of bewildering magnitude; and as the co-operative workshop had been open for several weeks before its earnings reached 20*l*., it is certain that at first wages were paid out of capital, as in any case they must have been for the first week of all. But if we pass on for a few months, the working shirtmaker's ability to pay wages on Saturday depends upon his having done, and having been paid for doing, work enough that week or previously to provide the money for wages along with other liabilities. If on any occasion it befell that the bank balance was low, and a despairing partner had to draw a cheque upon a private account to eke out the missing 20*l*., this would be either because work had been slack and earnings low during preceding weeks, or because the firm's debtors were wanting in punctuality. Practically in every industry, large or small, the payment of wages has to be advanced out of capital for just as long as it takes for the first returns to come in, according to the custom of the trade in question. A working shirtmaker is paid on Saturday for work done that week; a shipbuilder may stand out of his money for years, but if the normal period for building and selling a ship is, say, three years, the advance is not perpetual, but for that period only: the wages to the shipwrights employed on the second generation of ships are paid out of the money received for the sale of the first generation. And from the socialist point of view it may be argued that the real value of the advance is exhausted with the completion of the first sales. The profits earned by the joint efforts of capital and labour do not 'belong' to the capitalist before they have been earned, and it is a question to be reasoned or wrestled out between masters and men what share each shall take and transform into their own property for private consumption or saving. No economic law would be outraged, and capital would still seek to employ itself productively, even though wages came to swallow up so large a share of the gross profits that the capitalist did not, as at present, receive interest in perpetuity on the amount of the temporary advance made to his first set of labourers.

One word to justify this insistence upon wages and the need of increased expenditure under that head. For the moment the religious and charitable world is interested in the denizens of the slums; but will that world bear to be told that the slums are peopled by those whom they themselves help to send there? What about the shilling bibles and sixpenny or penny testaments which it is supposed to be a good work to disseminate? The women who fold and sew these books must live in slums, with the rest of the vast army whose life amongst us is a slow death upon starvation wages. Are the Bible societies or they to blame if they take to drinking? Ladies who 'work among the poor' think it right to save their money for charity, and buy cheap costumes, made far off by the same sisterhood; and who can tell the ladies that their so-called charity is a theft, and they themselves parties to more oppression than the district visiting of a lifetime can atone? Or among the well-to-do who make no pretensions to do more than meet the everyday claims of human honesty and kindness, what lady is there who will renounce a bargain or turn away from the fabulously cheap attractions of the juvenile outfitting warehouse (kept by 'Israelites not wholly without guile'), because it is physically impossible that the worker's share in the cheap price can represent a maintenance? Even the working classes themselves are not blameless in the matter; they buy slop goods themselves – what but slop goods can slop-workers ever buy with the pence scraped together by going without food and fire? Does not the State itself give the first example – laughable if it were not so tragic in its consequences – of political economy gone mad, and, seeking to buy services in the cheapest markets, have the clothing of its soldiers and police made (partly at least) by women whose earnings must be supplemented either by charity, poor rates, or occasional free quarters in hospital or gaol, because they are insufficient for the decent maintenance of a widow with children – a revival of the worst evils of the old poor-law system of rates in aid of wages?

At the present moment, when even ground landlords are credited with some duties and starving tenants with a few elementary rights, it is surely not too much to ask that wealthy and philanthropic dealers in the labour of the starving shall recognise their responsibility and be required by public opinion to assure themselves that they are not accomplices, willingly ignorant in the sacred name of competition, but none the less accomplices in that underpayment of honest industry which does more than drink, more than vice, more than improvidence to people our slums, and is itself the most fertile mother of all those three. Let the shop-keepers, the manufacturers, and most of all the respectable well-to-do public, which buys from both, look to it, and ascertain, as people would if they learned that there was stolen silver about in the market, that the wares offered to them for purchase have been honestly paid for at each stage in their production, and that the labourers employed, indirectly, in our service are not being starved and brutalised at the bidding of our heedless craving for an illusory cheapness.

Notes

1 Then, and still, honorary secretary of the Women's Protective and Provident League (36 Great Queen Street, W.C.), a society for promoting the formation of independent self-supporting trade and benefit associations of women.

2 Numbers xv. 38.

3 It was to meet this criticism, advanced by a Socialist workman, that Leclaire decided to let all hands without exception share in the division of the bonus to labour; but the advantages in the way of pensions, &c., enjoyed by members of the 'Mutual Aid Society' are still reserved for a select few.

31

ADA HEATHER-BIGG, 'WOMEN AND THE GLOVE TRADE'

The Nineteenth Century, Vol. 30 (December 1891), pp. 939–944, 946–947

THE glove trade in England gives employment to some 15,524 persons, of whom 13,261, or 85 per cent., are women.

The men's share in the manufacture consists in the preparation of the skins and in the all-important function of cutting the leather into pieces of the requisite length and width. They, too, punch out the glove-shapes, the pieces for the thumbs, and the forgets – *i.e.* the little side pieces of the fingers.

The next stages in the glove manufacture give employment to women; but the final processes again fall to men, since it is they, or, at any rate, boys, who, with the aid of a machine, punch in the buttons of the heavier make of gloves; while they also 'lay out' the gloves, and give them the final touches before packing them. This finishing work is done in the factories – the last process in a room called the 'laying-out,' or, more jocularly, the 'deceiving' room where the gloves are drawn on to heated iron lasts, so that the creases may get smoothed out.

The women's share in the manufacturing process begins when the glove-shapes have been distributed to them, either by an agent established in the villages, or by bag-women – women who travel from factory to village, and, in consideration of the small charge of 1*d.* a dozen, take in the completed work and bring out the fresh. Pointing – *i.e.* stitching the backs – is the first operation.

This was formerly done with the aid of an engine, more popularly known as the 'brass donkey.' This little apparatus – still used for the pointing of fabric gloves – is to be seen in many of the cottages. It consists of a flat stand, out of which springs an upright, wooden stem terminating in two brass clippers with little notches or teeth, through which the worker passes her needle. The work is firmly held between these teeth, and the clippers open and close by means of a spring worked with the foot. The worker sits on a low stool, the stem of the engine between her knees.

When tambour-pointing is in question, the procedure is altogether different. Holes having been previously perforated in the backs of the gloves, these are then stretched tightly in a tambouring-frame, and the tambourer, with a celerity which strikes the beholder as truly marvellous, works the silk or wool in and out of the holes with a sort of crochet-hook.

 DOI: 10.4324/9781315400105-36

After the gloves have been pointed, they are handed over to another set of women to be sewn. The 'forgets,' or side pieces of the fingers, and the thumb-stalls, have to be set in, and the seams closed up – an operation demanding, when it is done by hand, a skill only to be obtained by instruction in childhood.

Next in order come the welting and buttonholing processes. Little girls fell the welts and put on the buttonhole-pieces – the 'strengtheners,' as they are called. Buttons are mostly put on at factories, where also girls do various odds and ends – make and pack samples for special orders, &c.

But until lately it was only a small proportion of the women's work which was done at the factories. Most of it was carried on in the homes of the people, and in summer time little groups of girls and women could be seen sitting out in the tiny gardens stitching, their tongues keeping merry tune to the ceaseless clicking of the needles. All ages were represented in these groups: 'the child of eight, laboriously learning the trade; the little girl of ten, who ought to have been at school, bending wearily over the dull task; the young woman, in lively chat with a neighbour who had brought in her gloving; and the house-mother, with a sleeping baby on her knee, almost hidden by a little pile of forgets and snippings.'[1]

Introduction of machines

The glove manufacture, in short, was one which, like straw-plait and pillow-lace making, seemed destined to remain the permanent stronghold of hand labour, and to furnish the most satisfying instance of our old system of domestic manufactures. Machinery, which had so successfully encroached upon most cottage industries, seemed powerless to affect this one, and women, to all appearance, possessed an inalienable heritage in a mode of work peculiarly calculated to commend itself to believers in 'sex in industry' desirous of seeing women engaged only in light and cleanly occupations, carried on by the domestic hearth, in the midst of the infant workers of the future.

Little by little, however, the tide of mechanical invention set in. First, a French punch, or cutting-machine, shaped like a hand, was introduced, capable of cutting out gloves with speed and accuracy. Until this time all the slitting had been performed by hand with shears – a by no means occasional irregularity in the length of the fingers bearing full witness to this fact. Then a man named Köhler, of Chemnitz, invented and patented in all European countries a machine with two needles for doing the ornamental stitching at the backs of gloves. The sole right in England and a hundred of these machines were purchased from him by a manufacturer of Torrington, who in a month's time was laying on the point for 1½*d.* a dozen pairs, and doing 2,000 dozen a week.

It scarcely needs to be said that this particular individual rapidly made a fortune; but much temporary loss was entailed on those women who had previously worked at this branch at the rate of 7*d.* per dozen pairs.

The mass of workers, however, remained unaffected, for the simple reason that the sewing of the seams – the process which gave the women of the gloving districts their chief occupation, still resisted all endeavours to bring it under the domination of machinery. The first machines invented were practically useless, as they would not close up the fingers, and the good hands among the glovers naturally refused to finish machine-begun work. But in 1880 a machine called the 'looper' was invented, which at once revolutionised the whole system of production.[2]

The new machines were quickly adopted by the manufacturers of Yeovil and the adjacent districts, and centres for the gratuitous instruction of the glovers were formed in the principal villages, so that soon skilled machinists were springing up on all sides. As the glovers naturally were not in a position to purchase the necessary machines, a more or less uniform system was established under which the manufacturers supply them to the workers. Putting aside slight differences of detail, the prevailing tendency is to 'keep a hold on the workers by retaining ownership of the machines.' Messrs. Whitby, of Yeovil,[3] for instance, provide the machines and keep them in repair; while Messrs. Dent, Allcroft & Co., who began by taking a weekly payment, and allowing the machines in time to become the property of the workers, now lend them out in the same manner as the other masters. Although the manufacturers here mostly own the machines, there is always a section of the glovers shrewd enough to see that it is a manifest advantage to be themselves the owners, as they can then accept work wherever it is to be had, and can also refuse reductions in wages, without any dread of being told to 'send in their machines.'

Such far-seeing, thrifty, and independent personages get their sewing-machines for 8*l*., of which 1*l*. has to be paid before delivery, and the rest in monthly instalments. To the manufacturers, only 6*l*. 10*s*. (cash) is charged; but this seeming unfairness is to be explained by the fact that they purchase in large quantities, and that with them payment is certain.

Effect on handwork[4]

It was of course inevitable that the introduction of machines should affect adversely the wages of hand-workers.

Hand-gloving lasted on for a little while after the introduction of machines, but then there was no more given out from Somersetshire firms. Dent continued to give out a small amount of the best quality, 'but at much reduced pay – *i.e.* 4*s*. a dozen to 3*s*. 6*d*. for very fine work – and not much of it to be had either.'[5]

Now, in the days of handwork before 1880 the Vale of Blackmore glovers had work from Yeovil, Milborne Port, and Dent's factory in Worcestershire. Dent paid best, giving out the finest work at the rate of 5*s*. a dozen, down to 3*s*. 9*d*. a dozen. The Milborne Port factories paid as much as 5*s*. when the stitching of the backs was included in the work. The commoner gloves from Yeovil and Milborne Port brought the glovers in 3*s*. 6*d*. per dozen. A first-rate hand, working not less than twelve hours a day, could make three pairs daily of the 5*s*. per dozen work, and four of the 3*s*. 6*d*. per dozen kind, and so earn 7*s*. 6*d*. a week.

Nowadays, however, hand-sewing is scarcely worth undertaking, while buttonholing and tambouring, both processes which are still done by hand, are very poorly paid. One woman in Sturminster Newton told me that, working six hours regularly every day, she managed at buttonholing to make 2*s*. a week! On one never-to-be-forgotten occasion she had done four dozen and seven pairs in a week. The pay for four-buttoned gloves was 1*s*. 1*d*., for six-buttoned, 1*s*. 9*d*. a dozen.

Tambouring is generally done by hand in England, because English manufacturers are of opinion that machines tend to tear the leather. For four-row tambouring the women get 11*d*. per dozen, and for two-row are paid proportionately less. Pointing – *i.e.* stitching the backs, which before the introduction of machines used to be paid at the rate of 7½*d*. per dozen, has now fallen to 5½*d*. for the three-stitch pointing.

'How be I to live on that?' asked one of my informants, flushed and voluble, 'vor it takes me vive hours to meake that!'

Former earnings of machinists

But if the hand-workers suffered, the machinists, so long as they were thoroughly well supplied with work, flourished exceedingly. A good machinist who devoted a great deal of time to the work could make a dozen pairs a day of the four-buttoned gloves, for which she was paid 2*s*. 2*d*. a dozen, while single young women living at home with their parents, and having no domestic duties to perform, could turn out ten and even twelve dozen pairs in the course of the week, and thus earn from 20*s*. to 26*s*.[6]

But in 1886 the supply of work diminished, and the machinists complained bitterly that a material reduction was being effected in their wages. At the instance, therefore, of Miss Mary Lowndes, the Women's Trades' Union Provident League determined, if possible, to organise the glovers so as to retain for them the advantage which the introduction of machines had seemed to promise.

As a preliminary, however, one of the committee offered to visit the West of England gloving district, and report on the condition of the industry, and on the alleged fall of wages.

Present rate of wages

There are few things more difficult than to obtain reliable information about the earnings of any class of workers. Apart from the natural reluctance of those concerned to enlighten inquirers, there are innumerable unspecified considerations which diminish or increase the amount of wages actually earned; so that a perfectly true statement may yet convey a false impression.

It sounds excellent to be told that Mary Ann Fish earns 12*s*. a week, till one discovers that employment on these or any terms is only possible during so many days in the week or so many months in the year.

A first-rate machinist, whose case was brought under my notice, had not had more than three and a-half dozen pairs of gloves a week to make during the whole of one year; so that her total weekly earnings only amounted to 6*s*. 1½*d*. – 1*s*. 9*d*. a dozen pairs being the rate of payment.[7]

Very often, too, seeming discrepancies occur in the statements of those interrogated, for which the inquirer's ignorance of trade technicalities is chiefly responsible. Thus, two or three different sums will be mentioned as the wages paid for sewing, and it will turn out on investigation that the speakers severally were referring to the different lengths of gloves – prices varying according as the gloves are four-, six-, or eight-buttoned. Again, the actual wages earned are often less than one would suppose, in virtue of sundry deductions, about which little is said by employers, and which are so much a matter of knowledge to the *employés* that they fail to allude to them. In certain factories glovers have to pay for steam, silk or cotton, and needles, and these items, although small in themselves, cease to seem small when they mean a 10 or 15 per cent. reduction on the week's earnings.

Yet again, though the rate of pay per dozen pairs be the same, some change in the mode of doing the work may cause this pay to represent far more time and labour than formerly.

For instance, in one village I visited I found it was felt as a substantial grievance that an order had been issued to all the women making gloves for one firm 'to tie their ends.' As there are two ends to each forget (making four to each finger), the process of tying the ends of silk or cotton represented a great deal of additional labour, and there was a sense of brooding injury in one woman's voice as she told me that '2*s*. 6*d*. a dozen ought to be paid for theay – us tying the ends; 2*s*. 6*d*.,' she repeated – 'then three-dozen of theay would mean 7*s*. 6*d*. a week, and I could do on that.'

It is but fair to add, that sometimes innovations in methods of doing work are said to be justified by a want of conscientiousness on the part of the workers. Thus, in the case of one firm, I was told that the rule of sending in the gloves inside out had had to be imposed on the workers because often, instead of pressing and pulling the thumb-piece out into its proper shape, and sewing it in at the extreme edge, they sewed it in too high up, leaving a large edge, which they then pared off; the natural result being, that the thumb-stall was too small round, and the glove girted across the fleshy part of the hand.

However, weighing every point carefully, it was impossible to avoid the conclusion that the glovers had made out their case, and that Major Beadon, H.M. Inspector of Factories for the Southampton District, certainly took a somewhat over-roseate view of their financial position when he put their weekly earnings at from 10*s*. to 25*s*. a week. In all probability, in forming this estimate, Major Beadon confined his attention to the exceptionally flourishing branches of the industry, or perhaps failed to distinguish between the outdoor and the indoor workers; and, again, between those living in towns, such as Worcester and Yeovil, and in rural districts, such as the vales of Evesham and Blackmore.

Change in the character of the industry

Under any circumstances, there could be but little doubt but that the glove-manufacture would soon share the fate of most of our cottage industries. For, once introduce the sewing-machine into any branch of a manufacture, and it then becomes advantageous to drive the machines by power, in which case the workers get inevitably drawn into factories, and a great many married women lose their employment.

This consummation, I am aware, is one which commends itself to many, but personally I am of opinion that the disappearance of any of our few remaining cottage industries is matter for regret.

Particularly do I think this in the present instance. For gloving is work peculiarly suited to married women, as it can be taken up or laid down in obedience to the claims of domesticity, without any detriment to its satisfactory performance.

It might be well that married women should not work at all, but so long as the labour of the nominal bread-winner does not bring in enough for his family's support it is a distinct gain that the wife should be able to supplement his scanty earnings with the few shillings she can get from an accessory occupation carried on in her own home. Failing such methods of adding to their income as gloving affords, the women of these agricultural districts would have of necessity to take a much greater share of farm-work than they do at present. Even now, a good many of the glovers, in harvest-time, are to be found doing odd jobs for the farmers. This agricultural work can scarcely be considered as desirable for women as the gloving, nor is it as consistent with the maintenance of comfort in the home, though it would be rash to say that it is not as consistent with health.

Notes

1 Cf. *Women's Union Journal,* April, 1887: 'The Dorsetshire Glove Industry,' by 'South Country.'

2 The looper is the shuttle of a double-thread sewing-machine, which holds the under-thread; but, instead of working underneath the plate, it works in a slender upright rod, the length of a finger – the thread coming up out of its point. Over this point the machinist draws the glove-finger, working the machine with her feet, and the needle catches up the underthread from the point of the looper, at each stitch.

3 I must here express my acknowledgments to these gentlemen, who not only showed me all over their factory, but gave me much assistance in other ways.

4 Handwork still survives to a limited extent in particular villages, as, for instance, at Upton Sudbury, a village about six miles from Worcester.

5 Those of the Milanese glovers who sew by hand can do five or six pairs a week only. They are paid 5*s*. to 5*s*. 10*d*. a dozen for piqué sewn men's gloves.

6 It will be interesting to compare these prices with those paid on the Continent. In the Milanese gloving district the machinists are paid from 1*s*. 3*d*. to 1*s*. 10½*d*. a dozen. In France, glovers earn 1*s*. 8*d*. a day in the country generally, and 2*s*. 1*d*. to 2*s*. 6*d*. a day in Paris. In Brussels, girls earn 1*s*. 3*d*. a day, women 1*s*. 6*d*.

7 It was the year when silk gloves were suddenly taken up for evening wear, and when, consequently, those who worked at kid gloves were at a disadvantage.

2.3

Carpets

DOI: 10.4324/9781315400105-37

2.3 Carpets

'Carpets', *Reports by the Juries on the Subjects in the Thirty Classes into which the Exhibition was Divided*, Vol. 2 (London: Spicer Brothers; W. Clowes and Sons, 1852), pp. 1037–1045.

Professor Archer, 'On the Progress of our Art Industries: Textile Manufacturers – the Carpet Works of Messrs. J. Templeton & Co., Glasgow', *The Art Journal* (June 1875), pp. 177–178.

Harold Cox, 'How Real Axminster is Made – a Visit to the Only Factory in England', *Time: A Monthly Magazine* (October 1890), pp. 1067–1071.

David Paterson, *The Colour Printing of Carpet Yarns: A Useful Manual for Colour-Chemists and Textile Printers* (London: Scott and Greenwood, 1900), pp. 81–87.

The term 'carpet' in the following sources signifies a densely woven textile in which the threads stand proud, as distinct from floor cloths, woven matting, counterpanes and netting. Carpets were often associated in the Victorian period with bright colours, intricate designs, luxurious materials and expensive, labour-intensive manufacture; however, the sources here demonstrate the increasingly good quality of cheaper, machine-made carpets as the century progressed. At the Great Exhibition of 1851, as the extract from 'Carpets' in *Reports by the Juries* makes clear, prize medals were chiefly awarded to those manufacturers who could offer quality at an affordable price, with five medals awarded for 'patent' Axminster or Whytock carpets. Scotland was the centre of innovation in carpet manufacture, where scientific expertise resulted in improvements in quality and design. The Scottish company Henderson and Widnell gained a medal for their Whytock Patent Carpets, with the jury praising their innovative methods and the affordability of the carpets.

David Paterson's *The Colour Printing of Carpet Yarns* (1900) gives a history of the Whytock method from its inception in 1832. A Scottish innovation, the method improved the quality of the colour and the speed of carpet production by machine-printing colours on yarn, rather than a hand-blocking process. By 1900, the workers' input was minimal. One illustration depicts a boy 'boxer' and girl 'printer' staffing four enormous printing drums, three or four times human height. Paterson, a Fellow of the Chemical Society of London, is described as a 'colour chemist', an indication of the close relationship between science and industry in this period. Paterson tactfully suggests that the more garish carpets are intended 'for export', while emphasising that the Whytock method brought 'beautiful and inexpensive' textile items to consumers of all classes.

Other sources here recount visits to factories producing Axminster carpets, which are luxury seamless carpets made of wool, originally manufactured in Devon. Professor Archer's visit to Templeton & Co. in Glasgow sharply contrasts with Paterson's account of technical complexity; Archer offers only a short summary of the manufacturing process, focusing instead on aesthetic considerations. He sees Templeton's carpet works as demonstrating the beneficial effects of art training on design. Harold Cox's account, 'How Real Axminster is Made', written 15 years after Archer's article, suggests that machine-produced or mass-produced carpets were synonymous with 'cheap' or 'poorly made'. Published in *Time*, a left-leaning periodical edited at the time by Eleanor Marx (1855–1898), this article admits that the increased production time of hand-made manufacture results in carpets so expensive that only the aristocracy, royalty and grand hotels can afford them. Despite this, Cox is charmed by the skill and conditions of the workers he meets at the small factory in Wilton, Wiltshire. He is escorted by the manageress, and this is a rare reference to a woman in a managerial role in this period.

32

'CARPETS'

Reports by the Juries on the Subjects in the Thirty Classes into which the Exhibition was Divided, 2 vols. (London: Spicer Brothers, W. Clowes and Sons, 1852), pp. 1037–1040

In reviewing the existing state of the manufacture of carpets, the first specimens that claim our attention are those from India, Persia, Turkey, and Tunis.

However great may be the differences in quality amongst the carpets from the countries mentioned, they are all made upon the same principle, and that one of great simplicity; but which yet affords the means of producing a more perfect, beautiful, and durable description of carpeting than any other mode of manufacture more recently discovered or introduced.

The manufacture is not carried on in any large establishments; but in pastoral districts, where it is combined with occupations of that nature, and engages a portion of the time of the families employed in that pursuit.

The loom consists of two perpendicular pieces of wood, fixed at some distance apart, which support a beam or roller; at the top, upon which the warp or chain is wound, and about 2 feet from the floor, is another similar beam, upon which the carpet is rolled as it is made.

The work is done entirely by hand, and each tie passes across the face of two warp threads round the back, and has the ends drawn up between them.

When a row of ties has been completed, a shed is formed in the warp, and the shoot is then passed across from right to left, and returned, binding the whole together, and is beat down to a horizontal level by the hand-beaters. Upon this plan carpets of the largest dimensions are made in one piece. The number of shades or colours that can be used is unlimited, and any design can be copied with great accuracy.

The design and colours of several of the carpets from India, Turkey, and Persia are especially worthy of notice, and should be studied with a view to imitate their beauties by the manufacturers of other countries. There is one carpet from Cashmere, sent by GHOLAB-SINGH to the Exhibition, made entirely of silk, that cannot be too highly praised for the beauty of its texture, and the softness and harmony of its colouring. In this carpet there are at least 10,000 ties in every square foot. There are other specimens of carpets of small dimensions, but very beautiful, and

DOI: 10.4324/9781315400105-38

remarkable for richness and harmony of colours. The exceptions are where an attempt has been made to copy European designs; and there the failure is as great as is the success in those of the native eastern style.

The carpets from Turkey deserve especial notice, as there are, in addition to those made all in one piece, some in breadths, extremely well coloured and closely woven; and an attempt has been made at new designs with considerable success. The carpets from Tunis and Algiers are made upon precisely the same principle, and have the same peculiar character in colouring and design.

The most costly and magnificent carpets of Europe are made upon the same principle as those above described; and that large and beautiful carpet, sent from the manufactory of the Gobelins to the Exhibition, is made by the same process of weaving as the ordinary Turkey carpets; as also are those from Tournay, in Belgium; Deventer, in the Netherlands; Aubusson, in France; London, Wilton, and Millbridge, in Great Britain. The manufacture at Axminster in Devonshire, and Mirfield in Yorkshire, of this description of carpet, generally called "Axminster," ceased to exist about twenty years ago.

The chief seat of the carpet manufacture in France is the department of Creuze, at Aubusson, Felletin, and Maurissard, where there are probably not less than 5,000 persons engaged in the manufacture of carpets and tapestry.

With the exception of the kind referred to, when describing the carpets from the east, the Aubusson carpets are all made upon the same principle as tapestry, and are consequently too expensive to be purchased by any but the rich. The specimens of Aubusson tapestry and carpets exhibited by Mons. SALLANDROUZE DE LAMORNAIX are especially worthy of notice, being second only to those of the Gobelins and Beauvais. Their merits are not recompensed by a Medal, in consequence of M. Sallandrouze de Lamornaix, as Commissioner for France, having withdrawn from competition.

The manufacture is well represented in the Exhibition, and deserves, for its beauty of design and colours, the highest praise. There is a considerable demand for this manufacture by the noble and wealthy of European nations, and occasionally by the United States. At Turcoin, Nismes, and Amiens, the carpet manufacture is also carried on; there being at these three towns nearly 600 looms; and the production is increasing. One of the features of the Exhibition is the progress made by France in the manufacture of moquette or velvet-pile carpets. This branch is of recent introduction in that country, dating within the last twenty-five years; and the specimens exhibited by Messrs. REQUILLART, ROUSSEL, and CHOCQUEEL, of Paris and Turcoing-Nord, are pre-eminent for their artistic designs and beauty of colouring. Some of the specimens of 5-frame moquette, exhibited by FLAISSIER BROTHERS, of Nismes, are very good. The same manufacture is adapted for floors or for covering furniture; but for the latter purpose, it is made very fine to imitate tapestry, with a velvet surface.

Moquette, Wilton, or velvet-pile, and Brussels carpets, are all woven upon the same principle; the only difference being that in Brussels the wire, by which the pile is raised, is drawn out, and in velvet cut out, by a knife. The pattern is formed by having frames placed over each other, and filled with bobbins of worsted, each frame having for the ordinary width 260 bobbins.

The manufacture of Brussels carpets was first introduced at Kidderminster, about 90 years ago, by workmen brought from Tournay, and has been steadily increasing up to a recent period, when the introduction of Whytock's patent tapestry carpets, together with two other descriptions of carpet, put a stop to its further extension. It cannot be said, however, that the manufacture has been superseded to any extent, as nearly the same number of looms continue to be employed.

The colours in each frame are different, and some of the frames are striped, or planted, as it is technically called, with various colours, when the design to be executed requires it, as in flower patterns, and drawn up by the Jacquard machine now generally used, instead of the old mode of drawing up by hand.

The number of colours, or shades of colour that can be used in a line is limited to the number of frames of worsted, which rarely exceed five in England, but more frequently extend to six or seven in France. Within the last 20 years, three new kinds of carpet have been invented, and brought into extensive use in Great Britain, all of which are well represented in the Exhibition.

The first in order, is Whytock's Patent Tapestry, which has been brought to great perfection within the last five or six years, and now employs about 800 looms, which are not adequate to supply the existing demand. The peculiarity of this manufacture, is the unlimited number of shades or colours that can be introduced, so that the most elaborately-coloured designs, with flowers and scrolls, can be executed. The saving of worsted is also very important in an economical point of view. The appearance is the same or similar to Brussels carpet, but the manufacture is more simple, each thread being coloured separately at spaces, with the various shades as they follow each other in the design. The process by which this is accomplished is beautifully simple and ingenious, but requires much care in placing and arranging the threads, and putting them on the beam. It is also necessary to the economy of this manufacture, that a large quantity of each design should be made.

This invention was patented about 18 years since, and a renewal of the patent granted for a further term of five years, which expired on the 8th September, 1851.

The specimens exhibited by Messrs. HENDERSON and WIDNELL, and Messrs. CROSSLEY and SONS, show in an eminent degree the capabilities of the manufacture as regards design and colouring.

The next is the "Patent Axminster" of TEMPLETON and Co., of Glasgow, of which there are some excellent specimens exhibited in carpets, rugs, and table-covers.

The object of this invention was to give the beautiful appearance of Axminster, or Tournay, at less cost; and it has been very successfully and extensively applied to the manufacture of rugs, as well as carpets.

The last is a description of carpet, having the same appearance as Brussels, or tapestry, which is woven plain by steam power, and afterwards printed by the same agency.

It is woven at Rochdale by Bright and Co., under Sievier's patent, and printed near Macclesfield, by Burch and Co., by a machine invented and patented by Mr. Burch. This manufacture has already found large sale, more especially for exportation.

Another novelty in the Exhibition is a carpet, rugs, and hangings for walls, of patent wool mosaic, the carpet and rugs being well executed, and the surface or pile peculiarly close. As yet, there has not been sufficient time to see what position this manufacture is likely to take in the carpet trade.

The rapid extension of the carpet manufacture in Great Britain is proved by the fact, that within the last seven years, not less than 700 additional hand-looms have been put in operation, for one of the new fabrics referred to; and looms worked by steam-power, equal to the production of 300 hand-looms for another, without lessening the demand for former fabrics, being an increase of full 30 per cent. in seven years.

Not only has the home consumption greatly increased, but new foreign markets have been opened, and old ones extended.

Several patents have recently been taken for the application of steam-power to carpet weaving, in addition to that referred to of Sieviers, and no doubt now exists, of this having been successfully accomplished; at all events, for weaving patent tapestry carpets, if not for Brussels of the usual manufacture. This will tend to reduce the price, and, consequently still further stimulate consumption. In fact, there is scarcely any branch of our manufactures, that wears a more promising aspect for the future.

The principal seat of the carpet manufacture is Kidderminster, in which there are about 2,000 looms, chiefly occupied in weaving Brussels carpets; while the carpets called "Kidderminster" are made extensively in the neighbourhood of Glasgow, Kilmarnock, Bannockburn, and Aberdeen.

They are also made in Yorkshire, Durham, Lincolnshire, and Westmoreland; the largest carpet manufactory in Great Britain being at Halifax.

The number of looms of all kinds may be estimated at 4,000, and the value produced at upwards of 1,000,000*l*. sterling.

The average earnings of the operatives will vary from 16*s*. to 28*s*. per week.

The specimens of carpeting from Austria, Portugal, Sardinia, and Prussia, show that the manufacture is making progress in those countries, and is evidence of a growing taste that must ultimately lead to a large increase of consumption on the Continent of Europe.

The numerous exhibitors of Berlin work and their contributions, show that this is still a fashionable occupation among our fair countrywomen, and in addition to those who follow it for amusement, affords employment to a large number of females.

Some of the specimens exhibited are very beautiful; in fact, every description of needlework may be said to be well represented in the Exhibition, and one specimen worked from a cast, and another from a drawing, without the aid of ruled paper, exhibited by FAUDEL and PHILLIPS, are especially worthy of notice.

A specimen of tapestry by a lady (Mrs. ALDERSON) is also highly creditable to the taste and ingenuity of the exhibitor.

The contributions in embroidery of various kinds from India, Turkey, Tunis, and Persia, are extremely interesting, beautiful in taste, and displaying the highest degree of excellence in execution.

33

PROFESSOR ARCHER, 'ON THE PROGRESS OF OUR ART INDUSTRIES'

The Art Journal (June 1875), pp. 177–178

Textile manufactures. – the carpet works of Messrs. J. Templeton & Co., Glasgow

FEW, if any, of our Art-industries, show more fully the beneficial influence of the Schools of Design and the Art-Schools of this country than our great carpet-works. The British carpets made in the first quarter of the present century showed the lowest state of taste it is possible to imagine in a civilised country, and but for that universal stimulus given by the widespread Art-training through which the nation has since passed, there is good reason to believe no great advance would have been made.

In Glasgow there are two great manufactories of carpets of artistic character; they are carried on by members of the same family, the older – which will be described in this article – is that conducted by Messrs. J. Templeton & Co., and is almost entirely occupied by the manufacture of *pile*, or Axminster carpets, made by a patent process in a manner quite different from the old Axminster kinds; at the other, Messrs. J. and J. S. Templeton, manufacture the kind called Brussels carpets, and some other artistic fabrics, which we hope to describe in a future article.

The important and beautiful manufacture of patent Axminster carpeting, which forms the staple production of the works of Messrs. James Templeton & Co., is the result of an invention patented in 1839 by the present senior partner and Mr. William Quigley, we believe of Paisley; and in the hands of Mr. James Templeton has been improved and perfected to such a degree that it may now fairly claim to be considered one of the most complete and best of all carpet-making processes.

All processes for weaving by machinery are difficult to describe by mere words, and many of them are so puzzling that, even with the machine working before one, it is not easy to comprehend its quick and complicated movements; I will, however, try to explain the curious method used in making the patent Axminster carpets. First, then, the design has to be redrawn and coloured full size on paper covered by lines running across each other at right angles; the little square spaces formed by the intersection of the lines each represent a weft thread in the fabric. When complete, this copy of the original design receives what appears to be very

DOI: 10.4324/9781315400105-39

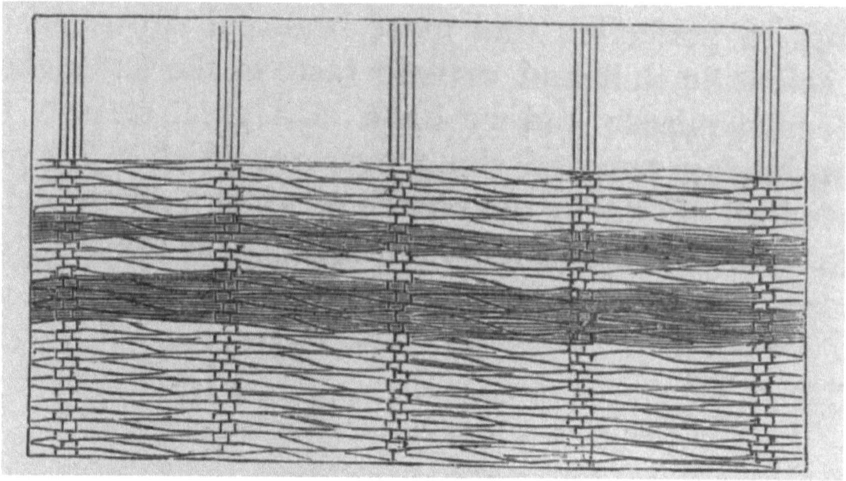

Figure 33.1

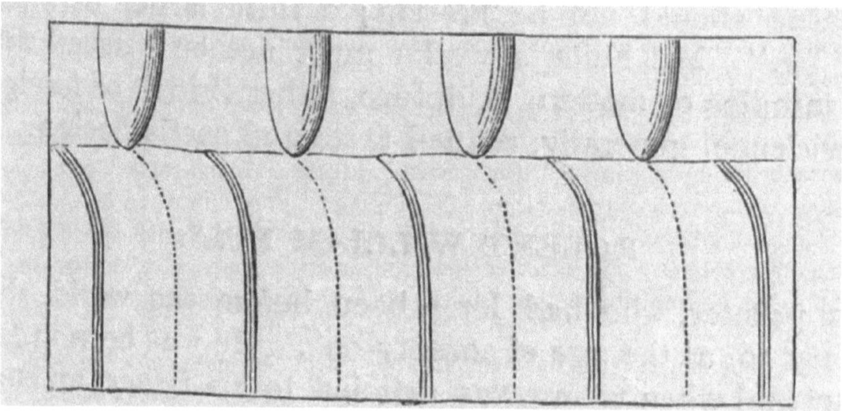

Figure 33.2

rough treatment, for it is cut up into transverse narrow strips, each representing one line across the whole pattern; and they form the guide to the weaver in the first weaving process. For this purpose the strips are placed in the opposite direction, so as to represent the direction of the warp threads in a small loom specially prepared. In this loom a series of warp threads are arranged in series of three or four, placed about half an inch apart, more or less according to the depth of pile desired, that is, between each series. The weaver then, following his pattern, weaves a web which, when complete, is like Figure 33.1; that is, it is only bound at intervals by the warps, between each series of which there is a space filled by the weft threads unwoven. This web, when complete, is a perfect medley of colours, without a trace of any pattern. It is next removed, rolled upon the beam, to the cutting machines, and when properly adjusted to another roller by its loose end, so that it can be wound off from one roller to the other, a series of cutting blades are brought to bear exactly on the middle of the space occupied by the unwoven threads of the weft; so that as the web passes under them, their blades cut through the web, leaving it in the end a series of very long strips of chenille. Figure 33.2 shows four of these blades cutting the web shown in Figure 33.1, as it runs off the beam, or roller, of the loom in which it was formed; the thicker dark lines show the binding warp threads, and the thinner lines meeting the points of the cutting blades mark the direction through which they cut the web. Figure 33.3 shows a small portion of one of the long strips so formed, being a fringe of threads of worsted tightly bound in the centre by the woven-in warp threads. Another operation gathers these threads up together, as in Figure 33.4; and in this state it now becomes the weft for the second and final weaving process. These figures, kindly lent by Messrs. J. M. Johnson and Sons (Limited), do not pretend to do more than convey an idea of what results from very complex arrangements and machinery, a description of which would be of too technical a character for this Journal. But if the description, aided by these woodcuts, has been sufficiently clear, it will be seen that in the next operation the carpet-weaver has, instead of a simple thread or yarn, to place in his shuttle a chenille the colours of which have been arranged exactly in accordance with the transverse strips into which the coloured pattern was cut; therefore if they are now laid side by side in proper order, the pattern will be again reconstructed. This is actually the case, and the skilled workmen who are employed in this work invariably place these chenille-wefts in correct succession, but in such a manner that the fringe of loose thread shall always be uppermost as they pass through the shed formed by the warps into which they are tightly interwoven and held by means of intermediate plain warps, which are concealed in the fabric by the raised pile formed by the chenille. These plain weft yarns, and also those of the warps, are, in the carpets woven by Messrs. Templeton, chosen with great care, as the durability of these fabrics, which is one of their best qualities, of course depends upon them and upon careful weaving. After each chenille weft has been laid, the operator gathers it up close along its whole length with a hand-comb; and when the weaving of the carpet is completed, then a cutting machine passes over the uneven surface of the pile until the whole is cut as level as a sheet of paper, and the pile so compact that it will bear considerable pressure without being flattened; in this respect, and in durability, greatly excelling, at much less cost, the old Axminsters. As the shuttles must be passed through the shed by hand to ensure sufficient care, there is hardly any limit to the size of such carpets, and some of gigantic dimensions have been made by Messrs. Templeton. One sent out to Siam, for one of the kings of that country, measured one hundred feet in length by thirty-four broad, the central ornament being a full-sized representation of the traditional three-headed white elephant emblematical of Siam. In going over the extensive manufactory I was shown a vast number of specimen-patterns

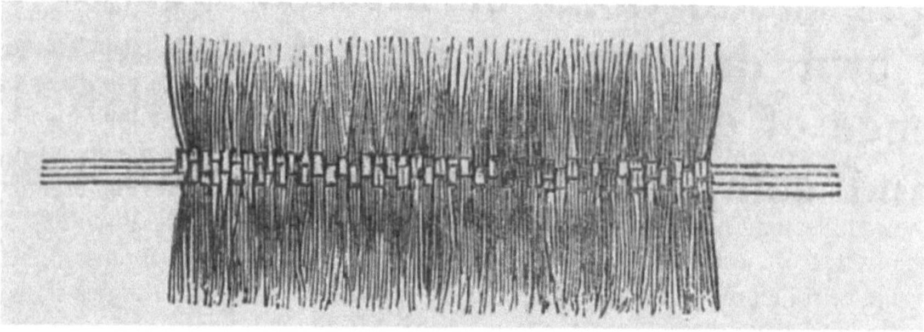

Figure 33.3

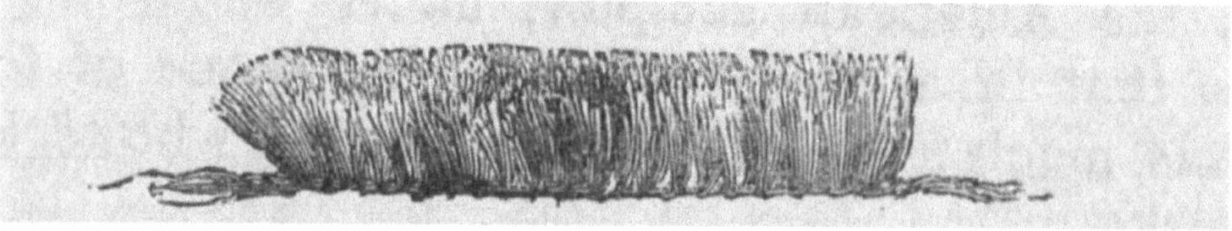

Figure 33.4

which had been made to order for all parts of the world, and for every imaginable purpose to which carpets can be applied. One, for instance, a present from a European sovereign, the King of Denmark, to the Tycoon of Japan, especially designed to show a perfect menagerie of animals forming a much-varied pattern. In many cases these specimens, as in the one mentioned, were simply grotesque, and marked the eccentricities of those for whom they were intended. But the staple productions of Messrs. Templeton's looms, in which their own designs are carried out, are remarkable for their excellence of quality as regards material; their closeness of texture and compactness, combined with softness of pile; for the brilliancy and skilful toning of their colours, of which they use not fewer than ten thousand shades; and, still more, for that great improvement in both designing and colouring which gained them the gold medal in the Paris Exhibition in 1867, and drew forth the highest encomiums which Sir M. Digby Wyatt, the British juror on that occasion, could bestow, and which has gone on unceasingly since then, until we, in this one speciality, feel warranted in saying that Messrs. Templeton have secured for Great Britain the highest position not only in that quality, which is not uncommon, excellence of manufacture, but in that very rare attribute of British work – high artistic taste.

They have wisely seen that the Orientals are *par excellence* the carpet-makers of the world, and have long since abandoned the meretricious ideas of French, and still more of the English carpet-weavers of the first half of this century, and have drawn their inspiration from the beautiful products of the looms of Persia, Cashmere, India, and Turkey, without too closely copying them. Some of their later productions are of so high a character that it is doubtful if they can be surpassed, especially in those designs which have been produced to meet the growing taste for low-toned colours and mediæval designs. Their success in these respects is in a great measure due to the great skill which directs, on the same premises, the dyeing of the wools, and afterwards in the close matching of the tints, which is done by a number of trained women, directed and supervised by a skilful artist. These matters, however, would not have been sufficient without that incessant devotion for, and attention to the business, which has led Mr. James Templeton on for more than a quarter of a century to work unceasingly in bringing to perfection this most beautiful Art-manufacture, in which scientific skill and artistic taste of the very highest order have been required; and we have in a great measure to thank him for having removed those eyesores which a few years ago frustrated all efforts by the choice of good furniture and decorations to make our apartments tolerable to the eye of taste.

34

HAROLD COX, 'HOW REAL AXMINSTER IS MADE – A VISIT TO THE ONLY FACTORY IN ENGLAND'

Time: A Monthly Magazine, October 1890, pp. 1067–1071

Just on the outskirts of the small town of Wilton (not long ago a parliamentary and still a municipal borough, three miles from the city of Salisbury), is an unimposing building eminently suggestive of a factory. In this building is carried on one of the most interesting of the hand industries that are still left in England. But before attempting to form an idea of this industry, it is necessary to dismiss from the mind the external aspect of the building in which it is housed. This is as bleak and forbidding as any of the hideous barracks that disfigure our northern towns. But go inside the gates and a very different spectacle presents itself. Instead of seeing a dirty yard deep in black mud, or covered with dull paving-stones, the visitor will find himself in a pretty little garden, surrounded by well-kept paths. Round three sides of the garden run the workrooms, built at different dates, and unrestrained by any fixed plan of architecture. On the fourth side is the house of the principal proprietor and manageress of the factory. It is a simple, two-storied, low-roomed building, that has outlived more than one generation. The dining-room opens with a glass door into the garden, so that the mistress is living literally within her factory. For the garden communicates directly with the workrooms, and indeed forms the main thoroughfare for the work people on their way from one part of the factory to another.

My visit is luckily made under the conduct of this lady-president of the factory. Stepping from her dining-room into the garden, and giving a brief glance at the flowers in the little greenhouse, we mount a few wooden steps and enter a long, low workroom filled with carpet frames, where scores of girls and women are busily at work, building up the deep-piled carpets.

This room which we first entered is the most typical room of the factory, and therefore it is worth while, before passing onwards, to give some description of the nature of the work by which the famous Axminster pile is produced. Let me take for my text the first frame I inspected, on which was being completed a carpet specially designed for a billiard room. The "frame" consists essentially of a large wooden roller or winch, about two feet six inches in diameter, and some twenty

 DOI: 10.4324/9781315400105-40

feet long, pinned at the ends to two uprights. The two uprights are joined together by a beam some four or five feet above the roller, and, of course, parallel to it. It is over this beam that pass long warp threads or strands of the carpet separated from one another by little pins or studs in the beam.

In order to set up the frame, these warp strands, which are made of the strongest linen thread, are fixed to the roller at one end, the other end being also secured. The girls then take their places in front of the frame, sitting beside one another on a long bench, each girl having her own width of work to attend to. She has two duties to perform: first, to fix the pile to the warp strands; secondly, to weave these strands into a solid backing.

First with regard to the pile: – Beside her, conveniently placed for her left hand to reach, hang a number of short lengths of different coloured wools; in front of her is pinned the coloured paper pattern by which she is working. Watching her pattern, she takes the appropriate wool, and with a few quick motions of her fingers ties it tightly on to the warp strand; then with a pair of scissors snips off the two ends within about an inch of the strand. In this way the two woollen tufts are left standing out from the warp, and by placing a succession of them side by side, the tuck pile of the carpet is gradually built up. So far, however, we have only got a number of separate threads with tufts of wool attached to them. The next process weaves them into a carpet. As soon as the girl has completed her row of tufts, she passes a shuttle carrying strong thread, once backwards and once forwards, between the strands, thus interweaving warp and tuft. Then comes another row of tufts, and then another row of weaving, and so on.

The process no doubt is a slow one, but the product is permanent. Each tuft of the pile goes through to the very back of the carpet, so that real Axminster cannot become threadbare until it has been worn right through. With that machine made article, on the other hand, known as patent Axminster, the backing and the pile are woven separately and then fastened together. Unfortunately, the two elements having thus distinct existences, are easily induced to part company.

So much for the nature of the work; now for the people who do it. In this little factory at Wilton were some two hundred girls and women, and, in all the factories I have visited at one time or another, I have seldom seen a higher general average of tidiness and good looks. Many of the girls were quite young – twelve or thirteen years old – and were learning their craft from elder girls sitting beside them. In these cases the firm pays the elder girl for teaching the junior, and the learner is paid something by her teacher for the work she does. Nearly all the wages are on the piece-work system, so that the weekly takings of the girls vary considerably. The highest amount taken seemed to be about 13s. a-week, and the average perhaps 9s. or 10s. This does not sound very high in a Londoner's ears. But all wages have a habit of being low in Wiltshire, and probably many a London factory girl who makes 15s. or 16s. a-week in the noise and dirt of the East End or the Borough, would find that she was a good deal better off on 10s. a-week in Wilton.

But I must not omit to mention the male part of the factory. Comparatively, only a few men are required, perhaps forty or fifty, and their work is merely supplementary to that of the women – for example, shifting the carpets, which are too heavy for the women to move. Men, too, are wanted for the engine-room, and there is a male machine department for making Brussels carpet and Wilton "velvet," where men and boys are employed. Also, the dyeing department is entirely given over to the male sex. The dyeing rooms, I think, delighted me more than almost any part of the factory. Nearly all the dyes employed are made from vegetable products, and great heaps of bright-coloured bark and chips were piled up in different bins waiting to be steeped. But my hostess and guide would not let me linger to examine these brilliant masses of colour, but led the way through the further door of the dye-room towards the next department. We were again in the open air, and, to my intense surprise and delight, standing on a little promontory of land, separated by two running streams from a wood, whose tall trees almost overhung the factory.

Of course, the streams were inky black, and vile to touch or smell, from the waste products of the dye-house! No, we are in Wilts, not in the West Riding of Yorkshire. The water was as pure and clear as any mountain stream, and, as it hurried by, murmuring against the stones, seemed to invite one to stoop down and drink.

From this open spot, a flight of wooden steps led to an upstairs room, where the girls, as they sat at their work, could look out through the open door on this fairy scene of wood and water.

Looking at this almost ideal, but quite unpretentious factory, with its garden in the centre and the woodland scenery at the back, the reflection arises: Why should not all factories be thus pleasantly situated, instead of being pent up amid dirty streets? The answer is, Because of the difficulty of getting a sufficient supply of labour in the country. At Wilton this single factory has used up all the available female labour in the district, and the proprietors have been obliged, reluctantly, to open a branch factory in Salisbury to meet the growing demand for their manufactures. And why cannot more labour be attracted to Wilton? For two reasons. First, because all the houses and cottages in the place are already full, and the nobleman who owns practically the whole of the district either will not, or, at any rate, does not allow more to be built. Secondly, because women will not go to live in a place where there is no work for their fathers and husbands.

The first of these causes is prevalent all over the country, but is obviously removable by the power of Parliament. The second is more serious. The tendency of machinery throughout Western Europe and America is to supplant male by female labour, at any rate in all textile industries. This tendency will certainly continue until women acquire the habit of insisting on wages at least as high as those of men engaged in similar work. And the effect will be, as is reported to be the case in the Eastern States of America, that the men will be driven abroad to new fields, while the women are left behind in "She-towns."

However, this is wandering a long way from Wilton. The carpet industry is firmly established there, even if economic and political causes prevent its further extension. The demand for real Axminster comes from quarters where more is attached to quality than to price – large London hotels, the City guilds, members of the Royal family, and the great land and money lords. It is by executing orders from these dignified personages and bodies corporate that the little factory at Wilton lives and thrives, and affords a healthful, happy livelihood to some twelve score persons.

35

DAVID PATERSON, *THE COLOUR PRINTING OF CARPET YARNS: A USEFUL MANUAL FOR COLOUR-CHEMISTS AND TEXTILE PRINTERS*

(London: Scott and Greenwood, 1900), pp. 81–87

As the process of printing tapestry carpet yarns differs so widely from all other methods of carpet making, it may be of interest, before entering into practical details, to consider a few notable features of the process. The method of printing the various colours on the yarn, which is most ingenious, was invented and patented by a Mr. Richard Whytock, of Edinburgh, in the year 1832. By his method carpets can be made of dyed or coloured warps without new blocks being required for each new pattern. The carpets may have a looped surface like the Brussels, or the loops may be cut in the weaving, giving a velvet pile like the Wilton carpets.

As very little information has been published regarding the early days of this invention, a few details may be of interest, gathered as they were by the present writer from those who were well acquainted with the inventor. Richard Whytock was the son of a minister in Dalkeith – a town near Edinburgh, and was born about the year 1775. Having a strong mechanical turn of mind, he spent much time in experimenting in a little workshop he had for the purpose. One day having accidentally drawn out a worsted thread from a piece of printed delaine, which was then fashionable for ladies' gowns, he observed that the single thread was coloured various colours at stated intervals according to the design printed on the delaine. The idea struck him, – could he not print single threads with colour in such a manner that, when a number of them were woven together, they would make a coloured carpet? By following out this idea he produced, after several years' experimenting, the process of carpet yarn printing known as the Whytock process, now employed in making tapestry carpets, velvet table-covers, sofas, rugs and similar fabrics.

Richard Whytock spent much of his time in quietly working out his mechanical ideas, and was well known for his charity. He died a bachelor in 1856, leaving £35,000 to be divided among his brother's family. The invention was first tried in Edinburgh in 1832 in a part of Queensberry House in the Canongate, and in 1833 it was removed to St. Ann's at Lasswade, which was formerly a brewery.

 DOI: 10.4324/9781315400105-41

About the year 1846 Messrs. John Crossley of Halifax bought the patent from Whytock for £10,000.

In 1841 a series of trials were made to print the colours on the yarn and steam it in one continuous process, but, after costing nearly £1000, the idea was abandoned.

Whytock's invention shows a sound knowledge of the arts of weaving and dyeing, as well as mathematics. Such a process, even though conceived, could not have been brought into practical work except by one thoroughly acquainted with these arts. Like many other useful inventions, its early progress was slow and disappointing. Manufacturers and dealers were not in favour of the new fabric, and printing drums were erected only a few at a time. After fifteen years, however, in 1847, we find fifty-six tapestry looms working, the greatest number of these being employed in the firm of Henderson & Widnell at Lasswade, near Edinburgh. The great success which has attended the tapestry carpet industry is owing principally to the energetic and enterprising manner in which the eminent carpet firm, Messrs. John Crossley & Sons, of Halifax, entered into its manufacture. It has now become an important branch of textile industry, extending over the whole world. By employing the same principle of printing and weaving, all kinds of beautiful and inexpensive velvet pile carpets, table-covers, sofas, rugs, etc., may be produced at a price within the reach of all. Many improvements in details have, of course, been made on Whytock's invention of 1832; but the principle of imparting to the yarns their various colours remains practically unaltered. In Brussels carpet manufacture all the yarns are dyed self-colours in the dye bath, each separate thread representing one colour in the carpet. In order to have a small piece of a colour in a Brussels a thread of that colour must traverse the *whole* pattern. The colours in Brussels are limited to five or six, and if another shade is desired, it can only be inserted by the process of planting, which is substituting it at the desired place for another colour already working in the carpet. Whytock's process overcomes this inconvenience. A single tapestry thread is printed various colours, and there is practically no limit to the variety of shades which can be employed. This, indeed, has been brought forward by some writers as a positive objection to the tapestry process, as the results are apt to become vulgar and "offensive to any one having artistic taste". But the fault here lies, not in the process itself, but in the taste of the colourist or designer. A soft, harmonious colouring, which would satisfy the most fastidious taste, can be employed with great effect in tapestry carpets. No doubt the colouring in many tapestries is crude and garish, but such are generally intended for foreign export where they have a ready market. With many nations there is a strong demand for bright, showy colours and glaring contrasts, which, to our eye, would appear offensive. This freedom in the employment of colours, then, instead of being a fault in the tapestry process, is indeed a positive advantage, as it enables the manufacturer to supply the demands of other nations, though their taste, perhaps, be not the most cultivated. Within late years tapestry carpets, as a whole, have greatly improved in colouring; the many excellent productions from our best firms have, no doubt, done much to elevate public taste. In a Brussels all the dyed threads lie in layers, one on top of another, under the surface of the carpet, and only reappear on the surface at the certain place where they are required to produce the design. In this way a large amount of dyed yarn must, of necessity, be concealed under the surface. In a Brussels of five colours, or a five-frame carpet, only about one-fifth of the dyed worsted forms the surface of the carpet and is visible; while, roughly speaking, about four-fifths lies under the surface and is lost to view. By Whytock's process this great loss of valuable material is altogether avoided, all the coloured yarn in the tapestry carpet being on the surface and visible. Another point of advantage is the saving of space with tapestry looms; a Brussels loom occupying three times the space in length that a tapestry one requires. In the early days of Whytock's invention the yarn was wound on the printing drum from bobbins, by rotating the drum by means of a hand crank, while a simple arrangement guided the threads across the breadth of the drum. At that time the colours were applied to the yarn, not by means of a printing pulley and colour box as now employed, but with straight wooden sticks or rulers which were dipped into the colour paste and then applied to the yarn across the drum. The edges of the printing sticks were covered with felt. Originally the printing drum seems to have been made of tin and covered over with waterproof cloth. The point at which these colour rulers were applied was midway up the drum, where a ledge or guiding shelf was erected to keep the ruler exactly parallel to the edge of the drum. The introduction of rollers or pulleys running in a small box and colour paste, and printing at the bottom of the drum instead of the side, was a great improvement on the old system.

Like the majority of clever inventions, Whytock's method of colouring tapestry carpets is very simple in theory; yet in actual practice, the many little important details requiring attention give it a complexity which renders it difficult to comprehend at first sight. To the reader who has never seen the printing drums, or the process in operation, a mere verbal explanation will be of little service. We have here in Figure 33.8

Figure 33.8 The Printing Drum.

an illustration of the modern tapestry printing drum with all its accessories in working order. This will give a clearer idea of the method of printing than any words can convey. The following explanation, combined with the assistance of the picture and diagrams, will give an intelligent idea of the tapestry process of carpet making to those unacquainted with it in actual work. The design of the carpet pattern is first painted on paper divided into little squares or parallelograms, each little oblong representing a loop in the finished carpet. This coloured design, which somewhat resembles a mosaic, is pasted on a board, and hung beside the printer. The design board is seen to the extreme right of the illustration, where a boy is pointing on it with his finger, evidently engaged in reading off the colours to the girl printer at the drum.

The circumference of the large cylinder or drum, which is made of wood, is first covered with varnished or glazed cloth to prevent the dyes from entering and staining the wood. It is then wound evenly round with one layer of the carpet yarn, giving it the appearance of an immense bobbin, covered with one layer of thread. The drum, as seen in our illustration, is covered only half-way across with yarn, thus making only half the number of carpets. Underneath the drum and running in the direction of its axis is a small set of rails, on which runs the carriage for the colour boxes for supplying the various colours to the yarn. A number of these boxes are seen around the boy – the "boxer" who is ready to supply any colour box which may be required.

2.4

Paper

DOI: 10.4324/9781315400105-42

2.4 Paper

Charles Dickens and Mark Lemon, 'A Paper-Mill', *Household Words*, Vol. 1 (31 August 1850), pp. 529–531.

Image: Wallpaper, *The Art Journal Illustrated Catalogue: The Industry of All Nations* (London, 1851), pp. 129, 143.

Harriet Martineau, 'Household Scenery', *Household Words*, Vol. 5 (14 August 1852), pp. 513–519.

'Cardboard', in *Tomlinson's Cyclopaedia of useful arts and manufactures*, Vol. 2, ed. Charles Tomlinson (London: George Virtue, 1852–1854), pp. 321–324.

Harriet Martineau, 'How to Get Paper', *Household Words*, Vol. 10 (28 October 1854), pp. 241–245.

Anon, 'Cigarette', *London Journal* (1 November 1869), p. 229.

Huge volumes of rags were needed for papermaking in Britain before the 1870s, and the recycling of cloth was perceived as a social duty. Later in the century, paper came to be manufactured more cheaply from wood pulp.[1] In the 1850s, however, British paper manufacturers were often hard pressed to source sufficient cloth because of excise duties imposed on the importation of rags from abroad. Harriet Martineau's anonymous article, 'How to Get Paper' (1854), decries the 'burden' imposed on British paper manufacturers. Unable to source rags from abroad, they find that 'precious tatters' in Britain are being bought cheaply by foreign manufacturers who do not have to pay the duty. 'How to Get Paper' highlights the high cost of paper in the mid-Victorian period, a time when the printing and publishing industries were expanding rapidly.

A similar message underpins 'A Paper-Mill', co-authored by Charles Dickens and Mark Lemon (1809–1870), which appeared anonymously in 1850. The narrator describes a visit to a paper mill in Dartford, Kent, which had been established in the Elizabethan period. The authors outline the processes whereby filthy rags are transformed into paper. Part way through the article, the account shifts into an 'it-narrative', where the first-person narrator states, 'I *am* rags', presenting the manufacturing process from the point of view of a bundle of rags.[2] This article also refers to the tax on rags having a 'depressing' effect on the paper industry. The entry on 'Cardboard' in *Tomlinson's Cyclopaedia of Useful Arts and Manufactures* (1852–1854) also details the processes of manufacturing, focusing in particular on the cardboard used for playing cards and address cards. Again, the excise duty on paper is referred to, with the author noting that the ace of spades in packs of cards for export acts as the 'duty card', costing the purchaser one shilling. The paper taxes are consistently presented as a serious impediment to British manufacturing in many of the sources in this section.

Harriet Martineau also wrote about wallpaper in 1852 in her anonymous article 'Household Scenery', in which she offers a history of the development of wallpaper. As in many of her other *Household Words* articles on manufactured goods, she bemoans the taxes which she sees as an impediment to British industry, arguing that if the Paper Tax is repealed, then everyone would be able to afford to have their homes ornamented with wallpaper. Recounting a visit to one of McCrie's factories in Edinburgh, which produces high-quality wallpaper, Martineau warns against buying cheaper paper made of buffalo skins, which can produce bad smells, papers that use arsenic to create the green colours, or those with wool flock which can disintegrate. The patterns in McCrie's factory are made both by machine and by hand, and Martineau indicates the importance of having a good designer because, she argues, intricate patterns can be wearisome and irritating, even precipitating illness. The two images in this section depicting wallpaper designs shown at the Great Exhibition were presented in the *Art Journal* in 1851 as examples of good taste, and it is hard to know whether Martineau found such designs 'irritating'.[3] In 1860, the Paper Tax was repealed and manufacturers were able to produce more paper at a lower price. An anonymous article, 'Cigarette', in the *London Journal* in 1869 reveals another dimension to paper manufacture. The author describes the importance of having the right paper for cigarette manufacture, extolling the superior quality of paper from the Mediterranean countries, particularly Turkey. From the 1870s, however, the problems associated with paper manufacture were alleviated when widely available wood pulp replaced rags as the basis of paper.

Notes

1 For a discussion of the history of textile recycling in the 1840s and 1850s, see Deborah Wynne, 'Reading Victorian Rags: Recycling, Redemption and Dickens's Ragged Children', *Journal of Victorian Culture*, 20:1 (2015), pp. 34–49.

2 For a discussion of the it-narrative see Freedgood, Elaine, 'What Objects Know: Circulation, Omniscience and the Comedy of Dispossession in Victorian It-Narratives', *Journal of Victorian Culture*, 15: 1 (April 2010), pp. 83–100. See also Leah Price, *How to Do Things With Books in Victorian Britain* (Princeton, NJ: Princeton University Press, 2012), pp. 107–136.

3 The issue of 'good taste' in design was discussed in Dickens' journal *Household Words*, both in Henry Morley's article, 'A House Full of Horrors', *Household Words*, Vol. 6 (4th December 1852), pp. 265–270, and in Dickens' serialised novel, *Hard Times*. The latter was serialised from April to August 1854, and the opening instalment depicts a disagreement over what is an appropriate design for a carpet between the utilitarian Gradgrind and the circus child Sissy Jupe.

36

CHARLES DICKENS AND MARK LEMON, 'A PAPER-MILL'

Household Words, Vol. 1 (31 August 1850), pp. 529–531

DOWN at Dartford in Kent, on a fine bright day, I strolled through the pleasant green lanes, on my way to a Paper-Mill. Accustomed, mainly, to associate Dartford with Gunpowder Mills, and formidable tin canisters, illustrated in copperplate, with the outpourings of a generous cornucopia of dead game, I found it pleasant to think, on a summer morning when all living creatures were enjoying life, that it was only paper in my mind – not powder.

Time was, in the old Saxon days, when there stood a Mill here, "held in ferm by a Reve," but *that* was not a Paper-Mill. Then, came a Nunnery, with kings' fair daughters in it; then, a Palace; then, Queen Elizabeth, in her sixteenth year, to sojourn at the Palace two days; then, in that reign, a Paper-Mill. In the church yonder, hidden behind the trees, with many rooks discoursing in their lofty houses between me and it, is the tomb of Sir John Spielman, jeweller to the Queen when she had grown to be a dame of a shrewd temper, aged fifty or so: who "built a Paper-Mill for the making of writing-paper," and to whom his Royal Mistress was pleased to grant a license "for the sole gathering for ten years of all rags, &c., necessary for the making of such paper." There is a legend that the same Sir John, in coming here from Germany, to build his Mill, did bring with him two young lime-trees – then unknown in England – which he set before his Dartford dwelling-house, and which did flourish exceedingly; so, that they fanned him with their shadows, when he lay asleep in the upper story, an ancient gentleman. Now, God rest the soul of Sir John Spielman, for the love of all the sweet-smelling lime-trees that have ever greeted me in the land, and all the writing-paper I have ever blotted!

But, as I turn down by the hawthorn hedge into the valley, a sound comes in my ears – like the murmuring and throbbing of a mighty giant, labouring hard – that would have unbraced all the Saxon bows, and shaken all the heads off Temple Bar and London Bridge, ever lifted to those heights from the always butchering, always craving, never sufficiently-to-be-regretted, brave old English Block. It is the noise of the Steam Engine. And now, before me, white and clean without, and radiant in the sun, with the sweet clear river tumbling merrily down to kiss it, and help in the work it does, is the Paper-Mill I have come to see!

DOI: 10.4324/9781315400105-43

It is like the Mill of the child's story, that ground old people young. Paper! White, pure, spick and span new paper, with that fresh smell which takes us back to school and school-books; can it ever come from rags like these? Is it from such bales of dusty rags, native and foreign, of every colour and of every kind, as now environ us, shutting out the summer air and putting cotton into our summer ears, that virgin paper, to be written on, and printed on, proceeds? We shall see presently. Enough to consider, at present, what a grave of dress this rag-store is; what a lesson of vanity it preaches. The coarse blouse of the Flemish labourer, and the fine cambric of the Parisian lady, the court dress of the Austrian jailer, and the miserable garb of the Italian peasant; the woollen petticoat of the Bavarian girl, the linen head-dress of the Neapolitan woman, the priest's vestment, the player's robe, the Cardinal's hat, and the ploughman's nightcap; all dwindle down to this, and bring their littleness or greatness in fractional portions here. As it is with the worn, it shall be with the wearers; but there shall be no dust in our eyes then, though there is plenty now. Not all the great ones of the earth will raise a grain of it, and nothing but the Truth will be.

My conductor leads the way into another room. I am to go, as the rags go, regularly and systematically through the Mill. I am to suppose myself a bale of rags. I *am* rags.

Here, in another room, are some three-score women at little tables, each with an awful scythe-shaped knife standing erect upon it, and looking like the veritable tooth of time. I am distributed among these women, and worried into smaller shreds – torn cross-wise at the knives. Already I begin to lose something of my grosser nature. The room is filled with my finest dust, and, as gratings of me drop from the knives, they fall through the perforated surface of the tables into receptacles beneath. When I am small enough, I am bundled up, carried away in baskets, and stowed in immense binns, until they want me in the Boiling-Room.

The Boiling-Room has enormous cauldrons in it, each with its own big lid, hanging to the beams of the roof, and put on by machinery when it is full. It is a very clean place, "coddled" by much boiling, like a washerwoman's fingers, and looks as if the kitchen of the Parish Union had gone into partnership with the Church Belfry. Here, I am pressed, and squeezed, and jammed, a dozen feet deep, I should think, into my own particular cauldron; where I simmer, boil, and stew, a long, long time. Then, I am a dense, tight mass, cut out in pieces like so much clay – very clean – faint as to my colour – greatly purified – and gradually becoming quite ethereal.

In this improved condition, I am taken to the Cutting-Room. I am very grateful to the clear fresh water, for the good it has done me; and I am glad to be put into some more of it, and subjected to the action of large rollers filled with transverse knives, revolving by steam power upon iron beds, which favour me with no fewer than two million cuts per minute, though, within the memory of man, the functions of this machine were performed by an ordinary pestle and mortar. Such a drumming and rattling, such a battering and clattering, such a delight in cutting and slashing, not even the Austrian part of me ever witnessed before. This continues, to my great satisfaction, until I look like shaving lather; when I am run off into chambers underneath, to have my friend the water, from whom I am unwilling to be separated, drained out of me.

At this tune, my colour is a light blue, if I have indigo in me, or a pale fawn, if I am rags from which the dyes have been expelled. As it is necessaiy to bleach the fawn-coloured pulp (the blue being used for paper of that tint), and as I *am* fawn-coloured pulp, I am placed in certain stone chambers, like catacombs, hermetically sealed, excepting the first compartment, which communicates with a gasometer containing manganese, vitriol, and salt. From these ingredients, a strong gas (not agreeable, I must say, to the sense of smell) is generated, and forced through all the chambers, each of which communicates with the other. These continue closed, if I remember right, some four-and-twenty hours, when a man opens them and takes to his heels immediately, to avoid the offensive gas that rushes out. After I have been aired a little, I am again conveyed (quite white now, and very spiritual indeed) to some more obliging rollers upstairs.

At it these grinders go, "Munch, munch, munch!" like the sailor's wife in MACBETH, who had chesnuts in her lap. I look, at first, as if I were the most delicious curds and whey; presently, I find that I am changed to gruel – not thin oatmeal gruel, but rich, creamy, tempting, exalted gruel! As if I had been made from pearls, which some voluptuous Mr. Emden had converted into groats!

And now, I am ready to undergo my last astounding transformation, and be made into paper by the machine. Oh what can I say of the wonderful machine, which receives me, at one end of a long room, gruel, and dismisses me at the other, paper!

Where is the subtle mind of this Leviathan lodged? It must be somewhere – in a cylinder, a pipe, a wheel – or how could it ever do with me the miracles it does! How could it receive me on a sheet of wire-gauze, in my gruel-form, and slide me on, gradually assuming consistency – gently becoming a little paper-like, a little more, a little more still, very paper-like, indeed – clinging to wet blankets, holding tight by other surfaces, smoothly ascending Witney hills, lightly coming down into a woolly open country, easily rolling over and under a planetary system of heated cylinders, large and small, and ever growing, as I proceed, stronger and more paper-like! How does the power that fights the wintry waves on the Atlantic, and cuts and drills adamantine slabs of metal like cheese, how does it draw me out, when I am frailest and most liable to tear, so tenderly and delicately, that a woman's hand – no, even though I were a man, very ill and helpless, and she my nurse who loved me – could never touch me with so light a touch, or with a movement so unerring! How can I believe, even on experience, that, being of itself insensible, and only informed with intellect at second hand, it changes me, in less time than I take to tell it, into any sort of paper that is wanted, dries me, cuts me into lengths, becomes charged, just before dismissing me, with electricity, and gathers up the hair of the attendant-watcher, as if with horror at the mischiefs and desertions from the right, in which I may be instrumental! Above all, how can I reconcile its being mere machinery, with its leaving off when it has cut me into sheets, and NOT conveying me to the Excise-man in the next room, whom it plainly thinks a most unnatural conclusion!

I am carried thither on trucks. I am examined, and my defective portions thrown out, for the Mill, again; I am made up into quires and reams; I am weighed and excised by the hundredweight; and I am ready for my work. Of my being made the subject of nonsensical defences of Excise duty, in the House of Commons, I need say nothing. All the world knows that when the Right Honourable the Chancellor of the Exchequer, for the time being, says I am only the worse by a duty of fifteen shillings per hundredweight, he is a Wrong Honourable, and either don't know, or don't care, anything about me. For, he leaves out of consideration all the vexatious, depressing, and preventing influences of Excise Duty on any trade, and all the extra cost and charge of packing and unpacking, carrying and re-carrying, imposed upon the manufacturer, and of course upon the public. But we must have it, in future, even with Right Honourables as with birds. The Chancellor of the Exchequer that can sing, and won't sing, must be made to sing – small.

My metamorphosis ends with the manufacture. I am rags no more, but a visitor to the Paper-Mill. I am a pleased visitor to see the Mill in such beautiful order, and the workpeople so thriving; and I think that my good friend the owner has reason for saying with an agreeable smile, as we come out upon the sparkling stream again, that he is never so contented, as when he is in rags.

Shining up in the blue sky, far above the Paper-Mill, a mere speck in the distance, is a Paper Kite. It is an appropriate thing at the moment – not to swear by (we have enough of that already) but to hope by, with a devout heart. May all the Paper that I sport with, soar as innocently upward as the paper kite, and be as harmless to the holder as the kite is to the boy! May it bring, to some few minds, such fresh associations; and to me no worse remembrances than the kite that once plucked at my own hand like an airy friend. May I always recollect that paper has a mighty Duty, set forth in no Schedule of Excise, and that its names are love, forbearance, mercy, progress, scorn of the Hydra Cant with all its million heads!

So, back by the green lanes, and the old Priory – a farm now, and none the worse for that – and away among the lime-trees, thinking of Sir John.

37

IMAGE: WALLPAPER

The Art Journal Illustrated Catalogue: The Industry of All Nations
(London, 1851) pp. 129, 143

Figure 37.1

DOI: 10.4324/9781315400105-44

Figure 37.2

38

HARRIET MARTINEAU, 'HOUSEHOLD SCENERY'

Household Words, Vol. 5
(14 August 1852), pp. 513–519

MOST people amuse themselves, at one time or other of their lives, by fancying what sort of house they would like to live in; what sort of house they would build for themselves, if they had opportunity for that very charming amusement. But the last thing that people seem to have any thought about is the walls of their rooms. Yet, what is there that we see so much of as the walls of the rooms we live in? Even those who have the blessing of a country residence – those even who dwell in one of the very few remaining parsonages in the North of England, where a spacious porch shelters the house-door from draughts and driving rains, and who resort to that porch, looking out upon a meadow or a flower-garden, – even these have to sit between four walls for at least three-fourths of the year; and certainly always to sleep within them. It is all very well to revel in fine views from terrace or window; but it is well, also, to consider what our eyes shall rest upon in all times of sickness, of bad weather, and when the sun is below the horizon. It is a charming speculation to a man about to build a house for his own residence, to plan what it shall look like externally – how many rooms it shall have, and how they shall be most conveniently arranged; but the aspect of the four walls of each room is worth mature consideration too. In old times, people thought more of this matter than we do, if we may judge by the pains taken to decorate the interior of ancient buildings; and those who attend to the signs of civilisation assure us that there will be a revival of such thought and pains – and very soon. Let us hope that this is true.

Tapestry hangings, those curtain-coverings for walls, are perhaps the most objectionable of all modes of decorating apartments.

This is downright heresy, no doubt, in the eyes of those who make the pursuit of tapestry an idolatry. Nobody doubts the vast amount of pains and care spent on tapestry as an art. Nobody doubts the skill which so directed the shuttle or the needle as that they rivalled the pencil and the brush in their delineations. In fact, no art could be despised which employed the talents of the greatest painters; and while the cartoons of Raffaelle are associated in our minds with tapestry hangings, it is impossible to speak with disrespect of such a representative of the art of a past

DOI: 10.4324/9781315400105-45

century. But we may be glad that it belonged to a past century, and that the present has done with tapestry. It might be necessary, in the days of imperfect building, to keep out draughts. King Alfred might have been glad of it before he invented his lantern, and when his candles were flaring and wasting so as to baffle him in his measurement of time by their burning; but we, in our tight houses, whose walls have no chinks and cracks, may better hang our apartments with clean, and light, and wholesome paper, which harbours no vermin, screens no thieves, and scares no fever patient with night-visions of perplexity and horror.

It was a great day when a Frenchman, bethought himself that, instead of hangings of wrought carpeting, or of velvet-flock, or stuff, a covering for walls might be made of figured paper – cheaper, lighter, cleaner – preferable in every way. It is said that this invention was made known in 1632, and that the first blocks used in making paper hangings are preserved in Paris. England followed so soon that there was some dispute as to which ought to have the credit of the invention, but it was doubtless due to France. James the First had lately given two thousand pounds – a large sum in those days – to encourage a manufacture of fine tapestry at Mortlake; but it was in a drawing-room of the Royal Palace at Kensington that the first specimen of English paper-hanging was seen. If anybody is curious to know whether that paper was like any that we see now, we can tell nothing more than that it was an imitation of the "velvet-flock" then in common use.

The "flock" order of paper seems to be: coming into fashion, more and more, after a long interval. Perhaps the truth is, that the reduction of the duty on paper hangings puts a higher class of papers within reach of a greater number of householders. Sir Robert Peel took off tenpence out of the shilling a yard duty on French paper hangings, which, before 1842, kept good decorations out of the reach of all but the wealthy. We remember the time – somewhere about 1818 – when stencilling came into fashion, and was thought a great, popular boon. Stencilling was done by splashing walls with colour through the interstices of tin patterns. The result was, a very coarse and untidy decoration of white-washed walls; the colours being bad, and the pattern never accurately made out for many consecutive feet of wall. But the work was so much cheaper than paper hangings, that people of small means were very glad of it; and, even in gentlemens' houses, the attics and servants' rooms were often thus coloured. Now, we seldom hear of stencilling; for papers of a tolerable quality and really good pattern may be had for less than a penny a yard, so that the abodes of the humble present a very different appearance now from any thing that could be seen even ten years ago. As for the taking off the duty, the story is the same that Free-traders are almost tired of telling about other articles. There were dismal prophecies that the French, who much excel us in the designs and preparations of paper hangings, would destroy the manufacture in England: and the wealthy did supply themselves – and perhaps do so still – almost exclusively from Paris; but, so much more extensively are paper hangings used, and so great is the improvement continually taking place through the emulation of the French by our manufacturers, that the manufacture is largely and steadily increasing. It only remains now to get the duty removed from the raw material, the paper, to give every body a fair chance of a neat set of walls to his dwelling-rooms, decorated according to his means.

Perhaps there are no gayer walls to be seen anywhere – in our country at least – than those we saw yesterday, on the premises of Her Majesty's Paper-stainer for Scotland, Mr. Wm. McCrie. This gentleman's walls – even the rough walls in the yards and passages – are as good as a rainbow for colours. The boys empty their brushes on the space next at hand, to save the trouble of washing them; and the result is a show which would make a little child – with its love of brilliant colours – scream for joy. There are things to be seen at Mr. McCrie's, which may please elderly people as much as rainbow hues can gratify a child. By means of studying there the process of paper-staining from beginning to end, glimpses are obtained into all classes of homes, from the Queen's palace, and the student's library, and aristocratic clubhouses, down to the humble abode of two or three rooms in town or country.

The paper used in this manufacture is made in Scotland, whence it is sent to England and Ireland, where more of the staining goes on than in Scotland. Mr. McCrie's establishment near Edinburgh, and one in Glasgow, are the only ones north of the Tweed. For ordinary patterns, the Scotch paper is about two feet wide. The French are narrower – a circumstance which should be remembered, when the cost of hangings is reckoned by the piece. Some of the granite papers for halls and staircases, and panel papers are of greater and various width. The pieces, of twelve yards, are tied up in bundles of ten; so that a bundle contains one hundred and twenty yards. The first thing that is done with the contents of a bundle, when it is untied, is to fit it for receiving a pattern by covering it smoothly and evenly with a coat of Paris white, or tint, for the ground, made of sulphate of lime and water, with size, which forms in fact a cement, and sets the pattern. This Paris white arrives from Hull and Leith: the size is made on the premises, as the observer's nose informs him; and in the yard, he sees the bundles of buffalo skins from which it is made, and the cauldron in which they are boiled. No part of the business is more serious than that of the preparation of the size – both for making the pattern on the paper, and for attaching the hanging to the wall. The size made in hot weather is never good; it runs, and the pattern is blotchy in places; and for this mischief there is no remedy. If the production must go on, without waiting for cooler weather, the patterns must suffer, and the sellers must have patience. A much more serious consideration for householders and decorators is, that none but the best size should be used for attaching the paper to the walls. Many a fever has been caused by the horrible nuisance of corrupt size used in paper-hanging in bed-rooms. The nausea which the sleeper is aware of on waking in the morning, in such a case should be a warning needing no repetition. Down should come the whole paper at any cost or inconvenience; for it is an evil which allows of no tampering. The careless decorator will say that time will set all right – that the smell will go off – that airing the room well in the day, and burning some pungent thing or other at night, in the meantime, will do very well. It will not do very well; for health, and even life may be lost in the interval. It is not worth while to have one's stomach impaired for life, or one's nerves shattered, for the sake of the cost and trouble of papering a room, or a whole house, if necessary. The smell is not the grievance, but the token of the grievance. The grievance is animal putridity, with which we are shut up, when this smell is perceptible in our chambers. Down should come the paper; and the wall behind should be scraped clear of every particle of its last covering. It is astonishing that so lazy a practice as that of putting a new paper over an old one should exist to the extent it does. Now and then an incident occurs which shows the effect of such absurd carelessness.

Not long ago, a handsome house in London became intolerable to a succession of residents, who could not endure a mysterious bad smell which pervaded it when shut up from the outer air. Consultations were held about drains, and all the particulars that could be thought of, and all in vain. At last, a clever young man, who examined the house from top to bottom, fixed his suspicions on a certain room, where he inserted a small slip of glass in the wall. It was presently covered, and that repeatedly, with a sort of putrid dew. The paper was torn down; and behind it was found a mass of old papers, an inch thick – stuck together with their layers of size, and exhibiting a spectacle which we will not sicken our readers by describing. A lesser evil, but still a vexatious one, may be mentioned here: that when there is not alum enough in the size, it will not hold. A family, sitting around a table, at dinner or at work, does not relish the incident of the entire papering of the room coming down at once, with a tearing, crashing sound, and a cloud of dust. Worse still is the trouble, when it is the pattern of the paper that is affected. A room was very prettily hung, not long ago, with a paper where a bright green trail of foliage was the most conspicuous part of the pattern. Day after day everything in the room was found covered with a green dust; and the pattern on the wall faded in proportion. The size had, in fact, been insufficient to fix the green powder, one ingredient of which, by the way, was arsenic. The decorator, being sent for, saw at once what was the matter, and, with expressions of shame and concern, pulled down the pretty paper, and put up another without charge – While on the subject of the mistakes that may be made in paper-hanging, we may mention one for which the householder is answerable, and not the manufacturer or decorator. While we are well, we ought to remember that we, and those belonging to us, shall some time or other be ill: and it is just as well to arrange the sleeping-rooms of our houses so as to give every advantage to invalids, when the day of sickness comes. It is of no consequence to the healthful, perhaps, how their beds stand; but it may make the difference to a sick person, of fever or tranquillity, of sleep or no sleep, whether his bed stands, as it should do, north and south, or east and west; and whether the window is opposite the foot of the bed, or in some less annoying direction. In the same way we may never think of the pattern on the wall of our room, while we go to bed only to sleep and rise the moment we awake; but it is certain that delirium in fever cases has been precipitated, and that frightful visions, or teasing images, have been excited by fantastic patterns on chintz bed-curtains, or on the hangings of the walls. The paper for bed-rooms should be of a rather light colour, and of a pattern as indefinite as can be had. For our part, we like nothing so well as a blank paper of some pleasant hue, with a dark border for a relief: but there are many papers now which do not present any of the everlasting forms and varieties of the square, the circle, and the diamond. A watered paper, or any trailing pattern is objectionable, because the eye of the invalid will trace human profiles in them. There are patterns in abundance which are pretty enough in a humble way – consisting of an aggregate of various small figures – so small and so various as to create nothing to the eye but a pleasantly-broken colour.

Having delivered our conscience of this admonition, out of the doctoring and sick-nursing part of our experience, we may return to our paper-staining.

The laying on the Paris white is done by a machine. The wet whiting is thrown into a trough, where it is licked up by a cylinder, which daubs it on a cylindrical brush, which transfers it to another cylinder, under which the paper is drawn, receiving the plaster as it goes. A wide brush, like a fringe of soft bristles, is fixed before the last cylinder, and sweeps the paper as the long sheet passes on, distributing the coating evenly, and smoothing the surface. The paper, in lengths of twelve yards, is drawn out by little boys, who carry it over little heaps of sticks, lifting up a stick, and of course the wet paper with it, and hoisting both on a pole, so that the paper can be carried to the drying place without being touched by human hands. Two boys thus carry away a piece in four folds, which of course do not touch each other. The lads, with their poles, lay the sticks across horizontal poles at some height from the ground; and there, still untouched, hangs the paper to dry.

If a polished ground is wanted, the paper – duly prepared by a chemical process in the open air – is rubbed with a lump of French chalk; then, with a surface of felt or flannel, and finally with a polishing brush; and from this treatment it comes out with a burnish like satin. The paper, with a polished or a dead ground, is now ready to receive the pattern.

There are three ways of giving it a pattern – by a printing machine, by block printing, and by marbling by hand. It appears that one machine does the work of about four block printers; that two persons may prepare the paper for fifteen printing tables; and that fifty workmen can, by great diligence, turn out three thousand pieces (of twelve yards each) per week. They are paid by the piece – from twenty-pence to two shillings per score, and a workman can easily earn from thirty to thirty-five shillings per week. The business is carried on in large airy rooms, and although much activity and strength of eye, foot, and hand are required for joining the pattern, lifting the heavy block, and stamping it, there is no pernicious fatigue, or perilous liability of any kind. It is altogether a favourable and fortunate kind of employment for a good workman.

In one part of the premises abides the designer, educated now, generally speaking, at one of our schools of design. He watches the French; he watches the English; he watches nature; and draws ideas from all for his patterns. Star patterns are eternal in popular favour; and so are lobby patterns – granites and marbles; but beyond these, all is uncertainty. A new set of designs must be made every year; and if a pattern does not pay its cost the first year, it never will. It may not be utterly lost, but it will never be remunerative. In one of the lower rooms at Mr. McCrie's, we trod upon wealth in a truly magnanimous manner. The floor was laid with obsolete blocks; and thus we trampled on many hundred pounds' worth of property.

The blocks are a pretty sight, from the beginning, when the block-cutter traces his pattern from oil paper upon the wood, and taps his chisel, sending it down to a certain depth in the wood (pine), and then clears out the spaces, up to the funeral ceremony of laying these memorials of departed fashions in the ground; that is, in the floor. Where little bits of the wood are broken away, they are supplied with brass or copper. The blocks for granite papers are stuck all over "with everything that will make a mark," as we were told; with odds and ends of copper and brass, and with common nail-heads. For the printing machine, the block is cylindrical, the process being just that of cylinder-printing of any kind. For the printing tables, the blocks are furnished with a strap at the back, to receive the workman's hand, and they are pressed down on the paper by a mallet driven by the workman's foot. Every time that he applies the block, he dips it on the surface of a stiff liquid in a trough by his side – the liquid being either the colour he wants to impress, or the oil which is to catch and retain the colour to be afterwards shed over it. For the best sort of gilding, gold leaf is applied: for the commoner gilding, bronze powder; for flock papers, the flock which is brought from the wool districts. The flock is wool, dyed of various colours, and reduced to powder, If the size or oil on which it is deposited be good, the flock cannot be rubbed off, or removed by any means short of scratching. The array of crimson flock papers is really superb in our day. One never tires of gazing at them in an establishment like this, and fancying how each would look in one's own study or dining-room. Of all charming rooms in a middle class house, the most bewitching, perhaps, is a library lined almost throughout with books, with the spaces between papered with a rich crimson flock paper, and affording room, between the book-cases, for a pedestal here and there, with a bust, or a good cast upon it, surmounted by a very few choice prints. The crimson makes a glorious ground for prints.

The workman has not always dismissed his piece when he has printed it from end to end. It may be a pattern of two colours, or of six, or even of twelve; and for each colour a fresh block and a fresh process are required, each repetition of course reckoning as a new piece in regard to his wages. The workman who does his work wholly by hand, he who marbles papers for lobbies and stair-walls, has also to go over it several times. The yellow polished ground is supplied to him ready for his brush. He veins it with a camel hair brush, dipped in a dark colour. One cannot but admire the decision with which he makes his strokes, and groups his veinings. We should stand hesitating which way to make our pencil wander, doubting whether we were making anything like marble; but the accustomed stainer wields his brush with as much purpose and decision as we do the pen, knowing as well where to go and wherefore. When he has thus veined a certain portion, he sprinkles, by jerking a brush, little drops of soap and turpentine, which make blotches, and give a marbled appearance to the whole surface. The coloured streaks, being diluted, spread into a perfect resemblance of the veins of marble; and nothing remains but to daub some white blotches into the centres of the groups of streaks. Of all the imitation papers this appeared to us the most perfect. The granite was good, with its glittering "frosting" which frosting is done by scattering, very sparingly, particles of the thinnest possible glass from the glass-houses. The graining of oak papers is done by putting an iron comb in the place of the smoothing brush, when the paper receives its first coat.

Among the papers shown in the warehouse, where the completed goods are deposited, the most beautiful in our eyes was a broad panelled paper of white, watered with a panel border of roses. We looked in vain for the sort of hanging which we must think will be in demand ere long; a hanging which, being dark near the floor, becomes gradually lighter towards the ceiling. At present, decorators depend on a dark carpet and a light ceiling to give the effect indicated by decorative principle and required by a trained eye, some aid being given by a dark skirting board, and a cornice of light and bright colours; but there seems to be no reason why the hangings on the walls should not do their part, and there can be no doubt that a wide new range of design would be opened by following out this principle.

What we owe to the designers of good paper hangings can hardly be estimated by those who have not travelled in countries which assume to be highly civilised, but have no time to get things done in the best manner. Even at home, and in good houses, one meets occasionally with a mistake in the choice of a pattern: a mistake which causes irritation and annoyance to the visitor, from hour to hour; as when a pattern, which is everything that could be wished in the single breadth, gives birth to an imperfect form when joined with the next breadth; a diamond, for instance, which turns out a little smaller on one side than the other, or a curve which is not freely carried out. But in some parts of the United States, among other places, where money is not spared in decorating dwellings, but workmen are scarce and ill-qualified, one sees extraordinary spectacles on the walls of good houses. We were once standing in perplexed contemplation of our chamber wall, when our hostess entered, and told us how vexed she had been about it. She had employed an emigrant paper-hanger, who had passed himself off as a first-rate workman. She gave him the papers, and left him to his work. In a wonderfully short time, he came to her, exulting: he had done the job – capitally – he would say that for himself; he had "made every crease show." And so he had – with the most perverse ingenuity – by now spoiling the pattern, and now leaving a white thread of space between the breadths. There was no upholsterer's store within many miles, and therefore no remedy. Our hostess was English, and annoyed accordingly. The Americans care less for such things, or do not even discover them, unless the blemish is very flagrant. We remember a curious instance of this difference between the American, and the English eye, which met our notice as far off as Lexington in Kentucky. We were taken, of course, to the Senate Chamber at Lexington – merely our own party – to see the room. A picture over the President's chair hanging awry, we naturally stepped upon a bench which stood below, and set it right with a touch; after which the party went home, to one of the best houses in the neighbourhood, where a young Englishman of rank and a Mr. Clay were to join us at dinner. Our hostess and her guests fell into conversation about furnishing drawing-rooms, and attention was drawn to the paper of the handsome room we were sitting in. All admired it; but we observed on the oddity of the workman having put up two breadths, in different parts of the room, upside down. The hostess laughingly doubted it, had never heard of it, could not see it now: would ask the young Englishman, and see if any body thought so but ourselves. Presently came a Mr. Moat with Mr. Clay. Mr. Moat was asked to look round the room, and say if he saw any blemish anywhere. He glanced round, and pointed to the two breadths that were topsyturvy, to the amusement of the good-humoured hostess, who said the English eye was something past her comprehension. Upon this, Mr. Clay related that he had just been taking Mr. Moat to see the Senate Chamber, and that he had mounted a bench to set straight a map which he declared to be hung awry, though nobody else could see it. The laugh was now louder than ever; and then followed a discussion whether it was a privilege or a misfortune to be so particular as we English had proved ourselves. Perhaps we should suffer more from our particularity in a new country than the thing is worth; but we should be sorry to lay it aside at home.

The omnipresent gutta-percha is among the paper hangings already. It presents itself in the form of consolation to the owners of houses which are cursed with a damp wall or corner. As for a generally damp house, one has only to quit it, if one has ever been foolish enough to go into it. But there are many excellent houses with some faulty bit – some corner or projection which got wet in the building, and could never be got dry; and here comes in the gutta-percha paper most consolingly. The housewife may have rubbed, and warmed, and dried, with toil and pain, every summer; but in winter, the stains come again, and, towards spring, the green moss. She may have battened that end or corner; but then, there was the uneasy thought that the damp and the moss were growing behind the screen. In case of damp from driving rains, in exposed situations, it may be true that there is nothing like a mantle of ivy, under whose leaves dry dust may be found at the end of the wettest winter. But, if the damp be incurred in the process of building, the ivy is not the appropriate cure; and besides, it takes some years to cover the end of a house. The gutta-percha paper confines the damp within the wall, at least, and compels it to evaporate externally, if at all. It thoroughly intercepts, if it cannot cure, a very great evil; and it will, no doubt, be in extensive use till all men are too sensible to have any damp corners in their houses at all.

39

'CARDBOARD'

Tomlinson's Cyclopaedia of useful arts and manufactures, Vol. 2, ed. Charles Tomlinson (London: George Virtue, 1852–1854), pp. 321–324

CARDBOARD. The manufacture of the cardboard which is used for playing cards and for address cards, contains a number of interesting processes, which we will describe in the order in which we recently witnessed them at the house of Messrs. Sabine, Poppin's Court, Fleet Street.

Cardboard consists of a number of thicknesses of paper pasted together, pressed and polished on the two surfaces. Ordinary cardboard consists of two sheets of white paper with a sheet of cartridge paper between them, and the thickness of the board is determined by the stoutness of the paper. For stout cards two or more sheets of cartridge paper are interposed. *Bristol-board*, which is used in sketching, is formed of two or more thicknesses of white paper only. Hence cardboards are known as *three-sheet, four, six*, or *eight-sheet* boards, either *white* or *coloured.* The outer surfaces may be white, blue, green, lavender, or pink, &c., the colours being produced by two outer surfaces of coloured paper. *Enamelled* cards are produced by a process which will be described presently.

For the sake of simplicity we will confine our attention to the manufacture of three-sheet board. The arranging of the paper for this is called *mingling*. That is, a ream of white demy paper is spread open, and between every two sheets, one sheet of cartridge paper is placed; and the pile when complete is called a *head*, consisting, of course, of a ream and a half of paper.

The next process is *pasting*. A man stands at a bench with a mahogany slab before him, the head of paper on his left hand, and a large tub of paste on his right. The paste-brush resembles the broom part of a long-handled hair broom. The operations are conducted as follows: – Pulling the first sheet from the head upon the mahogany slab with his left hand, the paster with his large brush saturated with thin smooth paste covers it with a layer by two or three skilful movements of the hand and arm. He then pulls down upon this pasted surface a sheet of cartridge paper, the top surface of which is in like manner pasted. He next pulls down upon the pasted cartridge surface *two* sheets of white paper, and covers the upper

DOI: 10.4324/9781315400105-46

surface only with paste. One sheet of cartridge paper is pulled down upon this and pasted; then two sheets of white paper, and so on until the whole head has been pasted. Now it is obvious that by pulling down two sheets of white paper upon a pasted surface, and then covering the upper surface of these two sheets with paste, two contiguous surfaces will be left unpasted, and these form the boundary between every two sheets of cardboard. One man will paste 4 heads of paper, or 7 gross of cardboards, in one day. This will consume about 14 lbs. or 16 lbs. of flour, reckoning 1 lb. of flour equal to 1 gallon of paste. It is not usual to damp the paper previously to pasting, unless papers are brought together which will not *marry*, as in the case of a hard hand-made paper, and a softer and more equable machine-made paper. In such a case the paper must be previously damped in order that the pasted surfaces may properly unite.

When the head has been pasted, it is put into an upright press, and condensed by the action of a well-oiled iron screw, and a long iron lever worked by two men. The water of the paste oozes out at the edges of the head, and falling into a channel in the lower bed of the press, escapes through a hole into a bucket, which becomes entirely filled with clear water from the produce of one man's work in the course of one day.

The next process is *drying*. Every evening before the men leave off work, each man takes out of the press the heads which he has pasted during the day, and placing one of the short sides of the heap before him, he pierces the boards close to the edge with a couple of holes. Then taking up two of the cardboards, he passes a piece of soft copper wire, about 1½ inch long, furnished with a little square of cardboard at one extremity, into each hole. In this way he goes on piercing and threading until the four heads are thus prepared. They are then taken to the drying-rooms, where a number of lines are stretched across near the ceiling, and bending the copper wires into the form of a hook, the boards are thus hung in pairs on the lines to dry. The room is heated artificially, and in the course of twenty-four hours, that is, on the next evening when the lines are wanted for the next day's work, the boards are sufficiently dry. On giving every pair a pull, the soft copper wire straightens, and releases them from the line. They are then separately brushed with a hair brush to remove any dust, &c.

The boards are now rough on the surface, warped and uneven. They are made smooth and even by passing them between a couple of powerful iron rollers in contact with thin sheets of smooth copper plate. The rollers very much resemble those used in bookbinding, and in order that the cardboards may be passed through the rollers square or without overlapping each other, they are placed in a three-sided frame very much like a small dinner tray with the front side left out. A cardboard is first placed in this frame, and upon it a sheet of copper, not quite so large as the board, then another cardboard, then a second sheet of copper, and so on alternately until about a dozen cardboards and as many sheets of copper have been piled up. The bottom roller is furnished with a handle and a fly wheel. The upper roller is movable upon a horizontal axis. A boy is kept turning the handle, and a man takes the pile from the frame and passes it between the rollers, and as soon as it gets within their grip, the resistance is too great for the boy to overcome. The man therefore takes hold of one of the radii of the fly wheel, and pulls it round; the pile passes through, and is received by a boy on the other side; who passes it over the top roller, and the man sends it a second time, and in some cases a third and a fourth time through the rollers. The effect of this rolling is very remarkable. The rough uneven cardboard is converted into a perfectly even board with a beautifully polished glazed surface. Each surface has in fact taken an impression of the smooth, hard, rigid surface of the copper plates, a species of *surface printing*, as simple in its operation as it is successful in its results. The rollers and copper plates are cold, but after passing through the rollers two or three times, the cardboards become sensibly warm to the touch in consequence of the enormous compression to which they have been subjected. While the rolling is going on, two boys are preparing another pile, and when one pile has been rolled, another boy takes out the sheets of copper and arranges the cardboards in a heap.

The cards are now ready for the *stenciller* if they are to be formed into playing cards, or for cutting up into sizes if for address cards. For the latter purpose there are various sizes known in the trade, such as *ladies' size, gentleman's size, trade-card size*, &c. The *large size* card is a parallelogram measuring 4 inches by 3 inches; *one-third large* or *gentleman's size*, is 3 in. by 1½ in.; *ladies' size* is 2¼ in. by 8¼ in. Then we have *large thirds*, 3 in. by 2¼ in.; *outsides*, also called *Cobourg, Town size* or *thirds, extra broad thirds, reduced half large*, all referring to a card which measures 3 in. by 2 in. Then there is *half large*, 3 in. by 2¼ in.

The cardboards are first cut into lengths or long strips 4 inches or 3 inches wide, according to the size required. These strips are then cut up with wonderful celerity into cards of one or other of the above dimensions. The cutting is performed by means of an apparatus very similar to the board-cutting machine described under Bookbinding, (Fig. 172, p. 157.) The cards are lastly tied up in packets ready for the copper-plate printer.

The enamelled surface of address cards is produced by means of a very pure variety of white lead, known as *China white, Krems*, or *Kremnitz white*, and *Silver white*. [See Lead.] It is imported into this country in cakes or lumps made up in sealed packets. This substance is stirred up with pure water containing fine sise, made from parchment cuttings boiled down, and rubbed through a sieve by the hand (a most dangerous practice), in order to reduce it to a state of minute mechanical division, and to separate any gritty particles. This mixture is brushed in a thin layer over one surface of the cardboards by means of a large *flat* and closely-set brush, and it is smoothed off by a circular brush made of badgers' hair, which leaves the enamel colour free from streaks or marks. The cardboards are then placed upon a rack to dry, and in the course of an hour or two, when all trace of moisture has disappeared, the dead white surface produced by the white lead is wrought into a glossy enamel by a very remarkable process. A piece of flannel dipped into the powder of talc (a silicate of magnesia) is rubbed lightly over the surface of the cardboard, the object apparently being to supply every portion thereof with a polishing material. If the flannel were rubbed with much pressure, the already dead white surface would remain so; but when the powder is once applied a strong pressure may be used, and this is given by means of a close-set brush similar to a scrubbing brush, the continued rubbing of which produces the well-known glossy enamelled surface. The great objection to this kind of card is its liability to turn black, the sulphur of the person or of the atmosphere, which is always present in minute quantities in the form of sulphuretted hydrogen, combining with the lead, and forming a sulphuret of that metal, the colour of which is black. On holding one of these cards in the flame of a candle metallic lead is produced in small beads.

Playing-cards are produced by the ancient art of *stencilling*, an art older, in Europe at least, than printing.[1] A stencil is a thin sheet of pasteboard, parchment, or metal, in which the outlines and general forms of the figures are cut out, for the purpose of being stencilled on cardboard or paper. By passing a brush charged with colour over the stencil, the colour enters into the *cut-out* lines, and imparts the figure to the material beneath. The *pips*, or common cards, require only one colour, either black or red; but the *têtes*, or court cards, require many colours. For the production of the former, a thin sheet of cardboard is divided into a number of spaces or parallelograms equal to the size of the playing-cards, and within the first of these spaces, exactly in the centre, the form of an ace, say of diamonds, is cut out; in the second space, a diamond is cut out, near the top and bottom; in the third space three diamonds, and so on up to the ten of diamonds. The stenciller places this stencil-plate upon one of the white cardboards, rolled and polished as above described, and holding it steady with his fingers, rubs in the colour with a large, heavy, circular brush, with closely-set bristles. A little of the colour, vermilion ground up with sise, is placed upon a board covered with parchment, and upon this the brush is worked until properly charged, and then it is worked upon the stencil with a rotatory dabbing sort of motion, until the forms are properly painted upon the card. For the court cards, several stencil-plates are used, one for each colour. Suppose the ground colour to be red. This goes over the cuffs, and belt, and coronet, and breeches of the knave; a stencil is then applied, which covers all the parts of the card except those which are to be painted yellow: in this stencil, therefore, the cut-out parts fall on the figure exactly where the yellow is to be produced, and this represents the gold lace, the jacket, &c.; a stencil is then applied, to allow of the application of the light brown which serves for the flesh colour; then another stencil for the dark brown that colours the hair: then there is a stencil for applying the light blue which forms orders of courtly dignities, baldrics, and shoe-strings. In this way the cardboards being covered with sets of cards, they are cut up in the same way as the address cards, and with such celerity, that a skilful workman can in two hours and a half cut up 200 packs, of 52 each, or 10,400 cards.

When the backs of the cards are ornamented with spots or small flowers, &c., these are printed in sheets from a stereotype plate, at a common hand-press, and the sheets are attached to the back of the card in the process of pasting.

The duty card, the ace of spades, is printed at the stamp-office, on sheets of thin paper, and supplied to the card-maker as he wants them. Each maker has his own plate, which is engraved at his expense by the Government authorities, and kept by them: he never being allowed even to see it. Each sheet containing aces is of course pasted to other sheets of paper, to make up the proper thickness. It forms the stamp of every pack of cards, and costs the purchaser one shilling. In cards for exportation, a drawback of the whole duty is allowed; in which case, the Stamp Office furnishes a different ace of spades, on which a notice is engraved, forbidding the use of such card in Great Britain and Ireland, under the penalty of 20*l*.

It does not appear, from the statements made to us by Mr. Sabine, that card-playing is on the decline. The export trade to the colonies is very large. Mr. Sabine frequently sends 500 dozen packs to one place, and there are other makers in the metropolis whose trade is equally large.

Cards are also produced by printing as well as by stencilling. In 1832, Mr. de la Rue took out a patent for improvements in manufacturing and ornamenting playing-cards; and since that date, other improvements have been introduced, some of which have been made the subject of patents. The following is a brief outline of the process as at present adopted: –

The polish which is communicated to ordinary paper by pressure merely is not sufficient to produce cards of the finest quality. The high finish which is afterwards imparted is produced by a previous preparation of white enamel mixed with size. For printing the pips, sets of blocks are prepared, each containing 40 engravings of one card; and as the ordinary method of letter-press printing is used, 40 impressions of one card are obtained at the same moment. As the pips are either black or red, they are worked at the hand-press, or at one of Cowper’s steam printing-machines. The têtes, however, contain five colours, including the outline, viz. dark blue, light blue, black, red, and yellow. These colours are printed separately from a series of blocks, which, if united, would form the intended figure complete: so that, by printing successively from these blocks, the colours fall into their proper places, each colour being made to *register* by means of points in the tympan of the press, or on the engraving.

The printing being completed, the sheets are left during three or four days in a room heated to about 80°, in order to fix the colours. It is of great importance to use such an ink as will not be liable to smear by repeated handling. The colours employed are prepared from the best French lamp-black, for the black, and Chinese vermilion, for the red. These are ground in oil by a machine consisting of cylinders revolving at regulated velocities.

The paper intended for the backs is tinted of the required colour, and printed in various devices by the hand-press or the steam-machine. The *plaid* or *tartan* backs are produced from a block engraved with straight lines, and printed in one colour, which is afterwards crossed with the same or any other colour by again placing the sheet on the block, so that the 2 sets of lines may cross at any required angle. Various other devices are produced by printing with blocks containing various patterns. In printing *gold backs*, size is used instead of ink: the face of the card is then powdered over with bronze-dust, and rubbed with a soft cotton dabber, by which the bronze is made to adhere to those parts only which have received the sise. The backs are also printed from wire woven into a variety of beautiful patterns: the wire is fastened at the ends by 2 pieces of wood, and stretched over a cast-iron block, to which it is fixed by screws. The printing is then conducted in the usual manner.

The pasting is performed after the printing. The printed sheets are either of double or single foolscap, and the cardboards are made 4 sheets thick; *i.e.* the front and the back, with 2 interior sheets of inferior quality. The paste is made as usual from flour and water, heated in a forty-gallon copper to the boiling-point by means of a steam-jacket: this prevents the paste from burning and acquiring a bad colour.

When the pasting is complete, a hydraulic press, of 100 tons, worked by a steam-engine, is used, to express the water from the paste. The cardboards are then hung up to dry, after which they are subjected to the pressure and friction of a brush-cylinder, in which the bristles are short and thick-set: these not only polish the surface, but penetrate into the interior. The best cards are waterproofed on the back at this stage with a varnish, to prevent them from being marked with the fingers in using. Such cards will bear washing without injury. The polishing is completed by passing the cardboards between rollers, one of iron and the other of paper, [see CALENDERING,] the former being kept moderately warm: they are then passed between 2 bright iron rollers, then milled between sheets of copper, as already described, and lastly flattened, by the pressure of a hydrostatic press of 800 tons. It has been found by experience that the beautiful polish, and perfect smoothness and flatness of these superior cards, can only be produced by a succession of processes, slow in action, and gradually increasing in power. Each cardboard is cut up as before described, first into 8 narrow slips, called *traverses*, each containing 5 cards: these are then cut up into single cards, to the amount of 30,000 daily. The cards, being properly sorted, are made up into packs, for which purpose a number of cards of the same name (probably 200) are arranged on a long table: these are then covered with other cards, and the process is repeated 52 times, with different cards, until the 200 packs are complete. They are then folded up in paper, and tied up. The best cards are known as *Moguls;* others are called *Harrys* and *Highlanders*.

Note

1 Mr. Chatto, in his ingenious and entertaining work on the "Origin and History of Playing-cards," (London, 1848,) says that in the oldest cards which he has had an opportunity of examining, and which appear to be of as early a date as the year 1440, the figures were evidently executed by means of a stencil. From the circumstance of so many women occurring as card-painters in the town books of Nuremberg, between 1433 and 1477, it seems probable that they were not wood-engravers, but stencillers. Mr. Chatto thus sums up the history of playing-cards: – "Admitting cards to be of Eastern invention – a fact which appears to be sufficiently established

by the evidence adduced in the first chapter – it would seem that they first became known in Europe as a popular game between 1360 and 1390. Covelluzzo, an Italian chronicler of the fifteenth century, says that the game was first brought into Viterbo in 1379; in 1393, three packs of cards were painted by Jacquemin Gringonnem for the amusement of Charles VI. of France; in 1397, the working people of Paris were forbid to play at cards on working days; and in the same year card-playing was prohibited by the magistrates of Ulm. Such are the principal facts relative to the introduction of cards into Europe. The game appears to have rapidly spread amongst all classes of people. The manufacture of cards was a regular business in Germany and Italy, prior to 1425; the importation of foreign cards into England was prohibited by Act of Parliament in 1463; and about 1484, cards, as at present, was a common Christmas game."

40

HARRIET MARTINEAU, 'HOW TO GET PAPER'

Household Words, Vol. 10 (28 October 1854), pp. 241–245

THERE never was such a country for variety as the United States. In all the great commercial countries of the world there is a collection of representatives from all nations who trade; but each country has a kind of uniformity about it which makes the various people collected within it appear – what indeed they are – foreigners. In the United States, the variety is, in addition to the aggregation of strangers, in the country itself, and in the people who inhabit it. To apprehend fully what the diversity is, perhaps no way is better than to survey the whole area, and see what the inhabitants are doing in any one particular, or how they are faring with regard to any one article of general use or convenience. We might observe on the nature of the dinner provided on any one day, from fishy Maine to sugary Louisiana, or the deserts where nothing is to be had but beef; or the forest clearings which yield nothing but corn. We might look in upon all the needlewomen of that continent, and see what dresses they are making, from the gossamer ball dress in Broadway to the leather fringes of the Potawatamies. But our attention happens to have been fixed – in the existing crisis of difficulty about the dearth of paper in England – on what the American people are writing and printing on, all through their thirty-one states and bordering territories.

In the more thickly inhabited parts of the United States the inhabitants use three times as much paper per head as we British do – three times as many pounds weight per head, even though the three millions of slaves are included, who cannot write or read. Except idiots, the blind, and slaves, everybody in that country reads and writes; and more persons appear in print than in any country since the alphabet was made. There, every child has its copy-book in its place at school. There, every log-house on the prairie has its shelf of books. Next to the church and the tavern, the printing-press is set up in every raw settlement; and a raw newspaper appears; probably on whity-brown paper, and in mixed type, with italics and Roman letters, capitals and diphthongs thrown together very curiously; but still – a newspaper. Books are printed in the great cities, not by the thousand or fifteen hundred, but by the five or ten thousand; for the readers are reckoned by millions. The Americans have cheapened their postage, as we have done; and the increase

DOI: 10.4324/9781315400105-47

of correspondence is in yet larger proportion, because families are more widely separated, and all are able to write. There is another reason for their larger consumption of paper (of a coarser kind than writing-paper) which is truly mortifying to us in England. There are manufactures in which we and they run so exactly abreast that neither can afford the slightest disadvantage in the sale without losing the market: our paper duty is a disadvantage; and we lose the market. The cost of the mere wrappers of a multitude of articles made at Birmingham and Sheffield precisely absorbs the profits to be obtained in African and Asiatic markets; and the Americans nearly sweep that market from us. Wanting all this paper, what do the Americans do to get it? This is a question of immense importance to us, because we cannot, by any means yet tried, get anything like enough paper; and the scarcity and dearness of it now constitute what may be called, without exaggeration, a national calamity. Our supply was short, the quality of our paper poor, and the price high, before the last doubling of our population; before the penny postage so immensely multiplied our population; before free trade expanded our commerce; before the advertisement duty was taken off. Now, while all this new demand is pressing upon us, and even the modified duty on paper remains, the injury to a multitude of minds and to a host of fortunes is so serious that we are impelled to the inquiry how it is that the Americans, with their threefold demand, get thoroughly well supplied.

We should add that we understate the truth when we call the consumption per head threefold. It is threefold by weight: but the Americans use a great deal of very thin paper, such as is rarely used by us. Consequently the threefold by weight could amount to hardly less than fourfold by surface. How is this vast quantity obtained?

Here again, in finding the answer to this question, we meet new evidence of the extraordinary variety of people and ways existing in the United States. A glance at the paper-makers of that country shows things as striking as our glance at the scribes round its outer circle. First, there is the great, the grand paper-manufacturer. His steam-engine puffs and pants like any other; his mills cover large spaces of ground; and his machinery is of the newest and best. One great difference between him and our manufacturers is, that he has the command of the world's rags, as far as they go, and of many substitutes, when there are no more rags. Our excise duty is such a burden on the manufacture that we cannot compete with him in the purchase of foreign rags; and he even comes here and buys up our precious tatters before our eyes. Another great difference between him and us is, that he can make any experiments he likes with new materials, at no other cost, in case of failure, than the partial loss of labour and material: whereas, we cannot try such experiments, because the excise authorities must claim the duty of from one hundred to three hundred per cent on all paper that is made, whether it turns out saleable or not. Our manufacture cannot improve, our mills cannot multiply, and the price of paper cannot come down, but must continue to rise, while that duty goes on to be levied. While our paper-makers are scolded by booksellers, authors, editors, printers, packers, and manufacturers, for the exorbitant price of their article, they are not growing rich, but very much the contrary. They are, in fact, the first victims of a monopoly which they have no desire whatever to preserve. Not only the duty makes the manufacture a monopoly, but the restrictions which attend the duty leave no freedom to any man's ingenuity or enterprise. So our manufacturers sink into low spirits, instead of rising into high fortunes, under the enormous prices of eighteen hundred and fifty-four. They are stormed by correspondents whom they cannot supply; they are scolded by customers for the amounts charged in their invoices; they pay a high price for material every month; the best kind of material becomes deficient; and if an inferior kind is used, down comes a deluge of complaints, to add to the sorrows of the involuntary monopolist, who is growing poor himself while giving satisfaction to nobody. He grows silent at his meals; he looks grave in the mill; he can hardly be civil to the excise collector; and he tells his wife after a vexatious day at the works, that he shall go to America. His American rival, meantime, is buying land, building houses, setting up his carriage; perpetually adorning his pattern-room with fresh specimens of paper of all colours; and often gratifying his customers with offers of a new article which makes a good substitute for one which is growing dearer.

What else do we see over there? Away from towns and steam engines, on some rapid near a new settlement in Ohio or Illinois, we see a humbler mill, worked by water-power. Here are no roods of drying-rooms for snow-white paper. There is not much snow-white paper made here, because the owner has not command of much material that will bear bleaching. In the sheds we see overhead all sorts of dingy hues; and in the packing-room a wide range of browns and yellows, with plenty of grays, and some greens and pinks. We never see such an assortment of tinted papers in England; where coloured paper is so little used that the Chancellor of the Exchequer might, as well as not, take off the duty from *coloured* papers.

This would cost the revenue a mere trifle, while it would be a vast boon to the public. Our American newspapers come to us in wrappers of brown and yellow, so tough, as never, by any accident, to arrive with the smallest rent in the edge, and bearing the ink as well as any paper whatever. This is made from the refuse of the Indian corn-plant. Our letters come to us in envelopes of pale yellow, gray, or green, – perfectly serviceable, and rather pretty than not. They are made of any one of half-a-dozen substances which have every good quality but that they will not bleach. The British manufacturers complain that we, their customers, are saucy about paper, and that we will use none but the whitest. We must have white envelopes, they say, a white surface for our washing bills, and snowy missives for the butcher and fishmonger. We, on the other hand, declare that we have never had a chance of showing a preference. Give us the option between white envelopes and tinted, at a difference of a few pence in the hundred, and see whether we do not buy the cheaper sort! But they are not to be had, and the reason why they are not to be had is that the excise will not allow experiments to be made, on fair conditions. We do not hesitate to say that the Chancellor of the Exchequer *must* repeal the duty on coloured papers at least, at the first possible moment. Prices are rising to an unendurable point; and so simple a palliative as setting free a portion of material that will bleach by a free use of that which will not, cannot be refused under the existing stress.

Let the government bear in mind that the increase in paper made in the kingdom within the last two years, under all the existing difficulties, is twenty-three million pounds; and that it would require, even at this rate, a dozen new average mills to be set up every year to meet the demands of the mere increase of our population; and they will see that the paper duty cannot be sustained.

What other variety do we see in our American survey? Is that a paper-mill on the banks of the Penobscot, in the midst of the forest clearings, far up in Maine? Yes, indeed, it is: and to whom do you suppose it belongs? An Englishman would never guess. It belongs to four or five lumberers (fellers and sellers of timber), who have put a part of their earnings into this form, and they believe they will not repent it. But why this form? Because paper is in increasing demand, and water-power and material are at hand. Here is the rushing river; here is the wood to build the mill of, and keep up the fires; and the metal work is easily got from the towns below; and the river is as good as a railway for carrying the paper to market. Well: but where are the rags? They do not use rags, except the few woollen ones that are bought up from Irish immigrants. Those, and some cotton-waste from the town-mills, are the only fibrous material of that sort used. The bulk of the substance required is on the spot, in the shape of marsh hay and wood shavings. Where there are clearings there are presently marshes; and where there are marshes, there is hay, too bad for the food of animals that are carefully treated. From this, from straw, from maize-stalks, from the shavings in the lumberers' sheds, together with a few Connaught tatters and sweepings of cotton-mills, our little company of speculators are making their fortunes. If they had not succeeded it would not have mattered much, because they put only as much of their earnings as they could well spare into the enterprise; for there is no unlimited liability of partnership there, to make a man risk his whole fortune in a partnership if he adventure the smallest fraction of it. And there is no exciseman, coming down upon them for eighty or ninety pounds a week, as his charge upon the six tons of paper which they send down the river weekly. If the English law and the English exciseman were there, there would be no mill on that spot on the Penobscot; there would be six tons of paper per week less in the market; and the partners would be making their fortunes at a much slower rate.

Turning from the extreme north to the south – even to the shores of the Gulf of Mexico – what do we find? There are negroes poking about in the swamps at the mouths of some of the great rivers. They twist about like water-snakes in the channels among the flowering reeds, gathering bundles of fibrous stalks; and they make themselves a way through acres of cane-brake, cutting the canes on either hand, to carry them to the paper-mill. The demand for paper must be pressing indeed to induce any one to set up a manufacture of it under the conditions of slave labour. But, before us lies at this moment a specimen of paper made from cane-brake. In colour it is a pretty good white, and in quality it is fair enough for all ordinary purposes. It would not do for the Queen's Speech. Macaulay would not write his History on it, nor Tennyson his lyrics; nor shall we order a stock of it for our next novel. But we should be glad to know that there was a supply of it in the next stationer's shop in the form of envelopes, large and small, and letter and note paper, so that we might do our part in saving the rags of the world.

About that saving – can none of us help in that way? Do any of us burn rags, or allow anybody under our roof to burn them? Never let such a thing happen again. Let the maids know that rags now fetch a pretty penny; and let them have a rag-bag as a regular part of the kitchen establishment. As for the parlour, the shop, the office – from the humblest tradesman's to the government bureau – do we not waste paper unconscionably? Is it not thought genteel and liberal to send as many blank pages as possible in an envelope? – to make our manuscript a rivulet of ink in wide banks of margin? This is foolish, and worse than foolish, when the evil is not merely dearness but scarcity. In a scarcity of flour, noblemen retrench their puddings and pastry, not because flour is dear, but because there is not enough, and the poor will be starved if the rich do not eat less of flour and more of other things. Thus it is with the present scarcity of rags. It is not meanness, but only justice to great social interests, if public men and rich men will enforce economy in the use of paper on all whom they can influence, until a remedy for the scarcity shall be found.

We do not insist very vehemently, or at great length, on this, because it is a minor matter. Any palliation from that method must be wholly insufficient for the occasion. It is good as far as it goes; but we must direct our exertions to obtain emancipation from two restrictions which are fatal to a fair supply of paper. Now that we are relieved of the soap and window duties, we must get rid of the paper duty – of the duty on coloured paper at all events, and of the whole if we can. We must also get rid of that unlimited liability in partnership which prevents ingenious men who are not rich, from placing their ingenuity at the public service; and which prevents men who are rich from devoting a sufficient portion of their capital, and no more, to rendering available the talent of the ingenious man.

41

ANON, 'CIGARETTE'

The London Journal and Weekly Record of Literature, Science, and Art (1 November 1869), p. 229

The cigarette

The Turkish is the most delicate and aromatic of all forms of the cigarette, but it is almost impossible to obtain them of good quality in this country. Even if you import the finest cut-tobacco, and procure the best of paper, there is something wanting in the flavour which it is difficult to describe. A cigarette on Mount Athos and a cigarette smoked in London may come from the same plant, but there will be a wide difference in the extent of the appreciation on the part of the smokers. There is no doubt the Turkish cigarette, made and smoked in the Mediterranean, is peculiar to the locality. The manner in which the leaf is cut by the native tobacco-cutter is primitive in the extreme. He sits on the ground, cross-legged, Turkish fashion, and placing a board on his knees, grasps a bundle of the assorted leaves, and proceeds to cut them with an unwieldy and awkward-looking knife. He uses this instrument with such dexterity that the tobacco falls away before him in delicate, silky flakes, cut with almost mathematical precision, and even more perfectly than if cut with an ordinary tobacco engine. Another important element in the preparation of the Turkish cigarette is the paper, and connoisseurs are often perplexed to procure a kind that shall answer their purpose. It should be light, yet tough, free from odour, and as nearly tasteless as possible. A good cigarette paper is one of the problems of the cigarette maker; and, like many other apparently simple matters, is extremely difficult of solution. The number of papers made by way of experiment and for sale may be reckoned by hundreds, and yet it would be hazardous to say that a first-rate cigarette paper can be obtained.

DOI: 10.4324/9781315400105-48

PART 3

Metal goods

3.1

Pins and needles

DOI: 10.4324/9781315400105-50

3.1 Pins and needles

Anon, 'Pin-Making (from Sir George Head's Home Tour)', *The Mirror*, Vol. 28 (9 July 1836), pp. 29–30.

Anon, 'A Second Day at the Birmingham Factories', *Penny Magazine of the Society for the Diffusion of Useful Knowledge*, Vol. 13 (28 December 1844), pp. 501–502.

Harriet Martineau, 'Needles', *Household Words*, Vol. 4 (28 February 1852), pp. 540–546.

Anon, 'Pins', *Belgravia: A London Magazine*, Vol. 6 (August 1868), pp. 300–302.

A. L. O. E., *The Story of a Needle* (London: T. Nelson and Sons, 1874), pp. 7–10.

'Needles' in *The Century Dictionary and Cyclopedia*, Vol. V. (New York: The Century Co., 1895) p. 3956.

The sources in this section reveal that pins and needles were both industrial and domestic objects, which could be pressed to ideological uses. Pins and needles characterised feminine industriousness, while the enormous quantities produced each year indicated Victorian Britain's might in manufacturing. Four of the five sources here give potted histories of needles and pins made in Britain, and these lionise Victorian technological progress by noting increases in production speed, improvements in quality and other innovations.

Descriptions of the manufacturing process are central to all examples cited here, suggesting a deep and abiding interest on the part of the Victorian reader in how ordinary objects were manufactured. As early as 1836, Sir George Head's 'Pin-Making' assumed the reader's familiarity with the manufacture of brass wire, describing a fine thread drawn 'in the usual manner'. The heat and violence of the manufacturing process is dramatically described in *The Story of a Needle* (1878), an it-narrative for children, which sketches a needle's journey from a 'rough mass of iron ore' to a young girl's workbox. Yet another audience is identified in 'A Second Day at the Birmingham Factories' in the *Penny Magazine* (1844) which offers technically precise descriptions for the working-class self-improver. The anonymous author illustrates the wire-drawing machines at the Birmingham Wire Works, describing how multiple male figures feed endless coils of iron around dual cylinders. In other articles, girls and boys are described as snipping and sharpening wire, while women 'papered' (that is, gathered pins into their paper packets). The variety of their output can be seen in *The Century Dictionary*'s illustration of its 'Needles' entry, which suggests that the 16 needles on show were in regular use even as late as 1895.

Victorian readers were encouraged to see their likeness as a laborious people reflected in the manufacture of needles and pins. Whether describing human or mechanised processes, each source in this section contains at least one passage which professes astonishment at the speed and proficiency of the production process. The quantities of pins produced numbered in the tens of thousands every day, astounding all of the authors of these sources and presumably their readers. Divided, specialised labour of precisely this kind underpins Marx's theory of the alienation of workers under capitalist production methods. Images of industriousness in the sources here reveal a complicated manufacturing process, along with the intended purpose of the pin and needle, which are consistently associated with women's labour as seamstresses. Needlework was represented as a desirable, even essential, feminine skill, a view represented here in *The Story of a Needle* (1878), in which a small girl learns patience and generosity by mending her frock instead of stitching a less useful pen wiper for her brother.

Harriet Martineau, in 'Needles' (1852), outlines a visit to the Victoria Works, in Redditch, Worcestershire. As with many other articles by Martineau for *Household Words*, her visit is discussed along with a history of the product and descriptions of the current processes of mass manufacture. Nationally, Warrington and Birmingham as well as Redditch were the principal towns in which needles and pins were manufactured. The global reach of the British needle trade encourages Martineau to reflect on the empire's role in facilitating manufacturing. When Martineau states that quills and fishbone are used elsewhere in the world as pins and needles, she positions the metal needle made in Britain as the pinnacle of technological progress and a symbol of British manufacturing supremacy.

By 1868, the rise of a middle class uneasy about associating itself with industry can be detected in *Belgravia*'s 'Pins', with its reluctance – suggested in its tone of ennui – to offer an educational technical guide to its readers. 'Pins' describes both the process of making pins by hand and the patenting of a machine in 1824, which 'during the revolution of a single wheel produced a perfect pin'. D. F. Tayler's packaging of pins boasted a picture of Queen Victoria and claimed to contain pins 'unlike those of any other manufacturer', suggesting that its solid-headed pins were a premium product.

42

ANON, 'PIN-MAKING (FROM SIR GEORGE HEAD'S HOME TOUR)'

The Mirror, Vol. 28 (9th July 1836), pp. 29–30

HAVING gone from Manchester to Warrington by the railway conveyance, I visited a large pin manufactory in the town. I had never an opportunity, either before or since, of witnessing this useful art and interesting process, but all the information I was enabled to glean during a hasty walk from chamber to chamber of the premises may be gathered from the following description: –

The brass-wire is received at the manufactory in hanks or rolls from Staffordshire, and these are, in the first place, drawn to a fine thread in the usual manner.

As the wire still retains a curved form, it is straightened by straining it between alternate rows of pegs inserted on a table; and when perfectly straight, it is cut into lengths of five or six inches; which lengths, however, are determinate, being intended to form the shafts of a certain number of pins. A handful of these is delivered to a workman sitting behind two wheels, like those of a scissor-grinder, excepting that, instead of stone, they are made of steel, one being of a surface finer than the other. This man performs the office of pointing with wonderful quickness. He no sooner receives the little bundle of wires, than in an instant they are assorted in his hand like a pack of cards in an even row; one touch on each wheel perfects the points of one end; and then, by a turn of the hand, the points of the other end are made in like manner, and the bundle handed to another operator, who, by the eye alone, snips off a pin's length from each end. The cutting is performed by a large pair of scissors fixed to the table, the blade of which is as big as a shoulder of mutton. The wires are now re-pointed as before; and so on re-cut by one man and re-pointed by the other, till the whole are subdivided into pins' shafts, and nothing is lost.

To make the heads, two little boys are employed, one of whom especially exercises in his vocation a degree of cunning workmanship hardly to be expected from an artist so young, and at all events exhibiting an interesting display of perfection in the faculties of sight and touch. From a piece of elastic wire, such as forms the covering of a fiddle-string, with an ordinary pair of scissors, he snips off, as quick as he can open and shut the scissors, just two threads of the spiral or *helix*, and no more. Were he to cut one thread or three, the head of the pin, which it is intended to form, being too large or too small, would be consequently rejected as waste metal and re-cast into wire. The elastic wire is prepared by another little boy in

DOI: 10.4324/9781315400105-51

the same apartment, who rolls it round a piece of straight brass-wire of the proper dimensions, and about three yards long, by the assistance of a large spinning-wheel. As the wheel hums round, the covering creeps along from one end to the other at the rate of two or three inches a second; and when the straight piece of wire is thus entirely covered, it being, I imagine, made purposely a little smaller at one end than the other, it is drawn out without any difficulty.

The pins are headed by little girls, and I was really astonished to perceive the rapidity with which every pin is taken up between the thumb and finger, and, after the head is strung upon the shaft, is placed in a small machine, which rivets it at one blow, and disgorges it at another. This machine is of rather complicated construction, but in general appearance like a small turning-lathe; that is to say, it is fixed on a table, and worked in a similar way. At a turn of the wheel two small iron slabs separate with a horizontal motion, and at another close again. The little girl sits behind the machine with a basin of pin's heads in her lap, which in that state resemble poppy seeds, and having threaded two shafts, gives the wheel a turn with her foot, when the aforesaid slabs diverge one from another; she then places the two pins in two small horizontal holes made to receive them, and turning the wheel again, the slabs close violently, and rivet the two heads in a moment. Every time the slabs open, the two new-made pins tumble out, and fall into a basin below.

In order to whiten the pins, they are boiled in a cauldron, in a composition of which I did not learn the ingredients, but of which the principal appeared to be tin broken into pieces the size of mustard seed.

After the pins are finished, it only remains to fix them upon paper in the usual way, and this is done in a separate apartment, where one woman doubles the paper, and at the same time superintends a number of girls who stick them in. The paper is doubled entirely by hand and by the eye, in parallel ridges, and then delivered to the girls, who sit at tables, each with a machine like a vice before her. The creased ridges or tucks of the paper being brought two and two, are introduced below into the machine which closes and leaves a narrow horizontal strip above. Into this the pins are inserted, and in order to guide them in a straight line, parallel transverse grooves are cut on the surface of the instrument, at equal distances, so that each pin cannot fail to enter exactly into its proper place, it not being possible for it, when pushed forward, to move in any other direction.

43

ANON, 'A SECOND DAY AT THE BIRMINGHAM FACTORIES'

Penny Magazine of the Society for the Diffusion of Useful Knowledge, Vol. 13 (28th December 1844), pp. 501–502

Wire

Wire-drawing, or the manufacture of wire from rods of iron, steel, or other metal, is extensively carried on at Birmingham, and is a process illustrating in a remarkable degree the ductility of metals. Unless a person has actually witnessed the operations, there is some difficulty in conceiving how the transformation takes place – how the diameter of the rod lessens and the length increases. There is no hammering or pressing or stamping, no cutting or dividing, no moulding or casting; and perhaps this is almost the only operation in the mechanical arts in which alteration of shape is produced without any one of the above agencies.

At the Wire-Works of Messrs. Carpenter and Co., to which we were favoured with access, the outline of the arrangements is such as may be here briefly described. The factory is situated in the western part of Birmingham, and consists of several buildings, of which some are occupied by wire-drawers, and the rest in a way afterwards to be noticed. There is considerable power required in the transformation of the iron rods into wire, and to provide this force there is a steam-engine employed. The other apparatus will come for notice as we proceed.

As nearly all wire is made pretty much in the same manner, it will suffice to confine our attention to that made of iron. The iron is brought to the Works in coils of rods, wrought to the state of what may perhaps be termed thick wire. In the Supplement for February, while describing the operations at a large Iron-Work, we explained how iron is brought into the form of rods and bars, by being drawn between two heavy revolving rollers while in a white-hot state. For wire-work this drawing is conducted to a greater extent than for most other purposes, until the lengthened rod is thin enough to be twisted up into a coil, and in that state to be transferred to the wire-factories.

The iron is covered with scale (the hard oxide produced by the heat necessary to roll the rods) when it comes to the Works; and to remove this scale the coils are put into large revolving cylinders containing gravel and water, the friction against

DOI: 10.4324/9781315400105-52

which effects the desired object. From these vessels the coils are taken to a large shop or room where the whole apparatus is contained for reducing the thickness of the metal. Previously to describing these, it may be well to notice the successive steps whereby the present system has been brought about.

Narrow filaments of metal have probably been employed for various purposes from very early times; but Beckmann supposes that, in the first instance, the metal was beaten with a hammer into thin plates or leaves, that these leaves were afterwards divided into small slips by a pair of shears or some similar instrument, and that the slips were hammered and filed to a tolerably round form. Respecting the subsequent change in the mode of operation Beckmann says, "As long as the work was prepared by the hammer, the artists at Nuremberg were called *wire-smiths;* but after the invention of the drawing-iron they were called *wire-drawers* and *wire-millers* (*Drahtzieher* and *Drahtmühler*). Both these appellations occur in the history of Augsburg so early as the year 1351, and in that of Nuremberg in 1369; so that, according to the best information I have been able to obtain, I must class the invention of the drawing-iron, or proper wire-drawing, among those of the fourteenth century." As respects our own country, it is supposed that all wire was made by the hammer till about 1565, when some German wire-drawers introduced an improved method. Even after the improved plan of drawing the wire was adopted, the preparatory processes were still very defective, for the iron rods were brought to the requisite thickness by means of the hammer. To this succeeded a plan by which the rods were drawn through a hole by sudden jerks, thereby reducing the thickness and increasing the length. Lastly came the improvement of passing the red-hot rods between grooved rollers, until such a thickness is attained as to be fit for the wire-drawer's operations; and in this state the art remains at present.

In the room of the factory to which our attention is now directed, and of which a sketch is given in the frontispiece, there is a double range of benches, on which are a number of wheels or drums rotating on vertical axes. All these axes are placed in connexion with the machinery of the steam-engine, and are so adjusted that the drums may be made to rotate or to remain stationary at pleasure. Near each drum is placed a 'drawing-plate,' pierced with holes for the reception of the wire. The plates are made of very hard steel, and have holes punched carefully through them. These holes have all intermediate diameters, between those corresponding with the thickest and the thinnest kinds of wire; and, as the plates are easily removed from the stand in which they rest, there are the means for employing draw-plates of any required kind.

The principle of wire-drawing consists in forcing the rod of metal to pass through a hole rather smaller than itself. This could not be done unless the metal possessed a yielding quality, for a portion of the diameter must be squeezed out of its place, and made to elongate the piece. The draw-plates, then, have the holes through which the metal is to be forced, and the drums give the necessary drawing-power. One end of a coil of wire is hammered or filed thinner, and inserted into one of the holes of a draw-plate, and after being pulled through it is held tight by an instrument attached to the drum; the drum is made to rotate rapidly, and in so doing draws the metal through the hole, and causes it to wind round the drum itself, the diameter of the wire being a little decreased by this agency. It is then passed similarly through a second hole somewhat smaller than the first, by exactly similar means, whereby a second stage of attenuation is brought about. Step by step does this continue, different draw-plates and different drums being employed, until the iron is brought to any required degree of fineness. It is by very small degrees that these changes are produced; for if an attempt were made to draw the wire through a hole much smaller than itself, it would break. There is a gauge employed, to determine the size of the wire; and the size so determined is indicated by numbers: for instance, wire No. 1 is about three-tenths of an inch in diameter, while No. 26 is not above one-fiftieth of an inch. There is, however, some little diversity in this matter in different factories, even to the extent of beginning with No. 1 at the smallest diameter, and going upwards to the largest. It would seem as if some designation which would give the actual diameter, such as the number of hundredths of an inch, would remove all ambiguity; but doubtless those concerned have a sufficient reason for their systems.

The mere act of drawing the wire through the holes does not comprise all that is to be done; for the metal becomes so hardened by the compression, that if it were not annealed from time to time it would be too hard for working. It also requires to be roughened by the application of sulphuric acid to facilitate the process of drawing. There is a kind of iron called 'charcoal'-iron (in which charcoal has been used instead of coal in the smelting) calculated to bear more drawing without annealing than common iron; and the number of annealings therefore depends partly on the thickness of the wire and partly on the quality of the metal. The arrangements for annealing are curious: in one of the buildings of the factory are annealing-kilns, cylindrical in form, three or four feet in diameter, and eight or ten in depth; they are made of iron, encased externally with brick. The coils of wire, as taken from the drums, are laid flat one on another in these kilns; the small coils being placed within the larger ones, so as to lose as little space as possible. After every aperture is closed, a fire is kindled, and the hot air circulates round the vessel, keeping the wire – amounting to twenty or thirty cwt. at once – at a red heat for twenty-four hours; or rather, the heating and the slow cooling together occupy this space of time. In the reduction of the metal to the state of very fine wire, this annealing is repeated several times, sometimes amounting to six or eight.

According to the hardness or softness of the metal, or the tenuity required to be attained, some or other of these arrangements are more or less modified; but the general principle is the same in all. Dr. Wollaston devised a mode of making exquisitely fine wire for micrometrical purposes by the following ingenious contrivance: he made some platinum wire, so small as 1–300th of an inch diameter, by a draw-plate of his own invention; then made a tiny cylinder or mould, down the centre of which he placed the wire; then poured melted silver into this mould, so as to form a sort of little ingot enveloping the platinum; then drew this ingot into the state of a wire nearly or quite as fine as the platinum had been; then immersed the wire thus produced into hot nitric acid, by which all the silver was dissolved, leaving a central fibre of platinum smaller perhaps than human eye had ever before (or since) seen: so fine, indeed, that in some instances he produced platinum wire less than one ten-thousandth part of an inch in diameter! For some fine and delicate purposes, in which the wearing away of the draw-holes would be a detriment, it was proposed some years ago to use diamonds, sapphires, or rubies as the material for draw-plates, on account of their excessive hardness; but this costly project is somewhat too startling for manufacturers in general.

44

HARRIET MARTINEAU, 'NEEDLES'

Household Words, Vol. 4 (28th February 1852), pp. 540–546

WE have been to Redditch, that remarkable little Worcestershire town, to see needles made. While on that perch – for Redditch crowns a high hill – while looking abroad, in all directions, over a true English country scene of hill and dale, orchard and sloping fallow, humble church-tower, and comfortable farmstead, we were compelled, by our errand, to contrast this with some very different places in which we had studied needles. People who invent and use such articles of convenience as needles must have a good deal in common, however widely different they must appear on the whole. How many wants and wishes, designs and plans, efforts and achievements, must be common to the minds of all sorts of persons who sew things together to make garments, and do it by means of the same invention, – of an instrument which shall pierce the material, and draw a thread after it, to tie two edges together! We could not but think, while on the table-land of Redditch, of the odd places in which, at intervals of years, we had observed this process, or the records of it.

In the Lebanon, high up among the defiles and rocky platforms, which succeed each other till the celebrated cedars are reached, there is a village, nestling among mulberry groves and orchards, called Eden, and believed by many people in the East to be the real first home of Adam and Eve. We did not, when we were there, see anybody sewing fig-leaves together; but we mention that place, not only because it is a wide-spread belief that the first sewing ever done was done there, but because we had, a little while before going there, seen a piece of sewing, of extremely old date. The work that we saw was a piece of darning, with the threaded needle still sticking in it, after the lapse of several thousand years. The old Egyptians had a custom of burying in their handsome, roomy rock tombs, specimens of the works and possessions of the deceased; and the cotton fabric that we saw, with the pretty unfinished darn (more like herring-bone stitch than our ordinary darning), and the needle sticking in it, was, no doubt, the property and the handiwork of the lady in whose tomb it was found. It may be seen in Dr. Abbott's collection of curiosities at Cairo. Those old Egyptians seem to have known the use of steel. They used it for armour; but not, we suppose, for needles; for this needle – the one remaining needle from the world of above five thousand years ago, is of wood. The wood is hard, and the needle is made as small,

DOI: 10.4324/9781315400105-53

probably, as it can be, but it is sadly clumsy; – harder to use, no doubt, than the sail-makers' needles we saw under the file at Redditch. It is a curious thing, however, to glance back, through all those thousands of years, to the Egyptian lady, sitting in her elegant chair, mending her muslin garment (whatever it might be), while surrounded by her children, – one of whom was playing with her doll (still in mummified existence), with a face and hair uncommonly like the Sphinx – and another, a baby, handling – not a woolly bow-wow dog like those that yelp in our nurseries – but a little snapping crocodile, of wood, with a loose under jaw. And then – what a long step it is over space and time! – to the place where we have seen another sort of needle, with its thread – no more to be compared with the Redditch needles than the Egyptian one; – the green shores of Mackinaw, in Lake Michigan, where, in some of the long row of wigwams, there are, at this day, Indian women, sewing with a needle of stout porcupine quill, and thread of the sinews of the deer. Again, among those that we have not seen, there are the fish-bones that the Greenlanders and the South Sea Islanders use; – the women of the one race sitting in their snow-burrow, stitching by the light of their oil-lamps; and the women of the other race wearing, while at work, a great palm-leaf on their heads for shade; and cooling themselves occasionally by a swim in the calm water within the coral reefs. Again, – but we must not stop to tell of all the different kinds of needles used in the world – though the list would now be a short one. It would be a short list, because our English needles of to-day are spreading all over the known world, wherever exchange of commodities is going on.

Some of us may feel uncomfortable at this thought; – uncomfortable at the recollection of a sad story about that. Do we not know of certain purchases, made of certain simple Africans – the purchase-money on our side being needles – "Whitechapel sharps," duly gilded at the head, – which were found, after the departure of the traders, to be without eyes? It is a sad story. The Redditch makers, who used to prepare gilt "Whitechapel sharps" for the African market, say that they don't believe it; that the needles were of a coarse and ill-finished kind; but that they were never "blind." Yet the testimony is so strong, and the effects of the cheat were so serious in damaging our commercial character among the savages, that we fear there can have been no mistake. It was, no doubt, a parallel case with that of the Anglo-Saxons, who sold a handful of gunpowder for a bale of furs, to the Red Indians, instructing their customers to sow the gunpowder in furrows, to get valuable crops next summer; and with that of the Dutch traders, who used their own hands and feet for weight, – the hand for half a pound, and the foot for a pound, and eternally astonished the Indians at the quantity of furs they had to heap up, and squeeze into the scale, to weigh down the Dutchman's pound. If we laugh at such stories, it is with a weeping heart; for tricks like these, done in any corner where new races are found, are a grave misfortune to the whole human race.

How is it that "Whitechapel sharps" are, or were, made at Redditch? It is supposed to be because Elias Krause lived in Whitechapel; giving a good name to needles, which they long preserved. And who was Elias Krause? He was a German, who came over in 1565, and was the first maker of needles in this country; – that is, of course, of the modern kind of needle. And who taught the Germans? The Spaniards, – if we may judge by the importation of "Spanish needles" into England and other countries before the Germans made them. And who taught the Spaniards? Nobody seems to know; so it is reported that they invented the true needle, – made of steel, with a point at one end, and an eye at the other.

What pains Elias Krause took with his work, we may judge by what some living persons could tell us of needle-making in their young days. Cyclopædias of the present century – within the last thirty years, even – give such an account of the formation of a needle, as appears quite piteous to one who was at Redditch yesterday. We read of such hammering, and rolling, such heating and cooling, such filing and punching, of each separate needle, that we wonder how any sempstress ever dared to break an eye, or turn the point, of a thing which had cost so much pains. And the needles of thirty, twenty, ten, five years ago, cost something much more serious than pains and toil. They cost human life, too, at a terrible rate. It never was true, as it is often said to have been, that needle-makers rarely lived beyond thirty years of age; but it was, for a long time, true that every needle that was pointed helped to shorten some man's life.

The facts were these. Needle-pointers lived, while at their work, in an atmosphere thick with stone-dust and steel-dust, generated by the dry grinding of the needles upon the wheel just under their noses. Instead of windows, there were many little doors in the places where they worked, in order to carry off as much dust as possible; and one consequence of this was that the men sat in a thorough draught. Their only precaution was to go out about once in an hour, and rinse their mouths; a poor device enough, while their noses, throats and windpipes were infested, like their dress and their skin, with myriads of sharp points of cruel steel. They died of consumption in a few years. If boys tried the work, they were gone before twenty. If men, with a consolidated frame, and good appetites, (for the largest eaters lived longest,) set to this work, they might possibly hold on to forty, – a case here and there occurring of a needle-pointer who reached forty-five. Bad morals always attend a permanent state of insecurity of life and bad health; and so it was in this case. Very high wages were given. Some men earned a guinea a-day; none less than two guineas a-week. It became an established fact, that the needle-pointers (then about forty men, in a population of one thousand five hundred, in Redditch; and in a similar proportion, as the population increased) were a set of debauched young men, who, tempted by the high wages, braved their doom, and entered upon the business at twenty, or soon after, – counting the years they supposed they might live, and declaring their desire for "a short life and a merry one." They married, and always left their widows and children to the parish. Following their notion of a merry life, they would at times drink ale, day and night, for two or three weeks together. Then, they would go back to their benches, raise a prodigious dust, and choke over it, almost without pause, for three weeks or a month, to clear off scores; then, they would have another drinking bout. This was a sight which no humane employer could endure; and many were the consultations and attempts entered upon by the masters to save or prolong life. All such attempts exasperated the victims themselves. They insisted upon their right to die early, if they chose; and they were sure their employers were in reality wanting to lower their wages. A good man invented a wire-gauze mask; which, being magnetised, must prevent the steel-dust from entering the mouth. The men would not wear it. This mask could be little or no protection against the dust from the grindstone. Another device was therefore joined with that of the mask; – a canvas cylinder, brought down close over the grindstone, up which, it was hoped, the dust would make its way, and be carried off. In one night, the canvas cylinders, throughout Redditch, were cut into strips, and the needle-pointers declared themselves under intimidation from their fellow-workers, about wearing the mask. It was pretty clear at the time, that the men agreed among themselves to cut one another's cylinders, and to threaten each other; – that it was a matter of collusion from end to end.

Other inventions were devised from time to time; but were never got into use. The new generation of needle-pointers (and an employer of fifty years old has seen four generations of them) was less ignorant, and somewhat less vicious than their predecessors; but still the sacrifice of life went on. It had become a point of honour, or of self-will, with the men, besides their dread of a lowering of wages, not to use any means of self-preservation; and on they went to their early graves, as fast as ever, until four years ago. Then there was a strike among the Redditch needle-makers. It lasted three months; at the end of which time the men became very hungry, very sad, and very humble. They made no objection to the terms offered by the employers; and the employers saw that now was the time to save the needle-pointers from their own folly; and they made it a prime condition of renewed connexion between masters and men, that a certain sanitary apparatus should be faithfully used. The promise was given; the trial was made; the men soon found the comfort and advantage of it; they seem, now, likely to live as long as other people; and the stranger observes that they seem to show off the arrangement with a certain complacency and pride, which prove that it works in excellent accordance with their will. What this arrangement is, we shall tell hereafter, when we have carried our commodity up to the need of being pointed. The number of needle-pointers in Redditch, now, is about one hundred and ten; a large company to be saved from an early and painful death!

It is not so very long since every needle of every size was made separately, from beginning to end, as sail-makers' needles and packing needles are made still. It is hard to say which is most perplexing to the imagination: the old method, by which nails, hooks and eyes, and needles, were separately fashioned by hand: or the present amount of production by machinery. We saw, the other day, hooks and eyes made by a machine, which gave us a strong impression of its being alive (some one said it could do everything but speak), by which one manufactory sends out a ton per week of hooks and eyes. No comment can add to the marvel of the thought – a ton of hooks and eyes per week! In needle-making there is no such marvellous machinery: the marvel consisting chiefly of the dexterity attainable by human fingers; but the monstrous numbers made are simply overwhelming. We saw, on a counter of a warehouse yesterday, a set of little parcels, such as a lady might carry home all at once in a hand-basket, and found that they contained a quarter of a million of needles! Comparing that set of parcels with what else the room contained, we gave up the attempt to comprehend what we saw. The room was surrounded by compartments, each of which was filled with similar packets. The effort to imagine their contents, when in use, was like undertaking to count the grains of a square yard of sea-beach. Yet this was only one room of one manufactory of one little town!

Needle-making is now, however, almost gone out everywhere else. There was, once, a famous manufacture at Long Crendon, in Oxfordshire; but it has languished so long that it has nearly expired. The people intermarried with remarkable exclusiveness; exchanged ideas with nobody else; heard, or would hear, of no improvement; chose to remain as they were; therefore, of course, they sank. The population of Redditch has, meantime, increased from fifteen hundred to nearly five thousand; of whom almost every man, woman, and child lives by needles. The neighbouring villages contain a population of from four thousand to five thousand more: a large proportion of whom are employed by the Redditch manufacturers. The lawyers' and doctors' fees were once needles; and the shopkeepers' profits, and the maid-servants' wages, and the houses, and the schools, and the land-allotments, and the flower-show prizes, and all the good things that may be found there now, were once needles too. Finding such things come of needles, let us see now how the needles come into being.

We are allowed to go over the Victoria Works, the manufactory of Mr. John James; and, moreover, into any of the houses of his work-people who carry on their business at home: which is the case with about three-fourths of them. Those who work on Mr. James's premises are well off for air, light, and cheerfulness. Some of the rooms overlook his pretty garden, and all have plenty of windows. When once we have left the furnaces and boilers, all the rest is clean; and there is no sign of ill health in any of the intelligent faces. Intelligent they are; for these people have had a good school education. Mr. James admits no children under ten years of age to his employment. He cannot prevent some of his people from hiring the help of children under that age; but his rule is enforced to the utmost of his power. Of the work-people, thirty-eight can read and write; fourteen read, but do not write; and only three can do neither. Those three are – a boy, just arrived from elsewhere; a man, of great natural intelligence, who earns two guineas a-week; and a half-wit, who can turn a wheel, but cannot learn his letters.

In going over the premises, we must pass hither and thither, and walk into the next street and back again, and even take a drive to a certain country mill and return, in order to present in their natural order the processes of needle-making.

The best wire comes from Yorkshire; the inferior from Birmingham. There is a small chamber, really pretty in its way, from being hung round with coils of bright wire, suspended from hooks. This wire is of all thicknesses, from the stout kind required for fish-hooks for Newfoundland cod, and for packing and sail-making needles, to the finest for cambric-needles. In the dark and dingy rooms below, bits of wire, each the length of two needles, are cut by a pair of vast shears, well fixed to the wall. The "measure" is a steel instrument, furnished with a screw, which determines the length of the bundle of wires cut at once. Two iron rings, about five inches in diameter, are placed on edge, and nearly filled with the cut wires, of which there is thus a pretty large faggot before us. These wires, having come off coils, are curved, and they must be straightened. A sort of hooked poker is thrust into the rings, and transports the faggot to the furnace, where it is presently heated red-hot. It is taken out; a curved iron bar is laid between the rings, and the bundle is rolled backwards and forwards on a table until the wires are straight. This is called "rubbing straight."

We now find ourselves in a mill in the country – a pretty place, with its pond, its unceasing gush of water, its little ravine, its cheerful farmstead, its fields with cows grazing, even at this season. There is a miller peeping out at us. What does *he* do here? One end of the mill is let for grinding flour; the other, for grinding needles. We go down some steps to a basement-room, where straps are revolving with all possible zeal. The water-wheel is under our feet; and round us are placed four grindstones. Each grindstone is furnished with a cap or cover, like a collapsing Dutch oven. It does not fit closely, but leaves a space, through which the deadly dust is blown. Here is the secret of the salvation of the dry-grinders. A comfortable-looking needle-pointer is seated on his bench. He takes up two dozen or so of wires, and applies the ends to the grindstone. While doing this, he has to roll every wire between his finger and thumb. Backwards and forwards he makes them revolve, in contact with the wheel; and off flies a shower of sparks. One end being done, he presents the other; for it must be remembered that these wires are of the length of two needles. As he works, we see the dust rushing under the cover, quite away from the workman's face; and we are invited to go and see what becomes of it. There is a covered fan-wheel in the middle of the chamber, turned by water-power; and this it is which sucks away the dust from all the four grindstones at once. We pass outside to the end of the building, and go down some more steps, to the brink of the stream which is flowing away down the little ravine. We observe that a patch of the opposite bank, some way down, is whitened – crusted over with dust; and, looking carefully, we see puffs, as of a thin smoke, coming from behind a grey stone on our side of the bank. Behind that stone is the outlet from the fan-wheel, and the whitening on the grass and brambles is the dust which would have hung about the men and within the men, if they had not consented to this saving measure.

It is a plan which costs a little money in the first instance; although it saves a vast deal in the end. That fan-wheel uses up a third of the water power appropriated to this chamber. The men have, nominally, the same wages as of old; but they pay their share of this loss, at the rate of about a shilling a-week. This is their toll for life and health. The masters bear a much larger share, and with extreme content. It may be mentioned here, that from the nominally high – extremely high – wages of this class of men, must be deducted the mill-rents they pay, and the cost of their tools – amounting altogether to ten or twelve shillings a-week.

We now have the wires straight, and pointed at both ends. We next find ourselves in a workshop, in the next street to Mr. James's. Here, we see a stamping machine and die, which flattens and prints a space precisely in the middle of each bit of wire. The print shows where the eye is to be, and at the same time the "guttering" is done – the forming the little channel seen in the heads of all needles. The workman strikes off five thousand of these in an hour; that is, he flattens and "gutters" the heads of ten thousand needles per hour – rather an advance upon the old method of doing each one by hand! Then comes the punching of the eyes. The punch is double, of course; and the boy who works it, perforates four thousand wires, or eight thousand needles per hour. This is dexterous work, the wires being laid and removed almost faster than the eye can follow.

The next boy we noticed was seven years old; a little fellow hired by the woman under whom he worked. "This boy," we were told, "earns his living by spitting. He is not an American; yet he passes his days in spitting." Before him lay bits of wire almost as fine as hairs: and these wires he was running through the eyes of the twin needles which had come from the punch. He ran a wire through each line of eyes, "spitting" two dozen or so on his two wires. A woman, whose wrists and arms were obviously of unusual strength, received these spitted needles, laid them on a prepared steel plate, and filed off all roughness on both sides. The twin needles had yet to be separated, and the fragments of flattened steel surrounding the heads to be removed. This was done by a woman close at hand, who sat before her little anvil, filing with precision between the rows of heads, so that they separated easily; and then, by another movement, clearing away all extraneous bits and sharp edges, delivering her spitsful of needles complete in form.

They are still rough and rusty-looking; and, what is worse, they are soft; – so soft as to bend with a touch. The hardening comes next. They are heated, in batches, in the furnace, and, when red hot, are soused into a pan of cold water. – Next, they must be tempered; and this is done by heaping them (all lying the same way) on a very hot metal plate, where a man with a metal slice, called "a knife," in each hand, shifts them incessantly backwards and forwards, upon each other, taking care that all get, as nearly as possible, an equal quantity of heat. If any get too little, they bend in the using; if too much, they break. As they turn blue upon this plate, they are removed, the shade of blueness showing when they are tempered enough.

The polishing remains to be done. The best needles are polished no less than six times; and there are three stages of polishing for all. The final scouring is the most emphatic affair. To see it, we must find ourselves at the mill again. The water power there appears to be moving half-a-dozen mangles: and very like mangling the process is. On a very coarse cloth, which lies upon another coarse cloth, needles are spread, to the number of forty or fifty thousand. Emery dust is strewed over them: oil is sprinkled upon them, and soft soap is daubed by spoonfuls on the cloth. The whole precious mess is then rolled up compactly, and tied at both ends, and round and round, as tight as packthread can bind it; and we have before us a disgusting black "roly-poly" dumpling. Several of these are put into one of the mangles, where they roll to and fro for eight hours. By that time, the emery is worn smooth, the packets are taken out, and the needles are dressed with fresh emery, oil, and soap; and another eight hours' mangling succeeds. From this, the needles come out dirty enough, and smelling horribly; but they are capable now of showing their brightness. They are washed with hot water and cleansing materials in iron pans, by boys, who seem to enjoy the shaking and boulting of the needles with real zest. When clean, the needles are tossed into sawdust, and tossed about in it, until they are dry, and then the sawdust is tossed out from them; they are tossed into bundles, and sent to the manufactory, to be sorted and put up for sale.

We shall not come back to the unsavoury mill any more; so we will ask what that boy is doing; and how any stone-breaking can be necessary to the making of needles? He is breaking into smaller pieces those not large white stones, from which emery powder comes. We follow his barrowful of pieces into a little shed, and find that the water power is working, up and down, the pestle of a great mortar, where the boy's fragments are broken into dust. A man is sifting what comes out of the mortar, and returning whatever will not go through his sieve.

Once more in the manufactory, we find the faulty needles separated from the perfect. Among so many, some must be broken, some bent, some with bad eyes or dull points. We inquire what becomes of the refuse, which is called "scrap;" and the answer appears to us so curious that we are glad we did not miss the information. The bright needles, which happen only to have lost their heads, are eagerly bought by picture-frame makers, and cabinet-makers. They are invaluable for delicate fastenings, for veneering, and where a nail is wanted of extreme fineness and without a head. The rest of the "scrap" is equally prized for another object, – for making gun-barrels. It is sold by cartloads, as the finest-tempered steel that gun-barrels can be made of. What an idea this gives, – or would give, if we could receive it, – of the extent of the manufacture!

The manufacture is now complete; but the making ready for sale exhibits a miracle of dexterity; at least, to unpractised eyes.

A handful of needles, lying all manner of ways, is put into a tray, which is shaken backwards and forwards, until the needles lie all one way. Those whose points lie left, from those whose points lie right, are separated. A little girl spreads a heap on her counter into a rough row, wraps a bit of cloth round the forefinger of her right hand, shakes the needles a little, and brings out a batch, with their points sticking lightly in the cloth, and their heads supported by her other forefinger. These she lays aside, and does the same thing again, until all are separated. A heap is thus separated more quickly than we can tell how it is done. But these needles are of different lengths. How should *we* set about sorting them? Certainly not in the actual way. The operation just described is called "heading." This is called "handling." A narrow piece of wood, like a thick flat ruler, is heaped with as many needles as will lie upon it, almost from end to end. A woman feels along both sides with the lower edge of her hands, and lifts from the rest, with her little fingers and the palms of her hands, the longest needles, which she places on one side. Then follow the next longest, which she places on the other side. It is altogether an affair of tact; and fine must be the touch, and long the experience, required to do such sorting with accuracy.

Then, we arrive at the seat of another wonderful woman, who is pronounced by her employer the most rapid worker he has ever seen. Her business is to count the needles into quarter hundreds, and paper them up. The squares of paper lie ready; the needles are before her. She separates twenty-five of them, whips them into a paper, and counts again with incredible rapidity; folding the filled papers when about half-a-dozen are ready. We are so persuaded that our readers could never believe how many packets this woman folds in a day, that we will not say how many thousands they number. That so many should go forth into the world from one house, is wonderful enough; that one woman should put them up for their journey, is more than any readers, not needle-makers, could be expected to believe on the declaration of an anonymous writer.

Next, we come among boys and girls. One little boy is cutting out the printed labels, which have had their figures neatly filled in by an older lad. A third is spreading the cut labels on a board smeared with paste. A girl is putting them on the packets of needles. Another is putting on the warranty ticket, in like manner. Another is "tucking;" slipping one end of the needle paper into the other. A lad is looking to the drying of the papers in the warm drying-closet, in the same room, where they remain about two hours; and he and another are tying up the papers into packets. Finally, we return into the warehouse, and see the piles of gay boxes, which are to be filled with an assortment of needles for presents, or for foreign sale. These boxes are a branch of industry in themselves; with their portraits of the Queen and Prince, and their copies from popular pictures, such as Raffaelle's Madonna in the Chair. As a further temptation, these pictures in the lids are so fitted as to be disengaged and hung up. They are probably to be seen on the walls of many a log cabin in America, and chalet in Switzerland, and bungalow in India, and home of exiles in Siberia. It seems as if all the world of needlewomen, of every clime, were supplied by England. One man has gone from among us to set up the business in the United States; but the Americans are not known yet to be making for themselves. In all directions, our hundredweights and tons of this delicate article are going forth.

We should have liked to know what the consumption of sail-makers' needles is at home: but this we could not learn. These formidable affairs are separately forged, as their finer companions once were. The flattening, and guttering, and filing of the heads, is done on grooved anvils; and so is the hammering of the lower half into a three-sided surface. The pointing is done by one at a time being held to a revolving cylinder of a grit-stone brought from Bristol; and then there is another rubbing against a "buff," – a cylinder covered with leather dressed with emery. The eyes are punched separately, and by repeated strokes; and pains are given to the finishing of the head, by flattening its sides, and filing all smooth. The process is nearly the same with packing-needles; but, as we know, their pointed ends are considerably flattened and bent.

We must deny ourselves the pleasure of describing the other manufacture which goes on in the same place, – that of fish-hooks. The pattern-books of the concern show specimens of all sorts, from the strong cod-hook, for the Newfoundland Banks, and the salmon-hook for the Norway cataracts, to the most delicate little barb that can be hidden under a streak of feather, to dance in the insidious character of a fly on the surface of an English rivulet. We find here sail-hooks, too, – like very large button-hooks. Without these the sailmaker could not hold together the edges of the uncommonly heavy fabric he has to sew.

The women and girls in this establishment are rather more numerous than the men and boys. Their employer accounts for the superiority of all in health, understanding, and morals, to the last generation, by citing the results of the Sunday schools of Redditch, and the good free-school there. He may be quite right: but there is something in the tone of the intercourse between himself and everybody on his premises, which convinces a stranger that there is also somebody else to thank for the improvement, which drives out all the stranger's preconceptions of the wretchedness of needle-makers. For our own part, we must say that a load has been removed from our mind – a burden of sorrow and commiseration – by our visit to the Victoria Needle-works at Redditch.

45

ANON, 'PINS'

Belgravia: A London Magazine, Vol. 6 (August 1868), pp. 300–302

IN the thorn Nature has provided man with the pattern and the first idea of the pin. When Adam and Eve, after their fall, but before their expulsion from Eden, made themselves aprons of fig-leaves, they doubtless used the thorn in the construction of their first garments. In the days of innocence there was no use for pins; and it was probably this fact which caused Byron to describe Juan when, metamorphosed into Juanna, he or she is unrobing in the seraglio, as

"Pricking her fingers with those cursed pins,
Which surely were invented for our sins, –
Making a woman like a porcupine,
Not to be rashly touch'd."

The pins thus anathematised by the poet are, however, comparatively a modern invention. In all the records which we have of man's past history we find evidence that articles for fastening clothes always existed, but very unlike the present. In the museums which have been formed out of the ruins of Herculaneum and Pompeii, or our own Uriconium, we find skewers of bone, of brass, of silver, or of gold, which were used for this purpose. In the representations of the life of the people found in the Egyptian hieroglyphics we discern the means which they employed for the like necessary purpose; but nowhere do we meet with a modern pin. In Strutt's illustrations we find ribbons, loop-holes, laces with points and tags, clasps, hooks and eyes, of every form, size, and variety of use, and often turned to very extraordinary and surprising account in completing the toilette of the ancient belle and the adornment of the ancient beau. The modern pin would have been of little use in sustaining that towering headdress; in fastening that wonderful cloak; in keeping up those curiously-slashed tunics; or in retaining the stiff uprightness of that extraordinary ruff. After pins came into use these eccentricities of costume and fashion were destined to give place to other fashions in which, perhaps, the modern pin has played tricks as fantastic as its many substitutes in the olden time.

History tells us that iron-wire pins were first introduced into this country in the year 1460. The finer examples of brass manufacture required a queen to procure them for us. They were brought from France by the beautiful Catherine Howard,

DOI: 10.4324/9781315400105-54

one of his wives whom the "great" Henry VIII. beheaded. But though introduced by a queen, and doubtless at first an article exclusively applied to aristocratic uses, they soon became a measure of value for things not valued at all. "Not worth a pin" is a proverb which we find in use soon after their introduction. Thomas Tusser, who wrote about 1550, writing of a not very reputable character, says:

> "His fetch is to flatter, to get what he can,
> His purpose once gotten, a pin for thee than."

And Shakespeare makes Hamlet show his utter indifference to life by saying:

> "I do not set my life at a pin's fee."

At the present time millions of these useful articles are wasted in a year.

We find pins first mentioned as an article of commerce in a statute of 1483. From a law passed in the reign of Henry VIII. we meet with some specific description of the kind of pins made – at least, of what they ought to have been. For instance, it is declared to be the will of the legislature that "no person should put to sale any pins but only such as shall be double-headed, and have the heads soldered fast to the shanks of the pins, well smoothed, the shanks well shapen, the points well and round filed, canted and sharpened." A pin possessing these qualities would not be a bad pin even now.

Birmingham is the centre of this industry, which, together with wire-drawing, was introduced there about the year 1750. The Rylands were amongst the earliest manufacturers who carried on this trade; but they gave up the business in or about the year 1785. In *Aris's Birmingham Gazette*, December 21, 1801, we read that "a pin-manufactory, on an extensive scale, is being established in this town under the firm of Lovell and Co." There are now about twelve pin-manufacturers in the town, the principal firm being Messrs. D. F. Tayler and Co. (the patentees of the solid-headed pin). As nearly as can be ascertained the making of this simple article affords employment to about five hundred persons – men, women, and children. At first pins were made entirely by hand, and the political philosophers employed them at once as a text and an illustration. These improvers of the occasion used to "quote the pin-manufacture as one of the most remarkable instances of the division of labour, a single pin requiring for its production the successive manual labour of no less than fourteen persons." There was the cutting, the pointing, the heading, the lackering, the whitening, the polishing, the sorting, the "sticking," and several other processes, each with its peculiar and technical name, now out of use and obsolete, and not to be understood even by pinmakers themselves. For *nous avons changé tout cela*. In 1824 an ingenious American inventor, of the name of Lemuel Wright, took out a patent in England for a machine, afterwards purchased by Messrs. D. F. Tayler and Co., which "during the revolution of a single wheel produced a perfect pin." This machine also produced a revolution in the pin-manufacture; and when steam was added the revolution was complete.

When we remember that by hand 1500 pins could be made in an hour, the rapidity with which they are now produced is something startling. This rapidity of production has, of course, lessened the price enormously; so much so, that the proverb, "not worth a pin," has increased in the same lowering proportion when applied as a measure of value either to person or thing. Soon after the introduction of Mr. Wright's machine, the change in the price was looked upon as something extraordinary. At that time Birmingham had no market-hall, and the sellers of goods had stalls in the Bull Ring – the name indicating the other purpose to which in the "good old times" it was put – upon which they exposed their wares for sale. One "Birmingham man" of the period, who afterwards attained wealth and rose to (local) fame, used to astonish prudent and economic housewives, and delight the *gamins*, by his peculiarity in announcing the wonderful fall in the price of pins. "Tell it not in Gath," said or rather shouted this original, – "tell it not in Gath, publish it not in the streets of Ascalon, pins seven rows a penny!" He must have been a lineal descendant of the genius who first delighted our Mohammedan brethren with the street-cry, "In the name of the Prophet – figs!"

It would be beyond the purpose of this paper, and would afford little edification, to give a verbal description of the way in which pins are now made. The patent machine, since it has been in the possession of Messrs. D. F. Tayler and Co., has undergone so many improvements and alterations that its own parent would no longer know the offspring of his inventive genius. Nothing is more tedious, as a rule, than the attempt to describe any working process in words. Suffice it that by this machine the wire goes in at one end, and comes out at the other a perfect pin. This machine cuts it at its proper length, "heads" it, points it, rough point and smooth point; after which process the pin drops into a receptacle below, and has only to be "whitened" and "stuck," to be ready to be sent to the dealer and the wearer in all parts of the world. Thus we have the pin, which a manufacturer has defined to be "a piece of polished brass-wire of variable length and thickness, having a point at one extremity and a head at the other, and entirely covered with a coating of metallic tin." Some notion of these variable sizes may be formed from the fact that the well-known blanket-pins are from three to four inches in length, while the ribbon-pins are made so small that 300,000 of them only weigh a pound.

Of the extent of this trade, and of the enormous number of pins made, a word or two may be said. In one manufactory in Birmingham (that of Messrs. D. F. Tayler and Co.) three and a half tons of brass wire are used every week for pins alone; and of the fineness and thinness of the wire from which they may be made, it may be stated that two miles and three-quarters of brass wire "have been produced from a three-quarter-inch brass strip." More than ten tons of pins are made in a week; and this country alone consumes in their manufacture from eleven to twelve tons of brass wire. The quality and make of a pin are no longer defined by statute. Competition, free-trade, and open markets have done for us what could never be effected by law; and the English pins are now classed among the best-made pins of commerce.

46

A. L. O. E., *THE STORY OF A NEEDLE*

(London: T. Nelson and Sons, 1874), pp. 7–10

My education

I REALLY can say nothing of my earliest days except from report. I have heard, but I can hardly believe it, that I was once part of a rough mass of iron ore, that had lain for ages in a dark mine in Cornwall; that I was dug out, and put into a huge furnace, and heated till I became red-hot, and melted; that I was made into part of an iron bar, and when in a fiery glow was suddenly plunged into cold water, which changed my whole constitution and name, for iron was thenceforth called steel. I can just fancy how the water fizzed and hissed, and how my fiery flush faded suddenly away, and I became again quite black in the face! I can fancy all this, as I said, but I really remember nothing about it.

Nor have I any recollection of being drawn out into wire, forced to push myself through little holes, smaller and smaller, till I was long enough and slim enough for the purpose for which the manufacturer designed me. My very earliest remembrance is of finding myself lying on an anvil, along with thousands of others of my species. But you must not fancy me then, gentle reader, in the least like the neat, trim, bright little article that now has the pleasure of addressing you. I fancy that I looked uncommonly like a bit of steel wire, neither useful nor ornamental.

While I lay quietly reflecting in a kind of dull, sleepy doze, for at that time I was not sharp at all, a violent blow on one end of me startled me not a little – I had been hit on that side as flat as a pancake!

"What next!" thought I. I had little time for thinking. I was popped into the fire in a minute, but taken out again before I had time to melt. Then down came another blow upon me, which had quite a different effect from the first. It pierced out a little hole in my flat head, and I received the advantage of having an eye. No sooner did I possess it than I began to use it; I peered around me with much curiosity, now on the long brick building in which I found myself, now on the rough careworn faces of the workmen, reddened by the glow of the fire-light, now on the multitude of baby needles around me, all looking up with their little round eyes.

I was now placed upon a block of lead, and my eye was punched to bring out the little bit of steel which was neither tidy nor convenient. Then, to improve the shape of my flat head, it was filed a little on both sides.

DOI: 10.4324/9781315400105-55

I felt now tolerably well satisfied with myself – something like a child (for I have since seen a good deal of the world) when it has mastered the first difficulties of learning, and begins to fancy itself a genius. But there was a good deal more of filing, and heating, and polishing before me; education is a slow and troublesome matter, whether to children or needles!

I am afraid that I should tire you, dear reader, were I to give you the whole story of how I was filed into a point; how I thought the file hard, disagreeable, and rough, as many young folk have thought their teachers; how I was then heated in a fire till I grew as red as naughty boys who have been caned by their master, then left to cool in a basin of cold water, like the same boys shut up to think over the matter.

Then I and a number of my companions were held in a shovel over the fire, and stirred about, and then straightened with blows of the hammer. I thought that I must now be quite perfect; but never was needle more mistaken. How could I go through linen, cloth, and silk, how could young gentlemen and ladies go through the world, without a proper degree of polish! Thousands of us were put on a piece of buckram, sprinkled with emery dust; more emery dust was thrown over us, and then a small quantity of oil; for I wish that every teacher would remember that though the emery of discipline is necessary enough, it works best when laid on with the sweet oil of kindness.

Oh, if I could only describe the rolling backwards and forwards, the rubbing and scrubbing again and again, the washing, the wiping, the smoothing on a stone, thought necessary to complete a good needle! Depend upon it, dear reader, your reading and writing, your sums and your tables, nay, even the terrible dog's-eared grammar, are nothing to what the smallest needle must go through before it is fit to appear in the world!

47

'NEEDLES'

The Century Dictionary and Cyclopedia, Vol. V (New York: The Century Co., 1895), p. 3956

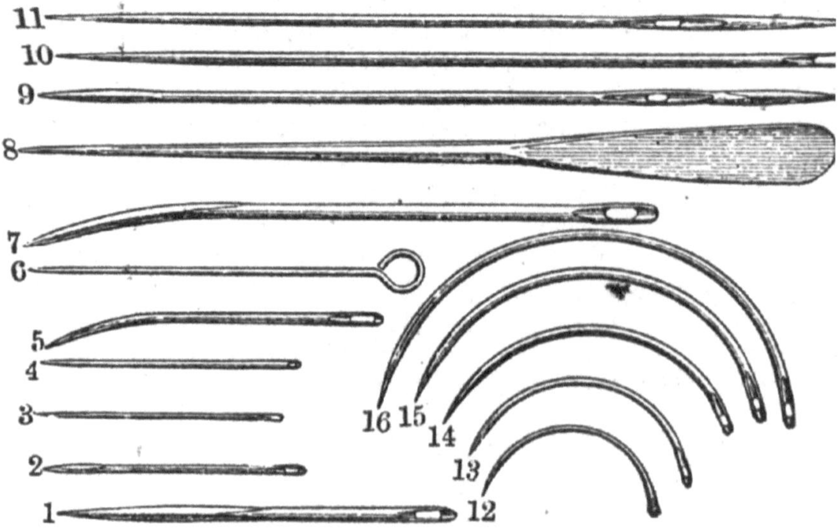

Figure 47.1

Upholsterers' and sailmakers' needles

1, 3½-inch sail; 2, 2⅝-inch spear-point carpet; 3, 1⅞-inch carpet; 4, 2¼-inch carpet; 5, 2½-inch speying; 6, upholsterers' skewer; 7, 5-inch packing; 8, 6-inch regulator; 9, 6-inch No. 14 gage, light spear double point; 10, 6-inch No. 13 gage, heavy round single point; 11, 6-inch No. 14 gage, light round double point; 12, 2-inch fine round tufting; 13, 2½-inch fine round tufting; 14, 3-inch flat single round curved; 15, 4-inch round single point curved; 16, 5-inch round single point curved.

DOI: 10.4324/9781315400105-56

3.2

Cutlery

DOI: 10.4324/9781315400105-57

3.2 Cutlery

Anon, 'A Day at the Sheffield Cutlery-Works', *The Penny Magazine of the Society for the Diffusion of Useful Knowledge*, Vol. 13 (27 April 1844), pp. 161–168.

Anon, 'Fraudulent Trade Marks', *Once a Week*, Vol. 8 (7 February 1863), pp. 177–179.

Anon, 'Joseph Rodgers & Sons, Limited', *The New Monthly Magazine*, Vol. 121 (July 1882), pp. 551–557.

Henry J. Palmer, 'Cutlery and Cutlers at Sheffield', *The English Illustrated Magazine*, Vol. 11 (August 1884), pp. 667–669.

Anon, 'Made in Germany', *The New Review*, Vol. 14 (March 1896), pp. 258–261.

Image: Joseph Rodgers & Sons, selections from the 'Old Table Day Book' (date approx. late 1800s), Museums Sheffield.

Image: 'Fish-slice and fork, and dessert-knife (Messrs. J. Rodgers & Sons, of Sheffield), *Art Journal Illustrated Catalogue of the Industry of All Nations* (London: Bradbury & Evans, George Virtue, n.d.), p. 278.

The sources in this section span the period 1844 to 1896 and use a domestic item to discuss British technological innovation, domestic habits and tastes, and Britain's place in the world. These accounts of cutlery production indicate hierarchies in the quality and prestige of the goods manufactured, the complications of social etiquette in dining, and the fraudulent, shady practices that beset the cutlery industry, which was based principally in Sheffield. The anonymous author of 'A Day at the Sheffield Cutlery-Works' (1844) focuses on descriptions of the production process. Forks are presented as simple to make, being forged from 'common steel' – unlike the fine gradients of steel that distinguish the quality of knives – with the prongs punched out by a powerful steam-powered hammer. The fork is then ground in a process similar to that of needle grinding. In sharp contrast, every step of knife production involves a hierarchy in the quality of the metal used. Blades can be made of iron or steel, with steel deemed to be of higher quality. The anonymous author of 'Joseph Rodgers & Sons, Limited' in the *New Monthly Magazine* (1882) refers to the quantities of ivory involved in the manufacture of knife handles, describing the annual 'destruction' of 1,280 elephants in order to keep just one firm supplied with ivory, a casual reference to the imperialist exploitation associated with this industry.

There is one firm of particular renown which is mentioned in several sources: Joseph Rodgers and Sons. This company, based in a large factory in Sheffield, manufactured and sold cutlery from their own premises. The factory covered 'an immense area', so large that even reading a description of it is said to be wearisome, according to the author of the 1882 article in the *New Monthly Magazine*. Rodgers' mark, a Maltese cross and a plain cross stamped upon the shoulder of the knife, was estimated in value at around £20,000 (approximately £1,182,584 today). Alongside the everyday cutlery manufactured by this company, visitors could also marvel at their special exhibition pieces. Both the *Penny Magazine* and *New Monthly Magazine* describe miniscule and outsize knives, all with huge numbers of folding blades. The most famous of these was the Norfolk knife, which was exhibited at the Great Exhibition, with its blades engraved with portraits of Victorian notables and famous views, such as Windsor Castle. The firm also exhibited more everyday designs, such as the knives and fork pictured here. Even self-described 'simple' designs show the Victorian taste for ornament, with the fish slice engraved with a riverside scene.

The Cutler's Company was established in 1624 to protect British dominance in the industry, its principal weapon being the trademark. In tones ranging from mild concern to utter outrage, each source in this section reports that Sheffield trademarks are forged, imitated and stolen, principally by German manufacturers. The author of 'Fraudulent Trade Marks' (1863) reaches for allegories of invasion to describe the 'seething mass of roguery', as 'the Northmen and the Danes who swept our coasts, . . . now . . . penetrate into the very heart of the country'. Threats to manufacturing industry are perceived as threats to British workers and the national revenue.

Henry Palmer in his visit to Sheffield, or 'Steelopolis', in 1884 noted the city's 'seamy' and dirty appearance, as well as its residents' inclinations towards 'sinister' trade unionism. In contrast, the hardening and tempering of steel are depicted by Palmer in aesthetic terms as a rainbow of brilliant colour: 'straw, gold, chocolate, purple, violet and blue'. He refers to John Ruskin (1819–1900), the Victorian art critic and educator who would establish his Guild of St. George in Sheffield, who insisted that ironwork is 'an art always necessary and useful to man; and English work in iron is masterful of its kind'. This article also condemns foreign imports as a nuisance which challenges both national pride and pride in the city.

The 'Old Table Day Book', or design repository, for Rodgers and Sons (one page reproduced here) contains patterns for over 2,700 knives and handles, revealing how one basic design could easily be tailored to differences in income, status and preferences of taste. Interestingly, given such a proliferation of choice, it is rare to find a Victorian conduct book or household management guide that specifies what type, and how much, cutlery a household should have. Nevertheless, the 'correct' laying of dining tables and use of cutlery could be associated with apprehension, and such anxieties are sometimes humorously depicted in Victorian fiction. In Dickens' *Great Expectations* (1861), for example, Pip's first lesson in gentlemanly behaviour takes place as he clumsily eats with a knife rather than using both knife and fork. International trade generated a different set of anxieties. British cutlery was in global demand, and all of the sources in this section note the cachet of a British-made knife. The author of 'Made in Germany' (1896) goes so far as to claim that 'the supreme merit of Sheffield steel is household knowledge in the remotest quarters of the earth'.

48

ANON, 'A DAY AT THE SHEFFIELD CUTLERY-WORKS'

The Penny Magazine of the Society for the Diffusion of Useful Knowledge, Vol. 13 (April 27 1844), pp. 161–165, 167–168

In the Supplement for March, relating to the Steel-Works of Sheffield, we had occasion to notice some of the peculiarities of that town as a centre of manufactures. But we must now view it more closely. We must regard it as one great workshop for the production of cutlery and edge-tools – a huge factory which scatters its separate departments in different parts of the town, but still retains them all, like so many links in a chain.

If we take a Directory of Sheffield as an index to the employments of its inhabitants, we shall see that, although the distinct occupations are very numerous, there is yet a tie which connects most of them together: cutting instruments, of some kind or other, being the objects to which most of the manufacturing arrangements relate. There are Cutlery Casters, Table-knife makers, Fork-makers, Penknife-makers, Lancet-makers, Razor-makers, Scythe-makers, Saw-makers, Edge-tool makers, Scissor-makers, Shear-makers, Spade and Shovel makers: preparatory to all these are the operations of the Steel-converters, and Tilters, and Rollers, and Casters; subsidiary to them are those connected with the making of handles, such as Ivory, Tortoiseshell, and Pearl-dealers, Ivory-cutters, Horn Merchants and Dealers, Horn-pressers, Bone Merchants and Dealers, Bone-pressers; and lastly, there are numberless minor occupations which contribute in various ways to the manufacture of cutlery, such as Casting-pot makers, Mark and Figure makers, Razor-strop makers, Studders and Handle-ornamenters, and many others. It is true that other manufactures are carried on to a considerable extent; for instance, the immense supply of steel at hand affords facilities for the production of various articles, such as fenders, wire, anvils, hammers; the large use of horn for handles has led to the settlement of the comb manufacture at Sheffield; the supply of bone for handles has given rise to button-mould making; and there are considerable manufactures in white metal, including silver and its various imitations. But still all these are so far outweighed by the arrangements connected with cutlery, that the latter must be deemed the staple, the characteristic, the distinguishing feature of Sheffield industry.

DOI: 10.4324/9781315400105-58

Like as in other instances, Sheffield has grown up to its present distinction by gradual advances. At the time when archery supplied the use of fire-arms throughout England, Sheffield is stated to have been celebrated for the manufacture of iron heads for arrows: and it was known by Chaucer as a place where blades of knives were made; for a character in one of his poems is mentioned as being furnished with a "*Sheffield thwytel*" (whittle), a kind of knife which used in those days to be carried about the person. Rather more than two centuries ago the principal cutlers formed themselves into a body corporate, for the protection of the trade, and especially for the protection of the 'marks' belonging to each individual, with a view to guard against the piracy of these marks by persons to whom they do not belong. It was about a century ago that the cutlery of Sheffield began to acquire such decided excellence as to raise it to a high rank. But it was not until the introduction of the mode of making cast-steel that this reputation reached its height; and at the present day it is not merely in the making of the steel, but also in the mechanical details of the manufacture, that the quality of the Sheffield steel goods is shown and appreciated.

Perhaps the mode in which we may best glance at the cutlery manufacture is to take, one by one, a few cutting instruments as examples, and see what are the chief processes which they undergo. The limited space at our command will not admit of all the varieties being noticed; nor is this necessary, since the broad features of manufacture are pretty much the same in all. We will commence with a notice of

Saws

which, whether included or not in what we generally term cutlery, hold an importance place among Sheffield manufactures.

Saws of the commoner kind are made of thin sheet-iron, planished, or hammered all over to give a certain degree of stiffness and elasticity. Those of a better quality are made of shear-steel; while the best are formed of cast-steel. We will suppose that the last-named are the object of our attention. The flat ingots of steel, as cast in the manner described in our former Supplement, are rolled between ponderous steel rollers, while red-hot, into the form of sheets the proper thickness for a saw. Many of the Sheffield firms carry on no other occupation than this of rolling bars of steel into sheets.

When the sheets of steel are brought to the workshops of the saw-maker, his first operation is to cut the sheets into pieces the proper size for the saws to be made. This operation of cutting is performed by means of a very stout pair of shears of peculiar form. A man holds the sheet of steel in such a position that the shears may act upon it, moving the sheet from time to time as the cut extends; while another works the shears. The edges of the pieces of steel are then made quite straight by means of a grindstone; and matters are ready for the making of the teeth. This is not done by a file, as some may suppose; nor by stamping out all the teeth at one blow, as others may imagine; but each tooth is punched out separately. There is a kind of flat bench so arranged that a steel cutter works vertically against a steel die; and by placing the saw-plate between the cutter and the die, one tooth is cut out at each movement of the fly-press connected with the cutter. The saw-plate is then shifted a little, and another tooth cut out in a similar manner, and so on until the whole of the teeth are formed. These teeth of course vary in size and shape according to the kind of saw to which they belong. In the saws for an ordinary saw-mill the teeth are generally right-angled triangles; in the pit-saw the teeth are so formed as to meet the fibres of the wood at an acuter angle; while hand-saws and the generality of carpenters' and joiners' saws have teeth midway in form between the two other kinds. The teeth, after being cut, are finished up with a file, and the burr, or raggedness of the edge, is removed. The steel then undergoes the process of 'hardening,' which, at some stage or other, is the case with nearly all steel goods. The saws are laid flat in a furnace fitted for their reception, and heated to a degree determined by experience. They are taken out of the furnace, and immediately plunged into cold oil (or into some prepared liquid), whereby they are quenched, and made to acquire a sudden and very considerable degree of hardness.

When the saws, or 'plates,' as they are called, are removed from the hardening-trough, part of the oily mixture is wiped from the surface, while the remainder is dissipated by holding the saw over a clear coke fire; this heating at the same time gives the proper degree of temper or elasticity to the steel. While yet warm, the steel is hammered at different parts, to remove any warping or bending which it might have suffered. Then follows one of the most noisy operations connected with the manufacture, viz. the 'planishing.' The saw is held in the left hand of the workman, rested on a small polished steel anvil, and hammered repeatedly on every part of the surface with a small hammer, whereby a clatter is produced from which a stranger gladly escapes. The object of this process is to make the saw true, even, and of equal elasticity in every part. The operation requires a great deal of dexterity; for the workman, by giving to the saw a kind of vibratory motion as he goes on, tests the elasticity and tension of the steel, and acquires by habit the tact of knowing where to strengthen the weaker parts by increasing the number of blows.

The saw is then carried to the 'wheel,' or grindstone, where both surfaces are ground all over, to reduce them to an even and regular state: this process having relation to the outer surface of the saw, while the planishing relates more to the internal texture. The grindstones employed for saws are of large size, sometimes as much as six or seven feet in diameter. The saw is too thin and flexible to be held against the grindstone as a knife would be; it is therefore fixed lightly to a board, and the board so held by the grinder (as sketched in our frontispiece) as to bring the saw in contact with the edge of the stone, shifting to and fro, until every part of both surfaces has been ground down level and true. As saws of the larger sizes could not be conveniently held in this way, they are suspended at both ends by cords from the ceiling, and swung backwards and forwards to bring them to the proper positions. The peculiarities attending this process are very exactly portrayed by Mr. Holland (in his Treatise on the Iron and Steel Manufacture), in the following words: – "It is not easy to conceive the idea of muscular exertion, imminent danger, and peculiarity of attitude presented to the eye; and the mind of an individual, who, unaccustomed to such a spectacle, looks at a saw-grinder when at work, standing on tiptoes over a great grindstone revolving with a fearful rapidity; his arms outstretched towards the extremities of the board under which lies the saw, and pressing against it with his knees to keep it in the closest contact with the surface of the stone; his person and dress appearing at the same time as if they had been dipped in an ochre-bed – present a picture of no common interest."

This grinding, though it gives one kind of regularity and equability to the saw, deranges it in respect to another; for the steel requires another planishing, or hammering on an anvil, to restore to it the flatness and straightness which the grinding had disturbed. After this second hammering, it is passed over a small coke fire till a particular and carefully tested degree of 'temper,' or elasticity, is given to it. Another grinding, but much slighter than the former, takes out the marks of the hammer, and gives a uniformity of appearance.

There next ensues a process so slight, so simple, and so soon ended, that it would seem hardly necessary to give it a separate place in the description; but it at the same time so remarkably illustrates the tact acquired by long practice, that a stranger is likely to be more struck with this than with any other part of the operations: If we look at the teeth of a saw, we shall see that half are bent in one direction, and half in the other; every alternate one being bent differently. This is done by the blows of a hammer, one blow to each tooth. The saw is rested flat on a steel anvil, and held by the left hand of the workman, who has a very small hammer in his other hand. With this hammer he strikes the sides of the teeth, one at a time; the weight of the hammer, the shape of the hammer-head, and the force of the blow, being just such as will enable one blow to give the required bending to the tooth. But the point worthy of note is the rapid and unerring manner in which the workman proceeds along the saw, *missing* every alternate tooth, striking one blow on each of the others, and yet advancing from one to another almost as fast as the eye can follow him. He then turns the saw over, and bends the other half of the teeth in a similar manner, but in an opposite direction. There is a kind of bevel or slope in the small anvil, to effect a bending in the teeth of the saw.

These are the main features, such as we witnessed at the Saw-manufactory of Messrs. Hoole and Unsworth. Several minor details we may pass over, and the making of the handles we shall slightly notice in a future page.

Table-knives

A table-knife is perhaps the most important of the different articles of cutlery – not from its quality, for a razor is more highly finished; not from its intricacy, for a clasp-knife has more detail about it – but from the large extent to which the use has risen. Every house in England, except the very humblest, has as many table-knives in it as there are inmates; and most houses have a great many more. When we consider, too, that table-knives, as well as other articles, have the art of wearing away, and that the industry and the brickdust of the housemaid greatly hasten this process; and when we look abroad to notice the avidity which all rude nations exhibit to gain possession of an English knife – we shall be prepared to regard this as a very extensive branch of Sheffield manufacture.

There is in most of the operations on steel goods a series of processes pretty constant in their general character. The forging, the hardening, the tempering, the grinding, the sharpening, the polishing – all form steps in most of the series, and bearing a certain resemblance in their general character. A table-knife, for instance, is forged out of a piece of steel of higher or lower quality according to the price at which it is to be sold. The very commonest are probably not steel at all, being simply bar iron; the next quality may be common steel, the next shear-steel, and the highest of all cast-steel. But whatever be the material, a length of bar is cut off, sufficient for one blade, and forged into shape. All the Sheffield forges are pretty much alike. They consist of a forge-fire kindled by bellows; and have a large block of stone or wood, serving as a bench, and provided with small steel anvils, stitheys, bosses, hammers, and other instruments necessary to the operation. The piece of steel is heated in the fire, placed on an anvil and hammered into form; being turned over and about in every direction, and the workman regulating his blows according to the form which he wishes to produce, reducing the thickness from one end to the other, and from one edge to the other. But this relates to the blade only; the 'tang,' or part which goes into the handle, is a separate part. To make this tang, the rudely formed blade is welded to a rod of iron, about half an inch square; and a sufficient length of this iron is cut off to form the tang, and also the 'shoulder,' or the projecting part between the tang and the blade. The end of the iron is heated and forged so as to be reduced in size sufficient to form the tang; and the shoulder is next brought into shape by hammering it in a kind of die or stamp called a 'swage.' The tang and the bolster being made, the whole is heated a second time, and the proper form and dimensions given to it. The blade is then heated red-hot, and plunged perpendicularly into cold water, by which a sudden hardening is effected; and a gradual heating afterwards to a certain point gives the 'temper' or degree of elasticity best fitted for the purpose to which table-knives are to be applied.

When the knives are thus far prepared, they are carried to the grinding wheels, where the blade is ground all over on a large revolving stone; whereby the surface is brought level, the edges made straight, or at least regular, the point rounded or tapered as the case may be, and the edge sharpened. The grindstones made use of for grinding table-knives are between three and four feet in diameter, and about six inches broad upon the face. They are formed of a species of sandstone, and revolve with great rapidity, without at the same time greatly heating the articles being ground. The knives are ground first upon this stone, and afterwards upon one of finer texture called the 'whitening stone.'

Here it may be well to notice the customary arrangements at Sheffield respecting the grinding of steel goods. As the town is dotted here and there with '*Tilts*,' so is it likewise with '*Wheels*;' and in the one case as well as in the other the name is an abbreviation well known among the townsmen. A 'wheel' is a building fitted up with a large number of grindstones, each hired at a weekly or yearly rental, by a grinder, who grinds some kinds or other of cutlery for other persons. Before the introduction of steam-power, the grinding wheels were in most cases situated by the side of a fall in one or other of the rivers of Sheffield, so as to obtain the action of a water-wheel; and these little structures often presented a picturesque appearance. But in modern times large buildings have been appropriated for this purpose, amply provided with steam-power. There is one building in particular, called the Castle Mills, situated near the junction of the Sheaf and the Don, which is especially calculated to illustrate this arrangement. It is a large castellated structure – open to the objection, perhaps, of exhibiting a style of architecture wholly inconsistent with the nature of the mechanical operations going on within. There is a central court-yard surrounded by buildings, and at different heights are galleries running round, with doors opening into numerous apartments on all sides. The south side of the building is adjacent to the river Don; but a steam-engine supplies the moving-power. If we go into the rooms of this building, we find men employed in grinding all the various kinds of Sheffield steel goods. In one room are men grinding saws, in another table-knives, in another pen and pocket knives, in another forks, in another scissors, in another razors; employing grindstones of all sizes from four inches to seven feet in diameter, and of varying quality. All are brought into connection with the moving power by means of the usual mechanism; and it is on these revolving stones that the grinding is effected.

In such places as this Castle Mill every man confines himself pretty nearly to one kind of work, and pays a rental to the proprietor for the use of the room and the steam-power; or sometimes a man hires a whole room containing several grindstones, and either employs others to work for him or sublets some of the room. When walking round the gallery, and looking in one room after another, we may see the men in their cramped attitudes (for it is never an easy one) bending over the grindstones, and engaged from morning till night in grinding articles of cutlery or other steel goods. These goods are not their own, but belong to others, who merely employ them as grinders.

But to return to our table-knives. When the knives are ground, they are ready for 'glazing' or 'polishing.' This is performed on a wheel called a 'glazer;' consisting of a circular piece of wood, fixed upon an iron axis, and coated on the edge either with leather, or with a ring of metal consisting of an alloy of lead and tin. The leather-faced glazers, used for glazing table-knives, are first covered with a solution of glue and then with emery powder; and it is by friction against this slightly roughened substance that the glazing of the knife-blade and shoulder is effected. The extent to which this process is carried on has led to the establishment of 'buff and glazer makers' among the trades of Sheffield.

Forks

Fork-making is not without its peculiarities among the departments of Sheffield industry. Most of the fork-makers live in the environs of the town; and indeed there are one or two villages almost wholly inhabited by these operatives. Forks are in most cases made of 'common steel,' that is, blister-steel which has been drawn out under the hammer, but neither sheared nor cast. They are forged out of rods about three-eighths of an inch square, in the following manner: – The tang and shank of the fork are first roughly formed, by hammering out the metal while in a red-hot state; and being again heated, the proper contour is given to them by means of a die and swage or stamp. The prongs are formed by stamping with a powerful punch acting on the principle of the pile-driving machine, but of course with a force proportionate to the work to be done. There is a large anvil fixed in a block of stone nearly on a level with the ground; to this are attached two rods of iron of considerable thickness, fixed about a foot asunder, perpendicular to the anvil, and reaching to the ceiling; the hammer or stamp, weighing about a hundred pounds, grooved on each side, slides up and down by means of the iron rods, which act as guides; a rope, passing from the hammer over a pulley, gives the workman the means of raising the hammer; and lastly, the lower surface of the hammer and the upper surface of the anvil are each provided with a die or stamp adapted to the cutting of the prongs. The blank fork, being heated to a certain degree of softness, is placed on the lower die, and the hammer containing the other die is made to fall upon it from a height of six or seven feet. This forms the prongs and the middle part of the fork, leaving a very thin substance of steel between the prongs, which is afterwards cut out by means of a fly-press. The forks thus brought to the form so familiar to us, are annealed by heating in an oven and then gradually cooling, so as to acquire a softness sufficient to enable them to be filed all round and between the prongs. After this they are hardened, by being heated and suddenly cooled.

The grinding of forks is one of the most lamentable operations in the whole series of manufacturing processes, from its deleterious effects on the health. Forks are ground upon a dry stone, called the 'fork-stone,' formed of sharp grit of a whitish colour, very similar to that of which millstones are formed. The stone is about half a yard in diameter and two inches broad at the edge. The grinder sits on a 'horse' or stool, bends over the stone, holds the fork crosswise against the stone, and grinds all the parts of the surface to a smooth and even condition. If the stone were wetted, as in most other cases, the inconvenience would not be great; but the stone is kept quite dry, whereby not only is there a profusion of sparks given out, but the face and head of the grinder are enveloped in an atmosphere loaded with small particles of steel and gritstone, which are inhaled into the lungs. Such is likewise the case in the process of needle-grinding; and in both instances the workmen infallibly fall victims to a distressing disease known as the 'grinders' asthma.' It is said that there are hardly any fork-grinders more than forty years of age, since the disease carries off most of them before they reach that time of life. When describing the Needle-manufacture at Redditch, in the Supplement for January, 1843, we alluded to the laudable endeavour of Mr. Abraham of Sheffield to devise a remedy for this sad evil, by placing a shield of magnets in front of the grinder's mouth, whereby the small particles should be arrested and prevented from entering the lungs. Another plan has been suggested by a Mr. Elliot; which consists in the adoption of a long box or wooden chimney, placed opposite to and partially covering the grindstone in front, while the other extremity is carried through a hole in the wall. In this arrangement it is said that such a current of air is excited by the mere revolution of the stone as to carry the dusty particles through this funnel into the open air outside the building. Yet both these plans have been rejected by the workmen, and so have all others having for their object the amelioration of this employment. Whether it is that the contrivances are very troublesome to arrange, or whether the grinders wish the occupation to remain unhealthy in order that wages may remain high (and both opinions have been expressed), certain it is that dry-grinding is still what it has ever been – one of the most disastrous occupations connected with the manufacturing arts; and it is equally certain that unless the men aid the attempts made for their comfort, all such attempts must be fruitless. [. . .]

Handles

We have more than once had to speak of the handles for knives, razors, and other articles of cutlery. These form an important and extensive department of Sheffield industry, leading to a vast consumption of material.

According to the technical phraseology applied, all handles are called *hafts* in which a tang of the knife passes into a hole in the handle, and is there fixed; while the handles which are formed of two flat pieces riveted to a central plate, as in penknives, are called *scales*. A 'haft and scale maker,' therefore (one of the trades of Sheffield), is in fact a handle-maker.

The workmen who engage in this employment confine themselves each pretty nearly to one kind of material. The pearl-handle makers procure the shells from the shores of India and Africa; these shells are about six inches in diameter, and are so extremely hard that they have to be wetted while being cut with a saw, to prevent the saw from being softened by the heat. This is a dirty occupation, and is accompanied by a

> "– very ancient and fish-like smell,"

elicited by the heat from the shell itself. The pearl, or rather mother-of-pearl, is cut up into thin slices, to be afterwards used for the scales for penknives, razors, &c. *Ivory* handles are made by sawing up elephants' tusks into the most useful pieces they can make, by means of a circular saw. If the ivory is for scales, it is cut into veneers; but if for hafts, it is cut into small oblong pieces, which are afterwards brought to shape by hand, polished, and pierced for the reception of the tang. *Bone* handles are similarly made by cutting with a small circular saw, and then filing into shape; and the same may be said of *ebony* and fancy-wood handles generally. *Saw-handles* are cut out of wood, which, after being planed to the proper thickness, is fixed in a vice, cut with a very fine saw, smoothed with files and glass-paper, pierced with rivet-holes, and riveted to the saws. *Metal* handles are, of course, made in a way similar to other articles of metal.

Horn handles have a peculiarity in their mode of manufacture, which places them in a distinct rank. When horn is made hot, it becomes so soft and ductile that it may be pressed into moulds; and this circumstance is taken advantage of to give an ornamental device to horn handles, except *stag's-horn*, which is left in its natural state. The tips or solid part of ox-horn and buffalo-horn are made into hafts, while the other parts are made into scales. The mould for pressing is in two halves, which close together like a pair of pincers; and this mould has the device on each of its halves. The mould is heated in a fire; the piece of horn is cut nearly to the requisite size, and put into it; and the mould is pressed in a powerful vice, whereby the horn receives the impress of the device.

There is also a good deal of skill shown in staining horn, bone, and ivory, or in bleaching them; as also in studding and ornamenting them in various ways.

System of manufacturing

All these departments of Sheffield manufacture, and others which we have not particularly noticed, are in themselves separate branches, and are only united in respect to the larger merchants and manufacturers. These manufacturers buy the steel from one or more firms, have it forged by another or several others, ground by others, and finished by others; or they will purchase ready-made goods from smaller manufacturers; or they sometimes advance money to workmen to purchase material, and then agree to give a certain price for the articles. In short, there are several modes of conducting the manufacture, but the *factory* system is not one of them. By this we mean, that there is no large building, under a central authority, in which a piece of steel goes in at one door, and comes out at another converted into knives, scissors, and razors. Nearly all the articles of cutlery made at Sheffield travel about the town several times before they are finished.

There are, however, a few large firms which, besides selling all the various kinds of cutlery, manufacture largely on their own premises. The firm of Messrs. Rodgers and Co. is one of these. On visiting the show-rooms of this establishment a stranger can hardly avoid being struck by the display of manufacturing skill which meets the eye. Sheffield has long been the head-quarters of the cutlery trade; and we here see examples of what Sheffield skill can produce. Besides the bulk of manufactured articles, such as we find a sale in the common course of business, there are three or four highly curious specimens of workmanship to be seen. One is a clasp-knife not more than an inch in length when closed, and yet containing seventy-five blades, all perfectly and properly formed, and resembling in shape such as are customarily used in clasp-knives, but on quite a miniature scale. Every blade has its spring, hinge, rivet, and other appendages, so that it forms altogether a tiny, yet multitudinous knife. Another specimen is about two feet in length, and contains the enormous number of eighteen hundred and forty-one blades! It was made a few years ago, and then contained blades corresponding in number with the year in which it was made; since then a few others have been added; and it is, we believe, contemplated to bring up arrears by shortly increasing the number to eighteen hundred and forty-four, so that this may be a sort of a Sheffield almanac and a specimen of Sheffield knife-making at the same time. The blades in this splendid group are about the usual size. A third specimen, though having less than this number of blades, eclipses the other two in beauty. It is placed in a glass case on a rotating stand, and is about thirty inches in height. It contains two hundred and twenty blades, all of large size, and most of them exquisitely engraved, or rather etched, with portraits of distinguished persons, views of the chief buildings in Sheffield, and other subjects. These pictures being of a dead white appearance, on steel having the most brilliant polish that art can impart to it, and being skilfully done in respect to drawing, the whole assemblage is strikingly beautiful. Such parts of the handle as present a flat surface are of pearl, studded with jewels; and it is said that a sum of between seven and eight hundred guineas was expended in wages alone in the production of the knife!

Many persons may perhaps occasionally have seen curious little specimens of cutlery, in which the object seems to be to try how much can be done in a small space. One such is included among the curiosities of this show-room. It consists of a group of ten pairs of scissors, each complete in itself, each about one-tenth of an inch in length, and the whole ten weighing rather less than a grain; or (to give a familiar standard) it would take nearly five hundred such pairs of scissors to weigh as much as a silver sixpence!

With respect to the workshops of this firm (excluding those relating to the manufacture of plate and plated goods, which we do not notice here), they exhibit many of the branches of manufacture which have been occupying our attention. There are ranges of forges, and other portions of the apparatus for manufacturing cutlery. Yet even in this establishment it would be impossible to trace the manufacturing history of a knife without following it to other workshops in Sheffield. And such may be said of the larger firms generally, as well as the smaller ones. Each class of manufacturers is so dependent on the others, and there is such a chain of links connecting them all, that we have found it convenient to speak of Sheffield as one huge workshop for steel goods.

49

ANON, 'FRAUDULENT TRADE MARKS'

Once a Week, Vol. 8 (February 7, 1863), pp. 177–179

WE have all heard of the tricks of our American cousins – of their wooden hams, fictitious nutmegs, and contract boots with the soles pasted on, and many of us have come to the belief that all the rascality is to be found on the other side of the herring-pond. This doctrine is comfortable, but unhappily it is not true. We have before us now a parliamentary report on Trade Marks and Merchandise Marks, two subjects on which our own Government lawyers are essaying to legislate. What a seething mass of roguery runs beneath the smooth surface of our so-called civilisation! If anybody doubts the truth of this remark, we recommend him to take a turn for an hour at the thin blue-book before us. Mr. Roebuck some time ago scared the nation with a recital of the manner in which foreigners were forging the Sheffield trade marks, and the evidence contained in this report fully warrants his statement. It appears that we are gradually losing our foreign cutlery and hardware trade, in consequence of pirates over the sea. We suffered of old from the Northmen and the Danes who swept our coasts, but now they penetrate into the very heart of the country, and snatch the bread from our working men. Our readers doubtless know that the excellence of our cutlery has long become famous throughout the world, and also that the seat of that trade is concentrated principally in Sheffield. The excellence of the wares there produced is guaranteed by the affixing of certain trade marks upon them by the different manufacturers of eminence belonging to the Cutlers' Company. Let us instance for example the knives of Rodgers and Son. If the reader possesses a pocket-knife of this maker, and opens it, he will see that, in addition to the name, there is a Maltese cross and a plain cross stamped upon the shoulder of the knife. This is the trade mark, the endorsement of the firm with respect to its excellence. This trade mark is very valuable; possibly the manufacturer would not sell it for 20,000*l*. There are other trade marks almost equally valuable. An adze maker will select as his mark or emblem a pipe, another will put on a hatchet, another a lion, a fourth a goat, according to the class of men whom the tool or implement is likely to reach. The reason why trade marks are stamped on this kind of "dry goods" is that they are often made for a distant market, where the peasantry can understand a simple

DOI: 10.4324/9781315400105-59

emblem, when they would not be able to read a maker's name. The Canadian backwoodsman, for example, has found that his old adze marked with a pipe was excellent; he therefore demands a new adze with a similar mark upon it. The name of the maker he may not be able to read, any more than the savage to whom these goods are sometimes sold.

Now here a fine field for forgery was open, and some of our friends across the water have not been long in availing themselves of it. Ramscheid and Solingen, in North Prussia, it appears, are the seat of this nefarious trade. The manufacturers in these towns keep a regular assortment of forged English marks, and send them out to the order of their customers, as a matter of course. The traveller for an English house happening to be in the former town a short time since, one of the manufacturers observing the name upon his card, remarked, "That is our trade mark, too," and illustrated his position by pulling down a parcel with the spurious articles thus stamped with the forged mark. He perfectly well knew that the article was spurious; but the roguery had been perpetrated so long, that he absolutely imagined that he had a right to the mark by proscription. No sooner, we are told, does an English trade mark become famous abroad, than the agents for the German houses immediately send word home to have it forged, and within six months a consignment of the spurious article enters the field, at a rate so low that the genuine article is driven out of the market. The roguish Prussian manufacturer not only destroys our Sheffield trade in this way, but he has the audacity to mark the rubbish he sells at a low rate with some celebrated English maker's name or emblem, and puts the name of his own firm upon a better-class article. He then goes to the customer, and says, "Here are the inferior English goods at a dear price, and here is our own make at a cheap one." In this manner many of our manufacturers who used to supply the South American market have been obliged to relinquish the trade. The shipment of these fraudulent goods is managed so adroitly, that our foreign customers are sure to fall into the trap. Thus, for instance, the goods are sent from abroad to Hull, and are there trans-shipped for some foreign market. When they have arrived, it is advertised that so many cases of Rodgers' cutlery, or of some other celebrated name, have just been landed from an English ship.

As far as Englishmen are concerned, there is now existing in Sheffield a system of trade marks which prevents piracy. These laws are, however, operative only in the county of Hallamshire, as the district including Sheffield and a radius of six miles around is called; but outside of Sheffield the only remedy against fraudulent imitations of trade marks is by an injunction and proceedings in Chancery; and we all know how very unsatisfactory such a method of obtaining justice generally is. The cutlers of London have also a law, by which the use of the word "London" is prohibited to any manufacturer of cutlery residing at a distance of ten miles from St. Paul's; but any article may be stamped with the address of any street in the metropolis, provided this word be omitted. The purchaser may therefore be certain that a knife marked "London" is "town made."

But it will be asked will not the Prussian Government – the Government which professes to rule over the best educated nation in the world – give us a remedy for this abominable system of forgery perpetrated by their manufacturers? Unfortunately no. There are excellent laws by which a Prussian can obtain redress against a Prussian for infringing his mark or forging his name, but this law does not extend to foreigners. On the other side, the Prussian can obtain justice in England against an Englishman committing the like offence; but then our process of proof is so expensive, and the result of law-suits is so uncertain, that foreigners do not care to put our laws in force. It might be otherwise if we had a treaty with the Prussians as we have with France, where we have absolute protection for the mere fee of registering, which only costs two francs; but if we hope for a treaty with Prussia, we must be able to offer them something in exchange for what we get: their Government would rightly say, if we give you the advantage of the cheap Prussian law to protect your manufactures, we must have something better than your cumbersome English law, which is practically inoperative to protect us Prussians. This is so reasonable that we trust the Bill about to be brought into Parliament will give us some cheap method of registration of trade marks which will protect us at home, and by reciprocity abroad, from the frauds of piratical manufacturers.

But we must not grow Pharisaical and thank God that we are not as other men, for the pages of this very blue-book unfortunately prove that we have just as much roguery going on in our tight little island as can be found abroad. We have all heard for instance of an operation called "shaving the ladies," yet we doubt if any lady is aware of the very clean shave she is constantly undergoing. If she is accustomed to frequent "cutting shops," where the stock is periodically thrown into a state of convulsions in its efforts to sell itself off, of course she expects to be done: but possibly she does not know that for years the trade in "small wares," as it is termed, has been losing its conscience in the most remarkable manner. There is, in short, a regular conspiracy to cheat between the manufacturers and the great wholesale dealers. If a lady, for instance, buys a reel of cotton marked a hundred yards, she imagines, possibly, that she gets that quantity. Miserable delusion! There are not more than seventy. All goods, again, that are sold in the piece, run short: "short-stick," in fact, is a slang term for insufficient lengths. Some of the wholesale middlemen will send up labels to the manufacturer indicating false lengths, and they are put on, as a matter of course, by many spinners. The Britisher is thus cheated out of 30 per cent. of his goods: but that is nothing to the way in which the Yankees plunder. Thus they will forge some well-known name, say in thread, and they will keep lowering the lengths on the reels from seventy until they touch thirty yards only, still retaining the hundred yards label. In this manner a good name is "run to death." Then a fresh one is selected, and brought into discredit in a similar manner.

Of old there used to be five hundred pins in a packet; now there are often only two hundred. Articles marked "worsted," again, often have 95 per cent. of cotton in them. The loss, it must be observed, always falls on the ultimate purchaser, as many of the articles cannot be unwound to be measured without being spoilt.

We can understand a petty tradesman perpetrating these contemptible frauds; but what shall we think of the integrity of British merchants, when we find that it is not at all an uncommon thing for them to send up to the manufacturers labels imitating those used by excellent makers, and stipulating that they shall be affixed to inferior goods of other makers? The Merchandise Marks Bill is aimed at this organised system of frauds perpetrated on our wives and daughters.

We may not be very deeply moved at the ladies being cleanly shaved, but the male Briton will not fail to feel indignant at the frauds perpetrated on his bitter beer. It will possibly be new to the public, that Bass does not bottle his own ale, but sells it in barrels, and supplies his customers with a sufficient number of labels marked with his trade mark (a red triangle) for the quantity of bottles which the cask will fill. So far, good; but these labelled bottles henceforth become the vehicles for a series of frauds. The publican round the corner, who supplies you, good reader, with your daily pint of Bass, stipulates for the return of the empty bottles, that he may fill them again with salted, sugared, filthy Burton; and again and again it is done, as long as the famous "red triangle" will keep decently clean upon the bottles. This is a matter which touches the thirsty Briton, and he should see to it. Mr. Bass evidently is unwittingly lending himself to a most detestable cheat. Imagine, good reader, the basket from Bunkum and Pott's, at your next pic-nic, duly unpacked by the river side in the charming month of June, and the tumblers held out by thirsty souls to John in attendance, only to receive, instead of the charming sparkling pale ale, sweet and clammy public-house beer! Would transportation be sufficient punishment for the rascal who has done that thing? It seems to us that if the labels were pasted over the cork, instead of on the bottles, and if the forging of this label were made a misdemeanor, punishable with imprisonment, as the Merchandise Marks Bill proposes, we might still rest in security as to the integrity of our Bass. As it is, even your black servant in India knows that he can get one coin more for an empty labelled bottle than for a plain one, and thus the swindle circulates round the world.

If we turn to arms, again, we find fraud pursuing us. Mr. Westley Richards complains that common rifles are stamped with his name, and sent into the market as genuine articles; and but too often the purchaser gets his hand blown off. It is always the English gentleman who has to pay the penalty of the fraud. We recommend this particular instance, therefore, to the attention of the sporting members of the House of Commons, and it will doubtless go some way towards obtaining their hearty concurrence in a measure which will put down a growing system of fraud which is sapping the integrity of the working and mercantile classes of the country.

A. W.

50

ANON, 'JOSEPH RODGERS & SONS, LIMITED'

The New Monthly Magazine, Vol. 121 (July 1882), pp. 551–557

The main buildings cover an immense area having a handsome frontage in Norfolk Street, skirting Milk Street, Sycamore Street and Flat Street, and to travel all round and describe what is there to be seen would be both wearisome to reader and to writer. We must therefore confine ourselves to a representative birds-eye view, and the first thing that attracts attention is the almost arbitrary sub-divisions into which the trade is cut up, each department being elevated to the dignity of and strictly regarded as a trade. A general example will suffice. Forging and grinding are necessarily different occupations, but the workman who forges or grinds a table blade will have nothing to do with a pocket knife, and the forger and grinder of the large blade of the pocket knife will have nothing to do with the pen blade of the same knife; and so it runs throughout. Our guide now conducts us to the forging shops, which are almost counterparts of the village smithy, the forger, or the maker as he is technically called, having before him his anvil fitted in proper style, to his left works his mate the striker, who is the servant of the maker, and who blows the fire and attends to the heating. At his right are hung upon the wall his various tools, which he takes down, uses, and hangs back again with surprising rapidity. The heating or firing the steel is one of the points that test the ability of the workman, for if the metal is insufficiently heated the forger cannot work it, and if too much it becomes "burnt" and changed into a sulphuret of iron, a condition unfitted for cutlery purposes. As we have already said, the best Sheffield blades are wrought by hand pretty much as in times of yore. Machinery has been introduced, but its application is at present very limited and it is problematical whether it can deal the few well-aimed blows requisite for the manipulation of the steel any better, or so well, as the practised muscle of the swarthy smith. At any rate, here we saw forgers dealing out their blows with wonderful alacrity, and fashioning the rude metal into blades of many sorts and sizes.

Pocket or penknives undergo the following processes: – 1st, "Mooding," or forging the rough ingot; 2nd, drawing the tang, that is, the piece that goes into the handle, a task achieved in as short a time as it takes to write about it; 3rd, the marking or stamping of the name and corporate mark upon the tang end or

DOI: 10.4324/9781315400105-60

the blade, which is done by softening the blade in the fire until it is brought to a dull red heat known as "worm red," in which state it is just heated enough to receive the impress of the stamp; 4th, the smithing or finishing, which includes the hardening and tempering, a very necessary process. This latter necessitates a further heating of the steel up to the dull red heat just mentioned, at which point it is removed from the hearth and thrust into water. It is then hardened, but useless, and it must be again heated until it assumes a bright blue tint. Taken out once more it is put aside to cool, by which time it has lost the brittleness given it by the hardening, and restored to its native pliability. Table blades pass through the same stage, but include the additional process of raising the "bolster," by the aid of "dies," "prints," or "bosses," as they are variously termed. The bolster, which is mostly of iron, is welded on to the end of the steel blade, and gives out the tang.

In these fundamental stages the worth or worthlessness of the knife is manifest, for no amount of grinding or subsequent processes can give to a blade the consistency denied it at the forge, or in the tempering, and sooner or later its imperfection will like murder reveal itself.

From the smithies and the preliminary filing shops, which latter practically belong to the former, the knives are taken to the grinders' wheel or "Hulls," and here a different scene is witnessed. In place of the harmonious ring of the forger's anvil, the air is rent with harsh and grating sounds arising from the stones, intermingled with the whirr and buzz of machinery. Little wonder is it that men of this trade are often devoid of the finer feelings which should characterise humanity – ordinary refinement and nerve being almost impossible amid such surroundings, yet, happily, there are many men who can and do throw off the associations of their trade as they divest themselves of their bespattered garments, taking their places as respectable and intelligent citizens. The term "wheel" applies to the grinding shops as a whole, and "hull" to each division in which a few men work. A dirty sandstone hue pervades the whole place, and often for yards around, and as the grinder dexterously holds his blade to the rapidly-revolving stone a continuous shower of sparks is emitted. It is the custom of the trade for the men to buy their own stones, which last on an average about six weeks, by which time they are worn down too small for table blade grinding, and are then "cleft" in two and passed on to the penknife grinders, who require much smaller stones. There is always a danger of the stones "flying," in which case fatal consequences often ensue; but these accidents are fortunately becoming less frequent. Rough and dirty as the work is, the grinder has to be a "skilled" man, whether he is engaged on running his blade over the first wheel, which is a sandstone, or over the second, a blue and harder stone, on which the edge is brought up. Penknives pass through the same processes with the exception of the small pen blades, which are ground on lead wheels to produce the concave.

The forging of the iron hafts or scales and springs is a simple matter which we may pass over, and to preserve the continuity of the manufacture we will leave this department and take a glance at the ivory store room, where the tusks of elephants, large and small, are seen in abundance. Now it is a well-known fact that pearl and ivory are every year becoming more and more scarce, and yet the consumption is on the increase. The African elephant yields the finest ivory. The destruction of the astonishing number of 1280 elephants would be involved to supply this firm with the twenty-four tons they require annually if they were not drawing on the hoards of byegone years. Most of the African ivory in the market is obtained from the collections made by dusky natives, who have had it buried in the sands for many years. Still, as civilization advances, the supply decreases, and there is little doubt that at some future time ivory will become an *article de luxe*, and that for general cutlery purposes a substitute will have to be found.

Costly as it is, particularly just now, and we believe we are correct in stating that it is over £1000 a ton, it can all be utilized, even the very saw dust and odd ends being sold for practical purposes. Half-a-dozen men are constantly employed in cutting it up into the various lengths and patterns, and their shop in appearance closely resembles a flour mill. In the stag horn room about 180 cwt. per annum of best horn is cut up, the common quality being purchased already cut. Germany supplies us with the finest quality, and England and Scotland come next, but in the words of the workmen, "when English and Scotch horn is good it is good, and very common when common." A good deal of horn also comes from Ceylon. Here also no waste occurs, as the refuse and ends are sold to spectacle and razor case makers, for whose purposes it appears to be admirably adapted.

Now, assuming that the blades, the hafts, the springs, and the scales are forged and cut, we will enter the cutler's shop, and it may be well to observe that the cutler is the workman who puts together the various parts and finishes the knife. Yet here, again, sub-divisions are the order of the day, for on one bench a man is balancing table knives, another is doing a special kind of grinding, whilst another is putting together the penknife. In the case of table knives the Bolster has to be smoothed down, but although the blade has gone through the hands of the grinder, he leaves this part for the cutler, who now passes it over a fine emery wheel, reducing the roughness in an incredibly short space of time. The "Buffers," or "Glazers," run the steel over a wooden wheel dressed with emery half-a-dozen times, and once more the knives are taken to the grinding wheel, where they receive a final polish on a Sea Horse leather, and are then ready for the warehouse, to be cleaned and packed for delivery.

With regard to razors and scissors, which now form no inconsiderable portion of Messrs. Rodgers and Son's trade, the process is in the main the same as just described, and we shall not tarry to go over the ground again. Our guide, however, pointed out the manufacture of hollow ground razors, as a refutation of the statement that such work is not nor cannot be done in Sheffield, but has to be sent to Germany.

There are many interesting points which we could dwell upon if space permitted, but we must hasten on to enumerate a few particulars which must not be omitted. In 1825 this firm adopted the experiment, at that time unprecedented, of opening a show room for the disposal of their goods, and set their fellow manufacturers an example which has been universally followed. In the two elegant rooms now set apart for this purpose some of the choicest specimens of cutlery work are to be seen. As a show knife they exhibit one containing as many distinct and different blades and instruments as the Christian era contains years, and then there is the "Norfolk Knife," which attracted so much attention at the great exhibition of 1851, and which was also exhibited at London in 1862, and in Paris and New York. The handle is of carved pearl, and on one side a stag hunt is represented, and on the other side a boar hunt. The backs of the blades are elaborately ornamented, and on their surface the Queen, the late Prince Consort, the President of the United States, views of Windsor Castle and other Royal Palaces, the White House at Washington, and such Sheffield local beauties as Haddon Hall, and the lovely Palace of the Peak, Chatsworth, all find representation.

Between 1700 and 1800 skilled workmen find employment here, and their weekly turn out is about 5000 dozen table knifes and forks, 1500 pairs of carvers, 1500 dozen of pocket knives, 1200 dozen of razors, and 1200 dozen of scissors. In the face of such figures, especially remembering the numerous other firms engaged in like manner, the enquiry, "Where do they all go?" is a very natural one, and the answer is partly found in the fact that in the last week of 1870 Messrs. Rodgers and Sons sent to America alone more than 10 tons of finished cutlery. Their market is the world, and it would perhaps be easier to specify the places with which they do not trade than detail the countries they supply. They have offices and warehouses in Cullum Street, London, New York, New Orleans, Montreal, and Toronto. Piratical and spurious work has been sent into the markets as Messrs. Rodgers and Sons', but their corporate mark, as already stated, is such a simple one – a Maltese cross and a star – that it would be well for the public to look for it when purchasing, and for their own protection to be on their guard against unscrupulous manufacturers who thrive on the simplicity and credulity of their customers. It is always the misfortune of really eminent manufacturers to have inferior articles passed off as their goods, but Messrs. Rodgers and Sons have been even more than usual the victims of this vicious practice. In the "dollar stores" of Colorado and the Far West, knives that are obviously like the countryman's razors, "made to sell" are unblushingly offered as "genuine Rodgerses," and the same tale is no doubt told in the Australian bush and on the pampas of South America. Where the name and trade mark are forged it is no doubt difficult for the unwary to escape the snare, but if they would all purchase from respectable tradesmen and look themselves to the name and mark they would be far less likely to have worthless cutlery foisted upon them.

It is well known that the atmosphere of Sheffield is not at all aesthetic. The odour of the lily is less palpable than that of smoke, and the glory of the sunflower is eclipsed by that of dusty grinding mills and grimy forges. The appearance of many of even large cutlery manufactures is one of unpicturesque dilapidation. Setting a good example in this as in so many other respects Messrs. Rodgers and Sons last year departed from the beaten track, and astonished the Sheffield world by new works in which attention was paid alike to utility, beauty, and health. The Pond Hill branch was where this revolution was effected, lofty ceilings, abundant light, good ventilation, revolving fans for the attraction and discharge of the injurious dust and filings here shame the imperfect provision made in too many places, and permit health and comfort to the five hundred men engaged within the walls. Every known improvement was added when these works were fitted. The gleaming steam-engines are so constructed that the sudden cessation of work throughout the place, would not incite a single wheel or band into undue velocity, and how important this is, may be judged from the known danger from the breaking of overstrained stones. The shops for scale-cutters, bolster hands, the forger's yard, the foundry, the rooms for drilling, countersinking, shaping and cross-cutting, the grinding hull, and indeed all parts of the premises have been planned and constructed in the best known way and with attention to the wants of both the employers and the employed.

51

HENRY J. PALMER, 'CUTLERY AND CUTLERS AT SHEFFIELD'

The English Illustrated Magazine, Vol. 11 (August 1884), pp. 667–669

The most interesting branch of cutlery manufacture, as a process, is the initial business of forging. For articles in which there is no welding to be done, such as scissors and pocket knives, a single hand is sufficient, but the forging of table-blades is a "double-handed" affair, the forger himself being assisted by a striker. The visitor to Sheffield will hear the ring of the forger's hammer not merely in the neighbourhood of the great manufactories, but in places where he least expects it. He will come across a "hearth" sandwiched between private dwellings in a quiet residential street, and he will sometimes catch the rasp of the cutler's file in the dwelling house itself. It may be as well to explain here that the term "cutler," now that the division of labour has given a specific title to every branch, is used in the trade in the restricted sense of a "putter together," that is, the man who fits the blade to the handle and produces the finished article. The solitary forger's hearth, discovered in a tranquil thoroughfare, might at first sight be easily mistaken for a small stable which had suffered a severe gunpowder explosion, but a second glance reveals the simple materials required to produce all that is essential in a good knife – a rod of steel, fire, hammer, water. Such are the elements out of which Mr. Ruskin's "masterful" magician will in a few moments present you with a table-blade, perfect in shape and symmetry, hard as adamant as to edge, pliable as a cane as to temper, and requiring only the grinder's touch and the cutler's hafting to be fit for the table. The forger's first operation is moulding ("mooding" as he calls it) or shaping, which is done before the length of blade required is severed from the strip of steel which he holds in his hand. The steel in a table knife ends at the base of the blade; at that point a small strip of wrought iron is welded to the steel, and forms what is called the "bolster" – that is the shoulder cap which meets the handle – and the "tang," or tail, which runs down the centre of the haft. Every person given to after-dinner meditation must have noticed at the base of the blade of his knife a shaded outline like a large thumb mark. This mark indicates the union of the iron with the steel, a process which is called "shooting," and is performed jointly by the forger and his assistant. The next stage is "tanging," and consists in shaping the bolster and tang by the aid of small dies and appliances

DOI: 10.4324/9781315400105-61

with which the anvil is fitted. The blade is now complete in shape, but has to be straightened, marked (with the manufacturer's name or other brand), hardened, and tempered, the whole operation being comprehensively called "smithing."

The straightening and marking are simple matters, but in the operation of hardening and tempering hand and eye have to be brought into delicate co-operation. Hardening is the process by which the steel blade is changed from the nature of lead to that of glass, from an obedient ductility to a petulant brittleness. This change is effected by plunging the heated blade into the vessel of dirty water which stands near the anvil. The operation appears ridiculous in its simplicity, but upon its performance in the right way and at the right time depends the value of your knife. For this you have to rely upon the trained judgment of the forger. Some tools will warp, or "skeller," if they are not plunged into the water in a certain way. Tools of one shape must cut the water like a knife; those of another must stab it like a dagger. Some implements, such as files, must be hardened in an old-standing solution of salt; others in a stream of running water; others again, like saws and scythes, in whale oil. The non-success of our American cousins in this mystery of hardening led some of them to the conclusion that Sheffield water was as necessary to the production of good cutlery as that of Burton is to the brewing of good beer. So a few years ago a party of enterprising persons went out to the West armed with several barrels of the mystic liquid of Sheffield and set up a razor manufactory at Bridgeport. But, alas! the precious virtue of the water evaporated in the strange land, the manufactory was closed, and Brother Jonathan, with characteristic fiscal logic, consoled himself by putting an extra 15 per cent. duty on Sheffield razors last July. As a matter of chemical analysis there is nothing more mysterious about the Sheffield water than an unusual deficiency of lime and an excessive proportion of iron, the one peculiarity being painfully obvious in the prevalence of bow legs in the town, and the other being indicated in the suggestive abundance of examples of the dentist's "dreadful trade." To return to the forge, the immersion of the knife into water is only momentary. When it is withdrawn the blade would snap like cast metal. A table-knife is required to bend like a hand-saw, and this property is obtained by "tempering," or passing the blade slowly over the fire until the elasticity required is achieved. The degrees of ductility acquired are successively indicated by the changing colours produced on the blade, these colours appearing consecutively as follows: straw, gold, chocolate, purple, violet, and blue. The bluish sheen to be observed on a table knife shows that the maximum temper is required for table-cutlery, but it may be noted that elasticity is always obtained at the expense of the hardness of the steel.

Much more might be said in a longer article than can be permitted here, of the cutlery trade of Sheffield, which, although at least six centuries old, may, if its custodians are wise, outlive six centuries more. "You may depend upon it," said Mr. Henry Seebohm, a leading Sheffield steel manufacturer, to an assembly which included Sir Henry Bessemer himself, in the London Cutlers' Hall on March 2nd, 1881, "there is nothing so dear as cheap steel;" and the same thing may be said of cheap cutlery. Sheffield has been forced into producing cheap cutlery, because the world abounds in persons who labour under the hallucination that because they can buy German scissors for sixpence a pair they have been scandalously cheated in being charged a shilling for the same article from Sheffield. But the great Sheffield firms can give all comers a long start in the competition for the permanent demand of the world for sterling cutlery. If proof were wanted, where could it be more conclusive than in the fact that America, which competes keenly in some of the neutral markets for common knives, is herself content to come to Sheffield for all her first-class cutlery and to pay a tax varying from 35 to 50 per cent. into the bargain?

Henry J. Palmer.

52

ANON, 'MADE IN GERMANY'

The New Review, Vol. 14 (March 1896), pp. 258–261

Cutlery

In the cutlery trades – an important and essentially English branch of English industry – the difficulty in obtaining statistics is exemplified with peculiar force. The Sheffield cutler hath a suspicious nature, with a rooted aversion from the collection of figures relating to his business. Accurate tables of production and sale are not, therefore, to be had; nor is much light to be got from the Government Export Returns, where razors, slop-pails, hairpins, lamps, brass bedsteads, with a multitude of other and various articles, are lumped together with catholic impartiality under the generic heading "Hardwares and Cutlery." Yet there are signs and to spare that the German is making himself felt in Hallamshire as elsewhere. He got a useful introduction to the market by inventing the hollow-ground razor, and he sedulously improved the advantage then and thus secured. Unfortunately for his commercial good name, his improvement of opportunities has not always been pursued with a due regard for commercial morality. The supreme merit of Sheffield steel is household knowledge in the remotest quarters of the earth; and that buyers may be assured that they are getting what they ask, and can identify the firm which sells, the goods are mostly branded with special trade-marks (as the famous star and cross of Rodgers and Son). Here was an opening for the German genius: and the world now glitters with German cutlery adorned with elegant suggestions (reproductions even) of the best praised Sheffield marks. Let me cite as a clamant and scandalous example, the Rodgers cutlery aforesaid. The makes of this firm have so exalted a reputation all over the globe that the Customs of more than one State have put them in a special category in their scale of import duties. Need I add that in Germany the Rodgers Brand has been steadily marked down for fraudulent trade? To say nothing of direct imitations – (and, considering that the firm has been spending £1,000 a year in fighting trade-mark thieves, we may assume that these are pretty extensive) – ingenious devices of a more indirect kind exist in shoals to testify to the German cutler's wit. To give an instance of the German commercial imagination: one firm has invented (for British India) a pretty trade-mark – a trade-mark figuring a pair of crossed dumb-bells and a wheel. It sounds original; but it looks so remarkably like the cross and star of the Sheffield

DOI: 10.4324/9781315400105-62

house that purchasers have bought large quantities wherever it is shown, under the agreeable delusion that they were stocking their houses with the finest Sheffield steel.[1] Other Germans have developed a taste for pseudonyms; and cutlery of their make may be met with bearing the legends, "Rudgens," "Rottgens," and the like, designed (I fear) "with intent to deceive" unwary customers in Oriental and other lands, where the niceties of European orthography are not known. Franker in thievery is a certain firm of sickle makers, which set itself to compete with a firm in the Sheffield district. The Sheffield firm was doing a very large business with Chili. The sickles, which were first quality, were stamped with an L.O. brand. The German firm soon found that "L.O." was a highly suitable mark; cargoes of L.O. sickles were shipped to Chili from German ports; they were sold there at a low figure; and now that Sheffield firm has lost its trade.

The commercial ability of the German cutler is further shown in his choice of goods for fraudulent marking. When he turns out good work, he subscribes to the dogma which proclaims the superior policy of honest dealing. It is when the stuff he produces is of the worst that its progress in the market is helped with English marks. So is Sheffield the victim of a double wrong: first, her good name is stolen; and next, it is ruined by being affixed to the nastiest cheap-German wares. In these circumstances it is not surprising that the Sheffield traders, unlike their colleagues in some other branches of commerce, should have taken unto their affections the Merchandise Marks Act; though how that Act is to protect them from German enterprise in foreign parts is not immediately apparent.

The German method of pushing business makes a pretty story. Unhappily that story lacks a moral. Retribution has yet to overtake the fraudulent. In the present they prosper exceedingly. A couple of instances will help to bring the flourishing character of the trade before my readers' minds in a concrete shape. In '93 Austria and Germany between them exported to Servia cutlery and tools to the value of £3,796, whereof £1,296 went to the credit of Germany. In that year the export of British cutlery to Servia was not worth a ten-pound note. Now, the contiguity of Austria sufficiently accounts for the magnitude of *her* export; but in view of the facts, that in '36 Lord Palmerston sent a British Consul to Servia for the purpose of encouraging commercial relations, and that England is not much farther off than Germany, but is as easily reached as Germany by sea, the figures of the two countries stand in startling contrast. My second example is from Russia. In '89 Germany exported to that country cutlery to the value of 21,000 r.; three years later her export was worth 67,677 r.: all this before the reduction in the duty made by the Russo-German Tariff Treaty, the operation of which is sending up the trade enormously! Contrast, now, this prosperity with what is virtually a decadence. As I have said, Board of Trade returns of cutlery exports are imbedded in a category which comprises many other articles; but statistics are compiled by other Governments, and they cast a cheerless ray upon the gloom. The authorities at Washington – most voluminous of statisticians – have separated cutlery from other steel goods; and I am indebted to the courtesy of the United States Consul at Sheffield for a table of the cutlery exports in recent years from the Sheffield district to the United States. It shows a decline from $1,307,540·85 in '90 to $407,379·13 in '94. Thanks to the new Tariff, there was better business in '95; but the fall in the years I have quoted is very great. The *Ironmonger's* Special Commissioner to the Antwerp Exhibition of '94, reviewing the matter with an expert's eye, was especially struck with the falling off in Sheffield cutlery in the Belgian city. English firms, he wrote, now "send a dozen where they formerly shipped a gross." In shop windows where some forty years before he remembered "a fine assortment of all sorts of English tools and cutlery, a few shipcarpenter's adzes and axes from Spear and Jackson and W. Greaves and Son are the remnants remaining." What wonder that this poor gentleman's visit impressed him with the belief that the great lesson of the Antwerp Exhibition was "the rapid decadence of England's industrial supremacy"?

Nor is it only German knives and razors, inferior in quality and fraudulent in mark, which compete successfully with English goods. The better class of German work is also in dangerous rivalry with ours; for, in truth, the despicable practices to which I have alluded are by no means the sole reason for Germany's success. There are many others. Those among them which are of application to our industries and commerce in general I shall deal with in another place; but there is one potent cause of successful competition in the cutler's trade which may conveniently be mentioned here. It is this: the magnificent quality of Sheffield work is in great part owing to the amount of "unseen work" which the Sheffield blade receives. Every blade made in a Sheffield shop gets a prolonged hammering in its unfinished state, a hammering whereby the molecules are driven out and the crystals arc smashed; with the result that it acquires a toughness not otherwise to be achieved, a toughness permitting continual use until it is worn to a mere wire. When it is finished it shows no trace whatever of this "unseen work," whose presence, indeed, not even an expert can detect. The German is wiser in his commercial generation. Why (in effect) put into an article a lot of work, which nobody can trace, and whose chief effect is to make the buyer independent of the cutler during many years? No: what is wanted is an article that will look perfect and cost as little as may be to make. Thus the German cutler to his soul; and thereafter he reduces his "unseen work" to the smallest possible proportions, and devotes himself to the achievement of a pleasing "finish": till even the Sheffield man is fain to admit that a German knife is a better looking article than an English one.

Note

1 The High Court of Saxony has discountenanced this particular expression of the German genius; but the penalty imposed (£15) is a mild deterrent. The robber gravely contended that the Hindoo's "highly developed sense for pictorial art" made confusion on his part "inconceivable."

53

IMAGE: JOSEPH RODGERS & SONS, SELECTIONS FROM THE 'OLD TABLE DAY BOOK'

(Date approx. late 1800s), Museums Sheffield

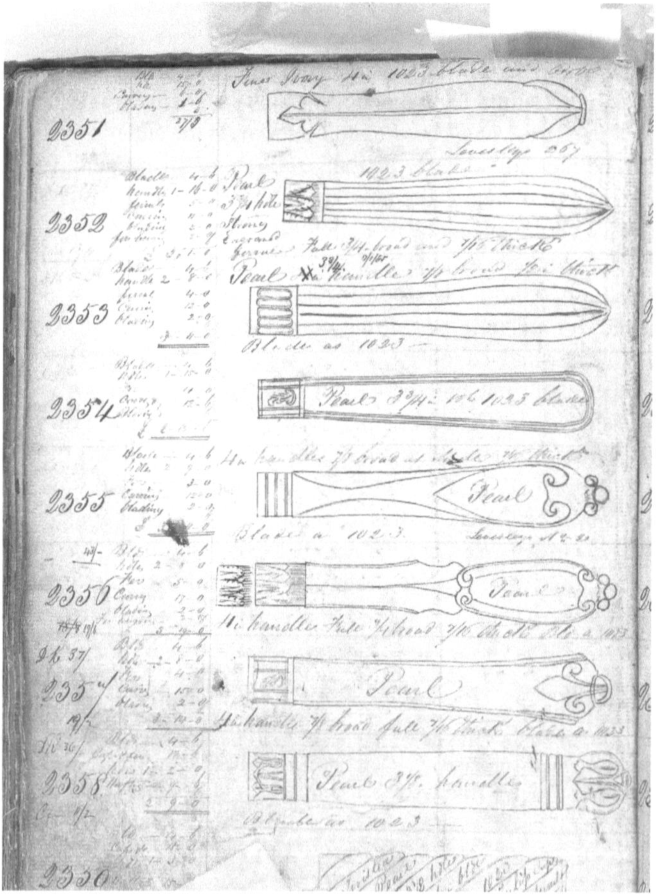

Figure 53.1

DOI: 10.4324/9781315400105-63

54

IMAGE: 'FISH-SLICE AND FORK, AND DESSERT-KNIFE' (MESSRS. J. RODGERS & SONS, OF SHEFFIELD)

Art Journal Illustrated Catalogue of the Industry of All Nations [n.d.] (London: Bradbury & Evans, George Virtue, n.d.), p. 278

The industry of all nations

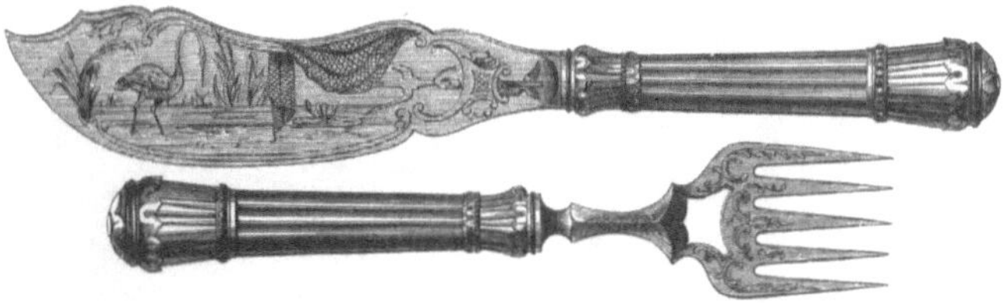

Figure 54.1 Messrs. J. RODGERS & SONS, of Sheffield, are the manufacturers of the FISH-SLICE and FORK, and DESSERT-KNIFE, which appear above. The blade of the first-named shows an engraving of a subject that is suggestive of the intended use of the article itself; a kingfisher is standing in a stream, surrounded by aqueous plants, while a fishing-net is tastefully brought into the composition. The handles are simply designed.

DOI: 10.4324/9781315400105-64

3.3

Locks and keys

DOI: 10.4324/9781315400105-65

3.3 Locks and keys

Charles Chubb, *Chubb's Improved Patent Detector Lock* ([n.p.], 1832), 4pp.
Benjamin Disraeli, *Sybil; or, the Two Nations* (London: Henry Colburn, 1845), Book III, pp. 54–57.
Samuel Smiles, *Industrial Biography: Iron Workers and Tool Makers* (London: John Murray, 1863), pp. 186–187.
Anon, 'A Few Thoughts on Keys', *Cornhill Magazine,* Vol. 12 (November 1865), pp. 623–628.
J. C. Tildesley, 'A Chapter on Locks and Keys', *Once a Week*, Vol. 4 (9 November 1867), pp. 560–563.
Anon, 'A Midland Tour; XVII – Wolverhampton', *The Leisure Hour: A Family Journal of Instruction and Recreation* (20 July 1872), pp. 462–463.
Image: 'Lock' [Plate], *The National Encyclopaedia: a Dictionary of Universal Knowledge*, Vol. 8 (London: n.p., c. 1870).

After the invention of the 'pin tumbler' lock in the late-eighteenth century, bitted keys became increasingly common. The most well-known pin tumbler locks were the designs manufactured by Jeremiah and Charles Chubb. Their 'patent detector lock' had four tumblers, which increased to six in the 1840s, and was unique in that any attempt to pick the lock, including use of an incorrect key, would cause it to jam. Chubb's advertising pamphlet of 1832 plays upon fears of burglary, noting a rise in burglaries and threats by 'depredators'. While the term 'burglar-alarm' was coined in 1840, suggesting a 'burglar' broke into homes, 'depredator' refers to a predator who plunders and pillages. Although the lock ostensibly protects property, the safety of the person was an important additional consideration. Inviolability was a lock's currency, and 'lock-picking' competitions became a craze.

Samuel Smiles' *Industrial Biography* (1863), an extract from which is reprinted here, describes Chubb's main rival, Joseph Bramah, famously submitting his lock to a trial. This extract, along with J. C. Tildesley's 'A Chapter on Locks and Keys' (1867), describes the 'lock controversy' at the 1851 Great Exhibition. The locks of Chubb and Bramah had been considered secure, until they were picked at the Exhibition by the American locksmith and inventor Alfred Charles Hobbs, a representative of the New York locksmiths Day & Newell. Unlike the Chubb lock, which was picked fairly quickly, Bramah's lock took Hobbs 16 days to pick and was pronounced, to all purposes, unpickable.

As with so many other metal goods, locks were chiefly manufactured in the Midlands. *The Leisure Hour*, an improving publication aimed at a Christian readership, sent a correspondent to Wolverhampton in 1872. The author of 'A Midland Tour; XVII – Wolverhampton' visited the highly skilled locksmiths working in the area, discovering that all locks are made by hand. The author comments on the variety of locks made; though this particular article is unillustrated, even a simple image from *The National Encyclopædia* (published around the same time and reproduced here) gives some idea of the range of locks and keys available. Almost 30 years earlier, Wolverhampton had inspired Benjamin Disraeli, in his Condition of England novel *Sybil; or, the Two Nations* (1845), to create Wodgate, an industrial town and the 'ugliest spot in England'. Disraeli intended to highlight the plight of many working people in the Midlands, and he depicts expensive locks being turned out in conditions of utter squalor. The Wodgate locksmiths are also shown to beat their apprentices mercilessly. So vivid are Disraeli's descriptions, that Tildesley's 'Chapter on Locks and Keys' quoted *Sybil* in order to describe the improving effects of education on this class of labourers. The article depicts youths working in unventilated, cramped workshops for extremely long hours for poor remuneration.

A more whimsical article, 'A Few Thoughts on Keys' (1865), reveals the widespread use of keys. The author parodies the solemn, comprehensive histories of objects which characterise many of the sources in this volume. The key becomes 'a mystic entity of diabolical powers', existing to frustrate human existence, yet so valuable that lavish quantities of gold are 'comparatively valueless' compared to the lost bunch of keys. Keys, according to the author, can be bright and alert or meek and embarrassed; they can lose themselves, wandering 'madly into the wrong pockets', and they can breed in kitchen drawers. The fear of burglars is related to the skeleton key, associated with 'secret murder' and 'the true burglarious rattle' contained in the very sound of its name. Different keys have different characters to match their looks: in particular, 'truculent and forbidding' house keys scare off the 'prowling depredator', a deft invocation of Chubb's fearful vocabulary of 30 years before.

55

CHARLES CHUBB, *CHUBB'S IMPROVED PATENT DETECTOR LOCK*

CHARLES CHUBB, *INVENTOR AND PATENTEE OF THE IMPROVED DETECTOR LOCK AND COMBINATION LATCH,*
LOCK MANUFACTURER TO HIS MAJESTY, H. R. H. THE DUKE OF CUMBEBLAND, THE SECRETARY OF STATE FOR FOREIGN AFFAIRS, THE HONOURABLE THE BOARD OF ORDNANCE, THE RIGHT HONOURABLE THE LORDS COMMISSIONERS OF THE ADMIRALTY, THE HONOURABLE THE NAVY BOARD, THE HONOURABLE THE GOVERNOR AND COMPANY OF THE BANK OF ENGLAND, THE WORSHIPFUL THE MAGISTRATES FOR THE COUNTY OF MIDDLESEX, &C. &C.

57, St. Paul's Church Yard, London

Respectfully calls the attention of the Public to the depredations on Property, which have lately been carried on to an alarming extent through the great insecurity of the Locks in general use, and the facility with which they are unlocked by means of picks and skeleton keys. Many Persons are not aware, that most of the Locks in common use present no obstruction to the ingenious depredator, and being made with wards which cannot be varied to any great extent, thousands are constantly on sale, the keys of which WILL PASS EACH OTHER; *consequently, those Persons who are disposed to be dishonest can, at all times, procure keys that will open nearly all the Locks to which they may have access. Complete security, however, may be obtained by the adoption of CHUBB's IMPROVED PATENT DETECTOR LOCKS, the combinations of which are so extensive, that many millions may be made, and not two alike.*

The Patentee solicits attention to the annexed description of his Detector Locks which CANNOT *be picked or opened by* ANY *false instruments; should even an attempt be made to pick them, immediate notice is thereby given, and the Lock thus rendered incalculably more secure.*

The Patent Detector Locks are made of every size, and adapted for all the purposes to which Locks are applied.

DOI: 10.4324/9781315400105-66

The Patent Detector Lock possesses in a much higher degree than any other, the four principal requisites of a good Lock; viz. SECURITY, SIMPLICITY, STRENGTH and DURABILITY. Its SECURITY, *particularly*, is increased beyond calculation, by an improvement, which not only renders it impossible to be picked or opened by *any* false Instruments, but also *detects the first attempt* to open it; thereby preventing those *repeated efforts*, to which even the best Locks hitherto invented are exposed. In these Locks, the combinations admit of so great variety, that many thousands of them may be made, and yet one Key shall not pass any two Locks: and the *Detector* renders that variety infinite; for the instant that one or more of the tumblers are lifted beyond the place where the bolt is at liberty to pass, it overlifts the Detector, which then hooks the tail of the bolt, preventing it from passing, and thus gives incalculable additional security, (as well as immediate notice, the first time the true Key is put into it to open it, that an attempt has been made to pick it,) and renders all farther attempts useless; it being *impossible* to discover the *first* combination, to disengage the Detector; or the *second* to remove the bolt; and nothing but the true Key can either release the Detector from its grasp on the bolt, or open the Lock.

In reference to its DURABILITY, it is not liable to be injured by constant use in any length of time; this has been ascertained, by an Iron-rimmed Lock having been attached to a Steam-Engine in the Dock-Yard, Portsmouth, (to try the effect of friction,) by which it was locked and unlocked upwards of four hundred and sixty thousand times, without receiving the least injury. The STRENGTH of its parts, and the SIMPLICITY of its construction, are such, that no false Key or other Instrument, introduced into it for the purpose of opening it, can (without very great violence) injure it.

☞ *To disengage the Detector from its hold on the bolt, when it has been overlifted by any attempt to pick the Lock, the Key must be turned the same way as in locking, as far as it will go.*

56

BENJAMIN DISRAELI, *SYBIL; OR, THE TWO NATIONS*

(London: Henry Colburn, 1845), Book III, pp. 54–57

[. . .] the inhabitants of Wodgate early acquired a celebrity as skilful workmen. This reputation so much increased, and in time spread so far, that for more than a quarter of a century, both in their skill and the economy of their labour, they have been unmatched throughout the country. As manufacturers of ironmongery, they carry the palm from the whole district; as founders of brass and workers of steel, they fear none; while as nailers and locksmiths, their fame has spread even to the European markets, whither their most skilful workmen have frequently been invited.

Invited in vain! No wages can tempt the Wodgate man from his native home, that squatters' seat which soon assumed the form of a large village, and then in turn soon expanded into a town, and at the present moment numbers its population by swarming thousands, lodged in the most miserable tenements in the most hideous burgh in the ugliest country in the world.

But it has its enduring spell. Notwithstanding the spread of its civic prosperity, it has lost none of the characteristics of its original society; on the contrary it has zealously preserved them. There are no landlords, head-lessees, main-masters, or butties in Wodgate. No church there has yet raised its spire; and as if the jealous spirit of Woden still haunted his ancient temple, even the conventicle scarcely dares show its humble front in some obscure corner. There is no municipality, no magistrate, no local acts, no vestries, no schools of any kind. The streets are never cleaned; every man lights his own house; nor does any one know anything except his business.

More than this, at Wodgate a factory or large establishment of any kind is unknown. Here Labour reigns supreme. Its division indeed is favoured by their manners, but the interference or influence of mere capital is instantly resisted. The business of Wodgate is carried on by master workmen in their own houses, each of whom possesses an unlimited number of what they call apprentices, by whom their affairs are principally conducted, and whom they treat as the Mamlouks treated the Egyptians.

DOI: 10.4324/9781315400105-67

These master workmen indeed form a powerful aristocracy, nor is it possible to conceive one apparently more oppressive. They are ruthless tyrants; they habitually inflict upon their subjects punishments more grievous than the slave population of our colonies were ever visited with; not content with beating them with sticks or flogging them with knotted ropes, they are in the habit of felling them with hammers, or cutting their heads open with a file or lock. The most usual punishment however, or rather stimulus to increase exertion, is to pull an apprentice's ears till they run with blood. These youths too are worked for sixteen and even twenty hours a day; they are often sold by one master to another; they are fed on carrion, and they sleep in lofts or cellars: yet whether it be that they are hardened by brutality, and really unconscious of their degradation and unusual sufferings, or whether they are supported by the belief that their day to be masters and oppressors will surely arrive, the aristocracy of Wodgate is by no means so unpopular as the aristocracy of most other places.

57

SAMUEL SMILES, *INDUSTRIAL BIOGRAPHY: IRON WORKERS AND TOOL MAKERS*

(London: John Murray, 1863), pp. 186–187

Yet locks are a very ancient invention, though, as in many other cases, the art of making them seems in a great measure to have become lost, and accordingly had to be found out anew. Thus the tumbler lock – which consists in the use of moveable impediments acted on by the proper key only, as contradistinguished from the ordinary ward locks, where the impediments are fixed – appears to have been well known to the ancient Egyptians, the representation of such a lock being found sculptured among the bas-reliefs which decorate the great temple at Karnak. This kind of lock was revived, or at least greatly improved, by a Mr. Barron in 1774, and it was shortly after this time that Bramah directed his attention to the subject. After much study and many experiments, he contrived a lock more simple, more serviceable, as well as more secure, than Barron's, as is proved by the fact that it has stood the test of nearly eighty years' experience,[1] and still holds its ground. For a long time, indeed, Bramah's lock was regarded as absolutely inviolable, and it remained unpicked for sixty-seven years, until Hobbs the American mastered it in 1851. A notice had long been exhibited in Bramah's shop-window in Piccadilly, offering 200*l*. to any one who should succeed in picking the patent lock. Many tried, and all failed, until Hobbs succeeded, after sixteen days' manipulation of it with various elaborate instruments. But the difficulty with which the lock was picked showed that, for all ordinary purposes, it might be pronounced impregnable.

The new locks were machines of the most delicate kind, the action of which depended in a great measure upon the precision with which the springs, sliders, levers, barrels, and other parts were finished. The merits of the invention being generally admitted, there was a considerable demand for the locks, and the necessity thus arose for inventing a series of original machine-tools to enable them to be manufactured in sufficient quantities to meet the demand. It is probable, indeed, that, but for the contrivance of such tools, the lock could never have come into general use, as the skill of hand-workmen, no matter how experienced, could not have been relied upon for turning out the article with that degree of accuracy and finish in all the parts which was indispensable for its proper action. In conducting

DOI: 10.4324/9781315400105-68

the manufacture throughout, Bramah was greatly assisted by Henry Maudslay, his foreman, to whom he was in no small degree indebted for the contrivance of those tool-machines which enabled him to carry on the business of lock-making with advantage and profit.

Note

1 The lock invented by Bramah was patented in 1784. Mr. Bramah himself fully set forth the specific merits of the invention in his *Dissertation on the Construction of Locks*. In a second patent, taken out by him in 1798, he amended his first with the object of preventing the counterfeiting of keys, and suspending the office of the lock until the key was again in the possession of the owner. This he effected by enabling the owner so to alter the sliders as to render the lock inaccessible to such key if applied by any other person but himself, or until the sliders had been rearranged so as to admit of its proper action. We may mention in passing that the security of Bramah's locks depends on the doctrine of combinations, or multiplication of numbers into each other, which is known to increase in the most rapid proportion. Thus, a lock of five slides admits of 3,000 variations, while one of eight will have no less than 1,935,360 changes; in other words, that number of attempts at making a key, or at picking it, may be made before it can be opened.

58

ANON, 'A FEW THOUGHTS ON KEYS'

Cornhill Magazine, Vol. 12, November 1865, pp. 623–628

Now, – this key was a fairy. – *History of Blue Beard*

It must be a flinty heart that can read without a sympathetic throb one of those plaintive advertisements, often seen in the second column of *The Times*' supplementary sheet, which offer lavish sums of comparatively valueless gold for the restoration of "A bunch of keys, on a steel ring." Those simple words touch a key-note which finds an echo in every bosom, not utterly destitute of feeling – and cupboards.

The wise and witty Sydney Smith instituted a "screaming-gate," at the verge of his parochial demesne, for the purpose of allowing due scope and expansion to the peculiar distress attending it; and, indeed, no family should be without some appropriate "wailing-place" of this sort; some monumental portal, or limitary grove, sacred to memory and the Dii Viales who are said to preside over luggage.

Although this particular misery is common to all, yet, for *man's* grosser nature, there are certain mitigations and tender assuagements (which his partner cannot share), that soften, if they do not remove, the sense of bereavement. He can kick his portmanteau, if he cannot open it; he can rip up and disembowel his carpet-bag; he can smash his despatch-box. Above all, *he can swear!* A hearty oath has been known to take the sting out of many such sorrows; it enters into the category of what are called "resources within one's self," and, as such, should not be altogether neglected.

But in the case of hapless woman, these safety-valves for legitimate emotion do not exist. In her keyless agony, she is like a lioness robbed of her cubs, yet denied the alleviation of a roar. Moreover, the amount of misery entailed on the two sexes by this loss admits of no comparison. Man has but a limited capacity of suffering, inasmuch as he is a creature of few keys. He probably possesses but *le stricte nécessaire*, – let us say, a latch-key, a watch-key, a desk-key, (perhaps) a cellaret-key; mere bagatelles. Woman, on the other hand, – especially woman of a methodical turn – is all keys. Not to mention that congeries of cares – the domestic bunch – she has all sorts of outlying and isolated keys; keys *in partibus infidelium;* colonial and collateral keys; keys that lock out, and lock in, and lock up – everything lockable – especially *keys:* which are in themselves susceptible of captivity, *custodes custodiunt.* When that fatal complication takes place, it is impossible to sound the depths of a woman's keylessness.

Thoughtless persons look upon keys in a merely subjective point of view – as suggestive of and subordinate to locks. "Under lock and key" is the usual careless way of speaking, putting (as it were) the cart before the horse. Persons of an analytic turn and discursive fancy will overleap the true object of reflection; they will wander from the matter in hand – the key, shut their eyes upon its concomitant, the key-hole, and, disdaining to linger even in that mediate region, the press, cupboard, closet, cellar, or store-room, under their bodily eyes, will mount (metaphorically) from shelf to shelf, till they lose themselves in bewildered contemplation of finite man's infinite faculties of acquisitiveness and retentiveness.

The antiquarian, again, will busy himself with the question – When did man first begin to lock up? "When wild in woods the noble savage ran," of course he carried no keys; a stone rolled to a cavern's mouth was probably the first rough expression of an art which has been so finely elaborated in later days. Boulders must have been precious stones in that golden age, when the rarity of property so simplified the duties and cares of possession.

The Greeks and Romans must have had but sorry methods of guarding their possessions. Would Grecian Aristippus have strewn the Libyan sands with his gold, when his over-burdened slaves found it too heavy for a hurried journey, – would miser Chremes have buried his money in the earth, – if either of them had possessed at home some decent lock-up place, or civilized strong-box? Who ever saw a Pompeiian cellar-key? Rusty nails from that locality are to be met with in museums, but where are the keys that guarded their curious vintages? Horace certainly uses the expression *servata centum clavibus*, but it is evidently a figure of speech, in honour of his friend Posthumus's genteel establishment; he never mentions the thing as in use in his own cozy bachelor household. Indeed, it puzzles one to guess how he managed about these matters. The Sabine *vin ordinaire* was probably left about in careless profusion; and it is possible that his Chian hogsheads may have been occasionally "on tap" in the atrium, as pipes of claret used to be in hospitable Irish drawing-rooms fifty or sixty years ago; but how about all that "choice Falernian" and "hoarded Cæcuban?" Pitching and plastering the mouths of the vessels was but a poor expedient. What was to prevent the abstraction of a fat amphora or two, if that ubiquitous "boy" of his had any taste for "care-dispelling Massic?"

But this is a digression. The *uses* of keys are no worthy subject for the true philosopher's contemplation; he looks upon the essences of things; he sees a key in its objective signification; he cares not for its qualifications as arbiter and agent of those vain attributes, "mine and thine;" he takes no interest in futile distinctions. He never locks anything up – knowing the inutility and peril of the act; it adds nothing to the security of property, but is apt to inspire others with too strong an interest in it. "Nothing venture, nothing have," is his favourite proverb, but with a more enlightened signification than it generally conveys. He looks upon a key as a mystic entity of diabolical powers – a talisman which can confer on inert matter, such as wood, iron, brass, leather, &c., the faculty of baffling and circumventing you in the effort to get at your own possessions.

This is, in fact, the only sound view of the subject. When once the mind has recognized this truth, every single key on your bunch will assume a peculiar physiognomy, even as it possesses a distinct idiosyncrasy. One key will come into your family with a certain malicious glitter about it – a defiant swagger and sparkle, that foretels the life-long struggle you are destined to have with it; you see at once that it will "rather bend than break," and rather break than open your box, desk, drawer, or portfolio, as the case may be. Another will wear a dull and gloomy air – a "here to-day and gone to-morrow" sort of aspect, as good as an epitaph and much more veracious.

House-door keys have been seen of so truculent and forbidding a countenance, that their very presence in the lock is supposed to have scared away the prowling depredator; one, indeed, has been known – on a remarkable occasion – to have "comprehended an auspicious person," and to have done good service in the capacity of a life-preserver.

What family has not, at times, possessed some meek little tea-caddy or perhaps cellaret key, which, however facile and effectual at other times, was liable – in any sudden exigency – to fall into so painful a state of hamper and embarrassment, as no effort of its owner could soothe, or politely feigned indifference on the part of visitors allay?

What household but has its own legendary reminiscences of keys strangely lost and mysteriously regained? – keys that have gone and *hung themselves* (for no human agency is ever traceable on these occasions) on wrong rings, and wandered madly into wrong pockets? Impulsive keys, that have been found apparently trying to open wrong locks of their own accord, and have broken short off in the effort to recover themselves? Industrious keys, which, on some favourable occasion, have so "improved the shining hour," that wax has been found in their wards. Precious keys (of tills and iron safes), each fondly supposed, by its possessor, to be as unique of its kind as the silver decadrachm of Alexander the Great, yet suddenly discovered to have twin brothers as experienced as themselves in the duties of their office.

The most careless observer will have been struck by a difference in the outward semblance of keys apparently subjected to the same external influences. Look, for instance, at the respective keys of your wine-cellar and your coal-cellar. What a bright, rollicking, jovial look the first wears – polished without effeminacy, forcible yet insinuating – evidently habituated to your butler's cordial grasp, and tenderly demonstrative of friction in his pocket. There is, indeed, a witching hour (about the fifth or sixth bottle, it is said), when that key assumes the figure of a miniature thyrsus – the very wards seem to drip with "blushful Hippocrene" – ivy-leaves seem to wreath its stalk, and the handle curls round the fervent fingers with the cool tender freshness of vinetendrils. In these subterranean regions "the atom darkness in its slow turmoil" perhaps disposes the senses to such hallucinations; but, strange to say, no similar transfiguration attends the coal-cellar key.

Visit that quiet retreat at what hour you will, no mysterious gnome peers at you from its cavernous depth – no swart cyclop "turns on" his one eye in your face with the obtrusive radiance of a policeman's lanthorn. A harmless, unnecessary cat, perhaps, pervades the gloomy precincts, but she is but a cat; Walpurgis' night itself could not invest her with solemnity, and the key remains a key to the end of the chapter. A hang-dog-looking, melancholy key it is – rusty, unamiable, antipathetic. How unlike "his wholesome brother" of the wine-cellar, though exercising his functions in such close proximity!

Observe, too, the engaging exterior of the area-gate key! Exposed to all the vicissitudes of weather, subjected to the temporary command of every scullion, yet ever bright, brisk, alert, and shining; alive to the meanest exigencies of domestic organization; cheerfully responsive to the call of butcher, baker, milkman, and fishmonger; not superciliously deaf to the voice of the humbler rag-merchant or sonorous dustman. How singular is its apt appreciation of the majesty of Themis, in the person of a policeman! with what oily alacrity it turns in the impassive lock to give him ingress, or discreet exit from the social seclusion of your kitchen! Thence, rising with rubicund visage, he goes forth, like a giant (doubtless refreshed) on his sternly beneficent career. His march eastward is, in fact, a modest "triumph" – not as madly clamorous, perhaps, as that of Indian Bacchus, but partaking in some degree of the god's privileges and attributes. Whispered "Evoes" from every area attend his steps; *Pan* is not entirely excluded from the pageant; the rattle of knife and fork will be heard, and the tinkle of the area-gate (and other) keys, instead of the clash of noisy cymbals.

The domestic latch-key, in full use, at the height of the season, is reported to have a worn and dissipated look. Those who are acquainted with its uses and habits affirm that it is apt to get muzzy and confused about four o'clock in the morning – incapable of key-holes, and altogether effete and idiotic.

No doubt there is an appropriate horror in the aspect of a "skeleton" key; the name imports it – secret murder is in the very sound. It has the *hiss* of caution, and the true burglarious rattle in it; there must be an evil harmony and coincidence between its countenance and its name. It leads the thoughts to another and a worse key –

The key of Newgate! Can the uninitiated realize its awful appearance? Viewed from the *outside*, no doubt, its peculiarities are less impressive; but we can conceive an aspect whose steely glitter might have the effect of Medusa's head!

The key of Bedlam is reported to work backwards, like a witch's prayer. Some say that it is always held by the ward end, and unlocks with the handle.

The Lord Chamberlain's key has a moral influence superior to that of any key in the kingdom – not excepting the Lord Chancellor's. It has the faculty of discrimination; and with the facility of a magic wand it separates the sheep from the goats in the fashionable herd.

But it would demand a greater space than these pages can afford to discuss the various attributes and powers of what may be called public keys; – from the Foreign-Office despatch-box key, to the keys of the Chancellor of the

Exchequer – which, we doubt not, are to be distinguished by a dignified reticence, and an alacrity in locking up. What we would especially recommend to general observation is, the generic tendency of *all* keys to spontaneous reproduction. This tendency is perhaps most remarkable in the *clavis domestica*, or key of private life, whose prolific qualities may be tested by a simple experiment. A very small bunch of them left in any confined space during a few months' absence on the part of their owner, will be found on his return to have colonized the whole drawer. In fact, single keys should never be left under these conditions for any time: they become family keys in no time. It is supposed that they sprout like asparagus in damp weather, or are produced like button-mushrooms in a hot-bed. It is a singular fact, that this reproductive faculty is to be found in no other metallic substance, however fashioned; locks never multiply of their own devices; you may leave any number of sovereigns or half-crowns together, yet never find an additional sixpence among them: sometimes quite the reverse.

The awkward consequences which may arise from this property of the key of domestic life may be easily imagined. You may come some day in a transport of anxious haste to the receptacle of your more important keys, to seek for (let us say) the key of the medicine-chest in some moment of an exquisitely emotional character – such as your infant's having gulped down its mother's thimble: – instead of the desired key, you find a mob of little nameless, objectless keys, staring you in the face, tripping up your fingers, and maddening you by their multiplicity and inane uniformity of aspect. Curiously enough, these "tadpole" keys, as they may be called, have at first no special physiognomy; it is only when launched into practical existence, and apportioned among the key-holes of real life, that they grow to be as distinct in appearance, and as diabolical in character, as their elders.

Such is the essential nature of these "shining mischiefs." Tricky, deceitful, capricious – never to be trusted out of your sight, and full of irritating associations when in it; informed by some devilish intelligence that only leads them wrong, and provocative of evil impulses in others: – "with all the rash dexterity of wit" for purposes of annoyance, yet powerless to do even the small good for which they were intended.

If man is wise, he will banish them from his pocket; if woman knows her own interests, she will lock them up for ever. If, however, the possession of great riches absolutely necessitates the employment of keys, let their hapless owner keep them well in hand, and allow no key to get the better of him; let there be no "master key" in his establishment, if he value his peace of mind. If he must use them, let him do so, in moderation; he will never want an occasion to abuse them. But the best thing that can happen to him, is to lose them. When that fortunate, and not improbable, circumstance occurs, let him not rush madly into the second column of *The Times* newspaper – let him not provoke fate by offering a reward for their restoration – but let him "call the watch together, and thank God he is rid of knaves."

In concluding this slight notice of the properties of an agent only too powerful in its influence on human affairs, we cannot avoid taking a side-glance at certain keys whose qualifications are universally alluded to, in polite conversation and refined literature, but which have never yet been collected, labelled, and catalogued, as they ought to be.

We are constantly hearing of "the key to So-and-so's extraordinary conduct," "the key to Miss Such-a-one's affections," "the key to a certain person's machinations," "the key of Lord Somebody's conscience," "the key to everybody's secret thoughts and private affairs." These things, no doubt, have a real existence; we cannot do without them; they are an important part of those rather threadbare "properties" which belong to the world's stage (as it is generally called), and "life's poor play." But, has anybody seen them? They are probably knocking about in that esthetic "green-room" of commonplace to which we all know our way; from whence we draw those slashing wooden swords and tin bucklers, that are so effective in all arguments; those spangled coats and jerkins in which our poor thoughts occasionally strut so bravely; those banners, with grand inscriptions, which look quite as well as opinions, at a little distance. There also may be found "all that useful lot" of hyperbolic essences, –

> The entities of things that are not yet:
> Subtleſt, but sureſt beings!

such as the wedge whose thin end is always being introduced into our most venerable institutions; the hinge on which momentous affairs habitually turn; the hypothetical leg which nobody has got to stand on, in all arguments; the other side to every question; in short, all the *matériel* for sensible conversation. These things are in constant requisition and daily use; but, like the mysteriously-circulating shoe in the game of "Hunt the Slipper," their existence is only made manifest to the senses by the sounding rap with which we shuffle them round in the polite intercourse of good society.

It would be a good deed to fix, substantiate, and classify these useful but volatile possessions, that they may be always at hand when wanted in public speech or private conversation; more especially the mystic keys to which we have referred. What a handy bunch *that* would be!

59

J. C. TILDESLEY, 'A CHAPTER ON LOCKS AND KEYS'

Once a Week, Vol. 4
(9 November 1867), pp. 560–563

If the time-honoured maxim, "Love laughs at locksmiths," has, like the Spanish proverb, "held good in every age and clime," the muscles of Cupid's chubby face, must have been relaxed toward that particular class of craftsmen, for a period not far short of forty centuries. The Egyptian locksmith as he fashioned his curious contrivance out of the world-renowned Damascus steel, was probably the first to excite the sly god's mirth. Next in order came the fabricator of the "doore fastenings of dyverse colours made of brass and ivory," of ancient Rome; followed by the maker of the still more elaborate *Serrure de Tabernacle* in the mediæval age, immortalised in early Christian Missals. The locksmith of the Celestial Empire then began to make his "strange instruments having wooden slides," the architecture of which was peculiarly adapted to the Summer House, in which the fair heroine of the "willow pattern" was kept in durance vile. Then the locksmith began to flourish in England; and by the time of good Queen Bess, the operations of the craft were so fully established "in the townes of Staffordshire: to wit, Wolverhampton, Willenhall, and Wednesbury," that Cupid must have indulged in peals of laughter worthy of the immortal Comus; and after all the enterprise of later years, with its levers, and wards, "detectors," and master keys, the Muse of Love is still able to chant even in the hearing of Hobbs and Chubb,

My father he has locked the door,
My mother keeps the key,
But neither bolts nor bars can part
My own true love and me.

The Egyptian lock, rude carvings of which are said to have embellished the walls of ancient Karnak's temple and the Herculaneum, is thus described by Mr. E. Beckett Denison, Q. C.: – "In this lock, three pins fall into a similar number of cavities in the bolt, and so hold it fast; they are raised again by putting in the key through the large key hole in the bolt, and raising it a little, so that the locking pins are pushed by the key out of the way of the bolt. The security afforded by this

DOI: 10.4324/9781315400105-70

lock is very small, as it is easy to find the places of the pins by pushing in a piece of wood covered with clay or tallow, on which the holes will leave their impress, and the depth can easily be ascertained by trial." These locks were first introduced into England by the merchants of Phœnicia, who gave them to the Cornish miners in exchange for tin. Strangely enough locks of similar construction, but evidently "home made," are still to be found on the doors of many of the peasantry in Cornwall and Devon.

The locks of ancient Greece and Rome are quaintly described by the philosophers and poets of the time. Aratus compares the constellation Cassiopeia to a Roman key, "having a curved stem," and a handle "shaped like the south stars," of the group. Curved stems were usual in the keys of that age, and the poet Ariston applies to one of those articles the epithet Βαθυκάμπη, or *deeply bent*. Eustathius says that these ancient keys resembled sickles, and were sometimes so large as to be carried on the shoulder, as reapers bear their sickles to the harvest field. This statement is confirmed by Callimachus in his *Hymn to Ceres*, where he represents the priestess of Nicippe carrying a key on her shoulders. Homer's allusion to the lock and key on the wardrobe of the fair Penelope, will probably be better known.[1] The passage is thus rendered by Pope: –

> A brazen key she held, the handle turned,
> With steel and polish'd ivory adorned.
> The bolt, obedient to the silken string,
> Forsakes the staple as she pulls the ring,
> The wards respondent to the key, turn round,
> The bars fly back, the flying valves resound,
> Loud as a bull, makes hill and valley ring,
> So reared the lock when it released the spring.

Eustathius, a Greek commentator on Homer, who flourished in the twelfth century, says that the key here referred to was very ancient, and was known as "the serpent key" from its resemblance of form. It was in use before the siege of Troy, although some writers persist in ascribing its invention to Theodore of Samos.

The mediæval locks were perhaps among the most elaborate and artistic specimens of those articles ever produced. Beads, scrolls, or floral wreaths exquisitely graven in steel, lined the edges. Angel-forms similarly wrought surmounted the escutcheon, like the twin guardians of the fairies' grotto in the pantomime; while the surface of the lock presented as great a variety of leaves and flowers all chased with the utmost skill, as Eugene Rimmel's beautiful bouquet. These locks were mostly found on the doors of the ancient continental cathedrals, or on the magnificent cabinets for which the middle ages were so famous, and Mr. Fairholt assures us, that in either case the lock constituted no mean part of the profuse decoration of the door to which it was affixed. The skill of continental locksmiths after a considerable slumber was revived in the seventeenth century in the person of M. Reignier, a French artizan, who acquired great fame as the maker of secret "letter locks," with which the couriers' despatch boxes were secured. A Dutch writer, Von Euse, passing over the claims of his own countrymen, ascribes to M. Reignier the invention of the letter lock, which is in reality of Dutch orgin, and was made a century before this French Chubb saw the light. An allusion to it is made in Beaumont and Fletcher's play, *The Noble Gentleman*, printed as early as the year 1615, which completely sets aside M. Reignier's claim to the invention: –

> A cap case for your linen and your plate,
> With a strange lock that opens with A. M. E. N.; –

and Carew, in some verses written five years later, has this reference: –

> As doth a lock that goes
> With letters, for till every one be known
> The lock's as fast as though you had found none.

The latter quotation partly explains the construction of the letter lock, with which M. Reignier's name will always be connected as their most famous manufacturer. The letters of the alphabet were engraved on four parallel revolving rings, which by pre-arrangement on the part of the owner were made to spell a certain word or number of words before the lock could be opened. If even the owner chanced to forget the *open sesame* on which he had determined; like the luckless youth in the story of Ali Baba, the door would remain closed against him, till the magic watchword was recalled.

The ancient Chinese lock verifies one of the wise sayings of King Solomon; "Men have sought out many inventions . . . there is nothing new under the sun." The fact has lately been disclosed that locks "having sliders and tumblers," have for centuries been made in China, on the identical principles of action which have been "re-invented" by English patentees at various periods during the last hundred years. Some of the very oldest locks made by Chinese workmen were constructed almost entirely of wood, and adorned with grotesque carvings of "Celestial scenes," such as those with which modern tea-caddies have made us so familiar.

Tradition assures us that locks were made in England as early as the reign of Alfred the Great, and some go so far as to say that the ingenious monarch himself, like Louis XIV. of France, was an amateur fabricator of those articles. It is true, no doubt, that even at so remote a period, ingenious blacksmiths were wont to construct clumsy locks and keys, together with other articles of domestic use, when occasion demanded; but lockmaking was not recognised as a distinct craft in England, until the fourteenth century; and two hundred years followed, before it assumed proportions at all equal to those attained in earlier times on the Continent, in China, and in Ancient Egypt. The locks produced in England in the fifteenth century were massive and strong; but chiefly of simple construction. Almost the only specimen now remaining, is to be found on the parish church of Snodland, in Kent. In the Sixteenth century commenced the display of ingenuity on the part of English locksmiths which has been uninterruptedly maintained since that time, and which forms an interesting chapter in the Curiosities of Industry. During Queen Elizabeth's reign, the bows of keys were usually ornamented by the insertion of a Cross, and the locks were frequently made of metal, sometimes imbedded in oak cases. Latch-keys – the terror of Mistress Caudle – also came into use about this period. Locks were for the first time made with alarum bells and chimes during the same period.

Some of these bells rang so loudly in case of any unlawful tampering with the lock as to arouse the whole street, and must have resembled the melodious bull already quoted. Bells with chimes warned the inmates and alarmed the burglar in a much more soothing way. No sooner was the skeleton-key of the intruder applied to the lock, than the latter began to chime some such plaintive air as,

> Home, sweet, home,
> Be it ever so humble
> There's no place like home;

a sentiment with which the chagrined housebreaker would doubtless concur as he took his precipitate flight. The Marquis of Worcester mentions a lock which he says "is so constructed that if a stranger attempt to open it, it catches his hand as a trap catches a fox, though so far from maiming him for life, yet so far marketh him that if suspected, he could be easily detected." This punishment was effected by a steel barb, concealed in the keyhole, ever ready to spring out at its victim on the slightest provocation. The patentee himself, we are told, was caught by it while testing the lock, after which he was inspired with implicit confidence in the efficacy of his invention. Perhaps as curious a specimen of a lock as is recorded, was made by Mark Scaliot, a noted blacksmith of Queen Elizabeth's time. This lock consisted of eleven pieces of iron, steel, and brass, all of which with a pipe key, weighed only two grains of gold. It might have suited the collar of the Queen of Lilliput's pet lap-dog.

The first Patent for a lock in England was granted to Mr. Robert Barron in 1774, immediately after the introduction of the Patent Laws, since which time the Patent Office has been besieged by not less than 150 locksmiths of the inventive class. Before Mr. Barron's day the security of locks was usually effected by fixed wards more or less intricate, through which the key had to pass before the locking-bolt could be moved in either direction. To these fixed wards Mr. Barron added lifting tumblers or levers, which had to be raised to a particular height of utmost exactness before the lock could be either opened or secured. The additional security of these levers is at once apparent to any one who has paid attention to the mechanism of a lock. The obstructions, however intricate, placed in warded locks, can be easily overcome by the application of a skeleton key, while a levered lock is only to be violated by pieces of curved steel, technically called "pickers," by which the levers may sometimes be raised, although the operation is always one of considerable difficulty. In 1784, Mr. Joseph Bramah of Piccadilly patented a lock which was declared, amidst a great flourish of trumpets, to supersede Barron's, especially in the matter of security. The leading feature of this invention was the introduction of a perpendicular bar or bolt in which were a number of small slides corresponding with notches in the key. These slides or springs effectually secured the bolt beneath, until they were pressed down a sufficient distance by the key, which having removed these obstacles, revolved, and opened the lock in the ordinary way. Mr. Bramah was so convinced of the absolute security of this lock, that he offered a large reward to "any artist who could make an instrument to pick or open it." The acceptance of this challenge by Mr. Hobbs, and his success in opening the lock at the Great Exhibition of 1851, are facts within the memory of our readers, and need not now be detailed. The victory of the young American, after sixteen days' persevering labour, was noised all the world over, and gave a stimulus to the lock trade such as it has never experienced either before or since. Chubb's locks were first heard of in the year 1818, when the original Patent was obtained by Mr. Jeremiah Chubb; but since that time many improvements have been added to the original invention by the present Mr. Chubb in conjunction with Mr. Ebenezer Hunter. The leading principle of Chubb's lock is what is called the "detector." This ingenious contrivance consists of a spring, which, so long as the levers are lifted with exactness by the true key, remains inactive; but should the levers, raised by a false key, vary in the slightest degree, this spring instantly falls and securing the bottom lever renders the bolt immovable. When the true key is applied while the detector spring is "on duty," the former has to be turned the reverse way, and the spring restored to its original position before the lever can be set at liberty. A more vigilant or reliable detector could not be found even in Scotland Yard. Some years ago, the late Mr. Chubb made 1100 locks for the Westminster Bridewell, forming one series, or suite, with keys for the master, sub-master, and warders. At any time the Governor has the power of stopping out the under keys, and in case of any surreptitious attempt being made to open a lock and the detector being "thrown," none of the under keys will regulate it, but the Governor must be made acquainted with it, he alone with his key having the power to restore the lock to its original state. So limitless are the combinations, that Mr. Chubb assures us it would be possible to make locks for all the doors of all the houses in London, with a distinct and different key to each lock, and yet there should be one master-key to pass the whole.

We can only just enumerate the other names of fame, in the annals of locks and keys: James Carpenter, the inventor of the "perpendicular-action" lock of world-wide renown, John Young, his coadjutor; Sanders with his sliding levers; Parsons, with his "changeable" lock; Hobbs, with his machine-made levered lock; and last, but not least, Chatwood of Bolton, the hero of the recent iron-safe lock contest at the Paris Exposition.

South Staffordshire worthily retains the position it has occupied for two hundred years as the principal seat of the lock trade in this country. Wolverhampton carries off the palm for levered locks, while warded locks are mostly made at Willenhall. In some outlying hamlets a great variety of cheap locks are manufactured at what Dickens would call "a ridiculously small sum." One of these village artizans was once twitted at having made some locks which a chapman declared would only lock once. "What did he pay for them?" asked the locksmith. "Twopence a piece," was the answer. "Then," rejoined the former, "it would be a shame if they *did* lock *twice* for that money!" The same locks are now sold for a half-penny each. So rapidly are they constructed that it is a common saying in the district, if a locksmith drops a lock in the process of manufacture, he does not stay to pick it up, he can make another in less time! But locks are also made as high as a guinea each, and below that at every price down to the smallest coin save one, in the realm. In size there is an equal diversity. There are caddy locks not measuring half-an-inch, and weighing not more than a quarter of an ounce, and there are massive contrivances three feet long, and approaching a hundred pounds in weight. Some we lately saw, intended for a Government fortress in Malta, measured six feet in length, and weighed 1 cwt. and a half each. The total weekly production of locks of all descriptions in this district has been estimated as follows: Pad, 24,000 dozens; cabinet, till, and chest, 3,000 dozens; rim, dead Mortice and Drawback, 3,000 dozens; fine-plate or stock locks, 1,000 dozens; levered locks and other descriptions, 500 dozens, being an aggregate of 31,500 dozens or 378,000 locks per week!

Unlike the textile manufactures, the lock trade, in common with other leading industries of South Staffordshire, is almost wholly in the hands of small capitalists, just a grade above the level of artizans, and not employing more than half a dozen, or at most a dozen work-people, and of these a good proportion are youths apprenticed to the craft. There are some large factories employing hundreds of "hands," but they are comparatively few and far between. This wide distribution of the lock trade is injurious both to the interests of the "journeyman," and to the progress of skilled handicraft. The approximate number of hands is 4,950, and of employers 450. Experienced workmen can earn from 30*s*. to 40*s*. per week, but the average earnings may be set down at 24*s*. for adults, and 15*s*. for youths between 17 and 21 years of age. Many of the workshops – the small ones more especially – are badly ventilated, dark, and unwholesome, often being in a confined yard at the rear of the master's house. The hours of labour, too, are unduly prolonged, especially in the winter months, when the locksmith's hammer may often be heard beating its monotonous music until almost midnight. These evils will, however, be to some extent removed by the extension of the Factory Act to this district, on the 1st of January next.

The condition of the locksmiths here has wonderfully improved during the last twenty or thirty years. For a true and graphic picture of their condition a quarter of a century ago, we cannot do better than refer the reader to "Sibyl," in which Mr. Disraeli details with great force the sufferings, the ignorance, and the coarse brutal tastes, which prevailed among this class of labourers at that time. Since then, however, education has found its way to almost every young disciple of Tubal Cain; and bull-baiting and "cocking," once so rampant in this district, have been supplanted by less revolting pastimes.

J. C. Tildesley.

Note

1 Odyssey xxi.

60

ANON, 'A MIDLAND TOUR; XVII – WOLVERHAMPTON'

The Leisure Hour: a family journal of instruction and recreation, 20 July 1872, pp. 462–463

It is about two centuries since Dud Dudley succeeded in establishing the use of pit coal in the manufacture of iron. Wilkinson lighted his first blast furnace in 1768, and built his first mill and forge three years afterwards. And now, while on the north and west – the "Green Border-Land" of Elihu Burritt – all is still, as we see, rural and picturesque – all about the south and east sides of this town are coal and iron mines, blast furnaces, forges, rolling mills, and foundries; and Wolverhampton produces iron in almost every shape, from pig-iron to finished iron, iron foundry goods, iron braziery and galvanised iron goods, iron tubes, steel, edge tools, and enamelled hollow wares, machinery, mills, cut nails, and, above all, *locks*, for in the production of locks more than 100 firms and 2,000 people find employment, and the town may be said literally to hold three-fourths of the habitable globe under lock and key. And the lock trade of Wolverhampton is quite distinct from that of other parts of South Staffordshire. Nearly two hundred years since it was said: "The artisans of Wolverhampton seem to be preferred to all others in lock-making, they making them in suites, six, eight, or more in a suite, according as the chapman bespeaks them, whereof the keys shall neither of them open the other's lock, yet one master-key shall open them all. Nay, so curious are they in lockwork that they can contrive a lock that the master or mistress of a family sending a servant into their closets, either with the master-key or their own, can certainly tell by the lock how many times that servant has been in, at any distance of time, or how many times the lock has been shot for a whole year together, some of them being made to show it 300, 500, or 1,000 times; nay, one of the chief workmen of the town told me he could make one that should show it 10,000 times. Further yet, I was told of a very fine lock, made in this town, sold for £20, that had a set of chimes in it, that could go at any hour the master should think fit. And these locks they make either with brass or iron boxes, so curiously polished, and the keys so finely wrought, that it is not reasonable to think they were ever exceeded, unless by Tubal Cain, the inspired artificer in brass and iron." It has been stated that in and around Wolverhampton "there are some five hundred distinct lock factories, some of them employing only a master workman and his

DOI: 10.4324/9781315400105-71

two or three apprentices, others boasting as many as a hundred or a hundred and fifty workpeople. There are probably five thousand locksmiths in the aggregate in the vicinity of this 'hardware village.'"

Messrs. Chubb and Son, of St. Paul's Churchyard, are among the foremost of our English lock manufacturers. Their works are situated at the entrance to the town, and attract the attention of the stranger immediately on his arrival. They inform us that they commenced business in Wolverhampton some forty years ago, and that they now employ about a hundred workpeople, and have room for many more. One peculiar feature – the "detector" – characterises, and has always distinguished, Chubb's locks; and, with the tumblers, is the basis of security against all attempts at "picking." The detector consists of a spring, which so long as the levers are lifted with exactness by the true key, remains inactive; but should the levers, raised by a false key, vary in the slightest degree, this spring instantly secures the bottom lever, and renders the bolt immovable. When the true key is applied while the detector spring is "on duty," the former has to be turned the reverse way, and the spring restored to its original position, and the lever is then set at liberty. All their locks are made in series, having a separate and different key to each, and a master-key for opening any number that may be required; moreover, all they manufacture in Wolverhampton are made by hand, and no machinery whatever is used in making them. They turn out about 40,000 locks a year, not one of which is sold at less than ten shillings, while the most expensive are five pounds each. Among the curiosities of manufacture in their possession is a lock and key in the Florentine style, the works being encased in walnut wood, and the ornamental steel-work cut out by hand; a key in Venetian Gothic style, adapted from some fine old specimens of ornamental ironwork at Venice, and beautifully wrought; another key, the bow of which is composed of nearly 2,000 pieces of steel; a detector padlock, made in gold, with four tumblers, detector, and springs, set in a finger-ring, the weight of the lock and two keys being only sixteen grains! – a gigantic rim-lock, weighing upwards of two hundred-weight, and as finely finished as a lady's watch; and "gunpowder-proof" locks for patent iron safes, which are manufactured in London.

To show the strength and durability of the locks, one was attached to a steam-engine in Portsmouth dockyard, and was locked and unlocked upwards of four hundred and sixty thousand times (to try the effect of friction), without receiving the least injury. Messrs. Chubb constructed a set of locks for the Westminster Bridewell, consisting of 1,100 locks, with separate keys for every lock, and master-keys that would open all. The whole of the locks on the external doors, and the principal inner doors, of the International Exhibition building of 1862, were made by the same firm. Although arranged in various divisions as regards their keys, all were under the command of one master-key, which was presented by the Chairman of the Commissioners to H.R.H. the Duke of Cambridge, her Majesty's representative, at the opening ceremony. And they tell us that so extensive are the combinations to be made in locks that it would be quite practicable to make locks for all the doors of all the houses in London, with a distinct and different key to each lock, and one master-key to pass the whole! Every lock they produce is entirely made by one man, whose name is recorded against it in a ledger, which also records that of the buyer; further, it bears a number; so that, by sending the number of a lock at any time, its history may be ascertained. Australia and India (especially Calcutta) are great markets for these locks, which are also supplied to the colonies generally.

61

IMAGES: 'LOCK'

The National Encyclopaedia: a Dictionary of Universal Knowledge, Vol. 8 (London: [n.p.], c. 1870)

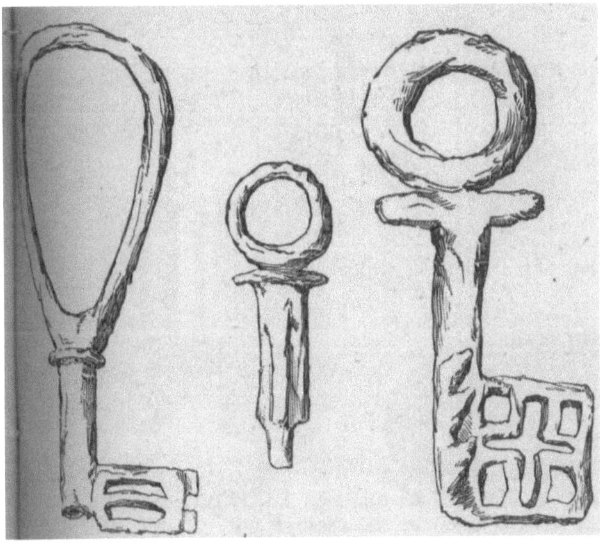

Figure 61.1 Specimens of keys in the British Museum from Pompeii and Herculaneum.

DOI: 10.4324/9781315400105-72

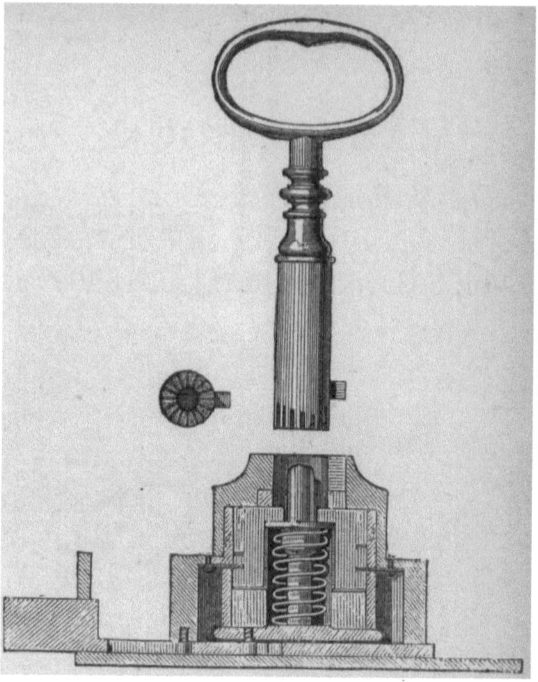

Figure 61.2 Section of bramah lock, with its key.

Figure 61.3 Two-bolt mortise door lock.

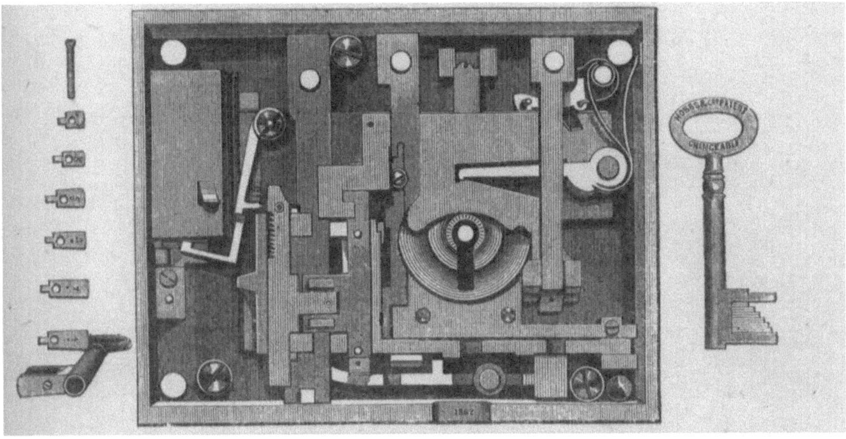

Figure 61.4 Hobbs & Co.'s patent changeable bank lock.

Figure 61.5 Puzzle or letter lock.

3.4

Fire ironmongery

DOI: 10.4324/9781315400105-73

3.4 Fire ironmongery

'Fire Irons' and 'Fenders, Grates, and Light Iron Castings', in Samuel Timmins (ed.), *The Resources, Products, and Industrial History of Birmingham and the Midland Hardware District; A series of reports, collected by the local industries committee of the British Association at Birmingham* (London: Robert Hardwicke, 1866), pp. 662–666.

Anon, 'William S. Burton, General Furnishing Ironmonger', *The Athenaeum*, no. 2171 (Jun 5, 1869), p. 780.

B. W. Richardson, 'Health at Home', *Good Words*, Vol. 21 (Jan 1880), pp. 98–101.

Anon, 'Musgrave & Co. (Limited), Stable Fitting and Stove Manufacturers, Belfast, London, Manchester, and Paris', in *Wyman's Commercial Encyclopædia of Leading Manufacturers of Great Britain and their Productions; Being a Guide to Merchant Buyers All Over the World* (London: Wyman, 1888), pp. 450–451.

With fireplaces in most rooms, including a hearth, range or stove in the kitchen and perhaps a copper in the scullery, domestic heat sources were highly visible features of the Victorian home. The majority were coal fuelled; although gas ranges were commercially available beginning mid-century for wealthy consumers, they remained rare throughout the Victorian period. Gas was more commonly used for light, as was electricity. However, electricity networks would remain rare in most British towns by 1900 and were initially used for light not heat. Even with improved technology and worries about unhealthy smog, for most of the population domestic warmth only ever came from a flickering coal fire.

An array of goods was available to fulfil needs for heating and cooking. Not all households could afford a stove or range, but open fires still needed equipment as coal will not burn without a grate. Bars and fenders protected soft furnishings from falling coals, while even the poorest households required some form of implement for stoking and tending a fire. Fire irons refers to a set of tools usually comprising a shovel, tongs and poker. The principal component of these was iron, with accents provided by steel, brass and bronze. Fire irons, fenders and grates were chiefly produced in the Midlands, while stoves were manufactured across the nation. The sources here demonstrate attitudes to domestic heating that range from a consumer's individual preferences to health anxieties.

The manufacture of irons, fenders and grates in the Midlands was, according to the entries on 'Fire Irons' and 'Fenders, Grates, and Light Iron Castings' in *The Resources, Products, and Industrial History of Birmingham and the Midland Hardware District* of 1866, a rough-and-ready process, easy to learn and conducted by a class of artisans who were not 'remarkable for intelligence or sobriety'. This extract details a process resembling blacksmithing, with irons bobbed, ground and shifted by hand before being polished by a woman with 'a palm-full of emery'. The range and variety of fire irons for sale belie the small number of workers in Birmingham, Dudley, Wolverhampton and Sheffield producing them. Only 500 workers are employed in manufacturing fire irons and fenders. The author's tone is practical, with no reference to luxury or ornamentation, suggesting that this book was aimed at technically minded readers.

The advertisement for 'William S. Burton's Show-Rooms' reveals the flourishing consumer market for domestic ironmongery, with boasts about the availability of 'an assortment of fenders, stoves, ranges, chimney-pieces, fire-irons and general ironmongery'. Like other manufactured goods included in this volume, the advertisement specifically invites readers to note the 'variety, novelty, beauty of design, or exquisiteness of workmanship'. An ornamented stove could cost anything from £3 to £33, with the quality of the ornamentation depending on the buyer's taste and budget. Fire irons were a much cheaper form of decoration, starting at 3*s* 3*d*; an affordable luxury. Burton's issued various illustrated advertisements between 1846 and 1883, showing the company's development from the modest Rippon and Son in 1820 to the possession of 20 large showrooms in London by the 1860s.

Anxieties about health problems associated with coal dust feature in 'Health at Home', written by the physician Benjamin Ward Richardson in 1880. This article focusing on heating appears at the end of a decade in which Richardson published *On Alcohol* (1875), *Disease of Modern Life* (1876), *Hygea, a City of Health* (1876) and *The Future of Sanitary Science* (1877). *Good Words* was an illustrated monthly magazine costing sixpence that was launched to rival *The Leisure Hour*. Both were illustrated, 'improving' publications aimed at Christian readers; 'Health at Home' appeared alongside Thomas Hardy's novel *The Trumpet Major* and an article on 'Lung Capacity and Tight Lacing'. In this article, Richardson argues that rapid changes in temperature threaten the health of 'enfeebled' people, particularly the very young or old. The best way of maintaining a steady heat, he suggests, is the 'Calorigen' stove, a system which simultaneously heats and ventilates and is sealed to limit dust.

Richardson's piece is unillustrated, but a similar model of stove is depicted in *Wyman's Commercial Encyclopædia* (1888). The 'Irish' or 'Patent Ulster' stove, developed by Musgrave & Co. in Belfast, claimed maximum heat with minimum fuel consumption and smoke. It was demonstrated at the Smoke Abatement Exhibition in South Kensington held in 1881 by the philanthropic Kyrle Society. Responding to Victorian smog, the event anticipated the founding in 1898 of the Coal Smoke Abatement Society.

62

'FIRE IRONS' AND 'FENDERS, GRATES, AND LIGHT IRON CASTINGS'

The Resources, Products, and Industrial History of Birmingham and the Midland Hardware District; A series of reports, collected by the local industries committee of the British Association at Birmingham
(London: Robert Hardwicke, 1866), pp. 662–666

FIRE-IRONS. – Fire-irons were originally made by simply heating bars of iron in the forge and hammering them into shape. The process, however, is now performed much more rapidly and accurately by "lapping," *i.e.*, turning a piece of hot iron round the heated rod wherever a swell or knob is required, placing the part thus thickened between two dies of the requisite form on the anvil, and striking the top die with a heavy hammer, thus welding the two pieces of iron together into one of the desired shape. The twisted shanks, now so much in fashion, are formed in the same way, the heated iron being drawn through a pair of dies about three inches long bearing the impression of the required twist. When cold the irons are filed all over, to remove the "scale," this operation being generally performed by boys. They are then case-hardened by exposure to great heat in an iron box filled with charcoal. They are next "bobbed," the "bob" being a wooden wheel covered at the circumference with glue and emery, which forms a substance so hard that the sparks fly as if the iron were ground on solid stone. Every set of irons has to pass over many bobs, shaped to fit the several parts of the outline, the length of plain shank being ground on a wheel not unlike a Somersetshire cheese, while the intricate portions of the pattern require narrow bobs with rounded edges. From the bobs the irons are removed to the "laps," or revolving wheels of white metal composed of tin and zinc, which have to be made of as many shapes as the bobs. When the scratches left by the bobs are all removed the final polish is given by hand, the fire-irons being placed in a lathe and a woman pressing a palm-full of emery against them. Those parts which cannot be polished in the lathe, such as the bows of the tongs, are rubbed by hand. The pans of the shovels are cut out of sheet

DOI: 10.4324/9781315400105-74

iron by a heavy press, worked either by a screw or by steam. If the pan is pierced the operation is performed in another press, the little bits cut out being sold to the gun-barrel makers. If required bright, the pans are then ground on a stone and bobbed. They are then hollowed by two blows from another press and are ready to be rivetted on to the shanks.

More fire-irons are sent to Germany than to any other European market. They are light and small. A few of the same character, but better finished, are shipped to France. Besides Birmingham, the manufacture is carried on at Dudley and Wolverhampton, and to a small extent in Sheffield. The number of comparatively large masters in Birmingham is now 12, and of working masters, 35. 260 men, 26 women, and 36 boys are employed. In Dudley, Wolverhampton, and the neighbourhood, there are 17 masters, 170 men, 26 women, and about 30 boys. In 1849, the number of masters in Birmingham was 35, but the small increase in this respect since that time by no means represents the progress of the trade, since in this manufacture, as in many others, large factories with increased capital and improved appliances are gradually supplanting the smaller ones. As any man who can wield a hammer can soon learn the trade, the class of artisans employed in this manufacture is not one remarkable for intelligence and sobriety, but there are many steady men in the trade who can earn full 60*s*. per week.

This is one of the Birmingham trades in which a workman may easily become a master; a loan of £5 being sufficient capital with which to start in business. Several such masters are to be found in shops, once may be stables or washhouses in a back court up an entry. The plant consists of a forge and anvil, a few pair of dies, three or four hammers, a vice and a file, and the casual visitor may stumble over the stock of iron in stooping to enter the door. The pans are bought from a "stamper and piercer," and the work is "bobbed" and "lapped" at "the mill," an institution common in many of the smaller trades of the town – where copper is "spun" into warming pans, spoons are "buffed," snuffers "coloured," &c. – kept by another tradesman who owns or hires steam-power and sublets it for temporary use to those who may require it.

Fenders, Grates, and Light Iron Castings. – The manufacture of cast-iron fenders appears to have been commenced in this town about forty years ago, when they began to supersede the elaborate and costly fender of steel, of rolled brass, or pierced sheet-iron. The first is still sometimes to be seen, its almost unlimited wear justifying the great price that was paid for it. The brass fender is now entirely extinct as an article of regular manufacture, and the pierced-iron very nearly so, there being but two makers of them in Birmingham. These changes have been effected by the gradual cheapening of the manufacture, combined with the increasing appreciation of the suitability of cast-iron for a purpose in which a certain amount of solid stability may be made ornamental at a slight cost.

At first, the fronts of fenders were cut in short lengths, and screwed together; but this plan was soon abandoned, as it was found that the screws often got loose and came out. The manufacturers then adopted the method now generally in use, of casting the fronts in one length, which saves much time in fitting, and makes a far better article. The rapidity with which fenders are now cast, filled with sheet-iron bottom plates, and blacked or bronzed, may be inferred from the fact, that one manufacturer making the cheapest class of work, and employing thirty people altogether, turns out no less than 100 dozen fenders a week. Perhaps a still more surprising statement is that, though he sells some of them at 11*s*. per dozen, his casters earn about £3 a week. This would be impossible if his arrangements were not so made that his men never have to stand still for anything, the materials required being always ready to their hands. Though so many of these cheap fenders are made, it is a satisfactory sign that there has lately been an increasing demand for the better class of work. Beyond Great Britain the chief markets for fenders are the British Colonies. A few are also sent to the free cities of Germany. Scarcely any go to France; partly because few are used there, and partly also on account of the difficulty of getting articles so large and yet so fragile to their destination, through various changes in transit, without breakage. Were it not for this risk we should be able to compete successfully with the French makers.

The stove grate trade was a very small branch of manufacture in Birmingham till within the last few years, but in that time it has made considerable advance. We are indebted to the tyranny of the Trades' Unions of Sheffield for the removal thence to Birmingham of a manufacturer who is making a reputation for our town in this branch of trade. Before 1855 he had works in Sheffield, where there is a union among the "casters," and another among the "grinders." The latter were especially stringent in their regulations. If, as sometimes happened, the master had so many orders on his books that he was actually obliged to refuse more, he could not take on another lad without consulting the men, who reported his wish to the committee of the union. This august body sent deputies to make enquiries whether in the plentitude of their grace they might vouchsafe to grant the humble petition of the employer. If the report were favourable he was permitted to take the desired youth into his service on condition that the lad was a son or near relation of some member of the union. Sometimes, however, the refusal of more orders by the master, from inability to execute them, was the inevitable consequence. Moreover, if it was found by the union that a man was working so steadily as to gain the highest possible wages, and thereby let the master see what very large sums could be earned if men lost none of their time, a deputation waited upon the man and carried him off to the nearest public house, where they kept him drinking for two or three days. It is not, then to be wondered at that a master should try to escape from the reach of influences so detrimental to his trade. The gentleman in question removed to Birmingham, and some of his steadfast men came with him, glad to be themselves out of the tyranny of the union. Other Sheffield manufacturers have followed his example. Some have gone to Rotheram, and one to Derby; and a once flourishing trade has been to this extent expelled from Sheffield by the folly of the men. Here, the materials used cost the same; good sand for ordinary castings can be obtained from the neighbourhood; and the fine loam sand of Mansfield, used for the best castings, is no dearer in Birmingham than Sheffield. Scotch iron is the same price in both places, and the Staffordshire iron is as good as the Yorkshire for best work. Owing to there being no union in Birmingham, the difference in wages makes a reduction in the cost of the finished article of about fifteen per cent., one process being actually forty per cent. cheaper than in Sheffield.

The continental countries to which most grates are sent are Spain and the German free cities. The Sultan of Turkey has lately taken a fancy to English grates, and has had some of elaborate and expensive style made in Birmingham; his example has been followed by the Pacha of Egypt. Some stoves are sent to France, but scarcely any to America, and none to Prussia, where the duty of 25 per cent. is prohibitive. The Palace at Brussels has been fitted up with grates large enough for an ample supply of the peat that warms the royal household of Belgium.

The approximate number of people employed in the fender and grate trade in Birmingham is 500, of whom about 50 are women, and 150 boys.

Amongst the miscellaneous articles made by the manufacturers in this trade are cast-iron hat and umbrella stands, door porters and knockers, garden seats and tables. One manufacturer has for some time past been making an almost incredible number of stands for patent sewing machines, the machines themselves being made in Canada; but as iron casting is so much cheaper here than there, the machines destined for the English trade are sent over and fitted on to their stands or tables here, thereby effecting a considerable saving of expense in freight.

63

ANON, 'WILLIAM S. BURTON, GENERAL FURNISHING IRONMONGER'

The Athenaeum, no. 2171 (Jun 5, 1869), p. 780

WILLIAM S. BURTON, GENERAL FURNISHING IRONMONGER, By Appointment to H.R.H. the Prince of Wales,
SENDS a CATALOGUE GRATIS and POST PAID.

IT CONTAINS UPWARDS OF 700 ILLUSTRATIONS OF HIS UNRIVALLED STOCK OF

ELECTRO-PLATE and
BRITANNIA METAL GOODS,
DISH COVERS,
HOT-WATER DISHES,
STOVES and FENDERS,
MARBLE CHIMNEY-PIECES,
KITCHEN RANGES,
LAMPS, GASELIERS,
TEA TRAYS,
URNS and KETTLES,
TABLE CUTLERY,
CLOCKS and CANDELABRA,
BATHS and TOILET WARE,
IRON and BRASS BEDSTEADS,
BEDDING and BED HANGINGS,
BEDROOM CABINET FURNITURE,
TURNERY GOODS,
KITCHEN UTENSILS,

WITH LISTS OF PRICES, AND PLANS OF THE TWENTY LARGE SHOW-ROOMS, At 39, Oxford-street; 1, 1a, 2, 3, and 4, Newman-street; 4, 5, and 6. Perry's-place; and 1, Newman-yard, London, W.

DOI: 10.4324/9781315400105-75

FENDERS, STOVES, KITCHEN RANGES, FIRE-IRONS, and CHIMNEY-PIECES – Buyers of the above are requested, before finally deciding, to visit WILLIAM S. BURTON'S SHOW-ROOMS. They contain such an assortment of Fenders, Stoves, Ranges, Chimney-Pieces, Fire-Irons, and General Ironmongery as cannot be approached elsewhere either for variety, novelty, beauty of design, or exquisiteness of workmanship. Bright Stoves with or-mulu ornaments, 3*l.* to 8*s.* to 33*l.* 10*s.*; Bronze Fenders, 3*s.* 9*d.* to 5*l.* 12*s.*; Steel Fenders, with rich or-mulu ornaments, from 2*l.* 18*s.* to 18*l.*; Chimney-Pieces, from 1l. *8s.* to 18*l.*; Fire-Irons, from 3*s.* 3*d.* the set to 4*l.* 10*s.*

The BURTON and all other PATENT STOVES, with radiating Hearth-plates.

64

B. W. RICHARDSON, 'HEALTH AT HOME'

Good Words, Vol. 21 (Jan 1880), pp. 98–101

III

It is always a matter of great moment to maintain an equable temperature in the bedroom. A bedroom, the air of which is subject to great, and frequent, and rapid changes of temperature, is always a trap for danger. To persons who are in the prime of life, and who are in robust health, this danger is less pronounced, but to the young and the feeble it is a most serious danger. It is specially dangerous to aged people to sleep in a room that is easily lowered in warmth. When the great waves of cold come on in these islands, in the winter season, our old people begin to drop off with a rapidity that is perfectly startling. We take up the list of deaths published in the *Times* during these seasons, and the most marked of facts is the number of deceased aged persons. It is like an epidemic of death by old age. The public mind accepts this record as indicative of a general change of external conditions, and of a mortality therefore that is necessary as a result of that change. I would not myself dispute that there is a line of truth and sound common sense and common observation in this view, but when we descend from the general to the particular we find that much of the mortality, seen in such excess amongst the aged, is induced by mistakes on the subject of warmth in the bedroom.

The fatal event comes about somewhat in this way. The room in which the enfeebled person has been sitting before going to bed has been warmed probably up to summer heat; a light meal has been taken before retiring to rest, and then the bedroom is entered. The bedroom perchance has no fire in it, or if a fire be lighted provision is not made to keep it alight for more than an hour or two. The result is that in the early part of the morning, from three to four o'clock, when the temperature of the air in all parts is lowest, the glow from the fire or stove which should warm the room has ceased, and the room is cold to an extreme degree. In country houses the water will often be found frozen in the hand-basins or ewers under these conditions.

Meanwhile the sleeper lies unconscious of the great change which is taking place in the air around him. Slowly and surely there is a decline of temperature to the extent, it may be, of thirty or forty degrees on the Fahrenheit scale; and though he may be fairly covered with bedclothes he is receiving into his lungs this cold air, by which the circulation through the lungs is materially modified.

DOI: 10.4324/9781315400105-76

The condition of the body itself is at this very time unfavourable for meeting any emergency. In the period between midnight and six in the morning, the animal vital processes are at their lowest ebb. It is in these times that those who are enfeebled from any cause most frequently die. We physicians often consider these hours as critical, and forewarn anxious friends in respect to them. From time immemorial those who have been accustomed to wait and attend on the sick have noted these hours most anxiously, so that they have been called by one of our old writers, "the hours of fate." In this space of time the influence of the life-giving sun has been longest withdrawn from man, and the hearts that are even the strongest beat then with subdued tone. Sleep is heaviest, and death is nearest to us all in "the hours of fate."

The feeble, therefore, are most exposed to danger during this period of time, and they are most exposed to one particular danger, that of congestion of the lungs, for it is the bronchial surface of the lungs that is most exposed to the action of the chilled air; and, in the aged, that exposure is hazardous. [. . .]

The practical question that comes out of this discussion is, How shall the danger of congestion of the lungs be avoided in the sleeping apartments of the enfeebled?

Our forefathers replied to this question in a very plain and striking manner. They shut themselves up in a warm tent. The old four-posters and the old tent bedsteads are the still extant witnesses of the ways and means for keeping out the cold in the old times. In country houses one sometimes finds still the massive four-post bedstead with its heavy damask curtains and snug enclosure. Advocate of fresh air as I am, I confess still to a lingering liking to this snug enclosure when I see it on a cold midwinter night. I met with it not very long ago and I crept into it with a sort of quiet glee as if feeling unusually safe and comfortable in so cosy a retreat.

I won't let mere likings tempt me to say that the plan is a good one. It is really not commendable, or only so when nothing better is at hand. If in a large room with cold walls and floors on a cold night I were obliged to sleep in a fireless room and had choice of two beds, one a curtained four-poster and the other a camp bedstead, I would no doubt, under the special circumstances, choose the four-poster, but not as a general principle by any means.

In our modern bedrooms, furnished according to modern taste and fashion, the best plan to adopt is that of admitting air freely to the sleeper, at the same time taking care that throughout the whole of the night the air shall be kept, within a few degrees, at the same temperature. I repeat, at the same temperature, for uniformity of warmth during all the hours of sleep is as essential as warmth. To have an overheated atmosphere at one time of the night and a low temperature at another, is just the kind of change that is attended with most hazard. Indeed, I doubt whether an equable cold atmosphere is not on the whole safer than one in which there is frequent and marked fluctuation.

The safest method is to have the air of the room, a short time before it is occupied, brought up to an uniform temperature of from 60° to 65° Fahr. It should never fall five degrees below 60° and never rise above 65° under ordinary circumstances. In cases where the occupant of the room is extremely enfeebled it may be necessary to raise the temperature to a higher point, but I am thinking at this moment of sleepers who are in fair health, and for whom no such special provision is required.

A mistake is sometimes made in observing the temperature. The reading of the thermometer is taken in one part of the room only, perhaps in the warmest part, that is to say, over the fireplace or from the mantle-shelf. This is not a fair observation, for a room at that part may be very warm while it is very cold in other parts. The temperature should, properly, be taken at the bed's head, about two feet above the pillow, and that is the best position in which to keep the thermometer, with which every bedroom ought to be furnished. An ordinary thermometer suffices as a general index, but a registering instrument is most advantageous when particular care is demanded in observation.

I now come to consider what is the best mode of warming the bedroom and of maintaining the equal warmth, on which so much has been insisted.

The simplest of all plans with which I am acquainted is that which brings air from the outside through a small chamber or pipe that can be heated by a fire or by gas, and which allows the air, after it has been warmed, to diffuse steadily into the room.

A stove called the Calorigen, invented by Mr. Webb George, is, in my opinion, best adapted for use in the bedroom. It burns either with coal gas or coal; or, more correctly speaking, a calorigen stove can be obtained either for gas or for coal. The stove has this great advantage, that it warms and ventilates at one and the same time. The stove contains within its outer cylinder or case a spiral iron tube, which by its lower end communicates with the outer air, and by its upper end opens into the room. The heat generated in the stove communicates heat to the spiral tube, and the air in the spiral is heated and ascends into the room. The ascension of warm air causes a draught from below, and so a current of warm air is at all times diffusing through the room so long as the fire of gas or coal is burning. At the same time the products of combustion from the stove are conveyed away by another pipe into a flue or chimney.

When one of these stoves is in good action the air of an apartment may be kept pure and warm for any length of time, and the temperature can be maintained at the same uniform degree all the while. There is also about the method the immense advantage that it secures freedom from cold draughts from doors and from windows. The copious influx of warm air from the stove is, indeed, so effective that when the stove is heated to its full, and the room is of moderate size, there is a draught or current of air out of the room by the doors when they are opened a little way, unless there be a provision for a fixed ventilating outlet. Properly there ought always to be a ventilating outlet, even when the room is steadily charged with fresh and warm air, for a current is always desirable.

My friend, Mr. Henry C. Stephens, in an excellent paper which he has written on Ventilation, maintains, with much force, that no mode of ventilation is actually perfect unless by precise mechanical means air be actually drawn into an apartment in duly measured quantities. He suggests a system of supply of air by a mechanism moved and regulated by weight and balance, so that the air through a house may be systematically supplied with all the accuracy of good and effective clockwork; or if this be not applicable, he favours the admirable waterwheel ventilation which has lately been brought out by Messrs. Verity, of Regent Street. There is much to be said in favour of Mr. Stephens's argument, and if I were constructing a house from the first I should introduce Verity's ventilating system into every room; but we have to deal with houses everywhere that were originally erected without the slightest regard to sanitary rules, and we must therefore adapt what is best and cheapest to improve if not to perfect. In the bedroom, the stove I refer to is of these adaptations the best I know of. It is really automatic in action when it is once started, and it can be put up anywhere where there is a chimney for the exit pipe for consumed air. Lastly, it is quite safe in the bedroom: the fire being enclosed no sparks can fly from it, and the fuel makes no dust within the room.

In my laboratory I have had one of the Calorigen stoves in work for several years, and I have found it so manageable and good I can recommend it on the best of all recommendations, its practical value. In the Annerley Industrial Schools, which I visited at the time of the Sanitary Congress, held last October, at Croydon, I found that the stoves were in common use, and that they were as much approved of by the school authorities as they are by my own experience of them.

There is one precaution which I would suggest to those who are going to introduce a Calorigen into their bedroom. When the stove is fixed it is usual for the man who fixes it to push the air-feeding pipe through the floor of the room so as to get the supply of air from under the floor. No arrangement can be better if due care be taken, but it is essential to make sure of three things in carrying out this plan. Firstly, it is essential to see that there is a free opening from the outer wall by a perforated brick or grating under the floor, so that the air chamber beneath gets a due supply of fresh air from without. Secondly, it is well to see that there is no gaspipe running beneath the floor from the joints of which gas could escape and be drawn by the stove into the air of the room above. Thirdly, it is important to have the space below the floor made quite free of old rubbish, and to have it made thoroughly dry. All these steps are really essential, for if there be no admission of air beneath the floor from without, the stove will exhaust, and the space will be recharged with air from the room through openings and chinks in the flooring; if there be any escape of gas beneath the floor the stove will diffuse the gas into the room; if there be decomposing matter or dust beneath the floor the stove will also diffuse them, and if there be damp it will diffuse the damp.

I name these possible errors because I have seen them all made, and, actually, in one instance, I saw removed from beneath the floor of a bedroom and dressing-room twenty barrow-loads of dust and débris which had been lying there for nearly a century. The workmen in building houses care little about leaving dust and rubbish on ceilings that are covered by floors. In this case the rubbish consisted of shavings, sawdust, and sundry other things, such as old slippers and shoes, which had been lying there ever since the house was built.

If it be impossible, or if it be too expensive, to lift up the floor-boards and clean the whole of the space beneath, the next best thing to do is to take up a floor-board and under it to carry a box one foot deep between the joists of the floor from the point where the air-pipe of the stove pierces the floor-board to the outlet in the wall in which the air-brick or grating is inserted. The floor-board will form as it were the lid of this box, and the air, drawn by the stove, will be through the box direct from the outside. The box should be made of pine wood, and neatly planed on its inner surface. That surface should be polished with beeswax and turpentine so soon as the box is laid in, and from time to time the floorboard should be removed and the polishing should be repeated. The air passing over the surface of wax and turpentine is made singularly healthy and pure. It is as if it had been subjected to ozone before entering the chamber, and if it enter the chamber at a temperature of 60° to 65° Fahr., the fresh odour is distinguishable in the room after it has been for a short time unoccupied. These plans are all very simple to carry out when they are simply explained, and as a bedroom that is well and easily warmed and well and easily ventilated is of priceless value, I make no apology for spending so much time on this one topic.

65

ANON, 'MUSGRAVE & CO. (LIMITED), STABLE FITTING AND STOVE MANUFACTURERS, BELFAST, LONDON, MANCHESTER, AND PARIS'

Wyman's Commercial Encyclopædia of Leading Manufacturers of Great Britain and their Productions; Being a Guide to Merchant Buyers All Over the World
(London: Wyman, 1888), pp. 450–451

OTHER towns may present more picturesque forms to the eye, but Belfast, the capital of the province of Ulster, stands out as one of the greatest and most flourishing seats of industry in the British Isles. In the graphic language of Lord Macaulay, the place of domes and spires is supplied by edifices, less pleasing to the taste, but not less indicative of prosperity – huge factories towering many stories above the chimneys of the houses, and resounding with the roar of machinery. Not only is Belfast the chief seat of the linen trade, but it has also become famous in several other branches of manufacture, and notably in those connected with shipbuilding, machinery, and ironwork. Although no native or other iron ores have down to the present been smelted in Ulster, its proximity to the enormous iron-producing districts of Scotland and its exceptional shipping facilities have placed Belfast in a most advantageous position for carrying on any business requiring a supply of crude or manufactured iron.

This fact has been recognised and taken advantage of in many ways, but in no case more energetically and successfully than by Messrs. Musgrave & Co. (Limited), of the Ann Street Iron Works, and Cromac Foundry, whose handsome and extensive premises are most conveniently situated close to the quays, and include commodious offices, show-rooms, and forwarding departments, from which latter the Firm's specialties are consigned to all countries of the world.

The present business was established many years ago by Messrs. Musgrave Brothers, a Firm which have been well-known in connexion with the iron industries of Ulster for close upon half a century. During the last fifteen years the concern has been carried on as a Limited Liability Company, the present directors

 DOI: 10.4324/9781315400105-77

being Mr. John R. Musgrave, J.P., D.L., Mr. John A. Hanna, and Mr. T. Foulkes Shillington. With the formation of the Company was ushered in a new era in the career of the business. Increased enterprise and vigour were brought to bear upon every branch; new and improved methods and appliances were introduced; and the works were extended by the building of the Cromac Iron Foundry. In addition to this, branch houses have been opened – in London, at 97, New Bond Street; in Manchester, at 40, Deansgate; and in Paris, at 240, Rue de Rivoli; all of which steps were rendered necessary by the continued growth of the business, and by the increasing demands made upon it by English, Continental, and Colonial customers. New branches of manufacture were added, and so the business has continued to grow and develop until it is now the largest in its own particular line of manufacture in the United Kingdom, if not in the whole world; and it takes, moreover, the leading position for originality of design and excellence of construction in its productions.

At a time when the comfort and health of horses and other animals received scant consideration from their owners, Messrs. Musgrave began to make the safe and sanitary housing of animals a subject of special study. This resulted in their designing and patenting a number of appliances for the purpose, and their specialties soon received highly favourable recognition from those interested in the subject. One of the earliest successes of the Firm was that they secured the patronage of the Royal Family, and it is worthy of note that the execution and fitting of the stables built in recent years for members of the Royal Family in this country have been carried out by Messrs. Musgrave & Co. For instance, they have entirely fitted up the magnificent stables at Sandringham for H.R.H. the Prince of Wales. Similarly the new stables of the Duke of Edinburgh and the Duke of Connaught have been fitted up by them.

Members of the nobility have not been slow to follow the example set by Royalty, and it may be worth while to enumerate a few of the more important contracts in this connexion which have been entrusted to the Firm. Fine specimens of their work can be seen at Eaton Hall, the seat of the Duke of Westminster; at Burghley House, seat of the Marquis of Exeter; at Aske Hall, the seat of the Earl of Zetland; at Ingestre Hall, the lately restored seat of the Earl of Shrewsbury; and at Buckminster Park, seat of the Earl of Dysart. On the Continent, too, their work is rightly held to be unrivalled, and the very extensive stables of Baron Adolphe Rothschild, Baron Edmond Rothschild, Baron Hirsch de Gereuth, of the Duchess de Medinaceli, Madrid, of the King of Holland, Prince Sciarra, Rome, and of many other foreign notabilities, have been fitted up by them. In each of the above cases, the special appropriateness of the designs and the utility and perfect workmanship of the fittings have been uniformly acknowledged. As typical of this class of work we give an illustration of a stable recently fitted by Messrs. Musgrave & Co.

Quite as important in its way as the housing of horses is the comfort and health of cattle, and to this subject the Firm have given equal attention, as is attested by some of the finest farm steadings in the kingdom. To particularise only two of these, the cattle houses on the estate of the late Sir Joseph Whitworth, and more recently on that of Chevalier Whitehead, of torpedo fame, have been fitted up by them. Both these gentlemen, be it remembered, were scientific engineers of the first standing, whose scrutiny nothing but the highest class of work would satisfy.

Flattering testimony of a like character to the quality of the productions of the Ann Street Iron Works is borne by the fact that Messrs. Musgrave have from time to time carried out important contracts for the War Office, and many of the best barracks in this country have been fitted up by them, including the new barracks at Knightsbridge and Maryhill.

As affording evidence of the exceptional capabilities of the works, it may be mentioned that in a recent case of emergency there were produced, in addition to the ordinary regular work, complete fittings for cavalry at the rate of two hundred and fifty stalls per week.

Intimately connected with the subject of fittings for horses is another specialty of the Firm, viz., the construction of grand stands for racecourses, &c., many of which have been erected on various courses.

Leaving now the subject of horses and their surroundings, and coming to matters more domestic, we find another special manufacture of world-wide celebrity, which like the foregoing owes its origin to Ulster genius – we refer to Musgrave's patent slow combustion "Ulster" stoves. For economy, durability, and convenience, these probably surpass anything of the kind ever introduced. It is not necessary to enter here into a description of the improvements effected in this stove to ensure the economical consumption of fuel, and the other advantages which have so markedly helped to popularise it and bring it into all but universal favour. From the time of its first invention repeated improvements have been made, until it is now in every respect perfect, insuring a maximum amount of heat, a minimum consumption of fuel, together with perfect combustion of the latter. As at present constructed the Musgrave stove embodies the result of five distinct patents. Its great advantages were fully demonstrated at the Smoke Abatement Exhibition held at South Kensington a few years ago.

The "Irish Stove" has become quite a household word on the Continent, where it is gradually replacing German and other stoves in competition with which it has been brought. Having been tested at an international trial conducted in Paris by an officer of high repute, it was found to be unsurpassed for heating power and economical consumption of fuel. The accompanying illustration shows one of these stoves with an exterior of handsomely designed iron and porcelain work.

From the foregoing it will be seen how by building up their immense business Messrs. Musgrave & Co. have benefited not only the manufacturing population of Ireland, but have also added to the commercial prosperity of the United Kingdom by establishing for British workmanship, in their own branch, an unrivalled reputation; and by thus creating a foreign demand they have been the means of extending our commerce in Continental as well as Colonial markets.

PART 4

Household goods

4.1

Ceramics

DOI: 10.4324/9781315400105-79

4.1 Ceramics

Beaver, Stanley H. 'The Potteries: A Study in the Evolution of a Cultural Landscape: Presidential Address' *Transactions and Papers* (Institute of British Geographers), No. 34 (June 1964), pp. 1–31.

Berg, Maxine, *Luxury and Pleasure in Eighteenth-Century Britain* (Oxford: Oxford University Press, 2007).

Cohen, Deborah, *Household Gods: The British and their Possessions* (New Haven and London: Yale University Press, 2006).

Moisley, H. A. 'The Industrial and Urban Development of the North Staffordshire Conurbation'. *Transactions and Papers, Institute of British Geographers*, Vol. 17 (1951), pp. 151–165.

Mokyr, Joel, *The Enlightened Economy: An Economic History of Britain, 1700–1850* (New Haven: Yale University Press, 2009).

Wynne, Deborah, 'Arnold Bennett and Material Culture' in *A Companion to Arnold Bennett* ed. John Shapcott (Leek: Churnet Valley Press, 2015), pp. 193–207.

The importance of the tea table in conceptions of domesticity for all classes ensured that mass-produced ceramics found a ready market at home, as well as being a major export product. The North Staffordshire Potteries where most ceramics were manufactured was a place of contrasts: emerging from the ugliness of its industrial landscape were beautiful objects, such as Wedgwood vases. The extracts here highlight the prejudices against and benefits of mass production. 'Leaves from the Mahogany Tree: Table Furniture' (1868) focuses on china epergnes for the dining table, with the anonymous author urging readers to seek original Pelissy china made in France in the sixteenth century or majolica ware from Spain from a century earlier, rather than to buy contemporary china from Dresden, a reference to a manufacturing district in the Potteries rather than the German town. The author, an aesthete and collector, dismisses mass-produced ceramics as 'common' and 'very mean and pitiful'. Connoisseurship became more fashionable as the century progressed, and the *Punch* cartoon of 1881 depicted here satirises aesthetes who are fixated on the beauty and rarity of their china. However, what the *All the Year Round* article fails to mention is that fine antique china was beyond the means of the majority of middle- and working-class people, most of whom would have found the cheapness of mass-produced ceramics from the Potteries very convenient.

There is a shift in attitude towards mass-produced items in the later article, 'China, China Everywhere', published in the trade journal *The Pottery Gazette* in 1899. This appeared at the height of the Arts and Crafts Movement, a time when ordinary readers sought advice on how to make their homes beautiful. The anonymous author recommends hunting around for ceramic items from a generation earlier, rather than collecting expensive antiques. These items would have been mass produced in their day and no doubt despised then as cheap by the arbiters of good taste, but they have since gained distinction over their 30 or 40 years of existence. The author asserts that there is little difference between the ceramics of the mid-Victorian period and old china from centuries earlier, urging readers to seek out the ceramic lamps, candlesticks, inkwells, call bells, creamers, lemonade jugs, scent bottles and chocolate pots owned by their parents and grandparents which had hitherto been rejected as old-fashioned. These items are now integral to the 'house beautiful', and many can be put to new uses. For example, tiny ceramic cups attached to their tiny saucers, originally created as an ornament, can now be placed on the dressing table to hold hairpins, while china salad dishes can be positioned on the hall table to receive the calling cards of visitors. The author asserts that 'Anything and everything which is china is worthy just now.'

Three years after this article appeared, *Anna of the Five Towns* (1902), a novel by Arnold Bennett, was published. Born in the Potteries, Bennett knew the region and its industry well and he finds extraordinary the fact that the local population is largely ignorant of the history and importance of the potter's craft. Set in the late-nineteenth century, the novel follows the fortunes of Anna Tellwright, a miser's daughter who lives in the heart of the Potteries. When she comes of age she inherits a 'pot bank' (the local name for a ceramics factory), and the extract here depicts Anna visiting the establishment for the first time. Mynors' pot bank is a state-of-the-art establishment specialising in cheap products, and Anna's questions about the processes of production allow the reader an opportunity to discover more about how raw clay is transformed into cups and saucers on an industrial scale. The image 'Ceramic Arts' depicts in detail the interior mechanisms of a pottery kiln. In Bennett's novel, the machinery and its operators are presented as engaged in a battle with a difficult raw material. By the time Anna sees the final product, the piles of tea sets in the warehouse, she finds it 'difficult even to conceive that, a fortnight or so before, they had been nothing but lumps of dirty clay'. This extract from *Anna of the Five Towns* offers a rare insight into the story behind virtually every cheap cup and plate used by most Victorians.

66

ANON, 'LEAVES FROM THE MAHOGANY TREE: TABLE FURNITURE (CHINA AND GLASS ETC.)'

All the Year Round, Vol. 20 (17 October 1868), pp. 441–443

If we were lucky enough to get a good bit of Palissy ware, well modelled, richly coloured, pleasant to the eye, and suggestive to the mind, we would try and also get a certain number of Palissy fruit and preserve dishes to match. These would not only have more individuality than Dresden or Worcester china, but the relievi would be sharper, the tints purer, the design less hackneyed, and the enamel colours and glaze more brilliant. The gay fruit will show all the pleasanter when contrasting with the deep indigo blues and chocolate browns of the French ware. If we had the choice, we would specially select those curious dishes, with rivulets in the centre, and shells and fish, spotted trout and lizards, frogs or efts, all round. Palissy used to search for these creatures in the ponds, brooks, and hazel coverts, round Fontainebleau; and they always show his patient love of nature, his industry, and his skill. He observed their colours, and reproduced them with most laborious care. The olive-green tints of a tench, the golden orange of a perch, the emerald armour of the lizard, the low-toned greenish greys of a miller's thumb – he took note of them all, and toiled at the furnace mouth until the stubborn clay glowed with the transmitted dyes. These Palissy dishes are quaint, but they are never repulsive, and, half hidden with fruit and vine leaves, would just sufficiently attract and rouse the attention, without too much occupying it. We have before us, photographs of two such dishes – the one has a translucent brook flowing round the bottom, while on an island in the centre are fish, shells, and pebbles. On the broad sloping bank of the margin, crawl one or two lizards; there, also lurk a coiled-up snake and a frog. The plants the artist has moulded, are ferns, ivy, oak leaves, and acorns.

In the second dish, the central island is studded with cockle shells, which are surrounded by a circle of small univalves. At each end is a large frog. In the circular rivulet disport a pike, two carp, and a miller's thumb: while on the raised border, artfully grouped, are two large lizards, two crayfish, a frog, and a death's

DOI: 10.4324/9781315400105-80

head moth, besides leaves and shells. Now, these objects coarsely executed and awkwardly placed by a dull workman, with no heart in his business, would be simply detestable. They would be stupid assertions of natural facts and so many incongruous and sometimes repelling objects stuck on a piece of pottery; but they are not so in Palissy's work. There, they come like glimpses of outer-world nature, and we seem when using his ware to be taking our fruit and conserves under the sunny green trees of a Boccaccio garden. The chief objection to using Palissy is that it is so precious, and so fragile, and it would be dangerous to entrust it to servants. We grant this, and we would remove this danger by mounting the Palissy plates in copper, and rendering their breakage almost impossible.

Men of fortune we would advise, when possible, to return, for dinner and dessert services, to some of those fine old styles of pottery that never can become obsolete. For instance, if Palissy appear to them too quaint, let them use Majolica. Many of our readers, not versed in antiquities, may not know the story of Majolica. It is a ware originally made by the Moors when they occupied Majorca, and it was exported into Italy from thence and from the potteries of the Spanish Arabs. About the middle of the fifteenth century, the Italians, probably aided by Italian workmen, began to make this beautiful ware for themselves, and soon the manufacturies of Faenza, Urbino, Castel-Durante, Gubbio, and Pesaro, became eminent for these iridescent plates – for which it was long supposed, in England, that Raphael, when young, had drawn designs. In due course, thanks to the patronage of the Italian princes, a great man arose, one Maestro Giorgio, a gentleman of Pavia, who about 1498 came to Gubbio, and either bought or succeeded to a manufactory that had the monopoly of the famed ruby lustre, the secret of which is now lost. Maestro Giorgio improved the yellow lustre into the golden, and purified the ruby from its previous orange tone. There is no discovering when ware like this was first made. It was probably one of the primeval discoveries. Mr. Layard found white enamelled pottery with lustre designs ten or twelve feet under the surface of ruins at Khorsabad.

These Majolica plates and dishes are often adorned with copies of Raphael's designs or fragments from Marc Antonio. Often they are what is called "amatoria," or love offerings. One, before us now, has an Amorino upon it, holding an eel which is sliding through his fingers, and the motto is, "Così fugge la vita nostra" – "So flies our life." In another there is a female bust portrait in profile, with a motto, "Chi a tempo non dorma." On the lady's sleeve is the device of a burning heart bound round with a cord, the whole executed entirely in ruby lustre, with blue outline and shading. Often in the centre of these plates Andromeda cries to Heaven from her rocky prison, or Mutius Scævola thrusts his bold hand into the flames. In the early periods, the yellow lustre, though dull in colour, has an extraordinary mother-of-pearl iridescence which is exquisitely beautiful. On these lovers' offerings – costly valentines of the sixteenth century – the usual emblems are the old common-place hearts pierced with daggers and darts. The arms of Urbino often appear upon them (these pieces of painted clay have survived the lovers and the princes who caused them to be made), and often they literally glow with ducal coronets, arabesques, warring dragons, intertwined serpents, sphinxes, masks, military and musical trophies, garlands, and inscribed cartouches, all radiant with gold and flame colour. After such ware as this, our common dinner-plates, with blue and maroon edges and a coat of arms or crest in the centre, or maybe a bunch of flowers or a timid landscape, appear very mean and pitiful.

We want more mind about our table furniture. If we must have few ideas, let them be repetitions of some fine type, like the Greek chair, the Greek tripod lamp, or the Greek amphora – let them be at least repetitions of beauty, not of dulness and ugliness. By all means use fine works of antiquity when practicable. The beautiful always assimilates, and Palissy and Majolica dishes would not lose, even by contrast with Sèvres plates. Buy harlequin suits; the variety is always pleasant. Designs from Raphael are more intellectual than barbaric wealth of mere gold or silver plate. Besides, metal is not pleasant to eat off. What we want in England is, not to produce a few masterpieces of art every year, but a better average of the ordinarily manufactured art articles. Mr. Cole did good work in this direction, but there is a vast deal still to do before a man of taste of the present day can dine surrounded by plates, cups, dishes, and glasses of beautiful shape and colour.

This deficiency ought not to exist. Our wealth is great, and our countrymen who have taste as well as means are numerous. The demand for tasteful table furniture is great. If our workmen cannot invent, let them imitate. In the fifteenth century, men had time to think, and patience to execute – they had love for their work, and spared no labour in thinking it out. Labour costs more now, but there are plenty who will pay labour. If material be dear, there are plenty who can afford to buy material. But there must be far more education of the eye, or people will still abound who will wish for nothing more beautiful than willow plates, stucco cornices, and tea-tray landscapes.

67

IMAGES: 'CERAMIC ARTS'

The National Encyclopaedia: a Dictionary of Universal Knowledge, Vol. 4 (London: c. 1870)

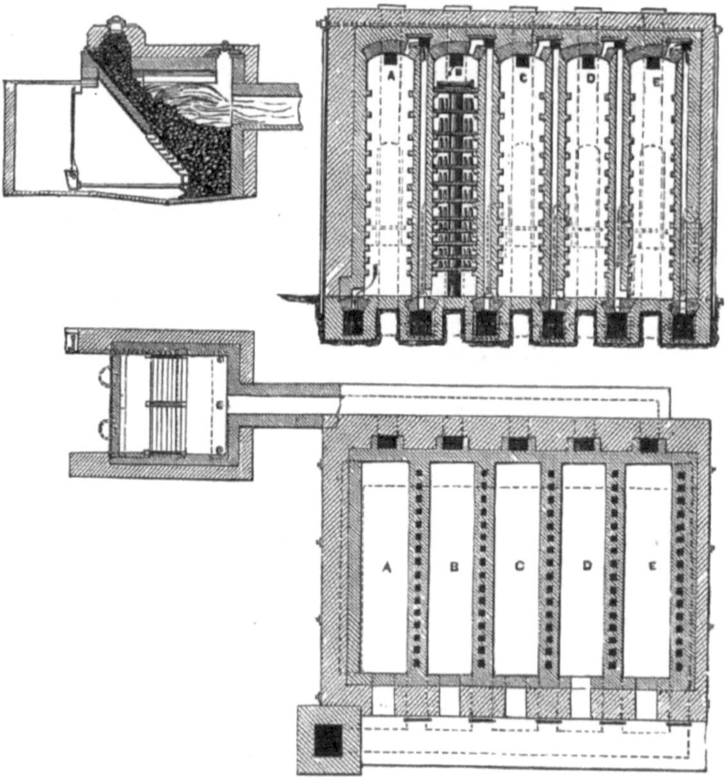

Figures 67.1, 67.2 Regenerative gas pottery kilns – vertical and horizontal sections.

DOI: 10.4324/9781315400105-81

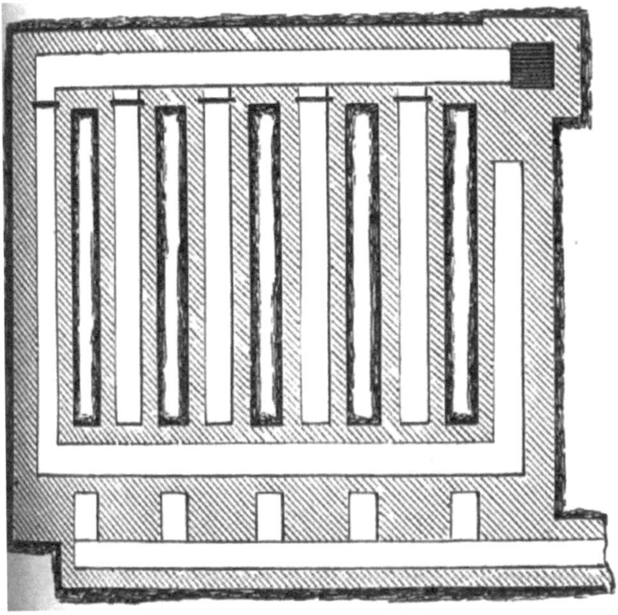

Figure 67.3 Sectional plan of the furnace and flues.

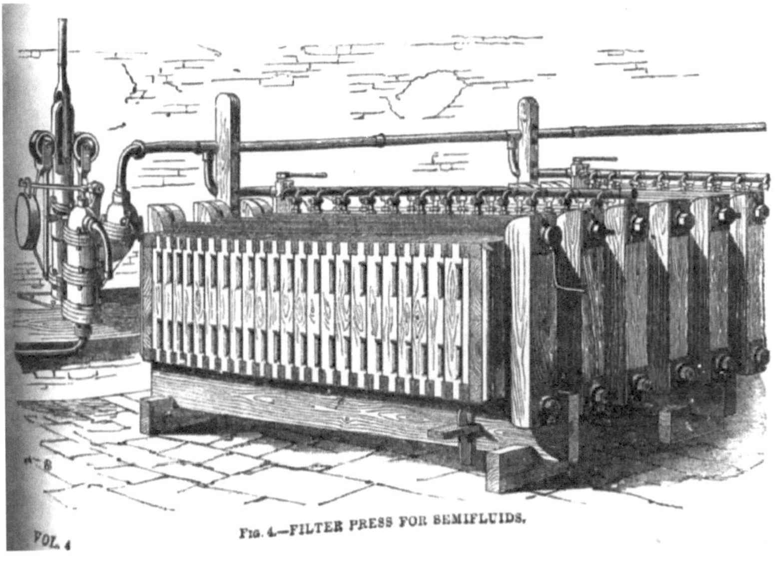

Figure 67.4 Filter press for semifluids.

68

IMAGE: GEORGE DU MAURIER, 'THE SIX-MARK TEA-POT'

Punch (30 October 1880) p. 194

THE SIX-MARK TEA-POT.

Æsthetic Bridegroom. "It is quite consummate, is it not?"
Intense Bride. "It is, indeed! Oh, Algernon, let us live up to it!"

DOI: 10.4324/9781315400105-82

69

ANON, 'CHINA, CHINA EVERYWHERE'

The Pottery Gazette (1 July 1899), pp. 824–825

An American writer says that there is a fad this season for having every article of china which can possibly be manufactured out of that material. Very beautiful are the dainty things made for the toilet table and the parlour, no less than for the ordinary dining-room and sideboard uses to which fine china is usually put.

Lamps of delicate ware, with the inevitable imitations, are brought out in the identical shapes and patterns which were relegated long ago to the farmhouse parlour and the city back bed-room. Though the new china may be a small degree more transparent, and the flower wreaths and Cupids more exquisitely coloured, there is still sufficient resemblance between the old and the new designs to render it hard to decide definitely and positively which is which. So the housekeeper who has been wise enough to save her lamps may now resurrect them from the top shelf of the pantry, and be fashionable, and therefore happy. She may use the porcelain shade which belongs to the lamp, she may embroider a silk or chiffon shade in colours which exactly match the pattern of the china, or she may provide herself with a dainty paper shade in the corresponding colours, before placing the lamp on the table in her front drawing-room, since parlours are no more.

Card-receivers are once more 'the thing' when made of fine, hand-painted china, and if one has not the money necessary to purchase one of these costly beauties, a pretty little cracker plate, a tiny individual salad-dish, or even the lower part of a soap dish have been known to do this duty in a well-appointed hall, and never a soul the wiser. The articles mentioned come in just as pretty and artistic designs, just as dainty colours, and just as graceful shapes as the card-holders sold for the purpose, and are much more reasonable in price. A pin-tray does very well for this use too; but since the useful fad of having a few pins, pretty and common, in every room in the house, from the best bedroom to the library, the little trays are in great demand for their original purpose. [. . .] [O]nce in a while a broken set of dinner or tea ware furnishes a few of these articles, which serve as birthday or souvenir presents.

An original fancy for the toilet-table consists of one of the tiny cups which, together with the saucer, were so much in vogue for gifts some years ago, and were so perfectly useless. The cup was glued firmly to the saucer, filled with the regulation curled hair, covered with coarse yellow net, with the joining hidden by

DOI: 10.4324/9781315400105-83

a ribbonruche, finished by a little bow and a few tiny velvet violets drawn through the knot, and struck full of hairpins of all sizes. The saucer was utilised for studs or any of the countless trifles which accumulate so easily and quickly, and are so hard to dispose of tidily. The bright girl who invented this arrangement was very proud of it, but it is not patented, and may be copied by any woman who has several of these pretty, useless articles in her stock of china. As a holder for burnt and unburnt matches, a cup and saucer could be arranged in this manner too; and in such a case a ribbon on the handle might be of a deep tobacco brown, and the china of the buff-coloured order.

Candelabra and single candlesticks of china are exceedingly popular, and the woman who understands china painting ever so slightly would better look after the decoration of her own candlesticks, for they are very high priced. The figures are necessarily so minute, and the care and time so great in proportion to their size, that they are exceedingly expensive. After all, they are easily painted, and as they are little used and in no great risk of breaking, they are popular with the home artist. Conventionalised wreaths, sprays or bunches of flowers, odd little faces of diminutive Cupids, are the most favoured decorations, and some of the prettiest are simply tinted in wave fashion – that is, with washes of colour, deepening softly towards a given point, and receding again until they are but little removed from pure white. This decoration is fashionable for the handles of fruit and fish knives, which are now made of china more frequently than of silver, and whose narrow surfaces present very little opportunity for more elaborate decoration. In fact, whole dinner sets are treated in the same manner. To be quite correct nowadays the entire furnishing of a table, from soup plates to fruit knives, relish dishes, lamps, favours, after-dinner coffee cups, the tiniest and least significant as well as the largest and most conspicuous article on the table, must be each parts of one harmonious whole, and must match religiously, not only in design and colouring but also in the materials from which they are made. A single odd dish is a blot on the escutcheon of the housekeeper. With this idea in view, and the knowledge that the fad is only just beginning, the wise woman will shun the lovely, flower-decked sets, and buy instead plain white, a fad for which is the natural outcome of the other whim. Unless she is an expert at china painting, it would be best to stick to the plainer variety.

All sorts of dainty things for the toilet table are brought out in fine china, and even in this kind of ware the set idea is followed. The hairpin holder, hair-receiver, pin-tray, manicure set and the small tray upon which it lies, powder boxes, cold-cream casket, lotion-bottles, rouge-pot, comb and brush, jewel boxes, frames of the hand and triple mirrors, bonbonnière, perfume bottles, sachet holders, and the cunning little barrel for small change, are all of china, and all match. These are usually decorated with small, isolated flowers – pansies, violets or daisies, scattered carelessly over the entire surface, and sometimes the insides are tinted. A recent fad, too costly and exclusive to prevail, save among brides, is to have each piece ornamented with a portrait either of as many persons as there are articles, or of one person seen in countless different ways. These sets are really works of art, and far too pretty to be actually used in everyday service. Those which a clever artist showed a while ago, however, and which were decorated with little scenes from nature, were just as lovely, and far easier to do. A pretty set of this kind can readily be obtained by purchasing the various items separately, and having them painted one by one, as taste and pocket book will allow. A very plain and scanty set may be elaborated in the same manner. If the owner has any idea of doing the fascinating work herself, however, she would better purchase a baking kiln outright, for it is the 'firing' which swells the bill for hand-painted china.

Silver and gold utensils for writing are quite passé now, for china is the only really stylish thing. The penholders and tray, inkwells, tiny candlestick and waterholder, case of sealing wax, matchsafe and receiver, stampbox, coinbox, case for postal cars, box for letter paper, corners for the blotter, holder for the sealing-wax and the seal, are all of the same fragile material, and a little receptacle for small candles is as much a part of the writing set as of the toilet appurtenances. These sets, too, come in pure white, ready for decoration, and more of this kind are purchased than any other.

Call bells are also made of porcelain, and give out a wonderfully sweet sound, more like a fairy bell than anything else which can be imagined. Water pitchers and creamers of china are an old-new wrinkle. So are frappe bowls, lemonade jugs, and water coolers. These are mostly seen in the old blue affected by Anglomaniacs. It is a thing quite apart from the real 'old blue', but lovely to see, and gives a most delicious idea of cool pleasantness. Perhaps this idea of suitability also explains why the cordial flasks prepared for travellers are so many of them of a warm, comforting red hue, and why the delicate, dainty smelling-bottles and scent-bottles are generally of old rose, old pink or lavender.

Sandwich and biscuit plates come decorated with quaint old mottoes, as do the mugs, tankards, and puncheons which for some occult reason are considered as absolutely necessary to a perfect set of ware. China tea and chocolate pots are also decorated with quaint letterings. After dinner coffee cups, afternoon tea cups, and plates and luncheon trays are often adorned with different single flowers, each framed by a narrow band of gold. The old fashioned green and gold, white and gold, pink and gold, and blue and white of our grandmothers is in again. So is the willow ware and basket china; and one fashionable woman looks almost daily into one drawer of her china closet in which reposes a set of mugs, an ale jug (dedicated at present to lemonade and fruit drinks), a bread and butter plate, and a limited number of smaller plates, and thinks with pride of how they will be the joy of her heart when standing upon the side-board in her dining-room. Not a few women have isolated articles of this kind which can be reclaimed from their latter-day uses of holding flowers or preserves; and the hideous old yellow bowls make most artistic and lively jardinières.

Anything and everything which is china is worthy just now and anything which is a generation or more old is guarded carefully and jealously as a teasure.

70

ARNOLD BENNETT, *ANNA OF THE FIVE TOWNS*

2nd ed. (New York: G. H. Doran, 1903), pp. 135–148

Probably no one in the Five Towns takes a conscious pride in the antiquity of the potter's craft, nor in its unique and intimate relation to human life, alike civilised and uncivilised. Man hardened clay into a bowl before he spun flax and made a garment, and the last lone man will want an earthen vessel after he has abandoned his ruined house for a cave, and his woven rags for an animal's skin. This supremacy of the most ancient of crafts is in the secret nature of things, and cannot be explained. History begins long after the period when Bursley was first the central seat of that honoured manufacture: it is the central seat still – "the mother of the Five Towns," in our local phrase – and though the townsmen, absorbed in a strenuous daily struggle, may forget their heirship to an unbroken tradition of countless centuries, the seal of their venerable calling is upon their foreheads. If no other relic of an immemorial past is to be seen in these modernised sordid streets, there is at least the living legacy of that extraordinary kinship between workman and work, that instinctive mastery of clay, which the past has bestowed upon the present. The horse is less to the Arab than clay is to the Bursley man. He exists in it and by it; it fills his lungs and blanches his cheek; it keeps him alive and it kills him. His fingers close round it as round the hand of a friend. He knows all its tricks and aptitudes; when to coax and when to force it, when to rely on it and when to distrust it. The weavers of Lancashire have dubbed him with an obscene epithet on account of it, an epithet whose hasty use has led to many a fight, but nothing could be more illuminatively descriptive than that epithet, which names his vocation in terms of another vocation. A dozen decades of applied science have of course resulted in the interposition of elaborate machinery between the clay and the man; but no great vulgar handicraft has lost less of the human than potting. Clay is always clay, and the steam-driven contrivance that will mould a basin while a man sits and watches has yet to be invented. Moreover, if in some coarser process the hands are superseded, the number of processes has been multiplied tenfold: the ware in which six men formerly collaborated is now produced by sixty; and thus, in one sense, the touch of finger on clay is more pervasive than ever before.

 DOI: 10.4324/9781315400105-84

Mynors' works was acknowledged to be one of the best, of its size, in the district – a model three-oven bank, and it must be remembered that of the hundreds of banks in the Five Towns the vast majority are small, like this: the large manufactory with its corps of jacket-men,[1] one of whom is detached to show visitors round so much of the works as it is deemed advisable for them to see, is the exception. Mynors paid three hundred pounds a year in rent, and produced nearly three hundred pounds' worth of work a week. He was his own manager, and there was only one jacket-man on the place, a clerk at eighteen shillings. He employed about a hundred hands, and devoted all his ingenuity to prevent that wastage which is at once the easiest to overlook and the most difficult to check, the wastage of labour. No pains were spared to keep all departments in full and regular activity, and owing to his judicious firmness the feast of St. Monday, that canker eternally eating at the root of the prosperity of the Five Towns, was less religiously observed on his bank than perhaps anywhere else in Bursley. He had realised that when a workshop stands empty the employer has not only ceased to make money, but has begun to lose it. The architect of "Providence Works" (Providence stands godfather to many commercial enterprises in the Five Towns) knew his business and the business of the potter, and he had designed the works with a view to the strictest economy of labour. The various shops were so arranged that in the course of its metamorphosis the clay travelled naturally in a circle from the slip-house by the canal to the packing-house by the canal: there was no carrying to and fro. The steam installation was complete: steam once generated had no respite; after it had exhausted itself in vitalising fifty machines, it was killed by inches in order to dry the unfired ware and warm the dinners of the workpeople.

Henry took Anna to the canal-entrance, because the buildings looked best from that side.

"Now how much is a crate worth?" she asked, pointing to a crate which was being swung on a crane direct from the packing-house into a boat.

"That?" Mynors answered. "A crateful of ware may be worth anything. At Minton's I have seen a crate worth three hundred pounds. But that one there is only worth eight or nine pounds. You see you and I make cheap stuff."

"But don't you make any really good pots – are they all cheap?"

"All cheap," he said.

"I suppose that's business?" He detected a note of regret in her voice.

"I don't know," he said, with the slightest impatient warmth. "We make the stuff as good as we can for the money. We supply what everyone wants. Don't you think it's better to please a thousand folks than to please ten? I like to feel that my ware is used all over the country and the colonies. I would sooner do as I do than make swagger ware for a handful of rich people."

"Oh, yes!" she exclaimed, eagerly accepting the point of view, "I quite agree with you." She had never heard him in that vein before, and was struck by his enthusiasm. And Mynors was in fact always very enthusiastic concerning the virtues of the general markets. He had no sympathy with specialities, artistic or otherwise. He found his satisfaction in honestly meeting the popular taste. He was born to be a manufacturer of cheap goods on a colossal scale. He could dream of fifty ovens, and his ambition blinded him to the present absurdity of talking about a three-oven bank spreading its productions all over the country and the colonies; it did not occur to him that there were yet scarcely enough plates to go round.

"I suppose we had better start at the start," he said, leading the way to the slip-house. He did not need to be told that Anna was perfectly ignorant of the craft of pottery, and that every detail of it, so stale to him, would acquire freshness under her naïve and enquiring gaze.

In the slip-house begins the long manipulation which transforms raw porous friable clay into the moulded, decorated, and glazed vessel. The large whitewashed place was occupied by ungainly machines and receptacles through which the four sorts of clay used in a common "body" – ball clay, China clay, flint clay, and stone clay – were compelled to pass before they became a white putty-like mixture meet for shaping by human hands. The blunger crushed the clay, the sifter extracted the iron from it by means of a magnet, the press expelled the water, and the pug-mill expelled the air. From the last reluctant mouth slowly emerged a solid stream nearly a foot in diameter, like a huge white snake. Already the clay had acquired the uniformity characteristic of a manufactured product.

Anna moved to touch the bolts of the enormous twenty-four-chambered press.

"Don't stand there," said Mynors. "The pressure is tremendous, and if the thing were to burst –"

She fled hastily. "But isn't it dangerous for the workmen?" she asked.

Eli Machin, the engineman, the oldest employee on the works, a moneyed man and the pattern of reliability, allowed a vague smile to flit across his face at this remark. He had ascended from the engine-house below in order to exhibit the tricks of the various machines, and that done he disappeared. Anna was awed by the sensation of being surrounded by terrific forces always straining for release and held in check by the power of a single will.

"Come and see a plate made: that is one of the simplest things, and the batting-machine is worth looking at," said Mynors, and they went into the nearest shop, a hot interior in the shape of four corridors round a solid square middle. Here men and women were working side by side, the women subordinate to the men. All were preoccupied, wrapped up in their respective operations, and there was the sound of irregular whirring movements from every part of the big room. The air was laden with a whitish dust, and clay was omnipresent – on the floor, the walls, the benches, the windows, on clothes, hands, and faces. It was in this shop, where both hollowware pressers and flat pressers were busy as only craftsmen on piece-work can be busy, that more than anywhere else clay was to be seen "in the hand of the potter." Near the door a stout man with a good-humoured face flung some clay on to a revolving disc, and even as Anna passed a jar sprang into existence. One instant the clay was an amorphous mass, the next it was a vessel perfectly circular, of a prescribed width and a prescribed depth; the fat and apparently clumsy fingers of the craftsman had seemed to lose themselves in the clay for a fraction of time, and the miracle was accomplished. The man threw these vessels with the rapidity of a Roman candle throwing off coloured stars, and one woman was kept busy in supplying him with material and relieving his bench of the finished articles. Mynors drew Anna along to the batting-machines for plate-makers, at that period rather a novelty and the latest invention of the dead genius whose brain has reconstituted a whole industry on new lines. Confronted with a piece of clay, the batting-machine descended upon it with the ferocity of a wild animal, worried it, stretched it, smoothed it into the width and thickness of a plate, and then desisted of itself and waited inactive for the flat presser to remove its victim to his more exact shaping machine. Several men were producing plates, but their rapid labours seemed less astonishing than the preliminary feat of the batting-machine. All the ware, as it was moulded, disappeared into the vast cupboards occupying the centre of the shop, where Mynors showed Anna innumerable rows of shelves full of pots in process of steam-drying. Neither time nor space nor material was wasted in this ant-heap of industry. In order to move to and fro, the women were compelled to insinuate themselves past the stationary bodies of the men. Anna marvelled at the careless accuracy with which they fed the batting-machines with lumps precisely calculated to form a plate of a given diameter. Everyone exerted himself as though the salvation of the world hung on the production of so much stuff by a certain hour; dust, heat, and the presence of a stranger were alike unheeded in the mad creative passion.

"Now," said Mynors the cicerone, opening another door which gave into the yard, "when all that stuff is dried and fettled – smoothed, you know – it goes into the biscuit oven: that's the first firing. There's the biscuit oven, but we can't inspect it because it's just being drawn."

He pointed to the oven near by, in whose dark interior the forms of men, naked to the waist, could dimly be seen struggling with the weight of saggars[2] full of ware. It seemed like some release of martyrs, this unpacking of the immense oven, which, after being flooded with a sea of flame for fifty-four hours, had cooled for two days, and was yet hotter than the Equator. The inertness and pallor of the saggars seemed to be the physical result of their fiery trial, and one wondered that they should have survived the trial. Mynors went into the place adjoining the oven and brought back a plate out of an open saggar; it was still quite warm. It had the *matt* surface of a biscuit, and adhered slightly to the fingers: it was now a "crook"; it had exchanged malleability for brittleness, and nothing mortal could undo what the fire had done. Mynors took the plate with him to the biscuit-warehouse, a long room where one was forced to keep to narrow alleys amid parterres of pots. A solitary biscuit-warehouseman was examining the ware, in order to determine the remuneration of the pressers.

They climbed a flight of stairs to the printing-shop, where, by means of copperplates, printing-presses, mineral colours, and transfer-papers, most of the decoration was done. The room was filled by a little crowd of people – oldish men, women, and girls, divided into printers, cutters, transferrers, and apprentices. Each interminably repeated some trifling process, and every article passed through a succession of hands until at length it was washed in a tank and rose dripping therefrom with its ornament of flowers and scrolls fully revealed. The room smelt of oil and flannel and humanity; the atmosphere was more languid, more like that of a family party, than in the pressers' shop: the old women looked stern and shrewish, the pretty young women pert and defiant, the younger girls meek. The few men seemed out of place. By what trick had they crept into the very centre of that mass of femineity? It seemed wrong, scandalous that they should remain. Contiguous with the printing-shop was the painting-shop, in which the labours of the former were taken to a finish by the brush of the paintress, who filled in outlines with flat colour, and thus converted mechanical printing into handiwork. The paintresses form the *noblesse* of the banks. Their task is a light one, demanding deftness first of all; they have delicate fingers, and enjoy a general reputation for beauty: the wages they earn may be estimated from their finery on Sundays. They come to business in cloth jackets, carrying dinner in little satchels; in the shop they wear white aprons, and look startlingly neat and tidy. Across the benches over which they bend their coquettish heads gossip flies and returns like a shuttle; they are the source of a thousand intrigues, and one or other of them is continually getting married or omitting to get married. On the bank they constitute "the sex." An infinitesimal proportion of them, from among the branch known as ground-layers, die of lead-poisoning – a fact which adds pathos to their frivolous charm. In a subsidiary room off the painting-shop a single girl was seated at a revolving table actuated by a treadle. She was doing the "band-and-line" on the rims of saucers. Mynors and Anna watched her as with her left hand she flicked saucer after saucer into the exact centre of the table, moved the treadle, and, holding a brush firmly against the rim of the piece, produced with infallible exactitude the band and the line. She was a brunette, about twenty-eight: she had a calm, vacuously contemplative face; but God alone knew whether she thought. Her work represented the summit of monotony; the regularity of it hypnotised the observer, and Mynors himself was impressed by this stupendous phenomenon of absolute sameness, involuntarily assuming towards it the attitude of a showman.

"She earns as much as eighteen shillings a week sometimes," he whispered.

"May I try?" Anna timidly asked of a sudden, curious to experience what the trick was like.

"Certainly," said Mynors, in eager assent. "Priscilla, let this lady have your seat a moment, please."

The girl got up, smiling politely. Anna took her place.

"Here, try on this," said Mynors, putting on the table the plate which he still carried.

"Take a full brush," the paintress suggested, not attempting to hide her amusement at Anna's unaccustomed efforts. "Now push the treadle. There! It isn't in the middle yet. Now!"

Anna produced a most creditable band, and a trembling but passable line, and rose, flushed with the small triumph.

"You have the gift," said Mynors; and the paintress respectfully applauded.

"I felt I could do it," Anna responded. "My mother's mother was a paintress, and it must be in the blood."

Mynors smiled indulgently. They descended again to the ground floor, and following the course of manufacture came to the "hardening-on" kiln, a minor oven where for twelve hours the oil is burnt out of the colour in decorated ware. A huge, jolly man in shirt and trousers, with an enormous apron, was in the act of drawing the kiln, assisted by two thin boys. He nodded a greeting to Mynors and exclaimed, "Warm!" The kiln was nearly emptied. As Anna stopped at the door, the man addressed her.

"Step inside, miss, and try it."

"No, thanks!" she laughed.

"Come now," he insisted, as if despising this hesitation. "An ounce of experience –" The two boys grinned and wiped their foreheads with their bare skeleton-like arms. Anna, challenged by the man's look, walked quickly into the kiln. A blasting heat seemed to assault her on every side, driving her back; it was incredible that any human being could support such a temperature.

"There!" said the jovial man, apparently summing her up with his bright, quizzical eyes. "You know summat as you didn't know afore, miss. Come along, lads," he added with brisk heartiness to the boys, and the drawing of the kiln proceeded.

Next came the dipping-house, where a middle-aged woman, enveloped in a protective garment from head to foot, was dipping jugs into a vat of lead-glaze, a boy assisting her. The woman's hands were covered with the grey slimy glaze. She alone of all the employees appeared to be cool.

"That is the last stage but one," said Mynors. "There is only the glost-firing," and they passed out into the yard once more. One of the glost-ovens was empty; they entered it and peered into the lofty inner chamber, which seemed like the cold crater of an exhausted volcano, or like a vault, or like the ruined seat of some forgotten activity. The other oven was firing, and Anna could only look at its exterior, catching glimpses of the red glow at its twelve mouths, and guess at the Tophet within, where the lead was being fused into glass.

"Now for the glost-warehouse, and you will have seen all," said Mynors, "except the mould-shop, and that doesn't matter."

The warehouse was the largest place on the works, a room sixty feet long and twenty broad, low, whitewashed, bare, and clean. Piles of ware occupied the whole of the walls and of the immense floor-space, but there was no trace here of the soilure and untidiness incident to manufacture; all processes were at one end, clay vanished into crock: and the calmness and the whiteness atoned for the disorder, noise, and squalor which had preceded. Here was a sample of the total and final achievement towards which the thousands of small, disjointed efforts that Anna had witnessed were directed. And it seemed a miraculous, almost impossible, result; so definite, precise, and regular after a series of acts apparently variable, inexact, and casual; so unhuman after all that intensely human labour; so vast in comparison with the minuteness of the separate endeavours. As Anna looked, for instance, at a pile of tea-sets, she found it difficult even to conceive that, a fortnight or so before, they had been nothing but lumps of dirty clay. No stage of the manufacture was incredible by itself, but the result was incredible. It was the result that appealed to the imagination, authenticating the adage that fools and children should never see anything till it is done.

Anna pondered over the organising power, the forethought, the wide vision, and the sheer ingenuity and cleverness which were implied by the contents of this warehouse. "What brains!" she thought, of Mynors; "what quantities of all sorts of things he must know!" It was a humble and deeply-felt admiration.

Her spoken words gave no clue to her thoughts. "You seem to make a fine lot of tea-sets," she remarked.

"Oh, no!" he said carelessly. "These few that you see here are a special order. I don't go in much for tea-sets: they don't pay; we lose fifteen per cent. of the pieces in making. It's toilet-ware that pays, and that is our leading line." He waved an arm vaguely towards rows and rows of ewers and basins in the distance. They walked to the end of the warehouse, glancing at everything.

Notes

1 *Jacket-man*: the artisan's satiric term for anyone who does not work in shirtsleeves, who is not actually a producer, such as a clerk or a pretentious foreman.

2 *Saggars:* large oval receptacles of coarse clay, in which the ware is placed for firing.

4.2

Glassware

DOI: 10.4324/9781315400105-85

4.2 Glassware

G. R. Porter, 'On the Manufacture of Crown-Glass, Broad Glass, and Bottle Glass', in *Treatise on the Origin, Progressive Improvement, and Present State of the Manufacture of Porcelain and Glass* (London: Longman, Brown and Green, 1832), pp. 182–187.

Luke Herbert, 'Glass' in *The Engineer's and Mechanics Encyclopeadia, Comprehending Practical Illustrations of the Machinery and Processes Employed in Every Description of Manufacture in the British Empire*, Vol. 1 (London: Thomas Kelly, 1836), pp. 635–639.

Anon, 'The Falcon Glass-Works' in *The Busy Hives Around Us: A Variety of Trips and Visits to the Mine*, the Workshop, and the Factory (London: James Hogg and Sons, c.1850), pp. 165–168.

Anon, 'A Glass Manufactory', pp. 197–201 [bound pamphlet].

The mass production of glass items increased following the repeal of glass duties in 1845. Glass windows were doubly taxed due to a notorious levy imposed in 1696, which was only repealed in 1851 to allow the construction of Victorian Britain's most significant glass structure, the Crystal Palace. Only one of the extracts in this section has a verifiable publication date, but the way in which the authors write about excise duties helps to date them. Herbert describes a late-Georgian arrangement whereby green bottle glass was taxed at 'one-eighth' the rate imposed on flint, crown and plate glass, while G. R. Porter's remarks on how taxes led to the rapid reduction of bottle glass suggests that this piece was published around the same time. *The Busy Hives Around Us* surely dates from a time when the taxes were lifted, probably around 1850; its description of a lavish warehouse overflowing with glass goods seems to celebrate the repeal of the duty. The pamphlet, 'A Glass Manufactory', refers to the recent removal of heavy taxes, with glass objects now being 'more plentiful and better than ever before', suggesting a publication date soon after 1845.

Each of the sources here offers detailed descriptions of glass production, including bottle glass, flint glass for drinking vessels and jars, and crown or plate glass for windows. Plate manufacture was an intensive and expensive process performed entirely by hand, while crown glass resulted in the distinctive 'bulls-eye' glass used for cheaper windows. By far the most common glass objects in everyday life were windows and bottles. Herbert suggests that, in the early nineteenth century, everyday glass objects were uncommon, although glass bottles were around, being cheaply cast in moulds. Innovation and quality are prized in all of the sources reprinted here. Porter notes the 'prodigious length of 160 inches', or just over four metres, attained by the British Plate Glass Company and proudly states that British flint is known abroad as 'crystal'.

Two of the extracts here are designed for children's reading. 'A Glass Manufactory' is a brief pamphlet with a simple, line-drawn title illustration. Its four pages give a basic explanation of the manufacture of glass, from the 'fritting' (drying) of raw materials to the blowing process and the final annealing, where the finished objects are cooled slowly in ovens. Not only is the main object in this narrative a domestic one, but, like *The Story of a Needle* (see Part 3.1, 'Pins and needles'), the reader is instructed that beautiful objects should also be useful. Although the pamphlet classifies different grades of glass, the reader is chiefly invited to admire the utility of window glass. 'Our houses', the pamphlet states, 'would be very uncomfortable if we had no glass for windows'. Despite its didactic, cautious tone, the pamphlet echoes other sources in this volume when it praises the artistic and philosophical outcome of manufacturing. Quoting Samuel Johnson it notes that those who produce glass enlarge the avenues of science.

The beauty of glass objects is emphasised in other sources. All extracts in this section reveal the variety of glass and glass items: scientific vessels and retorts, wine and beer bottles, artificial or 'paste' gemstones, thermometers and barometers, tubing of all kinds, watch and clock glass, glass beads and optical lenses. Occasionally, experimentation with raw materials produced new crazes for coloured glass: olive green or yellow glass bottles, ruby and purple colours, as well as brown and blue. 'The Falcon Glass Works' in *The Busy Hives Around Us* depicts manufacturing as a fairy-tale land through which the reader will frolic. The cover depicts the workshop, the mine and the factory, while the title page shows materials from across the globe pouring in to feed Victorian manufacturing industries. The seventh chapter recounts a visit to the Falcon Glass Works in Blackfriars, London, owned by Apsley Pellatt, the author of *Curiosities of Glass Making* (1849) and an innovator in the field of pressing and casting glass. Pellatt was known for his artistic taste and manufacturing skill. The Falcon Works are also referenced in Porter's book, where its reputation for innovation and design is mentioned.

71

G. R. PORTER, 'ON THE MANUFACTURE OF CROWN-GLASS, BROAD GLASS, AND BOTTLE GLASS'

Treatise on the Origin, Progressive Improvement, and Present State of the Manufacture of Porcelain and Glass (London: Longman, Brown and Green, 1832), pp. 182–187

When the materials are properly fused and refined by the removal of all the glass gall, the workman commences his blowing operations in exactly the same manner as has already been described in the process for making flint glass. By repeated dippings of the iron tube into the crucible, he gathers as much glass upon its end as experience teaches him will suffice for the formation of a sheet of glass of the usual size, and which generally weighs from ten to eleven pounds. This lump he allows to project beyond the extreme end of the tube; and first rolling it on the iron plane before described, to give the glass a cylindrical form, he commences blowing, when it assumes the shape of a pear. A fresh heating and a second blowing enlarge its dimensions, and render its shape more globular. A third operation of heating and blowing still further enlarges the size of the glass, and reduces its substance. The side opposite to the tube is then flattened by pressure against a plane surface; a small portion of melted glass is collected on the end of a punt, and is applied to the centre of this flattened side, forming an union with it exactly opposite to the hollow tube, which is then removed by wetting the glass near to their point of union, leaving a circular hole in the glass about two inches in diameter.

At this period the glass must be again held to one of the openings of the furnace until it has become sufficiently hot and ductile for the further alteration of its shape. The workman then dexterously twirls the punt in his hand, slowly at first, and then more and more quickly, when the glass yields to the centrifugal impulse; its diameter become greater and greater, the hole just mentioned expands proportionally; and when in this continued progression the doubled portion opposite to the iron rod, and between the periphery of the glass and the orifice, is diminished to an annulus or ring only a few inches wide, this in an unaccountable manner

DOI: 10.4324/9781315400105-86

Figure 71.1

Figure 71.2

Figure 71.3

Fig. 20.

Figure 71.4

Fig. 21.

Figure 71.5

instantly flies completely open, and the glass is converted into a plane disc of fifty to sixty inches diameter, having an uniform thickness throughout the entire plate, with the exception of the spot where it is attached to the iron rod, and where there is a knot or lump which is called a *bull's eye*. Twelve of these plates make up what is called a crate or side of glass.

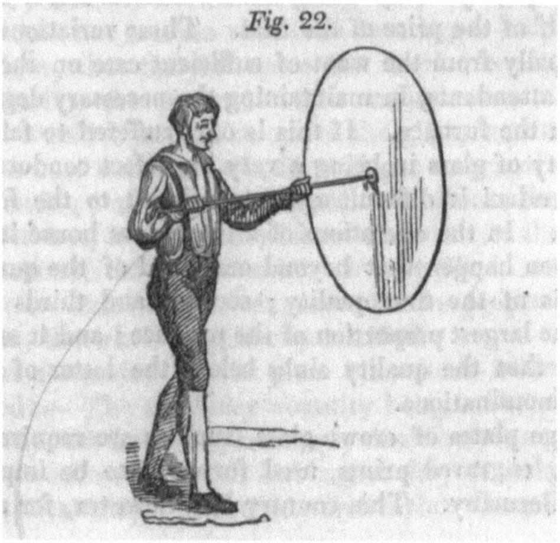

Figure 71.6

The effect of this operation upon persons who witness it for the first time is both pleasing and surprising in a high degree. The force wherewith the glass flies open at the close of the process would be sufficient, if its brittleness were not removed by heat, to break it into innumerable fragments.

The plate, when thus finished, is detached from the iron rod by the usual method, and placed resting on its edge in the annealing oven. Some considerable care is necessary for regulating the temperature at this stage; for if the heat be too great, the softened glass will bend, and for that reason will be lessened in value, while, if the oven be not sufficiently hot, the plates are very likely to crack; and if even this disaster should not happen, the glass will prove of inferior quality, and so brittle, that the glazier will be unable to cut it with any degree of certainty in the wished-for direction.

Crown glass is sold, according to its quality, under four different denominations – firsts, seconds, thirds, and fourths – at considerable difference of price; that of the fourth quality not yielding to the manufacturer nearly one half of the price of the first. These variations arise principally from the want of sufficient care on the part of the attendants, in maintaining the necessary degree of heat in the furnace. If this is once suffered to fall, the property of glass in being a very imperfect conductor of heat renders it difficult again to raise it to the former degree. In the operations of a large glass house it does not often happen that beyond one third of the quantity made is of the first quality; seconds and thirds compose the largest proportion of the produce; and it seldom occurs that the quality sinks below the latter of these two denominations.

Large plates of crown glass, such as are required for glazing engraved prints, used formerly to be imported from Germany. This country has, however, for a long time, been not only independent in this respect of all foreign manufacturers, but similar plates of English make are exported to a considerable extent.

72

LUKE HERBERT, 'GLASS'

The Engineer's and Mechanics Encyclopaedia, Comprehending Practical Illustrations of the Machinery and Processes Employed in Every Description of Manufacture in the British Empire, Vol. 1 (London: Thomas Kelly, 1836), pp. 635–639

GLASS. A well-known transparent and brittle factitious substance, of which the basis is silica, brought into complete fusion by the addition of one of the fixed alkalies. There are several different kinds of glass, adapted to different uses. The best and most beautiful, are the flint and the plate glass; these, when well made, are perfectly transparent and colourless, heavy and brilliant. They are composed of fixed alkali, pure silicious sand, calcined flints, and litharge, in different proportions. The flint glass contains, likewise, a large quantity of oxide of lead, which, by certain processes, is easily separated.

Crown glass is that used for windows, and is made without lead, chiefly of fixed alkali fused with silicious sand, to which is added some black oxide of manganese, which is apt to give the glass a tinge of purple.

Bottle glass is the coarsest and cheapest kind; into this little or no fixed alkali enters the composition: in this country it is composed of sand, and the refuse of the soap boiler, which consists of the lime employed to render his alkali caustic, and of the earthy matters with which the alkali was contaminated. The most fusible is flint glass, and the least fusible is bottle glass; flint glass melting at the temperature of 10° Wedgwood, crown glass at 30°, and bottle glass at 47°. Although glass when cold is exceedingly brittle, when heated to redness it becomes one of the most ductile bodies known, and may be drawn into threads so very delicate as to become almost invisible to the human eye: it is extremely elastic, and one of the most sonorous of bodies. In making glass, the materials undergo a preparatory process called *fritting*, which consists in mixing them in the proper proportions, and submitting them to a moderate heat for six hours, by which they are reduced to a pasty consistence, and form what is called frit, which is cut into squares, and stored up for use; and as the quality of the glass depends upon the age of the frit, the principal manufacturers endeavour always to keep a considerable stock of frit on hand. This frit is introduced into large pots made of prepared clay, and in

DOI: 10.4324/9781315400105-87

these is exposed to a heat sufficient to melt it completely. When the fusion has continued the proper time, the furnace is allowed to cool a little; in this state the glass is exceedingly ductile, and will assume any shape, according to the fancy of the workman. The vessels thus formed must not be permitted to cool very quickly; hence they are put into a furnace, that the heat may pass off very gradually, and this is called "annealing."

Having said thus much to give a general idea of the process, we shall now proceed to describe, somewhat in detail, the manual operations in the manufacture of glass; observing that, owing to the excise laws, the different branches of the manufacture, viz. crown, flint, plate, and bottle glass, are not carried on at the same works, but require to be in separate establishments; we shall, therefore, select for description the manufacture of flint glass, by which the various utensils in glass are produced. The other branches differ principally in the number and arrangement of the furnaces; but in all of them, with the exception of plate glass, the glass is brought into the desired form principally by means of a blowing pipe: the operation is exceedingly simple: the workman has a tube of iron, the end of which he dips into a pot of melted glass, and thus gathers a small quantity of it on the end of the tube; he then applies the other end of the tube to his mouth, and blows air through it; this air enters into the body of the fluid glass, and expands it out into a hollow globe similar to the soap bladders blown from a tobacco pipe, and by varied management of these globes while in a soft state, and with the aid of a few simple tools, they are reduced into the forms of the different vessels in common domestic use. The first thing to be described is the furnace: it consists of two large domes set one over the other; the lower one stands over a long grating, which is on a level with the ground; on this grating the fuel is laid, and beneath it is a large arch, by which the air is admitted, and by which the ashes may be removed. In the sides of the lower dome as many holes or mouths are made as there are workmen to make use of the furnace, and before each mouth a pot of melted glass is placed; the pots are very large, like crucibles, and will hold from three to four hundred-weight of liquid glass; they are supported upon three small piers of brickwork, resting on the floor of the furnace. The form reverberates the flame from the roof down upon the pots, and they are placed at some distance within the furnace, that the flame may get between the wall and the pots. The upper dome is built upon the other, and its floor made flat by filling up round the roof of the lower dome with brickwork; there is a small chimney opens from the top of the lower dome into the middle of the floor of the upper one, which conveys the smoke away from it, and a flue from the upper dome leads it completely from the furnace; the upper dome is used for annealing the glass, and is exactly similar to a large oven; it has three mouths, and in different parts a small flight of steps leads up to each. The implements employed in the formation of glass vessels are few and simple; the following are the principal: a blowing-pipe, which is simply a tube of wrought iron about three feet long, and covered with twine towards the mouth-piece, pliers and calliper compasses, a pair of common shears to cut the glass, a very coarse flat file, and several small iron rods; there is also a bench or stool with two arms, another stool or table with a smooth cast-iron plate upon it, and upon the ground behind this stool is another plate of iron.

We shall now proceed to describe, somewhat more minutely, the manufacture of flint glass. The melting pots are charged with frit, thrown in by shovelsful from time to time, allowing each portion to melt before a fresh quantity is added. When the whole is converted into a clear transparent glass, and is become perfectly pure and free from particles of sand or bubbles of air, the gatherers and blowers commence operations, and continue working night and day until the batch is exhausted. The process of blowing is varied according to the form of the piece to be manufactured; to illustrate it, it will be sufficient to describe the method in which a wine glass is formed. When the blower has received from the gatherer the blowing pipe charged with a sufficient quantity of metal, he seats himself in a chair provided with two arms or elbows, one of which is plated with iron, and placing the blow pipe across the elbows, so that the heated end may rest on the iron plate, having first formed the glass into a hollow ball, he rolls the pipe backwards and forwards, and laying hold of the glass on the farther side of the ball with a small pair of pliers, draws it out to form the stalk of the glass, while the part next the blow pipe is fashioned into the bowl. In the mean time another blower, having formed a smaller ball, opens it by a sharp cut, and presses it while red hot against the end of the stalk held by the former workman, to which it immediately adheres; the workman then with a piece of iron, which he wets with his mouth, touches the globe intended for the bowl of the glass, which is still very hot, although so much chilled as to retain its shape; in a second or two it cracks all round, and by giving it a gentle knock it is detached from the blowing pipe. The workman then instantly heats it, and with a pair of shears cuts the mouth smooth and even; but as the shears have put the glass out of the circular form, he heats it again, and by a dexterous twirl and swing round his head gives it the desired shape almost without the use of any tools. The wine glass now finished, the iron at the foot is detached by a smart blow, and the glass is carried by a boy, upon a long forked iron, to the annealing oven. After the glass is annealed it may be required to be cut before it is ready for sale: this, when the articles are small, and can be easily held in the hand, is performed upon small grit grindstones, or by circular plates of iron, revolving in troughs of sand and water; and for beaded mouldings, as upon decanters, a corresponding groove is formed upon the periphery of the plate. The operations are concluded by polishing the cut parts by means of revolving straps covered with polishing powder.

In the manufacture of bottle glass, after the metal is brought into fusion, which requires an intense heat during eighteen hours, it is reduced to the working temperature, which is steadily maintained by a due supply of fuel, and being scummed, is ready for blowing. For carboys and similar articles it is merely blown into a globular form; but for common wine bottles, or for square or octagonal bottles or jars, it is blown within moulds. Each piece, as it is blown, is handed over to the finisher, who forms the ring at the mouth of the neck, and delivers it to a boy, to be placed in the annealing oven.

In making crown glass, as soon as the metal is ready for blowing, a workman gathers on the blowing pipe a quantity of metal sufficient for forming a sheet or table of glass, which he blows, and, by frequent rolling on a polished table, brings it into a globular or cylindrical form; he then inflates it gently into an oblong ball called a *parisienne*, and immediately heats it again at the mouth of the furnace, in order farther to expand it; in this stage a solid iron rod, charged with melted glass, is made to adhere to the centre of the expanded part opposite the extremity of the blow pipe, and this latter is detached from the glass by a cold iron, leaving an orifice, which is gradually enlarged by heating the glass at the small hole of the flashing furnace, and afterwards at the larger hole of the same furnace, the workman all the while wheeling the rod which supports the glass on a hook in a cross wall, built to defend him from the heat. By degrees, in consequence of the heat and the centrifugal motion, the opening of the glass is continually enlarged, until it expands suddenly with great violence into the form of a large circular plate, four or five feet in diameter, and of uniform thickness, except at the centre, where it is attached to the supporting iron; from this iron it is separated by the application of cold, leaving in the centre a thick nodule called the bull's eye; and when the plate is sufficiently firm to prevent warping, it is carried to the annealing oven and placed on its edge in a proper frame, to keep it flat till all the tables are ready for removal into the crates in which they are kept.

Plate glass is formed either by blowing or casting: by the former method is made the glass for carriage windows; and by the latter, the large plates for looking glasses. Of late it is said that the art of blowing plate glass has been so much improved, that plates measuring 60 inches in length by 21 in breadth have been produced by this method; but by casting, much larger plates are produced, and the establishment at Ravenhead has exhibited at their warehouse near Blackfriars' Bridge plates of the extraordinary dimensions of 12 feet by 6. The most perfect furnace for manufacturing plate glass appears to be that which is employed in France. It consists of a central melting furnace of an oblong form, with a double arched roof; it is capable of containing, upon a raised bench on each side of the fire grate, two large melting pots and a cistern; in each angle of the furnace, and on each side, are two or three openings for introducing the materials, transferring the melted metal from the pots to the cistern, and withdrawing the latter when filled with metal: at each angle of the principal furnace is another of an oblong form communicating with the central one by flues, through which the flame reflecting from the arches of the melting furnace reverberates on their contents. Each of these smaller furnaces has two openings, a smaller one for producing a current of air, and a larger one for introducing and removing what is placed within them. Three of them are usually employed for burning the melting pots and cisterns, which are made of fire-clay; and the fourth is used for preparing the frit. Around the plate glass house are several annealing furnaces like baker's ovens, with capacious mouths. For receiving the melted metal from the pots, square cisterns of sufficient capacity to contain melted metal enough for one plate are used, and when these are filled they are withdrawn from the furnace by means of large iron tongs, supported upon an axle running upon two wheels; another pair of tongs made to encompass the cistern by entering a groove on its sides, and furnished at each end with a handle for the more convenient management of it, is attached by four chains to a sort of crane for suspending and raising the cistern into a proper position with regard to the table. The casting table consists of an oblong frame of wood, covered on its upper surface with a thick sheet of smooth copper, having at its sides two iron rulers of the thickness of the intended plate, their distance asunder being regulated by the proposed breadth of the plate. An iron roller of considerable weight, furnished with a handle at each end, resting on the iron rulers at one end of the table, is made to pass over the melted metal when poured upon the table, in order to form it into a plate of uniform thickness. The apparatus just described is used only for *casting* plate glass, that for blowing being so simple as to need no particular description. In preparing the materials for plate glass they are first reduced to powder, well mixed together and calcined in the fritting furnace before described; they are then removed as quickly as possible into the melting pots previously heated, and after being melted, which generally requires about ten hours, the heat is continued at its utmost degree till the metal becomes perfectly fine; it is then ladled from the pots into the cisterns, which are then drawn out on projecting ledges, and conveyed to the casting table, over which they are suspended by the crane, and by means of the handles of the tongs they are inclined so as to allow their contents to flow over the table: the iron roller is then immediately passed steadily over the surface of the melted metal, sweeping off the superfluous matter into troughs placed at the sides of the table; and when the roller reaches the further extremity of the table, it is expeditiously lowered on a tressel, which prevents its interfering with the plate. The operation of casting is performed before the mouth of the annealing oven, in which it remains exposed to a moderate heat for fourteen days, the heat being at last suffered to die away as gradually as possible. When quite cool it is withdrawn, carried to the magazine, examined, and cut square by a glazier's diamond, and is then ready for the operations of grinding and polishing. The casting table and tressel, as also the crane, are all mounted upon wheels, for the convenience of removing them from one annealing furnace to another. When plate glass is made by blowing instead of casting, after the materials have been fused as before described, and become fine, the further admission of air is prevented by closing all the openings of the furnace, and every thing is suffered to remain stationary for nine or ten hours. This gradual cooling has been found necessary, to enable the melted glass to adhere sufficiently to the blowing pipe. The mode of blowing plate glass greatly resembles that used in the manufacture of table glass, except in the quantity of metal gathered on the blowing pipe, which is sometimes nearly 100lbs. When plates of the largest size are to be formed, the metal is gradually blown and worked into the form of a cylinder, which is cut open at one side with a pair of shears, and the soft glass is spread on a heated floor, covered with a thick stratum of sand, and from thence is speedily conveyed to the annealing furnace. In grinding plate glass, two plates are always ground together, one being imbedded in plaster of Paris upon a table, whilst the other, also imbedded in plaster, is placed upon the former, and being loaded with great weights, is moved uniformly but pretty quickly over its surface. Sand moistened plentifully with water is from time to time sprinkled between the plates, and grinds away all the prominences of the glass until both plates become smooth and even. As the grinding proceeds, sand of greater fineness is employed; and towards the conclusion, it is exchanged for emery, also of varying fineness. As by grinding the surface is roughened and rendered incapable of transmitting the rays of light, it becomes necessary to restore its lustre by polishing, which is performed by rubbing the surface with a block of wood, covered on the lower side with a woollen cloth. The workman keeps it supplied with fine polishing powders, as tripoli and putty, changing from coarse to fine, as the polishing advances to a conclusion. To regulate the pressure a springing pole is put on the back of the block, which, being bent to a curve, is supported from the ceiling of the workshop.

73

ANON, 'THE FALCON GLASS-WORKS'

The Busy Hives Around Us: A Variety of Trips and Visits to the Mine, the Workshop, and the Factory (London: James Hogg and Sons, c. 1850), pp. 165–168

In one of the most dingy parts of the banks of the Thames is a great building, whose outside is duskier than the spot where it is to be found. Black bricks are too common in 'town' to act as loadstones, except to men in trade. We should, belike, pass by the dull corner of an out-of-the-way place, with no more to take our eye than a wall that goes round a tall shaft, like the rampart of an old fort to guard the central keep.

The only sign outside that it is worth while to go in is the board over the door, with the words of gold, 'APSLEY PELLATT'S WORKS.' We will use this door, and dive into the secrets of the place. At once we meet with bright objects. The path, on either hand, is hung with clear shining wares, such as might have crossed Aladdin in the cave of the genius of the ring. The ground is strewed with the same sorts of things. Counting-house and counters display samples likewise. Up-stairs we go, lighted with hues of the rainbow, and on and on we pass, fearful of damage at each step, through store-rooms and narrow lanes, till we reach the centre, and start with wonder. A well-lit hall greets our sight. Thick from the roof hang crystal drops, such as may be seen in the great caves of some parts of the world, but which prosy folks would call chandeliers. All round about the walls, the ceiling, and the floor, the most lustrous diamonds cluster, and send out their shoots of light. For a time we can enter into no details from the brilliancy round about. Like the sun which puts out the stars, so the one blaze hides here the sparkling points. Our eyes, getting used to the tremulous scintillations, begin to trace the walls, and look at the rich stores one by one. Join in our wonder, when the very first crystal we touch is the Koh-i-noor! Here it is, covered only with a glass shade, a solid lump of the first water, sending forth lines of fire, yet never burned up. No iron guard keeps a tingling finger from it as at the Great Exhibition; visitors to *this* crystal palace are so honest, that the tempting jewel is placed close to the door. We can now boast over our gracious Queen. She (may God ever bless her!) has the precious gem in its fresh cutting, but here we view it, not only thus, but in its pristine ugliness. The *little* attendants upon the 'Mountain of Light,' like priceless Indian ear-drops,

DOI: 10.4324/9781315400105-88

keep faithful service. The Koh-i-noor is itself but a trifle amongst the decorations of the place. Masses of pure carbon many times outvie this noted gem in size, and would make the queenly brow ache from their very weight. These, again, are only types of the treasures. Rubies and emeralds are commonplace beside brilliants which a king's crown could not buy. The *facets*, cut by a cunning hand, are made to cross each other through the clear medium, so that their sharp edges seem broken, and flash more numerous rays. One egg-shaped trophy of the diamond-cutter displays the genius of the artist in design, but, being in regular facets, appears as though bands went round. 'Play of light' is thus lost, which the Mentor whose beck has been our guide points out as a fault. Some such stores as these must Aladdin have had to give to the caliph, his future father-in-law, or to stud the windows of his magic palace. They increase as his did. All the diamond world is here (in copy); the 'Pitt,' the 'Regent,' and the 'Russian.' From this place came also the cases of the same gems in the Museum of Practical Geology. We begin to think that the reign of the genii is not over. Even they could not exceed the beauties above and around. Maybe, after all, it is in truth their palace. Aladdin, who sits at his desk making out bills, could feast a good party if his viands were as bountiful, and splendid, and costly, as the table services at his command. On his right are decanters and glasses of every fashion, to please the most fastidious taste. Coloured glasses, so giving flavour to some wines that the *connoisseur* could not endure plain glass again; long-leg negus and punch glasses with a mimic bowl at the top; and others so high and narrow that they seem nothing but spindle-shanks. Salts of 'prism cut,' so that the rays of light, in lieu of going through, may break upon the surface, and dart a myriad little fiery arrows like the diamond itself from every point of view; and spangling ornaments for the mantel-shelf. Some of the crystal wares are engraved, some are covered with a network of mazy line, some have curious, close spirals of two or three colours running up their legs; such would make London boys caper with joy to twist upon their palm, like a gimlet eating its way through their flesh.

74

ANON, 'A GLASS MANUFACTORY'

pp. 197–201 [bound pamphlet]

GLASS is a very useful, transparent substance, which is applied to many important purposes. Our houses would be very uncomfortable if we had no glass for windows; we should frequently have the wind and rain beating into them, or be without the light of the sun in them.

Pliny, an ancient writer, says, that the art of making glass was discovered in the following manner. A merchant vessel, laden with nitre, having been driven ashore on the coast of Palestine, near the river Belus, the crew went in search of provisions, and set the kettles in which they boiled their food on some lumps of nitre. Some of the nitre was dissolved by the fire, and mingled with the river sand, and formed a mass of glass. This suggested the mode of making this beautiful substance for useful purposes; and, by gradual improvements, its manufacture was brought to a high state of perfection.

The principal materials of which glass is composed are sand, or pulverised flints, mixed with soda, chiefly made from a sea-weed, or with pearl-ashes, made from the ashes of burnt wood; nitre, lime, and litharge of lead, are also employed to fuse and improve the mixed substances of which glass is made, and sometimes a small portion of the black oxide of manganese is added, to render the glass free from colour. In scientific language, glass is said to be compounded of silica, or flinty earth, fused with alkalies. Sand, and pulverised flints, are called silica. Nitre, soda, and pearl-ashes, are alkalies. Soap-boilers' waste, and kelp, are also used as alkalies in the manufacture of glass. The proportions of the different substances from which glass is made, vary according to the kind of glass required, and according to the judgment of the manufacturer.

The materials, before they are melted, are put into ovens to be freed from all moisture. In this process they are made very hot, but not sufficiently to dissolve them. This process is termed *fritting*, and occupies a considerable time. After this, the materials are thrown into the glass-pot, to be melted. In this they are subjected to a very intense heat. The furnace in which the materials are melted is closed up with wet clay, excepting a small hole for examining the progress of the melting. Soon after being placed in the melting-pots, the mass is in motion, and soon becomes a red-hot liquid body. The heat of the furnace has to be kept up for from twelve to eighteen hours; and during the process, samples are taken out of the pots,

DOI: 10.4324/9781315400105-89

to ascertain the state of the liquid mass. When it has become sufficiently melted, the heat of the furnace is reduced, and the mass, which is now called metal, is allowed to cool. Some particles of undissolved substances, which float on the top of the pots, are carefully skimmed off. When the metal has cooled sufficiently to be worked, it is still soft, and easily yields to the breath of the glass-worker, yet is so tenacious as to retain the shape into which it is formed. It is so soft and adhesive, that it may be drawn out in a fine thread, and wound round a reel.

When the metal is cooled into a state fit to be worked, a workman takes an iron tube, four or five feet long, called a blowing-iron, and dips it into the melting-pot, and turns it round, until a sufficient quantity of the metal adheres to the iron; he then takes it out, and hands it to the blower, who rolls the metal on a stone, or iron-plate, then puts the end of the blowing-iron, having the metal on it, towards the ground, and blows in at the other end of the iron, and thus the mass of glass becomes hollow, and is extended to its proper thickness and shape, by the blowing and skill of the workman. In making some articles, moulds are used to aid the blower in giving the articles their proper shape. A piece of cold wire, applied to the part where the glass is united to the blowing iron, causes the article which has been blown to break off from the blowing-iron, just as though it had been cut off. Some articles are made by putting the liquid glass into moulds. Common window-glass is made by blowing and twirling the metal, and plate-glass is made by pouring the metal upon iron tables, rolling it while fluid into sheets, which are afterwards ground to a face and polished.

Buildings for the making of glass are usually in the form of cones, from fifty to eighty feet in diameter, and from sixty to a hundred feet high. The furnace is in the middle, and under it is an open space, of a sufficient width to allow a workman, with a wheelbarrow, to go in and out to remove the rubbish. The crucibles, or melting-pots, are made of clay. The Stourbridge clay makes the best pots. Those used for bottles and window-glass are generally made about forty inches in diameter, and of about the same depth.

When glass has been put into the shape required, it has to be subjected to the process, termed *annealing*. This is done by putting it into ovens, in which it is heated and allowed gradually to cool; by this means it becomes less liable to be broken.

There are several kinds of glass. The coarsest is common bottle-glass; the next quality is common window-glass; another kind is called flint-glass, of which decanters and drinking-glasses are made; plate-glass is another description of fine glass. Besides these, a variety of coloured glasses are made; some of which are very beautiful. Formerly, glass was very expensive; some of the materials of which it is composed were dearer than they are now, and there was a heavy tax upon it, which, a few years' since, was removed.

It was not until near ten hundred years after the birth of Christ that window-glass was used in England. The windows of houses, and even of cathedrals, were either formed of lattice-work or horn, or covered with linen cloth. An English historian, who wrote in year 1584, says – "Of old time our country-houses instead of glass did use much lattice, and that made either of wicker or fine rifts of oak in checkerwise. I read also, that some of the better sort, in and before the time of the Saxons, did make panels of horne instead of glass, and fix them in wooden casements, but horne in windows is now quite laid down (or discontinued) in every place, because glass is come to be plentiful and good." It is, however, now more plentiful and better than ever it was before.

Dr. Johnson, in referring to glass, wrote as follows: "By some fortuitous liquefaction mankind was taught to produce a body at once in a high degree solid and transparent, which might admit the light of the sun, and exclude the violence of the wind; which might extend the sight of the philosopher to new ranges of existence, and charm him at one time with the unbounded extent of the material creation, and at another with the endless subordination of animal life; and, what is yet of more importance, might supply the decays of nature, and succour old age with subsidiary sight. Thus was the first artificer in glass employed, though without his own knowledge or expectation. He was facilitating and prolonging the enjoyment of light, enlarging the avenues of science, and conferring the highest and most lasting pleasures; he was enabling the student to contemplate nature, and the beauty to behold herself."

4.3

Plate

4.3 Plate

Alfred Crowquill, 'The Service of Plate', *Temple Bar*, Vol. 20 (May 1867), pp. 272–277.
Anon, 'The Age of the Electro-Plate', *Fun*, Vol. 5 (March 1867), p. 8.
Anon, 'Electro-Deposition', *The National Encyclopaedia: A Dictionary of Universal Knowledge*, Vol. 5 (London: [n.p], c.1870), pp. 782–786.

In 1867, the periodical *Fun* published a short ditty (reprinted in this section) called 'The Age of Electro-Plate', mocking all types of sham and show. The three verses present contemporary life in a gimcrack, morally bankrupt age. Examples include yards of 'dubious' hair, paper flowers, plagiarised theatre plays, cosmetics and blacking for men's bald patches, with the penultimate line referring to sexual trickery: 'dresses so low that our grandmothers faint'. The final line of each verse proclaims that the present is 'the Age of Electro-Plate!' The pride and quality of a previous 'gold and silver age' have been bartered for affordable, mass-produced trinkets. Concepts of quality and value, forgery and sham all feature in the discussions of electroplated articles in this section.

In many instances, however, 'silver plate' or 'plate' did not necessarily mean the impersonation by an inferior for a higher quality original. Silver plate referred to any thin, flat piece of silver or silver alloy, particularly in the form of a plate, vessel or utensil. The entry for silver in *Tomlinson's Cyclopœdia of Useful Arts* (1852) describes a complicated system of manufacturing alloys, accompanied by a strict regulatory system of hallmarks administered by the Goldsmith's Company. Particularly sought after were articles of Sheffield plate, a type of sterling silver made by rolling and fusing thin layers of copper and silver, which lent itself to intricate engraving and was hard wearing. Images of plated goods in the *Art Journal* depict jugs, mugs, teapots and sugar bowls with intricate leaf-and-fruit patterns, both raised and engraved. Electroplating was patented in the 1840s as a chemical process that allowed objects to be thinly coated with a layer of solid copper, silver or gold. By 1875, electroplating had almost entirely superseded Sheffield plate.

Electroplating used thin layers of pure silver, rather than alloy, so sham goods were probably manufactured by cheap gilding or leaf methods. Sham or not, copying was integral to the plating process. *The National Encyclopaedia's* section on electroplating reprinted here details multiple innovations in the process, including plating onto wax models. A perfect wax copy of the article to be plated was made; this was then plated thickly with copper. Once heated, the wax melted out of the now-hollow copper, which was then plated with precious metals. Similar processes were employed for making 'colossal' figures, including a life-sized copper statue of Malcolm Canmore (Mael Coluim Ceann Mór), otherwise known as Malcolm III of Scotland.

The distinctions between solid silver articles and those that were plated, as well as cheap articles posing as expensive ones, could easily be mapped onto Victorian notions of class. The 1867 comic story 'The Service of Plate' was published in

Temple Bar, a monthly magazine which sold for one shilling to a comfortably middle-class readership and was edited by George Augustus Sala. The story pokes gentle fun at the chaos caused by an expensive gift placed in the wrong hands. An unassuming office worker is rewarded for his charity work with the gift of a service of plate (given the story's date, it is very likely that 'plate' referred to electroplate), when he and his family have never wished for anything grander than their modest stock of teaspoons. So thrown are they by this unexpected gift that the narrator is two and a half minutes late to the office, an act so out of character that the porter comes searching for him. Frantic with worry about burglary, the family resort to ever-more absurd acts of security, but each act of protection results in more people knowing about the treasure within. After ruining the family holiday, they give in and display the plate, ruefully noting that the 'gift' ends up costing them a great deal in dinners and tea parties. The narrator's three quiet daughters are ultimately married to visitors who originally came to admire the plate: the men take not only a daughter but a share of the tea set, so that 'cares and anxieties' are over. In sharp contrast to *Fun*'s pessimistic view of plated goods, the *Temple Bar* story ends on a positive note.

75

ALFRED CROWQUILL, 'THE SERVICE OF PLATE'

Temple Bar, Vol. 20 (May 1867), pp. 272–277

I HAVE been in one situation forty years, and, like a squirrel in a cage, have progressed by going the same round every day; yet I have had my little ambitions, which, however, never interfered with the due digestion of my eight o'clock breakfast, one o'clock dinner, six o'clock tea, and nine o'clock supper; indeed, my life ran on in a calm, unruffled stream, devoid of precipices and atagonistic rocks; in fact, it could not be called a murmuring stream. I married at five and twenty, as my dear parents said that the proper age had arrived for me to settle. Knowing my timidity and unworldliness, they took upon themselves the onus of the courtship. By their foresight they secured me a prize in the mild daughter of remarkably mild parents, who were well to do, and had but that one treasure; thus the current of my true love was a smooth contradiction to the old adage. These few lines give an exact idea of my whole life, to write more would be positively repetition, until, alas! I became unfortunately fortunate; but, before I proceed, I must just mention that our union was blest with three girls. I really had nearly forgotten them, bless them! they were so quiet.

One morning – I tremble as I write it – a letter was handed to me. I borrowed my eldest girl's scissors to snip round the seal, for I am too methodical to tear anything. I read. Good heavens! my face flushed and my hand shook, my wife and daughters crowded round me, alarmed at my unwonted agitation. I read it aloud, and they partook of my excitement. It was to inform me that "a public charity, to which I had been honorary secretary for many years, proposed, as they were pleased to say, to present me, for my honour, probity, and usefulness, with a *service of plate!*"

Our five hearts throbbed tumultuously. What was "a service of plate?" Such was my confusion, that I believe I was two and a half minutes beyond my time at the office, and I found our old porter looking out for me at the end of the street, for the firm firmly believed that I must have met with some dreadful accident. I was bewildered, and muttered as I went, "a service of plate!" Our desires hitherto had been satisfied with the spoons and ladles of our deceased parents, and never for a moment entertained the most distant idea of adding to the stock, so that we were perfectly innocent of what a service of plate consisted of.

DOI: 10.4324/9781315400105-91

We soon knew what it was. I will pass over the intervening days between the letter and the presentation, the agony and disturbance of my system on the day thereof, and the speeches of the chairman and committee, and my reply. The secretary put something down in the minutes purporting to be a faithful report of that bit of eloquence, but as to my having spoken it, I have not even to this day been weak enough to believe. I remember nothing distinctly until I found myself rolling home in a carriage, half filled with packages – "The service of plate!"

Upon my arrival at home, my wife and daughters soon brought to light the magnificent present, first – a salver as large as a tea-tray, upon which was inscribed, as nearly as I could recollect, the substance of the chairman's speech, attributing to me all the virtues under the sun (here my wife and daughters kissed me, evidently astonished at possessing such a father and husband); next a tea-pot went the round of admiration, then a coffee-pot, milk-jug, sugar-basin, and tea-spoons, delightfully heavy, royal pattern, fiddle-head and handled, as I afterwards learned again and again, were they handled and admired; but we were not alone in our admiration, for, looking through the parlour-window at the glittering treasure, were two or three as ill-looking fellows as ever terrified a quiet family. We drew the window-curtains in their faces, and they sneaked off, but they had seen the service of plate, and our peace of mind was gone. A knock came at the door; one of the rascals wanted to know whether Mr. Thompson lived there, at the same time a large brass plate with my name thereon stared him in the face. Ah! we were marked down to be robbed.

What should we do? Why, lock it up in various closets; divide it in a way to distract the most experienced burglar; at least, by that stratagem we should not lose all at once. The servants had luckily been kept in ignorance of our acquisition, and, consequently, could not gossip in the neighbourhood.

I do not think that I, my wife, or daughters, slept a wink that night. The service of plate was galloping through our brains to the utter destruction of our usual calm repose.

The next morning arrived, and all was safe. I cut the morning paper, when, guess my horror, the first thing that caught my eye was: "Presentation of Plate;" there was my name at full length, even my residence was not forgotten, so that no one might be mistaken in the fortunate individual, or where this lump of silver was deposited. It was a positive invitation – a finger-post, one might say – to burglars; nothing less than "this is the way to the service of plate!"

I saw my own horror reflected in the faces of my family. I went to town an anxious, miserable man, the front gate and the front door were locked after me, and in my way to town I called on the carpenter to go immediately and secure the back door and shutters with extra bolts, &c.

As I deposited the office ledgers in the iron safe that evening, a happy thought crossed my brain: I would have an iron safe at home for my service of plate. This brilliant idea was canvassed after tea with my wife and daughters, and highly approved of, and carried *nem. con.*, to be instantly acted upon; for until the terrible present was in some safe depository, it would banish sleep.

The next morning I started somewhat earlier than usual, so that I might order the wished-for iron safe. Determined to have a good one, I disbursed some few pounds in the purchase of a most responsible-looking article, one that would bid defiance to the most expert thief.

As it was my Saturday half-holiday, I arrived at home very early, congratulating myself on my morning's purchase, and the relief it would prove to me and my anxious family. My pleasing reverie was broken into, as I turned into my street, by the appearance of a mob round my door. I hurried forward, and was soon in the midst of them, where I discovered my iron chest upon its back, waiting the decision of the wrangling carters, as to how it was to be got into the house, and placed into position, as it was of great weight, and more like a closet than a box. During this discussion, I had to bear the chaff of the surrounding mob. One fellow, winking his eye at a chum, and remarking, "that he undered vether the old cove was going to lock up his old woman or his suverains in that are iron coffin;" another observing, "that it voud take a precious swag of spoons and forks to fill it up." "Vot a plummy lot o' keyholes!" said a big boy to the last speaker. "Oh! they be blowed; a tap of a hammer voud open the lot on 'em, or a jemmy vith a screw!" replied he.

I actually burst out into a cold perspiration at the cool impudence of the vagabonds, but I held my tongue, as I always had a horror of what is called chaff.

I had at last to consent to receive the assistance of some of this motley crew, as the carmen must have left it in the street without such aid. After a great deal of swearing, scuffling, and noise, the ponderous closet was placed into a recess in the passage, from the utter impossibility of getting it into any of the upper rooms, without bringing the house about our ears.

Exhausted and distracted by the noise and bustle, we sat down to our tea, not in the most tranquil of moods, as it struck us all that the necessary public display of the troublesome chest must inform all whom it might or might not concern, that I had in some way acquired something that it was necessary to take extra precaution in locking up. Thus our very attempt for security had placed us in a worse position than before, as the provoking iron closet was a complete proclamation to every one entering the house, where to find "the service of plate!"

Again the carpenter was had recourse to, that he might continue the wainscoting over the recess, so as to deceive the eyes of the dustman, coal-man, brewer's-man, gas-meter man, and others, who must pass through the hall, and be struck at the sight of our ponderous safe. Safe, indeed! the folly and inappropriateness of this word I discovered that very morning, as if my evil genius delighted in tormenting me, for on my desk I found one of the periodicals, left by a careless junior, in which I discovered an article on burglary, illustrated with cuts, which plainly showed that iron safes or fire-doors, hitherto considered impregnable, could be as easily opened as a simple apple pudding, by taking out a large circular slice, with what is called a centre-bit, in the same way that we get to the interior of that domestic luxury. Then what was safe from such ingenuity, since iron and Mr. Bramah failed to circumvent these terrible inventions?

I, of course, in my nervousness, was foolish enough to borrow the book, and show it to my wife and daughters, who were thereby brought into a frightful state of nervousness surpassing my own. Then, again, the carpenter was so busy that he sent a strange man to proceed with our job: thus another stranger was let into the secret in the most unlooked-for manner, and we felt in our despair that our throats were not worth a week's purchase. Oh! how often did I think of my school copy, that I had written in a bold round hand in the days of threepence a-week pocket money, which never troubled me – "He who gathereth treasure often destroyeth sleep." Oh, how true had my juvenile round-hand proverb proved to me in my middle age, when I possessed a "service of plate!" and I was really desponding enough to wish that we could be robbed of it, without any fuss, and return to the simplicity of our original tea-spoons, counted up every night at bedtime and always right.

Our time for going out of town was fast approaching, but I saw no preparation being made for the usual month's absence and enjoyment by the sea-side. "We can't take the plate out of town with us," said my wife, "and how can we possibly leave it behind us, to the mercy of the thieves, who have no doubt read all about it in the newspaper, and only wait for our leaving, to pounce upon it, and perhaps murder old Sarah? I should never forgive myself."

Here was another dilemma, and I am sure I could not see how to get out of it. Then my good girls, to be deprived of the sea breezes, and the roses that they always brought back upon their cheeks to last them all the winter. To lose all this, was certainly paying very dearly for our "service of plate." After many counsels, it was at last finally settled that my wife was to go down to Brighton with the three girls, whilst I was to do Saturday, Sunday, and a little bit of Monday with them, and during my absence the gardener was to take care of the two servant-women and the plate.

I hardly like to recount what a wretched bachelor I made; how I wasted the tea, left the sugar-basin at the mercy of the sweet-toothed, forgot the keys, or took them with me to town, as I had been strictly enjoined by my careful wife, but discovered, on my return, that the cupboards were all open and at the full discretion of the servants. My responsibilities were too much for me. I was so positively unaccustomed to any domestic duties, as my dear kind old mother had handed me over to the care of my wife, so that I had had no interregnum of bachelorhood to break me in to the locking-up system.

After four weeks of anxiety, and much trouble to myself, we were once more seated at our own tea-table; and I assure you that I fully appreciated the blessings of home, and resigned the keys and *management* of household affairs with a sigh of relief. At last, my wife took courage – determined that my light should not be hid under a bushel – and placed the salver, in all its glory, on the sideboard, upon which my written character was emblazoned with many intricate flourishes and wonderfully imagined letters. Everybody in the house, however, deciphered it that day, and ever afterwards looked upon me as somebody who was somebody.

Dinner-parties were given for the sole purpose of showing the salver. The tea-pot, the coffee-pot, the sugar-basin, milk-ewer, and spoons, had the like honour paid to them, by having tea-parties given especially to bring them out; so that, all things considered, there was some cost attached to the possession of a service of plate.

In the course of time, one young man would bring music for my eldest daughter, another would most perseveringly bring his flute and practise duets with my second daughter; indeed, so persevering were they that my four-handed cribbage was entirely knocked on the head. Through all this strange innovation my wife would sit and smile in, to me, a most unaccountable manner. At last, one of the young men called before office hours, and made a very confused, garbled account of his feelings and his salary, which he wanted to share with my eldest girl. I rushed upstairs to my wife in a totally wild state to ask her to interfere.

"Why, you blind goose!" exclaimed she, laughing, "what do you suppose he has been here for, almost every night, for the last four months, for you may depend upon it he didn't come here to take away our service of plate? Go down again, do, and ask him to come to dinner this evening." I did so.

When I returned to dinner, somewhat confused, I found the bashful young gentleman helping my daughter to look over an album, whilst my other two girls were at a pitch of giggling that I had never observed before.

Before the week was out the flute gentleman had me in the front parlour with a tale not at all differing from the first gentleman, except in its object, which was my second daughter. The mother took it with the same astounding coolness that she had exhibited on the first occasion.

"Astonishing," said I; "here we have been bringing up these girls for the comfort of our age, and –"

"So they will be," said my wife; "go along, do, and put the young man out of his misery;" and I did so.

As both these young men were sons of old friends, I could not be but satisfied, although, I confess, I felt very strange at losing my children in this abrupt manner.

I mused as I went to town, wondering whether I should find another gentleman in the parlour requiring me to part with my third daughter. "No, no, not so bad as that, my little pet is only seventeen or eighteen, I don't exactly remember which. If such a preposterous thing were to occur, I think that I should knock the fellow down."

Before I had balanced my half-year's ledgers, I found myself in the midst of mantua makers, orange blossoms, and ribbons enough to decorate a Lord Mayor's show, whilst my poor wife was rushing about with a very indistinct idea of what she was about.

It may appear impertinent that I thrust my family affairs before the public, when this short paper is really dedicated to "a service of plate," but I can safely say that all this has to do with the subject, as the first proposer took away my eldest daughter and the silver tea-pot; the second, in the most polite manner, took away the coffee-pot and milk-jug with his bride, and a share of the spoons, and it was not long before my third daughter had occasion to take away the sugar-basin, sugar-tongs, and spoons to match. The salver remained with us until my eldest daughter's eldest son could decipher his grandfather's character, so elaborately displayed thereon for the credit and delectation of the rising posterity. Thus our cares and anxieties were over, and the iron safe sold at a loss; but we did not forget to look after the "service of plate," which we had continual opportunities of doing at my daughters' houses until they gave us something else to do in looking after, and borrowing, sundry rosy-cheeked little boys, and fair-haired girls, with eyes much brighter than our troublesome service of plate, for they are, without exception, the –

76

ANON, 'THE AGE OF THE ELECTRO-PLATE'

Fun, Vol. 5 (March 1867), p. 8

We sigh that the times are so terribly bad,
As we shut up our pockets and purse;
But it's easy to see how a "fashion" or "fad"
Makes them very decidedly worse.
We can tell, if we try to examine a page,
Of the book which is ticketed "Fate,"
We have bartered the gold and the silver age,
For an Age of Electro-Plate!

Who care for the cant of degenerate days
That of facts not theories sings,
We have authors of stolen Parisian plays,
And fingers for Brummagem rings.
The crosses and lockets for feminine throats,
May be purchased for "seven and eight."
There are flowers of paper to stick in our coats,
In the Age of Electro-Plate!

Not a barber exists but exhibits a yard
Of exceedingly dubious hair,
Which is twisted or plaited or shown on a card,
Ready dyed for the dark or the fair.
Soft faces are plastered with powder and paint
Bald patches made black as the grate,
The dresses so low that our grandmothers faint,
At the Age of Electro-Plate!

DOI: 10.4324/9781315400105-92

77

ANON, 'ELECTRO-DEPOSITION'

The National Encyclopaedia: a Dictionary of Universal Knowledge, Vol. 5 (London: [n.p.], c. 1870), pp. 782–786

ELECTRO-DEPOSITION, or ELECTRO-METALLURGY, called also *Electrotyping*, is the process by which, through electrolytic action excited by battery power in a solution of a metallic salt, objects immersed in that solution come to be coated over, or articles by means of a mould may be even wholly formed, by the precipitated metal. In the operations of this beautiful art, salts of copper, of silver, of gold, and of iron, are those ordinarily employed by the electro-depositor. The general nature of electro-deposition has been known to science since the beginning of the century, but it has been since 1838 only that its industrial application began to acquire any importance.

The term *Electrolysis* (which see) is applied to signify the electro-chemical decomposition of substances as a result of the electrical current. All compounds susceptible of direct decomposition by this means are called *electrolytes*, and when electro-chemically decomposed they are said to be *electrolysed.* Water slightly acidulated is an electrolyte, yielding oxygen and hydrogen; and so also are neutral salts electrolytes, yielding acids and alkalies. In these decompositions, the gases and proximate substances referred to severally appear at certain determinate poles of the battery. In the example of sulphate of copper, the sulphuric acid would show itself at one pole, and the metallic copper at the other. In using a solution of a salt of copper for electro-deposition, it was known at an early stage of this art, that if the pole at which the metal should appear were expanded into a mould or medal that naturally was or had been made a conductor of electricity, the article would shortly be covered over with a coating of pure metallic copper so completely as that a perfect counterpart of it would be formed, which, when stripped off, would present a reverse of every feature and line of the original mould. In 1838 the practice was introduced of coating military and other metal ornaments with gold and silver, by immersing them, under galvanic action, in solutions of salts of those metals.

In 1839 by the labours of two men, Professor Jacobi of St. Petersburg, and Mr. Thomas Spencer of Liverpool, the science and the trade application of electro-deposition were greatly advanced. An essential point to further progress was also

DOI: 10.4324/9781315400105-93

discovered about this time, known as the divergent current of the battery. The practical meaning of this distinction will be evident when the earlier and later modes of deposition are compared. Formerly the deposit of the metal took place on the enlarged battery pole proper to it, and the action was soon arrested in consequence, and only thin films of metallic coating could be procured; but by the later plan the battery pole was preserved clean, and the substance to be coated was suspended from the same wire conductor side by side with it in the solution, and the action could thereby be prolonged. The use of plumbago powder brushed on (1840) to render non-conducting surfaces conductible for electricity, and the invention by Smee of the platinised silver battery, were also great steps in the advance of the art.

The employment of the cyanides of the metals by Mr. Wright of Birmingham, in 1840, assisted forward electroplating as by a bound. The first attempts of this kind were made with chloride of silver dissolved in aqueous yellow prussiate of potash. The success attained was shown in the formation of a thick deposit of white silver by electrolytic action. Heretofore the deposition had been thin, imperfectly coherent, and dark-coloured; the chemical liquids now employed fulfilled almost completely the requirements of work in being thick, to choice, and of the proper metallic clearness and purity. Still, some minor difficulties had to be got over. The faults that recurred were blisters in the deposited silver, its aptness to peel off before the burnishing tool; sometimes also the silver was discolorised, and every new metal, whether iron, steel, tin, lead, or Britannia metal, as the foundation, presented its own difficulties.

Hitherto silver, on being deposited on a surface, had a snow-white or frost-like appearance, and it therefore required to be afterwards burnished, which was always expensive, and often troublesome or impracticable, from the intricacy of the forms of objects. The method of bright plating was another stride made towards the perfection of the art. This was effected by the use of bisulphide of carbon in small quantity in the deposit solutions, which had the effect of greatly reducing the necessity of mechanically polishing the surface of the deposited metal.

The *vat* or *trough* of the electro-depositor is usually a rectangular vessel (see Plate), traversed along its length at the top by two brass tubes set apart near to the sides and fixed in position. These tubes are crossed and connected by wires or by smaller tubes, which may be adjusted to and fro upon the first pair to suit the requirements of work. From these crossings the articles to be plated are hung by wire suspensions in the deposit solution with which the trough is charged. The long tubes extend beyond one end of the vat a little way, and are there provided each with a pinching screw for attaching to them the poles of the voltaic battery, or of the magneto-electric machine, when that form of electricity is used. The quantity of metal deposited depends on the amount of the electric current passing through the solution, and consequently upon the size and number of the elements or cells in the battery. It is customary to strike the first films of deposition with intensity, introducing more cells for this purpose than are afterwards used to continue and complete the process. The battery employed is ordinarily one of quantity, and not of intensity. The Plate represents two large stoneware jars, such as are commonly used; these contain dilute sulphuric acid, with an amalgamated plate of zinc and two plates of copper in each, or two amalgamated zinc plates, with a platinised silver plate between them. On the parts of this battery being connected together and with the conducting tubes of the vat, the galvanic current is established. The electricity in passing through the plating solution decomposes the elements of that liquid, viz., the cyanogen and the silver; the latter fixes itself to the article to be plated, and the free cyanogen combines instantly with plates of pure silver suspended in the solution, forming new cyanide of silver which is dissolved in the liquid; these sheets restore the waste of the silver caused by the deposition, and permits the latter to go on for an indefinite time. The articles to be plated must be made scrupulously clean, and clear of oxide or of any filth. The operation of cleaning is often much more tedious than that of plating them.

The method of solid deposits of copper or other metal is one of the latest improvements in the art. A wax model, exactly representing the article, is first made; this is brushed over most carefully and completely with plumbago powder. A thick layer of copper is then deposited upon it in the vat, so that when the wax is melted out of the interior of it, the article will retain its shape. The inside of the copper shell now represents the mould of the outside of the article to be manufactured. The exterior of the copper is now protected by varnish. The shell is then filled with the deposit solution, and one pole of the battery is inserted into it, and the other pole is connected with the outside of the shell. The operation goes on, whilst the solution is kept up at the proper strength, by plates of the metal suspended in the solution, until the deposit has acquired the proper thickness; if it be of gold or silver the copper shell is dissolved off by an acid, leaving the internal form free and entire.

For more massive forms, such as life or colossal sized statues, the method followed is that of first forming the figure in a plaster cast, which is soaked in boiled linseed oil. The surface on drying is coated over with a shining film of plumbago, and the figure is then transferred to the vat, and coated entirely with copper to the thickness of about one-sixteenth of an inch, or so thick as will enable its form to be preserved during the operations that follow. It is then removed from the vat, and the sulphate of lime matrix is excavated out of the interior with the utmost care and completeness. The shell is varnished outside, and on being restored to the vat the deposition takes place inside; and if the operation is prolonged over some weeks, a thickness of half an inch is often obtained. In the London Exhibition of 1862 there was shown a life-size statue in copper of Malcolm Canmore, executed by Messrs. Elkington of Birmingham. The same firm has produced several colossal statues of human forms, including one of the late Prince Consort, and another nine feet high, weighing a ton, by this process.

Among the latest applications of electro-deposition is that of copying engraved wood blocks and type by means of it. One method of this is the following: – The engraving to be copied is first carefully coated with plumbago; it is then surrounded with a shallow metal rim, or edging of plaster of Paris, to give it boundary. When the latter has hardened, a thick sheet of gutta percha, softened in hot water, is laid upon the blackened surface, and with increasing force pressed upon the engraving or type by the action of a screw, and left to cool. The reverse thus formed on the gutta percha is taken off and plumbagoed, and then coated with copper in the vat, or it may be with iron, in order that the surface may withstand still better the action of the printing-press. The metal mould, on being taken off, is heated upon a sand bath, and the back is then filled with melted stereotype metal, to give it strength and rigidity.

Another, and still better plan, and one extensively followed in the establishment from which the present work emanates, is that of using a preparation of wax for taking the moulds off wood-cuts or type. Our experience in this art leads us to expect that stereotyping, as at present followed, will by and by, to a great extent, be superseded by electrotyping.

Electro-deposition has extended to platinum, using the double chloride as the solution; to palladium, employing palladio-cyanide of potassium for this purpose. Zinc, cadmium, bismuth, and antimony have all been deposited by electrolytic action with greater or less success. The deposition of alloys was the subject of a patent in 1852. Brass is deposited from a mixed solution of the cyanides of zinc and of copper, using a large brass anode or deposit pole and a powerful battery, with the solution at 150° Fahr. Thick deposits of brass of uniform colour, and of any desired composition, can thus be obtained.

Nature-printing is one of the most beautiful applications of the electrotype. This is a method of producing impressions of plants and other natural objects in a manner so truthful, that only a close inspection reveals the fact of their being copies. A mould in the first place is taken of the object with gelatine or liquid gutta percha, the elasticity of which materials is favourable for flattening the mould without distortion, when separated from the original. The mould is rendered conducting by the application of plumbago, and copper is deposited of sufficient thickness to form a printing plate.

Copying Daguerreotype and Photographic Pictures. – This process is a further triumph of the art of electro-deposition. The method shortly is as follows: – Solder a wire to one corner of the daguerreotype plate; then varnish the back and edges of the plate, and hang it up to dry. Afterwards suspend it in a clean solution of copper or other salt, and connect it with one or two pairs of small Smee's batteries. In about 24 hours a sufficiently thick deposit will be found, which may be easily removed by the insertion of a knife edge, or tapering slip of hard wood, between the surfaces of the plate and the electrotype. When photographs are used for deposition, those taken on glass are employed in the process. By this means most beautiful and vivid copies of the original picture may be obtained. So delicate is the action of the electric current, that even a spider's web may be plated with gold and silver.

4.4

Soap

DOI: 10.4324/9781315400105-94

4.4 Soap

Anon, 'A Day at a Soap and Candle Factory', *Penny Magazine for the Diffusion of Useful Knowledge*, Vol. 11 (January 29, 1842), pp. 41–47.

Image: 'By Order of the Bath', Pears Soap, Unilever Archives, ref. GB1752.AFP 12/3/1 [n.d.], Unilever Collections, Unilever Art, Archives and Records Management, Port Sunlight.

'Some Good Reasons for Using Sunlight Soap', Wellcome Collection, Lever Brothers Ltd. [c. 1890].

Image: 'Vinolia Soap', Unilever Collections, Unilever Art, Archives and Records Management, Port Sunlight, Archive ref. GB1752. AFP 12/4/125 [c. 1890].

Throughout the nineteenth century, soap was manufactured in both factories and the home. Effective homemade soap could be made from ingredients as simple as fatty kitchen scraps saponified with lye made from wood ash. The average householder was easily able to manufacture soaps for cleaning, toilet use and laundry to avoid the heavy duties which had been levied on soap from the Restoration period to 1853, when William Gladstone repealed the tax. It is interesting to note that each of the sources here emphasises notions of the purity and consistency of factory-made soap, rather than its affordability. The laboratory and the factory, it is implied, offer what the home kitchen cannot. Ingredients include kitchen stuff (fatty scraps), pine resins, tallows, palm oil, potash and caustic soda: most are unpleasant and some are actively hazardous. This situation changed somewhat as the century progressed. A late-nineteenth-century advertisement for Pears soap, 'By Order of the Bath' (reprinted here), declares that consumers need the 'requisite knowledge of the manufacture of soap to guide them to a proper selection' and that ignorance may lead to their purchasing alkaline soap, suitable for laundry but damaging to skin.

Like much of Pears' advertising, 'The Order of the Bath' draws on imagery of children. Lever Brothers, manufacturers of Pears soap, famously used artworks by well-known painters in their advertising, most notably John Everett Millais' sentimental work *Bubbles* (1886), depicting a small boy blowing soap bubbles. In the source here, it is again infant skin which is emphasised, and the pamphlet's cover depicts two women washing a baby. At their feet are several bars of pure white soap, with the legend 'Use PEARS' SOAP for the Skin & Complexion'. The pamphlet's second page establishes the desirability of 'baby-skin', a fragile substance easily 'eaten away' by alkali soaps. Women and men can only obtain the 'charm' of baby skin through using 'emollient, non-irritant' Pears' soap. Around the time this advertisement appeared, domestic economy manuals carried a similar message, declaring the need for gentle toilet soap free from 'acid or alkali' or any other irritating substance. An American company called B. J. Johnson made similar complexion-based claims for their soap Palmolive. Factory-manufactured soap is thus presented as finer and more sophisticated than anything which can be made at home.

The scientific expertise associated with the late-Victorian environment of the factory also promised increased cleanliness. A similar four-page pamphlet for the Lever-produced Sunlight soap shows the more usual approach to soap advertising, in which the soap powerfully eradicates all traces of dirt in every conceivable situation. 'Some Good Reasons for Using Sunlight Soap' include washing dogs, caged birds and poultry, cheese vats and churns, horse's scratches and sores, 'everything in the house from cellar to garret', laundry (especially delicate items like lace) and finally the 'toilet' or washing the body. The rear page advertises Lifebuoy disinfectant soap, another Lever product. Where Pears' offered softness, Lifebuoy's selling point was health. 'How shall we save life?' the advertisement asks above a picture of a lifebuoy-wielding sailor. Like Sunlight, a single bar of soap will eliminate germs from multiple places. Soap was a beauty product, cleaning assistant and nurse. Lever's advertising presents the relationship between soap maker and consumer as one in which the manufacturer's expertise helps to maintain health. This relationship expanded into the concept of public health through practices such as the awarding of prize medals. Blondeau et Cie, the manufacturers of Vinolia Soap (pictured), won the prize medal at the 1892 Exhibition of Sanitary Apparatus and Appliances; the awarding body was The Sanitary Institute, known today as the Royal Society for Public Health.

As early as 1842, *The Penny Magazine* foreshadows Lever Brothers' presentation of soap as a complex technological product and the factory as a site of experimentation. The factory discussed in this extract is Messrs. B. T. and W. Hawes based in Lambeth. While there, the author witnesses a process close to full mechanisation. Only three workers are present; otherwise, the vats boil and bubble unwatched. The illustrations show workers engaged in low-skilled activities: stirring boilers, filling frames with liquid soap, cutting soap into slabs. In contrast to the magazine's other trips to cutlery and pin factories, there is a sense that this visitor does not fully understand the manufacturing process. When describing how soap is made, the author warns that 'there is a great deal of chemical nicety involved' and that the *Penny Magazine* 'is not the place where such matters can be . . . treated'; there is a palpable sense of relief when the article turns to the more straightforward processes of candle manufacture, 'a branch of art exceedingly simple and free from technical difficulties'.

78

ANON, 'A DAY AT A SOAP AND CANDLE FACTORY'

Penny Magazine for the Diffusion of Useful Knowledge, Vol. 11 (January 29, 1842), pp. 41–47

Figure 78.1 [Soap-Boiling Coppers.]

IF the reader will ramble some fine morning to that little green oasis in the great world of London – the Temple Gardens, and glance across the river, he will see immediately opposite to him a tall, black, bulky chimney, distinguishable from those which surround it by its large dimensions, and sending up its contribution to the smoky atmosphere of the metropolis. This chimney, and the buildings with which it is connected, point out the spot to which our attention will be directed in the present paper. It is true, the buildings present few of those attractions pertaining to "river scenery," nor do they add much to the famed beauties of the "banks of the Thames;" but they furnish an indication – one among many – of the commercial features of the metropolis, which are by no means devoid of interest.

We must quit the Temple Gardens, and cross Blackfriars Bridge to the Surrey side of the water, in order to reach the spot in question. The "way to wealth" in London, is generally through some narrow, dirty, dark, and crowded street, bounded on either side by ranges of factories, warehouses, or wharfs; with waggons and porters and cranes and bales of goods meeting the eye at every few steps. A street called Upper Ground Street, leading westward from Blackfriars Road at a short distance from the river, although it may not have a distinguished character as a "way to wealth," is certainly both narrow and dirty, and leads to many large factories and warehouses, most of which are situated in a part of the line called the Commercial Road, forming the communication between Upper Ground Street and the Waterloo Bridge Road. Among these factories, on the northern side of the Commercial Road, and occupying the space between it and the river, is the one to which our attention will be here directed, viz. the Soap and Candle Factory of Messrs. B. T. and W. Hawes; these gentlemen having with great courtesy permitted us to inspect and describe the operations conducted at this establishment.

This factory occupies the site where Queen Elizabeth's Barge-House formerly stood; a building wherein the state barge appears to have been kept, and to have undergone the necessary repairs. A creek or dock of some kind or other existed, into which the state barge was brought, but of which no vestiges now remain. A narrow pathway or passage leads down on the eastern side of the factory to the water's edge, and is known as 'Old Barge-house Stairs.' In the old maps of London, the 'Old Barge-house' is indicated as existing on this spot; but about a century ago the house ceased to be named, and we then find 'Old Barge-house Stairs' indicated. After the barge-house was removed, a glass-factory was established here; but about seventy or eighty years since, the manufacture of soap was commenced at this spot.

On entering the outer gates of the factory, we find ourselves in an open court, with a dwelling-house immediately on the left, a range of low buildings on the right, a counting-house and offices nearly in front, and adjacent to the latter the entrance to the main buildings of the factory. In the open court are waggons and carts, laden either with the raw materials from whence soap and candles are to be made, or with the manufactured articles about to leave the premises. Of the offices and counting-house we need say nothing; they contain the usual arrangements for the partners and clerks in the establishment. Contiguous to these offices is a small laboratory fitted up with a furnace, a sand-bath, a distilling apparatus, and other conveniences for conducting the chemical analysis of soap, and for making experiments incidental to the manufacture. The manufacture of soap is conducted in the warehouses westward and northward of the offices; the candle department eastward; and we will glance first through the former, and afterwards through the latter.

The building in which the main operations of the soap-manufacture are carried on, and which is represented in our frontispiece, covers a large area of ground, and is nearly filled with coppers and vessels of considerable dimensions. It is technically known in the factory as the 'Copper-side;' but we shall perhaps be better understood if we term it the 'boiling-house.' As we pass along the central avenue of this building from south to north, we have on the right hand a range of coppers or boilers, nearly a dozen in number, and averaging about eight or ten feet in diameter, the height being between four and five. These coppers are filled with soap or the materials for its formation, in various stages of progress. In one the soap is nearly in a finished state, and is about to be removed; in another the ingredients are boiling, and sending up a profuse volume of steam; into a third a supply of alkaline liquor is being conducted, from vats wherein it is prepared; from a fourth the spent ley or liquor is being pumped, after having imparted its alkaline property to the soap; some are for 'mottled' soap, some for 'yellow,' some for 'white' or 'curd' soap. According to the time when the 'boiling-house' is visited, so will these operations vary, but in general the contents of the coppers show the soap in many different degrees of formation. These coppers, as in many other instances, are oddly termed, for they are in reality iron vessels surrounded with brick. No flues or fires of any kind are connected with them; the boilers are heated by steam which is constantly passing from a large boiler which supplies all these vessels, and which is situated in another part of the factory. The introduction of the method of heating by steam instead of fire, in soap factories, sugar refineries, and other establishments, is one of the most important improvements of modern times; economizing space and fuel, maintaining an equable temperature, and lessening the liability to accidents by fire. In each copper is a pump, for removing the spent ley at a particular period in the process.

Along the left hand of the avenue, through the boiling-house and opposite the boilers, is a row of alkali vats, in which the alkali is brought into a purified and liquid state. The alkali employed in soap-making, and which is a crude carbonate of soda or of potash, is brought to the factory in a dry greyish powder; but before it can be used in the manufacture, the carbonic acid must be removed from the alkali, leaving the latter in a caustic state. This we shall explain further on; but we here merely observe, that the vats in which this purification takes place are situated a few feet to the left of the boiling-coppers, and that a shoot or trough conducts the liquid alkali from the vats to the coppers.

Adjoining the boiling-house on the left is a passage leading down to the water, through which is conveyed the carbonate of lime resulting from the purification of the alkalis, a residuum which is extensively used as a manure on stiff lands. Its beneficial effect is much increased by the small quantity of alkali and salt which it contains. Very interesting accounts have been published at various times exhibiting the effect of this manure on particular plants. A considerable quantity has been shipped to the West Indies since the abolition of slavery. On the right of the boiling-house, and communicating with it by a door, is the 'frame-room,' to which the soap is conveyed after being made; the name of *frame* being given to the vessel or receptacle into which the made soap is poured, and in which it remains till cold. The frame-room is full of these receptacles, nearly a hundred and fifty in number, lying in ranks or rows side by side, and the rows opposite each other. In walking between these rows of frames we see in one place a man filling a frame with liquid soap; in another, men taking a frame to pieces after the solidifying of the soap; in a third, other men cutting up a mass of hardened soap into slabs.

Near the frame-room is a range of warerooms, in which the slabs of soap are cut up into bars, and then piled up in tiers, like bricks in a wall. If "cleanliness is next to godliness," according to the old adage, we ought to have very pleasant thoughts while passing between these walls of soap – here 'mottled' – there 'yellow' – in another part 'curd,' and so on; but the truth is, that the odour from such a mass of soap, and the unavoidable absence of cleanliness in the manufacture, somewhat disturb the pleasure of contemplating the ulterior purpose to which the soap is to be applied.

In other parts of the factory, according to convenience, are placed the boiling-house for soft soap, and warehouses connected with it. The soft-soap copper is heated and managed in the same manner as the coppers for the hard soaps, and holds fourteen or fifteen thousand pounds of soap. As this kind of soap is not of such consistence as to enable it to be cut into slabs or bars, it is packed in barrels and sent from the factory in a pasty or semi-fluid state. In connection with this part of the factory too, are six or eight vats for de-carbonizing and purifying the carbonate of potash used as the alkali for soft soap. Some factories are built on such a regular plan, that the visitor retains a clear notion of the relative positions of the several parts; but in the present case the connecting doors, passages, and stories, between one part of the factory and another, are so tortuous and perplexing, that we cannot be properly topographical in our details. We can only say, therefore, in respect of other parts of the soap-department, that in one place is a storeroom or warehouse for tallow; in another, a similar depository for alkalis; in a third, for resin (an important ingredient in yellow soap); in a fourth, for oil; in another for 'kitchen-stuff,' an ingredient in the commoner kinds of soap. There is one room in which barrels of palm-oil are kept, and in which the oil – solid in our climate – is melted out of the cask through the bung-hole by means of steam. In another spot the oil thus melted is purified and bleached, and brought into a state fit for the soap-manufacture. Other rooms, or portions of rooms, are devoted to various subsidiary processes relating to the soap-manufacture; but to which we need not pay particular notice.

After having visited the various portions of the soap-department, we glanced through the candle-department, which, although much less considerable in size, presents many ingenious arrangements and many curious applications of the division of labour. The principal room in this department is that in which the 'dip' or 'store' candles are made, and which we may perhaps term the 'dipping-room.' This is, to the eye of a stranger, the most singular-looking room in the factory. It is of considerable height, having two stories or floors, one extending over the bottom in the usual way, and the other forming a kind of gallery round the four sides, at the height of about twelve feet from the floor. An inclined plane leads down from the gallery at one end to the floor at the other, consisting of a platform with ledges of wood at distances of about a foot asunder, forming a kind of an apology for a flight of stairs: it is, indeed, a kind of staircase, such as is used by ship-builders to ascend the sides of a ship, and is adapted by the smallness of its angle of elevation for the ascent of persons carrying loads. The floor or ground of the room is devoted to the manufacture of the candles, and the gallery to some subsequent operations. Along the middle of the floor is a row of cisterns, filled with tallow in a hot and melted state, which is kept at a proper temperature. Around the room on all four sides, and distant a few feet from the cisterns, are reservoirs or vessels of melted tallow, filled from the central cisterns, and consumed in the process of making candles. Between and above are candles, or the skeletons of candles, hanging in thousands; some having had only a single garment of tallow to cover the nakedness of the wicks; some more plentifully coated; and some nearly in a finished state. On three sides of the room men are making candles by the aid of the machines which we shall speak of by and bye; while in other parts of the room other men are 'dipping' according to the method in use before the invention of the machines. Here, a man is replenishing the supply of hot tallow in his dipping-cistern, from the cisterns in the middle of the room; there, is a boy removing the made candles from the machines, and fitting on a new supply of wicks; while other men and boys are busied in various parts of the manufacture.

On ascending the inclined plane to the gallery, we see near the outer edge of the gallery candles hanging on sticks; and round the gallery, next the wall, are a series of work-benches or tables, at each of which a man and a boy are engaged, the one to weigh the candles, according as they are 'eights,' 'tens,' 'twelves,' &c., – denominations too well known to every housewife to need explanation; and the other to fasten the candles on a string. In a small room attached to the candle department is kept the store of rushes for making rushlights; they are gathered in Lancashire, and brought to town in bundles weighing a few pounds each. In another room are sacks or bags filled with cotton, wound up in balls of about three pounds weight. There is also a beautiful machine, at which a man is engaged in making wicks for 'mould' and 'dip' candles. A third room, larger than those just alluded to, is the 'mould-room,' in which the mould candles are made, by the aid of an elaborate and ingenious machine. Connected with the candle department, also, are the requisite stores and warerooms for the commercial arrangements of the establishment.

Besides the various buildings and rooms belonging particularly to the soap or candle departments of the factory, there are mechanical and other arrangements of a general kind, which need not much description. In convenient parts of the factory are two steam-engines of different horse-power. Near these is a blacksmith's shop, for the repair and adjustment of various kinds of iron-work used in the factory. The smoke from the different flues and furnaces is conducted into a square or rather pyramidal chimney of large dimensions, being twenty-one feet square at the bottom, six feet square at the top, and a hundred and twenty feet in height. A carpenter's shop furnishes the conveniences for making packing-cases, boxes, &c. for the commercial department. Lastly, and perhaps to the manufacturers the least pleasant of all – there are rooms and offices fitted up for the Excise-officers, one or more of whom are in the factory day and night. It is a great blot upon the fiscal arrangements of this country, and one which seriously affects the manufacture of malt, of glass, of soap, and many other articles, that in order to collect the duties levied on these commodities, the officers of the Excise are empowered to control, as it were, every step of the processes, and to regulate the extent to which any improvement in the operations may be carried. It is not the amount of duty collected to which we here refer; this is another subject: it is the mode of collection which is so objectionable, by imposing impolitic checks to the natural course of improvement in manufacturing processes. Considerable ameliorations have, within a recent period, been made in the mode of collecting the revenue, and the survey of the premises of soap manufacturers; and under the able superintendence of the present chairman of the Excise (Mr. Wood), the manufacturers feel confident that, odious as the collection of the Excise revenue must be, every facility consistent with the security of the revenue will be afforded for the introduction of improvements and the protection of the fair trader.

It is almost impossible to calculate the benefits which would result to our manufactures if the Excise could be abolished, or the amount of the tax so reduced as to remove the temptation for the commission of frauds. The fair trader is doubly injured by them; he is injured by the reduction he is obliged to submit to in the price of his commodity, in consequence of the competition with the smuggler, and almost to a greater degree from the restrictions which are necessarily imposed upon him for the protection of the revenue. These oblige him to manufacture not according to his judgment, but as directed by law; the ignorant and intelligent are thus placed upon the same footing, and the dishonest or fraudulent trader is in a more advantageous position than either. The success which has attended the reduction of the duty from 28*l.* to 14*l.* 14*s.* per ton proves the truth of these observations, and could this amount be further reduced, so that, like the penny postage, soap should be within the reach of all, no one who has studied the statistics of this manufacture can doubt but that in a short time, by lessening fraud, and increasing consumption, a larger revenue would be produced. The quantity of soap charged with duty for *home consumption* had been decreasing from 1828 to 1832, the year preceding the reduction, when the duty was charged upon 91,000,000 lbs. In 1834, the year after the reduction, it increased to 104,796,000 lbs., showing an increase of 14 per cent. in two years. It has since gradually increased to 127,000,000 lbs. in 1840. This quantity, however, it is believed does not indicate accurately the total quantity made. The population of Great Britain is now 18,540,000. The most accurate calculations prove that the consumption of soap in the families of artizans earning from twenty to thirty shillings per week is 10 lb. per head per annum, and in families above this class from 12 lbs. to 25 lbs. per head. Now, the quantity used per head in 1840 was 6⅓ lbs., a smaller quantity than is used in workhouses or prisons, or than is allowed to soldiers; but if half only of the population are in such circumstances as to use the quantity ascertained, by very extended inquiry, to be used by artizans, and making no allowance for the extra quantity used by the other classes, we are driven to the conclusion either that nearly one-half of our population use no soap, or that a very large quantity is made and not charged with duty. To these facts the attention of the Excise is now directed. A superior class of officers is being introduced, and it appears likely that whilst the maker will no longer be subject to unnecessary or vexatious restrictions at the caprice of an exciseman, greater security will be afforded to the revenue.

We must now return to the factory, and having noticed the arrangement of coppers, boilers, engines, frames, moulds, cisterns, pumps, &c., it may be well to give such an account as the nature and object of this paper permit, of the operations conducted therein, and of the steps by which certain raw materials are converted into the well-known forms of soap and candles. Strictly speaking, there is a great deal of chemical nicety involved in the manufacture, both in theory and practice; but this is not the place where such matters can be consistently treated in a scientific manner. A rapid sketch of the nature and sources of the materials employed, and of their gradual transformation into the manufactured articles, will fill up the measure of our object.

Soap is designated in the 'Penny Cyclopædia' as a compound derived from the union between fat or oily substances and alkalis; and the nature of its formation is expressed in the following terms: – "It has been found by Chevreul that different varieties of fatty matter consist chiefly of two parts: one hard, to which he gave the name of stearin; and the other soft, which he termed olein. He also discovered that stearin is composed of stearic acid, and a peculiar principle, which, on account of its sweet taste, he named glycerin. When, in the manufacture of soap, an alkali (soda for example) is heated with tallow, the soda gradually dislodges the glycerin from combination with the stearic and oleic acids, and by combining with them, forms soap, or, in other words, a compound of stearate and oleate of soda, and the glycerin remains in solution." That the manufacture of this substance from the two classes of ingredients here mentioned has been long known is sufficiently indicated by a circumstance mentioned by Mr. Parkes in his 'Chemical Essays:' – "On examining the excavations that were made on the spot where this famous city (Pompeii) formerly stood, a complete soapboiler's shop was discovered, with soap in it, which had evidently been made by the combination of oil and an alkali. This soap was still perfect, though it had been manufactured more than seventeen hundred years."

There is a curious account of this trade in a small pamphlet, printed for Nicholas Bourne, in 1641, entitled 'A Short and True Narrative concerning the Soap

Business.' It contains an account of a patent granted to a Company for the exclusive manufacture of soap, under the title of the 'Governor, Assistants, and Fellows of the Society of Soapmakers of Westminster' (1622), on condition of their paying to his majesty 4*l*. per ton on 5000 tons annually. The manufacturers of that day (twenty in number) refused to join and acknowledge this Company; whereupon the Company obtained a proclamation forbidding, amongst other things, the sale of soap which had not been assayed by the Company. An information was then exhibited in the Star Chamber (1633) against sixteen London makers for opposing and affronting the letters patent; to which the defendants pleaded and demurred, &c., and after much discussion (all the defendants having been committed to prison for having put in their answer one day too late) the judges certified "all the answer except the first four words and last ten as fit to be expunged;" and it was decreed that the defendants be imprisoned during his majesty's pleasure, and fined in various sums from 1500*l*. to 500*l*. All were sent to prison. Fourteen remained there for forty weeks, and two died in prison. These tyrannical acts were followed by various proclamations and orders in council restricting the manufacture of soap except by the patentees, and fixing the price at which soap should be sold, and the materials from which it should be made. In 1635 many other soapmakers were committed to prison, and greater power was given by proclamation to the patentees upon their covenanting to pay 6*l*. per ton on five thousands tons annually. In a short time, however, the patentees, having "vexed the whole kingdom with their soap for three years," obtained a warrant from his majesty (1637) for 40,000*l*. for giving up the patent, and 3000*l*. for their houses, and obliged the soapmakers of London to pay them 20,000*l*. for their materials, so that they might have use of their trade again, of which they had been deprived. Little is known of the trade from this time to 1704, when Queen Anne imposed the first Excise duty. Several pamphlets and statements, on half-sheets, are to be found in the British Museum, containing petitions to be relieved from taxes, &c., but there is no account of the quantity manufactured.

As there are many kinds of fat and oil, and two very distinct kinds of alkali employed, it naturally follows that the soap will possess different qualities, and present different appearances, according to the ingredients.

Mottled soap is made from tallow, soda, a little 'kitchen-stuff,' a minute quantity of salt, and water. Its analysis is – alkali, 6·5; grease, 62·5; water, 31·0: total, 100. The tallow principally employed in the soap-factories of England is brought from Russia, and is exported from thence in a solid state in barrels. So large a quantity of this substance is used in England, that about thirteen hundred thousand cwts. are imported every year, yielding to the revenue somewhere about two hundred thousand pounds sterling. This supply is obtained principally from Russia, five-sevenths of whose exported tallow are sent to England. The tallow arrives in this country in a tolerably pure state, and requires no preparation previous to its employment in making soap. The heterogeneous substance known to domestic servants and 'dealers in marine-stores' by the name of kitchen-stuff, although very impure, is capable of being cleansed and refined, and used in the same manner and for the same purposes as tallow: it is heated in a copper, strained, and otherwise freed from the extraneous substances which are mingled with the tallow. It is only in the coarser kinds of soap that this material is used.

The alkali used for mottled soap is soda, the gradual changes in the production of which form a curious episode in the history of the soap manufacture. Although the form in which the alkali is used by the manufacturer is that of caustic soda, almost or entirely free from any acids, yet the state in which it is sold is that of a carbonate, more or less mingled with impurities. The barilla and kelp were until lately the only sources from which this alkali was derived; the one of foreign production, and the other British. Barilla is a kind of ash obtained by burning a South-European plant called the Salsola soda, which plant is cultivated with great care by the Spaniards and the Italians. A few years since there were 6000 tons imported annually from Spain, Sicily, and Sardinia; and formerly the quantity was much greater.

Kelp, another form of the carbonate of soda, alluded to above, is the ash remaining after the burning of sea-weed, and was introduced into the London market for the use of the soap trade by Mr. Hawes, the father of the members of the present firm. It contains only a little of the alkaline salt, but a large quantity of common salt, some salts of potash, and other substances. Previous to the year 1822, a duty of eleven or twelve shillings per cwt. being laid on barilla, a considerable quantity of kelp was made on the coasts of Ireland; and about a century ago from the present time the manufacture was begun in Scotland, where, in consequence, the land in certain localities by the sea-shore became greatly advanced in value, very large annual revenues being derived from estates which had previously been wholly unproductive. Dr. M'Culloch gives a graphic account of the kelp manufacture in its most flourishing state: – "The kelp season had now commenced, and the whole shore was one continued line of fires; the grey smoke streaming away from each on the surface of the water, till, mixing with the breeze, it diffused its odoriferous haze over all the surrounding atmosphere . . . The weeds, being cut by the sickle at low-water, are brought on shore by a very simple and ingenious process. A rope of heath or birch is laid beyond them, and the ends being carried up beyond the high-water mark, the whole floats as the tide rises, and thus, by shortening the ropes, is compelled to settle above the wash of the sea, whence it is conveyed to dry land on horseback. The more quickly it is dried the better the produce; and when dry it is burned in coffers, generally constructed with stone, sometimes merely excavated in the earth. In Orkney the latter are preferred. As twenty-four tons of weed at a medium are required to form a ton of kelp, it is easy to conceive the labour employed for this quantity in the several processes of cutting, landing, carrying, drying, stacking, and burning."

How strangely do variations in one branch of commerce affect the arrangements of another! Twenty years ago common table-salt was sold at four or five pence per pound; but when the duty was wholly removed, this price fell to one halfpenny. Manufacturers immediately turned their attention to this substance, as a source whence saleable commodities might be produced. Common salt is formed of chlorine and sodium, and by chemical agency the two can be separated, and each one made to combine with some other substance. Such has been the case in respect to the soda used in the soap-manufacture: by far the greater part of it is produced from the sodium which forms one of the ingredients in common salt, the decomposition of which in sufficient quantities to supply the soap and glass makers has for some years employed large capitals and many hundreds of workmen. This alkali, or 'white ash,' as it is called, made from salt, has driven kelp and barilla out of use. It is produced by treating common salt in a peculiar manner with sulphuric acid, from which there result muriatic acid and sulphate of soda; this sulphate is converted into a carbonate of soda by contact with carbon; and, lastly, the carbonic acid is driven from the carbonate, leaving the soda in a caustic state, and forming, when in solution with water, the liquor which soapmakers call a ley or lye. The ley is pumped out of the vats into the boilers, where it is mixed with the requisite quantity of tallow, and any other fatty substance which may be employed. The mixture is then heated by steam, and well boiled, an attendant stirring the mass occasionally. After a time the tallow is found to have combined with a portion of the ley, including all the alkali, and the remaining, or spent ley, is then of no further use in the process. It is pumped up from beneath the soap by a pump whose barrel descends to the bottom of the copper; and a fresh supply of ley is introduced. Again and again is this process repeated, new leys being introduced after the spent liquor is withdrawn, and the leys being used in a stronger or more alkaline state as the process advances towards completion. When the soap is nearly finished, that peculiar appearance to which it owes the name of 'mottled' soap is given to it by sprinkling upon the surface a small quantity of very dense and strong ley; this percolates slowly through the mass of soap, and leaves in its track those dark coloured veins which constitute mottling.

When the tallow and alkali have completely formed into soap, and have attained a proper consistency, the soap is laded from the coppers in buckets or pails, and conveyed to the frame-room, where it is poured into the frames. These frames have, until within the last few years, been made wholly of wood, but cast-iron frames are now occasionally used. The wooden frame is a kind of well or cistern, formed of a pile or heap of frames laid one on another. Each separate part consists of a rectangle of four bars of wood, measuring internally forty-five inches by fifteen; and these rectangles are laid one upon another to a height of ten or twelve feet. The bars of the rectangles are so neatly squared and smoothed, as to fit closely one upon another. The mottled soap is poured into these frames until full, and there allowed to remain till cold, which occupies more or less time according to the state of the weather.

When the mass of soap is cold and solidified, some iron fastenings, with which the rectangles of the frame were firmly bound together, are loosened, and the rectangles removed one by one, each one being lifted off the mass of soap. The soap is then presented to view as a compact body, whose dimensions are those of the interior cavity of the frame. Some of these masses of soap weigh three or four thousand pounds each. The next process is to cut the mass into slabs or slices

Figure 78.2 [Filling Soap-frames.]

Figure 78.3 [Cutting Soap.]

about three inches in thickness. To effect this a man marks the surface of the soap with parallel lines, by means of sharp points inserted in a gauge-stick; and two men draw a piece of wire through the soap in the direction of each mark, one man holding the wire by handles at the ends, and the other guiding the wire to the proper marks. The slabs are next taken to a machine in the form of a hollow box open at the top, with vertical crevices passing from the top nearly to the bottom of two opposite sides. The slabs being ranged horizontally in this box, a piece of wire is passed down each of the crevices in succession, cutting through the slabs in its progress. As the crevices are about three inches apart, it follows that the slabs are cut into bars about three inches wide and the same in depth, the length being about fifteen inches. These are the bars in which soap is sold in the shops. After the cutting, the bars of soap are piled one upon another in the form of a wall, and kept in that state for a certain time until required to be removed from the factory.

For curd or white soap the same general description will suffice as applies to mottled, with some minor exceptions. As its whiteness is one of its chief characteristics, the tallow is selected with more care, and no ingredients are introduced which will be liable to deteriorate the colour. The process of mottling is in this case dispensed with; but the general outline of processes, such as the de-carbonising of the alkali, the melting and boiling of the ingredients, the framing, the cutting, &c., is much the same as in the manufacture of mottled soap.

Yellow soap is less expensive than white or mottled; and it owes this cheapness, as well as its colour, and certain properties which it possesses, to the large employment of palm oil and resin in its composition. Although resin is in appearance very different from tallow, yet it possesses the same property of melting and combining with an alkali, and forming a soap by the combination. The analysis differs little in pure soap from that of mottled, and consists generally of 6 alkali, 62 grease, 32 water. Inferior soap, although in appearance nearly the same, contains from 10 to 20 per cent. more water, the knowledge of which will, we hope, be useful to our readers. The nature and source of resin are simply as follows: – From several species of the pine-tree there exudes, when an incision is made, a grey-coloured semi-fluid substance, known in commerce by the name of turpentine. This turpentine has the distinctive names of Venice, Strassburg, Carpathian, Canada, Cyprus, and common turpentine, according to the countries whence it is brought, and the species of pine from which it exudes. By distillation common turpentine yields the oil or essence of turpentine, and the solid residue constitutes resin.

Palm-oil is obtained from the oil-palm of Guinea, cultivated in the western parts of Africa. The fruit of this tree is ovoid, about the size of a pigeon's egg, with its outer fleshy covering of a golden yellow colour. The oil is obtained by bruising the fleshy part of the fruit, and subjecting the bruised paste to boiling water in wooden mortars: an oil of an orange-yellow colour separates, which concretes, when cool, to the consistence of butter, and has, when fresh, the smell of violets, and a slightly sweetish taste. The Africans use this oil in cookery, and for anointing the body; but when imported into England, it is used in soap-making, in perfumery, and in medicine, for which purposes two or three hundred thousand cwts. are used annually. When brought to the soap-factory it is in casks in a solid state; and the mode adopted for extracting it, is to place the cask over a trough with its bunghole downwards, and to pass a steam-pipe into the cask, by which means the palm-oil is brought to a liquid state and made to flow out of the cask. The oil is afterwards conveyed to a vat, where it is bleached by a chemical process. The use of this oil in soap, or wherever it can be introduced, is a matter of as much or more importance to the philanthropist and the statesman than to the soap manufacturer. The latter looks at it merely as a good and cheap ingredient; the philanthropist views it as the most powerful instrument he can employ in the abolition of the traffic in slaves; the statesman feels that it secures to our manufacturers a most lucrative barter trade, free from fiscal regulations, which impede our commerce with old states. Every cargo of oil bought with our manufactures does more to impede the traffic in slaves than a host of treaties and protocols with European states.

The mode of preparing the alkali for yellow soap, the process of melting and boiling it with the tallow and resin, and the general routine of manufacture, differ but little from those relating to mottled soap. The frames used are, however, very different. They are made of five pieces of cast-iron: one for the bottom, two for the sides, and two for the ends. By a simple mode of fastening at the edges, the whole can be quickly put together, so as to form a sort of well or cistern, between four and five feet high, forty-five inches long, and fifteen wide. Into these frames the yellow soap is poured, the contents of each being about fifteen cwt. These frames are not only put together and taken to pieces with more ease than the wooden frames, but the iron being a good conductor of heat, the process of cooling is effected more rapidly. The cutting of yellow soap into slabs and bars is effected in the same way as that of mottled.

Soft soap, a commodity which is almost exclusively used in the woollen manufacture, differs considerably from hard soap in its ingredients, its consistence, and its general appearance. Both the alkaline and the oleaginous ingredients are different from those employed in hard soaps; since potash is employed instead of soda, and oils are more largely used than tallow. This soap, when of good quality, consists of alkali 9, oil and tallow 42, water 49; total 100. The potash employed in the soap-manufacture is brought principally from Canada and the United States.[1] The carbonate of potash is rendered caustic, that is, free from carbonic acid, by a process similar to that adopted for the soda alkali; and several of the vats in the soap factory are employed for this purpose.

The oils employed in soft soap, whether whale, seal, olive, or linseed, are procured in the usual way, from the blubber of the two former, the fruit of the third, and the seed of the fourth, and need no particular description. Nor does the mode of combining the ingredients to form this kind of soap require any lengthened notice. It may, however, be remarked, that instead of supplying successive portions of alkaline ley to the boiler, and pumping out the spent ley at intervals, the whole of the ley is supplied at once, and kept boiling with the oils and tallow until the soap is made. The use of the tallow employed is to give consistency to the oil soap, the general quality of which is indicated by the gradual formation of white specks throughout the soap, which arise from the combination of the tallow with the salts of potash. Soft soap, as its name imports, has a consistence which renders useless the processes of framing and cutting: it is placed in barrels or casks, when finished, and in that state sent from the factory.

With respect to the large variety of soaps known as 'toilet,' 'fancy,' or 'perfumed' soaps, little need be said here. They are generally made from good white soap, which is remelted and modified in its form and appearance by perfumes and other substances. None of these fancy soaps are made at this factory; they are either the production of persons who devote their attention principally to the manufacture, or else of perfumers, who apply the fanciful terms – 'soap à la rose,' 'soap au bouquet,' 'cinnamon soap,' 'Windsor soap,' 'musk soap,' 'almond soap,' &c., to their manufactures.

Note

1 See 'Penny Magazine,' No. 573, for an account of the manufacture of potash.

79

'BY ORDER OF THE BATH', PEARS' SOAP

Unilever Archives, ref. AFP 12/3/1 [n.d.]

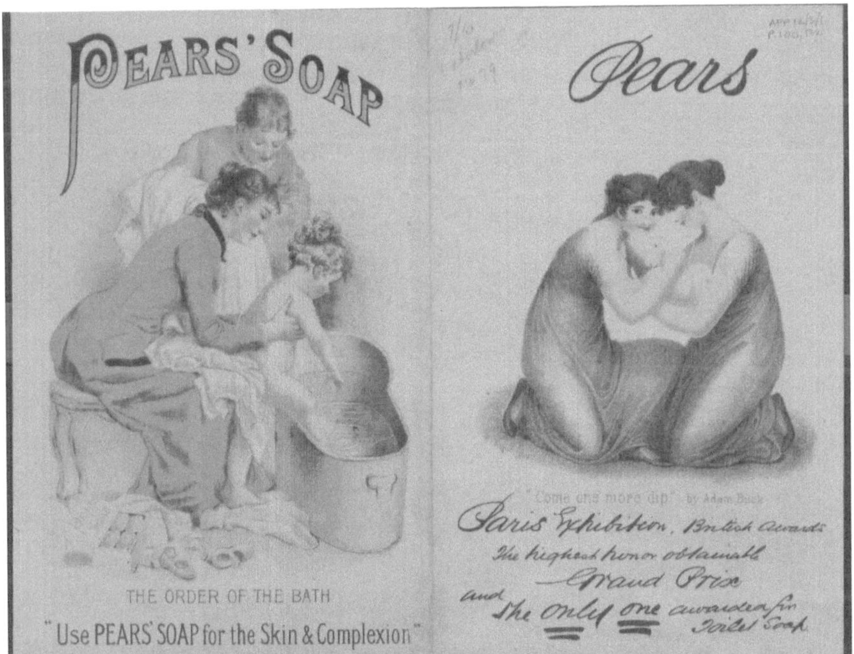

DOI: 10.4324/9781315400105-96

80

'SOME GOOD REASONS FOR USING SUNLIGHT SOAP'

Wellcome Collection, Unilever Archives, Lever Brothers, Ltd. [c. 1890]

Sunlight soap for washing dogs

Figure 80.1

DOI: 10.4324/9781315400105-97

The most successful Exhibitors and Prizewinners USE ONLY SUNLIGHT SOAP for preparing their dogs for Exhibition. *The Fanciers' Chronicle* for November 27th, 1891, says: – "As an article adapted for canine ablutions it knows no superior. It lathers very freely, cleanses the hair thoroughly, and does not injure the condition of the skin; three attributes which should certainly combine to make it popular amongst dog men."

Sunlight soap for cage birds and poultry

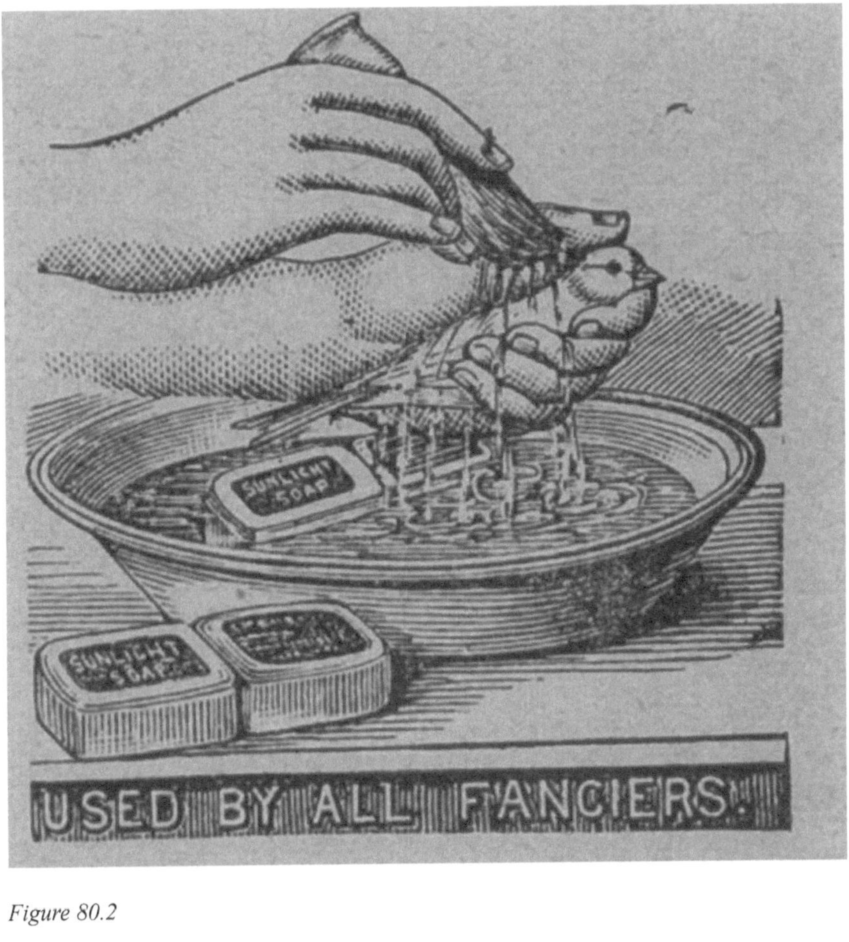

Figure 80.2

No other soap is used so largely for preparing our feathered pets for victory on the Show Bench. It does its work effectually in little time, and thus produces little or no fatigue to the birds. All who have tried it pronounce it best for the purpose.

The Sub-Editor of *Fur and Feather*, on October 5th, 1892, writes: – "I have used SUNLIGHT SOAP constantly for the past six years for preparing Poultry, Pigeons and Cage Birds for Exhibition, with the result that I have won many hundreds of prizes with birds washed with it."

Sunlight soap for the farm

Figure 80.3

Used in the Dairy it will keep Churns, Cheese Vats and Milk Pans beautifully bright and clean. Used in the Stable it will keep manes and tails clean and silky, and heal sores and scratches. Mr. Robert Evans, Stud Groom to Capt. Beckett, wrote us in November, 1890: – "I find SUNLIGHT SOAP is capital for Stable use, and strongly recommend it."

Sunlight soap for the household

Figure 80.4

The easiest method of performing the household duties should be considered by every good housewife, so that leisure for reading and social duties may be found. The use of SUNLIGHT SOAP brings Less Labour, Greater Comfort, and by its aid everything in the house from cellar to garret can be made as bright as a new pin. For Spring Cleaning it is invaluable. *The Young Ladies' Journal*, July, 1891, says: – "It is the best thing we know for household use."

Sunlight soap for the laundry

Those who use SUNLIGHT SOAP in the Laundry will find it all they could possibly desire. It gives the linen a beautifully white appearance, and is specially to be recommended for washing flannel goods, delicate cambrics and laces. *The Christian Herald* in its issue of January 26, 1893, says: – "Clothes which are washed with it have a peculiar freshness."

Figure 80.5

Sunlight soap for the toilet

Figure 80.6

Medical Men testify to its perfect suitability for the toilet. SIR CHARLES A. CAMERON, M.D., writes that he employs the soap himself. C. M. CAMPBELL, M.D., says: – "I find that SUNLIGHT SOAP fulfils all the indications required in a soap for toilet use." STANLEY WILDE, L.R.C.P., says he never used a pleasanter or more cleanly soap. *The People's Friend* for May 29th, 1893, writes as follows: – "It will not crack the skin, but will help to make the hands soft and beautiful."

81

IMAGE: 'VINOLIA SOAP'

Unilever Collections, Unilever Art, Archives and Records Management, Port Sunlight, Archive ref. AFP 12/4/125 [c. 1890]

Figure 81.1

DOI: 10.4324/9781315400105-98

4.5

Candles

DOI: 10.4324/9781315400105-99

4.5 Candles

Campbell Morfit, *A Treatise on Chemistry Applied to the Manufacture of Soap and Candles*, (Philadelphia: [n.p], 1856), pp. 17–21.

William Crookes, 'Preface' to Michael Faraday, *The Chemical History of a Candle: A Course of Lectures Delivered Before an Audience at the Royal Institution* (London: Chatto and Windus, 1875), pp. v–vii.

Joseph Hatton, 'Candle-Making', *The English Illustrated Magazine*, Vol. 105 (Jun 1892), pp. 703–712.

Image: James McNeill Whistler, 'Price's Candle-Works' 1876/77, The Metropolitan Museum of Art.

Like soap, candles were originally a homemade object improved and made cheap by industrial processes. Prior to the nineteenth century, illumination was largely supplied by candles made either at home or under the aegis of two guilds established in the Middle Ages: The Worshipful Company of Tallow Chandlers for candles made from animal fat and oil used domestically and The Worshipful Company of Wax Chandlers for the beeswax candles used by churches and the wealthy. Even cheaper, stronger smelling tallow was beyond the reach of labouring households, many of which would have relied on homemade rush lights.[1] The eighteenth-century whaling boom introduced spermaceti, which burned odourless and bright like beeswax but was much cheaper. The French scientist Michel Chevreul's pioneering work with animal fats in 1825 resulted in the production of stearic acid, followed in the 1850s by paraffin distilled by James Young. In the 1830s, Manchester pewterer Joseph Morgan patented a series of 'candle-mould' machines, which helped to transform the candle into a uniform, mass-produced object. The sources here present manufacturing as an established process but reveal different attitudes towards the candle: it is represented variously as aesthetic illumination, nostalgic simplicity and chemical innovation.

Morfit's *A Treatise on Chemistry* configures the candle as emblematic of scientific progress and perfection. Morfit was a significant chemist known to the public on both sides of the Atlantic. He studied in Georgetown before moving to Philadelphia and then London in 1861, where he became a fellow of the Chemical Society of London and the Institute of Chemistry. His *Treatise* is one of his many well-known books on the practical applications of chemistry. He produced similar guides to the chemical manufacture of perfume (1847), manures (1872) and fertilisers (1873), alongside more general guides to chemistry. His *Treatise* is aimed at general readers, perhaps inspired by the needs of working students at the Maryland Institute for the Promotion of the Mechanic Arts, where Morfit founded a Chemical Department in the early 1850s. Like the other sources in this section, technical terms are carefully explained and chapters on candles (dipped, moulded, stearin, spermaceti, wax, composite, paraffin and patent) are highly detailed. For Morfit, both soap and candle manufacture are 'useful arts' in the 'public interest'. Echoing John Ruskin (see 'Cutlery'), Morfit is lyrical on how 'the spark' of science is given lustre by the skilled hand of the artisan. The result is an object with the power to improve human experience and develop the human character.

For the journalist Joseph Hatton visiting Price's Patent Candles Limited for *The Illustrated English Magazine*, the candle becomes a cultural and aesthetic object steeped in 'English romance'. Hatton's travelogue is distinctive in that the bulk of his discussion is reserved for candles rather than soap, a reversal of the usual approach to the twin manufactures (as both Morfit and Hatton's texts demonstrate, candles and soap shared many of the same raw materials and processes and were often manufactured together; see also the preceding section on 'Soap' in this volume, particularly the extract from *The Penny Magazine*). Even in 1897, when oil lamps, gas lights and to a lesser extent electric lights were established, candlelight remains 'supreme', appealing to the aesthete and the housekeeper, as well as to the inventor and the 'mechanical expert'. He notes that candles no longer sputter but burn with a 'steady' light. As Hatton proceeds through the factory, his tone suggests that he is journeying through a chemical wonderland where scientists are hard at work in 'candleland'. They fight with paraffin and cocoanut oil, attacking them with sulphuric acid to extract glycerine or 'the Cinderella of Science, or the fairy of the autoclave'. The application of already known principles of stearin extraction to dark-coloured fats and oils was what made Price's famous and is, as Hatton patriotically notes, a British innovation not yet implemented in France. The perfect candle is 'white, transparent, brilliant', brought about by a careful blend of paraffin and stearin. The rate of production only adds to the sense of wonder; Price's was the largest candle manufacturer in the world at this time, with 400 varieties of candles made in the factory. The article is illustrated by William Henry Margetson in vignettes with soft, feathered edges, lending romance to the workers depicted; the factory itself was sketched by James McNeill Whistler (reproduced here) at the start of the period in which the artist would produce his famous Nocturnes.

A similarly romantic image can be found on the cover of *The Chemical History of a Candle*, the printed edition of one of Michael Faraday's Christmas lectures for 'juveniles' at the Royal Institution, which he launched in 1825. Shimmering golden light arcs from a lit candle, representing not candle manufacture but the chemistry of combustion. In this particular lecture series, his last, given in 1860, Faraday stated that left to his own inclination he would return to the subject of candle composition and history 'every year'. There is no better or more open door, he states, through which to enter the study of that great Victorian phenomenon: natural philosophy. William Crookes, a scientist who later became president of the Society for Psychical Research, focuses on the object itself in his 'Preface', gesturing towards the style of it-narratives by imagining the stories that candles could tell. Crookes' view that the candle flame is the Light of Science, a torch to light up the 'dark places of nature', echoes the articles by Hatton and Morfit.

82

CAMPBELL MORFIT, *A TREATISE ON CHEMISTRY APPLIED TO THE MANUFACTURE OF SOAP AND CANDLES*

(Philadelphia: [n.p.], 1856), pp. 17–21

The history of the art and its relations to science

THERE are no two articles bearing a more important and direct relation with the lighter range of domestic economy, than soap and candles. Their consumption throughout the globe amounts to thousands of millions of pounds annually, and extends to all classes, the high and the low, the rich and the poor. Though luxuries, indeed, they are alike necessities of life to all; and so closely are health, comfort, and even morality connected with cleanliness, that it has been aptly proposed by Liebig to estimate the wealth and civilization of a people by the quantity of soap which they consume. Neither soap nor candles leave any residue by which their value may be renewed, but are wholly exhausted in the use: the trade, therefore, which produces them becomes a subject of public interest; and no effort should be spared to rescue it from the slow progress of mere handicraft, and to perfect it by the rules of that science which is so intimately blended with its most practical details.

Improvements in the useful arts follow in proportion to their demand, or to that proper encouragement which is the stimulus to merit and industry to accomplish still more. The trades no longer now, as in former times, are viewed merely as mechanical operations, but labor and learning unite to work out subjects of beauty as well as utility. Science and art are, in fact, co-dependents – the one dealing in the mental and the other in the physical realities of life. It would be difficult to say which is most entitled to the common thanks of mankind, for if one begins the race, the other as surely carries it to its destined end. Scarcely an improvement in any of the great exhibitions of human ingenuity but can be traced to the operations of science; nor can a spark be struck from the mind of science to which the skilful hand of the artisan may not impart an additional lustre. Prometheus, who in fable made the mechanism of a human being, is the true figure of art; while the fire which he stole from heaven to animate its being may be said to represent the vitality of science.

DOI: 10.4324/9781315400105-100

The sciences would appear to be precursors of the arts, at least of those in the highest state of improvement, from the fact that it is their province to suggest or mark out those principles which it is the business of art to illustrate. Speculative discoveries may sometimes arise by chance, as the searcher in the quarry may light by surprise upon a vein of gold; but though the workman, whose right hand knoweth its cunning, may effect good results without his understanding the reason, yet they are invariably the consequence of fixed rules, which it would have greatly facilitated his progress to have known. The caprices and uncertainties in processes, so often complained of in manufactories, owe their origin to this very ignorance in regard to the theory or principles of the art.

There is no incongruity between occupations, however manual, and a knowledge of the principles which are interwoven with the work or its products. Artisans are like travellers, though on different roads; but in every route of life, whether operative or scientific, the course is the more facile as the instructed mind is enabled to shed its light upon the pathway. It is by continuing in the steady tracks of their calling that good men, aided by many helps from science and from study, have advanced themselves to high places among their fellow-men, and are enabled thus practically to illustrate the dignity of labor and the value of education.

The theory which accounts for the union of oils and alkalies in the formation of soaps, or the decomposition of fats into their crystalline acids, is as abstruse as that which expounds some of the most refined instances of affinities. The manufacture of soaps and candles is, therefore, strictly scientific, and they who desire to advance in that art must not merely make, but make understandingly; so that each result may be an advancing lesson for their own profit, while it enables them to repay the benefits they have derived from chemistry, by furnishing new lights to others who may be followers in the same path.

True, soap is a definite chemical compound of one or more of the fat acids, with an alkaline base, soda being the basis element of *hard*, and potassa of *soft* soaps; and both kinds were known to the ancients. Soap owes its cleansing property to what is called *detergency*, or, in other words, a power of aiding water to dissolve and remove the greasy dirt of the clothes and skin, for washing which it is almost exclusively used.

The term soap has its derivation from the Latin word *sapo*, which is corrupted from the German *sepe*, now written *seife*. The Germans derived their knowledge of the art from the Gauls, to whom Pliny ascribes its origin; for though, in periods anterior to the birth of Christ, the Hebrews, Egyptians, and Greeks washed their clothes, it was with free alkali, and by rubbing and stamping. From the Germans it passed probably to the Romans; and Miss Stark, in her letters from Italy, speaks of a complete soap-maker's shop being found in the ruins of Pompeii, destroyed by an eruption from Mount Vesuvius in the first Christian century.

The art, in more modern times, dates back, in England, to an unknown epoch prior to 1500. During Queen Anne's reign, about 1710, soap was made in London, it is said, very much after the method at present followed by some old-fashioned soap-makers – that is, with potash and salt; for barilla and kelp, two species of crude soda made by incinerating sea-shore plants, and much used previous to the introduction of soda ash, were not then known, for that purpose at least. At what time it was brought to this country is not stated; but certain it is that the great impulse which the art received originated in 1804, from the discovery of Leblanc, by which artificial soda, commercially known as soda ash, was economically supplied and introduced to the trade from the extensive chemical works of Mr. James Muspratt, England. This grand discovery, and the equally important investigations of Chevreul in 1811, by which the proximate constituents of the fats were exactly demonstrated, and their practical applications designated, gave to the soap and candle manufacture that consistence and method by which its present improved condition has been attained, and which elevates it to the distinction of a scientific art.

Much in the success of the chandler, as in other operative trades, depends upon his method and the economy of his processes. To the former he will be indebted for whatever approach he may make to perfection in his art, and to the latter for that saving in detail which, after all, is the element in the sum total of fortune. Saving is accomplished not merely by the careful use of the ingredients in a trade, because if it is not upon a good basis, a proper or scientific plan, no caution can realize a gain. It is by the completeness of the system, and the agencies of an instructed experience, and an intimate knowledge of what, as to time, labor, and materials, will produce the best results, that saving is reached. A mill per pound, in any article, is seemingly a small item when confined to a mere unit, but, when extended, it adds ten per centum in the general profit.

The advantages of the special mode by which a manufacturer advances the quality of his articles is perhaps of greater benefit, because reputation follows in proportion to that advance; and when to a high reputation is super-added the economy of a scientific system of working, the enterprising man has two prizes within his own command – good name and fortune.

It is for these reasons that the workman must seek all information he can conveniently find; he must study the reasonings and listen to the suggestions of others; and when he ascertains that the practice of his business may be improved from such sources, he must seize the lights held out to him by those workers, and apply and extend them, with the promulgation of his own improvements, to the rest of his fellow-laborers.

In this way a perpetual fund of benefits will be spread about, and, like a spirit of true humanity teaching by good example, it will descend in the form of a progressive benefit to distant generations.

Note

1 For a discussion of the profound impact that candles – particularly tallow – had on Victorian reading practices, see Simon Elliott, 'Reading by Artificial Light in the Victorian Age' in Matthew Bradley and Juliet John (eds.), *Reading and the Victorians* (Farnham: Ashgate, 2015), pp. 15–30. Anna Henchman also uses tallow candles to offer an olfactory reading of Dickens's *Bleak House*; see Anna Henchman, 'Tallow Candles and Meaty Air in *Bleak House*', *19: Interdisciplinary Studies in the Long Nineteenth Century*, 25, <doi: 10.16995/ntn.794> [accessed 12th January 2018].

83

WILLIAM CROOKES, 'PREFACE' TO MICHAEL FARADAY, *THE CHEMICAL HISTORY OF A CANDLE: A COURSE OF LECTURES DELIVERED BEFORE AN AUDIENCE AT THE ROYAL INSTITUTION*

(London: Chatto and Windus, 1875), pp. v–vii

Preface

FROM the primitive pine-torch to the paraffin candle, how wide an interval! between them how vast a contrast! The means adopted by man to illuminate his home at night, stamp at once his position in the scale of civilisation. The fluid bitumen of the far East, blazing in rude vessels of baked earth; the Etruscan lamp, exquisite in form, yet ill adapted to its office; the whale, seal, or bear fat, filling the hut of the Esquimaux or Lap with odour rather than light; the huge wax candle on the glittering altar, the range of gas lamps in our streets, – all have their stories to tell. All, if they could speak (and, after their own manner, they can), might warm our hearts in telling, how they have ministered to man's comfort, love of home, toil, and devotion.

Surely, among the millions of fire-worshippers and fire-users who have passed away in earlier ages, *some* have pondered over the mystery of fire; perhaps some clear minds have guessed shrewdly near the truth. Think of the time man has lived in hopeless ignorance: think that only during a period which might be spanned by the life of one man, has the truth been known.

Atom by atom, link by link, has the reasoning chain been forged. Some links, too quickly and too slightly made, have given way, and been replaced by better work; but now the great phenomena are known – the outline is correctly and firmly drawn – cunning artists are filling in the rest, and the child who masters these Lectures knows more of fire than Aristotle did.

The candle itself is now made to light up the dark places of nature; the blowpipe and the prism are adding to our knowledge of the earth's crust; but the torch must come first.

Among the readers of this book some few may devote themselves to increasing the stores of knowledge: the Lamp of Science *must* burn. "*Alere flammam.*"

W. CROOKES.

 DOI: 10.4324/9781315400105-101

84

JOSEPH HATTON, 'CANDLE-MAKING'

The English Illustrated Magazine,
Vol. 105 (Jun 1892), pp. 703–712

AT Battersea the Thames lays aside its holiday attire to become a strictly business river. Here we are on the outskirts of the capital. The pleasure boat backs water at Kew. Villas with flower gardens dipping into the stream itself have disappeared. Loungers on Battersea Bridge do not pause to gaze upon gaily-decorated house-boats and festive wherries. Trade and commerce and busy life occupy both sides of the river. The penny steamer is fussing up and down stream. Lighters packed with merchandise and labouring barges lumber along with the yellow tide. Everything indicates approximation to the great city of which Battersea is a quaint, picturesque suburb that still makes a sturdy if ineffectual struggle against the money-making encroachments of the time. Invaded by manufacturers, noisy with tram-car and omnibus, cut up with streets of sombre brick and stucco, blackened with fuel for the factories, Battersea still preserves landmarks of ancient house and garden, of literary state and social dignity. Quiet nooks for learned ease and contemplative leisure are still to be found in the village, with its church and schools, its spreading cedars, and its other grave old trees that look down from their umbrageous heights upon the changing world below them. The picturesqueness of the Thames itself seems to survive even the severest form of "modernity" about which the "realists" have so much to say. At low tide barges moored upon the mud, rickety boat-houses, informal landing stages, untidy hostelries that loom across the reeking banks, with here and there a sail creeping over the shallows, make up many a fascinating study of form and colour; and the innate romance that belongs to the English character may be trusted to keep alive the historic traditions of even the most unpromising surroundings, an instance of which struck me forcibly during a recent visit to the factories of Price's Patent Candle Company that have been so often mentioned in the scientific works of the day. Not attractive by reason of their tubular roofs and tall chimney stacks, the factory buildings are well known on the river. They cover an area of upwards of twelve acres, occupy two broad landing stages on the main stream, and have the advantage of being situated on both sides of a creek where the Company's lighters can ship and unship cargoes at their warehouse doors. Away on the Mersey at Bromborough pool the same firm have another extensive manufactory, but the variety of the operations at Battersea make the London works more interesting than those of Liverpool.

DOI: 10.4324/9781315400105-102

We were a little company of three, sometimes more; for during our tour of the works we made occasional fresh acquaintances with chiefs of departments and other officials, Mr. John Calderwood, the managing director, himself having courteously and with some useful suggestions started us on our way. A more difficult, albeit interesting, subject for popular literary treatment and illustration could hardly be selected than the manufacture of candles as it is carried on at Battersea, with an activity of experimental and practical science that exemplifies in a notable way the energy and skill necessary in these days to keep pace with competition, let alone the maintenance of a distinct supremacy in any art or manufacture.

The history of candles is the history of religion. The story of candle-making is a record of chemical and scientific progress. Candlemas Day originated with the Romans. They burnt candles in honour of the Goddess Februa, the mother of Mars. Pope Sergius, deeming it unwise to prohibit a practice of so long standing, made of it a Christian festival by enjoining a similar offering to the Virgin: hence Candlemas Day. An order in council under Queen Elizabeth prohibited this ceremony in the English Church. One who should sit down to fill in the details of the world's story between then and now would find himself engaged for a lifetime. It is bewildering to think of the varied illuminations that candles would shed upon his romantic and controversial pages.

On the other hand a volume might be compiled relating to the superstitions connected with candles. This would take us back to the once almost universal worship of the sun and fire. The splutter and "swealing" of candles, the curious process of combustion that goes on in the most primitive wicks, have given the world signs and omens from the earliest ages. A portion of the tallow rising up against the wick is still to many an omen of death; they call it a winding sheet. A disturbance of the flame without apparent cause is a sure harbinger of windy weather. The "corpse-candle" of the Welsh is, however, not a candle at all, but a gaseous exhalation that is said to start up from the earth, traversing without any visible agency the road upon which a man, whose death it presages, is walking.

When one thinks of "the good old days," so called, even the home-made rushlight that shed a glow upon the hearthstones of Gilbert White's classic village of Selborne is a star of the first magnitude compared with the smoky pine and reed torches and flambeaux with which palace and castle were illuminated in the middle ages. Small wax tapers were used in churches as early as the fourteenth century, "but," says Dr. John Yeats in his *Technical History of Commerce*, "they were considered even by princes as very costly." There were candles nevertheless in the thirteenth century, not equal to these clerical tapers but something of the character of the dip made by the old housewives of Selborne. The trade of the "tallow-chandler" is first mentioned in the reign of Edward I. By "the ancient laws" of gallant little Wales "the candle-bearer to royalty was allowed a piece of candle as long as the breadth of his hand and was entitled to the fragments, and enjoyed the delectable privilege of claiming all the tops on condition that he bit them off." In our own time a fortune that rose to the peerage began with the perquisite of candle-ends in a great official office. Travellers on the Continent even to-day have reason to know that large sums of money are made by foreign bonifaces out of *bougies*. I know a man, the soul of generosity in most things, who used to come home from his annual trip to France with a portmanteau full of candles, many of which had not been lighted, all of them having, however, been duly charged for in the bills at the highest possible rates. Gas and the electric light make no more difference to the Continental landlord touching that old tradition of *bougies* than they appear to make in respect of the general use of the light, which the Romans dedicated to Februa and Sergius rescued from heathenism to give artistic distinction to the altar and the sacred procession. One might have been forgiven for thinking that what the age of gas did not do in the destruction of the candle the new era of electricity would have completed. Not at all. The candle is still supreme. It has met competition with a remarkable power both of light and form. It has annexed in the way of manufacture the genius of the inventor and the art of the mechanical expert. It has appealed to the art-taste of the æsthete, and won the sympathy of the housekeeper. It has ceased to splutter; it has given up the gruesome habit of suggesting shrouds and coffins; it does not sweal; it gives a steady light; it is made in every size and shape. House-proud folk who love pictures, and cherish the colour of articles of *virtu*, have banished gas in favour of the candle, which is still to be seen in these days lighting the daintiest drawing-rooms, in cluster of sconce and chandelier. It would seem as if the more people use gas and electric lamps the more they require candles. This is no hap-hazard statement, no paradox thrown down in the course of a common-place essay: it is a fact attested by the severest statistics.

No firm in the world has done so much to maintain the popularity of the candle as that of Price's Patent Candle Company at Battersea. It is thirty years since Dr. Andrew Wynter in his *Social Bees* described candle-making at these works as "one of the most interesting sights in London." During that period the scientific production of candles had advanced as considerably as the demand for this varied class of manufacture, which now embraces between three and four hundred different kinds and sizes of lights, from the primitive dip to the finest hand-decorated wax.

Passing by busy shops where the firm's machines are made, taking no note of cooperages and box factories, turning his back upon stores of various kinds, and paying no heed to the steady rattle of printing machinery, our guide pilots us to the wharf where the paraffin is unloaded. It is brought from the docks by the company's lighters. Most notable are the barrels of crude yellow shale chiefly from America. It is of a light yellow colour, and contains about two to four per cent. of oil. From the quay the barrels go into the works, are broken open and the contents emptied into underground tanks that are heated by steam. When melted it is pumped into elevated tanks, and thence by pipes into the crystallising room. Here it is run into shallow pans and allowed to cool and crystallise. After crystallisation it is subjected to "the sweating process" (the only "sweating" the writer has yet encountered in his agreeable task of describing the national industries), invented by Mr. John Hodges, the foreman of this important department, and which is now generally adopted. The trays of crystallized blocks of paraffin are placed in steam-heated ovens. Here, packed in mats of cocoa-nut fibre, they are left to drain. The liquid that contains oil and colouring matter falls into underground tanks. The ovens are kept at a moderate temperature. Opened you see layers of cakes that are literally sweating through their fibrous packings, whitening and hardening. The liquid is carried off for further treatment, and the solid or purified paraffin is taken to the refinery, a great hall of tanks and retorts and mysterious pipes.

Here comes in one of those little romances of the laboratory that in works of this description must be continually cropping up to adorn what to the casual observer may appear very prosaic proceedings. Science has its fairy tales, and Battersea could supply more than one new subject for the ready and fanciful writer. Arrived at the refinery, it is found that certain impurities still cling to the seemingly regenerate paraffin; it has contracted objectionable associations which refuse to be shaken off. It is not allowable in human life to treat undesirable acquaintances as the chemist treats the debased associates of his purifying paraffin. To get rid of them the aid of certain chemical agents and allies are called in. They make short work of the intruder. But like the hired assassins of melodrama they seek to take advantage of their employers, and have, in turn, to be dealt with, and the fight is full of curious interest.

Passing on through what seem to us to be miles of sweating-rooms and refineries one after the other, we come to the blocking-room, where the finished paraffin is stacked in its great square pans ready for the candle-maker. The drainings from the sweating-room pass over to what is called the press-room, from the many elevated tanks of which department it flows into trays as before, but instead of being heated it is treated with cold air and submitted to hydraulic pressure. The residuary oil is now used for lubricating purposes. Both the paraffin and the oil are improved by these repeated processes of sweating and pressure. For the present this is the end of the paraffin process. We shall meet with the resultant cakes of purified and refined wax by and by, on its final introduction to candleland.

The machine oil department now intervenes between the paraffin factory and the neutral and fatty acid works. Here we are literally in a little world of oil. It is stored in tanks above us, it is collected in tanks beneath. It is being pumped hither and thither. The very floors are slippery with it. The atmosphere is oleaginous, but nowhere is it disagreeable, and everywhere, judging from the appearance of the work-people, its influences must be healthy. Cylinders oxidising oil, with the aid of steam air-pumps; agitators in tanks swirling to and fro and round and round; caldrons where it is boiled, separators, collectors – every kind of machine is at work. Have you ever witnessed the stage preparations for a great play? To the novice the entire business is one of confusion, doubt, and uncertainty. So it is to the unpractised eye in this oil factory that is incidental to candle-making; but as the curtain goes up on a series of most complete and perfect scenes in the theatre, so does the result of the busy factory come out in almost every variety of lubricating oil, from the delicate preparation used for the sewing-machine and the type-writer, to the lubricatory compounds used for marine engines. There is a point in respect of paraffin that it will be useful to explain. The light yellow shale which we saw in barrels on the wharf is denuded of its light oil before arrival. There is left a small percentage of heavy oil in the solid wax. This is not combustible. It does not ignite, burns only with a wick, and the idea of its inflammability is a popular fiction. Put a light to it and there is no flame; but let your light be a properly supported wick and it will float and burn and no more, even if you set it alight in a vat of the liquid.

Passing by closely packed stores of paraffin wax, we come to what is called the neutral fat department, to distinguish it from the fatty acid department. This opens up fresh vistas of men and machinery and presents new practical solutions of scientific problems. "All fats," remarks our guide, "consist of fatty acid and glycerine, that is to say when they undergo decomposition, but no glycerine is present in fats that are not rancid or decomposed, but we convert fats into this condition by artificial means." Fatty acid is developed with decomposition, and in the early days of candle-making the work was offensive, much rancid fat being used. In this department the solid matter is converted into soap, the liquid goes to make cloth oils, used in wool industries. It is a spacious place, with rows of smoking vats, each holding three and four tons of oil. It might be a floor in a brewery, or the storeroom of a vinegar works, but for the unmistakable oiliness of the atmosphere and the oleaginous grip of the pavement. This should be a fine atmosphere for any one suffering from bronchial trouble. The workmen have clear, healthy complexions. Some of them are old, and in other departments many of them have been employed here for a great number of years. Apart from the hygienic nature of their labour the work-people are well cared for in all other respects. Baths and wash-houses, libraries and reading-rooms, a new lecture-hall, with other privileges, belong to the industrial organisation of the establishment, and bring employer and employed into pleasant relationship. But this is by the way. Leaving the oil vats we come upon a department where cocoa-nut-oil is prepared for night-lights, the process of sweating being much the same as that already described in connection with paraffin, except that this product is so hard it has to be beaten into shape before it can be put into the presses.

And now we are on the other side of the creek which divides the main buildings of the great factory; and whereas when we started on our tour the tide was out, now the swelling water is rising, and on its bosom come forging in the lighters from the docks with cargoes of vegetable and other products for what is called the fatty acid department. And here our guide remarks that each side of the creek is known in the factory by their historic names, the one we have just left being known as the Sherwood House side; and that upon which we are now standing, the west side, being known as the York House side. Tradition rightly or wrongly has it that it was at York House where Cardinal Wolsey was surprised by Henry VIII. on the occasion of one of his luxurious entertainments, where for the first time he met Anne Boleyn as represented in Mr. Irving's production of Shakespeare's *Henry VIII.* at the Lyceum. Our guide discusses the probability of the truthful character of the story. "It was quite a palace," he said, "this York House, and within easy drive of Hampton Court; there is not the smallest reason that I can see why the cardinal should not have preferred to give certain of his receptions here; and I should say it was quite natural that the king should arrive by barge, and he could have landed where our lighters are lying a little outside the creek." It is no disparagement of his technical knowledge of candle-making to say that our guide was enthusiastic in his speculations about Wolsey, his court, and his king; he went so far as to refer to certain lines of Shakespeare that supported his contention, and he mentioned with admiration the historic play in which the Boleyn incident is given with so much artistic effect at the Lyceum. It is a pleasant thing to find the innate romance of our English character (reference to which has already been made in a passing note) breaking out in such an unexpected place, and it is quite possible, if we had followed it up, we might have found our guide ready with some equally interesting incidents of the historic use of candles in the pomp and pride of ecclesiastical procession, at the festive board of kings, and illuminating royal masques and festivals.

Coming down from these heights of poetry and romance, which we pause for a moment to contemplate with the consciousness that it would be difficult to develop such speculations in this present paper, we observe that whereas the paraffin oil in its solid state was easily tumbled into the underground tanks that await every cargo, the palm and other vegetable oils refuse to budge; they are solid in the barrels, and have to be coaxed by jets of steam which are directed into their bung-holes, with the result that in due course the coagulated masses melt and run into pipes, whence the oil is drawn off into elevated tanks similar to those in which the melted product of the paraffin wax is stored. Here, in the fatty acid department, the object is to separate the glycerine from the stearic acid, or stearine as it is popularly called; and this process is managed with a dexterity that is the result of many years of experiment and invention, and is the foundation of many patents.

M. E. Chevreul revealed to the world the foundation of our knowledge of the chemistry of the fatty or non-drying oils. His *Recherches Chimiques sur les Corps Gras d'Origine Animale* is well known, and though published in 1823 may – we have it on authority – be still profitably consulted. But it was left for the originators of Price's Patent Candles to practically apply the famous chemist's discoveries to dark-coloured fats such as palm-oil and greases. "The fatty oils," to quote Professor Mattieu Williams, "whether solid or liquid, animal or vegetable, are with one or two exceptions neutral compounds of glycerine, with substances to which the name of fatty acids has been applied. These acids are composed of carbon, hydrogen, and oxygen, united in varying proportions. Some are solid at ordinary temperatures, others liquid. The solids are pearly crystalline substances, smooth and unctuous to the touch, but not greasy, while all are fusible into oily liquids," and glycerine is produced as a secondary product in the manufacture of candles, and here at Battersea the method of production is on a highly scientific principle, and in such quantity that it has developed into many industrial uses "where its emollient properties and its maintenance of liquidity are due to its non-volatility and absorption of atmospheric moisture." It is used by the modeller to keep his clay soft; ordinary ink is made into copying ink by the addition of glycerine; it is used in paper pulp to make it soft; gas-meters are filled with a solution of glycerine, as it neither evaporates in summer nor freezes in winter; it is used for the sweetening of liqueurs; and treated with sulphuric and nitric acids, it enters into the deadly composition of dynamite. Now the great work of the fatty acid department is to separate the glycerine from the fatty acids, and although on a much more complicated and serious scale, this operation is in a way so much like the paraffin work we have already described that it is only necessary to say that the principal machine engaged in this work is called an autoclave, a construction as formidable as its name. It is, in appearance, a stupendous copper boiler, with mysteriously capped ends, and it goes down into the regions below, as far as it rises above us in this department of the fatty acid. In these curious boilers, or retorts, or autoclaves, the fat is charged with a percentage of lime in the presence of water, and subjected for five hours to the action of steam pressure of a hundred and twenty pounds to the square inch. The lime combines with the fat and forms a lime soap. The glycerine being set free combines with the water. The contents of the vessels are blown out by steam into tanks where a mechanical separation takes place, the glycerine or "sweet water," as it is technically called, being at the bottom, the lime-soap floating on the top. The sweet water is drawn off by taps, and the lime-soap is easily decomposed. It is attacked with sulphuric acid which now sets the fat free. Next comes another process of treatment with sulphuric acid, then water washing, followed by distillation, crystallisation and hydraulic pressing. Stearic acid is the result. It is a white, firm, clean, handsome product, the added value of which, when properly combined with paraffin in candle-making, the French have not yet learnt to fully appreciate in their own manufactures. Having been subjected to a similar process of refinement to that which we have noted in the matter of paraffin, we presently meet the stearine in its finished condition ready for its ultimate purpose of candle-making, and we meet it where it for the first time comes in contact with paraffin. While we have been watching the manufacture of these two products, paraffin-wax and stearine, they have been in careful training for formal and permanent introduction to each other. The meeting and marriage of the two chemical bodies takes place almost simultaneously, and with the happiest results. There are paraffin candles, and there are stearine, each made from the individual material; the one is apt to soften and bend as wax will, the other, wanting in that transparency which makes paraffin so attractive. A judicious blend of the two makes a perfect candle, white, transparent, brilliant. During the course of manufacture it will be noticed that these two materials never come in contact until they arrive in the great blending-room. On one hand we notice stacks of paraffin, on the other a store of stearine, the first in large crystallised stacks, the second in white cakes that break clean and dry. They are destined, in carefully calculated quantities, duly mixed, for the giant pans or caldrons, in which they are melted, for the moulding-rooms, that form another section of the factory.

Meanwhile, the glycerine, which we saw separated from its fatty acids, is marching on its way to perfect purification and white splendour, such as may well fit it to be called the Cinderella of Science, or the fairy of the autoclave. After filtration the sweet water is conducted to the concentrators, where it is converted from sweet water to the denser "candle glycerine," in which shape it goes to the refinery, where it is distilled, refiltered, and distilled again, until it is seen running slow and white and sweet from the stills, ready to be bottled in the warehouse, where it is packed, in company with oils and soaps and candles, in phials of many shapes and variety, in boxes of many colours, for conveyance to many distant lands, not forgetting the villages, towns, and cities of Great Britain herself. We are tempted to taste the liquid as it runs into its bright receptacles, with no unpleasant results, but with a full appreciation of its use in certain liqueurs.

The candle-moulding rooms contain a curious array of inverted mitrailleuse. The candle-moulding rooms are unlike any other part of the factory. Long lines of machines; an army of busy men. The machines, at first blush, might be anything you like to fancy, from the mitrailleuse to some new kind of barrel-organ. On closer inspection you find that the steel barrels are either being steadily filled with the oil from the blending-room, or that out of the barrels candles are being shot and collected for the packing-rooms. These ingeniously contrived moulds, with their cooling arrangements, turn out tons of candles a day, and of all sizes and classes. Nearly four hundred varieties are made, and so comprehensive is the scheme of the firm to satisfy customers, that in a small corner of the works, as we pass the packing-rooms, we come upon the very first method of candle-making, a kind of small chandlery where they are actually making dips. Time does not admit the opportunity of more than a passing mention of the stores, the packing, the box-making, or the engineering works, though we stop *en route* for the night-light and soap factories, to look into a department that is more like a room in a yarn factory. It is the wick-spinning room, where hundreds of bobbins are revolving with a sharp whirr and rattle that is in striking contrast with the repose of the autoclave and the silence of the sweating ovens.

There are few stairs to ascend at these Battersea works. Nearly every department is on the ground floor. Most of them are separated in such a way that they can be isolated in case of fire; but to the night-light casing-room we have to ascend to a floor above; and here we find for the first time a number of girls at work. They are all dressed in white linen frocks with aprons and sleeves. The room is bright and cheerful. There are three kinds of night-lights; two in paper cases, one in glass. In this room the paper cases are being made by nimble fingers aided by small automatic machines. Descending we see the cases filled. In one case a wick and metal sustainer has to be first placed; the material is then poured in; this is done with a dexterity that is remarkable. In another part of the room the other cased light is first moulded like a candle and then simply placed in its outer covering. While these operations are going on, two large drums at the extreme end of the room are revolving with a monotonous motion, making tapers. The wick – miles in length – is slowly wound and rewound about these drums, passing *en route* from one to the other through a melted waxy preparation that adheres on the principle of the repeated dipping of the original candle; and when the deposit is sufficient, the taper is cut into the required lengths. I have heard travellers speak of the usefulness of both tapers and night-lights, more especially on expeditions beyond the confines of civilisation. The paraffin-moulded light, which is simply fitted into its case and only requires lighting under any circumstances, is a very handy companion.

A long interesting day has almost come to an end. When we step once more into the open air, with a somewhat bewildered sense of a new knowledge of many things, our guide intimates that it might now be well to "take in the soap-works." "Why, that is a new industry altogether?" "Often goes with candles," our guide replies, smiling. "Don't you remember a certain combination in the neutral fat department that was reserved for soap?" "Why, certainly," we say, and as we chat, lo and behold we are in the boiling-room and the frame-room! Here are made several soaps – soft soap, carbolic soap, and some other ordinary soaps of commerce; but moving on to the next work of the soap-maker, we enter a clean well-lighted apartment, the atmosphere of which is sweet with a delicate perfume. We are in the toilet and fancy soap factory. The machines are turning out the "Regina" speciality, and very tempting it looks. In the ordinary method of scented soap manufacture, the perfumes are introduced while the soap is hot. The mode at Battersea is a great improvement on this. First the bars are torn into shreds, which are placed on trays, and put into ovens to dry. From the ovens the soap is packed into a machine with large solid granite rollers, between which it passes, getting crushed and ground, and coming out from the mill in continuous lengths of yellow tape. You may take it into your hands and it does not break, it is tender but quite solid. In this dry and cool condition the perfume is added; nothing is thus lost by heat and excessive evaporation; the perfume is retained, and at the same time the treatment which the soap undergoes serves to improve its quality in a remarkable way. But we came to Battersea to describe and illustrate candle-making; soap deserves separate and special treatment at some future day.

The rise of the candle trade in England may be said to date from 1831, when the manufacture was set free from Excise supervision. Soon after this date, Messrs. Price and Company established steam mills in Ceylon for crushing cocoa-nuts, to extract the oil as raw material for the London factory. In 1840 Mr. J. P. Wilson, a member of the firm, while endeavouring to produce a cheap self-snuffing candle for the illumination in honour of the marriage of Queen Victoria, succeeded in making the required light with a mixture of stearic acid and cocoa-nut stearine. This was the well-known "composite" candle. Then came the practical application of the Chevreul processes to which reference has already been made; and with numberless improvements arising out of these discoveries, the trade grew from year to year. From 1847 to 1851, the first five years of its existence, the Company sold 14,220 tons of finished produce. This amount has gone on increasing in a remarkable way; in the five years 1882 to 1886, it had risen to 80,205 tons, and in the five years ending 1890, the finished saleable produce amounted to 83,225 tons. But this great out-put was not the work of Battersea alone. In 1853 the Company bought an estate of sixty acres at Bromborough Pool, near Birkenhead, on which they erected a new factory. Liverpool being the chief palm-oil port, the Company found a great saving in the manufacture of this material in a large and exclusive way, where the material could be purchased without land carriage. Here the Company employs five hundred operatives who have some advantage over the workers at Battersea. Bromborough has a recreation ground and a set of allotment gardens. The growth of buildings at Battersea does not admit of this at the London factory, but each establishment has an efficient company of rifle volunteers. Football and cricket are among their outdoor games, and both in their sports and their work, there is an evident *esprit de corps* among the firm's employés, on the Thames and on the Mersey, which has no doubt been a valuable influence in the successful development of the candle industry.

85

IMAGE: JAMES MCNEILL WHISTLER, 'PRICE'S CANDLE-WORKS'

1876/1877, The Metropolitan Museum of Art

Figure 85.1

DOI: 10.4324/9781315400105-103

INDEX

Note: Numbers in *italics* indicate a figure.